Beginning
Data Structures
in C++

by Vic Broquard

Broquard eBooks

Beginning Data Structures in C++

4th Edition

Vic Broquard

Beginning Data Structures in C++
4th Edition
Vic Broquard
Copyright 2001, 2006, 2014 by Vic Broquard
Broquard eBooks
103 Timberlane
East Peoria, IL 61611
author@Broquard-eBooks.com

ISBN: 978-1-941415-54-2

To all of my dedicated, persevering students,
and to L. Ron Hubbard, who taught me to "Simplify"

Table of Contents

Preface

This book assumes you have had an introduction to C++ programming course. Specifically, you should be familiar with single dimension array processing, multiple-dimensioned array processing, and the use of structures in programming. If you are weak in these areas or are having trouble understanding the first few chapters, please study Appendix A before going further in this book.

Each chapter in some manner builds upon the previous material. One or more complete programming examples accompany each chapter. The book comes with a self-extracting zip file containing all of the sample programs in the book along with all of the test data required for the programming assignments. Download them at:
http://www.Broquard-eBooks.com/pb/beginningds and use the link there.

At the end of each chapter are **Review Exercises**, **Stop Exercises**, and **Programming Problems**. Before you tackle any programming assignments, you should do both the Review and Stop exercises. The Review Exercises are paper and pencil activities that assist in solidifying the basic design principles covered in the chapter. The Stop Exercises cover the new syntax of the language and the new principles of data structures. These illustrate many of the more common errors beginners make in coding or using the chapter's information. In some chapters, the Stop Exercises develop additional ways that the data structure can be applied or designed. If you dutifully do these two sets of exercises **before** you start in on your programming assignments, you will have a much better chance of success with drastically lower frustration level.

If you find any errors or have any suggestions or comments, please email me at author@Broquard-eBooks.com

Chapter 1—Functional Abstraction
Review of Two-dimensional Arrays

Introduction

Abstraction means "the formation of an abstract idea or concept." Abstract means "to think of a quality, such as color or weight, apart from any object or real thing having that quality or any actual instance."

If I say I have a "**red** car," then one can immediately visualize the color of my car. However, if twenty people visualized my car, there would likely be twenty different shades of red. Yet, if they were standing beside me and my car, then they would see the "real red" color of the car. If I say that I have "a hundred dollars" in my pocket, one can imagine what that represents. But if I pull out my wallet and lay five twenty-dollar bills on the table and say that I have "a hundred dollars," it is then the real object. We use forms of abstraction constantly in our daily lives as well as in programming.

Many simple programs that you have written up to now have undoubtedly consisted only of a **main()** function that performed all the necessary steps to solve that problem. Yet, you were always encouraged to break the problem down into one or more subprograms or functions. When you break a program down into a series of functions, you are doing what is called **functional abstraction**. This book begins with a formalization of this process of functional abstraction: its methods, techniques, benefits, and so on.

A program also has another form of abstraction—**data abstraction**. At a low level, we define two variables to "hold" the user's entered cost and quantity values and define another variable to hold the total cost of their order which can subsequently be calculated. In essence, these variables can be considered an abstraction as well. When the program executes and the user enters a quantity of 10 and cost of 42.00, the variables then hold a "real" value. However, from a program design point of view, most all of the variables you have defined and used in programs to this point are instances of the intrinsic built-in C++ data types, such as int, double, and long. (If you have studied the C++ structures, those are not intrinsic data types.)

Now when we speak of data abstraction, we normally do not mean this low level way of thinking about data. Rather the term **data abstraction** refers to larger scale ways and means of organizing and using data. To get a better idea of what we mean by data abstraction, consider writing a program to analyze the length of the lines of ticket buyers trying to get into the latest Star Wars movie. Certainly each potential buyer can be represented by several intrinsic variables such as ages and the number of people in that party trying to get tickets. But a program to analyze the line length must always process the current first group in the line; all newcomers must be added to the end of the line. (It is not nice to cut into a ticket line; it sometimes can be hazardous to your health.) Here we need a way to organize the sets of data and process them in the correct order. There is, in fact, just such a data abstraction that is totally designed for this precise application; it is called a queue. We examine queues and their operations in a later chapter.

Beginning Data Structures in C++

Next, suppose that you needed to write a program to manage the patients coming to visit a doctor. Here again comes a queue operation. When a patient arrives, he/she is placed at the end of the queue; when the doctor is ready for another patient, he/she generally comes from the head of the queue. Do we really want to invent and write all the coding for the ticket queue and then turn around and reinvent it all for the patient queue? If we learn how to properly build a queue data structure, then we only need to reuse it in this case. In fact, if you think about it for a minute, you can easily find other examples where a queue approach would be idea—just about any application that requires first in = first out type of processing.

This chapter covers functional abstraction and lays the ground work for the rest of the book which presents a first look at the broad topic of data abstraction. But first, let's examine the coding changes that the new Microsoft Visual Studio .NET 2005 makes to beginning C++ coding. Then we will take a quick review of two-dimensional array processing.

C++ Programming Changes Caused by the new Microsoft Visual Studio .NET 2005

Release executables now by default require three MS dll files in order to actually execute. Thus, if you intend to run a DOS C++ program on a machine that does not have .NET 2005 installed on it, you must install the three dlls. However, there is a way to avoid this and have a DOS C++ program that can execute on its own. In the Project Settings, C++ tab, Code Generation tab, Runtime Libs set this one to Multi Threaded /MT and rebuild. See Appendix B for details and screen shots of this setting.

At the beginning C++ level, and thus impacting all other courses, is Microsoft's re-write of the C Library. Their purpose is to make these basic functions "secure." However, their changes have not yet gotten ANSI standards approval, and are hence Microsoft only at this point. However, if you ignore this, compiles will generate tons of "function call is deprecated. Please use. . ." The area that impacts a beginning data structure's student is the string functions only. Yes, there are many other functions that have changed, but they will be covered in this course in the appropriate chapter.

First, let me explain the reasoning behind Microsoft's re-write of the standard C Library. A couple quick examples illustrate why. Suppose you had the following coding.

```
char string[5];
strcpy (string, "Hello World from Vic");
strcat (string, ". I forgot the .");
strcpy (0, "Hi");
strcpy (string, 0);
```

The first two instructions perform a core-override or a buffer overrun (to be politically correct), with wildly unpredictable results, potentially including a program crash. The last two instructions wipe out or read as a string the beginning part of the program's data segment where the C runtime globals are stored, equally disastrous.

With Microsoft's new library functions, all four of these instructions cause a program abort and do not wipe out any memory. No more security breaches is the idea. Over four hundred library functions have either been rewritten or replaced with new functions. It is my hunch that most all of these changes will eventually find their way into the ANSI standard for C++, given time.

Here is a summary of the changes at the beginning level of coding. The "big three" functions that most directly impact us are: string compare, string concatenation, and string copy.

```
Name-new: strcmp and _stricmp
Meaning: string compare, case sensitive and case insensitive
Prototype: int strcmp (const char* string1, const char* string2);
          int _stricmp (const char* string1, const char* string2);
Action done: strcmp does a case sensitive comparison of the two
             strings, beginning with the first character of each
             string. It returns 0 if all characters in both
             strings are the same. It returns a negative value if
             the different character in string1 is less than that
             in string2. It returns a positive value if it is
             larger. Both functions abort the program if the
             memory address is NULL or 0.
Example: char s1[10] = "Bcd";
         char s2[10] = "Bcd";
         char s3[10] = "Abc";
         char s4[10] = "Cde";
         char s5[10] = "bcd";
         strcmp (s1, s2) yields 0 - stings are equal
         _stricmp (s1, s5) yields 0 - strings are equal
         strcmp (s1, s3) yields a + value—s1 > s3
         strcmp (s1, s4) yields a - value—s1 < s4


Name-new: strcat_s
Meaning: string concatenation
Prototype: strcat (char* desString, size_t maxDestSize,
                   const char* srcString);
Action done: The srcString is appended onto the end of the
             desString. Aborts the program if dest is too small or either
pointer is NULL.
Example: char s1[20] = "Hello";
         char s2[10] = " World";
       strcat_s (s1, sizeof(s1), s2); yields "Hello World" in s1.


Name-new: strcpy_s
Meaning: string copy
Prototype: char* strcpy (char* desString, size_t maxDestSize,
                        const char* srcString);
Action done: All bytes of the srcString are copied into the
             destination string, including the null terminator.
             The function returns the desString memory address.
             It aborts the program if destination is too small or
```

```
                     either pointer is NULL.
Example: char s1[10];
         char s2[10] = "Sam";
         strcpy_s (s1, sizeof (s1), s2);
When done, s1 now contains "Sam".


Name-new: strlwr_s
Meaning: string to lowercase
Prototype: char* strlwr (char* string, size_t maxSizeOfString);
Action done: All uppercase letters in the string are converted
             to lowercase letters. All others are left untouched.
             Aborts the program if the pointer is NULL.
Example: char s1[10] = "Hello 123";
         strlwr_s (s1, sizeof (s1));
         Yields "hello 123" in s1 when done.


Name-new: strupr_s
Meaning: convert a string to uppercase
Prototype: char* strupr_s (char* string, size_t maxSizeOfString);
Action done: Any lowercase letters in the string are converted
             to uppercase; all others are untouched.
             Aborts the program if the pointer is NULL.
Example: char s1[10] = "Hello 123";
         strupr_s (s1, sizeof(s1));
         When done, s1 contains "HELLO 123"


Name-new: _strrev
Meaning: string reverse
Prototype: char* _strrev (char* string);
Action done: Reverses the characters in a string. It aborts the program
if the memory address passed is null or 0.
Example: char s1[10] = "Hello";
         _strrev (s1);
         When done, string contains "olleH"
```

Finally, when we pass a string to a function, we often encounter this situation.

```
     void Fun (char* string) {
         strcpy_s (string, sizeof (string), "Hello World!");
         // error sizeof(pointer) is 4 bytes

         // use the const int that was used to define the string
         // in the first place.
         strcpy_s (string, MAXARRAYSIZE, "Hello World!");
```

A Review of Two-dimensional Array Processing

Suppose that we had a two-dimensional array of numbers which is often called a matrix. Assume that it is defined in this manner.

```
const int MAX = 20;
int main () {
      int array[MAX][MAX];
```

Further, let's assume that we have inputted all twenty rows, each with twenty columns of data values. Concentrate on how one uses or manipulates the array.

Two of the most common actions are to sum the contents of one row or sum the contents of one column. To start, let's display the sum of each row.

```
int sum;
for (row=0; row<MAX; row++) {
      sum = 0;
      for (col=0; col<MAX; col++) {
            sum += array[row][col];
      }
      cout << "The sum of row " << row << " is "
            << sum << endl;
}
```

And next, let's sum each column and display it.

```
int sum;
for (col=0; col<MAX; col++) {
      sum = 0;
      for (row=0; row<MAX; row++) {
            sum += array[row][col];
      }
      cout << "The sum of col " << col << " is "
            << sum << endl;
}
```

Next examine some other things one can do with a matrix such as this. Let's add 1 to all column 1 items. The column subscript is therefore [0]. We need to traverse each row and perform the addition.

```
for (row=0; row<MAX; row++) {
      array[row][0]++;
}
```

Next, let's set all left diagonal elements to 0. The row and column subscripts must be the same values to be on the diagonal. Thus, again, only one loop is needed.

```
for (row=0; row<MAX; row++) {
      array[row][row] = 0;
}
```

Next, let's set all right diagonal elements to 0. In row 0, the corresponding column subscript is 19 (MAX - 1). In row 1, the subscript of the column is 18 (MAX - 1). Thus, again, only one loop is needed.

```
for (row=0; row<MAX; row++) {
```

```
          array[row][MAX - 1 - row] = 0;
     }
```

Next, let's swap the values in column 1 and column 20. In order to do a swap, a temporary integer is needed.

```
int temp;
for (row=0; row<MAX; row++) {
     temp = array[row][0];
     array[row][0] = array[row][MAX - 1];
     array[row][MAX - 1] = temp;
}
```

Next, let's swap all row 1 values with row 20.

```
int temp;
for (col=0; col<MAX; col++) {
     temp = array[0][col];
     array[0][col] = array[MAX - 1][col];
     array[MAX - 1][col] = temp;
}
```

Next, let's find the average of each row and display it as we go. Notice that we must remember to reset the sum back to 0 before we start in adding up the next row.

```
int sum;
for (row=0; row<MAX; row++) {
     sum = 0;
     for (col=0; col<MAX; col++) {
          sum += array[row][col];
     }
     cout << "Average of row " << row << " is "
          << sum / MAX << endl;
}
```

Finally, let's find the average of each column and display it as we go.

```
int sum;
for (col=0; col<MAX; col++) {
     sum = 0;
     for (row=0; row<MAX; row++) {
          sum += array[row][col];
     }
     cout << "Average of col " << col << " is "
          << sum / MAX << endl;
}
```

All right, now that you have got detailed manipulations reviewed, let's examine functional abstraction.

Functional Abstraction

Solving a problem with a computer program involves a method: an algorithm and some data. Every solution depends upon both the right data and the correct sequence of instructions. One could consider the right sequence of C++ instructions to solve a problem **control flow abstraction**.

Perhaps the "mantra" of a beginning programmer's use of control flow abstraction is the Cycle of Data Processing: IPO or Input a set of data, Process that set of data, Output the results of that set of data. And then repeat IPO until there are no more sets of data. Indeed, in my first book in this series, *C++ for Computer Science and Engineering*, that theme, IPO, was repeated over and over, from problem to problem.

Control flow abstraction can also be applied to such low level considerations as "Do I use a **for** loop or a **while** loop?" We know that every **for** loop can be rewritten as a **while** loop, and vice-versa. However, just because they are interchangeable does not mean that one should always use a **for** loop or always use a **while** loop! If the loop involves inputting an unknown number of sets of data from an input file, a **while** loop is far more understandable than its corresponding **for** loop! On the other hand, if one needed to add all elements in an array which contained **numElements**, a **for** loop is a better choice than a **while** loop. This book is not about control flow abstraction. But to give you some guidelines on coding style or methods, the major rule in industry is "readable code."

Rule: Your coding should be as readable by others as possible.

Why? In industry, someone has to maintain the programs you write. Usually, when the author of a program finishes that project, he/she gets moved on into another big critical project. Maintenance is normally left to the newly hired, "green" programmers who are just starting out on their programming career. If you have written a complex for loop with half the universe of processing steps buried inside that **for** statement, the maintenance programmers are destined for a wild time as they try to maintain it. Many errors can result. So in industry, maintainable code is vitally important. It saves them money, time and ill-will from their customers.

Thus, the only thing I will say regarding control flow abstraction is simply "write readable code so that someone else can maintain the program." Instead, let's examine the larger picture, functional abstraction.

When solving a more complex problem, we often break that problem down into subprograms or functions, each of which perform a specific task. Sometimes these tasks are unique and closely coupled to the immediate problem at hand, such as a function called **CalcTotals()** to find the totals of a customer's order. In all likelihood, such a function only has usefulness within this specific program. Indeed, programs can be written that only use functions specifically designed to meet the needs of that program alone. But again, this is not good design. Just how many times do you want to write the coding for a convert a date from mm/dd/yyyy into the nnn/yyyy format? How many times do you want to write the coding to produce some standardized company heading logo? How many times do you want to figure out the coding to sum all the values in a column of a two-dimensional array?

Reusable Software

In these times of ever-rising software development costs, a company is always looking for ways to reduce the cost of development of new programs. One approach is through careful program design in which attempts are made to reuse existing company libraries of useful functions. For example, if the date conversion was needed in many programs, one time only a pair of functions would be written: **ConvertDateToNumberForm()** and **ConvertNumberFormToDate()**. Then, every time any program needed a date conversion, it would call one of these standard company functions. Likewise, there could be a standard **PrintCompanyLogo()** function and perhaps even a **SumColumn()** function, though the latter would be more difficult to implement in total generality.

Creation of reusable functions requires a conscious effort on your part as you design and code a program. Reusable functions do not "just happen" ordinarily, but are carefully thought out to provide a generalized approach that can be reused. As you are coding or doing the program design, when you get to a function or a block of coding, ask yourself "Will anyone ever want to do something similar?" If the answer is yes or perhaps, see if you can make it into a generalized function that could be reused by other programs. To be reusable that function must be passed everything that it needs in order for it to accomplish its task in all circumstances.

Consider what would be needed to convert a date mm/dd/yyyy into a day of the year form, nnn/yyyy. Obviously it needs three values, month, day, and year. Should they be ints or longs? Realistically, they could even be shorts. However, since ints are more common, an int would be a better choice than a short since any calculation involving a short forces data conversion into an int. On a 32-bit platform an int is the same size as a long, 4-bytes, but it is not considered the same data type by the compiler and would generate warning messages about possible truncation at best. If you make them longs, then any integer type could be converted by the compiler into longs and passed. Thus, perhaps making the date to convert be specified by three longs might be a better approach if you think other programs might possibly be storing their dates in long variables. Otherwise, three ints would do fine. On the other hand, if one is storing the dates in vast quantities on disk, making them be two chars and a short would save disk space. Next, what about the resulting number form? It would need to return two values, the number of days in the year the date represents and the year. But the year is the same year that was passed. It really does not need to return that. Thus, we could simply return the number of days into the year the date represents. The following could represent the generalized **ConvertDateToNumber()** function.

```
int ConvertDateToNumber (int month, int day, int year);
```

Functional Decomposition

How are the functions that a program requires determined? The general process is called functional decomposition which means to break a problem down into smaller subprograms. What constitutes a good function? There is one vitally important guideline.

Rule: A function should perform a single task.

Imagine the coding steps that are needed for a function whose description was "Calculate your taxes, wash your clothes, and play ball with the kids." Chaos. Yet, I was once asked, in my role as consultant to a local company, to assist their programmers in trying to understand what one complex function was doing. And it indeed was trying to do three totally unrelated actions at the same time! When you try to describe the purpose of a function, you should use only one verb and one object of that verb. Print the company's heading logo. Convert the date into the number form. Calculate the weekly expenses. Compute the cost of goods sold. Load an array of cost records. Get the next random die roll. Print the report. You can have all the adjectives and adverbs and prepositional phrases desired. For example, calculate the weekly expenses quickly for company X.

How does one come up with the functions that are needed to break a problem down? There are two design tools available: Top-down design and Bottom-up design. There are pros and cons with each.

With Top-down design, one begins with a top, single box that representing the entire program. That function, the **main()** function, contains a clean statement of the problem to solve. One then asks oneself "What large scale major actions do I need to do to accomplish that task?" These become the first layer of functions. Then pick one of these and ask yourself what major steps do I need to do to accomplish this one smaller task. Those become the subfunctions to it. And so on. It is rather like peeling an onion, layer by layer. How does one know when to stop decomposing the problem? You create no more subfunctions for a given box or function when you can envision the simple sequence of programming steps that that function requires.

Let's illustrate this procedure by working out a design for the following problem. A file contains the company's month by month budget for the preceding twelve months. The first line contains the monthly income figures. Each of the subsequent lines contains the monthly cost of the various categories of expenses, such as phone bill, utilities, and so on. We are to display the income and expenses in columnar form with the first column containing the name of the income or expense and the next twelve columns containing the corresponding month's value of that income or expense. At the end of the report, display the totals of the monthly expenses and then a line showing the monthly net profit or loss. There are a number of ways the problem could be solved. Here is one way; see Figure 1.1.

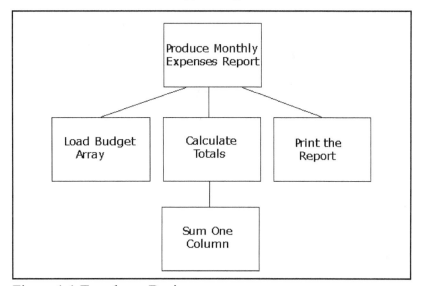

Figure 1.1 Top-down Design

Beginning Data Structures in C++

Notice that I chose to write a subfunction to add the contents of one column of the two-dimensional array. Presumably, the Calculate totals function would then call this function as many times as needed, twelve in this case. This avoids having to code nested loops within Calculate totals and makes it easier to comprehend:

```
for (col=0; col<12; col++)
    SumColumn(budget, startRow, endRow, col);
```

The major drawback of Top-down design is that the designer is often not fully aware of all the implementation details and steps needed as the initial design is done. Thus, as the programmer begins to implement the solution, function by function, new details appear that can alter the original Top-down design. This is particularly true with large programming projects.

The Bottom-up approach begins by identifying all of the lowest level functions that are going to be needed. Then, these pieces are joined together into larger units, building upwards toward the eventual top box representing the problem to be solved. The liability or major problem with this approach is that often the pieces when put together do not end up with the top box, the problem to be solved, but some alteration of it. The Bottom-up design of this problem looks exactly like Figure 1.1.

In actual practice in industry, program designers really use both at the same time. On large programs, they begin with Top-down design, peeling the onion until they cannot see what comes next. Then they switch to Bottom-up and put together a number of the low-level functions that are closely tied to the required processing steps. And then they try to merge the two designs into a unified whole. The analogy of a 5,000-piece jigsaw puzzle illustrates the real difference between these two approaches. With Top-down, one begins with the completed puzzle before them and splits large sections off into functions, such as separating all the sky chunks out, then the house, then the driveway, then the car from the driveway, and so on. With Bottom-up, one starts with all the pieces in a huge pile and begins assembling the blocks, such as putting together the car, and the driveway, and the house, and then try to figure out how to put the car, driveway and house sections together.

Let's create the design for another problem. Management at Acme TV has compiled a large file of viewer preferences. Each line in the input file contains the viewer's id number, the date (mm/dd/yyyy), the time (hh:mm) and the character string name of the show that was viewed. The data in the file are sorted into viewer id number order. Management wishes to have a real-time show analysis program developed to allow them to study the success ratio of various TV shows. The program should prompt the user to enter a show name or Ctrl-z to quit. When the show name is entered, the program should display the following informational results.

```
            Acme Show Analysis
    Show: nnnnnnnnnnnnn   Viewers: nnn.nn%

    Enter a new show or ctrl-z to quit
```
Management has agreed that the viewer percentage is found by counting how many viewers watched the show divided by the total number of viewers in their database.

Before we start inventing functions, we should examine the problem details and see how we wish to solve it. Since the file of data is very large, we cannot store every line in the file! We need to summarize the data as it is being input. We really need to create two arrays: one holds the show name and one holds the number of viewers. Also we need to accumulate the number of viewers as we go along. Given the fact that the file is sorted into viewer id order, to find the number of viewers we need to use control break logic. That is, when the current viewer id is not the same as the previous viewer id, then reset the previous viewer id and add one to the count of the total number of viewers. To load the arrays of show names and frequencies, we need to find out if the current show we have input is in our growing table or not. If not, we need to add that show to the table and increment the corresponding frequency count. If it is in the table, we need to increment the corresponding frequency count. Thus, the input process is fairly complex.

Once we have the two arrays loaded and the input file closed, we can then display the prompt message. When a show name to find has been entered, we must search the show names array looking for a match. If found, then it is a simple matter to calculate the percentage by multiplying the corresponding frequency count by 100 and dividing by the total number of viewers.

Now we can easily construct the Top-down design. Notice that we must match the show name in the array from both within the load array function as well as from normal main processing. Actually, the design is fairly simple because many of the processing steps are extremely short.

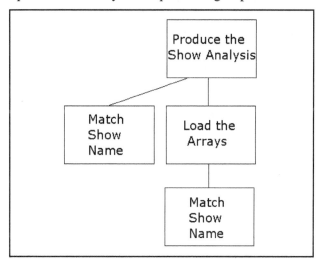

Figure 1.2 Top-down Design for Show Analysis

Thus, whenever you begin to tackle programming a new assignment, the very first step is to spend the time to functionally decompose the problem usually using Top-down design.

Coding the Functions

When actually coding for a function begins, five steps should be followed to achieve a finished function with the least problems.

      A. Code the function prototype
      B. Code the function header
      C. Code the function body
      D. Invoke or call the function
      E. Document the function fully

Let's examine these one by one.

Coding the Function Prototype—the Case of the Function Names

The action of coding the function prototype begins with the invention of a good name for the function. And at once the issue of the case of names arises. The objective is really to avoid what I call namespace pollution and still have a readable program. If you use case randomly, programs become very difficult to maintain because the case of an item does not give the reader a clue to the nature of the item whether it is a user variable, a constant/define name, a structure name/tag a function or a system function or name that cannot be altered. Thus, I follow these guidelines throughout the book. If an item is a variable name, it begins with a lowercase letter and if it is a compound name, the subsequent words are capitalized. For example, firstName. If the item is a constant or a #define name or is a structure tag or name, it is all uppercase. If it is the name of a function, it begins with a capital letter, for example, **CalculateTotals()**.

Let's code the function prototype needed for the Weekly Budget Report program we have just designed in Figure 1.1. Here are the names I chose: **LoadBudget()**, **CalculateTotals()**, **SumColumn()**, and **PrintReport()**. Here is a design consideration. The first row contains the income for the twelve months. Rather than make a separate array for the income, I chose to store it in the first row of the two-dimensional array budget. Further, after the last row of expenses comes the net profit for each month. Again, to avoid making another array of totals, I chose to store the twelve monthly totals in the row after the last expenses. Thus, if the budget array contains 100 rows, the maximum number of expense categories is thus 98. This simplification reduces the number of arrays to be passed from three to one to store the budget data.

Next, determine what parameters need to be passed so that the function can perform its desired processing steps, their data types and the order you wish to pass them. Finally, decide whether or not the function must return anything. If it is a single item being returned, have the function return it. However, if two or more values must be returned, then pass them both by reference. Here are the prototypes that I used for the four functions.

```
int LoadBudget (double budget[][NUMMONTHS], char names[][NAMELEN],
                int maxRows, int numMonths);
void CalculateTotals (double budget[][NUMMONTHS], int startRow,
                int totalsRow);
double SumColumn (double budget[][NUMMONTHS], int startRow,
                int endRow, int col);
void PrintReport (double budget[][NUMMONTHS], int totalsRow,
                char names[][NAMELEN]);
```

Let's review how parameters are passed. Normally variables, such as char, short, int, long, double, bool are always passed by value. That is, a copy of the caller's variable's contents are copied and placed in the function's parameter variable. Consider the following code.

In **main()**:
```
        int x = 4;
        Fun (x);
```
In **Fun()**:
```
void Fun (int y) {
        y = 42;
```

```
}
```
Where does the 42 go? It goes into **Fun()**'s parameter y, not **main()**'s x variable.

Arrays are always passed by address. Thus, the function has direct access to the calling function's array data. Consider the following code.

In **main()**:
```
int x[3] = {1, 2, 3};
Fun (x);
```
In **Fun()**:
```
void Fun (int y[]) {
     y[1] = 42;
}
```
Where does the 42 get stored? In **main()**'s x array in the second element. **Fun()**'s parameter y really contains the memory address of the first element in **main()**'s x array.

When you pass a variable by reference, you are allowing that function to have read and write access to that variable. That is, the function can use its value as well as change its value. A reference variable is nothing more than the memory address of the item, similar to that of a passed array. Consider the following coding.

In **main()**:
```
int x = 4;
Fun (x);
```
In **Fun()**:
```
void Fun (int& y) {
     y = 42;
}
```
Where does the 42 go this time? Since **Fun()**'s y is really the memory address of **main()**'s x variable, the 42 replaces the 4 that was in **main()**'s x.

Do not make indiscriminate usage of reference variables! In other words, a function should only pass by reference those variables that the function should be altering. If a function is not going to alter a variable's contents, pass it by value. When we cover structures, this guideline will be slightly modified. The following represents sloppy coding and poor design. Why?

```
double Fun (int& x, long& y, double& z) {
   double ansr = x / z * y;
   return ansr;
}
```
The reason for the poor design is Fun is being passed a reference to the caller's three variables but under no circumstances will be altering their contents. Use a reference when there is a situation in which the function will alter the original value.

Use of the const Qualifier

Let's review the prototypes we have coded thus far. They are

```
int LoadBudget (double budget[][NUMMONTHS],
                char names[][NAMELEN], int maxRows,
                int numMonths);
void CalculateTotals (double budget[][NUMMONTHS], int startRow,
                      int totalsRow);
double SumColumn (double budget[][NUMMONTHS], int startRow,
                  int endRow, int col);
void PrintReport (double budget[][NUMMONTHS], int totalsRow,
                  char names[][NAMELEN]);
```

Looking over **LoadBudget()**, the array we know is passed by address. Thus, **LoadBudget()** can alter values in the array. That is what is desired if we intend to input the data into the array. Likewise **CalculateTotals()** is passed the budget array and can alter its contents. That is also what we expect it to do as it calculates the net profit, storing it in the next unused row in the array. **SumColumn()** is also passed the budget array and can alter its contents. Whoa! This function is only summing the contents of a specific column and returning that sum. Under what circumstances would it change the passed array values? None. Likewise for **PrintReport()**. Neither of these two functions should alter the budget array's contents; yet the prototype is indicating that it has that right! Here is another use for the **const** qualifier.

The **const** qualifier specifies that this item is to be a constant and cannot be changed once it is given its initial value. We normally think of using it when defining constant values such as PI.

```
const double PI = 3.14159;
```

However, when used with a memory address, it also means that the data pointed to by that memory address is to be considered constant data as well. Thus, we need to revise the two errant prototypes as follows:

```
double SumColumn (const double budget[][NUMMONTHS], int startRow,
                  int endRow, int col);
void PrintReport (const double budget[][NUMMONTHS],
                  int totalsRow, const char names[][NAMELEN]);
```

Here again, we are making a bargain with the compiler. We are saying that within these functions, the data in the arrays cannot be altered in any way. And if we accidentally do so, the compiler will issue a compile-time error message.

What about making the other integers constants as well? This is one mistake beginners often make. Unsure of where **const** should be applied, they apply it everywhere.

```
double SillySumColumn (const double budget[][NUMMONTHS],
                       const int startRow,
                       const int endRow, const int col);
```

The three integers are already copies of the calling function's data. It is impossible for the function to be able to change the calling function's variables' contents. All that the use of the **const** qualifier does in this case is to prevent an accidental assignment into the function's parameter copies as shown here.

```
double SillySumColumn (const double budget[][NUMMONTHS],
                       const int startRow, const int endRow,
                       const int col) {
    col = 42; // errors out now
}
```

Trying to alter **col** above now generates a compiler error.

From a design point of view, the calling function could care less whether or not the function wants to clobber its own parameters. I jokingly say that nobody cares if you wish to shoot yourself in the foot; but please don't shoot my foot! In other words, if a function wishes to alter its parameter copies, that is the sole province of the function; it cannot harm the caller in any way.

The In/Out Aspects of a Function's Parameters

When we document a function, parameters that are passed by value only, that is where copies are passed, are said to be Input to the function only. However, parameters that are passed by address, such as arrays and those passed by reference, are called In/Out because they can be used both for inputting a value into a function as well as receiving the output of a function. The function can store a new result into them.

The Optional Variable Names in a Prototype

When coding a function prototype, the actual names of the parameters are optional. If coded, the compiler syntax checks them for valid names and then discards them. So if they are not really needed, why use them? They help document a program and reduce the chances for errors.

Consider the **SumColumn()** function prototype written this way.

```
double SumColumn (const double [][NUMMONTHS], int, int, int);
```

Yes, it certainly is shorter. But consider what happens when you need to actually call this function. All of these are possible.

```
result = SumColumn (budget, start, end, col);
result = SumColumn (budget, end, start, col);
result = SumColumn (budget, col, start, end);
result = SumColumn (budget, start, col, end);
result = SumColumn (budget, col, start, end);
result = SumColumn (budget, end, col, start);
```

So which one is the right way? And what happens if we choose one of the five wrong ways? We would have to scroll down and find the actual function header or trust our memory. Neither is optimum. Always provide good descriptive names in the prototypes.

Coding the Function Header

To avoid accidental errors, I recommend that you copy the function prototype and paste it where you want to begin to code the function body. Simply remove the trailing semicolon and replace it with the {} pair. Why do I recommend this approach?

Consider the results of the following coding.

```
double SumColumn (const double budget[][NUMMONTHS],
                  int startRow, int endRow, int col);
int main() {
  ...
  result = SumColumn (budget, start, end, col);
```

15

```
}

double SumColumn (const double budget[][NUMMONTHS],
                  long startRow, int endRow, int col) {
  ...
}
```

What happens when this program is built? A Linker error occurs, an unresolved external function error. The compiler uses the prototype as its model to follow when calling a function. In this case it is calling a function named **SumColumn()** which is passed the budget array along with three **int**s. However, the Linker, whose job is to actually find the required functions, can only find a function named **SumColumn()** that is passed the budget array and a **long** and two **int**s. Hence, it produces the error message. Tracking these down can be very frustrating indeed.

The way to totally avoid such errors is to simply copy the prototype and paste it and turn it into the function header. This way no accidental errors can occur.

Documenting a Function

In industry, you must document your coding. The first time you try to issue a program into production without any comments in it, you are likely in for a rude awakening. Someone at the company will have to provide maintenance on production programs. Unless you wish to spend the rest of your life maintaining the same programs you write, you will learn to fully document.

Function documentation usually consists of two parts. Either just before the function header or just after it, there must be a form of block comment that identifies the purpose of the function and the significance of what it is being passed and what it is being returned under what circumstances. I use visually strong block comments.

```
/*****************************************************************/
/*                                                               */
/* SumColumn: return the sum of a column in a 2-d array,         */
/*            beginning with startRow and ending before          */
/*            endRow; col specifies which column to sum          */
/*            No check is made for col being out of range        */
/*            or the rows being out of range                     */
/*                                                               */
/*****************************************************************/

double SumColumn (const double budget[][NUMMONTHS], int startRow,
                  int endRow, int col) {
```

Notice what is said in a block comment. It outlines what is being returned, what the function's purpose is, and points out any requirements or exceptions. From this comment, it is clear that it is the caller's responsibility to guarantee that the passed column number is within the array as well as the beginning and ending rows. It is also clear that the sum includes the **startRow** and continues through but not including the **endRow**.

16

Not everyone likes such visually acute style of block comments. Feel free to experiment with less dramatic forms. Try using +'s or ='s in place of the *'s or even simple C++ style comments: //.

The second form of documentation is instruction or section comment. The idea is to outline the higher level processing actions as well as any non-obvious instructions. This function is so short and so simple in nature that I choose not to add any further instruction comments.

```cpp
        double sum = 0;
        for (int row=startRow; row<endRow; row++) {
         sum += budget[row][col];
        }
        return sum;
      }
```

Here is how I chose to document the **PrintReport()** function.

```cpp
/*****************************************************************/
/*                                                             */
/* PrintReport: display the expense report                     */
/*          names contain the expense types and budget holds   */
/*          the numbers. row 0 is the income, rows 1 upto but   */
/*          not including endRow contain the expenses, while    */
/*          endRow contains the net profit                      */
/*                                                             */
/*****************************************************************/

void PrintReport (const double budget[][NUMMONTHS], int endRow,
                  const char names[][NAMELEN]) {
 // setup floating point output for dollars
 cout.setf(ios::fixed, ios::floatfield);
 cout.setf(ios::showpoint);
 cout << setprecision(2);

 // display the heading and column heading lines
 cout << " Acme Monthly Expenses Report\n\n";
 cout << " Item                    Jan        Feb        Mar"
         "         Apl      May      June       July       Aug"
         "         Sept     Oct      Nov      Dec\n\n ";

 // display all rows, the first is the income and last is profits
 for (int i=0; i<=endRow; i++) {
  cout.setf(ios::left, ios::adjustfield);
  cout << setw (20) << names[i] << " ";
  cout.setf(ios::right, ios::adjustfield);

  // display all 12 monthly values
  for (int j=0; j<NUMMONTHS; j++) {
   cout << setw(10) << budget[i][j];
  }
  cout << endl;
  if (i==0)                  // double space after the income line
```

```
  cout << endl;
 else if (i==endRow-1)  // double space before the net profit
  cout << endl;
 }
}
```

The complete program is shown below. When you review it, notice the effect of the comments on program readability.

Stub Testing

With the design done, coding begins. On larger programs, one should not write all of the coding for the entire program and then hit the compile button, unless you are either a perfect coder or a masochist. The sheer number of likely syntax errors is overwhelming. In addition, think of the runtime errors that occur! A larger program is developed a small portion at a time. Stub testing is the technique often used. Stub testing means to use fake function bodies that actually do nothing but perhaps display a message that we got to this function. One can then concentrate on debugging the higher level functions that are calling these stubs. Once the higher level coding is working, then code the function body for one of the stubs and test it. Any runtime or logic errors tend to be in that newly coded function or the way it is being used by the calling function.

One codes the **main()** function which should define the key variables and then call a series of functions that will eventually carry out the requisite processing steps. The function prototypes can all be coded at this point, or perhaps just the **LoadBudget()**. Instead of diving into the coding of the function bodies, instead, code only the function header and insert a dummy function body, such as this.

```
    int LoadBudget(double budget[][NUMMONTHS], char names[][NAMELEN],
                   int maxRows, int numMonths) {
        cout << "Loading the Budget\n ";
        return 0;
    }
```

Here **LoadBudget()** is called a stub because its actual body has not yet been coded. One can place "Killroy was here" type of messages to be displayed in the stubs. If you code all four of the prototypes and implement each function as a stub only, then you can actually build and run the program. The **main()** function can then be debugged and gotten to work properly.

If I were developing this program, I would next supply the function body for **LoadBudget()**. Now one could rebuild the program and run it. One could use the debugger to inspect the results. Is the number of rows correct? One could even insert an elementary loop to display each of the expense strings and maybe one month's numerical value from the budget array to verify the data is being loaded correctly. One can lower the maximum number of rows to see if the array bounds exceeded message works. One can insert the letter A in place of one of the budget expense digits and see if the bad data error message is triggered. In other words, you can easily verify that this function is working properly, and then move on to the next function to implement. Stub testing makes it easy to create and debug larger programs.

Testing Oracles

A test oracle is a collection of input values along with their expected output results. One ought to create the test oracles before you execute the program. Then, when you run the program with these values, observe if the program produces the expected results. If not, look for your logic error. Thorough debugging demands test oracles, especially on larger programs! I have been programming for more than thirty-five years. My one pet peeve, the one thing I hate the most in this industry, is "mostly working" software! I just lost a section of this chapter while I was writing it. I attempted to insert a six-line text file and WordPerfect chose instead to go into an infinite loop. Grrrr. Some have proclaimed that with really large programs, there is always another bug just over the horizon—that larger programs can never be error free. If you believe that, please contact me, I have a really wonderful bridge I would like to sell.

Seriously, there are many reasons why software is buggy. Perhaps there was an urgency to get the program delivered, perhaps management must save some dollars because the program development has exceeded the company's budget, perhaps the programmers were lazy, perhaps the programmers and designers had not even thought of using the program in the way that some user is doing so. There are many, many reasons. I, for one, have frequently been caught on the last excuse; it never ceases to amaze me the uses that some users find for my Image Collection Manager Program.

But good testing really boils down to having a solid, complete, thorough set of tests, which if the program passes, is a guarantee that the program performs according to the specifications. For simple programs, the test oracles are small and can easily be seen to prove the programs is perfect. Consider a program that prompts the user to enter a day of the week number and then displays the day name string, repeating the process until the end of file. What test sets would be needed to guarantee this program was perfect?

Enter 1 and display "Sunday" - verify spelling

...

Enter 7 and display "Saturday" - verify spelling

Enter 0 and get an out of range message

Enter 8 and get an out of range message

Enter 42 and get an out of range message

Enter -9 and get an out of range message

Enter A and get invalid data message

Enter ^Z and get a program complete message, program terminates

If such a program passed all of these tests, we could be fairly confident that it would work without any additional problems appearing.

However, when attempting to handle a large program, the sheer number of possibilities grows enormously. Couple that with users who find unexpected, new uses for the program and you have quite a challenge setting up a complete testing oracle.

After examining the complete Pgm01a Monthly Expense Report Program, see what additional test oracles should be tried. I provided a simple test file that contained an income line and five expense lines. Here are some that I tried.

Reduce the maximum number of rows to 4 and run; it should produce array size exceeded

Insert the letter A in place of one of the expense numbers and run; it should produce the bad data error message

Move the file to some other location and run; it should produce the file not found error

If you enter large numbers for any of the doubles, such as $1000000000.00 what will the program output look like?

See if you can find other tests that ought to be applied to Pgm01a to help guarantee that it is not "mostly working" software.

The Complete Program Pgm01a

Here is the complete listing for **Pgm01a**, the Monthly Expenses Program. Notice I boldfaced the **strcpy_s()** new function.

```
Listing of Pgm01a - Monthly Expenses Report

 1 #include <iostream>
 2 #include <fstream>
 3 #include <iomanip>
 4
 5 using namespace std;
 6
 7 const int NUMMONTHS = 12;   // the maximum number of columns
 8 const int MAXROWS = 1000;   // the maximum number of rows
 9 const int NAMELEN = 21;     // the max length of item names
10
11 int LoadBudget(double budget[][NUMMONTHS], char names[][NAMELEN],
12               int maxRows, int numMonths);
13
14 void CalculateTotals (double budget[][NUMMONTHS], int startRow,
15                   int totalsRow);
16
17 double SumColumn (const double budget[][NUMMONTHS], int startRow,
18             int endRow, int col);
19
20 void PrintReport(const double budget[][NUMMONTHS], int totalsRow,
21                 const char names[][NAMELEN]);
22
23 /***********************************************************/
24 /*                                                         */
25 /* Produce the Monthly Expenses Report Program             */
26 /*                                                         */
27 /***********************************************************/
28
29 int main () {
30
31  double budget[MAXROWS][NUMMONTHS];
32  char   names[MAXROWS][NAMELEN];
33  int    numItems;
```

```
34  int     startExpensesIdx = 1;
35
36  numItems = LoadBudget (budget, names, MAXROWS - 1, NUMMONTHS);
37  strcpy_s (names[numItems], NAMELEN, "Totals");
38  CalculateTotals (budget, startExpensesIdx, numItems);
39  PrintReport (budget, numItems, names);
40
41  return 0;
42  }
43
44  /******************************************************************/
45  /*                                                              */
46  /* LoadBudget: loads the budget and budget item names arrays,   */
47  /*   returning the number of rows input                         */
48  /*   An error is displayed if maxRows is exceeded, if the file  */
49  /*   cannot be opened, or if bad input data is encountered      */
50  /*   The item name strings are assumed to be delimited by " "   */
51  /*                                                              */
52  /******************************************************************/
53
54  int LoadBudget(double budget[][NUMMONTHS], char names[][NAMELEN],
55                  int maxRows, int numMonths){
56  int i = 0;      // the row subscript
57  ifstream infile ("MonthlyExpenses.txt");
58  if (!infile) {
59   cerr << "Error: unable to open file: MonthlyExpenses.txt\n";
60   exit (1);
61  }
62  char c; // to hold the leading " of the strings
63
64  while (i < maxRows && infile >> c) { // get the leading "
65   infile.getline (names[i], NAMELEN, '\"');
66   for (int j=0; j<numMonths; j++) {
67    infile >> budget[i][j];
68   }
69   i++;
70  }
71
72  // check for array bounds exceeded
73  if (i == maxRows && infile >> c) {
74   cerr << "Error: array bounds exceeded\n";
75   infile.close();
76   exit (2);
77  }
78  // check for bad input values
79  else if (!infile.eof() && infile.fail()) {
80   cerr << "Error: bad input data in the file at line "
81        << i << endl;
82   infile.close();
83   exit (3);
```

```
 84   }
 85   infile.close();
 86   return i;          // return the number of rows inputted
 87   }
 88
 89   /***************************************************************/
 90   /*                                                             */
 91   /*  CalculateTotals: compute the net profit for each month,    */
 92   /*   storing it in the first unused row after the last expense */
 93   /*   startRow specifies the index of the first expense and     */
 94   /*   endRow-1 represents the last expense; the net profit is   */
 95   /*   income - the sum of the expenses and is stored in endRow  */
 96   /*   No checks are made on for passed indexes being out of range*/
 97   /*                                                             */
 98   /***************************************************************/
 99
100   void CalculateTotals (double budget[][NUMMONTHS], int startRow,
101                       int endRow) {
102    for (int col=0; col<NUMMONTHS; col++) {
103     budget[endRow][col] = budget[0][col] -
104           SumColumn (budget, startRow, endRow, col);
105    }
106   }
107
108   /***************************************************************/
109   /*                                                             */
110   /*  SumColumn: return the sum of a column in a 2-d array,      */
111   /*            beginning with startRow and ending before        */
112   /*            endRow; col specifies which column to sum         */
113   /*            No check is made for col being out of range       */
114   /*            or the rows being out of range                    */
115   /*                                                             */
116   /***************************************************************/
117
118   double SumColumn (const double budget[][NUMMONTHS], int startRow,
119                     int endRow, int col) {
120    double sum = 0;
121    for (int row=startRow; row<endRow; row++) {
122     sum += budget[row][col];
123    }
124    return sum;
125   }
126
127   /***************************************************************/
128   /*                                                             */
129   /*  PrintReport: display the expense report                    */
130   /*            names contain the expense types and budget holds */
131   /*            the numbers. row 0 is the income, rows 1 up to    */
132   /*            but not including endRow contain the expenses,    */
133   /*            endRow contains the net profit                    */
```

```
134 /*                                                                  */
135 /******************************************************************/
136
137 void PrintReport (const double budget[][NUMMONTHS], int endRow,
138                   const char names[][NAMELEN]) {
139 // setup floating point output for dollars
140 cout << fixed << setprecision(2);
143
144 // display the heading and column heading lines
145 cout << "Acme Monthly Expenses Report\n\n";
146 cout << "Item                        Jan       Feb       Mar"
147          "       Apl       May       June       July      Aug"
148          "       Sept      Oct       Nov       Dec\n\n";
149
150 // display all rows, the first is the income and last is profits
151 for (int i=0; i<=endRow; i++) {
152   cout.setf(ios::left, ios::adjustfield);
153   cout << setw (20) << names[i] << " ";
154   cout.setf(ios::right, ios::adjustfield);
155
156   // display all 12 monthly values
157   for (int j=0; j<NUMMONTHS; j++) {
158     cout << setw(10) << budget[i][j];
159   }
160   cout << endl;
161   if (i==0)                   // double space after the income line
162     cout << endl;
163   else if (i==endRow-1)  // double space before the net profit
164     cout << endl;
165 }
166 }
```

Here is an abbreviated version of the program's output.

```
Acme Monthly Expenses Report

Item                    Jan        Feb        Mar        Apl        May

Monthly Income      10000.00   11000.00   13000.00   12000.00   10000.00

Studio Rental         500.00     550.00     600.00     500.00     550.00
Phone Lines           100.00     110.00     100.00     120.00     100.00
Office Supplies        42.00      55.00      60.00      55.00      50.00
Utilities             250.00     260.00     270.00     280.00     300.00
Wages                7000.00    7000.00    7500.00    7500.00    7500.00

Totals               2108.00    3025.00    4470.00    3545.00    1500.00
```

Additional Error Handling Functions

Two additional functions can be used to handle unusual input situations. Suppose that the user has entered bad data, that is, a letter instead of a numerical digit. We know that the **istream** goes into the fail state. Specifically, the fail bit is turned on prohibiting any further input operations. Until now, that left us with no choice but to abort the program.

It is possible to clear the I/O state flag, setting it back into the "good" state. However, it is mandatory that the offending data be removed from the stream before retrying the original input operations. The function that modifies a stream's state is called **clear** (). It takes one parameter which is the new state in which to place the stream. If no parameter is passed, the default is to place the stream back into the good state, which is exactly what we desire. It is coded this way.

```
cin.clear ();
infile.clear ();
```

Here is an example of its use. Suppose we need to input a menu choice which is a number from 1 to 4. The following accomplishes it, assuming that there is a function **DisplayMenu** which displays the menu.

```
int choice = 5;
char c; // for the offending characters
do {
        DisplayMenu ();
        cin >> choice;
        if (!cin) {
                cin.clear ();
                cin.get (c);
                choice = 5;
        }
}
while (choice < 1 || choice > 4);
```

Of course, if the user has entered several bad characters in a row on the line before the CRLF, then the menu gets displayed and that offending character removed several times. This is rather annoying. There is another way to handle this.

Another situation that can occur is the desire to ignore the remaining data on an input line. Suppose that the line contains the item number, quantity, product description and cost. Suppose further that in the problem we are solving, we only need the item number from the line. The remaining three field are not needed for the problem. True, one could define another three fields and also input them. But there is an easier way, the **ignore** function.

infile.ignore (100, '\n ');

This says to ignore or skip over all characters from the current position in the input stream until one of three things occurs: it reaches eof or the premature end of a corrupt file, it reaches a new line code or CRLF, it has ignore 100 characters. Here the 100 is an arbitrary number of characters which I conclude no line could contain that many characters.

So for the above example, one could code the following.

```
infile >> itemNumber;
infile.ignore (100, '\n');
```

And the current position should be on the CRLF or new line code that ends this line all ready for the next extraction of the next line.

Back to the menu problem in which the user has entered a number of bad characters in a row. The **ignore()** function can eliminate this mess this way.

```
int choice = 5;
char c; // for the offending characters
do {
        DisplayMenu ();
        cin >> choice;
        if (!cin) {
                cin.clear ();
                cin.ignore (100, '\n');
                choice = 5;
        }
}
while (choice < 1 || choice > 4);
```

Some Additional Screen Output Features

When showing menus, often we would like to clear the screen and show the menu. This can be done using the system() function which is passed a string. The string can contain any DOS command desired. The DOS command to clear the screen is CLS.

```
system ("CLS");
```

When the DOS Console window opens, we can install a nice title on its caption title bar using the DOS title command, which takes one parameter, the title string to be used. The following sets the window title to "Super Accounting Program."

```
system ("title Super Accounting Program");
```

The color scheme for the console window can be set as well, which makes a very nice effect. The DOS command to set the color scheme is:

COLOR   Sets the default console foreground and background colors.

COLOR [attr]

where attr specifies color attribute of console output

The color attributes are specified by two hex digits—the first corresponds to the background color; the second, the foreground. Each digit can be any of the following values:

```
0 = Black       8 = Gray
1 = Blue        9 = Light Blue
2 = Green       A = Light Green
3 = Aqua        B = Light Aqua
4 = Red         C = Light Red
```

```
5 = Purple        D = Light Purple
6 = Yellow        E = Light Yellow
7 = White         F = Bright White
```

Note that if no argument is given, this command restores the color to what it was when CMD.EXE started. This value either comes from the current console window, the /T command line switch or from the DefaultColor registry value.

My own preference for a color scheme is this one.
```
system ("color 1E");
```
which sets it to yellow on blue.

Review Questions

1. What is the difference between functional abstraction and data abstraction?

2. Why is this code segment not maintainable?
```
double x, a;
a = 3.14 * x * x;
```

3. A company is selling products in all 50 states. A new programmer needed to calculate the sales on the order his program is currently processing. The **stateCode** variable contains the state number from 1 to 50. What is wrong with this solution from the "Company's" point of view? How should the programmer have done this action? Hint: reusable code.
```
subtotal = qty * cost;
switch (stateCode) {
  case 1: rate = .065; break;
  case 2: rate = .075; break;
  ... etc
}
tax = subtotal * rate;
```

4. A programmer wrote the following function:
```
void SwitchRowsAndSumRow (double array[][NUMCOLS],
             int numRows, int switchRow1, int switchRow2,
             int sumThisRow);
```
What design criteria does this function violate? How could it be repaired?

5. A programmer wrote the following prototype to calculate the tax on a given sale. It is given the quantity, cost and stateCode variables. Why is it bad design? How can it be repaired?
```
double CalcTax (int, int, double);
```

6. Write a Top-down design for the following problem. Acme Graphics wants a program to calculate some properties of geometric shapes. Initially, the program displays a menu similar to the following:

> Acme Graphics Shape Properties Calculator
> 1. Rectangle Properties
> 2. Triangle Properties
> 3. Circle Properties
> 4. Sphere Properties
> 5. Pyramid Properties
> 6. Quit

Enter the number of your choice:

When a correct choice is made, then input the various measurements that define that shape, calculate and display the properties (such as area, circumference, perimeter and so on). Then after displaying a press any key to continue, re-show the main menu.

7. Consider the following function. What items are imported and what items are being exported?

```cpp
double FindMax (double array[][NUMCOLS], int numRows) {
    double biggest = array[0][0];
    for (int j=0; j<numRows; j++) {
        for (int k=0; k<NUMCOLS; k++) {
            if (biggest < array[j][k])
                biggest = array[j][k];
        }
    }
    return biggest;
}
```

8. Describe how stub testing could be applied to the program created in Review Question 6 above?

9. A program to find the roots of a quadratic equation has been written. You are to write a set of testing oracles with which to fully test the program. The program inputs values for **a**, **b** and **c**. The quadratic formula is

$$roots = \frac{-b \pm \sqrt{b^2 - 4ac}}{2a}$$

The input instruction from the program is

```cpp
cin >> a >> b >> c;
```

10. Consider the **FindMax()** function as given in Review Question 7. Write a good set of block comments to precede the function body. Consider what additional lines in the implementation need comments. Show also what other lines of documentation you should put within the function to make it easily maintainable.

Stop! Do These Exercises Before Programming

1. Consider the following problem. Acme Grocery Store desires to have a Price Planning Program written. It should input their master file of inventory. Each line contains an item number, a product description that is surrounded by double quote marks, the quantity on hand and the wholesale unit price. Once the basic data have been loaded, the program prompts the user to enter a markup percentage, such as 10.5%. The program then calculates and displays the total net profit to be made if all of the inventory is sold at this higher price. It then prompts for another markup percentage and continues until EOF is reached.

The programmer was very shaky on how to do Top-down designs. This is what he came up with.

```
Main while
            GetMarkup
                    InputMarkup
        LoadTheArray
        InputProductDescription
        TotalProfit
```

When he floundered while trying to implement the program, he asked for your aid. You wisely asked to see the design. You see at once that he has pseudo coding and designing mixed up. Draw a more nearly optimum Top-down design that would better fit this problem.

2. Grateful for helping him get a firmer grasp on design issues, the programmer next tries to follow the company practice of stub testing. Thus, he writes the **main()** function shown below.

```cpp
const int NAMELEN = 22;
const int MAXRECS = 10000;
struct COSTREC {
  int itemNum;
  char desc[NAMELEN];
  int qty;
  double cost;
};
int main () {
  COSTREC inventory[10000];
  int numRecs = LoadTheArray(inventory, MAXRECS);
  double markupPercentage;
  double profit;
  while (GetMarkUp (cin, markupPercentage)) {
   profit= CalculateTotalProfit(inventory,numRecs,markupPercentage);
  }
  return 0;
}
```

However, the programmer is unsure of what the functions' prototypes should be. Write the necessary prototypes for the needed functions that **main()** is calling.

3. Grateful for your assistance on the prototypes, he next discovers that he does not know how to implement stubs and asks you to help out. Write the needed stubs so that **main()** will actually run.

4. The programmer next ran into trouble while implementing the **LoadTheArray()** function. Here is what he has thus far. Correct his coding so that the function works according to the problem specifications.

```cpp
int LoadTheArray (COSTREC& array, int limit) {
    ifstream infile ("database.txt");
    if (!infile) {
        cerr << "Error: cannot open database.txt file\n";
        return 1;
    }
    int j = 0;
    char c;
    while (infile >> array[j].itemnum >> c && j<max) {
        infile.getline (array[j].desc, NAMELEN);
        infile >> array[j].qty >> array[j].cost;
    }
    if (j==max && !infile.eof() && infile >> c) {
        cerr << "Error: array bounds exceeded\n";
        return 2;
    }
    infile.close();
    return j;
}
```

5. Next, the programmer turned his attention to the profit calculation function. After much struggling, he once again turns to you for aid. Fix this function so that it works properly.

```cpp
double CalculateTotalProfit (COSTREC inventory[], int numRecs,
                             double markupPercentage) {
    double sum = 0;
    for (int j=0; j<numRecs; j++) {
        sum += inventory[j].qty * inventory[j].cost * markupPercentage;
    }
    return sum;
}
```

Programming Problems

Problem Pgm01-1 Day in the Week Program

Write a function called **DayInWeek()** that is passed the day of the week and an output stream. It displays the string name onto that output stream. For example, the function is passed the number 1 and it displays the string Sunday; 7, displays Saturday. On output, left align the string names in a field of width 10. The function should return the output stream it was passed. Bulletproof the function so that no matter what is passed the function does not crash.

Next, write a **main()** function to thoroughly test the function. Make up a set of test oracles which, if the function passes all the tests, guarantees the function works correctly in all circumstances. Make sure that the function is properly documented.

Problem Pgm01-2 Displaying Pet Types

Acme Pet Store handles several types of pets. Within the various programs that the company has, the pet's type is stored as an enumerated data type. Of course, with enums, the real problem is handling the input and output operations. Thus, it makes good sense to write a generic pair of functions to handle the pet type I/O. Then all programs can reuse these two functions.

The pet type enum is defined as follows.
```
enum PetType {Unknown, Dog, Cat, Gerbil, Rat, Snake, Hamster};
```
For input, the pet type is always a single letter, d for dog, C for cat and so on. Input should not be case dependent. For output, the character string types should be displayed using all lowercase letters left aligned in a 7-character width field. The prototypes of the two functions have been defined as shown.
```
istream& InputPetType (istream& in, PetType& pet);
ostream& OutputPetType (ostream& out, PetType pet);
```

Implement these two functions. Be sure to provide appropriate documentation of the functions. Then write a **main()** function to thoroughly test these two functions. Again, design a series testing oracles that fully test these functions. Place a major effort on ensuring that these functions work properly in all circumstances; avoid mostly working software.

Chapter 2—Mechanics of Functional Abstraction

Introduction

Having explored the concepts of functional abstraction in the last chapter, we are now prepared to extend those concepts to larger, more complex programs. It is one thing to handle the abstraction for a program that is to input a day of the week number and display the corresponding day name string and it is quite another thing to deal with the abstraction necessary for a larger program. One of my production programs available on the Internet, the Hunter Database Collection Manager, has an exe size of just over 1M. This is considered a "larger" program. The C++ source statements simply cannot be placed into a single cpp file. Instead, the source occupies nearly 500 file cpp files. The aim of this chapter is to understand how to handle the abstraction of larger programs including multiple source files. Programs that use multiple-dimensioned arrays and structures are used to illustrate these principles.

Larger programs are a collection of separate cpp files (that contain the source code implementations) and user-written header files (that contain the definitions of things). If you count the number of lines in the sample program from the previous chapter, it contains a respectful 166 lines! If you open up that source file in your Visual C++ editor window, to view it requires a significant amount of vertical scrolling!

Placing everything in a single source file creates two major problems when you implement larger programs. One, because of the huge size, you cannot **find** things; vast amounts of scrolling are required. Indeed, over the years I have discovered that there seems to be a relationship between the size of a file and the number of errors it contains. In my opinion, as the number of lines in a file increases, the number of errors in it goes up exponentially! For those of us that hate "mostly working" software, this is a serious consideration! Two, program compilation times become lengthy. If everything is contained in one huge file and if you make a tiny change in one small function, the compiler must recompile the entire huge file, not just the small portion that changed. Thus, because of the inability to rapidly find things and elongated compile times, we must find a way to break programs down into smaller physical units. Once you have gotten familiar with the process of making multi-file programs, you will not want to go back to writing monolithic source files.

User Written Header Files

You have been using system header files since you coded your first C++ "Hello World" program. We code
```
#include <iostream>
```
or if using the older iostreams,
```
#include <iostream.h>
```
The # sign indicates a command to the preprocessor. The **include** means to copy the contents of the following file and place them at this location in the source file. The <> signify that this is a system header file and to

look for this file in the **\include** folders located in the folder in which the compiler has been installed. The actual filename is coded between the angle brackets. Typically a header file has the extension of .h. However, the definitions of the newer iostreams that are used with the **namespace std** use **no** file extensions. This is because the .h extension was already in use. Rather than use some nonstandard file extension, the newer ones simply leave off the extension. If you look in the **\include** folder under the folder in which you installed the compiler, you will see files **iostream.h** and **iostream**.

A header file is a definition type of file. That is, it contains definitions of things such as constant ints, #defines, structure templates, function prototypes, includes for other header files and so on. A header file ideally should contain **no** actual coding—coding is implementation and should be in the cpp files.

To illustrate header files, let's examine the situation at Acme Hardware Stores, Inc. Acme owns a chain of stores. Each store has the potential to stock any number of company sanctioned items. The definition of an item is shown using the following structure template. Remember, a structure template is the model or blueprint that the compiler follows when actually making an instance of the structure. The structure groups a number of related fields of information into a single record of data. The name that we give the structure, its structure tag, becomes a **typedef** name with C++ compilers so that we can create instances of that structure by using the tag as a data type. Here is the inventory record that Acme uses.

```
const int DESCRLEN = 21;
struct INVREC {
   long    itemNum;
   char    description[DESCRLEN];
   int     qtyOnHand;
   double unitCost;
};
```

The **main()** function could create an instance of this structure by coding

```
INVREC invRec;
```

Recall that the members within a structure are accessed using the dot(.) operator.

```
invRec.qtyOnHand, invRec.description, invRec.itemNum
```

If a program for a single store wished to input all of the stock records that that store had, the program would define an array of **INVREC**s, where **MAXITEMS** contained the maximum number of possible items.

```
INVREC stock[MAXITEMS];
```

A subscript is then used to access the specific item in the array, such as

```
stock[i].itemNum, stock[i].description, stock[i].qtyOnHand.
```

However, if Acme Corporate Headquarters wished to have a program that inputted the stock contained in all four stores, a two-dimensional array would be defined.

```
INVREC stock[NUMSTORES][MAXITEMS];
```

Now two subscripts are needed to access a specific store's specific item data

```
stock[store][i].itemNum, stock[store][i].description,
stock[store][i].qtyOnHand.
```

With these basics in mind, here is the problem facing the Acme company. Obviously, there are likely to be many programs that use the inventory data. Thus, many programs are going to have to define this **INVREC** structure. For example, Acme may find that a total of twenty programs are going to need this structure. Certainly, it could be defined within each of the programs. However, if that were done, consider what would happen if management decided tomorrow to add a new field to the record, such as **retailCost**? What would happen if the length of the **description** was increased to 31 characters? The programming staff would have a miniature nightmare on their hands. They would have to find all the various definitions of the structure among all of the hundreds of programs in production and make the same change to every one of them. This is a tedious and very error prone task indeed. Think what would result if they forgot to change it in one or more programs? A disaster at production run time occurs.

Instead, suppose that Acme created a single header file that defined this **INVREC** structure and had all twenty programs simply include this single header file. If changes occur, one programmer can change the single header file and simply recompile the programs to implement the changes in all programs. What a difference in quality control! No more nightmares. Placing the definitions of items in header files and then including them in one or more programs goes a long way toward the "reuse of coding" that is so important in today's programming environment.

Mechanics of Header File Construction

The contents of the header file for the inventory records would be as shown.
file: InvRec.h

```
const int DESCRLEN = 21; // length of the description

/**************************************************/
/*                                                */
/* Acme Stock Inventory Record                    */
/*                                                */
/**************************************************/
struct INVREC {
  long   itemNum;                // Acme stock number
  char   description[DESCRLEN];  // product description
  int    qtyOnHand;             // store's qty on hand
  double unitCost;              // Acme's cost of the item
};
```

The next question is how would other cpp files include this new header file? The answer depends upon where the **InvRec.h** file is actually stored on disk. One will certainly **not** code the following.

```
#include <InvRec.h> // not this way
```

This is saying to look for **InvRec.h** in the \include folders where the compiler is installed! **Never** place user header files into the **include** folders of the compiler. Compilers get updated, replaced and moved. User-written header files are never ever placed into the compiler include folders. Thus, we cannot use the < > notation.

Instead we surround the filename with " " marks.

```
#include "InvRec.h"
```

The " " tell the compiler that this is a user header file located in the user's folders. Specifically, if no path information is included, the compiler looks for **InvRec.h** in the current project folder where the project cpp files are located. For most student programs this is precisely where the header files belong.

The compiler allows for an absolute or relative path as well. In the case of the Acme structure, since each of the twenty programs that need to use this header file would be located in its own separate project folders, the above technique needs to be refined. Otherwise, we would have to make twenty copies of that header file and put on into each of the twenty project folders, thereby losing most of the benefits of coding it once and reusing it twenty times! Instead, there should be one single company production header file folder, say **D:\AcmeProduction\Includes**. Now the **#include** would be coded in this manner.

```
#include "d:\\AcmeProduction\\Includes\\InvRec.h"
```
Don't forget the double \\; a single \ starts an escape sequence in C++.

Relative paths could also be used. Suppose that Pgm1 needs to use this header file and it is located in the **D:\AcmeProduction\Pgm1** folder. One could code a relative path as follows.

```
#include "..\\Includes\\InvRec.h"
```

All of the remaining examples in this text assume that user header files are located in the project folder with the cpp files that make up the program.

Placement of Header File Includes in a Cpp File

With the header file created and located in the project's folder. Let's see how to include it in the **main()** function's cpp file. Normally, any given cpp file begins with one or more **#include** statements that bring in the definitions and prototypes of the language elements and functions, such as **iostream.h**. One should always include one's own personal header files after including the any needed system headers. Thus, the coding for the **main()** function's cpp file begins

```
#include <iostream>
#include <iomanip>
#include <cmath>
using namespace std;

#include "InvRec.h"

int main () {
```

One should not include one's own header files before including those for the system definitions. Why? Namespace collisions can occur. To illustrate this, let us suppose that Acme began an Internet Online Service and our program decided to store the data in a structure. We store that structure definition in a personal header file called **ios.h** in our project's folder. The file looks like this.
File: ios.h

```
struct ios {
   ... // various member fields are defined here
};
```
Now we code the **main()** function's cpp file as follows, placing our header file first.

```
#include "ios.h"
#include <iostream>
```

```
using namespace std;
int main () {
```

What results? A huge number of compiler errors result, complaining about the **ios iostream** class. All the errors are on lines contained in the various system header files, like **iostream.h**. These are occurring because of a misfortunate choice of a structure name. There is an object-oriented iostream class called **ios** that is included and it is a part of all the **iostream** classes. Since we included our definition first, it overrides the C++ system header definitions and thus all of the subsequent **iostream** uses of **ios** end up referring to our new **ios** structure. Piles of errors result, giving the appearance that something is horribly wrong with our system header files! I have had students decide that their compiler must have some how gotten corrupted and totally reinstalled the compiler. Of course, it did not fix anything.

If you include your personal headers before the system header files, then any conflicts are reported as error messages within the system header files, not your header file. This makes tracking down the real cause very difficult indeed.

If we include our headers after the system headers, then the errors are reported within our coding. The real source of the error is then more readily found. Here is the proper way to handle the above example.

```
#include <iostream>
#include "ios.h"
using namespace std;
int main () {
```

All the errors point to our structure redefinition of the **ios** symbol.

#ifndef/#define Logic or #pragma once

So far, making our own header files to contain definitions of things looks straight forward. However, there is another vital detail that must be understood and circumvented. To see this problem in action, consider this situation of multiple structure definitions.

Acme uses dates frequently throughout their collections of programs. To standardize the way dates are stored, the following header file has been created and used by all programs.

File: date.h

```
struct Date {
    int month;
    int day;
    int year;
};
```

Next, a customer record structure is defined, but it needs to use an instance of the **Date** structure as one of its members. Oops. Thus, the **customer.h** file must include the **date.h** file. Also, since there can be some function prototypes in the customer header file, any needed system headers must be included. We have then the following for **customer.h**.

File: customer.h

Beginning Data Structures in C++

```
#include <iostream>
using namespace std;
#include "date.h"

struct Customer {
  Date serviceLaunchDate;
  Date warrantyExpirationDate;
  ... // many other field definitions
};


// needed function prototypes
istream& InputCustomer (istream& in, Customer& customer);
ostream& OutputCustomer (ostream& out, const Customer& cus);
```

Notice that the **iostream** header must be included because the function prototypes are using references to the streams. If you do not include the system **iostream** header, the compiler does not know what **istream** and **ostream** are and generates error messages. Likewise, without the inclusion of **date.h**, the compiler does not know what a **Date** object is that is. Finally, notice that the **OutputCustomer()** defines the customer as a constant reference to a **Customer** structure instance. Remember, an "output" function should not under any circumstances alter the contents of the data that it is to output.

Next, the company defines a service call structure which is generated in response to a technician visiting the customer and performing the needed repairs. The definition is stored in the **service.h** header file.
File: service.h

```
#include <iostream>
using namespace std;

#include "date.h"

struct ServiceCall {
  Date servicedDate;
  ... // many other field definitions
};

// needed function prototypes
istream& InputServiceCallData (istream& in,
                               ServiceCall& sc);
ostream& OutputServiceCallData (ostream& in,
                                const ServiceCall& sc);
```

Again, notice that the **date.h** header file must be included here because of the use of a **Date** instance in the **ServiceCall** structure.

Now let's look at the **main()** function of the Process Service Call Program. The coding begins as follows.

```
#include <iostream>
using namespace std;
#include "customer.h"
#include "service.h"
```

```
int main () {
  Customer    customer;
  ServiceCall serviceCall;

  InputCustomer (cin, customer);
  InputServiceCallData (cin, serviceCall);
  ...
```

As it stands, it looks well designed. However, it will not compile. Follow what the compiler does as it attempts to build the program. First, it is instructed to include the **customer.h** file. It does so, but that file instructs it to subsequently bring in the **date.h** file. It does so and now the compiler sees a **Date** structure definition and then a **Customer** structure definition. All is well. Next, the compiler is instructed to include the **service.h** file. It does so, but that file also instructs it to bring in the **date.h** file and it does that action. Now the compiler has the following structure definitions:

```
struct Date
struct Customer
struct Date
struct ServiceCall
```

And the compiler generates the error message that **Date** already exists: "error C2011: 'Date' : 'struct' type redefinition."

This situation, known as **circular headers**, occurs quite frequently in larger programs. So we must know how to deal with it. The solution is to instruct the compiler to only bring in one copy of the actual definition of the **Date** structure per cpp file. This is accomplished by using some additional preprocessor directives.

The directive **#ifndef** is a conditional if-then-else type logic command. It is saying if the following symbol is not yet defined and known to you, compiler, please include all of the following lines until you reach the **#endif** statement, and in any case, include all lines coded after the #**endif**. Thus, the **#ifndef** and **#endif** occur in pairs. If you forget your ending **#endif**, the compiler eats lines until it finds one. The symbol to be found is coded after the **#ifndef**. That symbol must be a unique one—one which would never conflict with any other name in the entire file. By convention, most programmers use a name that is some variation of the header file name using all uppercase letters. Thus, the **date.h** file must be rewritten as follows. File: date.h

```
#ifndef DATE_H
#define DATE_H

struct Date {
  int month;
  int day;
  int year;
};
#endif
```

Notice the vitally important second line, **#define DATE_H**. This is the first line that is actually included if the compiler has not yet seen the symbol **DATE_H**. This **#define** line then actually defines the symbol we are checking. Normally, we provide some value after the name such as **#define MAX 100**. Here, we give the symbol no value; however, the compiler provides a simple "true," the symbol is defined.

To understand better how this works, let's examine how compilers operate. When a compiler begins the compilation of a file, it creates a "**symbol dictionary**" whose entries contain the name of the symbol and other pertinent details. Initially, as it starts to compile **main.cpp** in this example, it is empty. The second line includes **customer.h**. The compiler copies that file into the program, but then discovers the include for **date.h**. It then copies in the **date.h** file contents. Now it sees, the **#ifndef** logic. It looks at its symbol table, which thus far has only the **iostream** definitions in it from the first line that included **iostream.h**. The symbol **DATE_H** is not there, so it places all of the contents of **date.h** down through the **#endif** statement along with any lines that come after the **#endif** into the main program for compilation. However, the second line in **date.h** tells the compiler to now define that symbol, **DATE_H**. So it makes an entry in its symbol dictionary for **DATE_H**. Next, it sees the include for **service.h** and copies that file into the program. Finally, it copies in the **date.h** file as instructed within **service.h.** However, the **#ifndef** logic is then processed. The **#ifndef** causes the compiler again to look to see if the symbol **DATE_H** is in its symbol dictionary. It is there this time. Thus, the compiler only includes all coding found in **date.h** after the **#endif**. Of course, there is no coding after that point. The result: only one copy of the structure definition for **Date** is included in the compilation.

#pragma once

The #pragma once is a new addition that greatly simplifies the process. It replaces the #ifndef logic entirely. One merely places this line as the first line in the header file and the compiler automatically only includes this file's content one time. This makes a more compact method.

File: date.h

```
#pragma once

struct Date {
  int month;
  int day;
  int year;
};
```

With header files, you often do not know all of the uses that a specific header file may have when you first write it. Thus, the following rule applies always.

Rule: The contents of every header file should be wrapped with #ifndef/#define logic or #pragma once.

Why? Imagine a large program with many header files and source cpp files. If the header files are not protected against multiple inclusions, then it is highly likely that multiple inclusions will occur. The resultant bombardment of compiler error messages can be terrific. It is no fun at all to try to guess long after writing the header files which ones absolutely must have the **#ifndef/#define or #pragma once** logic in them and then go back and put it in.

Thus, from this point forward in this text, all header files will be wrapped with **#ifndef/#define or #pragma once** logic. Then, there cannot be any surprises waiting at compile-time, no matter how the header files are included. Yes, in the above example, the customer and service header files should also be wrapped. Here is what they should be.

File: customer.h

```
#pragma once
#include <iostream>
using namespace std;
#include "date.h"

struct Customer {
  Date serviceLaunchDate;
  Date warrantyExpirationDate;
 ... // many other field definitions
};

// needed function prototypes
istream& InputCustomer (istream& in, Customer& customer);
ostream& OutputCustomer (ostream& out, const Customer& cus);
```

File: service.h

```
#pragma once
#include <iostream>
using namespace std;
#include "date.h"

struct ServiceCall {
  Date servicedDate;
 ... // many other field definitions
};

// needed function prototypes
istream& InputServiceCallData (istream& in,
                               ServiceCall& sc);
ostream& OutputServiceCallData (ostream& in,
                                const ServiceCall& sc);
```

Multiple Cpp Files in a Program

Larger programs often consist of several cpp source files as well as one or more user header files. There are many benefits from breaking a larger program into several smaller cpp files. Indeed, it is harder to envision the code reuse factor if that code is buried in a huge single cpp file. When splitting a large program into smaller cpp files, several key benefits occur at once. But to understand how these come about, let's see how the Visual C++ compiler handles the situation of multiple cpp files for a single program.

Microsoft's Visual C++ compiler requires a project file in order to build a program. The project file contains the compiler options required to make the program. It contains also what files make up the program. We know that to make a new project, we select File-New and then Project and select the Win32 Console Application type. We also know that once the empty project has been built, we do another File – New and choose cpp file. The compiler adds this file to the project. But what about multiple cpp files?

To add additional cpp files to the project, just continue to choose File – New cpp file and each of these are added to the project. Similarly with user header files, choose File – New and choose C++ header file.

If you have the various files on a floppy disk and wish to build the program, as usual, copy the files to a program folder on the hard disk and make a new project. Then right click on the Program Files label in the File View tab window and choose Add Files to Project as you normally would do. However, when the File Open dialog appears, multi-select all the cpp and header files desired. Click Ok. You should then see all of the cpp and header files listed in the tree view.

The first time you choose Build the program, all of the individual cpp files must be compiled into their corresponding obj files. Then, the Linker joins all the pieces, the obj files, into the single program exe file.

On larger programs, the initial build can be lengthy. However, the situation after that initial build is very different from the situation in which there is only one really large cpp file. To see this difference, imagine that you need to make one small change in one function. If this was the one giant cpp file, then to build the program, the compiler must recompile the whole file, even though there is only that one small change. However, if there are many smaller cpp files making up the program, then only that one file that contains the change must be recompiled and then the Linker joins the obj files into the exe. This can greatly decrease the total time it takes to rebuild a program! The larger the total program, the more significant this speed up becomes.

The second major benefit is a vast decrease in vertical scrolling required to view the source. Remember, the more you have to scroll to view the source, the greater the chances for errors appearing. Additionally, with multiple files, you can have several editor windows open at the same time. This allows you to look at the place in one file where a function that is contained in another file is actually called, while viewing that called function in another source window. This allows you to see how you are calling the function as you examine the function coding itself.

All programs in this text from now on will consist of multiple cpp files and one or more user header files.

Application Header Files

Normally, a header file is used so that its definitions can be shared among many programs. However, when one has say ten cpp files making up the larger program, a new situation arises. At the start of each file, one must include the necessary system headers, such as iostream, any needed const ints and such, any needed user header files such as invrec.h, and define all of the needed prototypes. Of course, these must be coded at the start of each cpp file. This creates a lot of typing and is hard to maintain if changes are needed, remembering to make the same change to all ten files.

This tedious situation is often resolved by making what's called an application specific header file. This header file contains nothing that is going to be shared among other programs, rather it contains what needs to be shared among all of the cpp files making up this program. An application header file usually contains all of the system includes, all of the const ints, all of the included user header files, and all of the function prototypes that the entire program needs. Then, each cpp file only needs to begin by including this one, single header file instead of all of the pieces it brings in with it. This makes maintenance much easier because there is only one place a change must be made, the application header file.

The program sample for this chapter makes use of just such an application header file as well as a user header file.

An Example: Stock On-hand Analysis Program

Let's return to the initial example of the Acme Stock Inventory problem at the beginning of this chapter. Recall that the structure definition was in the **InvRec.h** header file. Acme Corporate Headquarters, which owns four stores in our area, wants a program to produce a stock on-hand analysis report. Acme Corporation handles up to 1000 different items. However, each store does not necessarily have all 1000 items in stock at any one time. Each store has its own inventory database file that contains all of the items that it has in stock and each database file is sorted into item number order. There is a corporate master file that lists all of the item numbers and descriptions that the company handles; this file is also in increasing item number order.

The analysis report looks like this.

```
                Acme Stock Analysis Report

 Item     Total     Store 1      Store 2      Store 3      Store 4
Number   Quantity  Qty/Percent  Qty/Percent  Qty/Percent  Qty/Percent

12345      100      20/ 20%      50/ 50%      30/ 30%       0/  0%
```

Certainly, the **main()** function can define a two-dimensional array to store the data.
```
INVREC stock[NUMSTORES][MAXITEMS];
```
However, how can we load this array properly? We have four separate input files and any specific stock item may not be present in any specific file! We need an algorithm, a method, to handle the input operation.

Beginning Data Structures in C++

Since all files are sorted into increasing item number order, we could use a merge type of operation. That is, input the first inventory record from each of the four files. Then, compare the item numbers and insert the lowest item number into the array of the corresponding store. Then, if any of the others have that same item number, insert those records into the array. For stores which do not have that item, insert a dummy value of 0 for the quantity on hand. Then input another record for each of the stores that had that item. And repeat the operation. However, when one store runs out of data, we must continue with the remaining three stores, then the remaining two stores and then the last store, assuming they had different numbers of records. This approach would be exhaustive to code, error prone and lengthy. We need a better way, a faster way, one that is less error prone.

We can make use of the corporate master file. Suppose that we input it and store just the item numbers into a separate but parallel array called **itemToIndex**. We can use **itemToIndex** to convert any incoming item number from a specific store record into the corresponding subscript for that item in the main **stock** array. Illustration 2.1 shows the idea in operation.

Illustration 2.1

For a Store in the

stock Array	**itemToIndex**
[0] 12345	[0] 12345
[1] 23456	[1] 23456
[2] 34567	[2] 34567
[3] 45678	[3] 45678
[4] 56789	[4] 56789

For store 0, we input a stock inventory line. We match that item number in the **itemToIndex** array. Say that we input item number 23456 from store 0. We store that stock data in **stock[0][1].** We find the [1] by matching 23456 with the **itemToIndex** array and use the matching subscript to access the **stock** array. This makes a much nicer implementation.

Since there can be a rather large number of items, to speed up the matching process, let's take advantage of the fact that the master file is sorted into increasing numerical order on item numbers. We should use a binary search to find the matching item number in the **itemToIndex** array.

Next, do a Top-down design to decompose the problem into its major functions. Figure 2.1 shows the design I chose.

Here is the completed program, **Pgm02a**. Notice that the header file, **InvRec.h**, has been expanded to contain all of the system header files that the program needs, all the **const int** items and the prototypes of our functions. Each cpp file then includes this header to gain access to all of the definitions. On this program, I got a bit carried away with making each function reside in its own cpp file. I did this to illustrate how the process operates. However, **LoadStoresData()** and **LoadStore()** are so closely related, that I chose to put both in a single cpp file.

If you have trouble understanding the following coding, please go to the Appendix section entitled **A Review of Array and Structure Processing**.

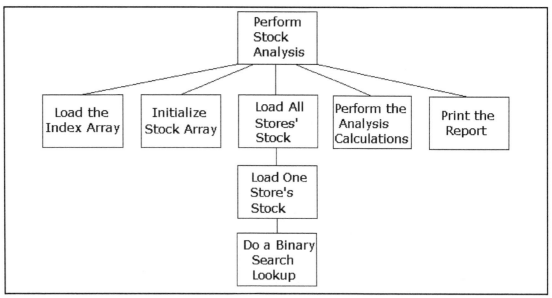

Figure 2.1 Top-down Design of the Stock Analysis Program

```
Inventory Record Definition (InvRec.h)

 1 #pragma once
 2
 3 const int DESCRLEN = 21; // length of the description
 4
 5 /******************************************************/
 6 /*                                                    */
 7 /* Acme Stock Inventory Record                        */
 8 /*                                                    */
 9 /******************************************************/
10
11 struct INVREC {
12   long    itemNum;              // Acme stock number
13   char    description[DESCRLEN]; // product description
14   int     qtyOnHand;            // store's qty on hand
15   double  unitCost;             // Acme's cost of the item
16 };
```

```
Application Header File (Pgm02a.h)

 1 #pragma once
 2 #include <iostream>
 3 #include <iomanip>
 4 #include <fstream>
 5 using namespace std;
```

```
 6
 7 #include "InvRec.h"
 8
 9 const int MAXSTORES = 4;    // 4 total Acme Stores
10 const int MAXITEMS = 1000; // max number of inventory items
11
12 int  LoadIndex (long itemToIndex[]);
13 void InitializeStockArray (INVREC stock[][MAXITEMS],
14                            long itemToIndex[], int numItems);
15 void LoadStoresData(INVREC stock[][MAXITEMS], long itemToIndex[],
16                     int numItems);
17 bool LoadStore (INVREC stock[][MAXITEMS], long itemToIndex[],
18                 int numItems, istream& infile, int store);
19 bool BinarySearch (const long id[], int num, long findId,
20                    int& foundIndex);
21 void PerformAnalysis (const INVREC stock[][MAXITEMS],
22     int numItems, long totalQty[], double percents[][MAXITEMS]);
23 void PrintReport (const INVREC stock[][MAXITEMS], int numItems,
24                   const long totalQty[],
25                   const double percents[][MAXITEMS]);
```

The Main Function (main.cpp)

```
 1 #include "Pgm02a.h"
 2
 3 /****************************************************/
 4 /*                                                  */
 5 /* Acme Stock Analysis Program                      */
 6 /*                                                  */
 7 /****************************************************/
 8
 9 int main () {
10  INVREC stock[MAXSTORES][MAXITEMS]; // the stock for each store
11  long   itemToIndex[MAXITEMS];      // the complete item numbers
12  int    numItems;                   // total number of items
13
14  // load the master list of stock item numbers
15  numItems = LoadIndex (itemToIndex);
16
17  // install all stock numebrs and set stores' qty to 0
18  InitializeStockArray (stock, itemToIndex, numItems);
19
20  // load all of the store data
21  LoadStoresData (stock, itemToIndex, numItems);
22
23  long   totalQty[MAXITEMS] = {0};            // company total qty
24  double percents[MAXSTORES][MAXITEMS] = {{0}}; // store percents
25
26  // perform the percentage analysis
```

```
27  PerformAnalysis (stock, numItems, totalQty, percents);
28
29  // display the final report of the analysis
30  PrintReport (stock, numItems, totalQty, percents);
31
32  return 0;
33 }
```

LoadIndex.cpp - Load the Corporate Item Numbers(Implementation)File

```
 1 #include "Pgm02a.h"
 2
 3 /***********************************************************/
 4 /*                                                       */
 5 /* LoadIndex: loads the master file of item numbers      */
 6 /*       fills itemToIndex array with the item numbers    */
 7 /*       from the master file                            */
 8 /*                                                       */
 9 /* returns the number of items in the itemToIndex array  */
10 /*                                                       */
11 /***********************************************************/
12
13 int LoadIndex (long itemToIndex[]) {
14  // open the master file
15  ifstream infile ("master.txt");
16  if (!infile) {
17   cerr << "Error: cannot open the master.txt file\n";
18   exit (1);
19  }
20
21  int i = 0;
22  while (i<MAXITEMS && infile >> itemToIndex[i]) {
23   infile.ignore(100, '\n'); // skip remaining fields
24   i++;
25  }
26
27  // guard against too much data
28  char c;
29  if (i == MAXITEMS && infile >> c) {
30   cerr << "Error: too many items in the master file\n";
31   infile.close();
32   exit (2);
33  }
34
35  // guard against bad data entry
36  if (!infile.eof()) {
37   cerr << "Error: bad input data in the master.txt file";
38   cerr << "It was on line " << i+1 << endl;
39   infile.close();
```

```
40    exit (3);
41    }
42    infile.close();
43
44    //return the number of items in the array
45    return i;
46  }
```

InitializeStockArray.cpp - Init Stock Array to Corp. Item Numbers

```
 1 #include "Pgm02a.h"
 2
 3 /*****************************************************/
 4 /*                                                   */
 5 /* InitializeStockArray: copies into each store's    */
 6 /*        itemNum the corresponding master itemNum    */
 7 /*        and sets the corresponding qtyOnHand to 0   */
 8 /*        it also clears decription and unitCost      */
 9 /*                                                   */
10 /*****************************************************/
11
12 void InitializeStockArray (INVREC stock[][MAXITEMS],
13                            long itemToIndex[], int numItems) {
14  for (int i=0; i<numItems; i++) {
15   for (int j=0; j<MAXSTORES; j++) {
16    stock[j][i].itemNum = itemToIndex[i];
17    stock[j][i].qtyOnHand = 0;
18    stock[j][i].description[0] = 0;
19    stock[j][i].unitCost = 0;
20   }
21  }
22 }
```

LoadStoresData.cpp - Load All the Stores' Data into Stock Array

```
 1 #include "Pgm02a.h"
 2
 3 /*****************************************************/
 4 /*                                                   */
 5 /* LoadStoresData: load all of the stores' data items */
 6 /*    for each store, it opens the data file and      */
 7 /*        calls LoadStore to input its data           */
 8 /*                                                   */
 9 /*****************************************************/
10
11 void LoadStoresData(INVREC stock[][MAXITEMS], long itemToIndex[],
12                     int numItems) {
13  char filenames[MAXSTORES][256] = {"store1.txt", "store2.txt",
```

```
14   "store3.txt", "store4.txt"};
15  for (int i=0; i<MAXSTORES; i++) {
16   ifstream infile (filenames[i]);
17   if (!infile) {
18    cerr << "Error: cannot open store file: " << filenames[i]
19         << endl;
20    exit (4);
21   }
22   if (!LoadStore (stock, itemToIndex, numItems, infile, i)) {
23    cerr << "The file was: " << filenames[i] << endl;
24    infile.close ();
25    exit (6);
26   }
27   infile.close();
28  }
29 }
30
31 /********************************************************/
32 /*                                                      */
33 /* LoadStore: loads a store data file into the          */
34 /*            corresponding items of the stock array    */
35 /*   The itemNum is matched to the itemToIndex set and  */
36 /*        the matching subscript is used to store the   */
37 /*        data into the stock array                     */
38 /*                                                      */
39 /********************************************************/
40
41 bool LoadStore (INVREC stock[][MAXITEMS], long itemToIndex[],
42                 int numItems, istream& infile, int store) {
43  INVREC in;
44  int index;
45  int line = 0;
46  while (infile >> in.itemNum >> ws) {
47   infile.get (in.description, sizeof (in.description));
48   infile >> in.qtyOnHand >> in.unitCost;
49   if (BinarySearch (itemToIndex, numItems, in.itemNum, index)) {
50    stock[store][index] = in;
51   }
52   else {
53    cerr << "Error: incorrect stock number in store " << store + 1
54         << "\nIt was: " << in.itemNum << endl;
55    return false;
56   }
57   line++;
58  }
59  if (!infile.eof()) {
60   cerr << "Error: bad data in line " << line + 1 << endl;
61   return false;
62  }
63  return true;
```

```
64 }
```

```
BinarySearch.cpp - Does a Binary Search for Matching Item Nums

 1 #include "Pgm02a.h"
 2
 3 /**********************************************************/
 4 /*                                                        */
 5 /* BinarySearch: finds a matching id                      */
 6 /*    returns true if findId is in id array and foundIndex*/
 7 /*                 contains the matching subscript        */
 8 /*                                                        */
 9 /*    returns false if findId is not in the id array      */
10 /*                 and foundIndex contains the subscript  */
11 /*                 of where it should be if it were there */
12 /*                                                        */
13 /**********************************************************/
14
15 bool  BinarySearch (const long id[], int num, long findId,
16                      int& foundIndex) {
17  int firstidx = 0;
18  int lastidx = num - 1;
19  int middleidx;
20  bool foundMatch = false;
21  while (lastidx >= firstidx && !foundMatch) {
22   middleidx = (firstidx + lastidx) / 2;
23   if (findId < id[middleidx])
24     lastidx = middleidx - 1;
25   else if (findId > id[middleidx])
26     firstidx = middleidx + 1;
27   else foundMatch = true;
28  }
29  foundIndex = middleidx;
30  return foundMatch;
31 }
```

```
PerformAnalysis.cpp - Does the Analysis Calculations

 1 #include "Pgm02a.h"
 2
 3 /**********************************************************/
 4 /*                                                        */
 5 /* PerformAnalysis: calculates the total quantity on hand */
 6 /*       from all stores and determines each store's      */
 7 /*       percentage of the total quantity on hand         */
 8 /*                                                        */
 9 /**********************************************************/
10
```

```
11 void PerformAnalysis (const INVREC stock[][MAXITEMS],
12                        int numItems, long totalQty[],
13                        double percents[][MAXITEMS]) {
14 int store, item;
15
16 // calculate the total quantity on hand for each item
17 for (store=0; store<MAXSTORES; store++) {
18  for (item=0; item<numItems; item++) {
19   totalQty[item] += stock[store][item].qtyOnHand;
20  }
21 }
22 for (store=0; store<MAXSTORES; store++) {
23  for (item=0; item<numItems; item++) {
24   percents[store][item] = stock[store][item].qtyOnHand * 100
25                          / totalQty[item];
26  }
27 }
28 }
```

PrintReport.cpp - Prints the Analysis Report

```
 1 #include "Pgm02a.h"
 2
 3 /*******************************************************/
 4 /*                                                     */
 5 /* PrintReport: displays on cout the Analysis Report   */
 6 /*                                                     */
 7 /*******************************************************/
 8
 9 void PrintReport (const INVREC stock[][MAXITEMS], int numItems,
10       const long totalQty[], const double percents[][MAXITEMS]) {
11 // print the heading and column headings
12 cout << "                 Acme Stock Analysis Report\n\n"
13       << " Item     Total     Store 1     Store 2     Store 3     "
14          "Store 4\n"
15       << "Number Quantity   Qty/Percent Qty/Percent Qty/Percent "
16          "Qty/Percent\n\n";
17 cout << fixed << setprecision(0);
19
20 // display one line for each item the company sells
21 for (int item=0; item<numItems; item++) {
22  // display the item number and total corporate quantity on hand
23  cout << setw(5) << stock[0][item].itemNum
24       << setw(8) << totalQty[item] << " ";
25  // display each store's quantity and percentage of the totalqty
26  for (int store=0; store<MAXSTORES; store++) {
27   cout << setw(7) << stock[store][item].qtyOnHand << "/"
28        << setw(3) << percents[store][item] << "%";
29  }
```

```
30    cout << endl;
31  }
32 }
```

A Set of Testing Oracles for Pgm02a

The next step is to design some testing oracles to verify the Stock Analysis Program works according to specifications. I approach testing this way. First, design one or more tests that can easily show that the program does what it is supposed to do, if everything goes as planned. Second, design a series of tests that represent unusual things happening that are not supposed to occur, such as too many items for the array, non-numeric data in the numeric fields and values that are out of range, for example.

In the accompanying samples, you should find several subfolders to **Pgm02a** called **TestSetn**, where n is a number. Each of these folders contains one of the following test oracles. To use them, simply copy the contents of the test folder and paste them into the project folder where the program expects to find the files. Then, run the program.

TestSet1 should show that the program does calculate the right results. I have inserted a description that is exactly 20 characters in length to verify we can handle a maximum length description. I have omitted some items from stores. I have used quantities that are easy to visually inspect as correct. Here is the output from **TestSet1**.

```
                  Acme Stock Analysis Report

  Item     Total    Store 1      Store 2      Store 3      Store 4
Number   Quantity  Qty/Percent  Qty/Percent  Qty/Percent  Qty/Percent

 12345      30     10/ 33%      10/ 33%      10/ 33%       0/  0%
 12347       6      2/ 33%       2/ 33%       0/  0%       2/ 33%
 23445       9      3/ 33%       0/  0%       3/ 33%       3/ 33%
 33434       8      4/ 50%       0/  0%       4/ 50%       0/  0%
 45345      15      5/ 33%       5/ 33%       0/  0%       5/ 33%
 45667      18      6/ 33%       6/ 33%       6/ 33%       0/  0%
 45678      28      7/ 25%       7/ 25%       7/ 25%       7/ 25%
 56756       8      2/ 25%       2/ 25%       2/ 25%       2/ 25%
 67565       2      1/ 50%       0/  0%       1/ 50%       0/  0%
```

TestSet2 has an item number in **store1.txt** that is not in the **master.txt** file. The program produces this output as expected.
```
Error: incorrect stock number in store 1
It was: 12348
```

TestSet3 has bad data, the letter a, where a quantity should be. The program produces this output as expected.
```
Error: bad data in line 3. The file was: store1.txt
```

50

TestSet4 tests exceeding array bounds. Rather than make up 1000+ test records, I ran TestSet1 but temporarily lowered **MAXITEM** to 5 in **Pgm02a.h**. The program produced

```
Error: too many items in the master file
```

One could devise additional tests of unusual things, such as what happens if the quantity is negative and so on. Certainly if the quantities were 5 digit numbers or larger, columnar alignment would suffer. But at least we can feel fairly confident we have a working program at this point.

Abstraction Barriers, Information Hiding, and Locality of Variables

The Stock Analysis Program illustrates many significant details. The first is the concept of an **abstraction barrier**. Conceptually, any function or module can be thought of as having an invisible wall or barrier around it, the abstraction barrier. The wall prevents the outside world from access to internal function items and prevents the internal function instructions from accessing the outside world. It acts like a black box. While a few functions could operate in a total vacuum from the outside world, in other words, the rest of the program, very few do so. For most functions to do their work, they need access to some information from the outside world (the rest of the program) and often need to provide some results to the outside world.

One way that we break down this abstraction barrier is by passing into the function copies of needed information through the parameter list. Another way is having the function return a value back to the outside world. By passing reference variables or memory addresses, as in the case of arrays, we also break down this abstraction barrier. Yet another way is to make key constants global in scope.

This break in the total abstraction barrier is called a **Module Interface**. A module interface illustrates the breach in the wall by showing what items are given as input to the function and what items are output from the function and what items the function has direct access to, such as reference variables and memory addresses of arrays. The items given as input are called **imports**. A function's parameters are an example of its imports. However, if a function has access to a global const int item, that item is also an import. The items that are available to the outside world, outside of a function, are called **exports**. The name of the function is an export. Header files often define what items are exported. For example, consider any function that we can code at this point in time (ignoring any object oriented classes). If we define any variable or enum within the function's body, can the outside world get any kind of access to that variable? Nope. However, via the function's prototype, the outside world could call the function, so hence the function's name is exported. If we create a header file that defines a **const int** or an enumerated data type, then any cpp file that includes that header file could use the value of the **const int** or create and use instances of the enumerated data type; thus, they are exported by the header file.

When designing a large program, sometimes a **module interface diagram** is drawn which shows each file's exported items and with lines drawn from them to the files that use those exported items. They greatly assist in the program's development. They can be done in a very fancy in 3-d style. Module interface diagrams are sometimes called **Booch** diagrams, named after Grady Booch, a leading figure in the software engineering field.

In this example, every cpp file is exporting only the name of the function(s) that it contains. The header file is exporting **DESCRLEN**, **INVREC**, **MAXSTORES** and **MAXITEMS**. On the import side, **main.cpp** is importing these three **const int**s as well as the function names (except **LoadStore()** and **BinarySearch()**). **InitializeStockArray.cpp**, **LoadStoresData.cpp**, **PerformAnalysis.cpp** and **PrintResults.cpp** are importing **INVREC**, **MAXSTORES** and **MAXITEMS**. **LoadStore.cpp** only imports **INVREC** and **MAXITEMS**. **BinarySearch.cpp** imports none of these. In addition, each of these cpp files also imports the parameter copies and addresses that they are passed.

The Locality of a Variable

We know from basic C++ principles that any variable that is defined as automatic within a function has a scope of from the point of definition to the end of the defining block, the } of the function. Such a variable is local to the function. Indeed, if we add the **static** keyword before the definition, so that the variable "remembers" its previous value from function invocation to invocation, that that variable is also local to the function. In both cases, no other function can access that local variable by using its name. However, we can control who can access its contents directly and modify it by passing a reference to it or by passing its memory address as in the case of arrays.

There is one type of data that does not share this locality, global data. In the **InvRec.h** file, three constant integers were defined. When that header file is included in a cpp file, the compiler creates three constant global variables with those specific names and values for our use. Thus, a global variable is not local but is in fact exported to anyone that wants to use it. As long as the variable is constant, this is totally acceptable. Global variables, on the other hand, are to be totally avoided, but that is another story.

However, the use of global constants raises another issue when header files are used. There are two locations that the three constant integers could have been defined. I chose the approach of placing them into the header file. Indeed, the **DESCRLEN** constant **must** be in the header file ahead of the structure definition because it is used in the definition of the length of the **description** string. The other two are there by choice. Why?

Since this header file, **InvRec.h**, is included in each cpp file, each cpp file gets its own set of constant integers. This simplifies things. To see why, let's consider the alternative approach, defining the three constant integers within the **main.cpp** file. It would appear as shown.

```
File: main.cpp
#include "InvRec.h"

const int MAXSTORES = 4;   // 4 total Acme Stores
const int MAXITEMS = 1000; // max number of inventory items

int main () {
  INVREC stock[MAXSTORES][MAXITEMS]; // the stock for each store
  long   itemToIndex[MAXITEMS];      // the complete item numbers
  int    numItems;                   // total number of items
```

If defined this way, how can the other cpp files gain access to these two global variables defined here in **main.cpp**? Only by use of the **extern** keyword. In each of the other cpp files, we would have to provide the following definitions.

```
extern const int MAXSTORES = 4;   // 4 total Acme Stores
extern const int MAXITEMS = 1000;// max number of inventory items
```

The **extern** keyword tells the compiler that these items are defined in another cpp file and that they are global in nature. It is the Linker program's job to later find where the actual definitions of the globals are and to tie them to their use in these other cpp files. If the Linker cannot find their definitions anywhere among all of the obj files of the project, it creates an "Unresolved external reference error" message.

This feature of global variables does have a drawback. And that is, **any** cpp file can insert an **extern** reference to the global variable or constant and then get access to it. Sometimes, that is not desirable. Suppose that **main.cpp** needed a value of **PI** but only required it to have two decimal places. It could define it as follows.

```
const double PI = 3.14;
int main() {
```

Now throughout this file, **PI** is 3.14 and all is well. The nature of the calculations among all of the functions within this file only require two digits of accuracy.

Now what happens if another cpp file needs **PI** and codes

```
extern const double PI;
```

and gets access to it? Suppose further that this file's functions need **PI** to 15 digits of accuracy? Oops.

The C++ language provides a mechanism for us to make a global item but restrict its use to only the defining file. In other words, to not export that global to the whole program. That is a **static** global.

When the **static** keyword is added to the definition of a global, the global is then not exported to any other file. It is a global only within the defining cpp file. Thus, in this example, **main.cpp** should define **PI** this way.

```
static const double PI = 3.14;
int main() {
```

Thus, we have a way to control the export of global items as well.

On Debugging a Larger Program—Using the assert Macro

Debugging a larger application can be challenging. The C++ language provides one additional tool to assist us called the **assert** macro. Its prototype is in the header file **assert.h**. The **assert** macro takes one parameter expression that results in a **bool** value. If the **bool** result of the expression is **false**, the assert macro displays a message and aborts the program. If the bool result is **true**, **assert** does nothing. The macro also does nothing at all when a Release build is made. It is strictly a Debug build macro.

Suppose that a program was solving the quadratic equation. A division by variable **a** is required. Also, the discriminant, **b*b – 4*a*c** must be greater than or equal to zero or the square root function would return an imaginary number error. The following coding shows how the **assert** macro could be inserted to assist in debugging.

```
cin >> a >> b >> c;
assert (a);
double discriminant = b * b - 4 * a * c;
assert (discriminant >= 0);
...
```

If **a** contains a zero, the assert then displays

Assertion failed: a, file: main.cpp, line 2

If the discriminant was a negative value, the assert displays

Assertion failed: discriminant >= 0, file: main.cpp line 4

In both cases, after displaying the error message, the program is halted.

Are assertions useful? It all depends. Personally, my own bias is against using asserts. Why? Consider the above coding. I hate mostly working software. When compiled in a Release or production run, the asserts are inert and not operational. Thus, if the user enters a zero, the program dies with a division by zero error while in production, hence "mostly working." Thus, I would have inserted real checking coding and alternative processing that would work in both the final Release build as well as while debugging. I would have coded it this way.

```
cin >> a >> b >> c;
double discriminant = b * b - 4 * a * c;
if (!a) {
   cerr << "Error: a is 0 yields division by 0"
        << " - please reenter a\n";
}
else if (discriminant < 0) {
   cerr << "Error: the discriminant is negative."
        << "Yields an imaginary square root. Please "
        << "reenter the values\n";
}
else {
   ... do the calc and show the result
```

In other words, I am always checking for those errors that can crash or otherwise cause problems at runtime and handling them in some fashion. Thus, there is no point or need for a Debug version only **assert** macro.

I would rather see beginning programmers insert error trapping coding into their programs so that the program works in both Release and Debug builds than use a simple **assert** that leaves their code wide open for runtime crashes when in production. I consider the use of the **assert** macro for advanced programmers. It has its place. In a complex situation where an error message is not easily displayed, an **assert** is fine as long as there is also coding to bypass the potential crash at runtime. In Windows programming, there are many such places where asserts are highly recommended.

Review Questions

Beginning Data Structures in C++

1. Outline the benefits a larger program that has many cpp files would gain by using user-written header files?

2. Why is the **#ifndef/#define** logic vitally important with header files?

3. What is the difference between the following two definitions? What is the impact in a program with multiple cpp files?
```
const int MAXROWS = 10;
static const int MAXCOLS = 5;

int main () {
```


4. What items can be found in a header file? What things should not be in a header file?

5. The user coded the following include and verified with Explorer that the file was in the proper folder. Yet it did not compile. Why?
```
#include "..\Include\AcmeDate.h"
```
6. Identify all of the items that are being exported from each of these files.
File: Dates.h
```
struct Date {
   int month;
   int day;
   int year;
};
struct Dates {
   Date startDate;
   Date endDate;
};

enum TriangleType {Scalene, Isosceles, Equilateral};
const double PI = acos (-1.);
```

File: Fun.cpp
```
double Fun (Date& d, Dates& elapsed, TriangleType type) {
   enum YN {No, Yes};
   return 42 * PI;
}
```


7. Code an assert statement that would allow the program to halt if the circumstances would lead to a crash or failure of the coding.

```
A. percentage = amount * 100 / total;
```

```
B.  z = sqrt (x - y);

C.  cout << "Enter an odd integer: ";
      cin >> num;
```

8. Use the following structure definitions and instances to answer the series of questions below.

```
struct EMPLOYEE {
   long    idNumber;
   char    firstName[21];
   char    lastName[31];
   char    payType;
   double  rate;
};

struct ACCOUNTREC {
   long    customerID;
   double  creditLimit;
   double  balance;
};

struct TIME {
   short hours;
   short minutes;
   short seconds;
};

struct CONTESTANT {
   long id;
   char name[50];
   TIME start;
   TIME finished;
   TIME elapsed;
};

EMPLOYEE    emp;
ACCOUNTREC  arec;
CONTESTANT  player1;
```

a. Place "John" into emp's first name field.

b. Place "Smith" into emp's last name field.

c. Place 42 into emp's id number field.

d. If emp's pay type is 'h' for hourly, calculate the pay as hours times emp's pay rate.

e. Place a balance of 5000.00 into arec's balance field.

f. Add 1000.00 to arec's credit limit.

g. Assign the name "Besty Smith" to player1.

h. Assign a starting time of 12:42:16 to player1.

i. Assign an ending time of 13:06:01 to player1.

j. Calculate the elapsed time for player1 based on the contents of player1's start and finish times.

9. Write the structure template that could hold the data defined in each of the following situations.

a. A cost of good sold structure contains the item number, the quantity, the unit cost, the tax, and the total cost.

b. A party record contains the name of a guest (up to 50 characters), the date and time of the party, and the number of people that that guest intends to bring.

c. A disco record contains the album id (a string of 20 characters), the album title of up to 50 characters, the number of songs, and the total play time.

d. A student grade record contains the social security number of the student, the first and last name (strings of 40 characters each), and the accumulated GPA.

e. A car maintenance record contains the customer id number, the car's make and model (both strings of 20 characters maximum), the car's year, and the date of last maintenance.

Stop! Do These Exercises Before Programming

1. The programmer wanted to define a two-dimensional array of grades. There are five sections of twenty-four students each. What must be done to the following to get it defined correctly?

```
const int Sections = 5;
const int Students = 24;
int main () {
  char grades[Students, Sections];
```

Which array bounds should come first, assuming that the normal processing handles all of the students within a given section at one time? Why?

2. Since not every section has 24 students in it, the programmer decided to have another array called **numberStudentsInThisSection** which is an array of five integers, one for each section. Thus,

numberStudentsInThisSection[0] contains the number of students in that section. With this defined, a **LoadStudentArrays()** function was written but does not compile or work. Why? What must be done to make this work properly?

```
const int Sections = 5;
const int Students = 24;
int LoadStudentArrays (char grades[][Students],
                       numberStudentsInThisSection[],
                       int maxSections, int maxStudents);
int main () {
 char grades[Sections, Students];
 int numberStudentsInThisSection[Sections];
 int numSections = LoadStudentArrays (grades[][Students],
       numberStudentsInThisSection[], Sections, Students);
 ...
int LoadStudentArrays (char grades[][Students],
                       numberStudentsInThisSection[],
                       int maxSections, int maxStudents){
 int j = 0;  // section subscript
 while (cin >> ws) {
  int k = 0; // student subscript
  while (cin >> grades[k][j]) {
   k++;
  }
  numberStudentsInThisSection[j] = j;
  j++;
 }
 return j;
}
```

3. Next the **main()** function attempted to printout all of the grades to see if they had been input properly. The following coding does not work properly. Why? What must be done to get it to properly print out the grades as entered?

```
const int Sections = 5;
const int Students = 24;
int LoadStudentArrays (char grades[][Students],
                       numberStudentsInThisSection[],
                       int maxSections, int maxStudents);
int main () {
 char grades[Sections, Students];
 int numberStudentsInThisSection[Sections];
 int numSections = LoadStudentArrays (grades[][Students],
       numberStudentsInThisSection[], Sections, Students);
 for (int j=0; j<numSections; j++) {
  cout << "\n\nSection: " << j << endl;
  for (int k=0; k<numberStudentsInThisSection[k]; k++) {
   cout << grades[k][j] << endl;
  }
```

```
        }
```

4. With the data properly input and printed, the next step is to calculate the average grade for each section. Since the grades are letter grades, assume that a 4.0 system is in use. That is, an A is worth 4 points, B is 3 and so on. The **FindAvgGrades()** function does not compile. Why? How can it be made to work properly?

```
        const int Sections = 5;
        const int Students = 24;
        void FindAvgGrades (char grades[][Students],
                            numberStudentsInThisSection[],
                            int numSections, double avgs[]);
        int main () {
         char grades[Sections, Students];
         int numberStudentsInThisSection[Sections];
         int numSections;
         double averages;
         ...
         FindAvgGrades (grades, numberStudentsInThisSection[],
                        int numSections, averages);
         ...
        void FindAvgGrades (char grades[][Students],
                            int numberStudentsInThisSection[],
                            int numSections, double avgs[]){
         double sum;
         for (j=0; j<numberStudentsInThisSection[j]; j++) {
          sum = 0;
          for (k=0; k<numberStudentsInThisSection[j]; k++) {
           switch (grades[j[k]) {
            case 'A':
             sum += 4;
            case 'B':
             sum += 3;
            case 'C':
             sum += 2;
            case 'D':
             sum += 1;
            case 'F':
             sum += 0;
          }
         }
         avgs[k] = sum / numberStudentsInThisSection[j];
         }
        }
```

5. Sorting of a two-dimensional array usually means sorting each row's worth of column values into order. Assume that there are 10 rows of raw scores and each row has 20 columns and that all elements are present. That is, there are 200 values in the array. The following coding to sort the array fails. Why? How can it be fixed so that the data are sorted properly?

```
const int Rows = 10;
const int Cols = 20;
double rawScores[Rows][Cols];
for (int j=0; j<Rows; j++) {
 double temp;
 for (int k=0; k<Cols; k++) {
  for (int m=k; m<Cols; m++) {
   if (rawScores[j][k] < rawScores[j][m]) {
    temp = rawScores[k][j];
    rawScores[j][k] = rawScores[j][m];
    rawScores[j][m] = temp;
   }
  }
 }
}
```

6. Consider the following files that are part of a programming project. When the cpp file is compiled, it generates an error. Why? What must be done to get this to work?

File: Point.h

```
struct POINT {
   int x;
   int y;
};
```

File: Rectangle.h

```
#include "Point.h"
struct RECTANGLE {
  POINT upperLeft;
  POINT lowerRight;
};
```

File: Circle.h

```
#include "Point.h"
struct CIRCLE {
  POINT center;
  double radius;
};
```

File: main.cpp

```
#include "Rectangle.h"
#include "Circle.h"
int main () {
  CIRCLE c;
  RECTANGLE r;
  return 0;
}
```

7. Consider the following program. Decide what items should be in a header file and what should be in the cpp file. Then, write the new header and cpp files.

```cpp
#include <iostream>
#include <fstream>
using namespace std;
const int MAXCUST = 1000;
const int NAMELEN = 31;
struct CUSTOMERORDER {
  long customerNumber;
  char name[NAMELEN];
  int itemNum;
  int quantity;
};
int main () {
  ifstream infile ("CustomerOrders.txt");
  CUSTOMERORDER orders[MAXCUST];
  int j = 0;
  while (j < MAXCUST && infile >> orders[j].customerNumber){
    infile.get(orders[j].name, NAMELEN);
    infile >> orders[j].itemNum >> orders[j].quantity;
    j++;
  }
  return 0;
}
```

8. Consider the following header file and **main.cpp** file.
File: password.h

```cpp
const int MAXPWS = 1000;  // max number of password records
const int MAXLEN = 51;    // max len of name and password
const int NoMatch = -1;   // no matching user found in tbl

// a password contains letters, numbers and blanks only
struct PASSWORD {
  char userName[MAXLEN];
  char password[MAXLEN];
};

// LoadPasswords inputs the name, pw pairs from a file
// called pw.txt. Both strings are delimited with " "
// it returns the number of records input into the array
// it aborts if array size is exceeded or on other errors
int LoadPasswords (PASSWORD pw[]);

// LogonUser prompts to cout and inputs from cin
// Enter UserId: and inputs it
// Enter Password: and gets it.
// if there is a match in the pw table, returns the index of
// the match; if no match, returns -1
```

```
int LogonUser (PASSWORD pw[], int numPws);

// ChangePassword displays the current password and then
// prompts for the new one. It changes the user's password
// in the table
void ChangePassword ((PASSWORD pw[], int thisIdx);
```
File: main.cpp
```
#include <iostream>
using namespace std;
#include "password.h"
int main () {
  PASSWORD pw[MAXPWS];
  int numPws = LoadPasswords (pw);
  int userIdx = LogonUser (pw, numPws);
  ChangePassword (pw, userIdx);
  return 0;
}
```
Write the implementations for **LoadPasswords()**, **LogonUser()**, and **ChangePassword()** functions. Place each function in its own cpp file.

Programming Problems

Problem Pgm02-1 Array Manipulations

The included file **Pgm02-1.cpp** provides the **main()** function and some helper functions that enable it to thoroughly test your coding. In this problem, you are going to practice various array manipulations. You are to write each of the six functions described below. Do NOT define any additional arrays inside your functions; work only with the array(s) passed as the argument(s).

1. Write the **LoadData()** function whose prototype is
```
int LoadData (istream &infile, int array[], int arraySize,
              int &count);
```

The **LoadData()** function reads integers from the passed stream and loads them into the successive elements of the array passed as the second argument. The third argument specifies the size of the array (number of elements). The function loads data into the array until the array is full or the end of the file is reached, whichever occurs first. The function assigns the count of integers stored into the array to the fourth argument. The function must not overflow the boundary of the array or read any more data after the array is full. The function returns a status code: 0 if the whole input file is successfully loaded into the array, 1 if the input file is too large to fully load into the array (the array is full but there are more data in the file), or –1 if there is invalid (non-integer) data in the input file. In all cases, the **count** parameter must be assigned the correct count of numbers stored in the array.

2. Write the **List()** function whose prototype is
```
void List (const int array[], int count);
```

Beginning Data Structures in C++

The **List()** function prints the numbers in the array passed as the first argument; the second argument is the count of numbers in the array. Print each number in a three-column field and print a newline character after each set of twenty numbers. After all the numbers are printed, print one blank line.

3. Write the **CopyArray()** function whose prototype is
```
void CopyArray (int destArray[], const int srcArray[], int count);
```
The **Copy()** function copies the contents of one array to another. The first argument is the destination array and the second argument is the source array. The third argument specifies the number of elements to copy.

4. Write the **RotateLeft()** function whose prototype is
```
void RotateLeft (int array[], int count);
```
The **RotateLeft()** function shifts each number in the array, except the first, one element to the "left" (the element with the next lower subscript). The first number in the array is shifted to the last element in the array.

5. Write the **RotateRight()** function whose prototype is
```
void RotateRight (int array[], int count);
```
The **RotateRight()** function shifts each number in the array, except the last, one element to the "right" (the element with the next higher subscript). The last number in the array is shifted to the first element. (Note: you can **RotateRight()** by repeating **RotateLeft()** for count − 1 times. However, this is extremely inefficient. Use an efficient method for rotating to the right; do not repeatedly rotate the array to left.)

6. Write the **Reverse()** function whose prototype is
```
void Reverse (int array[], int count);
```
The **Reverse()** function reverses the sequence of the numbers in the array. (Note: you can reverse an array by repeating **RotateLeft()** or **RotateRight()** for **count** − 1 times, while at the same time decreasing the count after each repetition. However, this is extremely inefficient. Use an efficient method for reversing; do not repeatedly rotate the array.)

Test your program on the provided test files **Pgm02-1a.txt**, **Pgm02-1b.txt**, **Pgm02-1c.txt**, **Pgm02-1d.txt** and **Pgm02-1e.txt**. Here are the outputs you should get (I have single-spaced the output to reduce lines here in the book.)

```
Enter input file name: Pgm02-1a.txt

status = 0   count = 9

load:      99 88 77 66 55 44 33 22 11
copy:      99 88 77 66 55 44 33 22 11
left:      88 77 66 55 44 33 22 11 99
right:     11 99 88 77 66 55 44 33 22
reverse:   11 22 33 44 55 66 77 88 99

Enter input file name: Pgm02-1b.txt

status = 0   count = 20

load:       1  2  3  4  5  6  7  8  9 10 11 12 13 14 15 16 17 18 19 20
copy:       1  2  3  4  5  6  7  8  9 10 11 12 13 14 15 16 17 18 19 20
```

```
left:        2  3  4  5  6  7  8  9 10 11 12 13 14 15 16 17 18 19 20  1
right:      20  1  2  3  4  5  6  7  8  9 10 11 12 13 14 15 16 17 18 19
reverse:    20 19 18 17 16 15 14 13 12 11 10  9  8  7  6  5  4  3  2  1

Enter input file name: Pgm02-1c.txt

status = 1  count = 20

load:        2  4  6  8 10 12 14 16 18 20 22 24 26 28 30 32 34 36 38 40
copy:        2  4  6  8 10 12 14 16 18 20 22 24 26 28 30 32 34 36 38 40
left:        4  6  8 10 12 14 16 18 20 22 24 26 28 30 32 34 36 38 40  2
right:      40  2  4  6  8 10 12 14 16 18 20 22 24 26 28 30 32 34 36 38
reverse:    40 38 36 34 32 30 28 26 24 22 20 18 16 14 12 10  8  6  4  2

Enter input file name: Pgm02-1d.txt

status = -1  count = 5

load:       90 80 70 60 50
copy:       90 80 70 60 50
left:       80 70 60 50 90
right:      50 90 80 70 60
reverse:    50 60 70 80 90
```

Problem Pgm02-2 A Matrix Math Package

A Quick Review of Matrix Algebra

Multiple dimensioned arrays open new vistas in the types of problems that can be solved. Specifically, matrices can be stored in two-dimensional arrays. Matrices can be used to solve linear simultaneous equations, such as **n** equations in **n** unknowns. The starting point is a brief review of the rules of Matrix Algebra.

Suppose that we had the following simultaneous equations.

$5x + 4y + 3z = 40$
$9y + 3z + 8x = 10$
$4z + 3x + 6y = 20$

They must be rearranged into the proper format.

$5x + 4y + 3z = 40$
$8x + 9y + 3z = 10$
$3x + 6y + 4z = 20$

In matrix notation, this becomes the following.

$$\begin{pmatrix} 5 & 4 & 3 \\ 9 & 3 & 8 \\ 4 & 3 & 6 \end{pmatrix} \times \begin{pmatrix} x \\ y \\ z \end{pmatrix} = \begin{pmatrix} 40 \\ 10 \\ 20 \end{pmatrix}$$

Or **A X** = **B**; so the solution is **X** = **B/A**

Beginning Data Structures in C++

The normal matrix notation for this case of 3 equations in 3 unknowns is shown below.

$$\begin{pmatrix} a11 & a12 & a13 \\ a21 & a22 & a23 \\ a31 & a32 & a33 \end{pmatrix} \begin{pmatrix} x1 \\ x2 \\ x3 \end{pmatrix} = \begin{pmatrix} b1 \\ b2 \\ b3 \end{pmatrix}$$

Notice that the math matrix notation parallels C++ subscripts, but begins with subscript 1 not 0. Always remember to subtract 1 from the matrix math indexes to get a C++ array subscript.

In this example, the **a** matrix is composed of 3 rows or row vectors, and 3 columns or column vectors. In general a matrix is said to be an **m** by **n** matrix, **m** rows and **n** columns. When **m** = **n**, it is called a **square** matrix. A matrix with only one row is a **row** matrix; one with only one column is a **column** matrix. The **x** and **b** matrices are both column matrices.

Matrix Math Operations Summary

1. Two matrices are said to be equal if and only if they have the same dimensions and all corresponding elements are equal.

aij = **bij** for all **i**=1,m and **j**=1,n

2. Addition and Subtraction operations require that the matrices involved have the same number of rows and columns. To compute **C** = **A** + **B** or **C** = **A** − **B**, simply add or subtract all corresponding elements. This can be implemented in C++ as follows.

```
for (int I=0; I<M; I++) {
  for (int J=0; J<N; J++) {
    C(I,J) = A(I,J) + B(I,J);
  }
}
```

3. Multiplication of a matrix by a number is commutative. That is, **rA** is the same as **Ar.** The result is given by **r** times each element.

```
for (int I=0; I<M; I++) {
  for (int J=0; J<N; J++) {
    A(I,J) = A(I,J) * r;
  }
}
```

For example, assume **A** is defined to be the following.

$$A = \begin{pmatrix} 2.7 & -1.8 \\ 0.9 & 3.6 \end{pmatrix}$$

Then 2**A** would be

$$A = \begin{pmatrix} 5.4 & -3.6 \\ 1.8 & 7.2 \end{pmatrix}$$

and 10/9**A** would be

$$A = \begin{pmatrix} 3 & -2 \\ 1 & 4 \end{pmatrix}$$

4. A **diagonal** matrix is one whose elements above and below the principal diagonal are 0: namely **aij**=0 for all **i!=j**

$$diagonal \begin{pmatrix} 3 & 0 & 0 \\ 0 & 4 & 0 \\ 0 & 0 & 5 \end{pmatrix}$$

5. An **identity** matrix is a diagonal matrix whose principal diagonal elements are all 1.

$$identity \begin{pmatrix} 1 & 0 & 0 \\ 0 & 1 & 0 \\ 0 & 0 & 1 \end{pmatrix}$$

6. Matrix multiplication says that the product of a square matrix times a column matrix is another column matrix. It is computed as follows: for each row in the square matrix, sum the products of each element in the square matrix's row by the corresponding element in the column matrix's column.

$$\begin{pmatrix} a11 & a12 & a13 \\ a21 & a22 & a23 \\ a31 & a32 & a33 \end{pmatrix} \cdot \begin{pmatrix} b1 \\ b2 \\ b3 \end{pmatrix} = \begin{pmatrix} a11*b1 + a12*b2 + a13*b3 \\ a21*b1 + a22*b2 + a23*b3 \\ a31*b1 + a32*b2 + a33*b3 \end{pmatrix}$$

For a square matrix times a square matrix, the result is a square matrix of the same dimensions, each element of the result is the sum of the products of each element of the corresponding row of one matrix times each element of the corresponding column of the other matrix

C = A * B

where **Cij** = ith row of **A** * jth column of **B** or in coding

```
for (int I=0; I<3; I++) {
 for (int J=0; J<3; J++) {
  C(I,J) = 0;
  for (int K=0; K<3; K++) {
   C(I,J) = C(I,J) + A(I,K)*B(K,J);
  }
 }
}
```

Program Pgm02-2 Specifications

1. Write an **IsEqual()** function that returns **true** if the two square matrices are equal. Its prototype should be

```
bool IsEqual (double A[MaxDim][MaxDim],
              double B[MaxDim][MaxDim], int limit);
```

66

2. Write an **Add()** function to add two square matrices **A** and **B**, placing the result in matrix **C**. Its prototype is

```
void Add (double A[MaxDim][MaxDim],
          double B[MaxDim][MaxDim],
          double C[MaxDim][MaxDim], int limit);
```

3. Write a **Subtract()** function to subtract two square matrices (**C** = **A** - **B**) placing the result in matrix **C**. Its prototype is

```
void Subtract (double A[MaxDim][MaxDim],
               double B[MaxDim][MaxDim],
               double C[MaxDim][MaxDim], int limit);
```

4. Write a **MultiplyByConstant()** function to multiply the matrix **A** by the value **b** and place the result in matrix **C**. The prototype is

```
void MultiplyByConstant (double A[MaxDim][MaxDim],
                         double b,
                         double C[MaxDim][MaxDim],
                         int limit);
```

5. Write a function **IsDiagonal()** that returns **true** if the matrix is a diagonal matrix. Its prototype is

```
bool IsDiagonal (double A[MaxDim][MaxDim], int limit);
```

6. Write a function **IsIdentity()** that returns **true** if the matrix is an identity matrix. Its prototype is

```
bool IsIdentity (double A[MaxDim][MaxDim], int limit);
```

7. Write a function **MatrixBySquare()** that multiplies the square matrix **A** by the column matrix **B** yielding the column matrix **C**. Its prototype is

```
void MatrixBySquare (double A[MaxDim][MaxDim],
                     double B[MaxDim],
                     double C[MaxDim], int limit);
```

8. Finally, write a function **MatrixByMatrix()** that multiplies the square matrix **A** by square matrix **B**, yielding square matrix **C**. Its prototype is

```
void MatrixByMatrix (double A[MaxDim][MaxDim],
          double B[MaxDim][MaxDim],
          double C[MaxDim][MaxDim], int limit);
```

9. Now write a main function to test all of these. Thoroughly test all functions.

Problem Pgm02-3 The Rhodes Magic Square

A Rhodes Magic Square is a rectangular figure of values such that the numbers in each row, the numbers in each column and the numbers in the main diagonal add up to the same value. The following logic creates a magic square of any odd number of rows and columns.

Rule 1. Place the initial value of 1 in the middle of the top row.

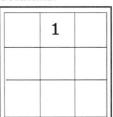

Rule 1

Rule 2. From this current square, move UP and Left subject to the following exceptions

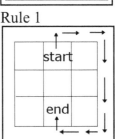

Rule 2

Rule 2a. If moving UP places you out of the rectangle, return to the bottom of the rectangle in the same column.

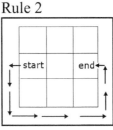

Rule 2a

Rule 2b. If moving LEFT places you out of the rectangle, return to the RIGHT side of the rectangle in the same row.

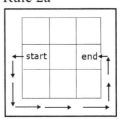

Rule 2b

Rule 3. If after moving UP and LEFT, the new square is blank, insert the new number here. Use this location as the new starting point and repeat Rule 2.

Rule 3a. If after moving to the new square, that new square is occupied, then return to the original square you started from and move DOWN.

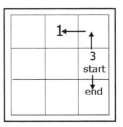

Rule 3a

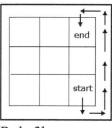

Rule 3b. If moving DOWN takes you out of the rectangle,
        move to the top of the same column.

Rule 3b

Part A.

Write a program to input the size of the magic square, which must always be an ODD number. The program should then create the square and display the square in some format that looks good to the user (you). Then perform the calculations necessary and display the following lines. Use as many functions as appropriate. (Note no credit will be given if there are no functions used except **main()**.)

For a magic square of nnn rows and columns:
The value in the upper-left hand corner is nnn.
The value in the upper-right hand corner is nnn.
The value in the bottom-right hand corner is nnn.
The value in the bottom-left hand corner is nnn.
The value in the middle is nnn.
The sum of the values in the bottom row is nnn.

Test the program with a value of 7 and then again with 15. The next figure illustrates the step-by-step process to construct a 3x3 magic square.

The Construction Steps for a 3x3 Magic Square

Part B.

Modify the program so that the magic square can be flipped in any of four directions. The four directions are:
 Horizontally - about the middle row
 Vertically - about the middle column
 Left diagonal - down the left diagonal
 Right diagonal - down the right diagonal

 Prompt the user for which of the four rotations to do, perform the rotation, reprint the resultant matrix and then prompt for another rotation. Provide a user choice to quit rotation process. Each of these should be performed in their own functions. You can have as many other functions as you deem appropriate. No credit is given if you merely display the results without actually modifying the array so that the array is now in the correct flipped order.

Original Matrix:

15	8	1	24	17
16	14	7	5	23
22	20	13	6	4
3	21	19	12	10
9	2	25	18	11

Horizontal Rotation of Original Matrix:

9	2	25	18	11
3	21	19	12	10
22	20	13	6	4
16	14	7	5	23
15	8	1	24	17

Vertical Rotation of Original Matrix:

17	24	1	8	15
23	5	7	14	16
4	6	13	20	22
10	12	19	21	3
11	18	25	2	9

Left Diagonal Rotation of Original Matrix:

15	16	22	3	9
8	14	20	21	2
1	7	13	19	25
24	5	6	12	18
17	23	4	10	11

Right Diagonal Rotation of Original Matrix:

11	10	4	23	17
18	12	6	5	24
25	19	13	7	1
2	21	20	14	8
9	3	22	16	15

Chapter 3–Pointers and Dynamic Memory Allocation

Introduction

A **pointer** is nothing more than the memory address of something, where in memory the item or thing begins. Addresses are essentially unsigned long numbers. The first byte of memory is given the number 0. Each byte's address is sequentially one larger than the previous byte's. On a Win32 platform, the maximum address is 4G. An address cannot be negative; if you said I want to see what is in address –5 that is saying to access the contents of the fifth byte before the computer's memory actually begins.

In actual fact, we have been using pointers already when we pass references to variables and arrays. However, with these data types, the compiler is responsible for their operation. When you use a pointer directly, you, the programmer must manually do the actions that the compiler does for you when you use a reference variable. Pointers are a powerful feature of the C++ language.

Until this point, the exact amount of memory a program required at any point in its execution is known at compile time. The compiler knows exactly the total amount of memory it must create as it enters each block of coding. Array bounds are fixed at constant, unchangeable values. Automatic and parameter variables are created and stored on the stack by the compiler upon block entry. Local static variables go into the static portion of the data segment of the program along with global variables that go into the global portion. However, the C++ language is far more flexible than this. It supports a method by which we can allocate some additional memory while the program is executing.

This is called **dynamic memory allocation** which is the action of allocating some additional memory that was not specifically specified as needed at compile time. Dynamic memory allocation allows a program to have a variable array bounds! That is, the number of elements in an array is not known until the program actually executes to some point in the program and determines then the array size. For example, the program asks the user how many elements they wish in an array. Then an array of that dimension is allocated. This removes the arbitrary upper limit to the number of items that can be input into an array! Arrays can be as big as they need to be at run time. This ability to dynamically allocate needed memory as the program is executing along is extremely important. In larger programs, a large percentage of variables are dynamically allocated as the program needs the space. It forms the basis for many of the data structures we will be studying in the later chapters of this text.

Pointer Basics

Defining Pointer Variables

The topic of pointers in general is the most difficult portion of the C++ language to learn and program well. It is error prone. Right from the start, I am going to name my pointer variables in a special way. Then, as we see how to use pointers, I will show you the tremendous benefit this naming convention has.

A pointer variable is defined by placing a * after the data type and before the variable name. The following all define pointer variables.

```
int*    ptrqty;
double* ptrcost;
char*   string;
```

The * in a data definition means "is a pointer to" whatever data type is involved.

These data definitions read backwards—**ptrqty** is a pointer to an **int**; **ptrcost** is a pointer to a **double**; **string** is a pointer to a **char**. Since a pointer is essentially an **unsigned long** on a 32-bit platform (they are an **unsigned int** or 2 bytes long under old DOS), a pointer takes up 4 bytes of memory.

The placement of the * in the definition is not critical from a syntax view point. These could have been defined this way.

```
int    *ptrqty;
double *ptrcost;
char   *ptrstring;
```

However, when the * is placed up against the variable name, the * tends to visually disappear from the reader's gaze. There is a huge difference between a **double** and the memory address of a **double**! Thus, I try to always place the * right after the data type where it is more prominently visible and not so easily missed.

More than one pointer can be defined on a single line. However, observe the syntax that is needed.

```
int *ptrqty, quantity, *ptrcount, count, *ptrtally;
```

Three pointers are defined along with two integers. The following would not yield the definition of two pointers.

```
int* ptrqty, ptrcount;
```

Here, **ptrcount** is assumed to be an integer!

A pointer can be of automatic storage type or it can be a parameter pointer or it can be a static pointer or even a global pointer. The following are all valid pointer definitions.

```
int*      ptrqty; // global pointer to an int
int main () {
   double* ptrcost;         // automatic storage pointer
   static char* string; // static storage pointer
...
double* Fun (double* ptrdata) {
        // parameter pointer and
        // a returned pointer from a function
...
```

Notice that every pointer is defined to point to some specific type of data, such as an **int**, **double**, or even an **INVREC** structure instance from the last chapter. When we use pointers, the compiler is very conscientious about making sure that our pointers match the kind of data to which they are supposed to be pointing. It does not allow one to access a **double** by using a pointer to an **int**, for example. There is one special kind of pointer that has no data type associated with it, a **void***. In order to make use of a **void*** type pointer, usually one must typecast it to the type of data to which it actually points or use the **mem**xxx string functions.

Ok. So we can define a pointer variable. But what is its starting value, its contents? At the moment, core garbage. The next step is vital. A pointer must be initialized with the memory address of the data to which it is supposed to point!

Initializing Pointers

Pointers must contain the address of what they are supposed to be pointing. How this is done depends upon the circumstances. The address operator, &, is sometimes used to obtain the memory address of the item that comes after it. So taking the address of something is one way to get the initial value for a pointer.

Suppose that we have defined the following variables.
```
int    qty;
double cost;
int* ptrqty;
double* ptrcost;
```
We could initialize these two pointers by coding
```
ptrqty = &qty;
ptrcost = &cost
```
Or they could be initialized as they are defined as follows.
```
int* ptrqty = &qty;
double* ptrcost = &cost;
```

However, the above is rather a contrived example. Why would one want an alternative way to access the function's **qty** and **cost** variables? In reality, you would not code the above two pointers. More frequently, the pointers are parameter variables. Suppose that we wanted to write a **Swap()** function that swapped two integers. Until now, how would you pass those two integers? Why by reference variables, of course. Here is how they could also be passed by pointers instead.

main():
```
int x;
int y;
Swap (&x, &y);
```

Swap():
```
void Swap (int* ptrx, int* ptry) {
```

Notice that we must manually pass the addresses of **x** and **y**, Again, while we could write **Swap()** this way, pointers are not really often used where a reference variable could and should be used. The reason pointers do not replace reference variables is that their use is more error prone in many ways. Reference variables are designed to remove many of the common causes of errors when pointers were used. What would have happened if **main()** had called **Swap()** this way?

```
Swap (x, y);
```

The compiler generates an error message, "cannot convert int to int*"—that is it cannot convert an integer into a memory address. In fact, this conversion error is one of the most common errors programmers new to pointers get—cannot convert double to double*, cannot convert long* to long, cannot convert INVREC to INVREC*.

A pointer variable can also be initialized to the name of a single dimensioned array. Suppose that a function defined the following array.

```
double grades[20];
```

What is the data type of the name of the array, in this case, **grades**? The name of an array is always a constant pointer to the first element. In this case, the symbol **grades** is a constant pointer to a **double**. Using this one can define and initialize **ptrthisgrade** as follows.

```
double* ptrthisgrade = grades;
```

Here, **ptrthisgrade** now points to the first element of the array **grades**, that is, it contains the address of **grades[0]**. One could have also initialized **ptrthisgrade** this way.

```
double* ptrthisgrade = &grades[0];
```

Dereferencing a Pointer

How can the contents of what the pointer points to be accessed? This is done by using the dereference operator, also a *. Assuming that **ptrqty** contains the address of the function's **qty** variable, then the following places a 42 into the **qty** variable.

```
*ptrqty = 42;
```

The * means go to the address pointed to by the pointer and access what is there. When it is on the left-hand side, it copying the right-hand value into the location pointed to by the pointer. When it is on the right-hand side, the compiler is accessing or reading the contents of the memory location pointed to by the pointer. Here **cost** is being multiplied by the **qty** field.

```
totalCost = *ptrqty * cost;
```

The dereference operator is needed to implement the **Swap()** function. It can be done as follows.

```
void Swap (int* ptrx, int* ptry) {
  int temp = *ptrx;
  *ptrx = *ptry;
  *ptry = temp;
}
```

Here the contents pointed to by **ptrx** are copied into the temporary integer, **temp**. Then the contents pointed to by **ptry** are stored in the memory location pointed to by **ptrx**. And finally, the temporary value in **temp** is copied into the memory location pointed to by **ptry**.

The Rules of Pointer Arithmetic

Pointer variables can be used in simple arithmetic expressions. Indeed, much of their benefits arise from these special abilities. But before we launch into these rules, let's see how a simple program could be written using all subscripts. Then, let's see how all subscripts could be completely replaced by pointers. Consider the following program to input an unknown number of grades, compute their average, and then print out the grades.

```
const int LIMIT = 5;
int main() {
  double grades[LIMIT];
  int j = 0;
  double sum = 0;
  while (j<LIMIT && cin >> grades[j]) {
    sum += grades[j];
    j++;
  }
  if (j == LIMIT && cin >> ws && cin.good()) {
    cerr << "Array bounds exceeded\n"
    return 1;
  }
  else if (!cin.eof() && cin.fail()) {
    cerr << "Error: bad data entered\n"
    return 2;
  }
  int numGrades = j;
  cout << "Average grade: " << sum / numGrades << endl;
  for (j=0; j<numGrades; j++) {
    cout << grades[j] << endl;
  }
  return 0;
}
```

Ok. Pointer notation and subscript notation can be interchanged. The goal is to eliminate all subscripts and counters in the above program. To do so, two pointers are needed, here called **ptrthisgrade** and **ptrlastgrade**. The **ptrthisgrade** always points to the current element to be utilized, either to be filled by an input operation or to be accessed in summing operations or displaying actions. The **ptrlastgrade** is used to point to the first byte that comes after the last element in the array. Thus, if the memory address in **ptrthisgrade** is strictly less than the memory address in **ptrlastgrade**, then there is still another element in the array that we can use. If **ptrthisgrade** ever becomes equal to or larger than **ptrlastgrade**, then the array bound is exceeded. Figure 3.1 illustrates this initial setup with these pointers.

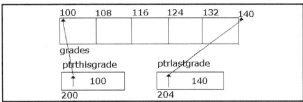

Figure 3.1 The Initial Pointer Setup

Assuming that the array **grades** begins at memory location 100 and that a double is 8 bytes in size, then if there are 5 elements in the array, memory address 140 marks the first byte that is not in the array **grades**. The two pointers are located at memory addresses 200 and 204 respectively. The initial state must have **ptrthisgrade** containing the address of the first element of the array, the address 100. The **ptrlastgrade** must contain the address of the first byte not in the array, the address 140 as shown above in Figure 3.1.

Recall that the name of an array is a constant pointer to the first element. Thus, we can define and initialize **ptrthisgrade** as follows.

```
const int LIMIT = 5;
int main() {
  double grades[LIMIT];
  double* ptrthisgrade = grades;
```

But how do we get the address 140 into **ptrlastgrade**?

An integer can be added to or subtracted from any pointer. However, that value is scaled by the **sizeof** the data type being pointed to, that is multiplied by the **sizeof** the data type. Thus, we can write

```
  double* ptrlastgrade = grades + LIMIT;
  double sum = 0;
```

To the right of the = sign, the symbol **grades** is really the memory address of the first element or 100. **LIMIT** has been defined to be 5. Thus, the equation appears as

```
  ptrlastgrade = 100 + 5;
```

However, if the compiler just added five bytes to 100, yielding 105, disaster would result since we would now be 5/8's of the way thru a **double**! Instead the compiler does the following.

```
  ptrlastgrade = 100 + 5 * sizeof (double);
```

or

```
  ptrlastgrade = 100 + 5 * 8;
```

or

```
  ptrlastgrade = 140;
```

Next, two pointers can be compared as long as they both point to the same type of data. Using this we can rewrite the **while** statement as follows.

```
    while (ptrthisgrade < ptrlastgrade
           && cin >> *ptrthisgrade) {
```

Notice also that the extraction operator needs a variable to fill and by dereferencing **ptrthisgrade**, we get it. Similarly, we can accumulate the score just inputted by coding

```
    sum += *ptrthisgrade;
```

Again, dereferencing the pointer gets to the value contained in this element in the array.

Then, **ptrthisgrade** must be incremented to point to the next element in the array or address 108. This is done by coding

```
    ptrthisgrade++;
```

Remember that an integer can be added to a pointer. The increment operator is adding 1, well, really 1 * sizeof (the data type) or 8 bytes in this case. However, the sum and the pointer increment lines are often combined into a single statement as shown below.

```
    sum += *ptrthisgrade++; // incs the pointer
  }
```

The postfix inc and dec operators have a higher precedence than the dereference operator. So the above expression reads, increment **ptrthisgrade** after any use is made of its current contents. If one wanted to

actually increment the grade being pointed to by the pointer, one would have to use () such as
```
sum = sum + (*ptrthisgrade)++; // incs the grade
```
This would add one grade point to the person's grade and add that new grade value into the sum.

Most of the coding to check for errors when the loop is done is exactly the same. The only difference in coding is how to check if we are at the end of the array. That is handled by comparing the two pointers:
```
if (ptrthisgrade == ptrlastgrade &&
    cin >> ws && cin.good()) {
  cerr << "Array bounds exceeded\n"
  return 1;
}
else if (!cin.eof() && cin.fail()) {
  cerr << "Error: bad data entered\n"
  return 2;
}
```

Next, a most important step must be done. With subscripts, we set the integer **numGrades** to the actual number of elements or grades that was input on this run. When using a pure pointer version, we reset **ptrlastgrade** to now point to the real end of the array on this run. The **ptrthisgrade** is pointing to the next available element that was not yet used. So we have

ptrlastgrade = ptrthisgrade;

The next action is to display the average, **sum / numGrades**. But wait, we do not know the number of grades that was input! We can easily calculate that value by subtraction of two pointers. Two pointers can be subtracted as long as they both point to the same type of data; the resulting integer is scaled by the **sizeof** the data type, divided by the **sizeof** the data type, in this case. To see this in operation, let's assume that three grades were input on this run. Figure 3.2 shows the state of our program at this point in its execution.

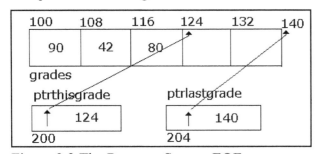

Figure 3.2 The Program State at EOF

If we write the expression,
ptrthisgrade - grades
this yields
    124 - 100 => 24
But it is then scaled by the size of a **double**
    24 / 8 => 3
This gives us the number of elements actually in the array on this run.

The way to think about what subtracting two pointers gives you is this: when you subtract the two pointers, it gives you the number of elements between these two points in the array. A pointer is just that a way of marking some point in an array in this case. So the program line becomes:

```
cout << "Average grade: " << sum / (ptrthisgrade - grades)
    << endl;
```

The final operation of the program is to display all of the grades as entered. That is, we must begin at the beginning of the array and move sequentially through all elements that were input accessing each one in turn. This is perhaps the most common coding found with array processing. The **for** loop is rewritten this way.

```
for (ptrthisgrade=grades; ptrthisgrade<ptrlastgrade;
    ptrthisgrade++) {
  cout << *ptrthisgrade << endl;
}
```

The working pointer, **ptrthisgrade**, is reinitialized back to the start of the array, it is tested each time through the loop to see that it is less than **ptrlastgrade** which marks the first element not actually used on this run. And it is incremented to get to the next element after each pass through the loop. Remember, to access the value that the pointer is pointing to, the dereference operator is needed. For your reference, here is the complete pointer replacement program.

```
const int LIMIT = 5;
int main() {
  double grades[LIMIT];
  double* ptrthisgrade = grades;
  double* ptrlastgrade = grades + LIMIT;
  double sum = 0;
  while (ptrthisgrade < ptrlastgrade
        && cin >> *ptrthisgrade) {
    sum += *ptrthisgrade++;
  }
  if (ptrthisgrade == ptrlastgrade &&
      cin >> ws && cin.good()) {
    cerr << "Array bounds exceeded\n"
    return 1;
  }
  else if (!cin.eof() && cin.fail()) {
    cerr << "Error: bad data entered\n"
    return 2;
  }
  ptrlastgrade = ptrthisgrade;
  cout << "Average grade: " << sum / (ptrthisgrade - grades)
      << endl;
  for (ptrthisgrade=grades; ptrthisgrade<ptrlastgrade;
      ptrthisgrade++) {
    cout << *ptrthisgrade << endl;
  }
  return 0;
}
```

Table 3.1 summarizes all of the rules for pointer arithmetic.

`ptrthisgrade = grades;`	The name of an array is a constant pointer to the first element.
`grades + 5 => 140, if grades contains 100 and points to doubles`	An integer can be added to or subtracted from any pointer. That integer is scaled by the sizeof the data type the pointer is pointing to, that is, multiplied by the sizeof the data type
`ptrthisgrade++`	Any pointer can be incremented or decremented. This is a variation of adding or subtracting an integer to/from a pointer.
`ptrthisgrade < ptrlastgrade`	Two pointers can be compared as long as they both point to the same type of data.
`ptrthisgrade - grades if ptrthisgrade contains 124 and grades has 100, this yields 24 / 8 => 3`	Two pointers can be subtracted as long as they both point to the same type of data. The resulting integer is scaled by the size of the data type, or divided by the size of the data type. Thus, when you subtract two pointers, you get the number of elements between these two points in the array.
`ptrthisgrade * n`	Pointer variables cannot be multiplied or divided.
`ptrthisgrade + 1.2345`	No floating point operations are allowed.
`*ptrthisgrade or *grades`	Any pointer can be dereferenced.
`grades[i] or ptrthisgrade[i]`	Any pointer can be subscripted.

Table 3.1 Summary of the Rules for Pointer Arithmetic

It is obvious that no multiplication or division is allowed. They would make no sense, such as **ptrthisgrade** * 100 for this would yield 100 * 100 or 10000! No floating point values can be used for obvious reasons. Pointers point to discrete locations, not fractional locations. Any pointer can be dereferenced. But look at this unusual one

```
*grades
```
Since the symbol **grades** is a constant pointer to the first element, it is a pointer and can be dereferenced. This accesses the first element in the array and is synonymous with writing

```
grades[0]
```

Even more peculiar is any pointer can be subscripted. No problem with writing

```
grades[i]
```
But what about

```
ptrthisgrade[i]
```
This unusual coding considers the origin point of the array to be at the location given by **ptrthisgrade**.

The Impact of Pointers on a Program

Why are pointers widely used with array processing instead of the more familiar subscript notation? Coding that uses pointers to process an array executes faster than coding that uses subscripts. Coding that uses subscripts generally requires fewer machine instructions and thus the program exe size is a bit smaller. Why?

To understand why there is a difference in execution speed, we need to examine how the computer actually does these actions. Let's say that we wrote

```
x = grades[i];
```

The compiler generates the following series of machine instructions to carry out this statement. I also show how many clock cycles that machine instruction might take. A clock cycle is the smallest unit of time in which a particular computer can perform units of work.

1. Look up the contents of variable **i** in memory, say it holds 1 => 1 clock cycle
2. Multiply that value by the size of the data type, 1 * 8 => 30+ clock cycles
3. Look up the contents of **grades**, 100 => 1 clock cycle
4. Add the 100 and the offset of 8, to get the memory address needed, 108 => 2 clock cycles
5. Go to that location and retrieve its contents, the grade of 42 in this case => 1 clock cycle

Total time is about 35 clock cycles.

For the pointer version

```
x = *ptrthisgrade;
```

we have the following machine instructions.

1. Look up the contents of the variable **ptrthisgrade**, say 108 => 1 clock cycle
2. Goto that location and retrieve its contents, the **grade** of 42 => 1 clock cycle

And the total time is about 2 clock cycles.

The difference between these two is 35 – 2 or 33 clock cycles. How fast is a clock cycle? In general it depends, in an overly simplified case, on the speed in MHz of your computer. To find the approximate clock speed of your computer, divide 1000 nanoseconds by the MHz speed rating of your computer. Suppose your machine had a speed rating of 500 MHz. Then a clock cycle would be 2 nanoseconds. A nanosecond is 10^{-9} of a second or one-trillionth of a second. Ok. So is this difference in speed of 33 clock cycles significant? The answer is that it all depends. If you had a single subscript access contained inside a loop that was executed 100 times, then the difference is minuscule. If you blink, you missed the difference in speed between these two versions of the program. On the other hand, if that single access was located within a loop that was done 100 times and that whole loop was within another loop done 10000 times, then you would certainly be able to observe the difference in run time speed between these two versions of the program.

Thus, pointers are widely used with array processing to gain speed of execution. But what about the pointer increment statement that must be part of such processing?

```
ptrthisgrade++;
```

The increment is always adding one to the pointer and the compiler knows at compile time what the size of the data type actually is. Hence, the compiler does not generate any multiply instructions, rather it generates an add instruction. The above expression becomes

```
ptrthisgrade + 8;
```

And speed of execution is maintained.

The Use of Hybrids and Dual Incrementing

There are two ways a programmer can misuse the pointer approach and thus lose much or all of the inherent speed benefits. The first of these is called using a hybrid expression—hybrid, in that both subscripts and pointers are used.

```
ptrthisgrade[i] = ptrthisgrade[i+1];
```

Here, although pointers are being used, a subscript is inserted. All speed benefits are lost as the slower subscript coding must be generated. Faster execution would be had by writing

```
*ptrthisgrade = *(ptrthisgrade + 1);
```

where **ptrthisgrade** is pointing to the ith element. The compiler handles the +1 term by simply generating +8 bytes to the pointer.

The second way to lose speed is to use a dual incrementing algorithm. Here is an example.

```
ptrthisgrade = grades;
for (i=0; i<numGrades; i++) {
  cout << *ptrthisgrade++ << endl;
}
```

Here, the pointer is dereferenced and dutifully incremented to get to the next element. However, the programmer cannot figure out how to terminate the loop and so uses another counter, **i** in this case. The program is incrementing the pointer and variable **i**—a dual increment.

Arrays of Pointers

Thus far, we have looked at various aspects of a pointer variable. But how about making an array of pointers? This is actually a very versatile type of an array as we will explore in this chapter and subsequent ones. Suppose that we wished to store an array of day name strings. If the user enters a day of 1, we can display the string "Sunday" on the screen. Here is how the array of pointers can be defined and initialized.

```
char* days[8] = {"", "Sunday", "Monday", "Tuesday",
                 "Wednesday", "Thursday", "Friday",
                 "Saturday"};
```

Each element of the array **days** contains the memory address of a null-terminated string. Figure 3.3 shows what this array looks like.

To use our array, one could code the following, ignoring the possibility of day values being out of range.

```
int day;
cin >> day;
cout << days[day];
```

If the user enters 1 for **day**, then **days[day]** is the element whose value is 101 which is the memory address of the string "Sunday."

It is just such a data layout that is used to pass the DOS command line parameters into the **main()** function of a program.

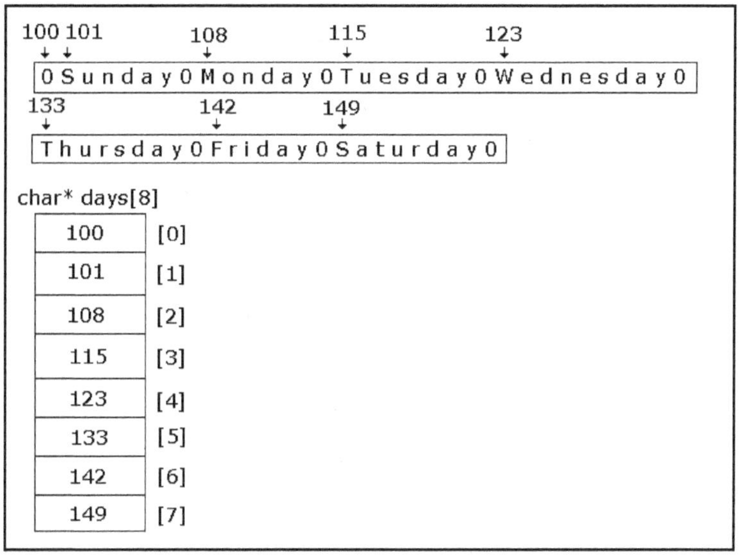

```
100 101        108         115          123
 ↓  ↓           ↓           ↓            ↓
| 0 S u n d a y 0 M o n d a y 0 T u e s d a y 0 W e d n e s d a y 0 |
 133          142         149
  ↓            ↓           ↓
| T h u r s d a y 0 F r i d a y 0 S a t u r d a y 0 |

char* days[8]
    | 100 |  [0]
    | 101 |  [1]
    | 108 |  [2]
    | 115 |  [3]
    | 123 |  [4]
    | 133 |  [5]
    | 142 |  [6]
    | 149 |  [7]
```

Figure 3.3 The Array of Pointers to Day Name Strings

Handling Command Line Parameters in the main() Function

When the **main()** function is called by the C runtime start up code, it is passed an array of **char*** items. Each **char*** element of the array points to one of the strings from the command line. As with any array, the number of items in the array is also passed. Here are the actual parameters that every **main()** function is passed.

```
int main (int argc, char* argv[]) {
```
The first parameter is the argument count or the number of items in the array. The second parameter an array of pointers, each pointer is the address of a string.

Let's review how a program can be launched. Assuming that the name of the program is pgm1.exe and that it is located in the \UserApps folder, the following represent various ways the program could be run.

```
    C:\>cd \UserApps
1   C:\UserApps>Pgm1
2   C:\UserApps>Pgm1 test.txt
3   C:\UserApps>Pgm1 test.txt result.txt
4   C:\UserApps>Pgm1 test.txt result.txt 10/12/2000
```

In the example on line 1, there are no parameters. However, since you cannot have an array with no elements in it, C++ always passes the full path to the program being run in element 0. Thus the content of **argv[0]** is always the program path that is being executed. In this case, **argv[0]** contains "C:\UserApps\Pgm1.exe" and the **argc** variable contains a 1, one item in the array.

In the example on line 4, the **argc** parameter contains 4 since there are 4 items in the **argv** array. The four strings contain:

argv[0] contains "C:\UserApps\Pgm1.exe"
argv[1] contains "test.txt"

83

argv[2] contains "result.txt"
argv[3] contains "10/12/2000"

Remember that on a command line, blanks are used to separate things. C++ places each item into a string for us.

This also is what happens if you create an icon from which to double click and launch the program. Remember that if you right click on the new icon and choose Properties, you can set a default path and also items to be on its command line.

Suppose that the program expected to be passed the input and output filenames from the command line. The following coding opens the two files.

```cpp
int main (int argc, char* argv[]) {
   if (argc != 3) {
      cerr << "Error: program is expecting the input and "
              "output filenames on the command line\n"
           << "Usage: Pgm1 infile.txt outfile.txt\n";
      return 1;
   }
   ifstream infile (argv[1]);
   ofstream outfile (argv[2]);
```

Dynamic Memory Allocation

During program execution, C++ provides a mechanism for a program to ask for additional memory for items. This is done with the **new** function. Of course, when the program is finished using that memory, it needs to free it up by using the **delete** function.

The **new** function is coded a bit differently. The basic syntax is

```cpp
new (std::nothrow) datatype_desired
```

The **new** function returns a pointer to the dynamically allocated memory if it is available. If there is no more memory with which to carry out the request, then **new** returns the null pointer, 0.

Note that the **new** function behaves differently under .NET versus VC6. Specifically, the behavior is what does the function do if the memory cannot be allocated? The function can do one of two things: return a 0 or NULL pointer or throw a C++ exception to be trapped by the caller. The C++ error handling system is beyond the scope of this text and is covered in the next course. So in this course, we need the **new** function returning a NULL pointer if it cannot allocate the memory.

In VC6, the default behavior of **new** was to return a NULL pointer if it was not successful. One needed to add an additional parameter if **new** should throw a C++ exception. However, in .NET or VC7, Microsoft reversed these; now the default is to throw the exception. Thus, we must pass the **new** function the **std::nothrow** parameter to get it to return a NULL or 0 pointer. If you are using VC6, you can omit the parameter entirely. Thus we have the following.

```cpp
new (std::nothrow) datatype_desired; // .NET users
new datatype_desired                 // VC6 and earlier
```

Suppose that we wished to allocate memory for a new **double** that represents a total. One could code

```
double* ptrtotal = new (std::nothrow) double;
```

The function allocates 8 bytes of memory (the size of a **double**) and returns its memory address which is then assigned to the automatic pointer variable, **ptrtotal**.

These are all valid.

```
int*  ptrtally = new (std::nothrow) int; // space for a new int
long* ptrlong = new (std::nothrow) long; // space for a new long
char* ptrtype = new (std::nothrow) char; // space for a new char
```

These four new variables can then be used in anyway a **double**, **int**, **long** or **char** could be used, just remember to use the dereference operator. One could code

```
*ptrtotal = 0      // set total to 0
*ptrtotal += cost * qty; // accumulate total of orders
*ptrtally = 0;     // set tally counter to 0
(*ptrtally)++;     // increment tally counter
*ptrlong = 42;     // assign 42 to the long
*ptrtype = 'F';    // place the letter F into the char
```

Finally, when the program is finished with the memory, the **delete** function is called.

```
delete ptrtotal;
delete ptrtally;
delete ptrlong;
delete ptrtype;
```

Now in practice, seldom does one dynamically allocate a new **double**, **int** or **long**. Much more frequently, one allocates a new instance of a structure. Suppose the program defined the following **INVREC** structure.

```
const int DESCRLEN = 21;
struct INVREC {
  long    itemNum;
  char    description[DESCRLEN];
  int     qtyOnHand;
  double unitCost;
};
```

One could now code a far more interesting allocation.

```
INVREC* ptrrec = new INVREC;
```

And the corresponding freeing of the memory would be

```
delete ptrrec;
```

The Location of the Heap

From where does the memory that is being allocated come? It is acquired from the local heap, which is, as its name indicates, a large pile of unallocated memory that is available for this use. Figure 3.4 shows the layout of memory of a C++ program and where the heap is located.

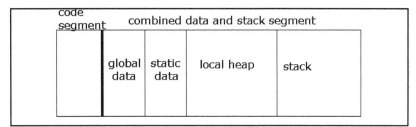

Figure 3.4 The Memory Layout of a Program

The heap is located between the static data section and the top of the stack section. On a Win32 platform, such as Windows 95/98/NT/2000/ME, if the stack section becomes full and more stack space is needed, Windows temporarily halts the program and resizes these areas making the stack larger. The same is true if the amount of memory needed on the heap exceeds the current size of the heap. Windows reallocates the heap larger dynamically on the fly as the program is running. How much can the stack and the heap grow? Any Win32 application can have a total memory usage of about 2G. However, being just a bit more practical since most of us do not have 2G of memory installed on our computers at this time, it is really the size of the Windows swap or paging file (virtual memory) plus the amount of free memory that determines the maximum size that the entire program can occupy. For example, on my programming machine that runs Win2000, I have a dedicated 500M swap file. Thus, no single application can use more than 500M + the amount of the free128M memory available on the machine.

Do We Need to Check for Successful Allocation?

Ideally, one should check the returned pointer for 0 and handle appropriately. That is, if the returned pointer is 0, the computer does not have sufficient memory to satisfy this request. Theoretically, one should code

```
double* ptrtotal = new (std::nothrow) double;
if (!ptrtotal) {
  cerr << "Error: out of memory\n";
  return 1;
}
*ptrtotal = 0;
. . .
*ptrtotal += cost * qty; // accumulate total of orders
```

In practice, this check is often not done. Consider what the status of the Windows system is if it cannot allocate a **double** for us. Long before we ever arrive at running totally out of memory so that it cannot even allocate 8 additional bytes, Windows has been displaying its famous message: "The system is dangerously low on resources; shut down some applications." In a simple allocation such as all of these are, most programmers do not bother to even check that returned pointer, figuring that if there is not sufficient memory left, Windows would already have told the user many times that it was running out of memory. By design, address 0, which would be the value returned if the computer was out of memory, actually is the very first byte of the global section of the data-stack segment. So they figure there is memory there somehow. Ah, mostly working programs arise from this. But with small amounts as the above four allocations are, it is probably a reasonable way to go, if the program was not a critical application.

Beginning Data Structures in C++

If the program is a critical application, such as customer billing, a real-time spaceflight simulator, an intensive-care health monitoring program, then **always** check on the success of the request for more memory. Also, if you are asking for a larger amount of memory as we will do here shortly, such as a new array or space to hold a graphical image, then by all means check that returned pointer for 0. These are often the two guidelines that seem to be followed by most working programmers on a Windows platform. However, to avoid mostly working software, one should always check that returned pointer for 0.

Dynamic Allocation of Arrays

Far more commonly an entire array of items is allocated. Suppose that the user has entered the number of points, **numPoints**, that they needed for a pair of x and y value arrays. We know that the following coding cannot compile.

```
int numPoints;
cin >> numPoints;
long x[numPoints];
long y[numPoints];
```

Remember, array bounds must be a constant known at compile time and are often **const int**s or **#define** symbols for ease of program maintenance. In the past, the only recourse was to make the array bounds sufficiently large to hold the worst case the programmer expected would arise. And if that limit was exceeded, the program would produce an array size exceeded message and abort.

Dynamic memory allocation totally removes this restriction on array limits. However, to dynamically allocate a single dimensioned array, changes must be made to both the **new** and **delete** function syntax.

```
new (std::nothrow) datatype_desired [arraysize];
delete [] arraypointer;
```

Thus, to handle the user inputting the number of points they need and then allocating a pair of **x** and **y** arrays sufficiently large, one could code the following.

```
int numPoints;
cin >> numPoints;
long* x = new (std::nothrow) long [numPoints];
long* y = new (std::nothrow) long [numPoints];
```

The **arraysize** parameter can be a constant, variable or integer expression. Here it is a variable. When the allocation is completed, memory appears as shown in Figure 3.5.

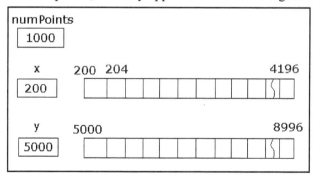

Figure 3.5 The x and y Arrays

87

Notice that **x** contains the address of the first element of the 1000 **long**s. Since each **long** is 4 bytes in size, the total array size is 4000 bytes, making the address of **x[999]** 4196. The array **y** begins at memory address 5000. Thus, the address of element **y[0]** is 5000. The address of **y[999]** is 8996.

Notice a subtle difference in the naming convention I have used with the two arrays. They are not called **ptrx** and **ptry** as have all of the other pointers. Why? I intend to use subscripts to access the elements in these arrays. Thus, one might expect to next see a sequence such as this.

```
for (int j=0; j<numPoints; j++) {
  cin >> x[j] >> y[j];
}
```

The following are all valid array allocations.

```
double*  totals = new (std::nothrow) double [maxTotals];
char* name = new (std::nothrow) char [currentNameLength];
INVREC* arec = new (std::nothrow) INVREC[maxInventoryItems];
```

What about passing these dynamically allocated arrays to a function? The prototype could be either of these two.

```
void DoCalcs (long x[], long y[], int numPoints);
void DoCalcs (long* x, long* y, int numPoints);
```

In either case, the function would be called this way.

```
DoCalcs (x, y, numPoints);
```

Remember, the name of an array is a pointer to the first element. Hence, there is no difference between coding **long x[]** and **long* x**; they are the same thing, the memory address of the first element. However, the reader of your program will naturally expect to see subscripts being used to access the elements when you use **long x[]**. Likewise, they will expect to see pointer notation being used when you use **long* x**.

Thus, dynamically allocated arrays open up vast new possibilities with array processing programs!

However, the deletion of dynamically allocated arrays is special too. Consider these two allocations.

```
long* ptrlong = new (std::nothrow) long;
long* x = new (std::nothrow) long [numPoints];
```

Notice one crucial, vital fact. Both **ptrlong** and **x** contain the memory address of a **long**. As far as the compiler is concerned, there is no difference whatsoever between these two pointers. They both point to the memory address of a **long**. However, there are also 999 more **long**s after that first one to which **x** points! And here is where a programmer can get into trouble with the **delete** function. These two dynamically allocated items must be deleted differently. The compiler must be told that pointer **x** is pointing to a whole array of **long**s!

```
delete ptrlong;
delete [] x;
```

What would happen if the programmer goofed and coded just

```
delete x;
```

The **delete** function would just free up storage occupied by one **long**, leaving the remaining 999 **long**s still marked as in use! This is called a memory leak. A **memory leak** means that some dynamically allocated memory has not been freed when the program terminates.

Memory Leaks

Failure to free up dynamically allocated memory is known as a memory leak. Is it serious? Well, it all depends. Under the Windows platform, when any application terminates, Windows automatically frees any and all memory that that program has ever allocated. In other words, Windows cleans up after you; it does not trust you.

However, being lazy and not freeing up dynamically allocated memory can sometimes get you and your program into deep trouble. Suppose that every time a new transaction was entered your program did something like

```
TRANSACTION* ptrtrans = new (std::nothrow) TRANSACTION;
```

And suppose that you forgot to free up the memory allocated when you were done processing that transaction. Suppose that an instance of this structure occupied 100 bytes. When the program is finally done processing today's transactions, suppose that it handled 100,000 of them. How much memory did the program ultimately consume and then leak? 10,000,000 or just under 10M.

Ah, but suppose your program in production is run on the company's network server. Servers are seldom rebooted for obvious reasons. And programs often run for days on servers. What do you suppose would happen after your program ran for 20 days consecutively? Now you have asked for 200M of server memory! You are going to eventually run the server completely out of memory, causing operations to have to deal with many "The server is dangerously low on resources; please shut down some applications." Once they discover which application has used up all of the server's memory, you will be asked not so politely to fix your program!

If you go on into Windows programming, you often need to allocate instances of Windows' system resources, such as brushes, pens, fonts, and so on. There are a limited, finite number of these items. If you ask for a new brush and do not give it back when you are done with it, eventually Windows runs out of brushes and crashes.

Thus, a program should never go into production with memory leaks. Period!

How can you tell if a program has a memory leak? Careful design aids along with verifying that every **new** has a corresponding **delete**. But there is another way. The Visual C++ compiler has an automatic way it can check for memory leaks and notify you of them if they occur.

Checking for Memory Leaks with Visual C++ 6.0 and .NET

The methods used to check for memory leaks are left up to the compiler manufacturer. Microsoft has developed a fairly easy way to check for them. To check for leaks, first include the header file **<crtdbg.h>**. Then, just before you return to DOS, call the **_CrtDumpMemoryLeaks()** function. This function takes no parameters but does two actions. It returns a **bool**; **true** if there are leaks, **false** if there are no leaks. Secondly, if there are leaks, then it dumps the memory addresses and contents of all memory that was leaked. The display is in the Output window after the program has terminated.

Beginning Data Structures in C++

Common coding of this function is in **main()** just before the **return 0;** instruction as shown below.

```
if (_CrtDumpMemoryLeaks())
  cerr << "Memory leaks occurred!\n";
else
  cerr << "No memory leaks.\n";
return 0;
}
```

There is one major caution here for the users of VC6 and earlier versions. Please note that the new iostream classes that are used with **namespace std** contain internal memory leaks as of VC6.0 Service Pack 3! Thus, if you use the **namespace std** you are guaranteed to get memory leaks. Try using the older iostream classes. They do not leak memory. Mostly working software.

Checking for Memory Leaks with Borland C++ 5.0

Borland does not have such a built-in method to check for leaks. Instead, we must provide a helper function to assist us in detecting leaks. Here is some coding that works for a Win32 Console application under BC5.0.

```
#include <alloc.h>

long HeapSize () {
 int result;
 if ((result = heapcheck ()) != _HEAPOK) {
  cout << "Corrupted heap: " << result << endl;
  return 0;
 }
 long hsize = 0;
 heapinfo info;
 info.ptr = 0;
 while (heapwalk (&info) == _HEAPOK)
  hsize += info.size;
 return hsize;
}

int main () {
 long beginsize =HeapSize  (), endsize = 0;
 ... now go allocate stuff
 ... now go free stuff
 endsize = HeapSize ();
 if (beginsize != endsize) cout << "Memory Leaks\n"
 else cout << "No Memory Leaks\n";
 return 0;
}
```

This coding and another version that can handle memory leak checking on other Borland platforms than just Win32 console applications are located in a BorlandOnly subfolder of Chapter03 folder in the sample programs for this chapter.

90

The Use of the const Keyword with Pointers

The **const** keyword when used with pointers and reference variables can have two meanings, depending upon its location within the data definition.

When the **const** precedes the data type, the data pointed to by that pointer or reference variable is constant. That is, the data itself cannot be changed. Consider the following definitions of functions.

```
void Fun1 (long* array, int numItems);
void Fun2 (const long* array, int numItems);
void Fun3 (long* const array, int numItems);
void Fun4 (const long* const array, int numItems);
```

In **Fun1()** one could say
```
array[0] = 42;
```
and one could say
```
array = new long[42];
```
This is because nothing is considered constant.

In **Fun2()**, the array data has been made constant. Thus if one coded
```
array[0] = 42;
```
it would generate a compile error. However, one could still say
```
array = new long[42];
```
This is because the parameter pointer is not considered constant.

In **Fun3()**, the parameter pointer is constant. Thus, one could say
```
array[0] = 42;
```
because the array has not been made constant. However, if you tried to do the following
```
array = new long[42];
```
This creates a compile error since the parameter pointer is constant.

In **Fun4()** both the array and the parameter pointer have been made constant. Thus both of the following would generate an error.
```
array[0] = 42;
array = new long[42];
```

Normally, only the array data is made constant to those functions that should not be granted rights to alter the array data.

A Complete Example Using Dynamic Memory Allocation

Pgm03a, Normal Body Temperatures, illustrates the use of dynamic memory allocation of an array. A health research institute has gathered a collection of the normal body temperatures for a large number of people. The first number in the file contains a count of the number of temperatures contained in that file. The program displays the average body temperature, the maximum and minimum temperatures, the mean temperature and the standard deviation. The program should accept the names of the input and output files from the command line.

Looking over the problem, we obviously need to dynamically allocate an array of **float**s to hold the temperatures. To get the mean, the one in the middle, the array must be sorted. To calculate the standard deviation, we must sum the square of the difference of each temperature from the average temperature, divide that sum by the number of temperatures – 1, and finally take the square root of that result.

As usual, the first step is to design a solution. Here is the Top-down design I chose.

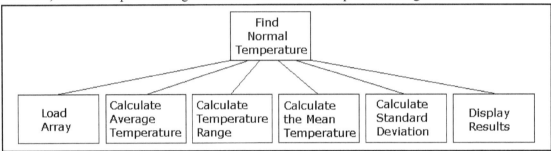

Figure 3.6 Top-down Design for Normal Temperatures Program

I have decided to use the C built-in **qsort()** function to handle the sorting aspect.

However, there is one significant detail that this design has upon the array processing. And that is the **LoadArray()** function. For obvious reasons, I prefer to encapsulate the inputting of an array thereby streamlining the **main()** function. In this situation, within **LoadArray()**, the first number in the data represents the actual array bounds. If I then dynamically allocate an array of that dimension, how do I get the address of that array back into a variable in the **main()** function? Here is what we have done up to this point.

```
int main () {
  float temps[MAX];
  int numValues = LoadArray (temps, MAX);
```
with
```
int LoadArray (float x[], int limit) {
```

LoadArray()'s **x** parameter is a pointer that contains a *__copy__* of the memory location of the first element of **main()**'s array **temps**.

In this case where **LoadArray()** actually allocates the memory for the array, the following cannot possibly work!

```
int main () {
 float* temps;
 int numValues = LoadArray (temps);
```
with
```
int LoadArray (float x[]) {
 int num;
 cin >> num;
 x = new (std::nothrow) float [num];
```
This is a very common error that programmers new to dynamic memory allocation make. What is wrong with this approach? Certainly, **LoadArray()** is allocating the needed array properly. But where does that address of the array get stored? It is placed into **LoadArray()**'s parameter _copy_ of the contents of **main()**'s **temps** variable (which is initially core garbage). So what is in **main()**'s **temps** pointer when **LoadArray()** returns? The same initial core garbage!

There are a number of ways this can be fixed. An easy one is to have the **LoadArray()** function simply return the pointer to the dynamically allocated memory. Here is the way I chose to handle this.
```
int main () {
 int numTemps;
 float* temps = LoadArray (numTemps);
```
with
```
float* LoadArray (int& numTemps) {
 float* temps;
 cin >> numTemps;
 temps = new (std::nothrow) float [numTemps];
 ...
 return temps;
}
```

The alternative is to pass the array as a reference to the address.
```
int main () {
 float* temps;
 int numValues = LoadArray (temps);
```
with
```
int LoadArray (float*& x) {
 int num;
 cin >> num;
 x = new (std::nothrow) float [num];
```
We allocate the new array but **x** is really a reference to main's **temps** pointer and the compiler stores the address of the new array back into main's **temps** variable.

C++ has a built-in function, **qsort()**, that can sort any array. Its simplified prototype is
```
qsort (array, number of elements, size of one element,
       the comparison function to use);
```
The array is obviously the memory address of the first element. The second parameter is the integer number of elements in the array. The third parameter is the integer size of one element. However, the function depends on the user to tell it which of two particular elements is the smaller. The fourth parameter is the memory address of a function, our comparison function that we provide. The comparison function must have

this prototype:
```
int compare (const void* ptritem1, const void* ptritem2);
```
And the return value is
```
0 if the two items are equal
1 if the first item is larger than the second item
-1 if the first item is smaller than the second item
```
Of course, when we implement the comparison function, the first action must be to typecast the **void** pointers back into usable pointers. In this case, the array is of type **float**; thus, a pointer to a specific element would be a **float***. So we can handle the conversion similar to this.
```
float* ptrt1 = (float*) ptritem1;
```

Here is the test1 input file and the results that the program produced.

```
Temps.txt - First Set of Test Data

 1 11
 2 98.6
 3 98.5
 4 98.7
 5 98.8
 6 98.4
 7 98.9
 8 98.3
 9 98.6
10 98.6
11 98.4
12 98.6
```

```
Results.txt - The Output of the Program on the First Test Set

1 Acme Health Studies - Average Body Temperatures
2
3 Number   Average   Maximum   Minimum   Median  Standard
4  Temps    Temp      Temp      Temp      Temp   Deviation
5
6   11      98.6      98.9      98.3      98.6     0.2
```

```
Pgm03a.h - Includes and Prototypes - Application Header

1 #pragma once
2 #include <iostream>
3 #include <iomanip>
4 #include <fstream>
5 //#include <stdlib.h> // for qsort if using VC6
6 #include <cmath>
7 #include <crtdbg.h>    // for memory leak checking
8 using namespace std;
```

```
 9
10 float* LoadArray (int& numTemps, const char* infileName);
11 float  CalcAvgTemp (const float temps[], int numTemps);
12 void   CalcTempRanges (const float temps[], int numTemps,
13                         float& minTemp, float& maxTemp);
14 float  CalcMeanTemp (const float temps[], int numTemps);
15 float  CalcStdDev (const float temps[], int numTemps,
16                 float avg);
17 void   DisplayResults (int numTemps, float avgTemp,
18                         float minTemp, float maxTemp,
19                         float meanTemp, float stdDev,
20                         const char* outfileName);
21 int    CmpTemps (const void* ptrtemp1, const void* ptrtemp2);
22
```

Pgm03a.cpp main() - Produce the Body Temperature Report

```
 1 #include "Pgm03a.h"
 2
 3 /*******************************************************/
 4 /*                                                     */
 5 /* Pgm03a: Compute the Average Body Temperature        */
 6 /*                                                     */
 7 /*******************************************************/
 8
 9 int main (int argc, char* argv[]) {
10
11  // verify we have the correct number of cmd line parms
12  if (argc != 3) {
13   cerr << "Error: the names of the input and output files "
14           "must be given\n"
15        << "Usage: Pgm03a temps.txt results.txt\n";
16   return 1;
17  }
18
19  int numTemps; // to store the number of temps in the array
20
21  // load the array, we are responsible for its deletion
22  float* temps = LoadArray (numTemps, argv[1]);
23
24  // find the average, maximum and minimum temperatures
25  float  avgTemp = CalcAvgTemp (temps, numTemps);
26  float  minTemp;
27  float  maxTemp;
28  CalcTempRanges (temps, numTemps, minTemp, maxTemp);
29
30  // sort the array so we can find the median temperature
31  qsort (temps, numTemps, sizeof (float), CmpTemps);
32
```

```
33  // find the median and standard deviation from the average
34  float   meanTemp = CalcMeanTemp (temps, numTemps);
35  float   stdDev = CalcStdDev (temps, numTemps, avgTemp);
36
37  // produce the final report
38  DisplayResults (numTemps, avgTemp, minTemp, maxTemp,
39                  meanTemp, stdDev, argv[2]);
40
41  // remove the dynamically allocated array
42  delete [] temps;
43
44  // check for memory leaks
45  if (_CrtDumpMemoryLeaks())
46   cerr << "Memory leaks occurred!\n";
47  else
48   cerr << "No memory leaks.\n";
49
50   return 0;
51  }
```

LoadArray.cpp - Dynamically Allocates the Array and Inputs It

```
 1  #include "Pgm03a.h"
 2
 3  /*****************************************************/
 4  /*                                                   */
 5  /*  LoadArray: dynamically allocates an array of     */
 6  /*             numTemps floats and inputs the array  */
 7  /*             if successful, returns the addr of the*/
 8  /*                array                              */
 9  /*             if it fails, array is removed and pgm */
10  /*                is aborted                         */
11  /*                                                   */
12  /*****************************************************/
13
14  float* LoadArray (int& numTemps, const char* infileName) {
15   ifstream infile (infileName);
16
17   if (!infile) {
18    cerr << "Error: cannot open input file: "
19         << infileName << endl;
20    exit (2);
21   }
22
23   infile >> numTemps; // input the number of temps in the file
24
25   if (!infile) {
26    cerr << "Error: cannot input the number of temperatures\n";
27    infile.close();
```

96

```
28   exit (3);
29  }
30
31  // abort if the number is not at least 1
32  if (numTemps <= 0) {
33   cerr << "Error: the number of temperatures cannot be 0 or less"
34        << "\nIt was: " << numTemps << endl;
35   infile.close();
36   exit (4);
37  }
38
39  // dynamically allocate the array to store the temperatures
40  float* temps = new (std::nothrow) float [numTemps];
41
42  // abort if out of memory
43  if (!temps) {
44   cerr << "Error: cannot allocate the memory for the array\n";
45   infile.close();
46   exit (5);
47  }
48  char junk;
49
50  // input the entire array of temperatures
51  for (int i=0; i<numTemps && infile >> temps[i]; i++) ;
52
53  // eof shoulf not have occurred yet
54  if (infile.eof()) {
55   cerr << "Error: premature EOF - too few temperatures in the "
56        << "file\nAborting the program\n";
57   delete [] temps;
58   infile.close();
59   exit (6);
60  }
61  else if (!infile) { // check for bad data on input
62   cerr << "Error: bad data in the input file\n"
63        << "Aborting the program\n";
64   delete [] temps;
65   infile.close();
66   exit(7);
67  }
68  else if (infile >> junk) { // check for extra temps remaining
69                             // in the file
70   cerr << "Error: there appears to be additional temperatures "
71        << "in the input file.\nCheck the count.\n"
72        << "Aborting the program\n";
73   delete [] temps;
74   infile.close();
75   exit(8);
76  }
77  infile.close();
```

```
78
79  // all went as planned, so return the address of the array
80  return temps;
81  }
82
```

CalcAvgTemp.cpp - Find the Average Temperature

```
 1  #include "Pgm03a.h"
 2
 3  /**************************************************/
 4  /*                                              */
 5  /*  CalcAvgTemp: find the average temperature from    */
 6  /*              an array of numTemps which as at least */
 7  /*              one element in it               */
 8  /*                                              */
 9  /**************************************************/
10
11  float  CalcAvgTemp (const float temps[], int numTemps) {
12   float sum = 0;
13   for (int i=0; i<numTemps; i++) {
14    sum += temps[i];
15   }
16   return sum / numTemps;
17  }
```

CalcTempRanges.cpp - Find the Max and Min Temperatures

```
 1  #include "Pgm03a.h"
 2
 3  /**************************************************/
 4  /*                                              */
 5  /*  CalcTempRanges: find the maximum and minimum temps */
 6  /*                 from an array of numTemps which    */
 7  /*                 has at least one element in it   */
 8  /*                                              */
 9  /**************************************************/
10
11  void   CalcTempRanges (const float temps[], int numTemps,
12                         float& minTemp, float& maxTemp) {
13   minTemp = maxTemp = temps[0];
14   for (int i=1; i<numTemps; i++) {
15    if (minTemp > temps[i])
16     minTemp = temps[i];
17    if (maxTemp < temps[i])
18     maxTemp = temps[i];
19   }
20  }
```

```
CmpTemps.cpp - qsort() Helper - Compares Two Temperatures

 1 #include "Pgm03a.h"
 2
 3 /****************************************************/
 4 /*                                                  */
 5 /* CmpTemps: qsort comparison function              */
 6 /*           compares two temperatures              */
 7 /*           returns 0 if temp1 = temp2             */
 8 /*                   1 if temp1 > temp2             */
 9 /*                  -1 if temp1 < temp2             */
10 /*                                                  */
11 /****************************************************/
12
13 int    CmpTemps (const void* ptrtemp1, const void* ptrtemp2) {
14  float* ptrt1 = (float*) ptrtemp1;
15  float* ptrt2 = (float*) ptrtemp2;
16  if (*ptrt1 < *ptrt2)
17    return -1;
18  if (*ptrt1 > *ptrt2)
19    return 1;
20  return 0;
21 }
```

```
CalcMeanTemp.cpp - Find the Median Temperature

 1 #include "Pgm03a.h"
 2
 3 /****************************************************/
 4 /*                                                  */
 5 /* CalcMeanTemp: find the median temperature from an */
 6 /*               array of temps that is sorted into */
 7 /*               increasing value order - numTemps  */
 8 /*               is at least 1                      */
 9 /*                                                  */
10 /****************************************************/
11
12 float  CalcMeanTemp (const float temps[], int numTemps) {
13  if (numTemps % 2) // odd number of temps
14    return temps[numTemps/2];
15  else // even number of temps
16    return (temps[numTemps/2] + temps[(numTemps-1)/2])/2;
17 }
```

```
CalcStdDev.cpp - Find the Standard Deviation
```

```
 1 #include "Pgm03a.h"
 2
 3 /*****************************************************/
 4 /*                                                 */
 5 /* CalcStdDev: find the standard deviation from the  */
 6 /*             average by summing the squares of the */
 7 /*             difference of each temp from the avg  */
 8 /*             and taking the sqrt of that over n-1  */
 9 /*                                                 */
10 /*****************************************************/
11
12 float  CalcStdDev (const float temps[],int numTemps, float avg) {
13  float sum = 0;
14  for (int i=0; i<numTemps; i++) {
15   float x = temps[i] - avg;
16   sum += x * x;
17  }
18  return (float) (sqrt (sum / (numTemps-1)));
19 }
```

DisplayResults.cpp - Print the Report

```
 1 #include "Pgm03a.h"
 2
 3 /*****************************************************/
 4 /*                                                 */
 5 /* DisplayResults: prints the final results         */
 6 /*                                                 */
 7 /*****************************************************/
 8
 9 void   DisplayResults (int numTemps, float avgTemp,
10                        float minTemp, float maxTemp,
11                        float meanTemp, float stdDev,
12                        const char* outfileName) {
13  ofstream outfile (outfileName);
14  if (!outfile) {
15   cerr << "Error: cannot open the output file whose name"
16        << " was: " << outfileName << endl;
17   exit (7);
18  }
19
20  outfile << fixed << setprecision (1);
22
23  outfile << "Acme Health Studies - Average Body Temperatures"
24          << endl << endl
25        << "Number   Average  Maximum  Minimum  Median  Standard"
26        << endl
27        << " Temps    Temp     Temp     Temp     Temp   Deviation"
28        << "\n\n";
```

```
29
30   outfile << setw(5) << numTemps << setw(9) << avgTemp
31          << setw(9) << maxTemp << setw(9) << minTemp
32          << setw(8) << meanTemp << setw(8) << stdDev
33          << endl;
34
35   outfile.close();
36 }
```

Notice that I placed all of the needed **#includes** in the program header file along with all of the function prototypes. This header is included in all of the cpp files.

Notice that most all of the functions are indeed very short. Indeed, we could have coded the whole program within the **main()** function. However, I did it this way for several reasons. One, we need more practice in seeing how a program can be composed of multiple cpp files. Two, by using many functions, the **main()** function becomes streamlined and shows the overall program flow or logic much better. Three, by developing larger programs in this fashion, stub testing becomes a breeze. That is, we can write **main()** and the **LoadArray()** functions and stub out the other functions and then run and test the program, guaranteeing that we have the array loaded properly. Then one by one, we can supply the missing function bodies and test each as we go along. The whole process of program development becomes much easier to handle this way.

What about test oracles? Notice that in the initial block comments of the functions, I outlined the incoming specifications. We can easily construct several testing oracles to verify all is working to specifications. However, I left a potential crash error in the program for you to find. The testing oracles that I created are as shown.

temps.txt	11 temperatures should work ok
temps-even.txt	10 temperatures should work ok
temps-baddata.txt	contains a letter where there should be a number
temps-extratemp.txt	contains an extra temperature, count is off
temps-missingdata.txt	lacking one temperature, count is off
temps-outmemory.txt	asks for too much memory
temps-zero.txt	asks for 0 elements in the array

There is still one situation, which if it occurs, will crash the program. Look over the coding and the testing oracles and create another testing oracle that would produce that error. The run the program with that oracle and prove that it does crash. Then, revise the program to be able to detect and handle that error.

Review Questions

1. If you have not yet done so, find the remaining error(s) in **Pgm03a** and create a testing oracle that would crash the program. Then sketch a fix that would allow the program to detect and handle that circumstance.

2. Assume that variable **x** is located at memory location 100 and that **ptrx** is located at address 104. Fill in the data types and value of the following expressions.

```
int x = 42;
int* ptrx = &x;
```

Expression	Data Type	Value
x		
&x		
* x		
ptrx		
&ptrx		
*ptrx		

3. A program defined the following.

```
double x;
double y;
double z;
double* prtx;
double* ptry;
double* ptrz;
```

Assume that the memory address of **x** is 100, **y** is 108, **z** is 116, **ptrx** is 124, **ptry** is 128 and **ptrz** is 132. Suppose that the following statements are executed sequentially in order so that their effects are cumulative. Show the new value of any expression whose value is changed by each assignment statement.

	Statement	x	ptrx	y	ptry	z	ptrz	*ptrx	*ptry	*ptrz
1	x = 1.23;									
2	ptry = & y;									
3	y = 42.5									
4	ptrx = &x;									
5	z = 99;									
6	ptrz = &z;									

7	z = *ptrx;									
8	*ptrx = y;									
9	*ptry = *ptrz;									
10	z = y;									
11	*ptrz = 0;									

4. Consider the **CalcAvgTemp()** function from **Pgm03a**.

```
float  CalcAvgTemp (float temps[], int numTemps) {
  float sum = 0;
  for (int i=0; i<numTemps; i++) {
   sum += temps[i];
  }
  return sum / numTemps;
}
```

Rewrite the function body using all pointers. That is, remove variable i and substitute some pointer variables instead.

5. Consider the **CalcTempRanges()** function from Pgm03a.

```
void  CalcTempRanges (float temps[], int numTemps,
                      float& minTemp, float& maxTemp) {
  minTemp = maxTemp = temps[0];
  for (int i=1; i<numTemps; i++) {
   if (minTemp > temps[i])
    minTemp = temps[i];
   if (maxTemp < temps[i])
    maxTemp = temps[i];
  }
}
```

Rewrite the function body using all pointers. That is, remove variable **i** and substitute some pointer variables instead.

6. Define an array of pointers to store the strings, "Ten," "Twenty," "Thirty" and so on up to "Ninety." Make sure the array is initialized to these strings.

7. Dynamically allocate memory for each of these and then delete that memory.
   A. a char
   B. an int
   C. an unsigned long

Beginning Data Structures in C++

D. a double
E. an array of 100 longs
F. an array of maxStore of doubles
G. an array of count + 2 characters

8. A programmer coded the following function. What is wrong with it and how would you fix it?

```
double fun (double x, int num) {
  double* array;
  array = new double [num];
  for (int j=0; j<num; j++) {
    array[j] = x + j;
    sum += array[j] / j;
  }
  return sum;
}
```

9. Rewrite the function in Review Question 8 above using all pointers and no subscripts. That is, remove all references to the subscript j. Use a couple of pointers instead.

Stop! Do These Exercises Before Programming

1. A program must be written to input all of the cash register sales receipts and perform some statistical studies on them. The first line in the input file contains the number of receipts that this file contains. The input file is produced as the output from another program and can be counted upon to contain no errors or discrepancies, such as missing a receipt.

 The programmer began the **main()** function by trying to create the array. The following does not compile. Why? How can it be fixed so that it works?

```
int main () {
  int count;
  double receipts = new double [count];
  cin >> count;
```

2. Frustrated by the failure of only 4 lines of code, the programmer then tried the following.

```
int main () {
  int count;
  cin >> count;
  double receipts = new double;
```

Likewise this did not compile. Why? How can it be repaired so that it would work?

3. Undaunted, the programmer guessed at his error and then tried the following coding. Memory became corrupted and the program did strange things and crashed. Why? How can it be repaired?

```
int main() {
  int count;
  cin >> count;
  double* receipts = new double;
  for (int k=0; k<count; k++)
   cin >> receipts[k];
```

4. Grateful for your assistance and with the idea of using modular development and stub testing, the programmer next decided to have a **FindAverageReceipt()** function. He created the prototype and a stub body. However, it did not compile. Why? How can it be fixed?

```
double FindAverageReceipt (double x[], int num);
int main () {
  int count;
  ...
  double* receipts;
  ...
  double avg = FindAverageReceipt (receipts[count], count);
```

5. Management has said that there can perhaps be many hundreds of thousands of receipts in the file and that the program should run as fast as possible. Thus, when the programmer got to the actual implementation of **FindAverageReceipt()**, he realized that a pure pointer version must be written, one that used no subscripts or counters. Realizing his lack of skill in this area, he has asked you for assistance in coding the function's body. Write the function's body.

```
double FindAverageReceipt (double x[], int num) {



}
```

6. Having learned a great deal from your assistance, the programmer successfully implemented several other functions. Now, however, he decided he should check for memory leaks. Sure enough, his program leaked memory. Where is the leak and how can this be repaired?

```
int main () {
  int count;
  ...
  double* receipts = new double [count];
  ... // loads it
  double avg = FindAverageReceipt (...
  SortIt (receipts, count);
  double mean = FindMean (receipts, count);
  DisplayResults (avg, mean, ...
  return 0;
}
```

Programming Problems

Problem Pgm03-1 Name Processing

A commonly entered field is a person's name. However, names vary greatly in their total length. Commonly, a program that needs to store names dynamically allocates a string that is exactly the right length to hold the current person's name. Often that string is a member of a structure. However, in this problem we are going to concentrate on the mechanics of how to construct the string in the first place.

Write a function **InputName()** that takes an **istream&** and returns a **char***. It defines a character string that is 100 characters long and inputs the next person's name into that string. The name in the input file is delimited by double quote marks. For example, "John Jones." Now, with the name inputted into the string that is fixed at 100 characters, dynamically allocate a new string that is sufficiently large enough to hold this new name. In this case, the new string's array size would be 11 - don't forget space for the null terminator. Then, copy the name into the new string and return the address of that new string.

Write a **main()** function that opens the file that I have given you called **names.txt**. Now write a loop that calls **InputName()** to retrieve the next name and then display's that name as shown below along with its **strlen()** value. When the end of file is reached, check for memory leaks.

```
string name
 len
  10    John Jones
  19    Samuel Addison, Jr.
```

Problem Pgm03-2 Customer Order Statistics

Acme wishes a program to perform a statistical study of their customer orders. Input the **orders.txt** file that I have provided and use the following structure.

```
struct ORDERS {
    long custNumber;
    char* name;
    double sales;
};
```

Each line of the data file gives the customer number, a 9-digit number, the customer's name surrounded by double quote marks (" ") and then that order's total sales.

Define an array that can hold 1000 orders. Then call a **LoadArray()** function to load the array from the data file, returning the number actually input on this run. When **LoadArray()** is ready to input the person's name, call the **InputName()** function from Pgm03-1 above. Store the returned pointer to the person's name string in the **name** variable of the current element in the array of orders.

Next, find the average sales, minimum sales, maximum sales, mean sales, and the standard deviation from the mean. Display the results similar to the following.

```
Acme Sales Analysis Report

Average   Minimum  Maximum       Mean   Standard
  Sales     Sales    Sales      Sales   Deviation
$1234.55  $   1.99  $2222.55  $ 500.50    1.22
Highest Sales: John Jones
Lowest Sales: Besty Smith
```

Finally, do not forget to delete all dynamically allocated memory. Before returning to DOS, check for memory leaks.

Problem Pgm03-3 Pre-owned Vehicle Finder Program

Your local automobile dealer has asked you to write a pre-owned vehicle finder program. Their problem is that they have a large number of pre-owned vehicles on the lot. When a potential customer arrives, the salesman asks them for information about what kind of used car they wish to buy. The salesmen would like to be able to key in the information and have the program display a list of possible matching pre-owned cars.

The Pre-owned Vehicle Master File Fields consists of the following. Create a Vehicle structure to hold these fields.

Field	Type of Information	Definition
Make	make of the car	a 15 character string
Model	model of the car	a 15 character string
Year	year of the car	four digits
NumDoors	number of doors	a number
Color	color of the car	0 is white, 1 is green, 2 is black, 3 is red, 4 is yellow, 5 is blue
EngineSize	the type of engine	a 15 character string, "4 barrel V8"
AirCond	does it have air conditioning	0 = no; 1 = yes
Stereo	the sound system	0 is radio, 1 is radio and tape player, 2 is radio, tape player and cd player
Mileage	number of miles on the odometer	a long number
OilLeak	yes or no	0 is no, 1 is yes
Tires	yes or no	0 is worn tires, 1 is good tires
Rust	yes or no	0 is no rust, 1 is yes significant rust visible

Beginning Data Structures in C++

First build a master.txt data file of at least 12 vehicles. One of these vehicles should have all 0's in every field except the character strings. One of these vehicles should have all of the information filled out (none containing 0). The remaining vehicles should have a variety of different fields supplied yet have a few fields still containing 0's.

The program first calls a **LoadArray()** function to load in the file of vehicle data into a vehicles array that can hold up to 100 records. Next, the program should display a message:
```
Try to match another vehicle? Enter Y or N: _
```
If an 'n' or 'N' is entered, the program terminates. If a 'y' or 'Y' is entered, then prompt and input the buyer's description of these fields. The data should be stored in another instance of Vehicle structure, called **request**.

When the buyer's data has been entered, then call a **MatchVehicle()** function giving it the database of vehicles and the **request**. For each vehicle in the database that matches one or more fields with the data in the **request**, display that vehicle in a format of your choosing. You should include an indicator of how close the match is by displaying a matching percentage. There are 12 items that could match. If all match, the percentage is 100%; do not display any that have a 0% of matching fields. Further, display the results sorted from high to low. That is, the first match shown should have the highest percentage.

Repeat the process until the user enters N at the prompt.

Design a solution before beginning to code. Notice that there is a lot of repetitive coding possible on this one. Try to create generalized functions to minimize the total amount of duplicative coding. As always, bulletproof your coding. Do not allow values out of range to be entered. You may use integers for the data types or define enumerated data types as you see fit.

Finally, create a set of testing oracles to thoroughly test your program.

Chapter 4—Recursive Functions

Introduction

Recursive functions are functions that call or invoke themselves. At first glance, this seems a bit unusual, a function as part of its function body in turn reinvoking itself. However, in the right circumstances, this can be very handy and a very simple way of a handling complex situation.

The starting point is to grasp the concept of a recursive definition. Then, using that as a guideline, we can tackle recursive functions.

Recursive Definitions

Consider a series of uniquely colored cars parked in a single line in a parking lot, each one bumper to bumper with the next. This gives us the following two definitions.

1. If the front of a car is not behind any car, then that car is not behind any other cars.
2. If the front of Car B is behind Car A, then Car B is behind Car A.
3. If the front of Car C is behind another Car B, and Car B is behind Car A, then Car C is also behind Car A.

For any two cars, if either 2 or 3 is true, then that car is behind Car A. However, if 1 is true, then that car is not behind Car A. It is the third definition above that is recursive. For example, if Car D is behind Car C, then we can apply the third definition again and ask if Car C is behind another car, and it is, Car B. So Car D is behind Car C which is behind Car B. And then on the next pass, the second definition becomes true. Thus, Car D is also behind Car A. Figure 4.1 illustrates the situation.

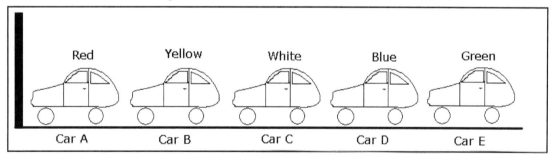

Figure 4.1 A Row of Cars and Their Colors

Next, let's assume each car has a unique color. Suppose that the question to be solved was is the Green Car behind the Red Car? How can we answer this question? We can reuse the original two definitions above. First we need to state the non-recursive color rule. This really ought to have two definitions.

1. If a car is not behind another car, then it is not behind the Red Car.
2. If a car is behind another car and if that car is the Red Car, then it is behind the Red Car.

Next we can add the recursive definition this way.

3. If a Car C is behind another Car B and Car B is behind the Red Car, then Car C is behind the Red Car.

Ok. So let's use these three rules to find out if the Green Car is behind the Red Car. The following represents the sequence of application of these three definitions.

Green Car: 1 false, 2 false, 3 true Green Car is behind Blue Car

    Blue Car: 1 false, 2 false, 3 true Blue is behind White Car

        White Car: 1 false, 2 false, 3 true White Car is behind Yellow Car

            Yellow Car 1 false, 2 is true Yellow Car is behind Red Car,

So yes, the Green Car is behind the Red Car.

Now let's try another one. Is the Blue Car behind the Green Car? Here is the sequence.

Blue Car: 1 false, 2 false, 3 true Blue Car is behind the Red Car

    Red Car: 1 false,

So no, the Blue Car is not behind the Green Car since we ran out of cars in the line.

Here is another question. Is the Blue Car behind the Yellow Car? By using the above definitions and substituting Yellow for Red, we get this sequence.

Blue Car: 1 false, 2 false, 3 true Blue Car is behind the White Car

    White Car: 1 false, 2 true so White Car is behind the Yellow Car

So yes, Blue Car is behind the Yellow Car.

And here is one final example. Is the Blue Car behind the Green Car? Again substituting Green for Red in the definitions, we get the following sequence.

Blue Car: 1 false, 2 false, 3 true Blue Car is behind the White Car

    White Car: 1 false, 2 false, 3 true White Car is behind the Yellow Car

        Yellow Car: 1 false, 2 false, 3 true Yellow Car is behind the Red Car

            Red Car: 1 true since we are out of cars again

So no, the Blue Car is not behind the Green Car.

Recursive Functions

A recursive function invokes itself to assist in solving the problem much like we repeatedly invoked the trio of definitions above with the car colors. There are two forms of function recursion. A function calling or invoking itself is called **direct recursion**. **Indirect recursion** occurs when a function calls some other function which in turn recalls the original function.

From my own many years of experience, recursion is a very difficult concept for programmers to understand and actually use. In more than 35 years in this business, I have only known two programmers who were totally comfortable and made good use of recursion. So take your time with this chapter and make sure you follow how recursion is done. The first few examples are very elementary and are designed to show you how it is done. Then, I will show you some excellent uses of recursion of which you might be able to make good use.

Recursion to Calculate N!

The first example of a recursive function shows how N! could be calculated. First, though, let's write a normal function that return the value of N! There are several ways such a function could be written; here is one way it can be done. Recall that 0! = 1. These functions assume that N is an integer and is not negative.

```
long Factorial (long N) {
   long factor = 1;
   for (long k=1; k<=N; k++) {
     factor = factor * k;
   }
   return factor;
}
```

How do we turn this into a recursive function? That means, somewhere within the body of **Factorial(), Factorial()** is called again. One way to do this is to write out a set of recursive definitions as we did with the cars. We might write the following Factorial definition.

1. if n is <= 1, then factor is 1
2. if n > 1, then factorial is the product of n and Factorial (n-1)

Ok. Let's test this using n = 5 and see how these definitions handle calculating 5!

n=5: 1 false, 2 true so factor = 5 * Factorial (4)

4!: 1 false, 2 true so factor = 4 * Factorial (3)

3!: 1 false, 2 true so factor = 3 * Factorial (2)

2!: 1 false, 2 true so factor = 2 * Factorial (1)

1!: 1 true, so factor is 1

So unwinding this we get 1 * 2 * 3 * 4 * 5 => 120 for 5!

Please note one **vital** aspect of this recursive definition: definition 1, which gives us a way to end the recursive use of definition 2. Without definition 1, the process would be endless. Now given this set of definitions, we can implement them as follows.

```
long Factorial (long N) {
   if (N <= 1)
     return 1;
   else
     return N * Factorial (N-1);
}
```

Next, let's examine what happens when this recursive **Factorial()** function is called by the user to calculate 5! The caller writes

```
long answer = Factorial (5);
```

Recall that when a function is called or invoked, the compiler places various items on the stack, such as the return address to go back to in the calling program, any parameters and any automatic storage that the called function needs. It then gives control to the first instruction of the function. The term **stack frame** is used to connote all of these items that the compiler places on the stack when a function is called. Further, we know that really the calling program's line above looks pictorially like this:

```
1. go call Factorial (5) and get its return value
2. copy that return value into answer
```

Figure 4.2 shows the successive call stack frames as the function is recursively called to find 5!

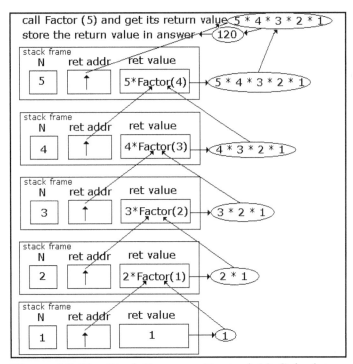

Figure 4.2 The Stack Frame as **Factorial()** Calculates 5!

As you look over Figure 4.2, notice how each stack frame's return address knows where to go back to and what value is returned.

Stack Overflow—Infinite Recursion

Now consider for a moment, what would happen if **Factorial()** was coded this way, without the Definition 1?

```
long Factorial (long N) {
   return N * Factorial (N-1);
}
```

With this version, there is no way for **Factorial()** to know when to stop reinvoking itself! It endlessly reinvokes itself, rather like an infinite loop. This is known as **infinite recursion**. When it happens, you will know it. There is a limit on how many times a function can call itself. Each function call builds a stack frame on the stack. Even with Window's marvelous ability to grow the stack when it gets full, there is a finite amount of memory available. Remember, it is 2G or the size of your swap file, whichever is smaller. Thus, such a program shortly crashes with stack size exceeded after tens of thousands of calls to itself!

Beginning Data Structures in C++

Thus, it is absolutely **vital** that every recursive function has some way to know when to stop calling itself. It must have an ending definition.

Reversing Characters Entered by the User

The next example of recursion illustrates a method reversing a series of characters entered by the user. For example, the user enters
```
cat
```
And when the enter key is pressed, on the next line we display the following.
```
tac.
```
How can this be accomplished? Without using recursion, we could input successive characters using the **get()** function and store them in an array of **char**. When the enter key is detected ('\n'), we could insert a null terminator in the next element of the array and then use the string **reverse()** function to reverse all characters in the string; then display the string. Simple, but it does have a serious limitation. Just how big do we make that array of char in which to store the user's characters? Ah, this would be an arbitrary decision on our part. Any number we pick could obviously be exceeded by the user!

If we use a recursive function, this arbitrary array size is eliminated. But first, let's define the definitions we need to solve the problem.

1. input a character
2. if that character is a '\n', then display the '\n' and quit.
3. if not a '\n', then {
       repeat the process
       and display our character
}

Ok. Let's test this definition using the "cat\n" as the user entry. We have then the following results.
first call: 1 'c', 2 false, 3 repeat
    second call: 1 'a', 2 false, 3 repeat
        third call: 1 't', 2 false, 3 repeat
            fourth call: 1 '\n', 2 true so we display '\n' and return
        third call: now displays 't' and returns
    second call: now displays 'a' and returns
first call: now displays 'c' and returns

Given our recursive definition, we can immediately code the **EchoReverse()** function.
```cpp
void EchoReverse () {
  char c;
  cin.get (c);
  if ( c == '\n' )
    cout << c;
  else {
    EchoReverse ();
    cout << c;
  }
}
```
Notice that we now have no arbitrary array bounds with the recursive version.

113

Summing all Even Integers from 2 to N

Now suppose that we wanted to write a function to sum all of the even integers from 2 to N. We could write a straightforward function **SumEven()** as follows.

```
long SumEven (long N) {
  long sum = 0;
  for (long k = 2;  k<=N;  k+=2)
    sum = sum + k;
  return sum;
}
```

To write a recursive version, we need to write a set of recursive definitions, at least one of which would cause the recursion process to stop. Notice that when k is 2, we are done and can return back a 2.

1. If n is a 2, return 2
2. If n is not a 2, then
      return back n + repeat the process for n-2

Once we have the recursion definition properly stated and tested, we can convert it into the recursive function.

```
long SumEven (long N) {
  if (N == 2)
    return 2;
  else
    return N + SumEven (N-2);
}
```

Notice this time that the function could go into infinite recursion if the user initially called **SumEven()** and passed it an odd number. How else could our function fail? What if the original N was sufficiently large, say 1,000,000? How many recursive function calls would need to be made to calculate this one? 500,000! This would surely cause a stack overflow because of the tremendous number of stack frames that must be allocated on the stack.

Speed Issues

Now that you have an idea of what recursive functions look like, how about their efficiency? Actually, recursive functions do indeed run slower than their direct counterparts. I timed both of these two versions of **Factorial()**. The simple non-recursive **Factorial()** executed over 3 times faster than did the recursive **Factorial()**!

One of the main reasons the recursive version runs much slower than a non-recursive version is the time that it takes to create all of the needed stack frames. And for the same reason, recursive functions will use more memory to carry out their task compared to a non-recursive version of that function.

The bottom line is simple. Recursive functions use more memory and run slower than their non-recursive counterparts. So why even bother using recursive functions in the first place?

Using Recursive Functions to Handle Situations Not Easily Programmed Otherwise

Pgm04a Making Folders

One use of recursive functions is suggested by the second example above, the **EchoReverse()**. Sometimes a recursive function can remove arbitrary barriers in a solution such as an array size. However, the major use of recursion is to handle situations that are not easily directly solved. Let's tackle one such problem.

Suppose that your program needed to guarantee that a path existed so that it could then save a file in that folder. However, if that path did not exist, the program was to make any and all folders so that the path did exist. For example, the user might have told the program to save the file here: **D:\testing\applications\database**. If all three folders existed, great, go ahead and save the file in the **database** subfolder. But what if the **database** subfolder did not exist? Or what if the applications subfolder did not exist? Or what if the testing folder did not exist? The program would have to make each of the missing folders. And the compounding problem is that we do not know in advance how many subfolders are going to be in the user's designated path! Tricky indeed!

First, we need to examine some C functions that can be used to make directories and related actions. These functions are not often found in basic textbooks. The C function to make a directory is **_mkdir()**.

```
int _mkdir(const char* path);
```

_mkdir() is given a string that contains the full path to actually make, including the drive letter portion. Remember, that DOS can only make one folder at a time. So if the database folder does not exist but the other two do exist, then the path string to **_mkdir()** would be "**D:\testing\applications\database**." If **_mkdir()** returns 0, it successfully made that directory. If it returns -1, then it failed to make it. In that case, a DOS variable **errno** contains the reason code for the failure. One of the reasons it could have failed to make the folder is that the folder already exists. We need to test for this result in the upcoming recursive function. That error value contained in **errno** is called **EEXIST**.

The recursive definitions needed for the **MakeDirectory()** recursive function are:
1. if path is the topmost folder {
    try to make the dir
    if the make was successful or the folder exists, return true
    else return false
2. if the path is not the top most folder, then
    remove this folder from the path
    repeat the process on the remaining path
    if the repeat was successful, {
        try to make this original path
        if the make was successful or the folder exists, return true
        else return false
    else return false

Thus, we have a simple design that handles any arbitrary number of folders in a path!

However, another complexity immediately arises. How are we going to "remove this folder from the path?" In other words, the user passes **D:\testing\applications\database** in the initial call. How do we extract **D:\testing\applications** to give to the recursive re-invocation of **MakeDirectory()**? This type of action is known as parsing a string looking for a token, here a '\\'. But there is a better way. The system provides another pair of functions to perform path string manipulations: **_splitpath_s()** and **_makepath_s()**. Both function prototypes are similar and they operate similarly. Although we only need **_splitpath_()** here, I will describe both of them.

Their prototypes are as follows.
```
_splitpath_s (const char* path,
              char* drive, size_t driveSize,
               char* dir, size_t dirSize,
               char* filename, size_t filenameSize,
               char* extension, size_t extSize);

_makepath_s (char* path, size_t pathSize,
              const char* drive, const char* dir,
              const char* filename, const char* extension);
```
For example, if the path was **D:\testing\applications\databases\mydatabase.db**, then after calling **_splitpath()**, the drive string contains **d:**, the dir string contains **\testing\applications\databases**, the filename contains **mydatabase**, and the extension contains **.db**. The **_makepath()** function would take these four strings and concatenate them together to form the complete path.

However, we do not have any filenames in the path we are given. What does **_splitpath_s()** yield if we give it **D:\testing\applications\databases**? It thinks that **databases** is the filename and that there is no file extension in this case. However, one tricky bit remains. What if we give it this messy path: **D:\testing\applications\database.mine**? Here database.mine is the folder name. Now **_splitpath_s()** yields a filename of database and an extension of .mine! Hence, in this special case where we are dealing solely with folder names, we need to rejoin the filename and extension strings.

There is one final detail that must be handled. Just exactly what should the array sizes be for all of these character path strings? The actual array bounds for paths and filenames are platform dependent. Since we are running under Windows as a Win32 Console Application, we should use that platform's array sizes. Filenames can be 256 characters long, for example. Conveniently, the new versions of these functions also provide such sizes. The const integer values are: **_MAX_DRIVE, _MAX_DIR, _MAX_FNAME**, and **_MAX_EXT**.

The recursive **MakeDirectory()** function then is a simple implementation of the above recursive definition. Here is the implementation which is in **MakePath.cpp** file.

```
Recursive MakePath Function

 1 #include "Pgm04a.h"
 2
 3 /**********************************************************/
 4 /*                                                       */
 5 /* MakeDirectory: make a directory by making all subdirs in   */
```

```
 6 /*                    this path                              */
 7 /*                    returns true if successful, false if not    */
 8 /* Note: if path exists, this is successful                  */
 9 /*                                                            */
10 /**************************************************************/
11
12 bool      MakeDirectory (const char *path) {
13  if (!path) return false;
14  if (strlen (path) == 0) {
15   cerr << "Error: trying to make a Null path\n";
16   return false;
17  }
18
19  char drive[_MAX_DRIVE] = "";
20  char dir [_MAX_DIR] = "";
21  char file[_MAX_FNAME] = "";
22  char y[_MAX_FNAME] = "";
23  char rest[_MAX_EXT ];
24
25 /* takes path that does NOT have file info in it and removes
26    the rightmost part
27      c:\path1\path2 yields  C:  \path1\  path2
28      c:\            yields  C:  \                    */
29
30  _splitpath_s (path, drive, _MAX_DRIVE, dir, _MAX_PATH,
31               file, _MAX_PATH, rest, _MAX_PATH);
32  // handle strange dirs, like mydir.data
33  strcat_s (file, _MAX_PATH, rest);
34
35  if (strlen (dir) <= 1) {       // are we at the root?
36   if (strlen (file) > 0) {      // yes, this is the topmost folder
37    if (_mkdir (path) == -1) { // try to make topmost folder
38     if (errno == EEXIST)       // failed because it exists?
39      return true;              // yes, so return true, its made
40     else {                     // no, so display error!
41      cerr << "Error: The desired folder cannot be created\n";
42      cerr << "The path was: " << path << endl;
43      return false;
44     }
45    }
46    return true;                // make of topmost folder successful
47   }
48   return true;                 // opps, no topmost folder
49  }
50
51  // here it is not the topmost folder, so try making the folder
52  // just above this one
53  // build the string with the path without the this subfolder
54  strcpy_s (y, _MAX_PATH, drive);
55  strcat_s (y, _MAX_PATH, dir);
```

```
56
57  // guard against a trailing backslash
58  if (y[strlen (y)-1] == '\\') y[strlen (y)-1] = 0;
59
60  // try making the folder above this folder
61  if (MakeDirectory (y)) {
62    if (_mkdir (path) == -1) { // was there an error?
63      if (errno == EEXIST)      // is folder already there?
64        return true;            // yes, return true folder made
65      else {                    // no, so display error message
66        cerr << "Error: The desired folder cannot be created\n";
67        cerr << "The path was: " << path << endl;
68        return false;
69      }
70    }
71    return true;     // successful folder creation, so return true
72  }
73  return false;     // unsuccessful folder creation, return false
74 }
```

What system header files are needed for all of these new DOS C functions? They are conveniently grouped into the file Pgm04a.h header file.

```
Pgm04a.h - Header with System Includes and Function Prototypes

1 #pragma once
2
3 #include <iostream>
4 #include <direct.h>
5 #include <errno.h>
6 using namespace std;
7
8 bool MakeDirectory (const char *path);
```

Notice that they are **direct.h** and **errno.h**. <iostream> handles the rest.

Finally, we need a tester **main()** function. It is called Pgm04a.cpp. It attempts to build a folder that is three levels deep on drive C: called **C:\\testing\\folder\\thisone.**

```
Pgm04a.cpp - main() Tester Function

1 #include "Pgm04a.h"
2
3 int main () {
4   char makethis[_MAX_PATH];
5   strcpy (makethis, "C:\\testing\\folder\\thisone");
6   if (MakeDirectory (makethis))
```

```
 7    cout << "Ok - made it\n";
 8   else
 9    cout << "Oops - failed to make path\n";
10   return 0;
11  }
```

Notice that we now have a particularly useful function in **MakeDirectory()**. It can be plugged into any application where a folder needs to be made for whatever reason. It is a good example of "reusable code."

Pgm04b Removing Empty Folders

If we can make directories, then we can also remove them. Again, this is ideal for recursion. In the previous example, several subfolders were created. Suppose that an application was given some path and asked to remove all empty folders beneath it. We certainly do not know how many empty subfolders and sub-subfolders could be present. But a recursive function could handle it fine. The recursive function's process would be to find a folder, then call itself to remove all folders in it. However, let's pass a **bool** in addition to the folder to empty; if it is true, we should also attempt to remove it as well. For documentation's sake, the **RemoveDir()** function returns a count of the number of folders actually removed.

Before we can write the **RemoveDir()** function, we must learn some additional DOS C functions that allow us to move through a directory and find all of the files and folders beneath it.

DOS C functions provide a trio of functions for this purpose, navigating through a directory. They are **_findfirst()**, **_findnext()** and **_findclose()**. One time only the **_findfirst()** function is called. This function sets up the initial hunt of the directory entries and gives us back the first directory item. Then, successive calls to **_findnext()** continues to iterate sequentially through the directory entries. When we are done with our search, a call to **_findclose()** closes down the action. The **_findfirst()** and **_findnext()** functions keep track of various directory searches through an integer value that **_findfirst()** returns and is then passed to each call of **_findnext()** and **_findclose()**.

The **_findfirst()** and **_findnext()** functions return useful directory information by filling up an instance of the **_finddata_t** structure that we must provide. This structure has several data members. However, we are interested in only two of them, the attribute of the item, called **attrib**, and the name of the item, called **name**. (The other members are **size** (file size) and **time_write**.)

If the **attrib** contains the flag **_A_SUBDIR**, then this entry is a folder. If not, this entry is a file. We only want folders in this case. Further, if you have ever done a DIR command within a DOS Prompt window, you know that every folder has two entries named . and .. The . represents this folder while the .. represents the parent of this folder. We must bypass processing these two entries.

Finally, when **name** contains the name of a folder that is eligible for removal, the DOS C function **_rmdir()** is used. **_rmdir()** is passed the folder to be removed and it returns 0 if it is successful. We do not care about any errors in this case. Only empty folders can be removed. We are counting only the ones that we can remove because they are empty.

The coding of the **RemoveDir()** recursive function is straightforward. Here is the coding for the **RemoveDir.cpp** file which is part of the Pgm04b project.

```
RemoveDir.cpp - The Recursive RemoveDir() Function

 1 #include "Pgm04b.h"
 2
 3 /*********************************************************/
 4 /*                                                       */
 5 /* RemoveDir: removes empty folders                      */
 6 /*     this function removes all empty folders under     */
 7 /*     the passed folder. If removethisone is true,      */
 8 /*     then it also removes this folder too, if empty    */
 9 /*     Returns the number of folders removed             */
10 /*                                                       */
11 /*********************************************************/
12
13 long RemoveDir (const char *dir, bool removethisonetoo) {
14  if (!dir) return 0;
15  if (strlen (dir) == 0) {
16   cerr << "Error: no folder to remove\n";
17   return 0;
18  }
19  char mdir[_MAX_PATH];
20  strcpy_s (mdir, _MAX_PATH, dir);
21  // guatantee no trailing backslash
22  if (mdir[strlen(mdir)-1] == '\\') mdir[strlen(mdir)-1] = 0;
23
24  long hFind;              // used by _findxxx functions
25  _finddata_t fd;         // filled in by _findxxx functions
26  char idir[_MAX_PATH];   // the search string with *.* appended
27  strcpy_s (idir, _MAX_PATH, mdir);
28  strcat_s (idir, _MAX_PATH, "\\*.*");
29  long ct = 0;            // the number of folders removed
30
31  // attempt to find the first entry in this folder
32  if ((hFind = _findfirst (idir, &fd)) == -1L )
33   return ct; // failed, so abort
34  // for each file found in this folder,
35  // check its file attributes - is it a subdir
36  // then if so, bypass . and .. system entries
37  do {
38   if (fd.attrib & _A_SUBDIR) { // is it a subdir?
39    if (fd.name[0] != '.') {    // yes, is it not . or ..
40     char xdir[_MAX_PATH];      // yes, so remove
41     strcpy_s (xdir, _MAX_PATH, mdir);        // anything under it
```

120

```
42        strcat_s (xdir, _MAX_PATH,"\\");
43        strcat_s (xdir, _MAX_PATH,fd.name);
44
45        ct += RemoveDir (xdir, false);  // remove under this folder
46        if  (_rmdir (xdir) == 0) ct ++; //remove this folder
47      }
48    }
49  } while (_findnext (hFind, &fd) == 0);
50  // repeat for all files in the folder
51
52  // now close the find operation
53  _findclose (hFind);
54
55  // finally see if we are to remove this folder too
56  if (removethisonetoo) {
57   if (_rmdir (mdir) == 0)
58     ct ++;
59  }
60  return ct;
61 }
```

The **Pgm04b.h** header file adds one more header file for the new DOS functions. It is `#include <io.h>`

The **Pgm04b.cpp** which contains our **main()** function contains just this coding.
```
long ct = RemoveDir ("C:\\testing", true);
cout << "Removed " << ct << " folders\n";
```

Thus, you now have two very useful, generic, reusable, recursive functions that can be used widely in applications that need the ability to make and remove folders.

Review Questions

1. Describe what is meant by a recursive definition. How does a recursive definition relate to a recursive function in programming?

2. What guidelines would you offer a new programmer as to when recursion should be used and when it should not be used?

3. Why must a recursive definition have some form of terminal, stopping or ending criteria?

4. Consider a vertical stack of colored children's blocks. The block on the bottom sitting on the table is a red block. Above it is a yellow block. Above it is a green block. And on top is a blue block. Write a set of recursive definitions that one could apply to find out if a block of a specific color was above the red block.

5. Review the recursive function presented above called **EchoReverse()**. What would the result be if the user pressed ^Z instead of the enter key? Would the result be any different if they had pressed the ^C key?

6. Consider the **SumEven()** recursive function above. What would occur if the user initially invoked it passing the function a –3? Would the result be any different had they passed it a 5 instead?

Stop! Do These Exercises Before Programming

1. A programmer was asked to write a recursive function that computes x^n, called **Power()**. Variable **x** is a **double** and the function should return a **double**. It was agreed that n would be a nonnegative integer. The programmer wrote the following function.

```
double Power (double x, int n) {
   return x * Power (x, n-1);
}
```

However, when he tested it with 10. for **x** and 2 for **n**, a stack overflow error message occurred. Baffled, he has asked you for some assistance. Explain to him what has occurred and how his function could be fixed so that it will work correctly.

2. Next, the programmer tried to write a recursive function called **Mul()** that would multiply two positive integers, j and k. He chose to use repetitive addition as the method. That is, in order to multiply 3 times 4, one would add 4 to itself 3 times. He wrote the following code for **Mul()**.

```
int Mul (int j, int k) {
  if (k==1)
    return j;
  return j + Mul (j, k);
}
```

Again, he received a stack overflow after thousands of iterations. After your assistance on the **Power()** function, he carefully verified that he had the correct ending criteria. Stumped he once again asks you for assistance. Why did it run endlessly? What must be done to get this function to work properly?

3. Excited by his recent successes with recursion, the programmer found this undocumented recursive function while surfing the web. Unfortunately, he cannot figure out what it does. You have offered to help. What does it do? And what are the ranges of **n** for which it works?

```
void Unknown (int n) {
  cout << n%10;
  if (n/10)
    Unknown (n/10);
}
```

Programming Problems

Problem Pgm04-1 City Sewer Flow Processing

Your city engineer has asked you to write a program to analyze the city's sewer system. The program maintains the city's water system connections in an array called **Junctions** which is an array of integers. Whenever two water pipes join, they form a junction. These junctions are numbered consecutively from 1 to N, where N is the number of junctions.

The **Junctions** matrix determines if water is able flow from one junction to another. A direct connection is indicated by a 1 in the matrix. If water cannot flow through that junction, the matrix contains a 0. Thus, if water can flow directly from point J to K, then **Junctions[J][K]** would contain a 1. On the other hand, if water flows from K to J (K is uphill from J) or these two junctions are not even connected, then **Junctions[J][K]** would contain a 0.

Here is the test matrix to use.

	1	2	3	4	5	6	7	8	9	10	11
1	0	1	0	0	0	0	0	0	0	0	0
2	0	0	0	1	0	1	0	0	0	0	0
3	0	1	0	0	0	0	0	0	0	0	0
4	0	0	0	0	0	0	1	0	0	0	0
5	0	0	0	1	0	0	0	0	0	0	0
6	0	0	0	1	0	0	0	1	0	0	0
7	0	0	0	0	0	0	0	1	1	0	0
8	0	0	0	0	0	0	0	0	0	0	0
9	0	0	0	0	0	0	0	0	0	1	0
10	0	0	0	0	0	0	0	0	0	0	1
11	0	0	0	0	0	0	0	0	0	0	0

Write a recursive function **CanWaterFlow()** that is passed the array **Junctions**, the array bounds of 11, and the two junction points, J and K. The function returns a **bool**, **true** if water can flow by any path from point J to point K and **false** if it cannot. Thus, if **CanWaterFlow()** was called like this,

```
CanWaterFlow (Junctions, 11, 3, 6)
```

It should return **true**, even though there is no direct connection between 3 and 6 because 3 can flow through 2 and then to 6. Likewise, if it was called like this,

```
CanWaterFlow (Junctions, 11, 6 , 2)
```

It should return **false**, since there is no way for water to flow by any means along this path.

Assume that no connection can be made such that water flows in a circle. Write a driver program that prompts the user to enter a pair of junction numbers from 1 through 11. Then call **CanWaterFlow()** and display whether or not water can flow between these two points. Repeat until the end of file is detected.

Place the tester program in a separate cpp file from the **CanWaterFlow()** function.

Your test runs should include at least these tests.

3 to 11	4 to 5	8 to 11	6 to 11	4 to 2
3 to 2	3 to 6	6 to 2		

The following illustration shows the graphical view from which the **Junctions** matrix was constructed.

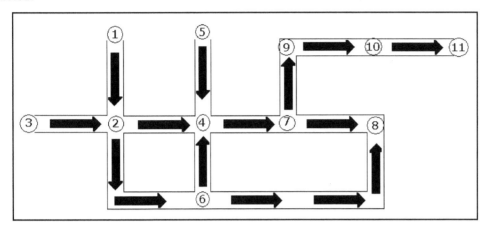

Problem Pgm04-2 The Fibonacci Series

The first seven numbers in the Fibonacci series are: 1, 1, 2, 3, 5, 8, 13, 21. The first two numbers are both 1. Each number after that is the sum of the previous two numbers. The 7th number in the series, denoted as Fibonacci(7), is 13. The 8th number, Fibonacci(8), is 21.

Write a recursive definition to compute Fibonacci (N). Then, write a function called **Fibonacci()** that is passed a **long** N and returns the **long** value of that number.

Write a **main()** function to test your **Fibonacci()** function. It should prompt the user to enter the requested number and then display its corresponding value. Repeat the process until EOF is reached. Your tests should include at least the following values for N; I have included the resulting values these should produce.

N	Value
1	1
2	1
3	2
4	3
5	5
6	8
7	13
8	21
10	55
20	6765

Chapter 5—Data Abstraction—an Overview

Introduction

Data abstraction represents ways and means of organizing the data into schemes that assists us in solving a problem on the computer. In the previous chapters, we have explored some simple techniques of data abstraction. By using functional modules, data can be encapsulated to hide data items. This allows the caller of such functions to be relatively independent of those hidden data items. Conversely, the localization of data items within functional modules prevents a function from indiscriminate access of the caller's data items. Only by passing a pointer or a reference that was not constant could the function gain the ability to directly alter the contents of the caller's data items. Together, these two aspects assist us in providing means of information hiding and implementation independence.

Structures play a significant role in data abstraction as well. From your first course in C++ through the first four chapters of this book, structures have allowed us to group a series of related fields together to form a record of data. By using arrays of structures and by passing references or pointers to structures to functions, greater simplification was gained in program design. For example, one nationwide auto insurance company has 1,500 fields in their Policy Master Record structure. Without using a structure, imagine coding the function prototypes and function calls to pass these data individually! However, there are some additional aspects of structures that are explored in chapter 6.

Historically, structures evolved into C++ classes. A class offers a design mechanism which encapsulates not only data items but also functions to manipulate those data. Like a structure template, a class is a template that the compiler uses when it needs to create an instance of that class in memory. For example, we could envision designing a **Car** class to simulate the operations of automobiles.

A **Car** class instance, called an **object**, would have a number of data items or **properties** such as its make and model, year, color, number of doors, size of the engine, miles per gallon, the size of its gas tank, the number of gallons of gas in its tank, whether or not the engine is started, and the car's current speed, for example. Additionally, a **Car** object would have many capabilities or functions or **methods** that operate on those member data. Among them might be **GetCarColor()**, **GetMpg()**, **GetSpeed()** and **SetSpeed()**. Notice that these functions provide the user of the Car object to retrieve or change the various properties and are known as **access** functions. Other functions perform operations on the **Car** object such as **StartMotor()**, **TurnCar()**, **LoadPassengers()**, and **FillUpGasTank()**. These are known as **operation** functions.

Classes are called **abstract data types** or **ADT** for short. Programming languages have built-in data types. In C++, we have **double** and **int**, for example. Each data type has two characteristics: a **set of values** it can hold and a collection of **permissible operations** that can be performed on those values. The **int** data type, remembering that under old DOS is limited to two bytes, can store any integer from -32,768 through +32,767. This is its range of values. The C++ language defines a multitude of operations that can be performed on an **int**, such as +, -, *, /, %, ++ and --, for example. An instance of such a built-in data type is, of course, called a variable.

C++ provides support for user-created data types, that is, abstract data types (ADT). The Car class is one example. Similarly, we could create a **Point** class to encapsulate the behavior of a geometric point. If we were in two-dimensional space, such a **Point** class would have two properties, an x and y coordinate. We can envision any number of operations or methods that could be performed on an instance of the **Point** class, such as **MovePoint()**, **ScalePoint()** and **PlotPoint()**. Even insertion and extraction functions would be reasonable to implement so the user could easily input and output a **Point** object.

One could envision a **ComplexNumber** class to encapsulate complex numbers. It would have two data members, the real and the imaginary parts. With an instance of a **ComplexNumber**, there would be a huge number of permissible operations that should be provided. Virtually all of the normal math operators should be made to work as well as the insertion and extraction operators and all of the comparison operators.

Construction of a class, then, requires a concrete data representation using existing data types (or instances of other ADTs that have been implemented already) and the implementation of all the allowable operations upon those data. We will examine class construction in chapters 7 and 8 in detail.

Data Types and Data Structures—the Relationship

We have seen that any data type has two characteristics:
1. the domain of its values or the set of all possible values it can contain
2. the collection of allowable operations on those values

This can be formalized for both the built-in data types (sometimes called intrinsic data types and also atomic data types) and the abstract data types we may design and write. Table 5.1 shows the definition of an **int** type and Table 5.2 shows the definition of a **Point** ADT. Notice the similarity between both these types of data.

Data Type	C++ **int**
Domain	The finite subset of integers—the least and greatest integers are platform dependent. Under old DOS, they are –32,768 through +32,767. On a Win32 platform, they are –2,147,483,648 through +2,147,483,647.
Operations	
=	Assignment
+	Addition
-	Subtraction
*	Multiplication
/	Division
%	Remainder or Mod

==	Equality Comparison
!=	Not Equal Comparison and so on
++	Increment
--	Decrement
<<	Insertion
>>	Extraction
etc	many other possibilities

Table 5.1 The Definition of an int Data Type

Data Type	Point ADT
Domain	Two-dimensional point coordinates (x,y) whose values are integers, each of which are of **int** data type and have the range of **int**s
Operations	
=	Assignment
MovePoint()	Move the location of the origin of the point
SetPoint()	Assign new (x,y) values
<<	Insertion
>>	Extraction
==	Equality Comparison
!=	Not Equal Comparison and so on
+	Addition, add a value to both x and y
-	Subtraction, subtract a value from both x and y
Polar()	Convert from x-y space into radius-angle space
Distance()	Distance from the origin of the coordinate system

Table 5.2 The Definition of a Point Abstract Data Type

A **data structure**, in contrast to these intrinsic data types and ADTs, has the following.

1. Component data items which may be intrinsic or ADT or even instances of other data structures.

127

2. A set of rules that define how these components interact with each other and to the structure as a unit or whole.

The C++ language has only one built-in data structure, the array. An array is sometimes called a vector. Table 5.3 shows the definition of a C++ built-in array.

Data Type	C++ Built-in Array
Domain	An array consists of: 1). A fixed number of values, each of which is of the same data type, whether a built-in data type or instances of ADTs 2). A set of index values(subscripts) that are nonnegative integers
Structure	There is a one-to-one relationship between each index and the corresponding array element. Always, index 0 accesses the first element in the array.
Operations	
[k] as a r-value	Retrieve the value of the array element at index k, when used as a r-value
[k] as a l-value	Store a value into the array element at index k, when used as a l-value

Table 5.3 The Definition of the C++ Built-in Array

The operations section defines actions that may be done to the data structure as a unit or whole and not to its internal components. The internal components are always subject to the set of allowable operations that can be performed on the types of data that they are, such as **int**s or **double**s or **Point**s. Assuming we have defined two arrays, **x** and **y** as shown below, the Operations on the arrays are dictated by the above definitions.

```
      double x[100];
      double y[100];
// allowable operations based upon [] operations and the data
//            type definitions of the elements themselves.
      cin >> x[k];
      x[k] = 42;
      x[k] = y[k];

// disallowed operations based upon the Operation rules
      cin >> x;
      y = x;
```

The structure, class and array are the only data structures that C++ provides. Using these components, many problems can be solved on the computer. However, the real-world that programs are often called upon to model or simulate is far more complex. For example, suppose that a movie theater wanted a program to monitor the length of the ticket purchasing lines. Or you wished to write a program to find the path through a maze. Or you wanted to determine the placement of chess pieces on a chess board subject to the rules of chess. Or you wanted to monitor the waiting room of a doctor's office. Or you just wanted to store all of the items in an array with no arbitrary maximum number of elements. Or you wanted to create your grocery shopping list. All of these would be difficult to implement with what we know just now. There are other organizations of data, other types of data structures, other ways of putting the data together, that mirrors more closely the real-world situation we are emulating in programming. Data structures can be thought of as the building blocks of a program.

An Overview of Data Structures

Caution: This is a beginning data structures text. Thus, I am limiting coverage to the fundamental data structures. Realize that there are many more types than are presented here. Also note that these data structures are often called container classes.

The different data structures differ from one another by their characteristics or properties. If we think broadly about organizations of data, much like we do with Top-down design, two broad categories emerge at once. Is the data **Linear** or **Nonlinear** in arrangement? **Linear** data structures arrange their data such that there is a unique first component, a unique last component, every component has a unique predecessor (except the first) and every component has a unique successor (except the last). It is a line of elements. Visualize a row of cars. There is a first and last car in the row. For any specific car (except the first and last one), there is a car in front of it and behind it. The C++ built-in array is an example of a linear data structure. The opposite of a linear data structure is a Nonlinear one. A **nonlinear** data structure, often called a **set** in mathematics, has no specific order; there is no designated first or last element, no rules about previous or successive elements. A **set** is thus a unique data structure.

Just specifying that a collection of data is linear is not sufficient. So we need to functionally decompose linear data further. Linear data can be broken down into two categories that depend upon how we wish to access that data, its access method: **direct access** and **sequential access**.

You are certainly familiar with applications that use **direct access**. If you wanted to know your grade for the course, you are asked to supply your student id number. Once the id number is inputted, the grades program then reads in your specific data and displays your grade. This type of a program is known as an **inquiry program**. The program inputs only your specific data based upon your id number; that is, it does a **direct access** of your information. It does not input sequentially every student, looking for a match on id number. Similarly, if you wanted to know the balance in your checking account, you provide your account number. The inquiry program then inputs and displays only your account information, based on your account number. This is direct access. Similarly, array processing is also direct access. Given a specific subscript, it is possible to immediately retrieve the data that corresponds to that index.

Sequential access is needed in other circumstances. If you wanted to simulate the line of ticket buyers at a movie theater, which is called a queue, processing is very different. With a queue, you do not suddenly sell a ticket to someone in the middle of the line! Here, one would access the data sequentially. Similarly, suppose that you wanted to implement an Undo operation for a program editor. When the user chooses the Undo action or menu, only the most recent operation is undone. It would be a nightmare to undo, say, the 10th previous one. You would have to undo the successive previous nine others.

Thus, linear arrangement breaks down into two subcategories based upon how we want to access the data components, direct or sequential. Next, we need to break down the direct linear access into its types. And then do likewise to the sequential linear access.

Direct linear access breaks down into two categories based upon whether all of the data components are homogeneous or heterogeneous. By homogeneous components, we mean that all data components are of the same data type. This is exactly how the C++ built-in array works. All elements of an array are of the same data type. By heterogeneous components, we mean that the elements are of differing data types. Consider a policy master record of an insurance company. There are a number of very different data types that compose the record of data. Character strings hold data such as the policy holder's name and car make and model. A **double** may store the premium due, while integers hold the premium due date and so on. Each of these are called **fields** of data. Some programming languages provide built-in support for records of data. C++ provides us with a structure by which we may group all of the fields into one larger aggregate and then create normal arrays of that aggregate, the structure. Alternatively, C++ allows us to create an ADT or class to encapsulate these fields and then we can construct arrays of class instances similar to arrays of structure instances. Thus, for C++ programming, the distinction between the array type of data structure and the record type of data structure is minimal.

Sequential access breaks down into categories based primarily on how we wish to access the components. A **stack** data structure, which is a last in (LIFO), first out type of data structure permits the retrieval only of that instance that is at the top of the stack. It allows for insertion of new components only at the top of the stack. The Undo operation is a prime example of a stack in operation. A **queue** data structure permits values to be retrieved only at the front and allows insertions only at the rear of the line. And finally, a **list** data structure allows one complete freedom of where components are inserted and removed and allows one to move sequentially through the list of components.

Figure 5.1 illustrates these different data structures and our hierarchy.

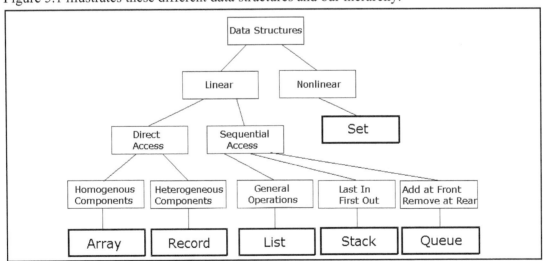

Figure 5.1 The Various Types of Common Data Structures

Let's examine the definitions and uses of each of these data structures in more detail.

Arrays

Arrays are a linear, direct access type of data structure whose elements are homogeneous. Table 5.4 shows the definition of the array data structure. Note that here I am using the array as an ADT, not as the built-in C++ array definition which is too limiting for our purposes. We really need an array that can grow in size, one that does not have an arbitrary upper limit on the number of elements that can be stored. The built-in arrays always have a finite, fixed upper limit on the array bounds. However, an ADT can remove that barrier yielding an array that can grow in bounds as the needs of the application changes. In practice, the amount of memory available to a program becomes the limiting factor on the number of elements in the array.

Data Type	Array as an Abstract Data Type
Domain	An array consists of 1). A collection of a fixed number of components that are of the same data type 2). A set of integer index values that permit a one-to-one correspondence with the array elements
Structure	It consists of a linear, direct access structure that has a one-to-one relationship between each integer index and an array element. The first subscript accesses the first element in the array. That first index does not have to be 0.
Operations	
[k] or GetAt(k)	Retrieve the value of the array element at the kth index
[k] or InsertAt(k)	Store a value in the array element at the kth index

Table 5.4 The Array Data Structure Definition

If one uses the C++ built-in array as the container, the language implementation supplies some additional considerations. In most programming languages, arrays are implemented by contiguous elements in memory. We know that if we define an array of 10 integers, that the second element comes immediately after the first element in memory in C++. Programs often make use of these implementation details. Using pointers instead of subscripts is one such technique which provides significantly faster array processing. However, this consideration is not necessarily going to hold true when we implement an ADT version of an array data structure. Array elements do not have to be in contiguous memory locations. But there must be a direct one-to-one correspondence between an index and its corresponding element.

In chapter 6, we will explore these principles in greater detail. And then after learning the basics of how to write classes (ADTs), we will see additional methods for array ADTs.

Records

The record data structure is a linear, direct access data structure whose elements are heterogeneous in nature. However, in C++ with the use of structures and classes (ADTs), the distinction between the array data structure and the record data structure becomes academic. Table 5.5 defines the record data structure.

Data Type	Record as an ADT
Domain	Each record consists of 1). A collection of a fixed number of field (component) values which may be intrinsic or instances of other ADTs 2). A set of identifiers (field names) for accessing each field
Structure	A linear, direct access data structure with a one-to-one relationship between the field name and a field in the record
Operations	
Get(fieldname)	Retrieve the contents of the field whose name is fieldname
Set(fieldname)	Store a new value into the field whose name is fieldname

Table 5.5 The Record Data Structure Definition

In the next chapter, we will examine how the C++ language handles records easily. Creating a record data structure is usually very straightforward because of the inherent language we are using, C++.

Lists

A list is a linear data structure that is accessed sequentially. The first item in the list is located at the **head** of the list, while the last item in the list is located at the **tail**. Each item in the list points to the next item in the list and in some lists. each item also points to the previous item in the list. There is no arbitrary maximum number of items in a list. Typical implementations of a list data structure maintain a pointer that points to the first item in the list, say called **headptr**. Each item in the list contains a pointer to the next item in the list, say called **fwdptr**. When an item's **fwdptr** is 0, there are no further items in the list. And in order to iterate sequentially through a list, the list data structure must maintain a pointer to the current item in the list, say called **currentptr**. This current item in the list pointer is called a **cursor**, which is something that marks a current location. The cursor can also be called an **iterator**.

In practice, the amount of memory available to a program becomes the limiting factor on the number of items that can be in a list.

Data Type	List Data Structure
Domain	Each list has 1). A collection of component values each of the same data type 2). A cursor to mark the current position in the list and whose values can range from 1 to N+1 where N is the number of items currently in the list.
Structure	A linear, sequential access data structure of varying length
Operations	Note: the C++ function names I have used can be called by many similar names.
Initialize()	Initialize to an empty list
AddAtHead()	Add an item at the head of the list
AddAtTail()	Add an item at the tail of the list
InsertAt()	Add an item at the cursor location
Next()	Move sequentially to the next item in the list
Previous()	Move sequentially to the previous item in the list
ResetToHead()	Reset the cursor to the beginning of the list
ResetToTail()	Reset the cursor to the last item in the list
IsHead()	Is the cursor at the head of the list?
IsTail()	Is the cursor at the tail of the list?
RemoveAt()	Remove the item at the cursor from the list
GetCurrent()	Get the item at the cursor
IsEmpty()	Is the list empty?
Empty()	Remove all items from the list

Table 5.6 The List Data Structure Definition

Note that I have provided quite a few operational functions. More robust applications might provide even more operations on the list. In simpler applications, not all of these operations I gave must be implemented. As you look over these functions, notice that it would be exceedingly difficult to permit a list to be accessed by direct methods. How would the list find the ith item? It would have to move the cursor sequentially forward through the list, counting items until it came to the ith one!

When a list is set up so that it can be traversed sequentially only in the forward direction, it is called a **single linked list**. No previous item pointers or a **tailptr** is maintained. If a list must be traversed both forwards and backwards, then a previous item pointer must be maintained with each item along with the forward to the next item pointer and a **tailptr** must be maintained as well. This is called a **double linked list** since each item is chained both forward to the next item and backwards to the previous item. Chapter 9 covers single linked lists while chapter 10 handles double linked lists.

Maintaining a class roster is an ideal application for a list. The list is maintained in alphabetical order on the student name. When a new student signs up, he/she is added into the list at the correct alphabetical position using the **InsertAt()** function. If a student drops a class, the item representing that student can be removed from the list using the **RemoveAt()** function. A roster can be displayed at anytime by calling **ResetToHead()** to reset the cursor back to the first item in the list. Then the list can be iterated sequentially using the **GetCurrent()** and **Next()** functions. Figure 5.2 shows a class roster list in action.

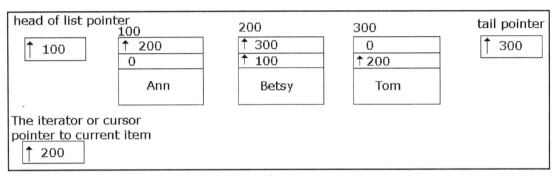

Figure 5.2 A List Data Structure in Operation

The head points to the item at location 100 which contains Ann. Ann's list item's forward pointer points to the next item in the list at location 200. Ann's back pointer is 0 indicating there are no other list items before her. At location 200 is the item containing Betsy. Notice that Betsy's item points forward to Tom and back to Ann. The tail pointer points to the last item in the list at location 300 which contains Tom. Tom's forward pointer is 0 indicating there are no items after this one. Finally, the current item in the list that the user is working with is at location 200 or Betsy.

When a patient visits a doctor, the visit information is stored in a patient record. The update program could use a list data structure to maintain the list of patients in alphabetical order. When a new patient visits for the first time, his/her data record can be added into the list at the appropriate alphabetical location.

Stacks

A stack is a linear, sequential access data structure. It has the property that the last item pushed or stored onto the stack is the first item that can be popped or removed from the stack. That is, a stack is LIFO. It is basically a very restricted version of a list in which all additions and removals occur at one end of the list.

If you make a tall stack of children's play blocks, new blocks are added at one spot only, the top. If you wish to remove a block, it must also be from the top of the stack.

Another place one often sees stacks in operation is at a buffet restaurant where the plates are on a recessed, spring loaded, stainless steel dispenser cart. The bottom plate rests upon a spring. Customers take a plate from the stack from the top and the spring pushes the stack up. New plates are added at the top of the stack, pushing the spring and whole stack down.

Beginning Data Structures in C++

A multiple car family with a single car-wide driveway has experienced stack operations. If your car is at the bottom of the stack that is closest to the garage, then you have to move all the other cars out of the way, that is, pop them off of the stack, so you can get yours out.

Automatic and parameter variables in C++ are stored on a stack data structure. Undo operations in word processing and paint programs are implemented by storing the changes onto a stack. Stacks also are used in "artificial intelligence" type programs. For example, the problem of finding your way through any maze by trial and error is inherently a stack problem.

The two major operations that a stack provides are called **Push()** and **Pop()** which puts a new item onto the top of the stack and removes the top item from the stack. Stacks are often implemented as a specialized single linked list. Table 5.7 shows the definition of a stack data structure.

Data Type	Stack
Domain	A stack is a collection of component whose values are all of the same data type
Structure	A list that is maintained in LIFO order so that only the most recently added item is available
Operations	
Initialize()	Creates an empty stack
Push()	Place a new item on the top of the stack
Pop()	Remove the current item from the top of the stack
IsEmpty()	Returns true if the stack is empty

Table 5.7 The Definition of the Stack Data Structure

Notice that the number of operations that can be performed on a stack is much smaller than the number that can be done on a list data structure. Stacks will be explored in depth in chapter 11. Figure 5.3 shows a stack in operation.

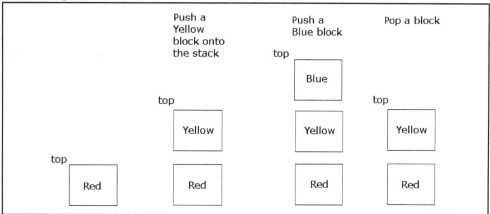

Figure 5.3 A Stack in Operation with Child's Colored Blocks

135

Initially the stack contains one red block which is at the top of the stack. Next, a yellow block is pushed onto the top of the stack. Then a blue block is pushed onto the top of the stack. Finally, a block is popped off from the top of the stack leaving the yellow and red blocks still on the stack.

Queues

The queue is a linear, sequential data structure with the properties that new items are added at one end of the list, the front, while items are removed from the other end of the list, the rear of the list. Queues are usually implemented as a variation of a linked list data structure. A queue supports two key operations, **Enqueue()** and **Dequeue()** for the insertion of a new item and the removal of an existing item.

Examples of queues abound in the real world. The line of ticket purchasers at a movie theater is a queue. New arrivals are enqueued at the rear of the line. Tickets are sold only to those at the front of the queue. It can be dangerous to your health to cut in front of others in such queues.

The waiting room of a doctor is a queue. When the next examination room is ready, the nurse takes the patient at the front of the queue. New arrivals are at the end of the queue. Often this is done by maintaining a "sign in upon arrival" list at the nurse's desk.

Programs that model assembly line operations use queues to simulate the line action. A new car's engine appears at the end of the line. Workers then do various actions to it as it moves along the line. It is then removed from the other end of the line when they are finished.

Farmers loading cattle into a cattle truck force the cows into a queue to enter the truck. Students registering for school classes are formed into queues. When you go to the drive in window of a bank to make a deposit or withdrawal, your car is forced into a queue behind the teller window.

Table 5.8 gives the definition of the queue data structure. Queues are often called FIFO, first in, first out lists.

Data Type	Queue
Domain	A queue is a collection of component whose values are all of the same data type
Structure	A queue is a list that is maintained in first in, first out order. That is, insertions are done at the rear of the list, and removals are done at the head of the list.
Operations	
Initialize()	Create an empty queue
Enqueue()	Add an item at the rear of the queue
Dequeue()	Remove an item from the head of the queue
IsEmpty()	Returns true if the queue is empty

Table 5.8 The Queue Data Structure Definition

Sometimes additional operations are provided with both stacks and queues. For debugging purposes, it is very convenient if some means of iterating through the items actually on the stack or in the queue is provided. Queues are discussed in depth in chapter 12. Figure 5.4 shows a queue in operation.

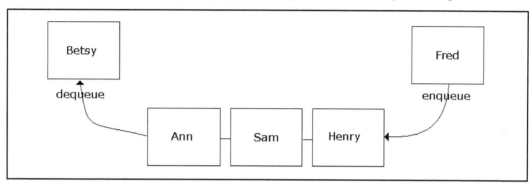

Figure 5.4 A Queue in Action

In Figure 5.4, Betsy has just purchased her ticket to the movie and is being dequeued from the queue of ticket purchasers. Fred has just arrived and is being enqueued at the end of the queue.

Sets

The final data structure, the set, is a basic building block of mathematics. A set is a nonlinear collection of objects called **elements**. The set of all positive even integers is an example. The **universe** consists of all possible positive even integers. The number 2, an object, would be a member of that set while the number 3 would not be a member. A set of items implies no specific ordering, just a pile of items that are in the set universe.

From set theory, we have three properties.

1. All elements of a set belong to some universe that represents all possible values that are potential elements.

2. For any given object, either it is a member or it is not a member of the universe.

3. There is no particular order of the elements within the set.

From property 2, a specific element can appear in the set only once. Thus, these two sets are the same set:

$\{2, 4, 6\} = \{4, 2, 6, 2, 6, 4, 4\}$

Remember, order does not matter. If a set is currently empty, it is denoted { }; it is also called the **null** set.

Another term associated with sets is the **cardinality** of a set. The cardinality is the number of distinct elements that are present in a particular set. The cardinality of a null set is 0. If a set has potentially an infinite number of elements, its cardinality is infinity. However, if the set has a finite number of elements, then its cardinality is finite and is expressed as a positive integer. Obviously, when we program a set, the cardinality must be finite since there is not an infinite amount of computer memory available to store an infinite number of elements.

A set has three binary operations that can be performed with it. Binary operations are those actions that involve two sets, in this case, two = binary. The **intersection** of two sets is those elements held in common between the two sets. For example, the intersection of the set of all integers from 1 to 10 with the set of all even integers between 4 and 8 would include the elements 4, 6, and 8. The **union** of two sets represents those elements that are in at least one of the two sets. For example, the union of the set of the integers 1 through 3 with the set of integers 3 through 5 would be the set of elements 1 through 5. The **difference** between set A and set B would be all elements of set A that are not in set B. The difference between the set of integers 1 through 3 and the set of integers 3 through 5 would be 1 and 2.

A set also has a couple of relational operations that can be performed. Set **equality** tests whether or not set A equals set B; two sets are equal if they contain the same elements. The other relational operation is the **subset**. Set B is considered a subset of set A if all of set B's elements are found in set A.

An element is a member of a set, if that set contains that element. This operation is called **membership**.

While this text is not concerned about writing mathematical applications where set theory abounds, there are some circumstances where a set data structure is useful in representing the real-world situation. Consider for a moment what classes you plan to take next semester. Obviously, you can only take those classes that are actually offered, for not every class a college has is taught each semester, particularly during the summer semester. Thus, we could use a set data structure to contain all of the classes that were to be offered in a given semester. Any given class the college potentially could offer either is in the set of offerings this semester or it is not.

Table 5.9 shows the definition of a set data structure.

Data Type	Set
Domain	A set is a collection of component whose values are all of the same data type
Structure	A nonlinear collection of items that correspond to a mathematical set
Operations	
Initialize()	Creates an empty set
Insert()	Add a new element to the set
Delete()	Remove an element from the set
IsAMember()	Is an item an element in the set
Intersection ()	Constructs a resultant set that represents the intersection of this set with another set
Union()	Constructs a resultant set that represents the union of this set with another set
IsEmpty()	Returns true if the set contains no elements
Difference()	Constructs a resultant set that represents the difference between this set and another set
Cardinality()	Returns the cardinality number of this set

Table 5.9 The Set Data Structure Definition

Memory Limitations

All of these data structures have one common theme, none are limited by an arbitrary array bounds or limit. Instead, an instance of these data structures is limited in the number of items it can store by overall available computer memory. On a Win32 platform, any application can use approximately 2G of memory, theoretically. No one that I know of has 2G of main memory on his/her computer; we are fortunate indeed if we can afford 256M of memory when running Win2000. Windows handles this shortfall of real memory versus the amount of memory required by the use of a swap file or virtual memory.

If an application requires more memory than is currently available, Windows places that memory onto its swap file and swaps into real memory only those locations that current instructions really need. Windows ensures that the memory any specific computer instruction is about to reference is actually located somewhere in real computer memory. If that memory was not in real memory, then Windows swaps some currently unreferenced memory out to the swap file and then swaps the needed memory into the now available real memory locations. This action is also called paging. Windows has a set of special file handling functions that permit it to access its swap file approximately 10 times faster than the fastest normal file input/output operations. (These functions are collectively known as Memory Mapped Files and are actually available for any Windows application to also use.)

Thus, in reality, the limitation on the maximum number of items in a data structure is defined by the size of the Windows swap file (plus the amount of free real memory at the moment the application is running). Under WinNT and Win2000, there can be multiple swap files located on multiple disk drives so that it is entirely possible for a machine to have a 2G swap file. Windows 95 and 98 have a more difficult time maintaining large swap files; their overall performance drops when one predefines a large swap file.

Implementation Details

The next question is how do we implement all these data structures? The answer is that there are many, many ways any one of these structures could be implemented.

One could use pure C style coding, forsaking ADTs (classes) making all of the data structure items global variables. But that is a terrible way to go.

Lying at the other extreme is the STL, Standard Template Library, that is provided by the compiler manufacturer. This library implements all of these data structures plus some additional ones. The STL makes use of ADTs (classes) but adds an additional piece of complexity. They are all implemented using template classes. A template is a blueprint for the compiler to follow when it needs to create a specific implementation of a data structure. The STL has the advantage of being reusable parts. That is, whenever you need a data structure, why you just create instances of it from the STL. However, template classes have the worst syntax I have ever seen and their coding rightfully belongs to advanced object-oriented programmers. My own experience with beginning programmers has shown me that dealing with template classes is a nightmare.

Thus, my approach is to use ADTs (classes) to implement the data structures. Even here, there is a huge range of possible implementations. If one knew that there were never going to be more than 5 items on a stack, ever, one could use an ordinary array with a bounds of 5 within the ADT (class) to contain the actual data. Simple, fast, clean and easy to follow. However, I am a firm believer in reusable coding. Why go to all the effort to write an ADT which has a fixed array size and then six months later discover you need another stack data structure for another application but this one needs to hold 100 items? I prefer to write the stack data structure one time and get it thoroughly debugged and then simply reuse it over and over when I need a stack. This means that I prefer implementations with no limits on the number of items in the structure, subject to available memory.

Next, when constructing the data structure ADT (class), one could make the implementation specific to the items that must be stored. For example, today you need a stack to store doubles. Then the ADT that is written stores doubles on its stack. But tomorrow you might need to store STUDENT structures on a stack. Oops. Now you need to make a new ADT (class) that stores STUDENT structures in its stack. In other words, the ADT (class) must know the kind of data that it is storing. Certainly, these are the simplest to write and we will begin out coding examples with ADTs of this type. However, this still is not optimum. You cannot easily reuse your nicely debugged double stack ADT without making major changes to get it to store STUDENT structure instances.

Thus, my point of view is to design the data structure in a more generalized manner such that it does not need to know or have any idea of what kind of items it is actually storing! If you can succeed at this, then you have a really reusable data structure ADT (class). However, when one makes the data structure container this general, it does place a greater workload on the user of the data structure. I consider this a small price to pay for being able to write the container class one time and then totally reuse it over and over without making the slightest change in that class.

So the direction of this text is down the road of making class (ADT) implementations of the various container classes. The first approach will be storing the specific data items the problem needs. Once we have the basic idea of how to write that container class, then let's see what can be done to make it a totally generalized container capable of total reuse.

Review Questions

1. What is meant by an ADT? How are they different than intrinsic data types? How are they similar to intrinsic types?

2. How does an array ADT differ from an intrinsic C++ array? How are they similar?

3. What is a double linked list? Describe two examples of real-world situations which would be best modeled by a linked list. Do not use those that were mentioned in this text.

4. What is a queue data structure? Describe two examples of real-world situations which would be best modeled by a queue. Do not use those that were mentioned in this text.

5. What is a stack data structure? Describe two examples of real-world situations which would be best modeled by a stack. Do not use those that were mentioned in this text.

6. What is a set data structure? Describe two examples of real-world situations which would be best modeled by a set. Do not use those that were mentioned in this text.

7. Describe the limiting factor that an instance of a queue data structure would have on the number of items that it could store.

Stop! Do These Exercises Before Programming

1. Using the table style definitions of data structures used throughout this chapter, write a definition for an ADT that would encapsulate a Rectangle object. Pay particular attention to the kinds of operations a user might like to perform on a Rectangle object.

2. Assume that **mylist** is an instance of a list data structure. Further, assume that the list contains the following character items in this order, from the front to the rear of the list:
  {A, B, C, D, E}
Further, assume that the current pointer or cursor is pointing to the D list item. Give the contents of the list after each of the following operations have been performed on the list. Also, assume each operation is done independently of the others, that is, always start the operation on the original list given above.

```
A. mylist.AddAtHead ('X');

B. mylist.AddAtTail ('X');

C. mylist.InsertAt ('X');

D. mylist.RemoveAt ();

E. mylist.Next();
   mylist.GetCurrent();

F. mylist.Previous();
   mylist.GetCurrent();

G. mylist.IsEmpty();
```

3. Assume that **myqueue** is an instance of a queue data structure and that it contains the following items from front to rear.

    {John, Ann, Betsy, Tom, Pete}

Give the contents of the queue after each of the following operations have been performed on the queue. Also, assume each operation is done independently of the others, that is, always start the operation on the original queue given above.

```
A. myqueue.Enqueue ("Ralph");

B. myqueue.Dequeue ();

C. myqueue.Dequeue ();
   myqueue.Dequeue ();

D. myqueue.Dequeue ();
   myqueue.Enqueue ("Sam");

E. myqueue.Enqueue ("Sam");
   myqueue.Enqueue ("Henry");
```

4. Assume that **mystack** is an instance of a stack data structure and that it contains the following items from top to bottom.

    {John, Ann, Betsy}

Further, assume that **mystack2** is also a stack structure but currently is empty: {}. Give the contents of the stack after each of the following operations have been performed on the stack. Also, assume each operation is done independently of the others, that is, always start the operation on the original stack given above.

```
A. name = mystack.Pop();

B. name = mystack.Pop();
   mystack2.Push(name);
   name = mystack.Pop();
   mystack2.Push(name);
   name = mystack.Pop();
   mystack2.Push(name);

C. mystack.Push("Tom");
   mystack2.Push("Tom");

D. mystack.Pop();
   mystack.Pop();
   mystack.Push("Tom");
```

Beginning Data Structures in C++

5. Assume that **set1** is an instance of a set data structure and that it contains the following items:
    {A, B, C, D, E}
Further, assume that **set2** is also a set structure and currently contains:
    {E, C, B}
Give the set results after each of the following operations have been performed. Also, assume each operation is done independently of the others, that is, always start the operation on the original set given above.


```
A.  set1.IsAMember (A);
    set2.IsAMember (A);

B.  set3 = set1.Intersection(set2);
    set4 = set2.Intersection(set1);

C.  set3 = set1.Union(set2);
    set4 = set2.Union(set1);

D.  set3 = set1.Difference(set2);
```

Chapter 6—Structures

Introduction

In your previous exposures to C++ programming, you probably have learned all about structures. If not, refer to Appendix A for the basics of structures. This chapter begins by providing a review of structures from the view point of how a structure handles the Record type of data structure by grouping a series of related fields together. Next, we will see how an array of structures can be designed in which the only limit on the number of elements in the array is the amount available memory on the computer. Finally, we examine some of the advanced features of structures.

Structures as a Record of Data

A structure provides a means to group a series of related fields of information into one entity. The structure template defines which fields are in this entity. Suppose that the program is to process cost records. Each cost record includes the item number, quantity on hand, product description and its cost. Here is what the structure template looks like.

```
const int DescrLen = 21; // max length of description

struct COSTREC {
   long   itemNum;         // item number
   short  qty;             // quantity on hand
   char   descr[DescrLen]; // item description
   double cost;            // item cost
};
```

The structure tag, **COSTREC** in this case, is used to identify this particular structure. Remember that by convention, all structure tags either are wholly uppercase names (usually) or are capitalized. The tag specifies that, when instances of the structure are built, four data members of these types and names are to be created. The member fields are always created and stored in the order shown in the template.

The order of the structure members can sometimes be important. If this program is part of a collection of programs, all sharing the same files, such as a payroll system of programs, or if the data file to be input is in binary format, then the structure members must be in the same order that the data is in the binary file. A **binary** file is one in which all data is stored in internal format; binary files cannot be viewed with text editors such as Notepad. They are discussed in detail in chapter 13. For most problems, the fields can be in any order you choose.

The following creates a structure variable called **costRec**.
```
COSTREC costRec;
```

Beginning Data Structures in C++

Figure 6.1 shows the memory layout of **costRec** and its member fields. Notice that the fields are in the same order as in the **COSTREC** template.

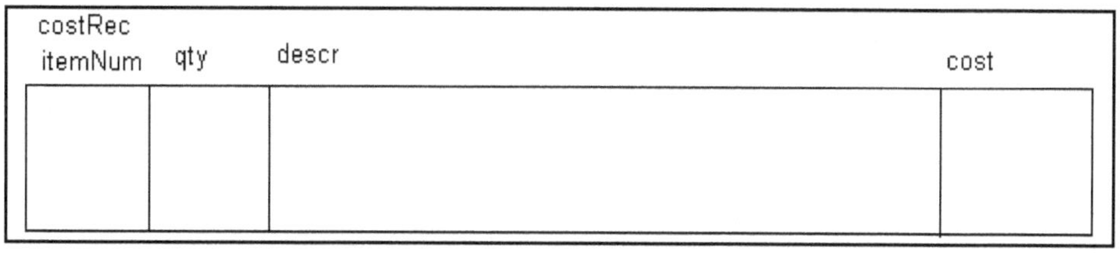

Figure 6.1 The **costRec** Memory Layout

One can have arrays of structures as well. Suppose that the program needed to store a maximum of 1000 cost records. The following defines the array and also shows the location of all the parts of the structure definitions.

File: CostRec.h

```
#pragma once
const int DescrLen = 21;   // max length of description
struct COSTREC {
  long    itemNum;          // item number
  short   qty;              // quantity on hand
  char    descr[DescrLen];  // item description
  double  cost;             // item cost
};
```

File: main.cpp

```
#include "CostRec.h"
const int MAXRECS = 1000;
int main () {
 COSTREC arec[MAXRECS];   // array of 1000 cost records
 ...
```

A structure can also contain instances of other structures and arrays of other structures. For example, consider a **DATE** structure which represents a calendar date. Using instances of a **DATE** structure would make passing dates very convenient. Further, consider an employee record that contained the employee's id number, his/her salary and the date that he/she was hired. The **EMPLOYEE** structure contains an instance of the **DATE** structure as shown below.

```
struct DATE {
  char month;
  char day;
  short year;
};

struct EMPLOYEE {
  long id;
  double salary;
  DATE hireDate;
};
```

Beginning Data Structures in C++

Suppose that a **CARMAINT** structure must be defined to represent the periodic maintenance requirements for a new car. Here the **CARMAINT** structure contains an array of **DATE** structures.

```
const int numMaint = 10;
struct CARMAINT {
 bool maintenanceDone[numMaint];    // true if the work was done
 int  maintenanceCode[numMaint];    // manufacturer's maint. codes
 DATE maintenanceDueDate[numMaint];// date maintenance is due
};
```

Having defined the structure template and an created instance of it, the next action is to utilize the members within the structure. This is done by using the **dot (.)** operator. To the left of the **dot** operator must be a structure variable and to the right must be a member variable of that structure. We know that to access the **qty** member of the **costRec** instance, one codes

```
costRec.qty
```

To calculate the **totalCost** using the **cost** and **qty** members of the **costRec** instance, do the following.

```
double totalCost = costRec.qty * costRec.cost;
```

To display the description, use

```
cout << costRec.descr;
```

To increment the **costRec**'s quantity member or add another variable to it, one can code

```
costRec.qty++;
costRec.qty += orderedQty;
```

To input a set of data into the **costRec** variable, there are a number of ways. Here is one.

```
cin >> costRec.itemNum >> costRec.qty >> ws;
cin.get (costRec.descr, DescrLen);
cin >> costRec.cost;
```

The above assumes that no description field in the input data contains all blanks. It also assumes that all descriptions contain **DescrLen – 1** number of characters.

Structures can also be dynamically allocated. Here a new **CARMAINT** instance is allocated dynamically.

```
CARMAINT* ptrcar = new CARMAINT;
```

The individual members are accessed using the **pointer operator, ->,** as shown.

```
ptrcar->maintenanceDone[i]
ptrcar->maintenanceCode[i]
ptrcar->maintenanceDueDate[i].month
```

Notice the syntax of the last one above. We desire to get at the ith due date's **month** field. The entire structure instance is pointed to by **prtcar**.

The **address** operator & returns the address of the structure variable. If one codes

```
&costRec
```

then the compiler provides the memory location where the instance begins. Normally, the compiler does this automatically for us when we use reference variables. Here &costRec would be a constant pointer to a **COSTREC** structure. Taking the address of a structure instance is sometimes needed when passing a pointer to the instance to a function.

Beginning Data Structures in C++

A structure variable can be passed to a function or a reference or pointer to one can be passed. Passing by reference is the best approach to take. However, passing by use of a pointer is also fine. The main issue here is to realize that we are passing the address of the data structure entity, the structure instance.

Suppose that the **main()** program defined the cost record structure as we have been using it thus far. Suppose further that the **main()** function then wanted to call a **PrintRec()** function whose task is to print the data nicely formatted. Of course, we would pass the instance either by reference or by its address to avoid forcing the compiler to make a duplicate copy of this instance. The **main()** function can do one of the following.

```
int main () {
COSTREC crec;

...
PrintRec (outfile, crec);
```
where the **PrintRec()** function begins this way
```
void PrintRec (ostream& outfile, const COSTREC& crec) {
   outfile << crec.itemNum...
```
or
```
int main () {
COSTREC crec;

...
PrintRec (outfile, &crec);
```
and the **PrintRec()** function begins as follows
```
void PrintRec (ostream& outfile, const COSTREC* ptrcrec) {
   outfile << ptrcrec->itemNum...
```

In both cases, the memory location of **crec** is passed to the function. Since **PrintRec()** is not going to modify the data, it is further qualified as being a constant address.

This brings up the **ReadRec()** function whose job it is to input the data and somehow fill up the **main()**'s **costRec** with that data. One way that the **ReadRec()** function can be defined is to have it return a **COSTREC** structure. This is not a good way to do it, because execution time is required to make duplicate copies to return and to copy the returned data into the designated instance in **main()**. We know that instead we should pass a reference to the instance to be filled or perhaps a pointer to that instance. The return value of such a **ReadRec()** function can then be used to return a reference to the input stream. We do this so that **main()** function has more ways that it can utilize the **ReadRec()** function.

```
istream& ReadRec (istream& infile, COSTREC& crec) {
 if (infile >> ws && !infile.good()) {
  return infile;
 }
 infile >> crec.itemNum >> and so on
 return infile;
}
```
Here the **main()** function can directly check on the input stream's status after an attempt has been made to input all of the fields.
```
int main () {
 COSTREC costRec;
 ...
```

```
while (ReadRec (infile, costRec)) {
```

This concept of encapsulating the action of inputting all of the data of a record within one function which then returns a reference to the input stream is a vital one. We will continue to make use of this concept when we write ATDs (classes).

The only obstacle we have faced thus far is with arrays of structure and the need for that constant fixed maximum number of elements in the array. So next, let's examine how an array of structures can be created such that it has no maximum upper bounds subject only to available memory.

A Growable Array of Structures

When writing applications, establishing the upper bounds for an array can often not be foretold with any degree of certainty. When you code

```
COSTREC arec[1000];
```

you are introducing an arbitrary, the maximum number of cost records that the program can handle. If the input contains even one additional record, the program has little choice but to terminate with an error stating the array bounds has been exceeded. With production programs, often a programmer can only make a wild guess at the maximum number that can be found in the input file(s) at run time. Indeed, as companies grow, their data bases likewise increase in volume. Sooner or later, a programmer can expect that he/she will be requested to make that arbitrary maximum number larger.

To counter this uncertainty, programmers sometimes make the array bounds way too large. That is, if the expected maximum is 100,000 elements, they make the array bounds 500,000 elements. Of course, this is self-defeating in that now the program itself always ties up vast amounts of memory that it never uses. However, if we design this array of records properly, no such limitation occurs. The array just gets larger and larger. This is called a growable array. A growable array just keeps increasing the number of elements in it and is subject only to the total amount of memory available on the computer.

Suppose that we are dealing with customer daily order records. Each week our program inputs a series of daily sales files and calculates weekly sales statistics. Assuming that we have a properly defined **ORDER** structure, the fixed array limit definition would be as follows.

```
const int MAXORDERS = 100000;
ORDER orders[MAXORDERS];
```

How can this fixed approach be converted into an array whose bounds can easily be increased?

The key is dynamic memory allocation. Let's change the constant **MAXORDERS** into a variable, **maxOrders**. Assuming that **maxOrders** has the value of 100 in it at the moment, we could create an array of this size as shown.

```
long maxOrders; // currently contains 100
ORDER* orders;
orders = new (std::nothrow) ORDER [maxOrders];
```

Here orders is an array of 100 **ORDER** structures. Now, suppose that we input one additional customer order so that the **orders** array needs to become an array of 101 elements?

Beginning Data Structures in C++

One way to accomplish this would be to allocate a new array of **maxOrders+1** elements, copy the old array of orders into this larger array, copy in the new order, delete the old array and assign the **orders** pointer to this newly allocated and filled array. The following represents these steps.

```
// assumes newOrderJustInput contains the new order info
// that is to be added to the array
ORDER* temp = new (std::nothrow) ORDER [maxOrders+1];
if (!temp) {
 cerr << "Error out of memory\n ";
 exit (1);
}
for (k=0; k<maxOrders; k++) {
 temp[k] = orders[k];
}
temp[maxOrders] = newOrderJustInput;
if (orders) delete [] orders;
orders = temp;
maxOrders++;
```

Figures 6.2 illustrates the copy operations and Figure 6.3 shows the results after the last three instructions in the above series are completed, that is the new state of the orders array.

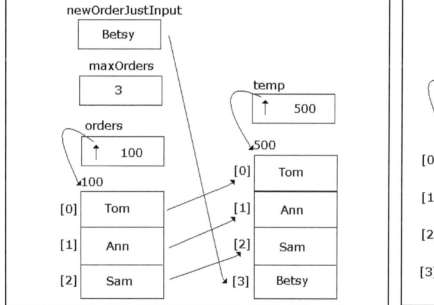 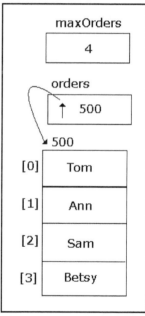

Figure 6.2 Growing the Orders Array — the Copy Operation   Figure 6.3 New orders

Thus, a simple sequence of allocating a new array one larger than the current array, copying over the current elements and adding the new element, reassigning the array pointer and incrementing the bounds counter allows the array to grow by one element. This simple approach will work just fine, but it has a serious performance problem. Can you spot the execution time inefficiency?

Assume that we start out with **maxOrders** at 0 and that each time the array grows as shown. Supposing that 10,000 orders are input. How many times will element at index 0 be copied into a larger

149

Beginning Data Structures in C++

array? 10,000 times! The element at index 1 is copied 9,999 times, and so on. If the order structure is large, our program's execution speed gets slower and slower and slower as more and more elements are added!

In this chapter, since this is our first look at growing an array dynamically at runtime, we will ignore this performance problem. Indeed, if the ultimate size is not too large and the size of the elements is not large, the performance degradation is not noticeably serious. In the ensuing chapters, we will examine alternate schemes to bypass this performance problem.

The next action to consider is how to encapsulate these array growing steps. The obvious choice is to place them into a function, **GrowArray()**. As a first attempt, let's code its prototype as follows.

```
void GrowArray (ORDER* orders, long& maxOrders,
                const ORDER& newOrderJustInput); // error
```

However, designing the function in this manner represents one of the most common errors programers new to pointers face. It is a very subtle bug. Can you spot the problem just by looking at the prototype? Extremely well done if you can! Ok. I'll give you a clue. Here is the proposed **GrowArray()** function implementation.

```
void GrowArray (ORDER* orders, long& maxOrders,
                const ORDER& newOrderJustInput) {
 ORDER* temp = new (std::nothrow) ORDER [maxOrders+1];
 if (!temp) {
  cerr << "Error out of memory\n ";
  exit (1);
 }
 for (long k=0; k<maxOrders; k++) {
  temp[k] = orders[k];
 }
 temp[maxOrders] = newOrderJustInput;
 if (orders) delete [] orders;
 orders = temp;
 maxOrders++;
}
```

Now, can you spot the insidious bug this design has created? If so, very good indeed. If not, here is a further clue. Here is how the **main()** function invokes **GrowArray()**.

```
ORDER* orders;
long   maxOrders;
ORDER  newOrderJustInput;
...
GrowArray (orders, maxOrders, newOrderJustInput);
```

Now can you spot the gross error? If so, good. If not, pay very close attention now.

All parameter variables in C++ are COPIES of what is sent by the caller. **GrowArray()**'s parameter **orders** is a COPY of the memory address of **main()**'s **order**. The error occurs on the second to last line of the **GrowArray()** function.

```
orders = temp;
```

Where does the new memory address of the new larger array get stored? It is stored in **GrowArray()**'s parameter **orders** variable and NOT in **main()**'s **orders** pointer!

150

There are several ways to bypass this potential error. We could pass a reference to the orders pointer or we could pass a pointer to the orders pointer. But there is a simpler way. Let's change the design of the function and have **GrowArray()** return the new memory address of the orders array. Here is the new prototype.

```
ORDER* GrowArray (ORDER* orders, long& maxOrders,
                  const ORDER& newOrderJustInput);
```

The **main()** function must now invoke **GrowArray()** this way:

```
ORDER* orders;
long   maxOrders;
ORDER  newOrderJustInput;
...
orders = GrowArray (orders, maxOrders, newOrderJustInput);
```

Here is the new implementation of **GrowArray()**.

```
ORDER* GrowArray (ORDER* orders, long& maxOrders,
                  const ORDER& newOrderJustInput) {
 ORDER* temp = new (std::nothrow) ORDER [maxOrders+1];
 if (!temp) {
  cerr << "Error out of memory\n ";
  exit (1);
 }
 for (long k=0; k<maxOrders; k++) {
  temp[k] = orders[k];
 }
 temp[maxOrders] = newOrderJustInput;
 if (orders) delete [] orders;
 maxOrders++;
 return temp;
}
```

The alternative method is to pass a reference to main's **orders** pointer;
The **main()** function would now invoke **GrowArray()** this way:

```
ORDER* orders;
long   maxOrders;
ORDER  newOrderJustInput;
...
GrowArray (orders, maxOrders, newOrderJustInput);
```

Here is the reference version implementation of **GrowArray()**.

```
void GrowArray (ORDER*& orders, long& maxOrders,
                const ORDER& newOrderJustInput) {
 ORDER* temp = new (std::nothrow) ORDER [maxOrders+1];
 if (!temp) {
  cerr << "Error out of memory\n ";
  exit (1);
 }
 for (long k=0; k<maxOrders; k++) {
  temp[k] = orders[k];
 }
 temp[maxOrders] = newOrderJustInput;
```

```
if (orders) delete [] orders;
maxOrders++;
orders = temp;
}
```

Handling a Variable Number of Command Line Arguments

Before we tackle the full order statistics program, another complexity must be examined. And that has to do with the actual input files themselves. Each day, Acme orders are stored in a daily sales file. This program must input those daily sales files. No problem, we can just open, input, and close each of the five input files. Designing like this is using tunnel vision. What happens on the weeks when the company is closed for a holiday, such as Christmas or Thanksgiving? And what happens on those weeks when the company extends its shopping hours and days to accommodate the expected rush of holiday shoppers? In other words, what I am suggesting is to think about the real-world situation before you dive into program design. Certainly this program will usually expect to input five daily files, but there obviously will be exceptions. Some weeks there will be fewer daily files; some weeks, more daily files.

Let's say that the filenames we need to use will be coded on the command line when the program is launched. The **main()** function has access to these via its parameters usually called **argc** and **argv**, the argument count and the array of string values. Now a design begins to suggest itself. We can write a loop that goes from 1 to **argc** and pass the corresponding filename in **argv** to a **LoadFile()** function whose task is to input that file of orders into the array.

Well, almost. Consider the situation in which the user mis-enters the last filename. If there are a large number of orders in each file, the program will have been executing for some time before it discovers that it cannot open that last file! This is very wasteful of computer and human resources. If a program expects to deal with five input files, then out of consideration for everyone, the program ought to let the user know immediately that one or more of the filenames is incorrect and not make them wait.

One way to do this is to have the **main()** function open and then close each of the proposed input files as its first action, just to verify that there are no user errors on filenames. However, it does take time to open and then close and then later on reopen each input file. So let's get a bit fancier. Let's make an array of **ifstream** objects, one for each of the input files the user has asked us to process. Then, we can open each in turn one time. If all is well, we can then pass those opened file streams on to the **LoadFile()** function. If we encounter an open error, we can notify the user at once.

Pgm06a Acme Weekly Sales Summary Report

Each of the daily sales order files contains the following fields: invoice number, customer account number, order date, item number, quantity, unit cost, tax and the total cost of the order
Presumably another company file contains the customer's personal details such as address and credit card information. The company assures us that these daily sales files do not contain any bad data, such as letters where a number should occur.

Beginning Data Structures in C++

The sales summary report the program is to create appears as follows. I have attempted to keep the report fairly simple so that we can concentrate on the new actions. Here is the output from the program using the set of sales files I have provided.

```
Output from Pgm06a

 1 Acme Weekly Sales Summary Report
 2
 3    Item        Qty            Total
 4   Number       Sold            Cost
 5
 6    23453       100      $   4250.00
 7     3453      1000      $  50100.00
 8     4354       100      $   6065.00
 9      253       200      $   2020.00
10    54333        50      $   1667.50
11    54453        50      $   1667.50
12                         ----------
13                         $  65770.00
```

Acme has two standard structure definitions that all programs must use. One defines their way of storing date objects and the other defines their order records. Here are those two files that we must use.

```
Date.h - Acme DATE Structure

 1 #pragma once
 2
 3 /*******************************/
 4 /*                             */
 5 /* Acme Standard DATE structure */
 6 /*                             */
 7 /*******************************/
 8
 9 struct DATE {
10   short month;
11   short day;
12   short year;
13 };
```

```
Order.h - Acme ORDER Structure

 1 #pragma once
 2
 3 #include "Date.h"  // needed for the orderDate member
 4
 5 /***********************************************************/
 6 /*                                                         */
 7 /* Acme Standard ORDER structure                           */
```

```
 8 /*                                                                   */
 9 /***********************************************************************/
10
11 struct ORDER {
12
13   long    invoiceNum;    // the customer's invoice number
14   long    customerNum;   // the customer's account number
15   DATE    orderDate;     // the date of this order
16   long    itemNum;       // the item number of the product purchased
17   short   quantity;      // the quantity purchased
18   double  unitCost;      // the price of one of these items
19   double  tax;           // the tax charged on this order
20   double  totalCost;     // the total cost of this order
21 };
```

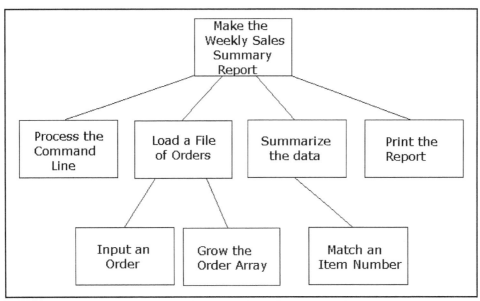

Figure 6.4 Top-down Design for Weekly Sales Report Program

As usual, after gaining an understanding of the problem, a Top-down design is created. Figure 6.4 shows the design that I am using.

The **main()** function first calls **ProcessCommandLine()** which dynamically allocates an array of **ifstream** objects and opens all of the user requested files. If one or more files fail to open, then error messages are displayed giving the name of each file that did not open properly and the program is aborted. If all is ok, the address of the array of files is returned to **main()**.

Next, **main()** calls **LoadFile()** for each of the input files. The logic loop for **LoadFile()** is very simple. Call **InputAnOrder()** to actually stream in the next order data. If there is another order, the **GrowArray()** is called to enlarge the array and add in this new order.

Finally, **main()** calls **SummarizeData()** and **PrintReport()** to perform the necessary calculations and display the results. Looking at the report we are to produce, three arrays are needed to store the item number, the corresponding total quantity purchased, and the total cost. However, I do not want to pass three arrays around to these functions much less worry about keeping them parallel arrays. A common simplification to such situations is to define a helper structure to encapsulate these three items. I called this new structure **SALESSUMMARY** and it contains three fields, the item number, quantity, and the cost. Now, **main()** can make a single array of this structure and pass it to the two functions. The maximum array bounds of this summary structure array is determined by the number of individual products the company sells. Here it is set to 100. Yes, this is an arbitrary being entered into the solution; it could very well also be a growable array of summary structures.

SummarizeData() sequentially accesses every order in turn and calls **MatchItemNumber()** to find out if this item number is already in the summary array. If it is, this order's quantity and total are added to the corresponding summary instance. If it is not yet in the summary array, then this item number is added to the summary array along with this order's quantity and total.

Here is the complete Pgm06a program.

```
Pgm06a.cpp Acme Weekly Sales Summary Program

 1 #include <iostream>
 2 #include <iomanip>
 3 #include <fstream>
 4 #include <crtdbg.h>    // for memory leak checking
 5 using namespace std;
 6
 7 #include "Order.h"
 8
 9 ifstream* ProcessCommandLine (int argc, char* argv[]);
10
11 ORDER*    LoadFile (ORDER* orders, long& maxOrders,
12                     ifstream& infile);
13
14 ifstream& InputAnOrder (ifstream& infile, ORDER& order);
15
16 ORDER*    GrowArray (ORDER* orders, long& maxOrders,
17                     const ORDER& newOrderJustInput);
18
19 // helper structure for summary totals
20 const int MAXITEMS = 100;
21
22 struct SALESSUMMARY {
23   long   itemnumber;
24   long   totalQty;
25   double totalCost;
26 };
27
28 void SummarizeData (const ORDER* orders, long numOrders,
```

```
29                        SALESSUMMARY totals[], int& numTotals);
30
31 int  MatchItemNumber (const SALESSUMMARY totals[], int numTotals,
32                        long matchItemNum);
33 const int NOMATCH = -1;
34
35 void  PrintReport (const SALESSUMMARY totals[], int numTotals);
36
37 /********************************************************************/
38 /*                                                                  */
39 /* Pgm06a: Produce Weekly Sales Summary Report                      */
40 /*                                                                  */
41 /********************************************************************/
42
43 int main (int argc, char* argv[]) {
44
45  // construct an array of opened daily sales files
46  ifstream* files = ProcessCommandLine (argc, argv);
47
48  int    numFiles = argc-1;  // the number of files to process
49  ORDER* orders = 0;         // the growable array of orders
50  long   maxOrders = 0;      // the current number of orders
51  int    i;
52
53  // load all of the orders from all of the files
54  for (i=0; i<numFiles; i++) {
55   orders = LoadFile (orders, maxOrders, files[i]);
56   files[i].close ();
57  }
58  //remove the files array as it is no longer needed
59  if (files) delete [] files;
60
61  // the summarized data helper structure
62  SALESSUMMARY totals[MAXITEMS];
63  int          numTotals = 0;
64
65  // go summarize all of the order data
66  SummarizeData (orders, maxOrders, totals, numTotals);
67  // remove the orders array as it is not needed further
68  if (orders) delete [] orders;
69
70  // finally, display the summarized data
71  PrintReport (totals, numTotals);
72
73  // check for memory leaks
74  if (_CrtDumpMemoryLeaks())
75   cerr << "Memory leaks occurred!\n";
76  else
77   cerr << "No memory leaks.\n";
78
```

```
 79  return 0;
 80  }
 81
 82  /***************************************************************/
 83  /*                                                           */
 84  /*  ProcessCommandLine: verify command line is a proper one  */
 85  /*    consisting of one or more daily sales filenames        */
 86  /*                                                           */
 87  /*    build an array of ifstream objects and attempt to open */
 88  /*    all of the files                                       */
 89  /*                                                           */
 90  /*    if any file cannot be opened, display an error message */
 91  /*    that includes that incorrect name and abort the program*/
 92  /*                                                           */
 93  /*    returns the address of the files array if all is ok    */
 94  /*                                                           */
 95  /***************************************************************/
 96
 97  ifstream* ProcessCommandLine (int argc, char* argv[]) {
 98   // guard against no command line files
 99   if (argc == 1) {
100    cerr << "Error: you must specify one or more daily sales"
101         << " filenames on the command line\n";
102    exit (1);
103   }
104
105   // allocate the array of file streams
106   ifstream* files = new (std::nothrow) ifstream [argc-1];
107   if (!files) {
108    cerr << "Error: out of memory for files\n";
109    exit (2);
110   }
111   int i;
112
113   // attempt to open each file
114   for (i=1; i<argc; i++) {
115    files[i-1].open (argv[i]);
116   }
117
118   // not display error messages for all that failed to open
119   bool ok = true;
120   for (i=1; i<argc; i++) {
121    if (!files[i-1]) {
122     cerr << "Error: unable to open daily sales file: "
123          << argv[i] << endl;
124     ok = false;
125    }
126   }
127
128   //if any failed to open, close all files and abort the program
```

```
129  if (!ok) {
130    for (i=1; i<argc; i++) {
131      files[i-1].close ();
132    }
133    delete [] files;
134    exit (2);
135  }
136
137  return files;
138 }
139
140 /****************************************************************/
141 /*                                                            */
142 /* LoadFile: input all order records in the file and add them*/
143 /*           to the growable orders array                     */
144 /*          return the address of the new larger orders array */
145 /*                                                            */
146 /****************************************************************/
147
148 ORDER*    LoadFile (ORDER* orders, long& maxOrders,
149                     ifstream& infile) {
150  infile >> dec;              // allow for numbers with leading 0's
151  ORDER newOrderJustInput;
152
153  while (InputAnOrder (infile, newOrderJustInput)) {
154    orders = GrowArray (orders, maxOrders, newOrderJustInput);
155  }
156  return orders;
157 }
158
159 /****************************************************************/
160 /*                                                            */
161 /* InputAnOrder: input another set of order data              */
162 /*                                                            */
163 /****************************************************************/
164
165 ifstream&  InputAnOrder (ifstream& infile, ORDER& order) {
166  char c; // for the / separating mm/dd/yyyy
167
168  infile >> order.invoiceNum >> order.customerNum
169         >> order.orderDate.month >> c
170         >> order.orderDate.day   >> c
171         >> order.orderDate.year
172         >> order.itemNum
173         >> order.quantity
174         >> order.unitCost
175         >> order.tax
176         >> order.totalCost;
177
178  return infile;
```

158

```
179 }
180
181 /****************************************************************/
182 /*                                                              */
183 /* GrowArray: make a new orders array that is one bigger than*/
184 /*            the current one, copy over all the existing      */
185 /*            orders, copy in the new order to be added,       */
186 /*            if the old array exists, delete it,              */
187 /*            increment the number in the array and return     */
188 /*            the address of the new larger array              */
189 /*                                                              */
190 /****************************************************************/
191
192 ORDER* GrowArray (ORDER* orders, long& maxOrders,
193                     const ORDER& newOrderJustInput) {
194
195   ORDER* temp = new (std::nothrow) ORDER [maxOrders+1];
196   if (!temp) {
197    cerr << "Error: out of memory\n";
198    exit (1);
199   }
200   for (long k=0; k<maxOrders; k++) {
201    temp[k] = orders[k];
202   }
203   temp[maxOrders] = newOrderJustInput;
204
205   if (orders) delete [] orders;
206   maxOrders++;
207   return temp;
208 }
209
210 /****************************************************************/
211 /*                                                              */
212 /* SummarizeData: summarize the daily sales information       */
213 /*    builds the sales summary array which contains the item */
214 /*    number and the corresponding quantity and total sales  */
215 /*                                                              */
216 /*    For each order, search the table for a matching item    */
217 /*    number. If not found, add this item. If found, add to   */
218 /*    its quantity and total sales.                           */
219 /*                                                              */
220 /****************************************************************/
221
222 void SummarizeData (const ORDER* orders, long numOrders,
223                     SALESSUMMARY totals[], int& numTotals) {
224   int match;
225   for (long i=0; i<numOrders; i++) {
226    match = MatchItemNumber (totals, numTotals, orders[i].itemNum);
227    if (match == NOMATCH) {
228     // avoid exceeding the fixed array size
```

```
229    if (numTotals >= MAXITEMS) {
230     cerr << "Summary array size exceeded!\n";
231     exit (1);
232    }
233    totals[numTotals].itemnumber = orders[i].itemNum;
234    totals[numTotals].totalQty = orders[i].quantity;
235    totals[numTotals].totalCost = orders[i].totalCost;
236    numTotals++;
237   }
238   else {
239    totals[match].totalQty += orders[i].quantity;
240    totals[match].totalCost += orders[i].totalCost;
241   }
242  }
243 }
244
245 /****************************************************************/
246 /*                                                              */
247 /* MatchItemNumber: match an item number with the array item   */
248 /*                  numbers - if no match because this item    */
249 /*                  is not in the array, return NOMATCH        */
250 /*                  otherwise return the subscript of match    */
251 /*                                                              */
252 /****************************************************************/
253
254 int  MatchItemNumber (const SALESSUMMARY totals[], int numTotals,
255                       long matchItemNum) {
256  for (int i=0; i<numTotals; i++) {
257   if (totals[i].itemnumber == matchItemNum) return i;
258  }
259  return NOMATCH;
260 }
261
262 /****************************************************************/
263 /*                                                              */
264 /* PrintReport: display the summary report                     */
265 /*                                                              */
266 /****************************************************************/
267
268 void  PrintReport (const SALESSUMMARY totals[], int numTotals) {
269  // setup floating point output for dollars and cents
270  cout << fixed << setprecision (2);
271
272  // display heading and two column heading lines
273  cout << "Acme Weekly Sales Summary Report\n\n";
274  cout << "  Item        Qty          Total\n"
275       << " Number       Sold          Cost\n\n";
276
277  // accumulator for grand total sales
278  double grandTotal = 0;
```

```
279
280  // display each summary line and accumulate the total dales
281  for (int i=0; i<numTotals; i++) {
282   cout << setw (7) << totals[i].itemnumber
283        << setw (10) << totals[i].totalQty
284        << "     $" << setw (9) << totals[i].totalCost << endl;
285   grandTotal += totals[i].totalCost;
286  }
287
288  // display the grand total sales
289  cout << "                        ----------\n";
290  cout << "                     $"
291       << setw (10) << grandTotal << endl;
292 }
```

Figure 6.1 below shows how I set the command line arguments for this test run.

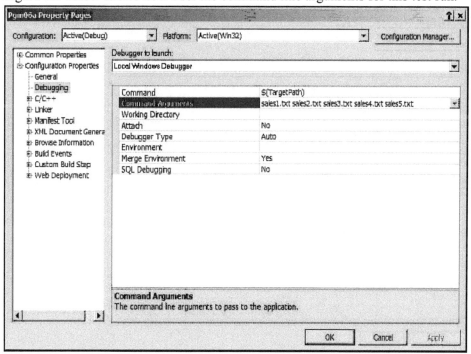

Figure 6.5 Setting the Command Line Arguments

What about testing oracles for **Pgm06a**? What tests would we need to perform to ensure that this program works perfectly? Test1—run the program with no command line arguments—it should abort with a proper message. Test2—run with several files that do not exist along with some that do—it should abort with messages on all of the files that do not exist. Test3—run with a number of files of known data values and see if the totals contain what they should hold. This is the test that I have provided above. Can you think of additional tests that should be performed on this program to ensure it works perfectly?

161

The String Stream Classes

There are two other iostream classes, the **istrstream** and the **ostrstream**. These encapsulate I/O into or from a null-terminated character string. The classes require the **<strstream>** header file.

Sometimes, one needs total control over the extraction of data, perhaps in a mission critical situation where one cannot afford to have the stream itself go into the fail state. In such cases, one can input an entire line of data into a character string and then input the data from the string in a totally controlled manner. For example, the user enters a date as 02/08/2003. We can input the string and then extract the date from the string.

```
char buffer[81];
cin.getline (buffer, sizeof (buffer));
istrstream is (buffer);
is >> dec >> month >> c >> day >> c >> year;
```

Other times, the user needs a character string filled with the desired output. Here, we must be careful to not overflow his string. Notice the constructor for the **ostrstream** class takes the maximum length of the user's string.

```
char buffer[81];
ostrstream os (buffer, sizeof(buffer));
os << setfill('0') << setw(2) << month << '/'
   << setw(2) << day << '/' << setw(4) << year << ends;
```

Notice that the **ends** manipulator function is used to append the null terminator onto the end of the string. Without it, the string has no end of string marker.

Unions—an Advanced Feature of Structures

A **union** is a special form of a structure which defines several members but in any given instances of the union, only one of those members is present. Memory for a union is always determined by the size of the largest member it could hold. Consider this union.

```
union Fun {
   int    x;
   long   y;
   double z;
   char   s[10];
};
```

When an instance of **Fun** is allocated, the compiler allocates a total of 10 bytes because member **s** occupies the largest amount of memory.

```
Fun someFun;
```

However, when the program that has allocated **someFun** executes, **someFun** can contain **x**, **y**, **z** or **s**. It can hold only one of these at any moment. But one can place any one of them in **someFun** at will as the following shows.

```
someFun.x = 42;   // it now holds an int x whose value is 42
someFun.z = 98.6; // it now holds the double z, 98.6
```

```
strcpy (someFun.s, "Hello"); // it now holds the string s
```

When the union's **x** member is assigned, only 4 bytes of the 10 available are used and contains the integer value of 42. When the union's **z** member is assigned, the contents of **someFun** are altered and now 8 bytes are used to store the double 98.6. When the union's **s** member is assigned, the **double** is overlaid with the string "hello." Notice that **x, y, z** and **s** all share the same memory area!

The real problem is knowing which variable is really in the memory at any given moment. But before we can see how this is commonly done, let's examine a special case of a union, called an **anonymous union**. An anonymous union is a union in which no tag and no specific instance is created as the union is being defined. Here is an anonymous union version of the Fun union above.

```
union {
   int    x;
   long   y;
   double z;
   char   s[10];
};
```

Since there is no tag, no other instances of this union can be created; there is no name to use as the data type.

Anonymous unions have a peculiar property. That is, the member names are not local to the union instance as are those in **Fun** above. Instead, the member names are treated as if they were defined immediately outside of the anonymous union and thus take on the definition aspects found there. That is, they act like they are members of the block that surrounds them. For example, here I have defined another structure around the anonymous one.

```
struct FUN {
        char which;
        union {
           int    x;
           long   y;
           double z;
           char   s[10];
        };
};
```

Here the structure **FUN** has two data members, which and either **x, y, z** or **s**; **FUN** occupies 11 bytes of memory, 1 for the **char** and 10 for the largest of the union members. Now if I create an instance of **FUN** called **fun**, we can get access to the union members because the act as if they were members of the surrounding block, **FUN** in this case.

```
FUN fun;
fun.which = 1;
fun.z = 42;
strcpy (fun.s, "Hello");
```

Variant Records

Ok, but what can we do with these unions? A union gives us the ability to store a single array of heterogenous data types! That is, we can now have an array whose elements are not of the same data type. We force the differences between data types to be in the union portion of a structure. However, with any specific instance of the outer structure, there must be a member outside the union that lets us know which one of the union members is in this specific instance. This concept is known as variant records. Variant records are a very powerful feature and very useful in advanced programming situations. They are widely used in Active-X and COM type programming.

Let's make a realistic example of a variant record. Suppose that our company has several forms that a date may take, depending upon the varying needs of applications. Further, the company wishes to have a uniform method for date processing across all applications. The forms the date may take are shown below.

"01/02/2000 " as a string

1 2 2000 as three shorts

155 2000 as two shorts representing the day of the year and the year

"January 2, 2000" as a string

The company can define a variant **DATE** structure which can hold any of these four forms. All applications can be passed an instance of this single **DATE** structure, independent of the precise format that it contains. Here could be that definition.

```
#ifndef DATE_H
#define DATE_H
enum DateFormat {MonthDayYear, DayYear,
                 StringFormat, EnglishString};

struct DATEMDY {
  short month;
  short day;
  short year;
};

struct DATEDY {
  short day;
  short year;
};

struct DATE {
  DateFormat type;
  union {
   DATEMDY dateMDY;
   DATEDY  dateDY;
   char    dateString[11];
   char    dateEnglish[19];
  };
};
#endif
```

164

A user program could then define an instance of **DATE** and store a month, day and year as shown below.

```
DATE d;
d.type = MonthDayYear;
d.dateMDY.month = 1;
d.dateMDY.day = 20;
d.dateMDY.year = 2001;
```

The important factor to note is this abstraction of a date yields a code reuse and commonality across all applications a company has. All applications that need a date object create instances of the **DATE** variant structure. All functions that are passed a date use an instance of this **DATE** structure.

Further code reuse can be achieved by writing a single function to handle all forms of date conversion. This is known as a utility function. In fact, that is precisely what our next application will be, a utility function to handle conversion of a date into the various forms.

Rather than make this utility function overly complex, let's make two assumptions that, while completely not valid in practice, will make this example easier to do so that we can follow this new variant record processing. I completely ignore leap years! No indication is given for the reason for a failure to perform the conversion.

The utility function should be called **ConvertDate()** and is passed a reference to a **DATE** object which holds the date to be converted and an instance of the enumerated data type that defines which conversion is to be performed. The answer will replace the original contents of the passed **DATE** instance, so the function returns a **bool**, **true** if the conversion was successful and **false** if it failed. The enum that defines the conversion is

```
enum DateConversion {ToMDY, ToDY, ToString, ToEnglish};
```

The function prototype is

```
bool ConvertDate (DATE& date, DateConversion which);
```

Here is the **Date.h** header file that is used in every Acme company application that processes a date.

```
Date.h - DATE Variant Record Definition

 1 #ifndef DATE_H
 2 #define DATE_H
 3
 4 /*******************************************************************/
 5 /*                                                                 */
 6 /* Acme Standard DATE Structure - variant records                 */
 7 /*                                                                 */
 8 /*******************************************************************/
 9
10 // DateFormat: identifies which type of data is in the variant
11 enum DateFormat {MonthDayYear, DayYear,
12                  StringFormat, EnglishString};
13
14 // the variant fields when in M D Y format
```

```
15 struct DATEMDY {
16   short month;
17   short day;
18   short year;
19 };
20
21 // the variant fields when in D Y format
22 struct DATEDY {
23   short day;
24   short year;
25 };
26
27 // the variant DATE structure
28 struct DATE {
29   DateFormat type; // tells which variant is present
30   union {
31     DATEMDY dateMDY;
32     DATEDY  dateDY;
33     char    dateString[11];
34     char    dateEnglish[19];
35   };
36 };
37
38 // DateConversion defines which type of date conversion
39 //                 is to be done
40 enum DateConversion {ToMDY, ToDY, ToString, ToEnglish};
41
42 // ConvertDate: converts date into the which form of date
43 // is requested. date is replaced with the new form if
44 // successful. Function returns true if conversion is ok
45 // false if it fails for any reason
46 bool ConvertDate (DATE& date, DateConversion which);
47
48 #endif
```

Notice how the member **type** is used to let us know which of the four variants is actually present in any given instance of **DATE**. Here is the **ConvertDate()** function. It is rather lengthy because of all of the possible conversion.

When running this code under the new .NET 2005 compiler, a bug in the compiler surfaced. When extracting an integer from a stream which is ended by a comma, the extraction fails! However, if a double is extracted instead, it works fine. Hopefully, this bug will get fixed soon. In the meantime, I have inserted a workaround function and commented out the coding that used to work on all previous compiler versions.

```
ConvertDate.cpp Converts a DATE into Another Format

 1 #include <iostream>
 2 #include <iomanip>
 3 #include <strstream>
```

```
 4 #include <string>
 5 using namespace std;
 6
 7 #include "Date.h"
 8
 9
10 const short daysInMonth[12] = {31, 28, 31, 30, 31, 30,
11                                31, 31, 30, 31, 30, 31};
12
13 const short daysYear[12] = {31, 59, 90, 120, 151, 181,
14                             212, 243, 273, 304, 334, 365};
15
16 const char monthNames[12][10] = {"January", "February", "March",
17         "April", "May", "June", "July", "August", "September",
18         "October", "November", "December"};
19
20 void BugFix2005 (char* source, char* mon, int& d, int& y);
21
22 /*****************************************************************/
23 /*                                                             */
24 /* ConvertDate: Utility function to convert a date from any of */
25 /*              four forms into any of four forms              */
26 /*              It returns true if successful, false if fails  */
27 /*                                                             */
28 /* It is passed the DATE object and the requested to conversion*/
29 /* If the converison is successful, it returns the new form in */
30 /*    the original passed DATE object                          */
31 /*                                                             */
32 /* From Forms: M D Y; D Y; "mm/dd/yyyy"; "mmmmmmmmmmm dd, yyyy" */
33 /*      as defined by DateFormat enum:                         */
34 /*      MonthDayYear, DayYear, StringFormat, EnglishString     */
35 /*                                                             */
36 /* To Forms the same as defined by DateConversion enum         */
37 /*      ToMDY, ToDY, ToString, ToEnglish                       */
38 /*                                                             */
39 /*****************************************************************/
40
41 bool ConvertDate (DATE& date, DateConversion which) {
42  // common workareas
43  int m, d, y;
44  char c;
45  char sm[10];
46  char ansr[11];
47  char ansrb[19];
48
49  /*****************************************************************/
50  /*                                                             */
51  /* Converting To the M D Y trio of numbers                     */
52  /*                                                             */
53  /*****************************************************************/
```

```
54
55   if (which == ToMDY) {
56    // original date already is in M D Y format
57    if (date.type == MonthDayYear)
58     return true;
59
60    // original date is in D Y format
61    if (date.type == DayYear) {
62     y = date.dateDY.year;
63     int i = 0;
64     // find the right month and day
65     while (i<12) {
66      if (date.dateDY.day <= daysYear[i]) {
67       m = i + 1;
68       if (i>0)
69        d = date.dateDY.day - daysYear[i-1];
70       else
71        d = date.dateDY.day;
72       // fill up the answer instance
73       date.type = MonthDayYear;
74       date.dateMDY.month = m;
75       date.dateMDY.day = d;
76       date.dateMDY.year = y;
77       return true;
78      }
79      i++;
80     }
81     return false; // invalid number of days in original date
82    }
83
84    // original date is in 01/01/2000 format
85    else if (date.type == StringFormat) {
86     istrstream is (date.dateString);
87     is >> dec >> m >> c >> d >> c >> y;
88     if (!is)
89      return false; // invalid digits in string date
90     // fill up the answer instance
91     date.type = MonthDayYear;
92     date.dateMDY.month = m;
93     date.dateMDY.day = d;
94     date.dateMDY.year = y;
95     return true;
96    }
97
98    // original date is in January 1, 2000 form
99    else if (date.type == EnglishString) {
100    BugFix2005 (date.dateEnglish, sm, d, y);
101    istrstream is (date.dateEnglish, sizeof(date.dateEnglish));
102 /*  is >> sm >> d >> c >> y;
103    if (!is)
```

```
104      return false; // invalid data in English date string*/
105     bool found = false;
106     int i=0;
107     while (i<12) {
108      if (_stricmp (sm, monthNames[i]) == 0) {
109       m = i + 1;
110       found = true;
111       break;
112      }
113      i++;
114     }
115     if (!found)
116      return false; // invalid month name spelling in string
117     // fill up the answer instance
118     date.type = MonthDayYear;
119     date.dateMDY.month = m;
120     date.dateMDY.day = d;
121     date.dateMDY.year = y;
122     return true;
123    }
124
125    // original date is an invalid form
126    else
127      return false;
128   }
129
130   /*****************************************************************/
131   /*                                                             */
132   /* Converting To the D Y pair of numbers                       */
133   /*                                                             */
134   /*****************************************************************/
135
136   else if (which == ToDY) {
137    // original date already is in D Y format
138    if (date.type == DayYear)
139     return true;
140
141    // original date is in M D Y form
142    if (date.type == MonthDayYear) {
143     d = date.dateMDY.day;
144     m = date.dateMDY.month;
145     y = date.dateMDY.year;
146     if (m != 1) {
147      d += daysYear[m-2];
148     }
149     // fill up the answer instance
150     date.type = DayYear;
151     date.dateDY.day = d;
152     date.dateDY.year = y;
153     return true;
```

```
154    }
155
156    // original date is in January 1, 2000 form
157    else if (date.type == EnglishString) {
158      BugFix2005 (date.dateEnglish, sm, d, y);
159 /*   istrstream is (date.dateEnglish);
160      is >> sm >> d >> c >> y;
161      if (!is)
162        return false; // invalid data in English string*/
163      bool found = false;
164      int i=0;
165      // find the month from the string name
166      while (i<12) {
167        if (_stricmp (sm, monthNames[i]) == 0) {
168          m = i + 1;
169          found = true;
170          break;
171        }
172        i++;
173      }
174      if (!found)
175        return false; // invalid month spelling
176      if (m != 1) {
177        d += daysYear[m-2];
178      }
179      // fill up the answer instance
180      date.type = DayYear;
181      date.dateDY.day = d;
182      date.dateDY.year = y;
183      return true;
184    }
185
186    // original string is in 01/01/2000 format
187    else if (date.type == StringFormat) {
188      istrstream is (date.dateString);
189      is >> dec >> m >> c >> d >> c >> y;
190      if (!is)
191        return false; // invalid digits in the date string
192      if (m != 1) {
193        d += daysYear[m-2];
194      }
195      // fill up the answer instance
196      date.type = DayYear;
197      date.dateDY.day = d;
198      date.dateDY.year = y;
199      return true;
200    }
201
202    // original date has an invalid format
203    else
```

```
204      return false;
205   }
206
207   /*******************************************************************/
208   /*                                                               */
209   /* Converting To string form of mm/dd/yyyy                       */
210   /*                                                               */
211   /*******************************************************************/
212
213   else if (which == ToString) {
214    // is original date already in string format?
215    if (date.type == StringFormat)
216     return true;
217
218    // original date is in M D Y form
219    if (date.type == MonthDayYear) {
220     ostrstream os (ansr, sizeof (ansr));
221     os << setfill('0') << setw (2) << date.dateMDY.month
222        << "/" << setw (2) << date.dateMDY.day
223        << "/" << setw (4) << date.dateMDY.year << ends;
224     // fill up the answer instance
225     date.type = StringFormat;
226     strcpy_s (date.dateString, sizeof(date.dateString), ansr);
227     return true;
228    }
229
230    // original date is in D Y form
231    else if (date.type == DayYear) {
232     d = date.dateDY.day;
233     y = date.dateDY.year;
234     int i = 0;
235     // find the month and day
236     while (i<12) {
237      if (d <= daysYear[i]) {
238       m = i + 1;
239       if (i>0)
240        d = date.dateDY.day - daysYear[i-1];
241       else
242        d = date.dateDY.day;
243       ostrstream os (ansr, sizeof (ansr));
244       os << setfill('0') << setw (2) << m
245          << "/" << setw (2) << d
246          << "/" << setw (4) << y << ends;
247       // fill up the answer instance
248       date.type = StringFormat;
249       strcpy_s (date.dateString, sizeof (date.dateString), ansr);
250       return true;
251      }
252      i++;
253     }
```

```
254      return false; // invalid number of days
255    }
256
257    // original date is in January 1, 2000 form
258    else if (date.type == EnglishString) {
259      BugFix2005 (date.dateEnglish, sm, d, y);
260 /*
261      istrstream is (date.dateEnglish);//date.dateEnglish);
262      is >> sm >> d >> c >> y;
263      if (!is)
264       return false; // invalid data in string date*/
265      bool found = false;
266      int i=0;
267      // find the month from the string month name
268      while (i<12) {
269       if (_stricmp (sm, monthNames[i]) == 0) {
270        m = i + 1;
271        found = true;
272        break;
273       }
274       i++;
275      }
276      if (!found)
277       return false; // invalid month spelling
278      ostrstream os (ansr, sizeof (ansr));
279      os << setfill('0') << setw (2) << m
280         << "/" << setw (2) << d
281         << "/" << setw (4) << y << ends;
282      // fill up the answer instance
283      date.type = StringFormat;
284      strcpy_s (date.dateString, sizeof(date.dateString), ansr);
285      return true;
286    }
287
288    // original date has an invalid format
289    else
290      return false;
291    }
292
293    /******************************************************************/
294    /*                                                                */
295    /* Converting To the string form of January 1, 2000              */
296    /*                                                                */
297    /******************************************************************/
298
299    else if (which == ToEnglish) {
300     // is it already in English format?
301     if (date.type == EnglishString)
302      return true;
303
```

172

```
304   // original date is M D Y form
305   if (date.type == MonthDayYear) {
306    ostrstream os (ansrb, sizeof (ansrb));
307    os << monthNames[date.dateMDY.month-1] << " "
308       << date.dateMDY.day << ", "
309       << date.dateMDY.year << ends;
310    date.type = EnglishString;
311    strcpy_s (date.dateEnglish, sizeof(date.dateEnglish), ansrb);
312    return true;
313   }
314
315   // original date is D Y form
316   else if (date.type == DayYear) {
317    y = date.dateDY.year;
318    int i = 0;
319    while (i<12) {
320     if (date.dateDY.day <= daysYear[i]) {
321      m = i + 1;
322      if (i>0)
323       d = date.dateDY.day - daysYear[i-1];
324      else
325       d = date.dateDY.day;
326      ostrstream os (ansrb, sizeof (ansrb));
327      os << monthNames[m-1] << " "
328         << d << ", " << y << ends;
329      date.type = EnglishString;
330      strcpy_s (date.dateEnglish, sizeof(date.dateEnglish),ansrb);
331      return true;
332     }
333     i++;
334    }
335    return false; // invalid number of days in original date
336   }
337
338   // original date is in string format 01/01/2000
339   else if (date.type == StringFormat) {
340    istrstream is (date.dateString);
341    is >> dec >> m >> c >> d >> c >> y;
342    if (!is)
343     return false; // invalid digits in string date
344    ostrstream os (ansrb, sizeof (ansrb));
345    os << monthNames[m-1] << " "
346       << d << ", " << y << ends;
347    date.type = EnglishString;
348    strcpy_s (date.dateEnglish, sizeof(date.dateEnglish), ansrb);
349    return true;
350   }
351
352   // invalid original format
353   else
```

```
354    return false;
355  }
356
357  // here invalid convert to format
358  else
359    return false;
360 }
361
362 void BugFix2005 (char* source, char* mon, int& d, int& y) {
363   double dd;
364   char c;
365   istrstream is (source);
366   is >> mon >> dd >> c >> y;
367   d = (int) (dd + .5);
368 }
```

Look over the **ConvertDate()** function. It could have been broken down into a number of subfunctions, one for each specific conversion. The logic is fairly simple; the length is due primarily to the fact the each of four possible conversions has three implementations for a total of twelve conversion sequences. However, they are in part very similar actions. Notice that I made extensive use of **istrstream** and **ostrstream** classes to conveniently extract or insert the data.

The overall logic is first split the conversion request into the four categories of conversion. Next, within a specific category, such as convert to MDY format, then split based upon the four possible current date formats. Of course, if the date is already in MDY format, then there is no conversion necessary, just return true. Let's look at two of these conversions.

One of the harder conversions is to get the month, day and year from a date in the form of day of the year and year.

```
// original date is in D Y format
if (date.type == DayYear) {
 y = date.dateDY.year;
 int i = 0;
```

My solution is to loop through the **daysYear** array and find that point where the given days is below the array value. There, the subscript plus one gives the month. The days is dependent on whether it is in January or not.

```
while (i<12) {
  if (date.dateDY.day <= daysYear[i]) {
   m = i + 1;
   if (i>0)
    d = date.dateDY.day - daysYear[i-1];
   else
    d = date.dateDY.day;
```

With the month, day and year now known, those values are then placed back into the date variant.

```
date.type = MonthDayYear;
date.dateMDY.month = m;
date.dateMDY.day = d;
```

```
      date.dateMDY.year = y;
      return true;
    }
    i++;
  }
  return false; // invalid number of days in original date
}
```

Next, let's see how I got the three numerical values from the English form, such as January 1, 2000. After constructing an **istrstream** on the variant string, the string month name is extracted along with the day and year.

```
  // original date is in January 1, 2000 form
  else if (date.type == EnglishString) {
    istrstream is (date.dateEnglish);
    is >> sm >> d >> c >> y;
    if (!is)
      return false; // invalid data in English date string
```

Then I loop through the array of **monthNames** looking for a string insensitive match. When found, the subscript plus one is the month and the assignment can be made.

```
    bool found = false;
    int i=0;
    while (i<12) {
      if (stricmp (sm, monthNames[i]) == 0) {
        m = i + 1;
        found = true;
        break;
      }
      i++;
    }
    if (!found)
      return false; // invalid month name spelling in string
    // fill up the answer instance
    date.type = MonthDayYear;
    date.dateMDY.month = m;
    date.dateMDY.day = d;
    date.dateMDY.year = y;
    return true;
  }
```

Finally, we need to devise a set of testing oracles. I created four test files with various dates in each of the four forms. A tester program can then input each date and attempt to convert that date into each of its three other forms, displaying the results. In this manner, we can more easily verify the results. Here is the tester program.

```
Pgm06b.cpp - Test Driver to Verify ConvertDate() Works

  1 #include <iostream>
  2 #include <iomanip>
  3 #include <fstream>
  4 #include <strstream>
```

175

```
 5 #include <string>
 6
 7 using namespace std;
 8
 9 #include "Date.h"
10
11 /**************************************************************/
12 /*                                                          */
13 /* Pgm06b: Testing driver for ConvertDate() function        */
14 /*                                                          */
15 /**************************************************************/
16
17 int main () {
18
19  /**************************************************************/
20  /*                                                          */
21  /* test forms of original date of M D Y shorts              */
22  /*                                                          */
23  /**************************************************************/
24
25  ifstream infile ("testMDY.txt");
26  if (!infile) {
27   cerr << "Error: cannot open testMDY.txt file\n";
28   return 1;
29  }
30
31  DATE originalMDY, d;
32  originalMDY.type = MonthDayYear;
33  infile >> dec;
34  while (infile >> originalMDY.dateMDY.month
35                >> originalMDY.dateMDY.day
36                >> originalMDY.dateMDY.year) {
37
38   d = originalMDY;
39   cout << "\nOriginal MDY Date from the file: "
40        << setfill('0') << setw(2) << d.dateMDY.month << "/"
41        << setw(2) << d.dateMDY.day << "/" << d.dateMDY.year
42        << setfill (' ') << endl;
43
44   if (ConvertDate (d, ToDY)) {
45    cout << "                                "
46         << d.dateDY.day << "/" << d.dateDY.year << endl;
47   }
48   else cout << "oops!\n";
49
50   d = originalMDY;
51   if (ConvertDate (d, ToString)) {
52    cout << "                                "
53         << d.dateString << endl;
54   }
```

176

```
55   else cout << "oops!\n";
56
57   d = originalMDY;
58   if (ConvertDate (d, ToEnglish)) {
59     cout << "                                        "
60          << d.dateEnglish << endl;
61   }
62   else cout << "oops!\n";
63 }
64
65 /****************************************************************/
66 /*                                                            */
67 /* test forms of original date of D Y shorts                  */
68 /*                                                            */
69 /****************************************************************/
70
71 infile.clear(); // clear eof flag
72
73 infile.close();
74 infile.open ("testDY.txt");
75 if (!infile) {
76   cerr << "Error: cannot open testDY.txt\n";
77   return 1;
78 }
79
80 DATE originalDY;
81 originalDY.type = DayYear;
82 infile >> dec;
83 while (infile >> originalDY.dateDY.day
84               >> originalDY.dateDY.year) {
85
86   d = originalDY;
87   cout << "\nOriginal DY Date from the file:  "
88        << d.dateDY.day << "/" << d.dateDY.year << endl;
89
90   if (ConvertDate (d, ToMDY)) {
91     cout << "                                        "
92          << setfill('0') << setw(2) << d.dateMDY.month << "/"
93          << setw(2) << d.dateMDY.day << "/" << d.dateMDY.year
94          << setfill (' ') << endl;
95   }
96   else cout << "oops!\n";
97
98   d = originalDY;
99   if (ConvertDate (d, ToString)) {
100    cout << "                                    "
101         << d.dateString << endl;
102  }
103  else cout << "oops!\n";
104
```

```
105   d = originalDY;
106   if (ConvertDate (d, ToEnglish)) {
107    cout << "                                         "
108         << d.dateEnglish << endl;
109   }
110   else cout << "oops!\n";
111  }
112
113  /****************************************************************/
114  /*                                                            */
115  /* test forms of original date of strings 01/01/2000         */
116  /*                                                            */
117  /****************************************************************/
118
119  infile.clear(); // clear eof flag
120
121  infile.close();
122  infile.open ("testString.txt", ios::in);
123  if (!infile) {
124   cerr << "Error: cannot open testString.txt\n";
125    return 1;
126  }
127
128  DATE originalString;
129  originalString.type = StringFormat;
130  infile >> dec;
131  while (infile >> originalString.dateString) {
132
133   d = originalString;
134   cout << "\nOriginal String from the file:    "
135        << d.dateString << endl;
136
137   if (ConvertDate (d, ToMDY)) {
138    cout << "                                         "
139         << setfill('0') << setw(2) << d.dateMDY.month << "/"
140         << setw(2) << d.dateMDY.day << "/" << d.dateMDY.year
141         << setfill (' ') << endl;
142   }
143   else cout << "oops!\n";
144
145   d = originalString;
146   if (ConvertDate (d, ToDY)) {
147    cout << "                                         "
148         << d.dateDY.day << "/" << d.dateDY.year << endl;
149   }
150   else cout << "oops!\n";
151
152   d = originalString;
153   if (ConvertDate (d, ToEnglish)) {
154    cout << "                                         "
```

```
155            << d.dateEnglish << endl;
156   }
157   else cout << "oops!\n";
158   }
159
160   /***********************************************************/
161   /*                                                         */
162   /* test forms of original date of English January 1, 2000  */
163   /*                                                         */
164   /***********************************************************/
165
166   infile.clear(); // clear eof flag
167
168   infile.close();
169   infile.open ("testEnglish.txt", ios::in);
170   if (!infile) {
171    cerr << "Error: cannot open testEnglish.txt\n";
172    return 1;
173   }
174
175   DATE originalEnglish;
176   originalEnglish.type = EnglishString;
177   while (infile.getline(originalEnglish.dateEnglish,
178                  sizeof(originalEnglish.dateEnglish))) {
179
180    d = originalEnglish;
181    cout << "\nOriginal English from the file:  "
182         << d.dateEnglish << endl;
183    if (ConvertDate (d, ToMDY)) {
184     cout << "                                    "
185          << setfill('0') << setw(2) << d.dateMDY.month << "/"
186          << setw(2) << d.dateMDY.day << "/" << d.dateMDY.year
187          << setfill (' ') << endl;
188    }
189    else cout << "oops!\n";
190
191    d = originalEnglish;
192    if (ConvertDate (d, ToDY)) {
193     cout << "                                    "
194          << d.dateDY.day << "/" << d.dateDY.year << endl;
195    }
196    else cout << "oops!\n";
197
198    d = originalEnglish;
199    if (ConvertDate (d, ToString)) {
200     cout << "                                    "
201          << d.dateString << endl;
202    }
203    else cout << "oops!\n";
204   }
```

```
205  infile.close();
206
207  return 0;
208 }
```

What dates should be checked? One could put all 365 possibilities in each of the files. However, I picked the extremes and several critical ones on either side of a month change. Here are the test results. After looking these over, are there other dates that should have been tested to help guarantee the function works as expected?

```
Pgm06b Output Results

 1
 2 Original MDY Date from the file: 01/01/2000
 3                                  1/2000
 4                                  01/01/2000
 5                                  January 1, 2000
 6
 7 Original MDY Date from the file: 01/31/2000
 8                                  31/2000
 9                                  01/31/2000
10                                  January 31, 2000
11
12 Original MDY Date from the file: 02/01/2000
13                                  32/2000
14                                  02/01/2000
15                                  February 1, 2000
16
17 Original MDY Date from the file: 02/28/2000
18                                  59/2000
19                                  02/28/2000
20                                  February 28, 2000
21
22 Original MDY Date from the file: 03/01/2000
23                                  60/2000
24                                  03/01/2000
25                                  March 1, 2000
26
27 Original MDY Date from the file: 12/01/2000
28                                  335/2000
29                                  12/01/2000
30                                  December 1, 2000
31
32 Original MDY Date from the file: 12/31/2000
33                                  365/2000
34                                  12/31/2000
35                                  December 31, 2000
36
37 Original DY Date from the file:  1/2000
```

```
38                                              01/01/2000
39                                              01/01/2000
40                    )                         January 1, 2000
41
42 Original DY Date from the file:             31/2000
43                                              01/31/2000
44                                              01/31/2000
45                                              January 31, 2000
46
47 Original DY Date from the file:             32/2000
48                                              02/01/2000
49                                              02/01/2000
50                                              February 1, 2000
51
52 Original DY Date from the file:             59/2000
53                                              02/28/2000
54                                              02/28/2000
55                                              February 28, 2000
56
57 Original DY Date from the file:             60/2000
58                                              03/01/2000
59                                              03/01/2000
60                                              March 1, 2000
61
62 Original DY Date from the file:             335/2000
63                                              12/01/2000
64                                              12/01/2000
65                                              December 1, 2000
66
67 Original DY Date from the file:             365/2000
68                                              12/31/2000
69                                              12/31/2000
70                                              December 31, 2000
71
72 Original String from the file:              01/01/2000
73                                              01/01/2000
74                                              1/2000
75                                              January 1, 2000
76
77 Original String from the file:              01/31/2000
78                                              01/31/2000
79                                              31/2000
80                                              January 31, 2000
81
82 Original String from the file:              02/01/2000
83                                              02/01/2000
84                                              32/2000
85                                              February 1, 2000
86
87 Original String from the file:              02/28/2000
```

```
 88                                      02/28/2000
 89                                      59/2000
 90                                      February 28, 2000
 91
 92 Original String from the file:       03/01/2000
 93                                      03/01/2000
 94                                      60/2000
 95                                      March 1, 2000
 96
 97 Original String from the file:       12/01/2000
 98                                      12/01/2000
 99                                      335/2000
100                                      December 1, 2000
101
102 Original String from the file:       12/31/2000
103                                      12/31/2000
104                                      365/2000
105                                      December 31, 2000
106
107 Original English from the file:      January 1, 2000
108                                      01/01/2000
109                                      1/2000
110                                      01/01/2000
111
112 Original English from the file:      January 31, 2000
113                                      01/31/2000
114                                      31/2000
115                                      01/31/2000
116
117 Original English from the file:      February 1, 2000
118                                      02/01/2000
119                                      32/2000
120                                      02/01/2000
121
122 Original English from the file:      February 28, 2000
123                                      02/28/2000
124                                      59/2000
125                                      02/28/2000
126
127 Original English from the file:      March 1, 2000
128                                      03/01/2000
129                                      60/2000
130                                      03/01/2000
131
132 Original English from the file:      December 1, 2000
133                                      12/01/2000
134                                      335/2000
135                                      12/01/2000
136
137 Original English from the file:      December 31, 2000
```

```
138                                    12/31/2000
139                                    365/2000
140                                    12/31/2000
```

Review Questions

1. Assume the following definitions.
```
struct EMPLOYEE {
    long    idNumber;
    char    firstName[21];
    char    lastName[31];
    char    payType;
    double  rate;
};
EMPLOYEE emp1;
EMPLOYEE emp2;
```

a. Copy emp1's first name into emp2.

b. Copy emp2's pay type into emp1.

c. Copy "Smith" into emp1's last name.

d. Place an 'h' into emp2's pay type.

e. Make emp1's pay rate the same as emp2's pay rate.

f. Write a prototype for an InputEmployee() function whose task is to input a set of employee data from the passed input stream.

g. Write a function to output an employee record to a file.

h. Make emp2 be a copy of emp1.

2. Use the **DATE** variant record defined in this chapter.

a. Create an instance of the date in month, day and year format storing Jan 21, 2002 in it.

b. Create an instance of the date in string format to store February 12, 1995.

c. Create an instance of the date in English format to store 03/04/1998.

d. Create an instance of the date in day-year form to store January 12, 1888.

3. Consider the following tax record. Write the coding sequences to solve the following problems.

```
struct DATE {
   short month;
   short day;
   short year;
};

enum TypeProperty {Home, Automobile, Computer, Appliance,
                   Stocks, Bonds};

enum TypeDepreciation {ThreeYear, FiveYear, TwentyFiveYear};

const double taxRates[3] = {.0789, .055, .000125};

struct ListedProperty {
   DATE               datePlacedIntoService;
   double             originalCost;
   double             depreciationCostThisYear;
   TypeProperty       typeProperty;
   TypeDepreciation   typeDepreciation;
};

ListedProperty item[100];
ListedProperty prop;
```

a. If the ith item is a home, set its depreciation type to 25-year.

b. Copy the ith item into prop.

c. If the ith item is a computer, set its depreciation type to 3-year.

d. If prop's depreciation type is 25-year, then calculate the depreciation cost this year by multiplying the corresponding tax rate by the original cost.

e. Assign type appliance to the ith item's type of property.

f. Write the sequence of statements that would make the 5th element of item be an automobile purchased on March 21, 2000 that originally cost $25,000 and depreciates using the 5 year rule.

g. Write the sequence of statements that would make prop be a computer purchased on 27 June, 1999 that depreciates using the 3-year rule.

Stop! Do These Exercises Before Programming

1. An Acme programmer was given the task to design a phone book structure. He presented the following to the design staff for review. It was not passed by the reviewers because of errors and poor design features.

```
struct NAME {
  char firstName[50];
  char lastName[50];
};
struct ADDRESS {
  char street1[80];
  char street2[80];
  char city[20];
  char state[2];
  char zip[5];
};
struct PHONE {
  short area;    // such as 309
  short prefix;  // such as 699
  short number;  // such as 9999
};
struct PHONEBOOK {
  NAME    name;
  ADDRESS addr;
  PHONE   phone;
  char    type; // 0 = normal, 1 = business listing
};
```

Point out the two actual errors in the design. Then, point out the many poor design features. Write an improved definition for PHONEBOOK.

2. Write the function **InputPhoneBookEntry()** that is passed a reference to a **PHONEBOOK** instance and an **istream** reference. The function returns an **istream** reference. On input, all character strings are surrounded by double quote marks, such as "John." The phone number on input appears as (309) 699-9999. Assume that all fields are in the order of occurrence in the PHONEBOOK and other structures.

3. Write the function **LookUpPhoneNumber()** that is passed an array of **PHONEBOOK** objects, the count of the number in the array and a constant reference to a **PHONE** structure to match. The function returns the subscript of the matching entry or –1 if no match occurs.

4. Write a structure definition for a COIN that has four data members. The first member is the count of the number of this coin type. The second is the number of pennies this coin type is worth. The last two members are string pointers, that is, **char***—one for the English name for one of this coin type and the other for the English plural name of this coin type. For example, if one created an instance of COIN to hold a dime, the count field is 0, the denomination field contains 10. The two **char*** pointers point to the strings "Dime" and "Dimes". Now create and initialize instances to hold a dime, nickel, and a quarter.

5. Write a structure to hold the information for a bank account. The fields include the account number, the person's name (an array of 60 characters), the current balance, the average daily balance, and the date (stored as three integers). Next write an **InputAccount()** function to input a single bank account record. Assume that the name is surrounded by double quote marks.

Programming Problems

Problem Pgm06-1 The Suspect Matcher Program

Your local law enforcement agency has requested that you write them a suspect matcher program. The program should load a file of suspect information into an array of Suspect structures. Then, the program prompts the user to enter the characteristics of the perpetrator of the crime as described by the witness. The program then displays the suspects that match the perpetrator's characteristics. After waiting for an "Ok to Continue" message, the program prompts for another set of perpetrator characteristics and so on until the end of file is signaled.

The Suspect structure should contain the following fields.

Field	Type	Description
First Name	first name of a person	a 12-character string including the null terminator
Last Name	last name of a person	a 25-character string including the null terminator
Height	height in inches	0 is unknown, 44 to 90 is valid
Eye Color	eye color	0 is unknown, 1 is brown, 2 is blue, 3 is hazel
Hair Color	hair color	0 is unknown, 1 is brown, 2 is black, 3 is red, 4 is gray, 5 blonde
Hat Size	an integer	0 is unknown
Shoe Size	an integer	0 is unknown
Teeth Marks	a characteristic	0 is unknown, 1 is normal, 2 is crooked, 3 is gold filled, 4 is partial, 5 is missing
Facial Scar	a yes/no field	0 is unknown, 1 is yes, 2 is no
Hand Scar	a yes/no field	0 is unknown, 1 is yes, 2 is no
Eye Patch	a yes/no field	0 is unknown, 1 is yes, 2 is no
Bald Patch	a yes/no field	0 is unknown, 1 is yes, 2 is no
Leg Limp	a yes/no field	0 is unknown, 1 is yes, 2 is no

Beginning Data Structures in C++

Tattoo	a yes/no field	0 is unknown, 1 is yes, 2 is no

First, make up a test **suspects.txt** data file. The file should contain at least 12 suspect records. One of the records should have all information filled out with none marked as unknown; one should contain all 0's except the first and last name fields. The remainder should contain a variety of values. Assume that all information in the **suspects.txt** file is correct—there can be no invalid data in this data file.

This is in part a major design problem. You are faced with data entry of a lot of fields that are very similar in nature. You should try to write "generic" or reusable functions to minimize the volume of coding. If you do not, you will be writing volumes of lines of code!

You may use enumerated data types for program maintenance purposes or you may use **#define** values or **const int** values. While the program does not have to check for invalid data in the input file, it will have to detect invalid perpetrator entries being entered and re-prompt the user accordingly.

The matching process is done on all fields except the first and last names. No one characteristic is given more weight than another. If the perpetrator's twelve items match a particular suspect record, then the matching percentage is 100%. If none match, it is 0%. After calculating the matching percentage of the perpetrator to all of the suspects, display first the perpetrator's data followed by the suspects that match with a percentage above 0% in percentage order from highest to lowest. Your output should allow the user to see at a glance which characteristics are matching and which are not. There are many ways this can be done; columnar aligned fields is one way.

Problem Pgm06-2 The TIME Variant Record

Acme Corporation wishes to handle times in a similar manner to the **DATE** variant records discussed in this chapter. That is, times in Acme applications can be stored in several ways.
long total seconds since midnight
three shorts: hours, minutes and seconds
hh.hhhhhh in a double
a string "hh:mm:ss" such as "09:03:06" based on a 24-hour time
All times are 24-hour based beginning at midnight. Thus, the range of values go from 00:00:00 through and including 24:00:00.

Construct a TIME structure to store these variants similar to the DATE structure presented in this chapter. Then create a conversion function called **ConvertTime()** that is passed a reference to a TIME structure instance and a conversion type enum instance that indicates which conversion is to be performed. The conversion enum values should be
TimeToTotalSeconds, TimeToHMS, TimeToFraction, and TimeToString

Also provide a **VerifyTime()** function that is passed three short integers representing the hours, minutes, and seconds. It returns **true** if the time is valid and **false** if it is not valid. This function is intended for the user to call upon inputting a time from the user. Once the data has been stored in a TIME structure instance, assume that it is a valid time. In other words, when in the **ConvertTime()** function, always assume that the time stored is valid; you do not need to continually re-verify it.

When the **ConvertTime()** function is written, design a testing program to thoroughly test the function. Provide a testing oracle along with the testing program to ensure the function works perfectly in all cases. That is, the testing program should implement your testing oracle.

Problem Pgm06-3 Bank Account Processing

Acme Consolidated Bank wishes a new bank transaction processing program. Their database consists of up to 10,000 accounts. Each record contains the long account number, the current balance, the cumulative daily balance, a count of the number of days in this monthly period that have elapsed and an indicator that defines whether this is a checking (a 1 digit) or savings account (a 0 digit). At the end of each day's processing, that day's current balance is added to the cumulative daily balance field and the count of the number of days is incremented for every bank account. Then, at the end of a monthly period, the cumulative balance is divided by the count of the number of days to find the average daily balance for each account.

The transactions program begins by loading an array with the bank account database called **bankaccount.txt**. Next, the daily transactions file, **trans.txt**, should be processed. The first character of each transaction line contains a C for check or a D for deposit. This is followed by the bank account number and then a monetary amount to be added or subtracted accordingly. If this transaction is a check, then a third number contains the check number.

The following rules apply to each account processed. If the current balance is below $500 and if this transaction is a check, there is a $0.15 service charge to be debited as well. No check can be subtracted if that would lower the balance below 0. If such would occur, the check is bounced. However, if a check bounces, there is an automatic $25.00 service charge debited immediately which could make the balance fall below zero. If this is a deposit, a service charge of $0.10 is applied.

When the end of the transaction file occurs, then add one day to every bank account's count of the number of days that have elapsed. Also add each account's current balance to its cumulative balance member. Finally, the bank account database, **bankaccount.txt**, is re-written to disk. Two reports are generated: the Transactions Log (**TranLog.txt**) and the Accounts Summary (**AcctSum.txt**). These are shown below.

```
Acme Daily Transaction Log
```

Trans Type	Account Number	Current Balance	--Transaction-- Amount check	Service Charge	New Balance
Check	12345	$1000.00	$ 100.00 (1234)	$ 0.00	$ 900.00
Check	23445	$ 200.00	$ 100.00 (444)	$ 0.15	$ 99.85
Check	45346	$ 100.00	$ 100.00B(333)	$25.00	$ 75.00
Check	56423	$ 10.00	$ 100.00B(1211)	$25.00	$ -15.00
Deposit	23454	$2000.00	$ 500.00	$ 0.10	$2499.90

Beginning Data Structures in C++

```
Acme Daily Account Summary Report

Account    Current  Average Daily Number
Number     Balance     Balance     Days
 12345   $  900.00  $1900.00        2
 23445   $   99.85  $  299.85       2
 45346   $   75.00  $  175.00       2
 56423   $  -15.00  $   -5.00       2
 23454   $  500.99  $4499.90        2
```

Chapter 7—Classes (ADT)—I

Introduction

The definition of an **object** is a thing, an entity. Take a car, for example. In an abstract sense, a car can be thought of as having a set of **properties** (or data members) associated with it. These properties could include the number of doors, its color, its engine size, its miles per gallon, the size of its gas tank in gallons, an isTurnedOn switch and its current speed. A car also has **capabilities** (member functions). A car object might have the capabilities of: start, stop, drive, speed up, slow down, turn left, and turn right. Thus, an abstract data type or class has both **data members** that define its various properties and **member functions** that perform requested actions.

Specifically, a class is a model or blueprint for the compiler to follow in order to create a specific instance of an object. When one creates a specific instance of the car class in memory, one has then a real computer simulation of that object. This action of creating an instance of a class is known as **instantiating an object**. Now with a real instance of a car, we can then request that object to perform various actions, such as starting up and driving.

Encapsulation means to enclose in a capsule or a black box. A class's data members and its functions that operate on the member data are joined into an inseparable whole. The outside world can utilize the object through its provided member functions. How those actions are actually implemented are totally hidden from the outside world. Internally, the object itself knows how to carry out those actions. Hence, we have the idea of a black box. Ideally, one should be able to completely rework the internal algorithms of a class and yet never have to modify the user's original coding. This also means that the user of the object usually cannot access directly the data members of an object.

With the car, the user might invoke a member function called **StartCar()**. How the car is actually started is **never** known to the user nor is it a concern of the user. The benefits of encapsulation are major. Perhaps the biggest benefit is code reusability.

The member data and member functions have a user **access attribute** which controls who can directly access that data or function. The access attributes are public, private, and protected. The **public access** attribute on a data item or function allows the user of the class to use and refer to it. Only public data and public functions can be accessed directly by the user of the object. Most of the time, we do not wish the user to be able to directly access the class member data because then we can never change it in any way without breaking the user's program. Thus, for the member data and few member functions for which we wish to restrict user access, we can use either **protected** or **private access**; these are for our own internal use. Both totally restrict a user of a class from accessing such data and functions.

For example, the method by which we wish to keep track of whether the car is started or not is our own business. The user should not be given public access to that data member. Instead we provide him with a function **IsStarted()** which returns either **true** or **false**. If we do not like the way we are internally storing the "started state," we can change it without affecting the user's code because we adjust **IsStarted()** to continue returning a **bool**. Similarly, we would not give public access to the speed of the car data item. Instead, we provide two functions for the user to access the speed of the car: **GetSpeed()** and **SetSpeed()**.

It is unwise to make data members public because that allows the user to be able to change the object state and it removes a bit of the black box. Also, we cannot then change these public data members without impacting the user. On the other hand, member functions are usually made public so the user can perform actions with the object by calling them. Hence, the following two rules usually apply:
1. Make class data members protected.
2. Make class function members public.
(We will examine the subtle difference between protected and private access shortly.)

Another term associated with object oriented programming (ADTs or classes) is **polymorphism** which means having many forms. Polymorphism allows a single name to be used to handle a set of similar actions. For example in C, we have the three conversion functions: **atoi()**, **atol()**, **atof()** which convert a string to an **int**, **long** or **double**. Polymorphism permits us to create one function name, called say **convert()**, and then based on the actual arguments passed, determine which conversion function is needed:

```
convert (int& x);
convert (long& y);
convert (double& z);
```

This is also called **function overloading**. We use one function name but have several versions of that function to carry out the similar actions. The overloaded functions must differ in either the number of arguments or their data types. The return data type alone is not sufficient to distinguish between overridden functions. The following functions create compile errors as there is no way for the compiler to tell them apart in user coding as shown below.

```
int    convert ();
long   convert ();
double convert ();
...
x = convert (); // error: which convert is requested?
```

Polymorphism means we can have one interface for a generic class of action. The + (add) operation is an example; the parameter to be added could be a **short**, **int**, **long**, **double**, **unsigned long** and so on. The compiler determines which version of the add (+) function to call based upon the data type in the actual add instruction. **Operator overloading** is the name that is used to describe class functions such as operator+. Nearly all of the C++ operators can be overloaded in an ADT.

Another term found in object oriented programming is **inheritance** which is an extremely powerful concept denoting a hierarchical relationship of classes where one class builds upon another.

One could create a base, parent class, **Vehicle**, that has properties such as **isMoving**, **speed**, **weight**, and **color**. It has member functions such as **IncreaseSpeed()**, **Start()**, and **Stop()**. Now with a properly working **Vehicle** class, we can derived a new class, **Car**, based upon the **Vehicle** class. A **Car** would inherit **Vehicle**'s data and functions because a **Car** is a **Vehicle** but with extras. So **Car** would inherit **Vehicle**'s **isMoving**, **speed**, **weight**, and **color** data members along with any member functions, such as **IncreaseSpeed()**, **Start()** and **Stop()**. In turn, the **Car** class might wish to add some additional data members such as **numberOfDoors**, **mpg** and **totalGallons**. Also, the **Car** class can add some new member functions, modify inherited functions and disable inherited functions that are not appropriated in the derived class. Next, one could derive class **Truck** from **Car**, adding perhaps **cargoWeight** to the object.

Thus, one writes the code for moving the **Vehicle** base class object. Then, in the **Car** and **Truck** classes, one does not have to reinvent the wheel—just use the inherited move function. Of course, if the **Vehicle** function does not do what is needed in the **Car** or **Truck** class, it can be completely overridden in the **Car** or **Truck** class, that is, given a new implementation.

The protected and private access qualifiers impact who can access items in derived classes. If items are public or protected in the base class, say **Vehicle**, then the **Car** class itself can directly access them as needed. However, any items that are private in the **Vehicle** class cannot be directly accessed in the **Car** class. Making items private in the base class forces any derived class to have to call the public member functions of the base class to access in any way those private members. This is a severe restriction on a derived class. If you have done a really good job in writing a class, almost certainly someone else will desire to extend your class to their situation, that is, they will desire to derive another class from yours, inheriting your good work. If the items they need to access are private, they will not think too kindly of you! Hence, use protected access instead of private and everyone wins.

In this book or course of study, full coverage of classes or ADTs or object oriented programming (OOP) cannot be done because OOP is really a complete course or book in and of itself. Specifically, this book does not cover operator overloading or inheritance. Those should be covered either in the advanced data structures class or in an OOP class. Here we are after the basics of writing classes.

C++ Class Syntax Summary

A class defines a new kind of data type, called an abstract data type. A class encapsulates data items, called member data, and functions to operate on that data, called member functions or methods. The class is created in two files: a definition file (.h) and an implementation file (.cpp).

The class header file (the definition file) defines the class, providing the blueprint for how to create an instance of it. The class cpp file provides the implementation of the class functions. The user of the class is called the client. The client often creates instances of the class and calls member functions to perform various operations on these instances to solve their problem. Thus in the client's cpp files, the class header file must be included so that the compiler knows what the class is. The client program project has the class implementation cpp file as part of the project so that the actual implementation is available for use. If this class is part of a production system, then the project would not include the cpp implementation files but would rather link to the production .lib file provided by the manufacturer of the class.

Here is the general syntax of the class header file.

```
#includes as needed in this header file
```

```
/*******************************************************/
/*                                                   */
/* name: purpose, etc                                */
/*                                                   */
/*******************************************************/

class name {

  /*******************************************************/
  /*                                                   */
  /* class data                                        */
  /*                                                   */
  /*******************************************************/

  public:    // these can be used freely before each data
  protected: // member as desired - private is the default
  private:   // if nothing is coded

    Ordinary data definitions or instances of other classes

  /*********************************************************/
  /*                                                     */
  /* class function                                      */
  /*                                                     */
  /*********************************************************/

  public:
  protected:
  private:
    function prototypes
};
```

Most data definitions are protected. Note that if you do not code any access qualifier, private is the default; so one usually has to code protected before coding the ordinary data definitions for the member data. Conversely, one codes public before the actual member function prototypes because most functions are public except those internal only helper functions which are often protected. Notice the overall syntax is parallel to that of a structure definition.

For example, consider defining a **Vehicle** class:

```
class Vehicle {
  // here the default access is private unless qualified
};
```

Also notice that I used lots of comment blocks in the header file. The users of your class will have access to this file. Make it very understandable for them. Similarly, organize the class definition. I usually place all data members first followed by all of the functions. Here is how the beginning of the **Vehicle** class might be coded.
File: vehicle.h

```
// no #includes needed at this point

/***************************************************/
/*                                                 */
/* Vehicle: encapsulates the actions of a wheeled vehicle*/
/*                                                 */
/***************************************************/

class Vehicle {

  /***************************************************/
  /*                                                 */
  /* class data                                      */
  /*                                                 */
  /***************************************************/

  protected:
    bool isMoving;
    int  speed;

  /***************************************************/
  /*                                                 */
  /* class function                                  */
  /*                                                 */
  /***************************************************/

  public:
    function prototypes
};
```
Thus, every instance of a Vehicle that the user allocates will have two data items, an **isMoving** bool and a **speed** of motion.

Next, notice the use of capitalization. The guidelines that many of us follow are to capitalize the name of the class and all member functions. We use member names that begin with lowercase letters for the data member names.

The next step is to determine what member functions are needed. When the user or client creates an instance of the class, how do these member data get their initial starting values?

Constructor and Destructor Functions

Generally, a class has one or more **constructor** functions and one and only one **destructor** function. The constructor function is called by the compiler when the object is being created and its job is usually to give initial values to this instance's data members. The destructor function is called by the compiler when the object is being destroyed. Its purpose is usually to remove allocated memory items, if any. Both functions have the same name as the class, except that the destructor has a ~ character before its name. Neither a constructor nor a destructor function can ever return any value of any kind, not even **void**. A destructor function cannot ever be passed any parameters, ever, and thus cannot ever be overloaded with multiple versions. However, the constructor function can have as many parameters as desired and often is overloaded so that the class can be initialized in a variety of ways. Note that "constructor" is often abbreviated as "**ctor**." Likewise, "destructor" is often called "**dtor**."

> **Rule: All classes must have at least one constructor function whose job is to initialize this instance's member data. It can be overloaded.**

> **Rule: Also when the compiler or client deletes the object or instance, all classes must have a destructor function whose job is to perform cleanup activities.** This usually means to delete any dynamically allocated memory this instance has used. It cannot be overloaded.

> **Rule: If a class has either no constructor or destructor function, the compiler provides a default constructor or destructor function for you.** The provided constructor and destructor do nothing but issue a return instruction.

Remember that overloaded functions are functions whose names are the same but differ in the number and types of parameters being passed to the function. Return data types do not count. Here in the **Vehicle** class the constructor function and destructor function prototypes could be

```
Vehicle ();
~Vehicle ();
```

When designing the constructor functions, give some thought to how the user might like to create instances of your class. With a **Vehicle**, the user might want to create a default vehicle or they might like to create a specific vehicle that is moving down the road at 42 miles an hour. Thus, we should provide two different constructor functions in this case. Here is the class definition with the new functions added. Note that since there is no dynamic memory allocation involved in this class, there is no need to code the destructor function. Let the compiler create a default one which does nothing because there is nothing to delete.

File: vehicle.h

```
class Vehicle {

 protected:
  bool isMoving;
  int speed;

 public:
        Vehicle ();
        Vehicle (bool move, int sped);
};
```

The constructor that takes no parameters is called the **default constructor**. A class should always provide a default constructor as a matter of good practice. This default constructor is called when the user wishes to create a default instance. These functions are actually implemented in the **Vehicle.cpp** file; they are only defined in the header file.

The Implementation File

In the class cpp file, the member functions are implemented. However, you cannot just code
```
Vehicle () {
 ...
}
```
Why? The compiler thinks that this is an ordinary C function whose name is **Vehicle**! It does not know that this function actually belongs to the **Vehicle** class. To show that a data member or a member function is part of a class, we use the **class qualifier** which is the name of the class followed by a double colon—**classname::** To notify the compiler that this function belongs to the **Vehicle** class, we code
```
Vehicle::Vehicle () {
 ...
}
```

Rule: When you define the member function body, include the classname::
```
returntype  classname::functionname (parameter list) {
 ....
}
```

Here is how we could implement the two constructor functions of the **Vehicle** class.

File: vehicle.cpp
```
Vehicle::Vehicle () {
 isMoving = false;
 speed = 0;
}

Vehicle::Vehicle (bool move, int sped) {
 isMoving = move;
 speed = sped;
}
```

One must be a bit careful of parameter variable names. Suppose that we had coded it this way. Notice all of the errors that result.
```
Vehicle::Vehicle (bool isMoving, int speed) {
 isMoving = isMoving; // error
 speed = speed;       // error
}
```
What is happening is that the parameter variables hide the class member variables of the same name. Of course you can indicate it properly by using the class qualifier as shown below.
```
Vehicle::Vehicle (bool isMoving, int speed) {
 Vehicle::isMoving = isMoving;
 Vehicle::speed = speed;
}
```

Access Functions

Because we do not want the user directly accessing any of the protected data members, we must provide some means for the user to access this protected data that we are storing for them. Functions that permit the user to retrieve and change protected data members are called **access functions**. Such functions commonly begin with the prefixes Get... and Set... If a class is encapsulating a lot of data, then there are a large number of these access type functions.

Consider our **Vehicle** class. What access functions do we need to provide? What data that we are storing would a user need to retrieve or change? In this example, a user of a **Vehicle** object probably needs to access the **isMoving** state and the vehicle's **speed**. Thus, the definition is expanded to include four more functions.

File: vehicle.h
```
class Vehicle {

  protected:
   bool isMoving;
   int speed;

  public:
        Vehicle  ();
        Vehicle  (bool move, int sped);

    // the access functions
    bool IsMoving ();
    void SetMoving(bool move);

    int  GetSpeed ();
    void SetSpeed (int sped);
};
```

Rule: any member function has complete access to all member data and functions. Outside that class, only public members are available (except with derived classes and friend functions).

These four new functions are implemented as follows.

File: vehicle.cpp
```
bool Vehicle::IsMoving () {
 return isMoving;
}

void Vehicle::SetMoving(bool move) {
 isMoving = move;
}

int Vehicle::GetSpeed () {
 return speed;
}
```

```
void Vehicle::SetSpeed (int sped) {
  speed = sped;
}
```

Finally, have you noticed anything rather unusual about OOP coding? Quite frequently, the implementation of a class consists of a rather large number of extremely short functions, many of which are one-liners!

Instantiating Classes

How are instances of a class instantiated or created in client programs? An instance is defined just like any other data type—just like you would create an instance of a structure.

File: main.cpp
```
#include "vehicle.h"
int main () {
 Vehicle a;              // calls the default constructor
 Vehicle b (true, 42); // calls the overloaded version to create
                        // a vehicle that is moving at 42 mph
 Vehicle c[100];   // array of vehicles
```

The next action is to access public data members and call public member functions. The syntax parallels that of structures. How is a member of a structure accessed? By using the dot (.) operator. The same is true with classes. We use **object_instance.function** or **object_instance.data_item**. The client program can now perform the following actions on its newly created **Vehicle a**.

```
a.SetSpeed (100);     // get the car moving
a.SetMoving (true);   // at 100 miles per hour
cout << a.GetSpeed (); // display a's speed
```

Just as one structure instance can be assigned to another structure instance as long as they both have the same structure tag, objects can be assigned as long as they are instances of the same class. Thus, the client program could make a copy of **Vehicle b** as follows.

```
a = b;
```

When an assignment is done, all data members are copied as is; constructors are not called. The compiler does a byte-by-byte copy of all of **b**'s data into instance **a**, replacing all of the data stored in object **a**. In the case of the **Vehicle** class, this is just what is desired.

However, if a class has dynamically allocated memory, such as an array, then catastrophic trouble arises, because only the pointer to the memory is copied, not the array itself. Be extra careful when the constructor allocates memory and a destructor frees that memory. This problem is discussed later on along with the solution to the problem.

Objects (Instances of a Class) Can Be Passed to Functions and Returned

A function can return an instance of a class. A function can be passed a copy of a class instance. This is exactly the same as structures.

We saw with structures, that returning a structure instance or passing a copy of a structure to a function is inherently inefficient in terms of both speed of execution and of memory usage. The same holds true when passing or returning class instances. With structures, we removed these inefficiencies by passing pointers or references to a structure instance. The same is true when passing instances of classes to functions.

Consider the following client C function. Notice how it is passed a copy of a **Vehicle** object and also returns a copy of a **Vehicle** object.

```
Vehicle fun (Vehicle a) { // Vehicle a is a copy of the
                          // object that was passed
  Vehicle b = a;   // copy Vehicle a
  b.SetSpeed (42); // and change its speed
  return b;        // return a copy of b on the stack
}
```

And the **main()** function might call **fun()** as follows.

```
Vehicle newvehicle = fun (b);
```

Initializing Arrays of Objects

The client program can allocate an array of objects. In the example a few pages above, the **main()** function created an array called **c** as follows.

```
Vehicle c[100];   // array of vehicles
```

In a similar manner, one can create arrays of structures or intrinsic data types, such as **temps** shown below.

```
double temps[100];
```

However, there is a significant difference between these two allocations. What is the content of each element in the array **temps** after it is defined above? No initialization is done and so all elements contain core garbage. Instances of classes behave differently.

> **Rule: When the compiler allocates each instance of a class, it also calls that instance's constructor function to permit that instance to initialize itself!**

Thus, when the compiler allocates the memory for the array **c** above, it then calls the default **Vehicle()** constructor 100 times, once for each instance in the array. Whenever an instance of a class is created, the compiler always gives it a chance to initialize itself.

It is also possible to specify which constructor function is to be called during array initialization. **Vehicle** has a second constructor that allows the user to specify the initial state. The syntax is shown below.

```
Vehicle d[3] = {Vehicle(false,0), Vehicle(true,50),
                Vehicle(true,30)};
```

Within braces {}, one specifically invokes the desired constructor function passing it the desired parameters. However, if one had a large array to initialize, the syntax would be cumbersome to say the least.

Function Overloading

We have seen that functions can be overloaded. That is, the same function name can be used but with different parameters. In the **Vehicle** class, the constructor is overloaded—there are two versions of this function. Very often, constructors are overloaded.

Other member functions can also have several versions of them as well. At this point, the Vehicle class provides a single **SetSpeed()** function. Recall that its prototype was

```
void SetSpeed (int);
```

and its implementation was

```
void Vehicle::SetSpeed (int sped) {
 speed = sped;
}
```

Can you spot anything amiss in this function's implementation? Consider all the possibilities. Suppose the vehicle was currently stationary and the user calls the function to get the vehicle moving at 42 miles per hour. What would the state of the object be? It would have **speed** at 42 but **isMoving** would be **false**! Likewise, if a vehicle that was initialized to **true** and 42 miles per hour had its **SetSpeed()** function invoked passing 0 miles per hour, again the state would be **true** it is moving but at 0 mph! We ought to rework the actual implementation of this function.

```
void Vehicle::SetSpeed (int sped) {
 if (sped) {
  speed = sped;
  isMoving = true;
 }
 else {
  speed = 0;
  isMoving = false;
 }
}
```

However, the client might like to call **SetSpeed()** and be more specific. An alternate form of **SetSpeed()** could be

```
void SetSpeed (bool move, int sped);
```

In this version, the client specifies both values. This is an example of overloading the access functions. Member functions can be overloaded; however, the destructor (**~Vehicle()**) cannot be overloaded. If we insert this version of **SetSpeed()** into our class, we have the following

File: vehicle.h

```
class Vehicle {
 protected:
  bool isMoving;
  int speed;

 public:
```

```
            Vehicle  ();
            Vehicle  (bool move, int sped);

        // the access functions
        bool IsMoving ();
        void SetMoving(bool move);

        int  GetSpeed ();
        void SetSpeed (int sped);
        void SetSpeed (bool move, int sped);
    };
```

However, another mechanism sometimes allows us to reduce the number of overloaded functions.

Default Arguments

C++ gives us the ability to specify default values for arguments to be used when an argument is not be specified by the caller. In the function prototype ONLY, after coding the data type and the name of the argument, code an equal sign (=) followed by the default value the parameter is to have if the caller omits that argument. **Vehicle**'s **SetSpeed()** function is a prime candidate for default arguments. It could be coded as follows

```
        void  SetSpeed (bool move = false, int sped = 0);
```
The implementation does not specify these default values.
```
        void Vehicle::SetSpeed (bool move, int sped) {
         isMoving = move;
         speed = sped;
        }
```

There is a reason that the default values are not coded on the function header. When the compiler is compiling the client program, which has included the class header file, when it encounters the client call to the function, the compiler must know about the default values so that it can create temporary variables with those default values to pass to the function. While compiling the client program, it only sees the class header, thus coding the default values in the class implementation file does not work.

> **Rule: Once one begins coding default values, all arguments after that must have a default value.**

Given the above default values for **SetSpeed()**, the client program can invoke **SetSpeed()** in three ways.
```
    Vehicle a;
    a.SetSpeed ();
    a.SetSpeed (true);
    a.SetSpeed (true, 55);
```
Rule: There is NO way to take a default for the first parameter and supply a second.

This creates a compiler error:
```
    a.SetSpeed (, 55); // errors out
```

201

Beginning Data Structures in C++

In other words, as soon as you force the compiler to begin using the supplied default values, all remaining parameters MUST have and use the default values!
The following would be illegal:

```
void fun (int a = 0, long b, double c = 42.); // error
```

This creates a compile time error because once **a** is given a default, all subsequent arguments must also have a default value. Here argument **b** does not have one. If one really did not have any possible default that one could assign to argument **b**, then rearrange the parameters as follows.

```
void fun (long b, int a = 0, double c = 42.);// correct
```

Thus, we commonly organize the argument list by placing non-default arguments before the defaulted ones.

The default values must be constants or global variables. They cannot be local variables or other parameters.

However, be careful in your use of overloaded functions and the use of default values. When you have overloaded functions that have default values, you can introduce "function ambiguity." Consider the following C style functions.

```
long   fun (long i) {
 return i/42;
}

int    fun (int i){
 return i/10;
}
```

Here is the client coding.

```
long   a = 50;
int    b = 22;
float c = 55.;
short d = 42;

cout << fun (a); // calls the long fun version
cout << fun (b); // calls the int fun version
cout << fun (c); // ambiguous function call error
cout << fun (d); // ambiguous function call error
```

In the last two instructions, the compiler cannot find a version of function **fun()** that takes a **float** or a **short**. However, the **short** could be converted to either a **long** or an **int** equally well. Thus, you are inadvertently asking the compiler to make a choice from two equally valid possibilities. It refuses to do so and generates the compile time error. Similarly, the **float** creates an error.

In this next example, the two versions are inherently ambiguous.

```
// these two are inherently ambiguous
int morefun (int a, int b) {
 return a*b;
}

int morefun (int a, int&b) {
 return a/b;
}
```

Why? Consider these two client lines.

```
int a = 5;
int b = 10;
int c = morefun (a, b); // error which morefun??
```
Both versions of **morefun()** are equally plausible for the compiler to use, hence the ambiguity error message.

Sometimes, the use of default arguments can introduce ambiguity as well. Consider the next situation.
```
int morefun2 (int a) {
  return a*2;
}

int morefun2 (int a, int b = 1) {
  return a/b;
}
```
The client codes the following.
```
int a = 5;
int b = 10;
int c = morefun2 (a);     // error which morefun??
int d = morefun2 (a, b); // is ok - calls second version
```
In the first call to **morefun2()**, either version would be applicable because of the presence of the default value. Thus, this one creates a compile time error. The second call to **morefun2()** is fine as there is only one possible candidate, the second version that takes two parameters.

Constant Member Functions

Consider the Get... type of access functions. A Get... function's purpose is simply to return the value of the indicated property that the class is encapsulating for the user. Under what circumstances could such a Get... type access function ever change the data that it is retrieving for the user? None! Therefore, those member functions that do not in any way alter the data being stored in this class instance **MUST** be made constant member functions.

Only member functions can be constant. They are so indicated by placing the keyword **const** after the end of the parameter list. In the **Vehicle** class, the **GetSpeed()** and **IsMoving()** functions should be constant functions. I have highlighted the new keyword in the header file below.

File: vehicle.h
```
class Vehicle {
 protected:
   bool isMoving;
   int speed;

 public:
        Vehicle  ();
        Vehicle  (bool move, int sped);

   // the access functions
   bool IsMoving () const;
   void SetMoving(bool move);
```

```
    int  GetSpeed () const;
    void SetSpeed (int sped);
};
```

Also, these functions must be specified as constant in the implementation file. I have highlighted this addition below.

```
bool Vehicle::IsMoving () const {
 return isMoving;
}

int Vehicle::GetSpeed () const {
 return speed;
}
```

Why do they have to be made constant functions? Users sometimes create constant objects whose properties are supposed to be held constant under all situations. In the case of a **Vehicle** class, suppose the user has created the "pace car" at a race track. Its properties are to be constant, since it is setting the initial launching of the race. The user might code

```
const Vehicle paceCar (true, 80);
cout << paceCar.GetSpeed();
```

If the user now calls **GetSpeed()** on this object, the compiler will generate an error unless this **GetSpeed()** member function has been made constant.

If one does not specify **const** in the prototype (and function header), it does not matter whether or not you actually change any member data in the actual implementation file. When compiling the client program, the compiler sees only the **Vehicle** definition file with the prototype; it cannot look ahead into another cpp file to see if you are really not changing anything; it must use the class function prototype.

Another way a constant object occurs is when the client program passes a constant reference (or pointer) to an object to a function that should not be altering that passed object. For example, suppose that the client race track program had an array of **Vehicle** objects and wanted to call a function, **CalcAverageSpeed()**. It might do so as follows.

```
Vehicle array[100];
int numCars; // current array bounds
double avgSpeed = CalcAverageSpeed (array, numCars);
```

The function is coded as follows.

```
double CalcAverageSpeed  (const Vehicle* array,
                              int numCars) {
 double sum = 0;
 if (!numCars) return 0;
 for (int j=0; j<numCars; j++) {
  sum += array[j].GetSpeed();
 }
 return sum / numCars;
}
```

Here the call to **GetSpeed()** is made on a series of constant objects. If **GetSpeed()** was not a constant function, the compiler would issue an error message about this.

Handling I/O Operations—a First Look

The final question is how can an object be input or output to/from a text file? The insertion and extraction operators are certainly convenient with intrinsic data types, such as longs. However, those operators are discussed in the next chapter. There is an alternate approach that is often used in place of and/or in addition to the insertion/extraction operators. Such member functions are commonly called **Input()** and **Output()**.

An **Input()** member function has access to all of the member data. Thus, if it is passed the **istream&** from which to input the data, it can do so, filling up all the member data. Likewise, for the **Output()** function. If it is passed the **ostream&** on which to display, it can display the data members as desired. However, would any output type function ever alter the member data being displayed? No. Thus, the **Output()** function must be made constant.

For our Vehicle class, here are the two new prototypes in the header file.

File: vehicle.h

```
#include <iostream>
using namespace std;
class Vehicle {

 protected:
  bool isMoving;
  int speed;

 public:
        Vehicle  ();
        Vehicle  (bool move, int sped);

   // the access functions
   bool IsMoving () const;
   void SetMoving(bool move);

   int  GetSpeed () const;
   void SetSpeed (int sped);

   istream& Input (istream& is);
   ostream& Output (ostream& os) const;
};
```

The implementation of **Input()** has the additional problem of how to input the **bool isMoving**. The best way is not to input it at all, but input only the **speed**. Then set **isMoving** based upon whether or not the vehicle is moving.

```
istream& Vehicle::Input (istream& is) {
 is >> speed;
 if (!is) {
  cerr << "Error on inputting vehicle's speed\n";
  speed = 0;
```

```
  isMoving = false;
  return is;
 }
 isMoving = speed ? true : false;
 return is;
}
```

The **Output()** function can be written to match the form of display that the client desires. Let's say that the user wishes to see output similar to the following.

The vehicle is not moving.

The vehicle is moving at 42 miles per hour.

Then the **Output()** function would be as shown below.

```
ostream& Vehicle::Output (ostream& os) const {
 if (isMoving)
   os << "The vehicle is moving at " << speed
      << " miles per hour.\n";
 else
   os << "The vehicle is not moving.\n";
 return os;
}
```

A Practical Example—The Class Rectangle

Let's encapsulate a rectangle. First, we must decide upon what properties we should store. I have chosen to save the length and the width as **double**s. Additionally, I store the name of the rectangle as a character string.

Next, examine how a user might wish to construct an instance of a **Rectangle** class. Certainly, there must be a default constructor that takes no parameters. But also we should provide one that is passed the length and the width the user desires. Let's default the name to just "Rectangle" should the user not be interested in naming the instances.

Now examine what user access functions should be provided to allow the client to retrieve and alter the length and width we are storing for them. I have chosen to create Get/Set functions for both the length and the width. And I also chose to allow the user to change them both by providing **GetDimensions()** and **SetDimensions()** functions.

Some means must be provided for I/O operations. Thus, I have an **Input()** and **Output()** pair of functions. Since a name could contain blanks, the input and output will surround the name string with double quotes. However, the client also wishes to have a fancier form of output that looks like this: Rectangle [10.5, 22.5]. This function I called **OutputFormatted()**.

Now many of these functions must guard against various errors, such as entering a negative length or too long of a name string. Thus, I have added two helper functions that are protected. One validates a numerical value; it is passed a constant string identifying which value is being verified: length or width. So if an error occurs, it can display which is being called. The other validates the name. We must guard against the user entering a null pointer, that is a 0, for the parameter or against too long a string.

Beginning Data Structures in C++

Finally, what operations would you expect a user to wish to do with a rectangle? Most likely they wish to find the area or the perimeter of the rectangle. Hence, I added **GetArea()** and **GetPerimeter()**.

The next step is to code the **Rectangle** definition file. When all of the function prototypes have been coded, look them over and decide which functions must be made constant member functions and add that **const** keyword to them. Here is the **Rectangle** definition file from Pgm07a.

```
Rectangle Definition .h File

 1 #pragma once
 2 #include <iostream>
 3 using namespace std;
 4
 5 /******************************************************/
 6 /*                                                    */
 7 /* Rectangle: encapsulates a rectangle                */
 8 /*                                                    */
 9 /******************************************************/
10
11 const int MAXNAMELEN = 21;
12
13 class Rectangle {
14
15   /******************************************************/
16   /*                                                    */
17   /* class data                                         */
18   /*                                                    */
19   /******************************************************/
20
21 protected:
22   double length;
23   double width;
24   char   name[MAXNAMELEN];
25
26   /******************************************************/
27   /*                                                    */
28   /* class function                                     */
29   /*                                                    */
30   /******************************************************/
31
32 public:
33   // constructors
34   Rectangle ();
35   Rectangle (double len, double wid,
36             const char* nam = "Rectangle");
37
38   ~Rectangle ();
39
40   // Access Functions
```

```
41  const char* GetName () const;
42  void    SetName (const char* nam);
43
44  double GetLength () const;
45  void    SetLength (double len);
46
47  double GetWidth () const;
48  void    SetWidth (double wid);
49
50  void    GetDimensions (double& len, double& wid) const;
51  void    SetDimensions (double len, double wid);
52
53  // Operational Functions
54  double GetArea () const;
55  double GetPerimeter () const;
56
57  // I/O Functions
58  istream& Input (istream& is);
59  ostream& OutputFormatted (ostream& os) const;
60  ostream& Output (ostream& os) const;
61
62 protected:
63  // helper functions
64  void VerifyNumber (double& number, double val, const char* who);
65  void VerifyName (const char* newname);
66 };
67
```

Next, start the cpp file by copying all of the prototypes into the **Rectangle.cpp** file and removing the semicolons and inserting { } braces. Do not forget to add the **Rectangle::** qualifier to all functions. In this implementation, I chose to log an error message to **cerr** whenever I encountered a negative length or width. And I inserted a value of zero in its place in the corresponding data member. All of the coding is very simple and quite straightforward. Here is the **Rectangle.cpp** file. Notice the generic nature of the **VerifyNumber** function. Also, pay attention to the error handling in **VerifyName**.

```
Rectangle Implementation File .cpp

 1 #include <iostream>
 2 #include <iomanip>
 3 using namespace std;
 4
 5 #include "Rectangle.h"
 6
 7 /****************************************************/
 8 /*                                                  */
 9 /* Rectangle: default constructor - sets all to 0   */
10 /*                                                  */
11 /****************************************************/
12
```

```
13 Rectangle::Rectangle () {
14  length = width = 0;
15  name[0] = 0;
16 }
17
18 /***********************************************************/
19 /*                                                         */
20 /* VerifyNumber: helper function to verify val is not      */
21 /*               negative - displays error msg if so       */
22 /*                                                         */
23 /***********************************************************/
24
25 void Rectangle::VerifyNumber (double& number, double val,
26                                 const char* who) {
27  if (val >= 0)
28   number = val;
29  else {
30   number = 0;
31   cerr << "Error: a rectangle's " << who
32       << " cannot be less than 0\n";
33  }
34 }
35
36 /***********************************************************/
37 /*                                                         */
38 /* VerifyName:   helper function to verify new name string*/
39 /*               is not 0 or too long - fills up name      */
40 /*                                                         */
41 /***********************************************************/
42
43 void Rectangle::VerifyName (const char* newname) {
44  if (!newname) {
45   cerr << "Error: a null pointer was passed for the name"
46       << " instead of a character string\n";
47   name[0]  = 0;
48   return;
49  }
50  if (strlen (newname) > MAXNAMELEN - 1) {
51   cerr << "Error: name exceeds " << MAXNAMELEN -1
52       << " characters - truncation occurred\n";
53   strncpy_s (name, sizeof(name), newname, MAXNAMELEN -1);
54   name[MAXNAMELEN-1] = 0;
55   return;
56  }
57  strcpy_s (name, sizeof (name), newname);
58 }
59
60 /***********************************************************/
61 /*                                                         */
62 /* Rectangle: makes a rectangle from user's data           */
```

```
63 /*              displays error if either is < 0        */
64 /*                                                     */
65 /*****************************************************/
66
67 Rectangle::Rectangle (double len, double wid,
68                       const char* nam) {
69  VerifyNumber (length, len, "length");
70  VerifyNumber (width, wid, "width");
71  VerifyName (nam);
72 }
73
74 /*****************************************************/
75 /*                                                     */
76 /* ~Rectangle: destructor - does nothing              */
77 /*                                                     */
78 /*****************************************************/
79
80 Rectangle::~Rectangle () { }
81
82 /*****************************************************/
83 /*                                                     */
84 /* GetName: returns the name property                 */
85 /*                                                     */
86 /*****************************************************/
87
88 const char* Rectangle::GetName () const {
89  return name;
90 }
91
92 /*****************************************************/
93 /*                                                     */
94 /* SetName: sets our name property to a new string    */
95 /*                                                     */
96 /*****************************************************/
97
98 void Rectangle::SetName (const char* nam) {
99  VerifyName (nam);
100 }
101
102 /*****************************************************/
103 /*                                                     */
104 /* GetLength: returns the length of a rectangle       */
105 /*                                                     */
106 /*****************************************************/
107
108 double Rectangle::GetLength () const {
109  return length;
110 }
111
112 /*****************************************************/
```

```
113 /*                                                      */
114 /* SetLength: sets the length, displays error if < 0    */
115 /*                                                      */
116 /*****************************************************/
117
118 void    Rectangle::SetLength (double len) {
119  VerifyNumber (length, len, "length");
120 }
121
122 /*****************************************************/
123 /*                                                      */
124 /* GetWidth: returns the width of the rectangle         */
125 /*                                                      */
126 /*****************************************************/
127
128 double Rectangle::GetWidth () const {
129  return width;
130 }
131
132 /*****************************************************/
133 /*                                                      */
134 /* SetWidth: sets the width - displays error if < 0     */
135 /*                                                      */
136 /*****************************************************/
137
138 void    Rectangle::SetWidth (double wid) {
139  VerifyNumber (width, wid, "width");
140 }
141
142 /*****************************************************/
143 /*                                                      */
144 /* GetDimensions: updates user's fields with length/width*/
145 /*                                                      */
146 /*****************************************************/
147
148 void Rectangle::GetDimensions (double& len, double& wid) const {
149  len = length;
150  wid = width;
151 }
152
153 /*****************************************************/
154 /*                                                      */
155 /* SetDimensions: sets the length and width - errors are */
156 /*              displayed if either is < 0              */
157 /*                                                      */
158 /*****************************************************/
159
160 void    Rectangle::SetDimensions (double len, double wid) {
161  VerifyNumber (length, len, "length");
162  VerifyNumber (width, wid, "width");
```

```
163 }
164
165 /*****************************************************************/
166 /*                                                             */
167 /* GetArea: returns the area of a rectangle                    */
168 /*                                                             */
169 /*****************************************************************/
170
171 double Rectangle::GetArea () const {
172  return length * width;
173 }
174
175 /*****************************************************************/
176 /*                                                             */
177 /* GetPerimeter: returns the perimeter of a rectangle          */
178 /*                                                             */
179 /*****************************************************************/
180
181 double Rectangle::GetPerimeter () const {
182  return length * 2 + width * 2;
183 }
184
185 /*****************************************************************/
186 /*                                                             */
187 /* Input: "name" len wid is the format expected                */
188 /*                                                             */
189 /*****************************************************************/
190
191 istream& Rectangle::Input (istream& is) {
192  char nam[MAXNAMELEN];
193  char c;
194  double val1, val2;
195  is >> c;
196  if (!is) return is;
197  is.get (nam, sizeof (nam), '\"');
198  is >> c >> val1 >> val2;
199  if (!is) return is;
200
201  VerifyName (nam);
202  VerifyNumber (length, val1, "length");
203  VerifyNumber (width, val2, "width");
204
205  return is;
206 }
207
208 /*****************************************************************/
209 /*                                                             */
210 /* OutputFormatted: displays as name [length, width]           */
211 /*                                                             */
212 /*****************************************************************/
```

```
213
214 ostream& Rectangle::OutputFormatted (ostream& os) const {
215   os.setf (ios::fixed, ios::floatfield);
216   os << left << setw (MAXNAMELEN + 2) << name << right << " ["
217       << setprecision (2) << length << ", " << width << "]";
218   return os;
219 }
220
221 /***********************************************************/
222 /*                                                         */
223 /* Output: displays the name surrounded with " " and      */
224 /*         the length and width with 2 decimals            */
225 /*         separated by a blank                            */
226 /*                                                         */
227 /***********************************************************/
228
229 ostream& Rectangle::Output (ostream& os) const {
230   os.setf (ios::fixed, ios::floatfield);
231   os << '\"' << name << "\" " << setprecision (2)
232       << length << " " << width;
233   return os;
234 }
```

The last step is to design a testing program to **thoroughly** test the class before placing it into production by giving it to the user. Once again, a testing oracle is highly desirable. Ideally, one should test out all circumstances of the class usage. Specifically, this means at least testing every one of the member functions. In the case of those functions which can report an error or run into execution errors, such as inputting bad data from the input stream, several tests are needed. Please carefully examine the output from the tester program and the tester program (**Pgm07a.cpp**) and see if I did indeed test all of the possibilities. (In actual fact, I did not; I failed to thoroughly test this one. However, that is the topic of a Stop Exercise below.)

```
Pgm07a - Tester Program for Rectangle Class

 1 #include <iostream>
 2 #include <iomanip>
 3 #include <fstream>
 4 #include <strstream>
 5
 6 #include "Rectangle.h"
 7
 8 using namespace std;
 9
10 int main () {
11   Rectangle a;                    // test default ctor
12   cout << "Default ctor (0,0): " << a.GetLength() << " "
13       << a.GetWidth() << endl;
14
15   Rectangle b (42.42, 84.84); // test overloaded ctor
```

```
16  cout << "b's overloaded ctor (should be 42.42, 84.84): "
17       << b.GetLength() << " " << b.GetWidth() << endl << endl;
18
19  double l, w;                   // test GetDimensions
20  b.GetDimensions (l, w);
21  cout << "GetDimemsions: should be the same: "
22       << l << " " << w << endl;
23
24  Rectangle c;                   // test assignment
25  c = b;
26  cout << "Rectangle c should be as b: " << c.GetLength()
27       << " " << c.GetWidth() << endl;
28
29  Rectangle d (1, 2);            // test integers
30  cout << "Rectangle d should be 1,2: " << d.GetLength()
31       << " " << d.GetWidth() << endl << endl;
32
33  Rectangle e (-1., 4);          // test error length
34  Rectangle f (1, -4.4);         // test error width
35  Rectangle g (-2, -4);          // test error both
36  a.SetLength (-1.1);            // test error length
37  a.SetWidth (-2);               // test error width
38  a.SetDimensions (-1, -2);      // test error both
39  cout << endl;
40
41  a.SetLength (4);               // test SetLength and SetWidth
42  a.SetWidth (8);
43  cout << "SetLen and width check (should be 4,8): "
44       << a.GetLength() << " " << a.GetWidth() << endl;
45
46  a.SetDimensions (9, 10);       // test SetDimensions
47  cout << "SetLen and width check (should be 9,10): "
48       << a.GetLength() << " " << a.GetWidth() << endl << endl;
49
50  // test GetArea and GetPerimeter
51  cout << "Check area (should be 90): " << a.GetArea()
52       << endl;
53  cout << "Check perimeter (should be 38): "
54       << a.GetPerimeter() << endl << endl;
55
56  // test Input function for good and bad data
57  char string[] = "\"Test Input 1\" 10.10 20.20   ";
58  istrstream is (string);
59  a.Input (is);
60  if (!is) {
61   cerr << "Oops: input should be good\n"
62        << a.GetName () << " " << a.GetLength() << " "
63        << a.GetWidth() << endl;
64  }
65  cout << "Input test (should be Test Input 1 10.1 20.2):\n "
```

```
66         << a.GetName () << " " << a.GetLength() << " "
67         << a.GetWidth() << endl;
68
69    // test bad input
70    char stringbad[] = "\"Test Input 2\" 30 A";
71    istrstream isbad (stringbad);
72    if (a.Input (isbad).fail()) {
73     cout << "bad data was correctly found\n";
74    }
75    else {
76     cerr << "Oops - bad data not detected in Input function\n"
77           << a.GetName () << " " << a.GetLength() << " "
78           << a.GetWidth() << endl;
79    }
80
81    // testing Output function
82    cout << "\nTest Output: ";
83    b.Output (cout) << endl;
84
85    // testing OutputFormatted function
86    cout << "Test OutputFormatted: ";
87    b.OutputFormatted (cout) << endl << endl;
88
89    Rectangle m (42,42, "Test name");
90    m.Output (cout) << endl;
91
92    Rectangle n (42, 42, "too long a nameeeeeeeeeeeeeeeeee");
93    n.Output (cout) << endl;
94
95    cout << "n's truncated name is |" << n.GetName () << "|" <<endl;
96    n.SetName (0);
97    cout << "Should have seen null pointer for name error\n";
98    n.SetName ("A new Name");
99    cout << "n's new name is |" << n.GetName () << "|" << endl;
100
101
102   // test file operations
103   cout << "\nTest reading a file\n";
104   ifstream infile ("RectangleTest.txt");
105   while (a.Input (infile)) {
106    a.OutputFormatted (cout) << endl;
107   }
108   infile.close ();
109   cout << "tests done\n";
110
111   return 0;
112
```

Output of the Tester Program

215

```
 1 Default ctor (0,0): 0 0
 2 b's overloaded ctor (should be 42.42, 84.84): 42.42 84.84
 3
 4 GetDimemsions: should be the same: 42.42 84.84
 5 Rectangle c should be as b: 42.42 84.84
 6 Rectangle d should be 1,2: 1 2
 7
 8 Error: a rectangle's length cannot be less than 0
 9 Error: a rectangle's width cannot be less than 0
10 Error: a rectangle's length cannot be less than 0
11 Error: a rectangle's width cannot be less than 0
12 Error: a rectangle's length cannot be less than 0
13 Error: a rectangle's width cannot be less than 0
14 Error: a rectangle's length cannot be less than 0
15 Error: a rectangle's width cannot be less than 0
16
17 SetLen and width check (should be 4,8): 4 8
18 SetLen and width check (should be 9,10): 9 10
19
20 Check area (should be 90): 90
21 Check perimeter (should be 38): 38
22
23 Input test (should be Test Input 1 10.1 20.2):
24  Test Input 1 10.1 20.2
25 bad data was correctly found
26
27 Test Output: "Rectangle" 42.42 84.84
28 Test OutputFormatted: Rectangle                 [42.42, 84.84]
29
30 "Test name" 42.00 42.00
31 Error: name exceeds 20 characters - truncation occurred
32 "too long a nameeeeee" 42.00 42.00
33 n's truncated name is |too long a nameeeeee|
34 Error: a null pointer was passed for the name instead of a charac
35 Should have seen null pointer for name error
36 n's new name is |A new Name|
37
38 Test reading a file
39 Rectangle 1             [1.00, 2.00]
40 Rectangle 2             [3.00, 4.00]
41 Rectangle 3             [5.00, 6.00]
42 Rectangle 4             [0.50, 0.50]
43 Rectangle 5             [123.00, 45.00]
44 Rectangle 6             [678.00, 99.00]
45 tests done
```

Practical Example 2—The Interval Timer Class (Pgm07b)

Suppose that we wished to time how long some action took to execute. The C Standard Library has built-in support for timing. The function **clock()** returns the number of clock cycles that have taken place since the computer was started. The returned data type is **clock_t** which is a **typedef** name for a **long**. The library also provides a constant, **CLOCKS_PER_SEC**, which, if divided into a **clock_t** value, converts it into seconds. The header files are **ctime** or **time.h**.

To construct an interval timer class, what data items are required? It should store the start and ending **clock_t** times. The class constructor can initialize these to 0 or perhaps the current time. The operational functions are **StartTiming()**, **EndTiming()**, and **GetInterval()**. The idea is to invoke **StartTiming()** to initialize the start time member. Then, do the processing we wish to time. When it is finished, invoke **EndTiming()** to set the end time. And call **GetInterval()** to obtain the number of seconds the process required. With these functions, one only needs to allocate a single instance of the **Timer** class in order to be able to time many events.

Here are the **Timer** class definition and implementation files. It is a very simple class but highly useful for timing things.

```
Timer Class Definition - an Interval Timer

 1 #pragma once
 2 #include <ctime>
 3 using namespace std;
 5
 6 /*****************************************************/
 7 /*                                                   */
 8 /* Timer: encapsulates an elapsed time in clock cycles */
 9 /*                                                   */
10 /*****************************************************/
11
12 class Timer {
13
14 protected:
15   clock_t startTime;    // the starting time of the interval
16   clock_t endTime;      // the ending time of the interval
17
18 public:
19   Timer();              // initializes the two times to 0
20
21   // reset the starting time value to begin monitoring
22   void StartTiming ();
23
24   // resets the ending time value at the end of the interval
25   void EndTiming ();
26
27   // returns the measured interval in seconds
```

```
28  double GetInterval () const;
29
30 };
31
32 #endif
```

Timer Class Implementation - an Interval Timer

```
 1 #include "Timer.h"
 2
 3 /****************************************************************/
 4 /*                                                            */
 5 /* Timer: ctor that sets the two times to 0 clock cycles    */
 6 /*                                                            */
 7 /****************************************************************/
 8
 9 Timer::Timer() {
10   startTime = endTime = 0;
11 }
12
13 /****************************************************************/
14 /*                                                            */
15 /* StartTiming: sets startTime to the current time at the    */
16 /*              beginning of the interval to monitor         */
17 /*                                                            */
18 /****************************************************************/
19
20 void Timer::StartTiming () {
21   startTime = clock ();
22 }
23
24 /****************************************************************/
25 /*                                                            */
26 /* EndTiming: sets endTime to the current time at the end    */
27 /*            of the interval to be monitored                */
28 /*                                                            */
29 /****************************************************************/
30
31 void Timer::EndTiming () {
32   endTime = clock ();
33 }
34
35 /****************************************************************/
36 /*                                                            */
37 /* GetInterval: returns the interval just timed in seconds   */
38 /*                                                            */
39 /****************************************************************/
40
41 double Timer::GetInterval () const {
```

```
42  return ((double) (endTime - startTime)) / CLOCKS_PER_SEC;
43 }
```

Next, we need something to time. I have chosen to find out just how much faster it is to use a pointer to access the elements in an array of objects than using the traditional subscript approach. The objects are rectangles. I have simply copied the **Rectangle** class definition and implementation files from **Pgm07a** into this new project folder, **Pgm07b**. No changes are required in the **Rectangle** class.

The code to time consists of setting the dimensions of 1000 **Rectangle** objects and outputting the resultant area. The first version uses subscripts to access each element in the **Rectangle** array. The second version uses a pointer to point to each successive element; to move to the next element in the array, I use **ptrThis++**.

I create a single instance of the **Timer** class and invoke the **StartTiming()** method. After the subscript processing loop is finished, I call the **EndTiming()** method to set the ending time and invoke **GetInterval()** to acquire the total elapsed time for the loop in seconds. Then, the process is repeated for the pointer version. When that loop has finished and its interval acquired, the program then prints a short report of the results.

Here is **Pgm07b** and a sample output run that is abbreviated showing the last few lines. Are the results what you expected? The actual values will depend on your particular computer and its speed.

```
Pgm07b - Timing Subscript Versus Pointer Array Access

 1 #include <iostream>
 2 #include <iomanip>
 3 using namespace std;
 4
 5 #include "Timer.h"
 6 #include "Rectangle.h"
 7
 8 /*****************************************************************/
 9 /*                                                               */
10 /* Pgm07b: measure the difference in execution speed            */
11 /*         between using subscript array accesses and           */
12 /*         using pointer array accessing methods                */
13 /*                                                               */
14 /*****************************************************************/
15
16 const int MAXRECTS = 1000; // maximum number of rectangles
17
18 int main () {
19   Rectangle array[MAXRECTS];
20   int i;
21
22   Timer timer;              // the single Timer object
23   timer.StartTiming ();     // begin timing the subscript version
24
```

219

```
25  for (i=0; i<MAXRECTS; i++) {
26   array[i].SetDimensions (i, i);
27   cout << array[i].GetArea() << endl;
28  }
29
30  timer.EndTiming ();        // mark the end of the subscript timing
31  double subscripts = timer.GetInterval (); // get its duration
32
33  timer.StartTiming ();     // begin timing the pointer version
34
35  i = 0;
36  Rectangle* ptrThis = array;
37  Rectangle* ptrEnd = array + MAXRECTS;
38  while (ptrThis < ptrEnd) {
39   ptrThis->SetDimensions (i, i);
40   cout << ptrThis->GetArea () << endl;
41   ptrThis++;
42   i++;
43  }
44
45  timer.EndTiming ();        // mark the end of the pointer timing
46  double pointers = timer.GetInterval (); // get its duration
47
48  // display a simple report of the results
49  cout << endl << "Release Build Run Timings\n";
50  cout << "Subscripts version total time: " << subscripts
51       << " seconds\n";
52  cout << "Pointers version total time:   " << pointers
53       << " seconds\n";
54  cout << "Elapsed time difference:       " << subscripts-pointers
55       << " seconds\n";
56
57  return 0;
58 }
```

```
Results of Timing Subscript Versus Pointer Array Access

1 ...
2 996004
3 998001
4
5 Release Build Run Timings
6 Subscripts version total time: 3.424 seconds
7 Pointers version total time:   0.902 seconds
8 Elapsed time difference:       2.522 seconds
```

The above results were using a 1.6GHz cpu and version 2002. On a 3GHz machine in a Release Build using 2005, the timings were:

```
6 Subscripts version total time: 0.468 seconds
7 Pointers version total time:  0.250 seconds
8 Elapsed time difference:      0.218 seconds
```

Review Questions

1. Reflecting upon member data and member functions, how do member data obviate the need for global variables or the passing a large amounts of data to a series of functions?

2. Why should most member data have the protected (or private) access qualifier?

3. How does encapsulation impact class design? What is its benefit to the programmer of a class and to the client of the class?

4. What is meant by polymorphism? Of what use is it in class function design?

5. What are the parallels in coding syntax between **struct CostRec** and **class CostRec**?

6. What is a constructor function? What is its purpose? How many constructors can a class have?

7. What is a destructor? What is its purpose? How many destructors can a class have? Why?

8. Why is the class qualifier, such as Vehicle::, needed in the implementation file?

9. What is the purpose of access type member functions? Give an example.

10. Ignoring the initialization aspect, compare how a client program can create instances of a structure called **CostRec** and a class called **InventoryRec**.

11. Why is the use of default arguments useful? What problems does the use of default arguments pose when such functions are overloaded?

12. What is the difference between the two uses of the const key word shown below?

```
class Point {
protected:
 int x;
 int y;
public:
 Point ();
 long AvgPoints (const Point& p);
 long SumPoints () const;
};
```

Stop! Do These Exercises Before Programming

1. Look over the **Pgm07a** testing program. What major feature covered in this chapter concerning the use of instances of objects did I fail to test in any way whatsoever? What about constant objects? Sketch out some additional tests and perhaps a client function call that would guarantee that **Rectangle** is properly supporting constant objects.

2. A programmer decided to encapsulate a geometric point object by writing a class called **Point**. He began with the following design. There are several design flaws with what has been actually coded thus far. Point out these flaws and show a more optimum way to code the definition.

Point.h
```
Class Point {
  int x;
  int y;
 public:
  Point ();
  Point (int x, int y);

  Point GetPoint ();
  void  SetPoint (int x, int y);
  void  SetPoint (Point& p);
 }
```

3. The programmer decided to add the ability to I/O a point. He added the following two member function prototypes. What is wrong with them and how should they be corrected?
```
class Point {
 ...
  void InputPoint (istream infile, int x, int y);
  void OutputPoint (ostream outfile, Point& p);
```

4. The programmer decided to use overloaded functions with default arguments. He added the following member prototypes. What is inherently non-optimum with these new functions as coded? Could they be repaired to be productive?

```
class Point {
...
  void SetPoint (int xx, int yy);
  void SetPoint (int xx, int yy = 0);
  void SetPoint (int xx = 0, int yy = 0);
```

5. The programmer created two tester functions to be called from the **main()** function. What is non-optimum about the coding? How can it be repaired?

```
void SumPoints (Point& p, long& totalX, long& totalY,
                long& count) {
  totalX += p.x;
  totalY += p.y;
  count++;
}

Point MakePoint (int x, int y) {
  Point p (x+42, y+42);
  return p;
}
```

6. The programmer gave up on overloaded functions and wrote the following implementations. What is wrong with the coding and how can it be fixed?

Point.cpp

```
void SetPoint (int xx, int yy) {
  x = xx;
  y = yy;
}

void GetPoint (int xx, int yy) const {
  xx = x;
  yy = y;
}
```

7. Next the programmer attempted to implement the constructors but failed. How can they be corrected so that the constructors work fine?

Point.cpp

```
void Point::Point (int x, int y) {
  x = x;
  y = y;
}

void Point::Point () {
  x = y = 0;
}
```

Programming Problems

Problem Pgm07-1 A Circle Class

Design and implement and test a class that encapsulates a **Circle** object. It should have three data members: its radius and the integer x, y coordinates of its center. There should be a default constructor and a constructor that takes the necessary three parameters to define a circle object. Provide proper access functions for the user to retrieve and modify the three properties. **Circle** operations include obtaining the area of the circle, its circumference, and the ability to input and output a **Circle** object.

The input stream containing a **Circle** object consists of two integers for the coordinates (x,y) followed by a **double** representing the radius. The output is more formalized. It should appear as follows:
```
Circle at [xxx, yyy] of radius rrrr.rr
```
Always show two decimals in the radius.

Next, add a function, **CompareRadius()**, which returns an **int** as follows.
0 means the two circles have the same radius
+ means the member circle has a larger radius than the passed circle
− means the member circle has a smaller radius than the passed circle
Its prototype is
```
int CompareRadius (const Circle& c) const;
```
Now write a tester program to thoroughly test the **Circle** class.

Problem Pgm07-2 An Employee Class

Acme Corporation wishes a class to encapsulate their employee workforce. The **Employee** class contains the employee first and last name strings which should include a maximum of 10 and 20 characters respectively. The date he/she was hired should be stored as three **short**s. His/her job title is a string of up to 20 characters. His/her age and sex should be stored as **char** fields. His/her pay rate is stored in a **double** and the pay type is a **char** containing an H or S for hourly or salaried. If he/she is an hourly worker, the pay rate is the hourly rate. If he/she is a salaried worker, the pay rate is the uniform amount that he/she is paid each week. Finally, his/her employee id number is stored as a **long**.

The class should have a default constructor and a constructor that is passed all of the relevant data needed to initialize an employee object. Provide access functions for all of the data members.

Write an **Input()** function that is passed a reference to an **istream** from which to input the data. One blank separates each field on input. All strings are padded with blanks to the maximum length of that particular string. That is, if the first name was Sam, on the input it would appear as Sambbbbbb where the b represents a blank. The order of the fields on input are:
id number, first name, last name, job title, mm/dd/yyyy, age, sex, pay rate, pay type
Note that there are / separating the elements of the hired date.

Write a **Pay()** function that calculates and returns the employee's weekly pay. Its prototype should be

```
double Pay () const;
```

Write a tester program to thoroughly test the class functions. When that is working properly, then write the client Weekly Pay program. Use the file that came with the book called **Problem7-2-WeeklyPay.txt** as the input file. The pay program inputs all of the employee records into an array of **Employee** objects. Allow for a maximum of 50 employees in the array. Then, for each employee in the array, calculate and print their pay as shown below.

```
                Acme Weekly Payroll Report
Employee   First      Last                  Date        Weekly
    Id     Name       Name                  Hired       Pay

 1123123   John       Jones                 05/12/1994 $9999.99
...
Total Payroll ------------------------------------> $999999.99
```

The last line represents the total amount that all of the employees are paid. For this assignment, assume that all employees worked exactly 40 hours this week.

Problem Pgm07-3 A Bank Account Class

Acme First National Bank wishes a new basic **BankAccount** class to be written. The class contains a long account number, the current balance and the accumulated total fees for this month.

Provide a default constructor and one that takes the three parameters necessary to properly initialize an account. Create access functions to get and set each of the three properties. Create input and output functions to handle I/O of a bank account. On input, the account number comes first, followed by the balance and fees. On output, display the fields in the same order, but with each field 10 columns wide and separated by five blanks.

The operations member functions consist of **Deposit()** and **Withdrawal()**. We are ignoring any possible interest in this overly simplified problem. The **Deposit()** function is passed a positive amount to be added to the current balance and it returns the new balance.

The **Withdrawal()**function is more complicated; it is passed the withdrawal amount and a reference to the service charge that will be applied to the account for this transaction. The function returns **true** if the withdrawal was successful or **false** if there are insufficient funds for this transaction. The service charge is $0.10 per withdrawal as long as the balance is below $500.00. There is no service charge if the balance is $500.00 or above. If the withdrawn amount plus any service charge would take the balance below $0.00, then the withdrawal is not made; instead a service charge of $25.00 is applied to the account and the function returns false. Note that the service charges are always applied to the balance with each transaction. They are accumulated as well for later monthly display. The service charge for this transaction is stored in the passed reference variable for the client program's use.

Next, write a tester program to thoroughly test the new class.

When you are satisfied that the class is working correctly, write the client program to process a day's transactions. There are two files provided with this text. The first file, **Problem7-3-BankAccounts.txt**, contains the initial bank accounts at the start of the day. The program should load these into an array of up to 50 bank account objects. Next, the program should input the transactions file, **Problem7-3-Transactions.txt**. Each line in the transactions file contains a character, D for deposit or W for withdrawal. This letter is followed by the account number and then the monetary amount to be deposited or withdrawn. For each transaction, attempt to process it. Display the results in a report as shown below. When the end of the file is reached, then output a new version of the bank accounts for use in the next day's processing.

```
Account   Type Amount    Status   Service Charge
1234567   W    $ 100.00   Ok      $ 0.10
1234546   D    $  50.00   Ok      $ 0.00
1234556   W    $1000.00   Failed  $25.00
```

Chapter 8—Classes (ADT) II—A Growable Array

Introduction

Back in chapter 2 we discovered the need for **#ifndef-#define** or **#pragma once** logic in header files. This same need is carried forward into class definition files as well. Next, we must examine just how a member function can actually find the member data on which to operate. Knowing this detail, we can then expand our discussion of classes into the area of operator overloaded functions. That is, most all of the C++ operators can be overloaded by a class. Among the more common ones frequently supported by ADTs are <<, >>, +, -, *, /, ==, !=, = and so on. Once our classes provide for these types of operations, the classes become quite convenient and very usable by client programs.

Enumerated data types are extremely useful for adding clarity to a program. An **enum** can be physically a part of a class definition. That is, the **enum** itself may belong to a class and is called a class **enum**. In OOP programming, the use of class **enums** is widespread and becomes a very powerful feature.

Our use of overloaded operators for this book centers on just three key operators: <<, >> and =. Why? We do need to be able to input and output an instance easily. However, the key reason that we must support the assignment operator is because most of our data structure classes are going to have dynamically allocated data members. Thus, if one assigns an instance of such a class to another class, only the pointer data member gets copied. We must overload the assignment operator to provide a way to actually copy the dynamically allocated data to which the pointer is pointing.

All this leads to the construction of a growable array class. In this chapter, we examine just how we can create a generic class of growable array that can be reused in any application and array that is independent of what kind of information it is actually storing!

Using #ifndef-#define or #pragma once Logic in Class Header Files

Back in chapter 2, we discovered the need to guarantee that a specific definition, then of a structure, was copied only one time into a given cpp implementation file. The same is even more true when dealing with class definitions. A very common practice in OOP is to include instances or references to instances of other classes or structures within a given class definition.

Consider for example, designing an **Employee** class. One of its data members would likely be a date, such as their hired date. Very often, a company already has an existing **Date** class to encapsulate a date and provide standardized support for date operations. Thus, duplicate **Date** class definitions can very easily occur when **#ifndef** logic is not used. Consider the following skeletal class coding.

File: Date.h
```
class Date {
...
};
```
File: Employee.h
```
#include "Date.h"
class Employee {
...
 Date hiredDate;
...
};
```
File: main.cpp
```
#include "Date.h"
#include "Employee.h"
int main () {
 Date today;
 Employee employee;
...
}
```

As you can see, in **main.cpp**, two copies of the definition of the **Date** class are brought in by the compiler which results in a compile-time error. Ok, in this overly simplified example, main does not need to include **Date.h** because it is coming in from **Employee.h**. True. However, let's add another class to **main.cpp**, **YTDPay** (year to date pay), which encapsulates the yearly accumulated pay of the employees. This class would also have one or more **Date** instances as data members and would be also including **Date.h** in its header. Now, **main.cpp** has no way to avoid duplicate definitions when it includes **Employee.h** and **YTDPay.h**.

The solution is use **#ifndef** or **#pragma once** logic around the entire class definition.

> **Rule: Always wrap a class definition with #ifndef or #pragma once logic to avoid any future possibility of duplicate definitions.**

Thus, the above example should have been coded as follows.

File: Date.h
```
#pragma once

class Date {
...
};
```

File: Employee.h
```
#pragma once

#include "Date.h"
class Employee {
...
 Date hiredDate;
```

```
...
};
```

File: main.cpp
```
#include "Date.h"
#include "Employee.h"
int main () {
 Date today;
 Employee employee;
...
}
```
Now only one copy of the **Date** class definition is included by the compiler in **main.cpp**.

The `this` Pointer

Suppose I had four instances of the **Vehicle** class from chapter 7 called, **a**, **b**, **c** and **d**. There is only one code area for each of the member function; the machine instructions of the functions are the same for every instance of the class. However, there must be four separate member data areas, one for each of the four **Vehicle** objects. It does not make sense to carry along a copy of constant code (member functions) with each object instance. Figure 8.1 shows the layout of memory for these four **Vehicle** objects.

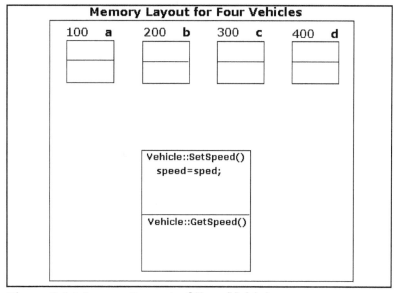

Figure 8.1 Memory Layout of Four Vehicles

Here **Vehicle a** is located at memory location 100. Its two member data, **isMoving** and **speed**, are shown. Similarly the other three vehicles are at locations 200, 300 and 400. Consider what happens when the **main()** function does
```
a.SetSpeed (50);
```

How does that common code, the **SetSpeed()** member function in this case, know where to find the data for object **a** - that is to set **a**'s **speed**? Without some help, it cannot know where object **a** is located and thus cannot place a new value into **a**'s **speed**!

The C++ language handles this situation by defining and passing a very special constant pointer that contains the memory location of the object in question. The pointer is called **this** and it is automatically passed to any member functions by the compiler. Actually, it is a hidden first parameter to member functions. When we code

```
a.SetSpeed (50);
```

The compiler obtains the address of **Vehicle a**, here location 100, and passes that address into the **this** parameter of the **SetSpeed()** function. Our prototype for this function is

```
void SetSpeed (int sped);
```

But when the compiler compiles the class, it modifies our prototypes of member functions to include the **this** parameter. What the compiler actually creates is shown below with the additions by the compiler in bold/italics.

```
void SetSpeed (Vehicle* const this, int sped);
```

Now in the implementation of **SetSpeed()**, we code

```
void Vehicle::SetSpeed (int sped) {
  speed = sped;
}
```

But the compiler alters our coding as follows.

```
void Vehicle::SetSpeed (Vehicle* const this, int sped) {
  this->speed = sped;
}
```

This clever scheme allows the compiler to automatically access the member data of any object from within member functions. In fact, the **this** parameter is also available for our use as well, when the need arises. We could also have implemented the function this way.

```
void Vehicle::SetSpeed (int sped) {
  this->speed = sped;
}
```

But why do the compiler's work for it? However, suppose that we had called the parameter **speed** instead of **sped**? We saw in the last chapter that we cannot just code

```
void Vehicle::SetSpeed (int speed) {
  speed = speed;
}
```

But now we have two ways to specify the member data **speed**. Either of the following is correct.

```
void Vehicle::SetSpeed (int speed) {
  Vehicle::speed = speed;
  this->speed = speed;
}
```

When the situation of conflicting parameters and member names occur, programmers use either one of these methods to avoid the name conflict. However, the major use of the **this** pointer occurs when we implement operator overloading.

Operator Overloading

C++ operators, such as +, -, [], ==, >>, and << can be overloaded just as ordinary functions can be overloaded. These are called **operator overloaded functions**. The syntax is a bit unusual because of the "name of the function" is + for instance. The general syntax is

```
return type   classname::operatorZ (argument list);
```
where "Z" is the operator.

The only operators that cannot be overridden are : .* ? preprocessor directives. Yes, [] and even () function call operators can be overridden!

Rule: Maintain the spirit of C++ usage of operators when overloading them.

If you are overloading the + operator, it should do some form of addition, not output the data to a file. If you overload the [] operator, it should access the indicated element in an array, not add 42 to every element or sum the ith column of the array, for instance.

Rule: Operator functions cannot have default arguments.

This is invalid:
```
double operator+ (double millimeters = 1.); // error
```

The overloading of operators breaks down into two major categories: the **unary** operators and the **binary** operators. The unary operator functions do not have any parameters. Examples of these include -x, x++ and --x, for example. The vast majority of operators have the binary form because two items are involved. For example, the add + operator adds the item on its right to the item on its left, as in
```
x = y + 5;
```
The relational operators are another example, such as
```
if (x == 42)
```
Even the insertion, extraction and assignment operators are binary in nature.
```
cin >> x;
x = y;
```
Let's begin with the simpler operators, the binary operators.

Overloading Binary Operators (such as + and –)

Suppose we had a **Point** class whose definition was
```
class Point {
 protected:
   int x;
   int y;
 public:
     Point ();
     Point (int xx, int yy);
};
```

231

The basic implementation is

```
Point::Point () {
  x = 0;   y = 0;
}

Point::Point (int xx, int yy) {
  x = xx; y = yy;
}
```

And we want to be able to write such operations as these.

```
Point a (5, 10);
Point b (10, 20);

Point c;
c = a + b;
c = c + 1;
c = 1 + c;
```

Rule: When overloading binary operators, there is **only** one parameter and that parameter is the operand that is **to the right** of the operator +. It is the object on the **left** side of the operator that generates the function call. The **this** parameter is used by the compiler to pass the left side object to the function **operator+()**.

First, let's examine this **operator+()** function.

```
c = a + b;
```

In this example, it is **Point** object **a** that invokes the **operator+()** member function of the **Point** class. Object **b** is passed as the single parameter to the **operator+()** member function. So within the **Point::operator+()** function, **this** points to object **a**. Thus, we would expect to need a prototype of

```
Point   operator+ (Point b);
```

However, this would be very inefficient indeed. Would the addition function every change the contents of **Point b**? Never! Thus, always consider passing a constant reference to the objects. Our revised prototype is now

```
Point   operator+ (const Point& b);
```

Next consider the actual behavior of the addition with respect to object **a** itself. Does the addition itself alter object **a**? Never! The only way to alter object **a** is to code

```
a = a + b;
```

Here it is the assignment operator that is actually altering object **a**. Thus, the whole **operator+()** function is constant as well, since object **a**, or the object that **this** is pointing to does not change. Our prototype is now revised to the following.

```
Point   operator+ (const Point& b) const;
```

Finally, what about the return value? Since the function is not changing either object **a** or **b** and is to compute the sum of the two, an automatic storage local **Point** instance must be created to hold the result. Since automatic storage items are discarded as the function ends, we must return a copy of that temporary **Point**. Hence, the return type of **Point** is correct.

What does the implementation look like? We must first decide what it means to "add" two **Point** objects together. Let's assume that the add operation is to add the two x coordinates together and then the two y coordinates. If this is correct, here is the implementation.

```
Point    Point::operator+ (const Point& b) const {
 Point t = b;
 t.x += x;
 t.y += y;
 return t;
}
```

It can also be implemented this way.

```
Point    Point::operator+ (const Point& b) const {
 Point t;
 t.x = x + b.x;
 t.y = y + b.y;
 return t;
}
```

Since we have a constructor that takes two coordinates, it can also be implemented this way.

```
Point    Point::operator+ (const Point& b) const {
 Point t (x + b.x, y + b.y);
 return t;
}
```

Finally, one can just return a temporary object this way.

```
Point    Point::operator+ (const Point& b) const {
 return Point (x + b.x, y + b.y);
}
```

Which implementation do you prefer? Which is the easiest for you to understand?

Now let's examine the second case.

```
 c = c + 1;
```

Here object **c** is passed with the **this** parameter and the integer 1 is passed as the single argument. Thus, we would expect to need a prototype of

```
 Point    operator+ (int i) const;
```

The actual implementation might be as follows, assuming that the integer is to be added to both the x and y coordinates.

```
 Point    Point::operator+ (int i) const {
 Point t (x + i, y + i);
 return t;
}
```

Using Friend Functions to Handle Overloading Normal Data Types

The third case that we need to implement poses a significant problem in design.

```
 c = 1 + c;
```

Here, following the rule for determining the **this** parameter and the **operator+()** parameter, we would have the **integer** class's **operator+()** function being invoked with the **this** parameter being the 1 and the function would be passed **Point c** as its parameter! Oops. There is no integer OOP class! To handle this situation, which occurs with some frequency in class design, we must write an ordinary C style function that takes the integer as the first parameter and the **Point c** as the second parameter. The prototype is as follows.

```
 Point operator+ (int j, const Point& p);
```

This is **not** a member function. However, this function must be able to get at the private and protected data of the **Point** class in order for it to perform its needed actions.

Rule: Any C function can be granted access to a class's private and protected data if it is designated as a **friend** of that class. These are known as **friend functions**.

A friend function is **not** a member of the class of which it is a friend. But it is granted the rights to access private member data as if it were. Its primary use is to aid operator overloading and I/O streaming. It also is a means for a function to be able to access member data of several classes to be able to do its work.

The syntax is simple. The C function prototype is contained in the class definition file and has the keyword **friend** prefixed to its prototype. Thus, its correct prototype is as follows.

File: Point.h

```
class Point {
 protected:
   int x;
   int y;
 public:
    Point ();
    Point (int xx, int yy);

    // operator overloaded functions
        Point  operator+ (const Point& b) const;
        Point  operator+ (int i) const;
    friend Point  operator+ (int j, const Point& p);
};
```

Notice that it is **not** a member function; yet as a **friend** function, it is granted all of the rights and privileges that are due a member function.

Its implementation would be as shown below.

```
Point operator+ (int i, const Point& p) {
 Point ret (p.x + i, p.y + i);
 return ret;
}
```

Note that there is no class qualifier, **Point::**, on the function header since it is not a member function.

If a class is providing support for all of the math operators, usually each will need one or more friend functions to handle the cases in which there is an intrinsic data type to the left of the math operator. The implementation of other math operator overloaded functions is entirely parallel to these addition functions.

Beginning Data Structures in C++

Overloading the Relational Operators

When overloading ==, <, >, and so on, the **this** parameter points to this instance that is to the left of the operator and the single parameter is what is to the right of the operator. For runtime efficiency, try to use a reference to the class parameters when possible. The return values can be the usual integer type or even a **bool**, if a true/false result makes more sense.

Let's implement the test for equality. The user expects to code the following.
```
Point a;
Point b;
if (a == b) {
```
Applying the rule for constructing the prototype for the **operator==()** function, we have object **a** being passed as the **this** parameter and a constant reference to object **b** as the main parameter.
```
bool   operator== (const Point& p) const;
```
Its implementation might be as follows.
```
bool   Point::operator== (const Point& p) const {
 return x == p.x && y == p.y;
}
```

Overloading the I/O Insertion and Extraction Operators (<< and >>)

For the convenience of client programmers, a class ought to overload the insertion and extraction operators to provide a convenient method for an object's input or output. Typical coding for our **Point** class is as follows.
```
Point p;
cin >> p;
cout << p;
```
From our knowledge of overloaded operators, we can predict that the **iostream** class's **operator<<()** and **operator>>()** functions are being invoked with the **this** parameter pointing to either **cin** or **cout**. The single parameter to these functions is our **Point** object **p**. This is no good because we are not going to alter Microsoft's **ostream** libraries! Thus, once again, we must resort to using **friend** functions to implement these two functions.

Their prototypes are as follows.

File: Point.h
```
#pragma once
#include <iostream>
using namespace std;
class Point {
 protected:
   int x;
   int y;
 public:
    Point ();
    Point (int xx, int yy);
```

```
    // operator overloaded functions
        Point   operator+ (const Point& b) const;
        Point   operator+ (int i) const;
  friend Point   operator+ (int j, const Point& p);

  friend istream& operator>> (istream& is, Point &p);
  friend ostream& operator<< (ostream& os, const Point &p);
};
```

Notice that both functions must return a reference to the passed **iostream**. Further, to compile, we must include <iostream> so that the compiler knows what the identifiers are. Let's see how these two functions for our **Point** class might be coded.

```
ostream&   operator<< (ostream& os, const Point &p) {
 os << p.x << " " << p.y;
 return os;
}

istream&   operator>> (istream& is, Point &p) {
 is >> p.x >> p.y;
 return is;
}
```

Overloading the Assignment Operator

When a class has dynamic memory allocation as part of its basis of operation, the copying and assignment of such objects pose a major problem. To illustrate the problem, consider a simple class to encapsulate a string.

Here is the proposed simple class which dynamically allocates the memory needed to store the client's string.

File: str.h

```
class String {
 protected:
  char* string;
 public:
  String ();
  String (const char* str);
 ~String();
};
```

And here is the basic implementation of the class thus far.

```
String::String () {
 string = new char [1];
 string[0] = 0;
}

String::String (const char* str) {
 if (!str) {
  string = new char [1];
```

```
  string[0] = 0;
 }
 else {
  string = new char [ strlen (str) + 1];
  strcpy (string, str);
 }
}

String::~String() {
 delete [] string;
}
```

Now consider some user coding.
```
String Fun (String s);
int main () {
 String a ("Hello World");
 String b ("Good Bye");
 String c (a);              // problem 1
 String d = a;              // problem 2
 b = a;                     // problem 3
 Fun (a);                   // problem 4
 return 0;
}
String Fun (String s) {
 String d ("Hi there");
 return d;                  // problem 5
}
```

At the instructions labeled "problem 1, 2, 4 and 5," the compiler must make a duplicate copy of another string as it is constructing the new String. With only the coding that we have provided in the class thus far, the compiler simply copies the data item, the pointer to string. Thus, **c.string** points to **a.string**. **d.string** also points to **a.string**. The parameter of **Fun()**, **s.string**, also points to **a.string**. And the returned temporary string also points to **d.string**. When the destructor of these objects are called, the compiler will try to delete the array pointed to by **a.string** many times causing a runtime crash. Worse still, as soon as one of these destructors is called, the memory for **a.string** gone, but the other objects are still pointing to the now deleted memory! Figure 8.2 illustrates the problem. Additionally, when the assignment to **String b** is done, the compiler also copies the pointer so that **b.string** also points to **a.string**! Worse still, the memory originally allocated to store **b**'s string has not been deleted, causing a memory leak.

When a copy of an object is made, the data member's contents are duplicated. When that member is a pointer, only the pointer's contents are duplicated. This is sometimes called a shallow copy. Look over Figure 8.2 below to see the effect of the shallow copy.

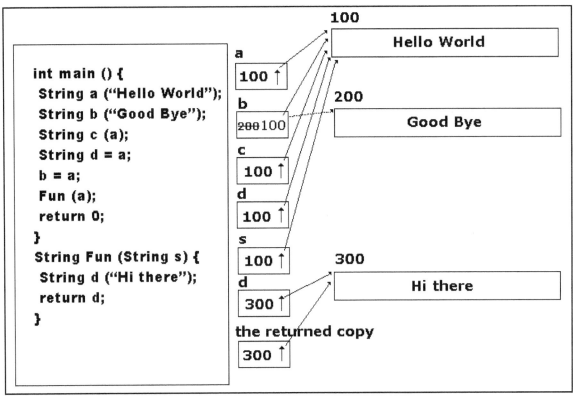

```
int main () {
  String a ("Hello World");
  String b ("Good Bye");
  String c (a);
  String d = a;
  b = a;
  Fun (a);
  return 0;
}
String Fun (String s) {
  String d ("Hi there");
  return d;
}
```

Figure 8.2 Effects of a Shallow Copy with Dynamic Memory Allocations

When **String c** is initialized, the memory location of **a**'s **string**, here location 100, is copied. So now two objects point to the same dynamically allocated memory. When the objects go out of scope, in this example the } brace of **main()**, the compiler calls the destructors in the reverse order that they were constructed—automatic storage is on the stack as last in – first out. Thus, destruction of object **c** removes the memory allocated at location 100. Then, when object **a**'s destructor is called, it also attempts to delete memory at location 100, and a runtime crash occurs. The same holds true for the other occurrences. However, it is worse when the assignment operator is called, assigning **a** to **b**. Here, the assignment is shallow and only copied the pointer but in the process the memory currently pointed to at location 200 is not deleted. A memory leak results.

> **Rule: When a class uses dynamic memory, that class should define and implement a copy constructor, the assignment operator and the class destructor functions.**

> **Rule: The copy constructor and assignment operator functions should perform a deep copy by deleting any already allocated memory and making a duplicate copy of the actual dynamically allocated data.**

> **Rule: If you do not want the client making a copy in any way, then define the copy constructor and assignment operator and make their access private. Then the compiler cannot call them and it will error out a client program's attempts to make duplicate copies of these objects.**

The **copy constructor** has a special prototype. It is always a constructor that is passed a constant reference to an instance of that class. The two missing functions from our **String** class prototypes are as follows. (Note we already have the destructor function.)

```
String (const String& s);
String& operator= (const String& s);
```

When we implement the copy constructor, the current instance is just being created so that there is nothing yet existing to delete. However, when we implement the assignment operator, the object to which we are assigning already exists; we must first delete its dynamically allocated string and then make the duplicate copy. Further, in C++ assignments can be chained, as in

```
a = b = c = d = 0;
```

Thus, we need to return a **String** object. However, since we are assigning to us or the **this** parameter instance, we are not going out of scope when the function returns, we can return us. Use a reference to us to avoid making additional copies of us. Alternatively, since we are now a copy of the passed **String s**, one could return **s** as well.

Here is how the copy constructor can be coded.

```
String::String (const String& s) {
  string = new char [ strlen (s.string) + 1];
  strcpy (string, s.string);
}
```

And here is a first attempt at the assignment operator; it is not totally correct yet.

```
String& String::operator= (const String& s) {
  delete [] string;
  string = new char [ strlen (s.string) + 1];
  strcpy (string, s.string);
  return *this;
}
```

Notice the clever ***this** coding; **this** is a pointer to a **String** while the return type is a **String&**. Both are the memory of this instance of the **String**. However, the compiler will not make the assignment because one is a pointer (**this**) and the other a reference. We can force the compiler to make the assignment by coding ***this** which then becomes us, the **String** object, and the compiler then takes our address for the return reference.

But what is the problem with the assignment operator's coding? Can you spot it? The code works well in all cases but one. What happens in the following ordinary code?

```
int a = 42;
a = a;
```

The value of **a** is still 42. Now consider what the above assignment does in this case.

```
String a ("Hello");
a = a;
```

Our assignment operator begins by deleting the memory to which the **this** parameter is pointing which is **String a**. Oops. In this case, s is a reference to a! So now there is no more **s.string** to copy! It's gone. The fix then is simply to check that **this** and the passed object **s** are not the same. Here is the revised version.

```
String& String::operator= (const String& s) {
 if (this == &s) return *this;
 delete [] string;
 string = new char [strlen(s.string) + 1];
 strcpy (string, s.string);
 return *this;
}
```

Using Class enums

Suppose that we desired to make a class to encapsulate pets for a pet store. One of the data members would have to be the pet's type, such as dog, cat, snake, hamster or mouse. While one could use #**define**s or **const int**s to create good identifiers for the pet types, we know that an **enum** is a much better approach. We could easily define **PetType** as follows.

```
enum PetType {Dog, Cat, Snake, Hamster, Mouse};
```

From a design point of view, this new **PetType** really belongs with our new **Pet** class. It does not likely make any sense if used outside of the **Pet** class and such operations. So if we just defined the **enum** as above, then there is nothing to show that it really is used in conjunction with **Pet** objects.

A **class enum** is an enumerated data type that is defined within the class definition and thus belongs to the class. As such, all uses outside the class require the class qualifier. Usually, a class **enum** has the public access qualifier so that it can be broadly used. Here is how the **Pet** class could be defined.

File: Pet.h

```
#pragma once
class Pet {
 public:
   enum PetType {Dog, Cat, Snake, Hamster, Mouse};
   enum Gender {Male, Female};
 protected:
   PetType type;
   Gender  sex;

 public:
   Pet ();
   Pet (PetType t, Gender g);
   PetType GetPetType () const;
   Gender  GetPetGender () const;
};
```

And here is how it could be implemented. Notice how the **Pet::** class qualifier is used with both the return data types and with actual **enum** values.

File: Pet.cpp

```
Pet::Pet () {
 type = Dog;
 sex = Female;
}
```

Beginning Data Structures in C++

```
Pet::Pet (Pet::PetType t, Pet::Gender g) {
 type = t;
 sex = g;
}

Pet::PetType Pet::GetPetType () const {
 return type;
}

Pet::Gender Pet::GetPetGender () const {
 return sex;
}
```

Here is how a client program may use the class **enum**s. Since the **enum** is **public**, it can even allocate instances of the **enum**.

```
int main () {
 Pet::PetType t = Pet::Cat;
 Pet p (Pet::Dog, Pet::Male);
 if (p.GetPetGender() == Pet::Male &&
     P.GetPetType() == Pet::Cat) {
```

Class **enum**s are widely used in class designs. All of the **ios::** identifiers you have been coding are class **ios enum**s! Try opening up the **ios.h** header file and there you will find all of the **ios::** identifiers you are familiar with—all are **ios** class **enum**s.

Designing a Generic Growable Array Class

It's time to create the first of our totally reusable container classes. A **container class** is a data structure which holds items for the user. In this case, the container is an array that grows in size as the number of items are added. The limit, as before, is the amount of memory available. The key feature is reusability. While one could easily envision a class devoted to holding an array of cost records, inventory records and so on, such would not be portable to the next programming project that needed an array of other items. I am always in favor of writing something once and then being able to use it in many different programs.

What should the specifications of an array class be? Obviously, there are going to be two data members of the class, the array of items and the count of the number of elements in the array. But what should the data type of the array be? This is the critical design aspect. If we make the array of some specific data type, such as a **CostRec** structure, then at once the container class cannot be reused except in another program that deals with cost records. In fact, I hope that it is abundantly clear to you at this point that if we specify any kind of intrinsic data type or structure as the array data type, the container cannot easily be reused.

However, there is one type of data that is independent of data type and that is a **void***, a pointer to **void**. Such pointers cannot be dereferenced. However, if all that our class is doing is maintaining an array of such pointers and providing access to those pointers, we do not need to dereference such pointers. Thus, to make the array reusable, our class stores a resizeable array of **void** pointers. Note that our member data

241

type is thus
```
void** array; // an array of void*
```

When a user wishes to gain access to a specific element and calls say **GetAt (i)** to acquire the ith one, our function returns to the user a **void***. For the user to be able to do anything with that data, he or she must typecast the pointer back to the specific data type to which it is pointing. The user, of course, knows what kind of data to which it is supposed to be pointing. This, of course, places an extra burden on the programmer. However, the benefits of using a generic array container are many.

There is also a significant side effect of storing only **void** pointers. To see the impact of that side effect, let's examine the alternative approach, say storing an array of **CostRec** structures. The class name might be **CostRecArray** and its data members might be as shown.
```
CostRec* array;
long      numElements:
```
When the user wants to add a new instance to the array, he or she calls our **Add()** function which might be coded similarly to the following.
```
void CostRecArray::Add (const CostRec& crec) {
 CostRec* temp = new CostRec [numElements + 1];
 if (!temp) {
  cerr << "Array: Add Error - out of memory\n";
  return;
 }
 for (long i=0; i<numElements; i++) {
  temp[i] = array[i];
 }
 temp[numElements] = crec;
 numElements++;
 delete [] array;
 array = temp;
}
```
The sequence is simple: allocate space for a new array of **CostRec** structures that is one element larger than the current array. Then copy all of the **CostRec** structures in the old array into the new array. Next, copy the new one into the last element. After incrementing the number of elements in the array, delete the old array and assign the address of the new array to our **array** member.

When the destructor is called, we must delete all of the **CostRec** structures we are storing. Since we are storing an array of them, it is a simple task.
```
delete [] array;
```
Thus, the programmers never have to concern themselves with any clean up activities. The class handles the destruction of the array and its contents.

Ok. So what is the side effect of having the class store **void** pointers? The programmer must allocate the items they wish the container to store and they must delete those items before any class destructor is called. When the programmer calls the **Add()** function, they must pass the address of the item to be stored. Frequently, they will have already dynamically allocated that item and filled it up with relevant data. Later, **before** any destructor of the **Array** class is called, they must traverse all elements in the array, retrieve each pointer from the **Array** and then delete the memory occupied by that item.

This is really not too high a price to pay for a totally reuseable array container. In fact, in Windows programming (MFC—Microsoft Foundation Classes), this is quite commonly done since the MFC provides just such a **void*** array called **CPtrArray**. (In advanced data structures, an alternative implementation can be made by using a template class.)

When designing the **Array** class, what member functions are needed? The default constructor sets the array pointer to zero along with the number of elements in the array. The destructor should delete the array. How would a client want to add elements to an array? If the data is coming from a file, most likely, the programmer would just want to add the next item at the end of the array. Let's call that the **Add()** function. However, a programmer might wish to add an item at the beginning or after some specific index. Let's call that function **InsertAt()**. Certainly, the need the ability to get at an item located at a specific index, function **GetAt()**. On the removal side, they might wish to remove an item at a specific index or perhaps empty the array to reuse it; this gives us **RemoveAt()** and **RemoveAll()**. A client program certainly must be able to find out the number of elements currently in the array—the **GetNumberOfElements()** function.

Given these few member functions, a client program can make effective use of an **Array** class. However, since there is dynamic memory allocation involved, we know that we must guard against shallow copy operations. Consider a client program that does the following.

```
Array a;
Array b = a;
Array c;
c = a;
Fun (a);
```

where

```
void Fun (Array a);
```

In the above cases, disaster results. We must provide a copy constructor and the assignment operator implementations. Since both functions make a duplicate copy of the array of **void** pointers, let's use a common helper function called **Copy()** to do that common work.

Finally, if there are any errors, let's display them to the **cerr** device. Here is the **Array** class definition. Notice the extensive use of comments alerting the programmer to class usage notes. It is sometimes helpful to insert a bit of client coding in the comments to illustrate what a client program must do that might not be clear to all programmers. I did just this to illustrate how a client program should clean up the array before the destructor gets called. I also documented the expected behavior of certain functions such as **InsertAt()**, **GetAt()** and **RemoveAt()**.

```
Array.h Definition - Growable Array Class

 1 #pragma once
 2
 3 /*****************************************************/
 4 /*                                                   */
 5 /* Array:  container for growable array of void* items */
 6 /*         it can store a variable number of elements  */
 7 /*                                                   */
 8 /*         since elements stored are void*, they can   */
 9 /*         point to anything desired, intrinsic types, */
```

```
10 /*         structures, other classes, for example         */
11 /*                                                          */
12 /*   limited by amount of memory and swap drive size        */
13 /*                                                          */
14 /*   errors are logged to cerr device                      */
15 /*                                                          */
16 /*   Note on destruction: before calling RemoveAt or       */
17 /*   RemoveAll or the destructor, the user is responsible   */
18 /*   for the actual deletion of the items the void*         */
19 /*   pointers are actually pointing to                      */
20 /*                                                          */
21 /*   Typical clean up coding might be as follows:           */
22 /*   MyData* ptrd;                                          */
23 /*   for (i=0; i<array.GetNumberOfElements(); i++) {        */
24 /*    ptrd = (MyData*) array.GetAt (i);                     */
25 /*    if (ptrd)                                             */
26 /*      delete ptrd;                                        */
27 /*   }                                                      */
28 /*   array.RemoveAll ();                                    */
29 /*                                                          */
30 /***********************************************************/
31
32 class Array {
33
34   /***********************************************************/
35   /*                                                        */
36   /* class data                                             */
37   /*                                                        */
38   /***********************************************************/
39
40 protected:
41  void** array;
42  long  numElements;
43
44   /***********************************************************/
45   /*                                                        */
46   /* class functions                                        */
47   /*                                                        */
48   /***********************************************************/
49
50 public:
51  Array ();     // default constructor - makes an empty array
52  ~Array ();    // be sure to delete what the void* are pointing
53                // to before the destructor is called
54
55  bool Add (void* ptrNewElement);
56    // add the element to array end returns true if successful
57
58  bool InsertAt (long i, void* ptrNewElement);
59      // adds this element at subscript i
```

244

```
60          // if i < 0, it is added at the front
61          // if i >= numElements, it is added at the end
62          // otherwise, it is added at the ith position
63          // returns true if successful
64
65  void* GetAt (long i) const; // returns element at the ith pos
66                    // If i is out of range, it returns 0
67
68  bool RemoveAt (long i); // removes the element at subscript i
69                    // if i is out of range, an error is
70                    // displayed on cerr - Note what the
71                    // element actually points to is not deleted
72                    // returns true if successful
73
74  void RemoveAll (); // removes all elements - Note what the
75                    // elements actually point to are not deleted
76
77  long GetNumberOfElements () const; // returns the number of
78                                      // elements in the array
79
80  Array (const Array& a);              // copy constructor
81  Array& operator= (const Array& a); // duplicates the array
82  // Note that neither the copy constructor or the assignment op
83  // makes a copy of what the pointer elements are actually
84  // pointing to. Displays an error msg to cerr if out of memory
85
86 protected:
87  void Copy (const Array& a); // performs the actual deep copy
88 };
89
```

From the implementation viewpoint, I chose to return **bool** values to indicate success or failure of the add and remove functions. With the **Add()** and **InsertAt()** functions, the only way **false** can be returned is if the computer is out of memory. The implementation of **InsertAt()** reflects my own personal consideration that a function should try to do its job in all cases. If the index is out of range, I still add the item. If the index is negative, I insert it at the front of the array; if the index is too large, I insert it at the end of the array. **RemoveAt()** must return false if the index is out of range because there is no way to second-guess the programmer's intention.

Look over the implementation of the **Array** class. The coding is actually quite simple and heavily documented.

```
Array.cpp Implementation - Growable Array Class

1 #include <iostream>
2 using namespace std;
3
4 #include "Array.h"
5
```

```
 6  /***********************************************************/
 7  /*                                                         */
 8  /* Array: constructs an empty array                        */
 9  /*                                                         */
10  /***********************************************************/
11
12  Array::Array () {
13   numElements = 0;
14   array = 0;
15  }
16
17  /***********************************************************/
18  /*                                                         */
19  /* ~Array: deletes dynamically allocated memory            */
20  /*         It is the client's responsibility  to delete    */
21  /*         what the void* are pointing to before the       */
22  /*         destructor is called                            */
23  /*                                                         */
24  /***********************************************************/
25
26  Array::~Array () {
27   RemoveAll ();
28  }
29
30  /***********************************************************/
31  /*                                                         */
32  /* Add: Adds this new element to the end of the array      */
33  /*      if out of memory, displays error message to cerr   */
34  /*                                                         */
35  /***********************************************************/
36
37  bool Array::Add (void* ptrNewElement) {
38   // allocate new temporary array one element larger
39   void** temp = new (std::nothrow) void* [numElements + 1];
40
41   // check for out of memory
42   if (!temp) {
43    cerr << "Array: Add Error - out of memory\n";
44    return false;
45   }
46
47   // copy all existing elements into the new temp array
48   for (long i=0; i<numElements; i++) {
49    temp[i] = array[i];
50   }
51
52   // copy in the new element to be added
53   temp[numElements] = ptrNewElement;
54
55   numElements++;  // increment the number of elements in the array
```

```
56   if (array) delete [] array; // delete the old array
57   array = temp;   // point out array to the new array
58   return true;
59  }
60
61  /*******************************************************/
62  /*                                                     */
63  /*  InsertAt: adds the new element to the array at index i*/
64  /*   if i is in range, it is inserted at subscript i      */
65  /*   if i is negative, it is inserted at the front        */
66  /*   if i is greater than or equal to the number of       */
67  /*      elements, then it is added at the end of the array*/
68  /*                                                     */
69  /*   if there is insufficient memory, an error message    */
70  /*      is displayed to cerr                              */
71  /*                                                     */
72  /*******************************************************/
73
74  bool Array::InsertAt (long i, void* ptrNewElement) {
75   void** temp;
76   long j;
77   // allocate a new array one element larger
78   temp = new (std::nothrow) void* [numElements + 1];
79
80   // check if out of memory
81   if (!temp) {
82    cerr << "Array: InsertAt - Error out of memory\n";
83    return false;
84   }
85
86   // this case handles an insertion that is within range
87   if (i < numElements && i >= 0) {
88    for (j=0; j<i; j++) { // copy all elements below insertion
89     temp[j] = array[j];  // point
90    }
91    temp[i] = ptrNewElement; // insert new element
92    for (j=i; j<numElements; j++) { // copy remaining elements
93     temp[j+1] = array[j];
94    }
95   }
96
97   // this case handles an insertion when the index is too large
98   else if (i >= numElements) {
99    for (j=0; j<numElements; j++) { // copy all existing elements
100    temp[j] = array[j];
101   }
102   temp[numElements] = ptrNewElement; // add new one at end
103  }
104
105  // this case handles an insertion when the index is too small
```

```
106  else {
107   temp[0] = ptrNewElement;        // insert new on at front
108   for (j=0; j<numElements; j++) { // copy all others after it
109    temp[j+1] = array[j];
110   }
111  }
112
113  // for all cases, delete current array, assign new one and
114  // increment the number of elements in the array
115  if (array) delete [] array;
116  array = temp;
117  numElements++;
118  return true;
119 }
120
121 /*******************************************************/
122 /*                                                     */
123 /* GetAt: returns the element at index i               */
124 /*        if i is out of range, returns 0              */
125 /*                                                     */
126 /*******************************************************/
127
128 void* Array::GetAt (long i) const {
129  if (i < numElements && i >=0)
130   return array[i];
131  else
132   return 0;
133 }
134
135 /*******************************************************/
136 /*                                                     */
137 /* RemoveAt: removes the element at subscript i        */
138 /*                                                     */
139 /* If i is out of range, an error is displayed on cerr */
140 /*                                                     */
141 /* Note that what the element actually points to is not*/
142 /*       deleted                                       */
143 /*                                                     */
144 /*******************************************************/
145
146 bool Array::RemoveAt (long i) {
147  if (i < 0 || i >= numElements) {
148   cerr << "Array: RemoveAt Error: - element out of range\n"
149        << "        It was " << i << " and numElements is "
150        << numElements << endl;
151   return false;
152  }
153  if (numElements > 1) { // resize one smaller
154   void** temp;
155   temp = new (std::nothrow) void* [numElements - 1];
```

```
156   if (!temp) {
157    cerr << "Array: RemoveAt Error: out of memory\n";
158    return false;
159   }
160   long j;
161   for (j=0; j<i; j++) {              // copy all elements up to
162    temp[j] = array[j];              // the desired one to be
163   }                                 // removed
164   for (j=i+1; j<numElements; j++) { // then copy all the elements
165    temp[j-1] = array[j];            // that remain
166   }
167   numElements--;                    // decrement the number of elements
168   if (array) delete [] array; // delete the old array
169   array = temp;                     // and assign the new one
170   return true;
171   }
172   // here, numElements is one, so delete everything
173   if (array) delete [] array;
174   array = 0;
175   numElements = 0;
176   return true;
177 }
178
179 /************************************************************/
180 /*                                                          */
181 /* RemoveAll: empties the entire array, resetting it to     */
182 /*            an empty state ready for reuse                 */
183 /*                                                          */
184 /* Note that what the elements actually points to are       */
185 /*      not deleted                                         */
186 /*                                                          */
187 /************************************************************/
188
189 void Array::RemoveAll () {
190   if (array) delete [] array; // remove all elements
191   numElements = 0;                  // reset number of elements
192   array = 0;                        // and reset array to 0
193 }
194
195 /************************************************************/
196 /*                                                          */
197 /* GetNumberOfElements: returns the number of elements      */
198 /*                      currently in the array              */
199 /*                                                          */
200 /************************************************************/
201
202 long Array::GetNumberOfElements () const {
203   return numElements;
204 }
205
```

```
206 /************************************************************/
207 /*                                                          */
208 /* Array: copy constructor, makes a duplicate copy of a     */
209 /*                                                          */
210 /* Note: what the elements actually point to are not        */
211 /* duplicated only our pointers are duplicated              */
212 /*                                                          */
213 /************************************************************/
214
215 Array::Array (const Array& a) {
216  Copy (a);
217 }
218
219 /************************************************************/
220 /*                                                          */
221 /* operator=: makes a duplicate array of passed array a     */
222 /*                                                          */
223 /* Note: what the elements actually point to are not        */
224 /* duplicated only our pointers are duplicated              */
225 /*                                                          */
226 /************************************************************/
227
228 Array& Array::operator= (const Array& a) {
229  if (this == &a) // avoids silly a = a assignemnts
230   return *this;
231  if (array) delete [] array; // remove existing array
232  Copy (a);        // duplicate array a
233  return *this;    // return us for chaining assignments
234 }
235
236 /************************************************************/
237 /*                                                          */
238 /* Copy: helper function to actual perform the copy         */
239 /*                                                          */
240 /************************************************************/
241
242 void Array::Copy (const Array& a) {
243  if (a.numElements) { // be sure array a is not empty
244   numElements = a.numElements;
245   // allocate a new array the size of a
246   array = new void* [numElements];
247
248   // check for out of memory condition
249   if (!array) {
250    cerr << "Array: Copy function - Error out of memory\n";
251    numElements = 0;
252    return;
253   }
254
255   // copy all of a's pointers into our array
```

250

```
256    for (long i=0; i<numElements; i++) {
257     array[i] = a.array[i];
258    }
259   }
260   else { // a is empty, so make ours empty too
261    numElements = 0;
262    array = 0;
263   }
264  }
```

Next, let's examine how a client program might use the **Array** container. Here is some shell coding that illustrates its use.

```
struct MyData {
 ...
};

ostream& PrintRec (ostream& os, const MyData& rec);
istream& ReadRec (istream& is, MyData& rec);

int main () {
 Array a;
 MyData* ptrd;
 ptrd = new MyData;
 while (ReadRec (cin, *ptrd)) {
  a.Add (ptrd);
  ptrd = new MyData;
 }
 for (i=0; i<a.GetNumberOfElements(); i++) {
  ptrd = (MyData*) a.GetAt (i);
  if (ptrd)
    PrintRec (cout, *ptrd);
 }
 for (i=0; i<a.GetNumberOfElements(); i++) {
  ptrd = (MyData*) a.GetAt (i);
  if (ptrd)
    delete ptrd;
 }
 a.RemoveAll ();
}
```

Next, we must thoroughly test the **Array** implementation. Once again, construct testing oracles. To avoid the extra complexity of the client's tester program allocating and deleting all of the items, I have chosen a simpler route. I allocate an automatic storage array of integers, each element is given an increasing value from zero on up. What is stored in the **Array** instances are the addresses of specific elements in this integer array? This makes the testing an easier proposition to implement. Before you look at my tester program's detailed coding, sketch out what kind of tests you think should be done to ensure **Array** works perfectly. Then, check to see if I tested for them. See if I missed any situations.

Here are the tester program and its output. Please note how I created a uniform **PrintArray()** function that prints a test id string along with the theoretical output that we should see and the actual contents of the **Array** at this point. This way, errors are trivial to spot.

```
Pgm08a - Tester Program for Growable Array Class

 1 #include <iostream>
 2 #include <iomanip>
 3 #include <crtdbg.h> // for memory leak checking
 4 using namespace std;
 5 #include "Array.h"
 6
 7 // common results display function
 8 void PrintArray (const Array& a, const char* title,
 9                  const char* shouldBe);
10
11 // function to test passing a copy and returning a copy
12 Array Fun (Array f);
13
14 /****************************************************/
15 /*                                                */
16 /* Pgm08a: tester program to test the Array class  */
17 /*                                                */
18 /****************************************************/
19
20 int main () {
21  // an array of some items whose addresses can be stored in the
22  // growable array - this avoids our having to constantly
23  // allocate and delete items as they are added and removed
24  int test[50];
25  int i;
26  for (i=0; i<50; i++) {
27   test[i] = i;
28  }
29
30  // wrap the Array processing in a block so that the destructors
31  // are called before we check for memory leaks
32  {
33   Array a;
34
35   // Add testing
36   for (i=0; i<10; i++)  {
37    a.Add (&test[i+1]);
38   }
39   PrintArray (a, "Testing Add", "1 2 3 4 5 6 7 8 9 10");
40
41   // InsertAt testing
42   a.InsertAt (0, &test[0]);
43   a.InsertAt (11, &test[12]);
```

```
44   a.InsertAt (11, &test[11]);
45   a.InsertAt (1, &test[49]);
46   PrintArray (a, "Testing InsertAt",
47                "0 49 1 2 3 4 5 6 7 8 9 10 11 12");
48
49   // RemoveAt testing
50   a.RemoveAt (0);
51   a.RemoveAt (a.GetNumberOfElements()-1);
52   a.RemoveAt (5);
53   PrintArray (a, "Testing RemoveAt", "49 1 2 3 4 6 7 8 9 10 11");
54
55   // RemoveAll testing
56   a.RemoveAll ();
57   PrintArray (a, "Testing RemoveAll", "empty ");
58
59   // some special cases of RemoveAt and RemoveAll
60   a.RemoveAt (42);
61   a.RemoveAll ();
62   PrintArray (a, "Testing Empty Array", "empty ");
63
64   // InsertAt the beginning test with negative subscript
65   for (i=0; i<10; i++)  {
66    a.InsertAt (-1, &test[i]);
67   }
68   PrintArray (a, "Testing InsertAt", "9 8 7 6 5 4 3 2 1 0");
69
70   // InsertAt the beginning test with constant 0 subscript
71   a.RemoveAll ();
72   for (i=0; i<10; i++)  {
73    a.InsertAt (0, &test[i]);
74   }
75   PrintArray (a, "Testing InsertAt", "9 8 7 6 5 4 3 2 1 0");
76
77   // InsertAt the end test with out of bounds high subscript
78   a.RemoveAll ();
79   for (i=0; i<10; i++)  {
80    a.InsertAt (42, &test[i]);
81   }
82   PrintArray (a, "Testing InsertAt", "0 1 2 3 4 5 6 7 8 9");
83
84   // testing copy constructors
85   Array b (a);
86   PrintArray (b, "Testing Copy Ctor", "0 1 2 3 4 5 6 7 8 9");
87
88   Array c = a;
89   PrintArray (c, "Testing Copy Ctor", "0 1 2 3 4 5 6 7 8 9");
90
91   // testing assignment operator
92   Array d;
93   d = a;
```

253

```
 94    PrintArray (d, "Testing Assignmment", "0 1 2 3 4 5 6 7 8 9");
 95
 96    // testing passing and returning copies of the array
 97    Array e = Fun (a);
 98    PrintArray (e, "Testing Returned Array", "1 2 3 4 5 6 7 8 9");
 99
100    // testing dumb assignment
101    e = e;
102    PrintArray (e, "Testing e = e assignment",
103              "1 2 3 4 5 6 7 8 9");
104
105    // testing assignment of empty arrays
106    Array h, j;
107    j = h;
108    PrintArray (h,
109        "Testing assignment of empty arrays - Original Array",
110        "empty");
111    PrintArray (j,
112        "Testing assignment of empty arrays - Duplicate Array",
113        "empty");
114
115  }
116
117  // check for memory leaks
118  if (_CrtDumpMemoryLeaks())
119   cerr << "Memory leaks occurred!\n";
120  else
121   cerr << "No memory leaks.\n";
122
123  return 0;
124 }
125
126 /**********************************************************/
127 /*                                                        */
128 /* PrintArray: helper function to create a standard       */
129 /*             display of results                         */
130 /*                                                        */
131 /**********************************************************/
132
133 void PrintArray (const Array& a, const char* title,
134                  const char* shouldBe) {
135  cout << endl << title << endl
136      << "Should Be:   " << shouldBe << endl
137      << "Actually Is: ";
138  int* ptrInt;
139  long i;
140  if (a.GetNumberOfElements () == 0) {
141   cout << "empty\n";
142   return;
143  }
```

```
144   for (i=0; i<a.GetNumberOfElements (); i++) {
145    ptrInt = (int*) a.GetAt (i);
146    if (!ptrInt)
147     cout << "Error Invalid ptr at" << i << endl;
148    else
149     cout << *ptrInt << " ";
150   }
151   cout << endl;
152  }
153
154  /************************************************************/
155  /*                                                        */
156  /* Fun: function that is passed a copy of an Array and    */
157  /*               that returns a copy of an Array          */
158  /*                                                        */
159  /************************************************************/
160
161  Array Fun (Array f) {
162   PrintArray (f, "Testing Fun's Parameter Copy of Array",
163             "0 1 2 3 4 5 6 7 8 9");
164   Array g;
165   g = f;
166   g.RemoveAt (0);
167   PrintArray (g, "Testing Fun's To Be Returned Array",
168             "1 2 3 4 5 6 7 8 9");
169   return g;
170  }
171
```

Here is the output from the tester program.

```
Tester Program Results

 1
 2 Testing Add
 3 Should Be:   1 2 3 4 5 6 7 8 9 10
 4 Actually Is: 1 2 3 4 5 6 7 8 9 10
 5
 6 Testing InsertAt
 7 Should Be:   0 49 1 2 3 4 5 6 7 8 9 10 11 12
 8 Actually Is: 0 49 1 2 3 4 5 6 7 8 9 10 11 12
 9
10 Testing RemoveAt
11 Should Be:   49 1 2 3 4 6 7 8 9 10 11
12 Actually Is: 49 1 2 3 4 6 7 8 9 10 11
13
14 Testing RemoveAll
15 Should Be:   empty
16 Actually Is: empty
17 Array: RemoveAt Error - element out of range
```

```
18          It was 42 and numElements is 0
19
20 Testing Empty Array
21 Should Be:   empty
22 Actually Is: empty
23
24 Testing InsertAt
25 Should Be:   9 8 7 6 5 4 3 2 1 0
26 Actually Is: 9 8 7 6 5 4 3 2 1 0
27
28 Testing InsertAt
29 Should Be:   9 8 7 6 5 4 3 2 1 0
30 Actually Is: 9 8 7 6 5 4 3 2 1 0
31
32 Testing InsertAt
33 Should Be:   0 1 2 3 4 5 6 7 8 9
34 Actually Is: 0 1 2 3 4 5 6 7 8 9
35
36 Testing Copy Ctor
37 Should Be:   0 1 2 3 4 5 6 7 8 9
38 Actually Is: 0 1 2 3 4 5 6 7 8 9
39
40 Testing Copy Ctor
41 Should Be:   0 1 2 3 4 5 6 7 8 9
42 Actually Is: 0 1 2 3 4 5 6 7 8 9
43
44 Testing Assignmment
45 Should Be:   0 1 2 3 4 5 6 7 8 9
46 Actually Is: 0 1 2 3 4 5 6 7 8 9
47
48 Testing Fun's Parameter Copy of Array
49 Should Be:   0 1 2 3 4 5 6 7 8 9
50 Actually Is: 0 1 2 3 4 5 6 7 8 9
51
52 Testing Fun's To Be Returned Array
53 Should Be:   1 2 3 4 5 6 7 8 9
54 Actually Is: 1 2 3 4 5 6 7 8 9
55
56 Testing Returned Array
57 Should Be:   1 2 3 4 5 6 7 8 9
58 Actually Is: 1 2 3 4 5 6 7 8 9
59
60 Testing e = e assignment
61 Should Be:   1 2 3 4 5 6 7 8 9
62 Actually Is: 1 2 3 4 5 6 7 8 9
63
64 Testing assignment of empty arrays - Original Array
65 Should Be:   empty
66 Actually Is: empty
67
```

```
68 Testing assignment of empty arrays - Duplicate Array
69 Should Be:    empty
70 Actually Is: empty
71 No memory leaks.
```

We now have a very useful class. Any time any program needs to store an array of items, no matter what those items actually are, we can use an instance of **Array** to hold them. One never again needs to worry about exceeding an arbitrary array bounds.

However, this class is very inefficient when storing large numbers of items. Consider the **Add()** function implementation. Suppose that 10,000 items were consecutively added by the client program. How many times will the temporary array be allocated and all previous items copied? Worse still, during the add process, we have allocated in memory both the current array and the temporary larger array before the current array gets deleted. Done so many times, this can fragment the free memory pool. The result is that as the number of items in the array increases, the poorer the performance of our **Array** class add operations.

This serious design problem can be rectified by adding two new members to the class. If a user knew that there were likely to be at least 10,000 items to be added, when they initially allocate the array, allow them to specify an initial size for the array. Further, every time the array needs to be grown, we are adding only one element. Suppose we let the user specify a grow by value. Here is how the default constructor's prototype could be redesigned.

```
Array (long initialSize = 0, long growBy = 1);
```

By using the default arguments, the client can create instances as follows.

```
Array a;               // initial size = 1, grow by 1
Array b (10000);       // initial size = 10000, grow by 1
Array c (10000, 100);  // initial size = 10000, grow by 100
```

Naturally, the revised **Array** class would be a bit more complex to implement. This is the topic of one of the programming exercises below.

Inline Functions

An **inline** function is a function for which the compiler actually substitutes the function body in the calling program and does not actually create a function of that name in the resulting program. In other words, the compiler bypasses all of the function calling overhead by placing what would have been the function's body directly in the client's code at the point the function would have been invoked. The idea is to speed up the client program by reducing the function calling overhead of that function. However, please use caution with inline functions. In the client program, wherever that inline function is used, the compiler places another copy of the function body. Thus, if the client calls an inline function from 100 locations, then there are 100 copies of that function's body in the client program. Its exe size has grown but it runs faster.

Inlining should only be used on very short functions, such as **GetNumberOfElements()** in our **Array** class. Inlining is only a request of the compiler. If the compiler feels it is not worth it or is too complex a body to inline, it will not inline that function.

Beginning Data Structures in C++

A function can be inlined in one of two ways. One is to code its body right there in the header file. In the industry, this is frowned upon because the clients of the class are going to have a copy of the header file. Thus, part of the actual class implementation is visible to the customers of the class. Further, the inclusion of coding details, clutters up the definition file which your users are studying. Inlining by coding the body directly in the header file is found in short magazine articles, academic areas and book examples. It is not done in the real world of production. The second method of inlining is used in production as shown shortly.

Here is an example of how inlining can be done in a header file.

File: Array.h

```
class Array {
...
Array () {
 numElements = 0;
 array = 0;
}
...
long GetNumberOfElements () const {
 return numElements;
}
...
~Array () {
 RemoveAll ();
}
...
```

The second method uses the **inline** keyword in the header file function prototypes. Note that the **inline** keyword is not found in the implementation file function headers. Also note that you must include a separate file that contains these inline function's implementations. So you now have three Array files.

File: Array.h

```
class Array {
...
inline Array ();
...
inline long GetNumberOfElements () const;
...
inline ~Array ();
...
};
#include "Array.inl"
```

And here is the corresponding inline implementation file.

File: Array.inl

```
Array::Array () {
 numElements = 0;
 array = 0;
}
...
long Array::GetNumberOfElements () const {
```

```
 return numElements;
}
...
Array::~Array () {
 RemoveAll ();
}
...
```

All non-inlined functions are found in the normal Array.cpp file.

If you want to use **inline** functions, first get the entire class fully operational and error free. Then simply add the **inline** keyword before the function prototypes that you wish to inline (in the header file).

Making Production Libraries

When a class is fully operational, it is often put into production in a shared library of classes. The file extension of these is .lib. Users are given the header file and the lib file which with to link. The Visual C++ compiler can make such a lib file for us. When you choose File-New Project, instead of choosing Win32 Console Application, choose instead Win32 Static Library. Make the folder as usual and then copy the header and implementation files that you desire to be part of the library package into that project folder. Right click on the project in Project View and choose Add Files to Project. (In the series of dialogs that appear, do not check Pre-compiled Header or MFC Support. Build the project. Then use Explorer to examine the Debug or Release folders of the project. There you will find the .lib file.

One would copy the .lib file and place it in the company production lib folder. In the case of student programs, copy it and place it in the project folder of the program that wishes to use it.

On the samples disk, in folder **Pgm08b**, there is a project setup to build the .lib version of our **Array** class.

Also in folder **Pgm08c**, I have created a project that uses our new .lib file. You must use Project Options-Link tab and add this new .lib file to the Object/library modules edit box. Since it is now in the project folder, I just used the name **Pgm08b.lib**. Please examine these projects and see how this is done, especially how the lib file is specified in the Link tab of Project Options.

A Practical Example Illustrating How Client Programs Must Use the Array Class (Pgm08d)

Finally, we need to examine just how a real client program would make use of the Array class and its void pointers, in particular. Let's rework the Orders Processing Program from Chapter 6, **Pgm06a**. Recall that the data contained in a variable number of daily sales input files needed to be summarized. We used a growable array of **ORDER** structures in program 6, so now we replace that array with an instance of our new Array class. I've highlighted in bold face the changes needed.

First, here is the output form the program.

```
Output from Pgm08d

 1 Acme Weekly Sales Summary Report
 2
 3    Item        Qty           Total
 4   Number       Sold           Cost
 5
 6   23453        100      $  4250.00
 7    3453       1000      $ 50100.00
 8    4354        100      $  6065.00
 9     253        200      $  2020.00
10   54333         50      $  1667.50
11   54453         50      $  1667.50
12                         ----------
13                         $ 65770.00
14 No memory leaks.
```

Here are the two header files.

```
Date.h

 1 #pragma once
 2
 3 /******************************/
 4 /*                            */
 5 /* Acme Standard DATE structure */
 6 /*                            */
 7 /******************************/
 8
 9 struct DATE {
10   short month;
11   short day;
12   short year;
13 };
14
```

```
Order.h

 1 #pragma once
 2
 3 #include "Date.h"  // needed for the orderDate member
 4
 5 /**********************************************************/
 6 /*                                                        */
 7 /* Acme Standard ORDER structure                          */
```

260

```
 8 /*                                                              */
 9 /**************************************************************/
10
11 struct ORDER {
12
13   long    invoiceNum;   // the customer's invoice number
14   long    customerNum;  // the customer's account number
15   DATE    orderDate;    // the date of this order
16   long    itemNum;      // the item number of the product purchased
17   short   quantity;     // the quantity purchased
18   double  unitCost;     // the price of one of these items
19   double  tax;          // the tax charged on this order
20   double  totalCost;    // the total cost of this order
21 };
22
```

Here is **Pgm08d**. Note bold face changes.

```
Pgm08d.cpp
```

```
 1 #include <iostream>
 2 #include <iomanip>
 3 #include <fstream>
 4 #include <crtdbg.h>
 5 using namespace std;
 6
 7 #include "Order.h"
 8 #include "Array.h"
 9
10 ifstream* ProcessCommandLine (int argc, char* argv[]);
11
12 void       LoadFile (Array& orders, ifstream& infile);
13
14 ifstream& InputAnOrder (ifstream& infile, ORDER& order);
15
16
17 // helper structure for summary totals
18 const int MAXITEMS = 100;
19
20 struct SALESSUMMARY {
21   long    itemnumber;
22   long    totalQty;
23   double totalCost;
24 };
25
26 void SummarizeData (const Array& orders, SALESSUMMARY totals[],
27                     int& numTotals);
28
```

```
29 int  MatchItemNumber (const SALESSUMMARY totals[], int numTotals,
30                        long matchItemNum);
31 const int NOMATCH = -1;
32
33 void  PrintReport (const SALESSUMMARY totals[], int numTotals);
34
35 /*****************************************************************/
36 /*                                                               */
37 /* Pgm08d: Produce Weekly Sales Summary Report                   */
38 /*                                                               */
39 /*****************************************************************/
40
41 int main (int argc, char* argv[]) {
42 { // extra block to force all destructors to be called before
43   // checking for memory leaks
44
45   // construct an array of opened daily sales files
46   ifstream* files = ProcessCommandLine (argc, argv);
47
48   int   numFiles = argc-1;  // the number of files to process
49   Array orders;             // the growable array of orders
50   int   i;
51
52   // load all of the orders from all of the files
53   for (i=0; i<numFiles; i++) {
54    LoadFile (orders, files[i]);
55    files[i].close ();
56   }
57   //remove the files array as it is no longer needed
58   delete [] files;
59
60   // the summarized data helper structure
61   SALESSUMMARY totals[MAXITEMS];
62   int          numTotals = 0;
63
64   // go summarize all of the order data
65   SummarizeData (orders, totals, numTotals);
66   // remove the orders array as it is not needed further
67   ORDER* ptrorder;
68   for (i=0; i<orders.GetNumberOfElements(); i++) {
69    ptrorder = (ORDER*) orders.GetAt (i);
70    if (ptrorder) delete ptrorder;
71   }
72   orders.RemoveAll ();
73
74   // finally, display the summarized data
75   PrintReport (totals, numTotals);
76 }
77
```

```
 78  // check for memory leaks
 79  if (_CrtDumpMemoryLeaks())
 80   cerr << "Memory leaks occurred!\n";
 81  else
 82   cerr << "No memory leaks.\n";
 83
 84  return 0;
 85  }
 86
 87  /****************************************************************/
 88  /*                                                            */
 89  /* ProcessCommandLine: verify command line is a proper one    */
 90  /*    consisting of one or more daily sales filenames         */
 91  /*                                                            */
 92  /*    build an array of ifstream objects and attempt to open  */
 93  /*    all of the files                                        */
 94  /*                                                            */
 95  /*    if any file cannot be opened, display an error message  */
 96  /*    that includes that incorrect name and abort the program */
 97  /*                                                            */
 98  /*    returns the address of the files array if all is ok     */
 99  /*                                                            */
100  /****************************************************************/
101
102  ifstream* ProcessCommandLine (int argc, char* argv[]) {
103  // guard against no command line files
104  if (argc == 1) {
105   cerr << "Error: you must specify one or more daily sales"
106        << " filenames on the command line\n";
107   exit (1);
108  }
109
110  // allocate the array of file streams
111  ifstream* files = new (std::nothrow) ifstream [argc-1];
112  if (!files) {
113   cerr << "Error: out of memory for files\n";
114   exit (2);
115  }
116
117  int i;
118  // attempt to open each file
119  for (i=1; i<argc; i++) {
120   files[i-1].open (argv[i]);
121  }
122
123  // not display error messages for all that failed to open
124  bool ok = true;
125  for (i=1; i<argc; i++) {
126   if (!files[i-1]) {
127    cerr << "Error: unable to open daily sales file: "
```

```
128               << argv[i] << endl;
129    ok = false;
130    }
131  }
132
133  //if any failed to open, close all files and abort the program
134  if (!ok) {
135   for (i=1; i<argc; i++) {
136    files[i-1].close ();
137   }
138   delete [] files;
139   exit (2);
140  }
141
142  return files;
143 }
144
145 /*****************************************************************/
146 /*                                                             */
147 /* LoadFile: input all order records in the file and add them*/
148 /*           to the growable orders array                     */
149 /*         return the address of the new larger orders array  */
150 /*                                                             */
151 /*****************************************************************/
152
153 void    LoadFile (Array& orders, ifstream& infile) {
154  infile >> dec;            // allow for numbers with leading 0's
155  ORDER* ptrNewOrderJustInput = new (std::nothrow) ORDER;
156  if (!ptrNewOrderJustInput) {
157   cerr << "Error out of memory\n";
158   exit (1);
159  }
160
161  while (InputAnOrder (infile, *ptrNewOrderJustInput)) {
162   orders.Add (ptrNewOrderJustInput);
163   ptrNewOrderJustInput = new (std::nothrow) ORDER;
163a  if (!ptrNewOrderJustInput) {
163b   cerr << "Error out of memory\n";
163c   exit (1);
163d  }
164  }
165  delete ptrNewOrderJustInput;
166 }
167
168 /*****************************************************************/
169 /*                                                             */
170 /* InputAnOrder: input another set of order data               */
171 /*                                                             */
172 /*****************************************************************/
```

```
173
174  ifstream&  InputAnOrder (ifstream& infile, ORDER& order) {
175   char c; // for the / separating mm/dd/yyyy
176
177   infile >> order.invoiceNum >> order.customerNum
178          >> order.orderDate.month >> c
179          >> order.orderDate.day   >> c
180          >> order.orderDate.year
181          >> order.itemNum
182          >> order.quantity
183          >> order.unitCost
184          >> order.tax
185          >> order.totalCost;
186
187   return infile;
188  }
189
190  /***************************************************************/
191  /*                                                           */
192  /* SummarizeData: summarize the daily sales information      */
193  /*    builds the sales summary array which contains the item */
194  /*    number and the corresponding quantity and total sales  */
195  /*                                                           */
196  /*    For each order, search the table for a matching item   */
197  /*    number. If not found, add this item. If found, add to  */
198  /*    its quantity and total sales.                          */
199  /*                                                           */
200  /***************************************************************/
201
202  void SummarizeData (const Array& orders,
203                      SALESSUMMARY totals[], int& numTotals) {
204   int match;
205   for (long i=0; i<orders.GetNumberOfElements(); i++) {
206    ORDER* ptrorder = (ORDER*) orders.GetAt (i);
207    if (!ptrorder) continue;
208    match = MatchItemNumber (totals, numTotals, ptrorder->itemNum);
209    if (match == NOMATCH) {
209a    if (numTotals >= MAXITEMS) {
209b     cerr << "Summary array size exceeded!\n";
209c     exit (1);
209d    }
210    totals[numTotals].itemnumber = ptrorder->itemNum;
211    totals[numTotals].totalQty = ptrorder->quantity;
212    totals[numTotals].totalCost = ptrorder->totalCost;
213    numTotals++;
214    }
215    else {
216     totals[match].totalQty += ptrorder->quantity;
```

```
217      totals[match].totalCost += ptrorder->totalCost;
218    }
219  }
220 }
221
222 /****************************************************************/
223 /*                                                            */
224 /* MatchItemNumber: match an item number with the array item  */
225 /*                  numbers - if no match because this item   */
226 /*                  is not in the array, return NOMATCH       */
227 /*                  otherwise return the subscript of match   */
228 /*                                                            */
229 /****************************************************************/
230
231 int  MatchItemNumber (const SALESSUMMARY totals[], int numTotals,
232                       long matchItemNum) {
233  for (int i=0; i<numTotals; i++) {
234   if (totals[i].itemnumber == matchItemNum) return i;
235  }
236  return NOMATCH;
237 }
238
239 /****************************************************************/
240 /*                                                            */
241 /* PrintReport: display the summary report                    */
242 /*                                                            */
243 /****************************************************************/
244
245 void  PrintReport (const SALESSUMMARY totals[], int numTotals) {
246  // setup floating point output for dollars and cents
247  cout << fixed << setprecision (2);
249
250  // display heading and two column heading lines
251  cout << "Acme Weekly Sales Summary Report\n\n";
252  cout << "  Item         Qty           Total\n"
253       << " Number       Sold           Cost\n\n";
254
255  // accumulator for grand total sales
256  double grandTotal = 0;
257
258  // display each summary line and accumulate the total dales
259  for (int i=0; i<numTotals; i++) {
260   cout << setw (7) << totals[i].itemnumber
261        << setw (10) << totals[i].totalQty
262        << "      $" << setw (9) << totals[i].totalCost << endl;
263   grandTotal += totals[i].totalCost;
264  }
265
266  // display the grand total sales
267  cout << "                         ----------\n";
```

```
268  cout << "                         $"
269        << setw (10) << grandTotal << endl;
270 }
```

Review Questions

1. Why is **#ifndef/#define** logic used in header files? Show an example of circular headers that absolutely must have this logic in them or **main.cpp** will not compile.

2. What is the significance of the **this** pointer? What is its purpose? What use can we make of it in coding class member functions? What happens if the client program codes the following?
```
Point p;
this->SetCoordinates (42,10);
```

3. What is meant by operator overloading? Why is it needed? Which operators can be overloaded?

4. What is the difference between binary and unary operators? Give two examples of each.

5. For a class **Distance** that is to encapsulate a linear measurement, write the prototypes for the function required to allow the client to do the following.
```
Distance a, b, c;
a = b + 5;
c = a + b;
c = 1 + a;
```

6. For the **Distance** class above, assume that the only data member in the **Distance** class is called distance, a **double**. Write out the implementation for the three functions.

7. For the **Distance** class above, write the prototypes for the functions **operator==** and **operator+=**.

8. For the **Distance** class above, write the implementation of **operator+=**.

9. What is a friend function? Why are they needed? Show two very different situations in which friend functions are mandatory.

10. For the **Distance** class above, write the prototype for **operator>>** which inputs a single **double**.

11. What is meant by a copy constructor? Under what circumstances must a class provide an implementation of the copy constructor and the assignment operator? Why?

12. What is a class **enum**? How is it different than a normal C **enum**? Why are class **enums** useful?

13. Write a class **enum** called **Month** for use in a **Date** class. The **enum** values contain three letter abbreviations for the 12 month names such as Jan for example.

14. What is meant by a growable array? Why does storing the data as **void*** lead to a generic reuseable class?

Stop! Do These Exercises Before Programming

1. A programmer decided to implement a class called **Line**. He began with a simple header file shown below. What is syntactically wrong with it and what is non-optimum about the header file? Show how these can be corrected.
Line.h
```
struct Point {
  double x;
  double y;
}
class Line {
protected
  Point left;
  Point right;
public
  Line ();
  Line (const Point& l, const Point r);
}
```

2. The client program intends to use **Line** in the following manner only. No other variations are to be allowed.
```
Line a, b, c;
Point p;
a = b + 5;
a = b + p;
a = b - 4;
a = b - p;
```
When the addition operator is passed a number, it should add that value to both coordinates of the right

Point. When it is passed a **Point**, it should add the corresponding **Point** x and y values to the right **Point**. When the subtraction operator is called, it should subtract that value from both coordinates of the left **Point**. When it is passed a **Point**, it should subtract that **Point**'s x and y values from the corresponding values of the left **Point**. The programmer wrote the following four prototypes.

```
Line& operator+ (Point p);
Line& operator+ (double x);
Line& operator- (Point& p);
Line& operator- (const double x);
```

None of these is correct nor optimum in terms of efficiency. Correct all errors and inefficiencies in these prototypes.

3. The programmer went ahead and coded the following which does not work. Use the revised prototype from question 2 above and correct his errors.

```
Line& Line::operator+ (Point p) {
  Line a (*this);
  a.right += p;
  return a;
}
```

4. Similarly correct the following programmer coding.

```
Line& operator+ (double x) {
  Line a;
  a.left = left + x;
  a.right = right;
  return a;
}
```

5. Similarly correct the following programmer coding.

```
Line& Line::operator- (Point& p) {
  Line a (left, right);
  a.left.x += p.x;
  a.left.y += p.y;
  return *this;
}
```

6. Similarly correct the following programmer coding.

```
Line& Line::operator- (const double x) {
  Line a;
  a.left = left;
  a.right = right;
  left.x -= x;
  left.y -= x;
  return a;
}
```

7. Next, the programmer added prototypes for the insertion and extraction operators. His prototypes are in error. Correct them.

```
istream Operator>> (Line& l);
ostream operator<< (Line& l);
```

8. This time, the programmer believes he found his errors in his insertion operator and began its implementation as follows. Correct his errors.

```
ostream& Line::operator<< (const ostream& os,
            const Line& l) const {
  os.setf (ios::fixed, ios::floatfield);
  os << setprecision (2);
  os << "[(" << l.left.x << ", " << l.left.y << ")-("
     << l.right.y, << ", " << l.right.x << ")]";
}
```

9. After much work the programmer finally has this **Line** class operational. Now he turns his attention to the client drafting program which must store an unknown number of lines. He decides to use our **Array** container. Here is his beginning of the client program. When it runs, there is a massive memory leak. Correct his errors.

```
...
#include "Array.h"
int main () {
 {
  Array a;
  Line* ptrl;
  for (int k=0; k<100; k++) {
   ptrl = new Line;
   a.Add (ptrl);
  }
  a.RemoveAll();
 }
 memory leak checking here
```

Programming Problems

Problem Pgm08-1 The Piggy Bank Class

Write a class to encapsulate a child's piggy bank. Allow for pennies, nickels, dimes, quarters, half dollars and dollar coins. Also allow for unknown type coins because children often insert any kind of coin token into their piggy banks. Create a class **enum** called **CoinType** that defines a coin's type (dime, nickel and so on). The **PiggyBank** class needs to keep track of the number of each type of coin in the bank. Thus, you can make a **Coin** structure that contains the coin type, number of those coins and string name of the coin type and store an array of these in the **PiggyBank** class. Or you can design a class **Coin** that encapsulates this same information and store an array of **Coin** objects in the **PiggyBank** class.

Next, decide what member functions the **PiggyBank** class would need to have. Certainly it must have an **AddCoin()** function and some means of displaying the entire contents of the **PiggyBank**. There must also be some way to remove a coin from the **PiggyBank**. See what other functions a **PiggyBank** ought to have.

After writing the class, create a testing oracle. Then write a client program to thoroughly test your **PiggyBank** class.

Problem Pgm08-2 The Revised Array Container Class

The **Array** class as presented in this chapter is very inefficient when storing large numbers of items. Consider the **Add()** function implementation. Suppose that 10,000 items were consecutively added by the client program. How many times is the temporary array allocated and all previous items copied? Worse still, during the add process, we have allocated in memory both the current array and the temporary larger array before the current array gets deleted. The result is that as the number of items in the array increases, the poorer the performance of our **Array** class add operations.

This serious design problem can be rectified by adding two new members to the class. If a user knew that there were likely to be at least 10,000 items to be added when they initially allocate the array, allow them to specify an initial size for the array. Further, every time the array needs to be grown, we are adding only one element. Suppose we let the user specify a grow by value. Here is how the default constructor's prototype should be redesigned.
```
Array (long initialSize = 0, long growBy = 1);
```
By using the default arguments, the client can create instances as follows.
```
Array a;              // initial size = 0, grow by 1
Array b (10000);      // initial size = 10000, grow by 1
Array c (10000, 100); // initial size = 10000, grow by 100
```
Redesign the **Array** class to store two additional member variables, **initialSize** and **growBy**. After you have implemented these changes to all necessary functions, test it with the **Pgm08a.cpp** tester program. If it passes that test, then retest it by specifying various initial sizes and grow by values.

Once you are convinced that the new **Array** class is fully functional, then let's compare just how much more efficient the new version actually is. In the **TestDataForAssignments' Chapter08** folder, find the program **Pgm08d.cpp**. Make a new project and copy **Pgm08d.cpp** and your **Array.h** and **Array.cpp** files into this new project folder. Make a Release build and run the program. It displays the total amount of time in seconds that it takes to construct an array of 10,000 items. It compares an initial size of 0 and grow by of 1 with 1000, 100 and 10000, 100. You should be able to see the difference your implementation has made, hopefully for the better.

Problem Pgm08-3 A Checkbook Class

With electronic checking becoming more popular, design a Checkbook class to manage an account electronically.

Assume that a check contains the person's name and account number, the check number, to whom the check is written, the date, and the amount. A deposit slip contains the person's name and account number, the deposit number, the date, and the amount.

The default constructor, **Checkbook()**, initializes all fields to reasonable defaults, such as zero. Additionally, no other operations on an account whose account number is 0 are permitted until **Setup()** is called. **Setup()** is passed the person's name, account number, and the initial deposit. Provide an overloaded constructor that takes the person's name, account number, and the initial deposit.

With all financial type operations, a transaction's log is essential to maintain an account's history. Thus, the overloaded constructor and **Setup()** must take an additional parameter, the name of this customer's transaction log file. The first line in the log file should contain the information passed to **Setup()** or the overloaded constructor. Thus, after initializing the member data, these functions should open the transaction's log file and write that first line of data and then close the file.

Assume check and deposit numbers begin with number 100. Member operational functions consist of **GetBalance()**, **MakeDeposit()** and **WriteCheck()**. These functions should perform the indicated actions. In addition, **MakeDeposit()** and **WriteCheck()** must also reopen the transaction's log and append an additional line with the relevant deposit or check information.

Another operation is **DisplayHistory()**. This function opens the transaction log file and displays a report of the initial state and the account activities.

Write a tester program that thoroughly tests the **Checkbook** class.

Problem Pgm08-4 A Distance Class

A linear distance is to be encapsulated in a **Distance** class. The only data member is the distance stored as a double in millimeters. Users frequently will wish to use other units of measurement than millimeters. Create a class enum **DistType** that contains **Millimeters, Meters, Kilometers, Inches, Feet, Yards**, and **Miles**. Note that the distance stored in the data member is always in millimeters. Your functions must convert to and from the desired user units.

There should be two constructors. The default constructor stores zero millimeters. The overloaded constructor takes a distance and the **DistType**. Clients could code the following for example.

```
Distance a;
Distance b (1, Distance::Miles);
Distance c (42.6, Distance::Kilometers);
```

The constructor must convert the distance from the indicated units into millimeters and store it in the data member.

Provide a **GetDistance()** function which is passed an instance of **DistType**. The function returns the distance that is stored converted into whatever units are specified in the **DistType** parameter. For example, the user might code

```
cout << a.GetDistance (Distance::Miles);
```

Here the function must return the stored distance in millimeters converted temporarily into miles.

Provide a **SetDistance()** function that is passed a distance and an instance of **DistType** which tells what units this passed distance is in. For example, the caller might code

```
a.SetDistance (42.1, Distance::Kilometers);
```

And you need to convert the 42.1 from kilometers into millimeters and store it in the data member.

Implement the following overloaded operator functions, +. -. >> and <<. The following are all correct usage of these operators.

```
Distance a, b, c, d;
a = b + 5;
c = d + b;
a = b - 5;
c = a - b;
cin >> a;
cout << b;
```

Do not implement this version:

```
a = 1 + b;
```

The extraction operator inputs a double that is always assumed to be in millimeters. The insertion operator always outputs the distance in millimeters using a precision of 6 digits.

Design a testing oracle and write a tester program to thoroughly test the **Distance** class. You may use whatever conversion constants you desire. If nothing else, there are 25.4 millimeters in an inch.

Problem Pgm08-5 Using the Array Container Class

In chapter 7, you may have written the **Employee** class. Recall that Acme Corporation wanted a class to encapsulate their employee workforce. The **Employee** class contains the employee first and last name strings which should include a maximum of 10 and 20 characters respectively. The date he/she was hired should be stored as three **short**s. His/her job title is a string of up to 20 characters. His/her age and sex should be stored as **char** fields. His/her pay rate is stored in a **double** and the pay type is a **char** containing an H or S for hourly or salaried. If he/she is an hourly worker, the pay rate is the hourly rate. If he/she is a salaried worker, the pay rate is the uniform amount that he/she is paid each week. Finally, hie/her employee id number is stored as a **long**.

If you did write that class, you may reuse the entire class as-is with **no** alterations whatsoever in this problem. If you did not write that class, then define a structure called **EMPLOYEE** that contains the above information.

In this problem you are to write the client program only that produces the client Weekly Pay Report. Use the file that came with the book called **Problem7-2-WeeklyPay.txt** as the input file. The pay program inputs all of the employee records into an array of **Employee** objects. Use the **Array** class from this chapter with **no** changes whatsoever made to it. With the array loaded, for each employee in the array, calculate and print their pay as shown below.

```
                  Acme Weekly Payroll Report
Employee  First      Last               Date        Weekly
   Id     Name       Name               Hired       Pay

 1123123  John       Jones              05/12/1994 $9999.99
...
Total Payroll -------------------------------> $999999.99
```
The last line represents the total amount that all of the employees are paid. Again, assume that each employee worked 40 hours this week.

Finally, add in memory leak checking to make very sure that your program has no memory leaks.

Chapter 9—Linked Lists—Single

Introduction

In chapter 5 the basic concepts of linked lists were presented. Let's review what we know about them. A list is a linear data structure that is accessed sequentially. The first item in the list is located at the **head** of the list, while the last item in the list is located at the **tail**. Each item in the list points to the next item in the list by some means. These are known as **single linked lists**. In other lists, each item also points to the previous item in the list. These are known as **double linked lists** and are the topic of the next chapter. There are no arbitrary maximum number of items in a list.

Each item in the list is called a **node**. A node contains the client's data in some manner and the physical linking mechanism forward to the next node in the list and is known as **chaining**. Figure 9.1 shows the general nature of a single linked list.

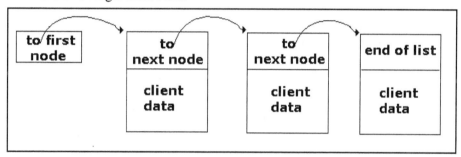

Figure 9.1 General Single Linked List

A way to find the first node in the list must always exist. A number of mechanisms are available for tracking the next node. Likewise there are different ways that the client's data can be stored. One could implement the entire list as an array and use subscripts for the "to next node" implementation. However, since this text is an introduction to data structures and not a compendium on all possibilities, I focus solely on using pointers to handle the "to next node" situation and use dynamic memory allocation to create the nodes. This specific choice does not introduce an arbitrary upper limit to the number of nodes in the list and makes the list very flexible and extensible.

Typical implementations of a list data structure maintain a pointer, often called **headptr**, that points to the first node in the list. Each node in the list contains a pointer, often called **fwdptr**, that points to the next node in the list. When a node's **fwdptr** is 0, there are no further items in the list. Figure 9.2 illustrates the pointer mechanism for chaining.

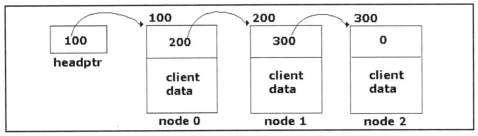

Figure 9.2 Using Pointers to Point to the Next Node

In order to iterate sequentially through a list, the list data structure must maintain a pointer to the current node in the list, for example, called **currentptr**. This current node in the list pointer is called a **cursor**, something that marks a current location. The cursor can also be called an **iterator** in the literature.

In practice, the amount of memory available to a program becomes the limiting factor on the number of items that can be in a list. Here is the definition of single linked list data structure.

Data Type	List Data Structure
Domain	Each list has 1). A collection of component values each of the same data type 2). A cursor to mark the current position in the list and whose values can range from 1 to N+1 where N is the number of items currently in the list.
Structure	A linear, sequential access data structure of varying length
Operations	Note: the C++ function names I have used can be called by many similar names.
Initialize()	Initialize to an empty list (In an ADT, this is usually done in the constructor.)
AddAtHead()	Add an item at the head of the list
InsertAt()	Add an item at the cursor location
Next()	Move sequentially to the next item in the list
ResetToHead()	Reset the cursor to the beginning of the list
IsHead()	Is the cursor at the head of the list?
RemoveAt()	Remove the item at the cursor from the list Sometimes this function is called EmptyList().
GetCurrent()	Get the item at the cursor
IsEmpty()	Is the list empty?
Empty()	Remove all items from the list

Table 9.1 The Single Linked List Data Structure Definition

I have provided quite a few operational functions. More robust applications might provide even more operations on the list. In simpler applications, not all of these operations I gave must be implemented. Further, I tried to use reasonably descriptive names for the functions. The actual names used in specific implementations vary considerably; their purpose and functionality do not. As you look over these functions and the figures, notice that it would be exceedingly difficult to permit a list to be accessed by direct methods. How would the list find the ith item? It would have to move the cursor sequentially forward through the list, counting items until it came to the ith one!

How are single linked lists structurally built? Perhaps the crudest method that uses pointers would be to use straight C style coding with the head pointer stored as a global variable so that all the operations functions can easily access it. However, I use ADTs or classes to encapsulate the linked list. A class is an ideal tool because the head pointer and current node pointers can be protected data members and thus easily access by all of the operational member functions.

We are going to begin with a very simplified single linked list class written specifically for one single application. This way, the actual implementation details can be more readily understood by the beginner. Then, we will experiment with ways to improve the implementation. Our goal, as always, is to arrive at a generic, reusable linked list class.

Maintaining a Student Class Roster as a Single Linked List

Maintaining a class roster is an ideal application for a list. In this sample, the class called **StudentRoster** is built to meet the specifics of the problem and is anything but generic. The problem is fairly simple in nature. A file of the students that are currently enrolled in a class is loaded into a list. Then, throughout the day, when new students sign up for the class, they are added to the list. When other students drop the class, they are removed from the list. At the end of the day, an updated roster file is written. At any point in time, a complete class roster can be displayed. Figure 9.3 shows the roster list after three students have been added.

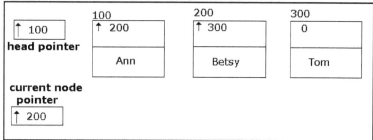

Figure 9.3 Student Roster Single Linked List

Let's begin our design examining how we can store the data. There are many approaches that can be used. Let's use the simplest. Define a **Student** structure to hold the information about one student as follows.

```
const int NAME_LEN = 21;
struct Student {
 char name[NAME_LEN];
```

```
 long ssno;
 char grade;
};
```
The data that the client program wishes to store is contained in the **Student** structure.

What would be the simplest node definition? Again, using a structure works well. The simplest practical definition of the student link list node would be given by **StudentNode**:
```
struct StudentNode {
 StudentNode* fwdptr;
 Student      student;
};
```
Note the data type for the forward pointer. It is a pointer to one of these same **StudentNode** structures.

Now given these structures, what would be the single data member of the **StudentRoster** link list class? It is the member **headptr** and it must point to the first node in the list. This member pointer is of data type **StudentNode**. In this first example, we do not even need a current pointer. With just this one data member, we can totally solve the problem. The only action that the **StudentRoster()** constructor must do is set **headptr** to 0 indicating an empty list.

The first action that the client program is likely to request is to load the list from a file of students already enrolled in the class. Note that I make the assumption that all data in the file are correct - that the program does need not to check for bad input from the file. (In the real world, this is not always a wise thing to assume, but it helps simplify this program so we can concentrate on the link list portion.) What information would the member function **LoadAllStudents()** function likely need? The filename that contains the student information is required. That is its only parameter. How do we design **LoadAllStudents()**? It involves a fairly complex series of actions, so let's functionally decompose this member function. Notice that Top-down design or functional decomposition applies equally to class member functions.

LoadAllStudents() involved opening and reading a file of data until EOF is detected. Each student record must be input. Each student must be added to the list. So logically, two subfunctions appear: **InputStudentData()** and **AddStudentAtHead()**. The first function is responsible for the actual file input of a single student's data into a **Student** structure instance. The second function is then passed that structure instance and adds that student to the list.

The large scale processing steps of **LoadAllStudents()** are as shown below.
```
void StudentRoster::LoadAllStudents (const char* filename) {
 Student s;
 ... open the file, etc.
 while (InputStudentData (infile, s)) {
  AddStudentAtHead (s);
 }
 infile.close ();
}
```

The implementation of **InputStudentData()** is just a straightforward input from a file operation. What steps does the function **AddStudentAtHead(),** which is passed the just inputted **Student** structure instance, involve? The first action must be to acquire a new **StudentNode** instance. Then, that instance's **Student** portion should be filled with the passed new student data. Finally, the new node must be added at the head of the list. Notice how easy it is to copy the entire structure's data in one line of coding.

```
void StudentRoster::AddStudentAtHead (const Student& s) {
// allocate a new node
StudentNode* ptrnew = new (std::nothrow) StudentNode;

ptrnew->student = s; // copy the passed student information
ptrnew->fwdptr = 0;  // set the forward pointer to 0

// now chain this one into the list
// if headptr exists, then our new fwdptr contains the
// address of the previous one in the list
if (headptr)
 ptrnew->fwdptr = headptr;

// set the headptr to this newly added
headptr = ptrnew;   one
}
```

Figure 9.4 shows this chaining operation for the first two students that were input and added to the list.

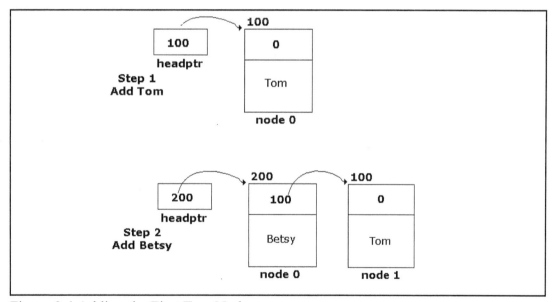

Figure 9.4 Adding the First Two Nodes

Next, let's examine perhaps the hardest function to implement—the **InsertAfter()** function. The function is given the social security number on which to match. If a match is found, the function is to insert the passed student data after this matching one. This, in effect, appears to move all those nodes that are to the right of the matching node on down to the right by one node. However, two situations can arise. If the list is empty, we cannot find a matching number. Also, if the number to match is not in the list, what do we do? In this case, to simplify matters for the client program, I have adopted the approach that **InsertAfter()** will always insert the new node somewhere. Thus, if the list is empty or no matching number is found, I add the new node at the head. In reality, one could return an error code and let the client program work out what it wishes to do next. However, doing so here overly complicates the program. I wish our full attention to be on the list construction.

The **InsertAfter()** function illustrates how a list can be traversed as well as how matching criteria can be handled. Here is the start of the function. Notice how I leverage already existing coding by invoking **AddStudentAtHead()**.

```
void StudentRoster::InsertAfter (long ssn,
                                    const Student& s) {
  // if list is empty, add at head
  if (!headptr)
    AddStudentAtHead (s);
  else {
  // traverse the list looking for this ssn
```

To traverse the list without having a current pointer and a **Next()** function, we must have a working pointer, here called **ptrstudent**, which is a pointer to the **StudentNode** structure. It is initialized to **headptr** which is non-zero at this point. As long as **ptrstudent** is non-zero, we have another node to check. When it finally becomes zero, we have reached the end of the list.

```
    StudentNode* ptrstudent = headptr; // set to start of list
    while (ptrstudent) {   // repeat if not at the end of list
```

Within the loop, check for a matching number. Notice the syntax required to access the structure member.

```
      if (ptrstudent->student.ssno == ssn) // have we found it?
        break;                          // yes, end the loop
```

If the student at this node does not match, move down one node in the list by resetting **ptrstudent** to the forward pointer.

```
      ptrstudent = ptrstudent->fwdptr; // no, point to next one
      }
```

When the loop ends, one of two situations must exist. If **ptrstudent** is zero, then we did not find any matching number. Alternatively, if **ptrstudent** is not zero, then it is pointing to the matching node. If none was found, simply add the new student to the head. Alternatively, you could report an error situation at this point.

```
    if (!ptrstudent)      // did not find this ssn in the list
      AddStudentAtHead (s);// so add it at the head
    else {
    // we have found the matching ssn pointed to by ptrstudent
```

The next step is to allocate a new **StudentNode** and fill it up with the new student data to be added.

```
    StudentNode* ptrnew = new (std::nothrow) StudentNode;
    ptrnew->student = s;
```

And finally, we must chain the new node into the list. The new node's forward pointer must be what was in the matching node's forward pointer. Then the matching node's forward pointer must point to this new node.

```
    ptrnew->fwdptr = ptrstudent->fwdptr;
    ptrstudent->fwdptr = ptrnew;
```

These steps are illustrated in Figure 9.5 below. Notice how the new node Ann is chained into the list's forward pointers.

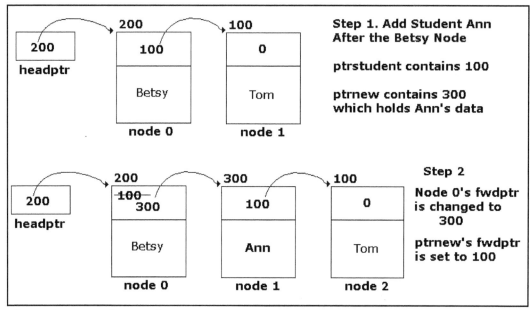

Figure 9.5 Inserting Node Ann After Node Betsy

Next, let's examine how the destructor is coded. We already have seen how to traverse the list. The destructor must traverse the list and delete each node in turn. However, we must check for an empty list.

```
StudentRoster::~StudentRoster () {
 if (!headptr) return;
 StudentNode* ptrnext = headptr; // ptr to traverse the list
 StudentNode* ptrdel;            // the node to delete
 // traverse the list - ends when there are no more nodes
 while (ptrnext) {
  ptrdel = ptrnext;         // save current one to be deleted
  ptrnext = ptrdel->fwdptr;// point to the next node
   delete ptrdel;           // and delete the previous node
```

Notice that we must save the current node to be deleted because we must reset **ptrnext** to its **fwdptr** before we delete it.

Finally, let's examine how the client can process a student who drops the course. The **DeleteThisStudent()** function is called and is passed the social security number of the student to find and delete from the list. Again, do nothing if the list is empty. We must again traverse the list looking for a match on the number. The coding begins as follows.

```
void StudentRoster::DeleteThisStudent (long ssn) {
 // check for an empty list and do nothing if empty
 if (!headptr) return;
 // iterate through list looking for this ssn
 StudentNode* ptrThisStudent = headptr;
 StudentNode* ptrPrevStudent = 0;
```

```
    while (ptrThisStudent) {
      if (ptrThisStudent->student.ssno == ssn)
        break;
```

However, there is a complication. Examine Figure 9.5 once more. Suppose that we are to delete the Ann-node. When we find that node, its address is in **ptrThisStudent**. However, we cannot just delete this node. What about the forward chain? The previous Betsy-node is still pointing to the Ann-node. We must reset the Betsy-node's forward pointer to Ann's forward pointer which is to the Tom-node. Thus as we iterate through the list, I keep track of the previous node as shown.

```
      ptrPrevStudent = ptrThisStudent;
      ptrThisStudent = ptrThisStudent->fwdptr;
    }
    // if ptrThisStudent is 0, it was not found, do nothing
    if (!ptrThisStudent) return; // there is no matching node
```

At this point, I sort out whether or not there is a previous node.

```
 if (headptr == ptrThisStudent) // at head, so no previous Node
  headptr = ptrThisStudent->fwdptr;
 else // set previous fwdptr to this's fwdptr to rechain
  ptrPrevStudent->fwdptr = ptrThisStudent->fwdptr;
 // now delete this found Node
 delete ptrThisStudent;
```

Here are the completed **StudentRoster** definition and implementation files. Look them over and then we will examine the client program that uses this class.

```
StudentRoster.h Definition of StudentRoster Class

 1 #pragma once
 2
 3 /************************************************************/
 4 /*                                                        */
 5 /* StudentRoster class                                    */
 6 /*                                                        */
 7 /* Maintain a list of students who are enrolled in a      */
 8 /* course                                                 */
 9 /*                                                        */
10 /* No checking is done for any out of memory errors       */
11 /*                                                        */
12 /************************************************************/
13
14 const int NAME_LEN = 21;
15
16 /************************************************************/
17 /*                                                        */
18 /* Student: contains the client's student data            */
19 /*                                                        */
20 /************************************************************/
21
22 struct Student {
23   char name[NAME_LEN];
```

```
24  long ssno;
25  char grade;
26 };
27
28 /*****************************************************/
29 /*                                               */
30 /* StudentNode: the list node structure          */
31 /*                                               */
32 /*****************************************************/
33
34 struct StudentNode {
35  StudentNode* fwdptr;  // points to the next node in the list
36  Student      student; // contains the actual client data
37 };
38
39 class StudentRoster {
40
41  /*****************************************************/
42  /*                                               */
43  /* class data                                    */
44  /*                                               */
45  /*****************************************************/
46
47 private:
48  StudentNode* headptr;
49
50  /*****************************************************/
51  /*                                               */
52  /* class functions                               */
53  /*                                               */
54  /*****************************************************/
55
56 public:
57          StudentRoster ();
58          ~StudentRoster ();
59
60  void    LoadAllStudents (const char* filename);
61  void    AddStudentAtHead (const Student& s);
62 protected:
63  istream& InputStudentData (istream& infile, Student& s);
64
65 public:
66  void PrintAllStudents (ostream& outfile) const;
67  void PrintThisStudent (ostream& outfile, const Student& s)const;
68  void WriteNewFile (const char* filename) const;
69
70  Student* FindThisStudent (long ssn) const;
71  void    InsertAfter (long ssn, const Student& s);
72  void    DeleteThisStudent (long ssn);
73 };
```

283

```
StudentRoster.cpp Implementation of StudentRoster Class

 1 #include <iostream>
 2 #include <iomanip>
 3 #include <fstream>
 4 using namespace std;
 5 #include "StudentRoster.h"
 6
 7 /*****************************************************/
 8 /*                                                   */
 9 /* StudentRoster: constructor to set list to empty   */
10 /*                                                   */
11 /*****************************************************/
12
13 StudentRoster::StudentRoster () {
14   headptr = 0;
15 }
16
17 /*****************************************************/
18 /*                                                   */
19 /* ~StudentRoster: destructor to empty the list      */
20 /*                                                   */
21 /*****************************************************/
22
23 StudentRoster::~StudentRoster () {
24   if (!headptr) return;
25   StudentNode* ptrnext = headptr; // pointer to traverse the list
26   StudentNode* ptrdel;            // the node to delete
27   // traverse the list - ends when there are no more nodes
28   while (ptrnext) {
29     ptrdel = ptrnext;          // save the current one to be deleted
30     ptrnext = ptrdel->fwdptr;  // point to the next node
31     delete ptrdel;             // and delete the previous node
32   }
33 }
34
35 /*****************************************************/
36 /*                                                   */
37 /* LoadAllStudents: input a file of students into the list */
38 /*                                                   */
39 /*****************************************************/
40
41 void StudentRoster::LoadAllStudents (const char* filename) {
42   Student s;
43   ifstream infile (filename);
44   if (!infile) {
45     cerr << "StudentRoster Error - cannot open file "
```

```
46              << filename << endl;
47     return; // assume data is correct in the file
48     }
49     while (InputStudentData (infile, s)) {
50      AddStudentAtHead (s);
51     }
52     infile.close ();
53    }
54
55    /************************************************************/
56    /*                                                          */
57    /* InputStudentData: read in one set of student data        */
58    /*                                                          */
59    /************************************************************/
60
61    istream& StudentRoster::InputStudentData (istream& infile,
62                                              Student& s) {
63     // assumes that the file contains no bad data
64     infile >> ws;
65     if (!infile) return infile;
66     infile.get (s.name, sizeof (s.name));
67     if (!infile) return infile;
68     infile >> s.ssno >> s.grade;
69     return infile;
70    }
71
72    /************************************************************/
73    /*                                                          */
74    /* AddStudentAtHead: add this student at the head of list */
75    /*                                                          */
76    /************************************************************/
77
78    void StudentRoster::AddStudentAtHead (const Student& s) {
79     // allocate a new node and fill it up
80     StudentNode* ptrnew = new (std::nothrow) StudentNode;
81     if (!ptrnew) {
82      cerr << "Error: out of memory in AddStudentAtHead\n";
83      exit (1);
84     }
85     ptrnew->student = s; // copy the passed student information
86     ptrnew->fwdptr = 0;  // set the forward pointer to 0
87     // now chain this one into the list
88     if (headptr)                 // if headptr exists, then the new
89      ptrnew->fwdptr = headptr; // fwdptr contains the previous one
90     headptr = ptrnew;  // set the headptr to this newly added one
91    }
92
93    /************************************************************/
94    /*                                                          */
95    /* PrintAllStudents: display all of the students in list */
```

```
 96 /*                                                      */
 97 /*******************************************************/
 98
 99 void StudentRoster::PrintAllStudents (ostream& outfile) const {
100  StudentNode* ptrstudent = headptr;
101  while (ptrstudent) {
102   PrintThisStudent (outfile, ptrstudent->student);
103   ptrstudent = ptrstudent->fwdptr;
104  }
105 }
106
107 /*******************************************************/
108 /*                                                      */
109 /* PrintThisStudent: displays one set of student data  */
110 /*                                                      */
111 /*******************************************************/
112
113 void StudentRoster::PrintThisStudent (ostream& outfile,
114                                       const Student& s) const {
115  outfile << left << "     " << setw (25) << s.name
117          << right << setw (12) << s.ssno << setw (5)
118          << s.grade << endl;
119 }
120
121 /*******************************************************/
122 /*                                                      */
123 /* FindThisStudent: match ssn with an item in the list */
124 /*                                                      */
125 /* returns a pointer to the matching student or 0      */
126 /*                                                      */
127 /*******************************************************/
128
129 Student*  StudentRoster::FindThisStudent (long ssn) const {
130  StudentNode* ptrstudent = headptr;
131  while (ptrstudent) {
132   if (ptrstudent->student.ssno == ssn)
133    return &ptrstudent->student;
134   ptrstudent = ptrstudent->fwdptr;
135  }
136  return 0;
137 }
138
139 /*******************************************************/
140 /*                                                      */
141 /* InsertAfter: adds this student to list after ssn Node */
142 /*                                                      */
143 /* if no match or empty list, it is added at the head  */
144 /* of the list                                          */
145 /*                                                      */
146 /*******************************************************/
```

```
147
148 void StudentRoster::InsertAfter (long ssn, const Student& s) {
149  // if list is empty, add at head
150  if (!headptr)
151   AddStudentAtHead (s);
152  else {
153   // traverse the list looking for this ssn
154   StudentNode* ptrstudent = headptr; // set to start of list
155   while (ptrstudent) {          // repeat if not at the end of list
156    if (ptrstudent->student.ssno == ssn) // have we found it?
157     break;                     // yes, end the loop
158    ptrstudent = ptrstudent->fwdptr;    // no, point to next one
159   }
160   // here, ptrstudent is 0 (not found) or non-zero (found match)
161   if (!ptrstudent)       // did not find this ssn in the list
162    AddStudentAtHead (s); // so add it at the head
163   else {
164    // we have found the matching ssn pointed to by ptrstudent
165    StudentNode* ptrnew = new (std::nothrow) StudentNode;
166    if (!ptrnew) {
167     cerr << "Error: out of memory in InsertAfter\n";
168     exit (2);
169    }
170    ptrnew->student = s;                    // copy the new data
171    // set new node's fwdptr to matching one's fwdptr
172    ptrnew->fwdptr = ptrstudent->fwdptr;
173    // set matching one's fwdptr to point to the new added node
174    ptrstudent->fwdptr = ptrnew;
175   }
176  }
177 }
178
179 /*****************************************************/
180 /*                                                   */
181 /* DeleteThisStudent: deletes this student from the list */
182 /*                                                   */
183 /* does not return an error code if the ssn is not found */
184 /*                                                   */
185 /*****************************************************/
186
187 void StudentRoster::DeleteThisStudent (long ssn) {
188  // check for an empty list and do nothing if empty
189  if (!headptr) return;
190  // iterate through list looking for this ssn
191  StudentNode* ptrThisStudent = headptr;
192  StudentNode* ptrPrevStudent = 0;
193  while (ptrThisStudent) {
194   if (ptrThisStudent->student.ssno == ssn)
195    break;
196   ptrPrevStudent = ptrThisStudent;
```

```
197    ptrThisStudent = ptrThisStudent->fwdptr;
198  }
199  // here, if ptrThisStudent is 0, it was not found, do nothing
200  if (!ptrThisStudent) return;
201
202  // sort out whether this one to delete is at the head which has
203  // no previous node - if it is not at the head, then this one
204  // does have a previous node whose fwdptr must be altered.
205  if (headptr == ptrThisStudent) // at head, so no previous Node
206    headptr = ptrThisStudent->fwdptr;
207  else // set previous fwdptr to this's fwdptr to rechain
208    ptrPrevStudent->fwdptr = ptrThisStudent->fwdptr;
209  // now delete this found Node
210  delete ptrThisStudent;
211  }
212
213  /***********************************************************/
214  /*                                                         */
215  /* WriteNewFile: writes all students in list to a file     */
216  /*                                                         */
217  /***********************************************************/
218
219  void StudentRoster::WriteNewFile (const char* filename) const {
220    ofstream os (filename);
221    if (!os) {
222      cerr << "StudentRoster Error: cannot open output file "
223          << filename << endl;
224      return;
225    }
226    // traverse list and write each one to the file
227    StudentNode* ptrstudent = headptr;
228    while (ptrstudent) {
229      os << setw (sizeof (ptrstudent->student.name))
230          << ptrstudent->student.name << " "
231          << ptrstudent->student.ssno << " "
232          << ptrstudent->student.grade << endl;
233      ptrstudent = ptrstudent->fwdptr;
234    }
235    os.close ();
236  }
237
```

As you look over this class, can you spot its deficiencies and oversights and oversimplifications? They are abundant. **LoadAllStudents()** should probably return a **bool** to let the user easily determine that the file could not be opened. **InputStudentData()** should check for bad data and report such to the client by some means. **PrintAllStudents()** should display a message if the list is empty. **InsertAfter()** and **DeleteThisStudent()** should probably return an error code if the list is empty or if no matching node can be found. **WriteNewFile()** should return an error code if the output file cannot be opened. There are no checks

288

for having duplicate student social security numbers in the list. I neglected these mostly to streamline the main coding of the linked list.

More crucial is the repetitive coding for a list traversal. We keep seeing the same repetitious coding to move through the list. This repetitious coding is removed in the next sample program. Now let's examine an actual client program that uses this class, **Pgm09a.cpp**. Many of the functions of **StudentRoster** should be tested by requesting the node at the head of the list, the node at the tail of the list and a node in the middle of the list. Thus, the client program specifically tests for these situations.

Pgm09a performs basic tests on all of the **StudentRoster** member functions. With those functions that require matching a specific student id number, it matches the first in the list, the last in the list, one in the middle of the list and one that is not in the list at all. The program also displays a crude this is "what is to be expected" so that one can check for correctness at a glance.

Here are the basic tester, Pgm09a and the output results.

```
Pgm09a - Tests the StudentRoster Functions

 1 #include <iostream>
 2 #include <iomanip>
 3 #include <crtdbg.h>
 4 #include <string>
 5 using namespace std;
 6
 7 #include "StudentRoster.h"
 8
 9 /*****************************************************/
10 /*                                                 */
11 /* Pgm09a: Process a day's student roster activities */
12 /*                                                 */
13 /* Loads the initial roster and then adds new students */
14 /* and deletes students who have dropped. Finds students.*/
15 /* At day's end, writes a new roster file          */
16 /*                                                 */
17 /* Basic test of all StudentRoster functions       */
18 /*                                                 */
19 /*****************************************************/
20
21 int main () {
22
23   {
24     StudentRoster r; // tests destruction of an empty list
25   }
26   {
27     StudentRoster roster;
28     // test LoadAllStudents and its subfunctions
29     // test PrintAllStudents and PrintThisStudent
30     roster.LoadAllStudents ("Roster.txt");
31     cout << "          My Class Roster - tests loading the file\n\n"
```

```
32          << "       Name                          StudentID  Grade\n\n";
33     roster.PrintAllStudents (cout);
34     cout << "order should be Jennifer Smallville, Allan Adaire,\n"
35          << " Thomas J. Jones, Annie Smith, Sam Spade, Betsy \n\n";
36
37     cout << endl;
38
39     // tests FindThisStudent
40     cout << "Testing FindThisStudent()\n";
41     Student* ptrFoundStudent;
42     long idToFind[4]= {123456789, 234565677, 234234333, 987654321};
43     char fnames[4][14] = {"Betsy", "Sam Spade", "Jennifer",
44                           "not on roster"};
45     long id;
46     for (id=0; id<4; id++) {
47      if ((ptrFoundStudent = roster.FindThisStudent (idToFind[id])))
48       roster.PrintThisStudent (cout, *ptrFoundStudent);
49      else
50       cout << "Student not on my roster: id is " << id << endl;
51      cout << "Should find: " << fnames[id] << endl;
52     }
53
54     // tests InsertAfter
55     Student s[4] = { {"After Betsy", 123456799, 'B'},
56     {"after Thomas", 1231231, 'C'},
57     {"after Jennifer", 3423222, 'D'},
58     {"before Jennifer", 8888888, 'A'}};
59     long afters[5] = {123456789, 345344344, 234234333, 777777};
60     for (id=0; id<4; id++) {
61      roster.InsertAfter (afters[id], s[id]);
62     }
63     cout << "\nTesting InsertAfter() - should be\n"
64        << "before Jennifer, Jennifer, after Jennifer, Allen,\n"
65        << "Thomas, after Thomas, Annie, Sam, Betsy, after Betsy\n";
66     roster.PrintAllStudents (cout);
67
68     // tests DeleteThisStudent
69     cout << "\nTesting Delete - should be the original list\n";
70     for (id=0; id<4; id++) {
71      roster.DeleteThisStudent (s[id].ssno);
72     }
73     roster.PrintAllStudents (cout);
74
75     // tests WriteNewFile
76     cout << "\nTesting WriteNewFile()\n";
77     roster.WriteNewFile ("NewMaster.txt");
78     StudentRoster n;
79     n.LoadAllStudents ("NewMaster.txt");
80     n.PrintAllStudents (cout);
81     cout << "Above list from new master should be in reverse\n"
```

```
82              << "Order from the original list\n";
83  }
84
85  if (_CrtDumpMemoryLeaks())
86    cout << "\nOops! Memory Leaks!!\n";
87  else
88    cout << "\nNo Memory Leaks\n";
89
90  return 0;
91  }
```

```
Output from Pgm09a - Tests the StudentRoster Functions

 1         My Class Roster - tests loading the file
 2
 3    Name                         StudentID  Grade
 4
 5    Jennifer Smallville          234234333    A
 6    Allan Adaire                 324234234    C
 7    Thomas J. Jones              345344344    A
 8    Annie Smith                  324233456    A
 9    Sam Spade                    234565677    B
10    Betsy                        123456789    A
11 order should be Jennifer Smallville, Allan Adaire,
12  Thomas J. Jones, Annie Smith, Sam Spade, Betsy
13
14
15 Testing FindThisStudent()
16    Betsy                        123456789    A
17 Should find: Betsy
18    Sam Spade                    234565677    B
19 Should find: Sam Spade
20    Jennifer Smallville          234234333    A
21 Should find: Jennifer
22 Student not on my roster: id is 3
23 Should find: not on roster
24
25 Testing InsertAfter() - should be
26 before Jennifer, Jennifer, after Jennifer, Allen,
27 Thomas, after Thomas, Annie, Sam, Betsy, after Betsy
28    before Jennifer                8888888    A
29    Jennifer Smallville          234234333    A
30    after Jennifer                 3423222    D
31    Allan Adaire                 324234234    C
32    Thomas J. Jones              345344344    A
33    after Thomas                   1231231    C
34    Annie Smith                  324233456    A
35    Sam Spade                    234565677    B
36    Betsy                        123456789    A
```

291

```
37      After Betsy                    123456799     B
38
39  Testing Delete - should be the original list
40      Jennifer Smallville            234234333     A
41      Allan Adaire                   324234234     C
42      Thomas J. Jones                345344344     A
43      Annie Smith                    324233456     A
44      Sam Spade                      234565677     B
45      Betsy                          123456789     A
46
47  Testing WriteNewFile()
48      Betsy                          123456789     A
49      Sam Spade                      234565677     B
50      Annie Smith                    324233456     A
51      Thomas J. Jones                345344344     A
52      Allan Adaire                   324234234     C
53      Jennifer Smallville            234234333     A
54  Above list from new master should be in reverse
55  Order from the original list
56
57  No Memory Leaks
```

The real question one should now ask is "What additional tests should be made to ensure that **StudentRoster** functions completely correctly?" Take a few minutes to inspect the situation and see if you can recommend some additional testing oracles that ought to be run on this class. For example, how do the various functions that require a student id to match perform when there are no items in the list or with just a single item in the list?

The Revised Student Roster Class—Pgm09b

In the above **StudentRoster** class, the urgent need for list iteration should be abundantly clear. Over and over, the member functions needed to begin at the beginning of the list and traverse sequentially through the list. This revision adds the iterator functions to the class.

To iterate a list, a current pointer must be maintained, here called **currentptr**. Its purpose is to point to the current node in the list. When it is 0, then there are no more nodes in the list; the end of the list has been reached. The new function, **GetCurrentStudent()**, has been added to allow the user to get access to the current student pointed to by **currentptr**.

To maintain this current node pointer, two additional functions are added: **ResetToHead()** and **Next()**. **ResetToHead()** sets **currentptr** back to the start of the list, **headptr**. **Next()** does the actual iteration from node to node. It assigns to **currentptr** whatever is contained in the current node's forward pointer.

Given these new functions, most of the previous member functions can be rewritten to use these iteration functions. Thus, the class implementation begins to have a good measure of internal code reuse.

The second area of near-duplicate coding is that of finding a matching node. In this version, I added a protected function called **Find()** whose purpose is to traverse the list looking for a match. It returns a pointer to the found node or 0 if none is found. **FindThisStudent()**, **InsertAfter()** and **DeleteThisStudent()**—all use the **Find()** function. Additionally, since in some situations the previous pointer is also needed, **Find()** returns the previous node pointer as a reference variable. That parameter is defined as

```
StudentNode* &ptrprevstud
```

Notice that it is a reference to the caller's pointer. If we merely passed this pointer this way

```
StudentNode* ptrprevstud
```

Then the **Find()** function would receive a copy of the value in the caller's pointer. And when **Find()** set **ptrprevstud** to its new value, the new value would only be stored in **Find()**'s parameter copy, not in the caller's pointer.

With the addition of these changes, the client program can now also iterate the list as it chooses. I took the liberty of adding the following list traversal coding to the **Pgm09b** testing program.

```
// Testing Client Iteration through the list
cout << "Testing client iteration thru list\nList should the "
    << "same as the previous listing\n";
roster.ResetToHead ();
Student* ptrstudent; ;
while ((ptrstudent = roster.GetCurrentStudent ()) != 0) {
  roster.PrintThisStudent (cout, *ptrstudent);
  roster.Next ();
}
cout << endl;
```

Here is the revised **StudentRoster.h** definition file. I boldfaced the new additions. Because the iterator functions alter **currentptr**, many of the previous constant functions are now not constant. Also, look over each function in the implementation for the new changes in coding to use the new iterator functions. The complete coding is found in the **Samples** folder under **Pgm09b**.

```
Revised StudentRoster Definition

 1 #pragma once
 2 #include <iostream>
 3 using namespace std;
 4
 5 /****************************************************************/
 6 /*                                                            */
 7 /* StudentRoster class                                        */
 8 /*                                                            */
 9 /* Maintain a list of students who are enrolled in a          */
10 /* course                                                     */
11 /*                                                            */
12 /* No checking is done for any out of memory errors           */
13 /*                                                            */
14 /****************************************************************/
15
```

```
16 const int NAME_LEN = 21;
17
18 /*******************************************************/
19 /*                                                     */
20 /* Student: contains the client's student data         */
21 /*                                                     */
22 /*******************************************************/
23
24 struct Student {
25   char name[NAME_LEN];
26   long ssno;
27   char grade;
28 };
29
30 /*******************************************************/
31 /*                                                     */
32 /* StudentNode: the list node structure                */
33 /*                                                     */
34 /*******************************************************/
35
36 struct StudentNode {
37   StudentNode* fwdptr;  // points to the next node in the list
38   Student      student; // contains the actual client data
39 };
40
41 class StudentRoster {
42
43   /*******************************************************/
44   /*                                                     */
45   /* class data                                          */
46   /*                                                     */
47   /*******************************************************/
48
49 private:
50   StudentNode* headptr;     // the list pointer
51
52   StudentNode* currentptr;  // the pointer to the current node
53
54   /*******************************************************/
55   /*                                                     */
56   /* class functions                                     */
57   /*                                                     */
58   /*******************************************************/
59
60 public:
61          StudentRoster ();
62          ~StudentRoster ();
63
64   void   LoadAllStudents (const char* filename);
65   void   AddStudentAtHead (const Student& s);
```

```
66 protected:
67  istream& InputStudentData (istream& infile, Student& s);
68
69 public:
70  void PrintAllStudents (ostream& outfile);
71  void PrintThisStudent (ostream& outfile, const Student& s)const;
72  void WriteNewFile (const char* filename);
73
74  Student* FindThisStudent (long ssn);
75 protected:
76  StudentNode* Find (long ssn, StudentNode* &ptrprevstud);
77
78 public:
79  void       InsertAfter (long ssn, const Student& s);
80  void       DeleteThisStudent (long ssn);
81
82  // list iterator functions
83  void       ResetToHead ();
84  void       Next ();
85  Student* GetCurrentStudent () const;
86 };
87
```

Revised StudentRoster Implementation

```
 1 #include <iostream>
 2 #include <iomanip>
 3 #include <fstream>
 4 using namespace std;
 5
 6 #include "StudentRoster.h"
 7
 8 /****************************************************/
 9 /*                                                  */
10 /* StudentRoster: constructor to set list to empty  */
11 /*                                                  */
12 /****************************************************/
13
14 StudentRoster::StudentRoster () {
15  headptr = currentptr = 0;
16 }
17
18 /****************************************************/
19 /*                                                  */
20 /* ~StudentRoster: destructor to empty the list     */
21 /*                                                  */
22 /****************************************************/
23
```

```
24 StudentRoster::~StudentRoster () {
25  if (!headptr) return;
26  StudentNode* ptrnext = headptr; // pointer to traverse the list
27  StudentNode* ptrdel;            // the node to delete
28  // traverse the list - ends when there are no more nodes
29  while (ptrnext) {
30   ptrdel = ptrnext;         // save the current one to be deleted
31   ptrnext = ptrdel->fwdptr; // point to the next node
32   delete ptrdel;            // and delete the previous node
33  }
34 }
35
36 /*****************************************************************/
37 /*                                                             */
38 /* LoadAllStudents: input a file of students into the list */
39 /*                                                             */
40 /*****************************************************************/
41
42 void StudentRoster::LoadAllStudents (const char* filename) {
43  Student s;
44  ifstream infile (filename);
45  if (!infile) {
46   cerr << "StudentRoster Error - cannot open file "
47        << filename << endl;
48   return; // assume data is correct in the file
49  }
50  while (InputStudentData (infile, s)) {
51   AddStudentAtHead (s);
52  }
53  infile.close ();
54  ResetToHead ();          // leave currentptr stable
55 }
56
57 /*****************************************************************/
58 /*                                                             */
59 /* InputStudentData: read in one set of student data       */
60 /*                                                             */
61 /*****************************************************************/
62
63 istream& StudentRoster::InputStudentData (istream& infile,
64                                            Student& s) {
65  // assumes that the file contains no bad data
66  infile >> ws;
67  if (!infile) return infile;
68  infile.get (s.name, sizeof (s.name));
69  if (!infile) return infile;
70  infile >> s.ssno >> s.grade;
71  return infile;
72 }
73
```

```
74  /**************************************************/
75  /*                                                */
76  /* AddStudentAtHead: add this student at the head of list */
77  /*                                                */
78  /**************************************************/
79
80  void StudentRoster::AddStudentAtHead (const Student& s) {
81   // allocate a new node and fill it up
82   StudentNode* ptrnew = new (std::nothrow) StudentNode;
83   if (!ptrnew) {
84    cerr << "Error: out of memory in AddStudentAtHead\n";
85    exit (1);
86   }
87   ptrnew->student = s; // copy the passed student information
88   ptrnew->fwdptr = 0;  // set the forward pointer to 0
89   // now chain this one into the list
90   if (headptr)                 // if headptr exists, then the new
91    ptrnew->fwdptr = headptr; // fwdptr contains the previous one
92   headptr = ptrnew;  // set the headptr to this newly added one
93   currentptr = ptrnew; // leave the current one at the new one
94  }
95
96  /**************************************************/
97  /*                                                */
98  /* PrintAllStudents: display all of the students in list */
99  /*                                                */
100 /**************************************************/
101
102 void StudentRoster::PrintAllStudents (ostream& outfile) {
103  ResetToHead ();
104  while (currentptr) {
105   PrintThisStudent (outfile, currentptr->student);
106   Next ();
107  }
108  ResetToHead ();         // leave currentptr stable
109 }
110
111 /**************************************************/
112 /*                                                */
113 /* PrintThisStudent: displays one set of student data  */
114 /*                                                */
115 /**************************************************/
116
117 void StudentRoster::PrintThisStudent (ostream& outfile,
118                                        const Student& s) const {
119  outfile << left << "    " << setw (25) << s.name
120          << right << setw (12) << s.ssno << setw (5)
121          << s.grade << endl;
122 }
```

297

```
124
125 /***********************************************************/
126 /*                                                         */
127 /* FindThisStudent: match ssn with an item in the list    */
128 /*                                                         */
129 /* returns a pointer to the matching student or 0          */
130 /*                                                         */
131 /***********************************************************/
132
133 Student*  StudentRoster::FindThisStudent (long ssn) {
134  StudentNode* ptrprevstud;
135  StudentNode* ptrstudent = Find (ssn, ptrprevstud);
136  return ptrstudent ? &ptrstudent->student : 0;
137 }
138
139 /***********************************************************/
140 /*                                                         */
141 /* InsertAfter: adds this student to list after ssn Node */
142 /*                                                         */
143 /* if no match or empty list, it is added at the head     */
144 /* of the list                                            */
145 /*                                                         */
146 /***********************************************************/
147
148 void StudentRoster::InsertAfter (long ssn, const Student& s) {
149  // if list is empty, add at head
150  if (!headptr)
151   AddStudentAtHead (s);
152  else { // look for matching ssn
153    StudentNode* ptrprevstud;
154    StudentNode* ptrmatched = Find (ssn, ptrprevstud);
155    if (ptrmatched == 0)   // no matching ssn, so
156     AddStudentAtHead (s); // add this one at head
157    else { // here it matches, so allocate new node and fill it
158     StudentNode* ptrnew = new (std::nothrow) StudentNode;
159     if (!ptrnew) {
160      cerr << "Error: out of memory in InsertAfter\n";
161      exit (2);
162     }
163     ptrnew->student = s;
164     // set new node's fwdptr to matching one's fwdptr
165     ptrnew->fwdptr = ptrmatched->fwdptr;
166     // set matching one's fwdptr to point to the new added node
167     ptrmatched->fwdptr = ptrnew;
168    }
169  }
170  ResetToHead ();           // leave currentptr stable
171 }
172
```

```
173 /*****************************************************************/
174 /*                                                               */
175 /* DeleteThisStudent: deletes this student from the list */
176 /*                                                               */
177 /* does not return an error code if the ssn is not found */
178 /*                                                               */
179 /*****************************************************************/
180
181 void StudentRoster::DeleteThisStudent (long ssn) {
182  // check for an empty list and do nothing if empty
183  if (!headptr) return;
184  StudentNode* ptrprevstud;
185  StudentNode* ptrmatched = Find (ssn, ptrprevstud);
186  if (!ptrmatched) return; // this ssn was not found
187
188  // Handle chaining, is this one to delete at the head of list?
189  if (headptr == ptrmatched)      // yes is at head
190   headptr = ptrmatched->fwdptr; // reset head to next
191  else      // no, so set previous node to point to next node
192   ptrprevstud->fwdptr = ptrmatched->fwdptr;
193
194  // now delete the found node
195  delete ptrmatched;
196  ResetToHead ();        // leave currentptr stable
197 }
198
199 /*****************************************************************/
200 /*                                                               */
201 /* WriteNewFile: writes all students in list to a file   */
202 /*                                                               */
203 /*****************************************************************/
204
205 void StudentRoster::WriteNewFile (const char* filename) {
206  ofstream os (filename);
207  if (!os) {
208   cerr << "StudentRoster Error: cannot open output file "
209        << filename << endl;
210   return;
211  }
212  // traverse list and write each one to the file
213  ResetToHead ();
214  while (currentptr) {
215   os << setw (sizeof (currentptr->student.name))
216      << currentptr->student.name << " "
217      << currentptr->student.ssno << " "
218      << currentptr->student.grade << endl;
219   Next ();
220  }
```

```
221  os.close ();
222  ResetToHead ();          // leave currentptr stable
223  }
224
225  /******************************************************/
226  /*                                                  */
227  /* Find: matches a ssn with a list node             */
228  /*                                                  */
229  /******************************************************/
230
231  StudentNode* StudentRoster::Find (long ssn,
232                                   StudentNode* &ptrprevstud) {
233   ResetToHead ();          // start at the beginning again
234   ptrprevstud = 0;         // set no previous node found yet
235   while (currentptr) {     // continue through all nodes
236    if (currentptr->student.ssno == ssn)
237     return currentptr;     // return matching one with previous set
238    // save the previous node in case the next one matches
239    ptrprevstud = currentptr;
240    Next ();                // go to next mode
241   }
242   ResetToHead ();          // leave currentptr stable
243   return 0;                // return no matching node
244  }
245
246  /******************************************************/
247  /*                                                  */
248  /* ResetToHead: sets currentptr to the first node in list*/
249  /*                                                  */
250  /******************************************************/
251
252  void StudentRoster::ResetToHead () {
253   currentptr = headptr;
254  }
255
256  /******************************************************/
257  /*                                                  */
258  /* GetCurrentStudent: returns ptr to the current student */
259  /*                                                  */
260  /******************************************************/
261
262  Student* StudentRoster::GetCurrentStudent () const {
263   return currentptr ? &currentptr->student : 0;
264  }
265
266  /******************************************************/
267  /*                                                  */
268  /* Next: sets currentptr to the next node in the list     */
```

```
269 /*                                                        */
270 /**********************************************************/
271
272 void StudentRoster::Next () {
273   if (currentptr)
274     currentptr = currentptr->fwdptr;
275 }
```

However, one serious problem remains. Consider the following user coding.

```
StudentRoster roster;
StudentRoster newRoster;
...
newRoster = roster;
StudentRoster save (roster);
```

Ah ha. Here the copy constructor and the assignment operator come into play once again. What does our implementation do in these circumstances? Since we provided neither function, the compiler provides them for us and does a shallow copy. That is, the contents of **headptr** and **currentptr** are copied. And we now have two or more class instances pointing to the same dynamically allocated memory. When the destructors are called, runtime errors will occur from attempting to delete previously deleted memory. It would be even worse if the client deletes only one of these instances and then attempts to use the remaining instances whose pointers now would point to garbage!

Adding Support for the Copy Constructor and Assignment Operator—Pgm09c

Actually, it is fairly simple to add support for the copy constructor and assignment operator. And only one other function must be modified. When implementing the assignment operator, we need to empty the current list before we can make the copy. Currently the destructor is emptying the list. So I have added a new public function, **EmptyList()** which can be called by client programs as well as our destructor and assignment operator functions. Finally, since both the copy constructor and assignment operators must make a duplicate copy of a list, I created a helper function that both can call, **CopyList()** which is a protected member function.

With all the new functions added to the class header file, I added more comments to aid in understanding how to use the many functions. Here is the header for the final version of **StudentRoster**.

```
Revised StudentRoster Definition - Copy Ctor and op=

1 #pragma once
2 #include <iostream>
3 using namespace std;
4
5 /**********************************************************/
6 /*                                                        */
7 /* StudentRoster class                                    */
8 /*                                                        */
```

```
 9  /* Maintain a list of students who are enrolled in a      */
10  /* course                                                 */
11  /*                                                         */
12  /* No checking is done for any out of memory errors        */
13  /*                                                         */
14  /**********************************************************/
15
16  const int NAME_LEN = 21;
17
18  /**********************************************************/
19  /*                                                         */
20  /* Student: contains the client's student data             */
21  /*                                                         */
22  /**********************************************************/
23
24  struct Student {
25   char name[NAME_LEN];
26   long ssno;
27   char grade;
28  };
29
30  /**********************************************************/
31  /*                                                         */
32  /* StudentNode: the list node structure                    */
33  /*                                                         */
34  /**********************************************************/
35
36  struct StudentNode {
37   StudentNode* fwdptr;  // points to the next node in the list
38   Student       student; // contains the actual client data
39  };
40
41  class StudentRoster {
42
43   /**********************************************************/
44   /*                                                         */
45   /* class data                                              */
46   /*                                                         */
47   /**********************************************************/
48
49  private:
50   StudentNode* headptr;     // the list pointer
51
52   StudentNode* currentptr;  // the pointer to the current node
53
54   /**********************************************************/
55   /*                                                         */
56   /* class functions                                         */
57   /*                                                         */
58   /**********************************************************/
```

```
59
60 public:
61          StudentRoster ();  // constructs an empty roster
62          StudentRoster (const StudentRoster& r);  // copy roster
63 StudentRoster& operator= (const StudentRoster& r); // copy roster
64          ~StudentRoster ();  // deletes the roster
65 void     EmptyList ();       // removes all items from the list
66
67 // loads all students from a file - items are in reverse order
68 void     LoadAllStudents (const char* filename);
69 // adds a new student to the list at the head of the list
70 void     AddStudentAtHead (const Student& s);
71
72 // displays all students in the list
73 void PrintAllStudents (ostream& outfile);
74 // displays a single student
75 void PrintThisStudent (ostream& outfile, const Student& s)const;
76 // outputs the whole list to a new student roster file
77 void WriteNewFile (const char* filename);
78
79 // finds a specific student, returns 0 if ssn is not found
80 Student* FindThisStudent (long ssn);
81
82 // inserts a new student into list after this specific student
83 // or inserts the new one at the head if this ssn is not found
84 void     InsertAfter (long ssn, const Student& s);
85 // remove this student from the list, does nothing if not found
86 void     DeleteThisStudent (long ssn);
87
88 // list iterator functions
89 void     ResetToHead ();            // set to start of the list
90 void     Next ();                   // moves to the next item
91 Student* GetCurrentStudent () const; // gets the current student
92                                     // or 0 if there is none
93 protected:
94 StudentNode* Find (long ssn, StudentNode* &ptrprevstud);
95 istream&     InputStudentData (istream& infile, Student& s);
96 void         CopyList (const StudentRoster& r);
97
98 };
99
```

```
Revised StudentRoster Implementation - Copy Ctor and op=

  1 #include <iostream>
289 /*********************************************************/
290 /*                                                       */
291 /* StudentRoster: copy constructor - make duplicate list */
```

303

```
292 /*                                                        */
293 /************************************************************/
294
295 StudentRoster::StudentRoster (const StudentRoster& r) {
296  CopyList (r);
297 }
298
299 /************************************************************/
300 /*                                                        */
301 /* operator= makes a duplicate list                      */
302 /*                                                        */
303 /************************************************************/
304
305 StudentRoster& StudentRoster::operator= (const StudentRoster& r){
306  if (this == &r) return *this;
307  EmptyList ();
308  CopyList (r);
309  return *this;
310 }
311
312 /************************************************************/
313 /*                                                        */
314 /* CopyList: helper function to copy a list              */
315 /*                                                        */
316 /************************************************************/
317
318 void StudentRoster::CopyList (const StudentRoster& r) {
319  // handle the empty list first
320  if (!r.headptr) {
321   headptr = currentptr = 0;
322   return;
323  }
324  StudentNode* srcCurrentPtr = r.headptr;
325  // previousptr tracks our prior node so we can set its
326  // forward pointer to the next new one
327  StudentNode* previousptr = 0;
328  // prime the loop so headptr can be set one time
329  currentptr = new (std::nothrow) StudentNode;
330  if (!currentptr) {
331   cerr << "Error out of memory in CopyList\n";
332   exit (3);
333  }
334  headptr = currentptr;  // assign this one to the headptr
335
336  // traverse list r's nodes
337  while (srcCurrentPtr) {
338   // copy r's student info into our new node
339   currentptr->student = srcCurrentPtr->student;
340   currentptr->fwdptr = 0;  // set our forward ptr to 0
341   // if previous node exists, set its forward ptr to the new one
```

```
342    if (previousptr)
343     previousptr->fwdptr = currentptr;
344    // save this node as the prevous node
345    previousptr = currentptr;
346    // and get a new node for the next iteration
347    currentptr = new (std::nothrow) StudentNode;
348    if (!currentptr) {
349     cerr << "Error out of memory in CopyList\n";
350     exit (3);
351    }
352    // move to r's next node
353    srcCurrentPtr = srcCurrentPtr->fwdptr;
354   }
355   delete currentptr; // delete the extra unneeded node
356   // leave both lists at the beginning
357   ResetToHead ();
358  }
```

A Linked List Written for a Specific Program Versus a Generic Reusable Single Linked List Container

At this point, we now have a respectable **StudentRoster** single linked list class. The class has all of the features most often needed in a linked list. However, suppose that we now needed to write a program that used a linked list of cars? Suppose we needed to write a program that needed a list of boats docked in our harbor or that needed a list of computer parts that our store stocks. How could we proceed to solve those problems?

The key issue here is that while the **StudentRoster** ADT is a good example of how to implement a single linked list, it is **not** a generic container. There is no way that we can "reuse" this class in other applications! Why?

The first issue is that **StudentRoster** is tightly coupled to the actual data being stored. That is, each node holds an instance of the **Student** data structure. Think about the steps you need to do to alter it to contain a list of computer parts or boats docking in a harbor. The Student structure would have to be replaced by another structure instance.

Next, the **LoadAllStudents()** and **PrintAllStudents()** functions are totally coupled to the actual data to be input. These would have to be drastically altered to handle boat or computer parts objects.

While the above changes are doable, they require extensive rewriting of most every function in the class. Only a few would be exempt, such as the constructor and **Next()** for example.

How could we proceed to make a generic list container? Based upon what you already know, using a **void*** to store the user's data in the nodes would be the obvious answer. In other words, the **StudentNode** structure would be altered to **ListNode** as follows.

```
struct ListNode {
  ListNode* fwdptr;
  void*     dataptr;
};
```

If this were done, then the class could not have any LoadAll... or PrintAll... type of functions because we would not know what the actual user data was. It would be the client program's responsibility to input an instance of their data and give us the address to store in the nodes. Again, this is not a problem, really. But if we did just this, there remains a very real problem that the **ListNode** class would indeed have. And this is the second major problem, second only to the fact that we are storing user-specific data by having a **Student** structure instance directly in the node. Can you spot this second major hurdle?

What is the one action that is called from a number of member functions that would still be directly dependent on the client's data? The **Find()** function! In the **Find()** function, we are given the **long ssn** to match in the data. If we switch to storing boats or computer parts, we would have to completely rewrite the **Find()** function to match on some new identification, such as boat name or id or computer part id number.

However, if we convert to a generic container that is storing **void** pointers, how could we ever possibly hope to know how to find a matching list item? There is absolutely no way we could do so without locking our coding into the specific data of the client program thereby destroying the general nature of the list container. But there is a way around even this barrier. And that is to use a call back function just like the **qsort()** function does.

As you recall, **qsort()** is a function that sorts an array of any kind of data. It is given the address of the array, the number of elements in the array, the size of one element in the array and the address of a user-written call back comparison function. Only the user knows what kind of data the array actually contains. It is the calling application that must perform the actual comparison.

Thus, to turn this list class into a truly reusable container, we must insist that the calling application provide us with a function that will compare two items that the list is storing for them and tell us the comparison results (=, > or <). This is explored in depth in the next chapter which deals with double linked lists because it makes more sense to write a generic double linked list. Why? Double linked lists have a broader usage in the real world of applications because programs frequently need the ability to back up a node or two in a list, something that is very difficult to do with a single linked list.

Until the next chapter, we will have to be content to extensively modify **StudentRoster** to create other single linked list applications.

Review Questions

1. Why are linked lists useful programming tools? Give three examples in which a linked list would be an idea way to store the data. The examples should not be ones that I have mentioned in this chapter, of course.

2. In a linked list, what is the purpose of a "headptr?" How can one node know where the next node is located? Show a sketch of how this works.

3. What is meant by iterators? Explain how a current pointer works with a **ResetToHead()** and **Next()** functions. What happens if a node in the middle of the list has its forward pointer clobbered?

4. Explain how an **InsertAt()** function could insert a new node at a specific point in the list. Show a sketch of how this works. What two different circumstances must be allowed for in the coding?

5. Outline the programming steps needed to empty a list.

6. In the **StudentRoster** class, the **StudentNode** structure contains an instance of the **Student** structure. Show how this could be changed to store a pointer to a **Student** structure. What, if any, benefits to the class would the storing a pointer to a **Student** instance make? Would there be any difference needed in the client program? Be specific in your comments.

7. Compare the coding needed to add a new node at the head of the list versus the general case of **InsertAt()** function. Are there any circumstances in which they are doing the same sequence of instructions?

8. It has been said that a list class is an excellent example of encapsulation leading to great coding benefits. How does having **headptr** be a member data item assist in the implementation of a linked list? Contrast how the linked list would have to be implemented using straight C-style coding—that is, without using classes.

9. What is the benefit of providing iterator functions in the list class with respect to the other functions in the list class? What effect does the presence of iterator functions have on the clients of the list class?

10. Why should a linked list class have a destructor?

11. Explain why a linked list class should provide a copy constructor and the assignment operator functions.

Stop! Do These Exercises Before Programming

1. A programmer has decided to use the **StudentRoster** class as a basis for his linked list class **PetsList**. He has defined the following as the beginnings of his class.

PetsList.h
```
const int NAME_LEN = 21;

struct Pets {
 char name[NAME_LEN]; // pets name
 char type[12];       // dog, cat and so on
 char sex;            // m or f
 short age;           // pet's age
}

struct PetsNode {
 PetsNode* fwdptr;  // points to the next node in the list
 Pet       pet;     // contains the actual client data
}

class PetsList {

private:
 Pets* headptr;       // the list pointer
 Pets* currentptr;    // the pointer to the current node

public:
          PetsList ();  // constructs an empty roster
         ~PetsList ();  // deletes all the nodes
}
```
It does not compile correctly. Correct his coding and logical errors thus far.

2. Grateful for your assistance, he coded the following for his constructor, destructor and added a function to add a new Pet at the head of the list. Unfortunately, this does not compile or work properly either. You are called upon to assist him once more. Correct his errors in these functions.

PetsList.cpp
```
PetsList::PetsList () {
 headptr = currentptr = 0;
}

PetsList::~PetsList () {
 if (headptr) return;
 PetsNode* ptrnext = headptr;
 PetsNode* ptrdel;
 while (ptrnext) {
  delete ptrdel;
```

308

```
    ptrnext = ptrdel->fwdptr;
    ptrdel = ptrnext;
   }
  headptr = currentptr = 0;
 }


void PetsList::AddAtHead (const Pet& p) {
 PetsNode* ptrnew = new Pet;
 ptrnew->pet = p;
 ptrnew->fwdptr = 0;
 if (!headptr) {
  ptrnew->fwdptr = headptr;
  headptr = ptrnew;
 }
 currentptr = ptrnew;
}
```

3. The programmer swears that he has learned a lot from your assistance and is now ready to solo on his next function. He has coded the following for **InsertAfter()**. As expected, it also does not work properly. Correct once again his errors.

```
void PetsList::InsertAfter (long ssn, const Pets* s) {
 if (headptr) AddAtHead (s);
 else {
  PetsNode* ptrnode = headptr;
  while (ptrnode) {
   if (ptrnode->student.ssno == ssn) {
    ptrnode = ptrnode->fwdptr;
   }
  }
  if (ptrnode) AddAtHead (s);
  else {
   PetNode* ptrnew = new PetNode;
   ptrnew->pet = s;
   ptrnew->fwdptr = ptrnode;
   ptrnode->fwdptr = ptrnew->fwdptr;
  }
 }
}
```

4. Convinced that he now understands what he is doing, the programmer charges into the **DeleteThisPet()** function. He claims that it is nearly working but cannot find his remaining bug. You offer to help him find this last error.

```
void PetsList::DeleteThisPet (long ssn) {
 if (!headptr) return;
 PetsNode* ptrThisPet = headptr;
 PetsNode* ptrPrevPet = 0;
 while (ptrThisPet) {
```

```
 if (ptrThisPet->pet.ssno == ssn)
   break;
 ptrPrevPet = ptrThisPet;
 ptrThisPet = ptrThisPet->fwdptr;
 }
 if (!ptrThisPet) return;
 if (headptr == ptrThisPet)
  headptr = ptrThisPet->fwdptr;
 else
  ptrPrevPet->fwdptr = ptrThisPet->fwdptr;
 delete ptrThisPet;
}
```

Caution. This error is not obvious or easy to fix. Look this one over carefully.

5. Another programmer was called in to assist on the trickier portions of the new **PetsList** class. This programmer implemented the assignment operator and copy constructor. When these functions are called, memory leaks are reported and the copy constructor crashes as well. You are once again called in to fix the situation. Fix the coding so that they work properly.

```
PetsList::PetsList (const PetsList& r) {
 delete [] headptr;
 CopyList (r);
}

PetsList& PetsList::operator= (const PetsList& r){
 if (this == &r) return *this;
 CopyList (r);
 return *this;
}

void PetsList::CopyList (const PetsList& r) {
 if (!r.headptr) {
  headptr = currentptr = 0;
  return;
 }
 PetsNode* ptrRcurrent = r.headptr;
 PetsNode* previousptr = 0;
 currentptr = new PetsNode;
 headptr = currentptr;
 while (ptrRcurrent) {
  currentptr->pet = ptrRcurrent->pet;
  currentptr->fwdptr = 0;
  if (previousptr)
   previousptr->fwdptr = currentptr;
  previousptr = currentptr;
  currentptr = new PetsNode;
  ptrRcurrent = ptrRcurrent->fwdptr;
 }
 ResetToHead ();
}
```

Programming Problems

Problem Pgm09-1 The Boat Docking Application

Acme Holiday Harbor needs a list application written to assist them in managing small crafts that are docking at their harbor. The harbor has assigned slip numbers to all docking areas. They have a total of 200 slips available which limits them to docking a maximum of 200 boats at one time.

When a boat is docked, they need to store the following information:
           boat name—a string of 20 characters maximum
           boat id—a string of 10 characters
           owner's name—a string of 30 characters
Create a **BOAT** structure to store this information or create a **Boat** class to store the data.

Next, revise the **StudentRoster** class to store either **BOAT** or **Boat** nodes. Call the new list class **BoatList**.

When the program begins, it calls the **LoadAllBoats()** function passing it the name of the file to load. This function then inputs the file of boat data, storing each in a list node. Then the program goes into its main processing loop.

The program displays a small menu as follows.
```
Acme Holiday Harbor

     1. Dock a new boat
     2. Undock an existing boat
     3. Display all docked boats
     4. Write new master file
     5. Terminate the program

Enter the number of your choice: __
```

When "Dock a new boat" is chosen, prompt the user for the three data fields and then add that boat to the list. Keep in mind that there cannot ever be more than 200 boats docked at any one time. When "Undock an existing boat" is chosen, prompt for the boat id number and then delete that boat from the list. When "Display all docked boats" is made, traverse the boat list and display a nicely formatted report. For convenience, send the output to a file on disk to later print. When "Write new master file" is chosen, prompt the user for the new file name and pass it to the corresponding function.

The file **boatMaster.txt** located in the **TestDataForAssignments\Chapter09** folder contains the initial series of boats that are docked when the program begins.

Problem Pgm09-2 The Third Grade Roster

Acme Consolidated School is experimenting with using a new list application to maintain their third grade class roster. Mrs. Applebee, the teacher, will run the program from her laptop on her desk. At the start of the school year, the administration uploads a beginning roster file to her laptop. The roster file called **ThirdGradeRoster.txt**, is located in the **TestDataForAssignments Chapter09** folder. The initial file contains the student id number, their name and a placeholder grade for this six-week grading period. The placeholder character is N for not reported yet. Note that for your assistance, the file **ThirdGradeRosterBackUp.txt** is a duplicate of the original file.

Use the **StudentRoster** class as given in **Pgm09c** as is with **no** modifications to solve this problem. You are to write the client application that used the roster list class.

When Mrs. Applebee launches the program, the program initially loads the list automatically from the **ThirdGradeRoster.txt** file. Then it displays the following menu.

```
Third Grade Roster Menu

    1. Change a grade
    2. Add a new student
    3. Drop a student
    4. Display all grades
    5. Save and Exit

Enter the number of your choice: __
```

When "Change a grade" is chosen, prompt the user for the student id number and the new grade letter. Find that student and alter his/her grade.

When "Add a new student" is chosen, prompt the user for that information and add the student to the list.

When "Drop a student" is chosen, prompt the user for the student id, find out if that id is in the list. If the student is not in the list, display an error message and handle accordingly. If the student is in the list, display a prompt "Confirm deletion of student" and display all that student's information. If yes is chosen, delete that student from the list.

When "Display all grades" is chosen, show a nicely formatted display to the screen.

Finally, when "Save and Exit" is chosen, automatically rewrite the original file with the current list contents and terminate the program. Note that to repeatedly rerun the program from its initial state, you will need to use the Explorer program to copy the backup file back into the original file.

Problem Pgm09-3 The Parking Lot Survey Program

Acme Parking Deck wishes you to write them a survey analysis program. Their problem is tracking the number of cars actually parked in their fancy new lot throughout the day. The survey will help them answer when is the peak load and similar questions. Rewrite the **StudentRoster** class from **Pgm09c** to provide the new list class **ParkingList**.

The car data to be stored consists of the license plate number, 7 characters maximum, and initial time the car was parked in the deck. The time is stored as two short integers, hours and minutes.

When the program loads, it automatically loads the starting data file containing the cars already parked in the deck. This file is called **carsInDeck.txt** and is located in the **TestDataForAssignments Chapter09** folder. Count the number of cars initially parked in the deck.

Next, input the transaction's file called **carsInDeckTransactions.txt**. This file contains a character code followed by the license number and the time (hour and minute integers). The code is **a** for add new car and **d** for depart car. If this transaction is an add car, add it to the list. If this is a depart, remove it from the list.

The statistical numbers to track on an hourly basis consist of the number of cars in the deck at the start and end of the hour along with the number of actions (the sum of all adds and departs). The tracking hours begin at 7 a.m. and end at 6 p.m. When the end of the file occurs at 6 p.m., display an analysis such as the following.

```
        Acme Parking Deck Analysis

   hour     total    number    percent of
  begins     cars       of        total
    at     in deck    actions    actions

   7:00      nnn        nn        nn.n%
   8:00      nnn        nn        nn.n%
   9:00      nnn        nn        nn.n%
  10:00      nnn        nn        nn.n%
  11:00      nnn        nn        nn.n%
  12:00      nnn        nn        nn.n%
   1:00      nnn        nn        nn.n%
   2:00      nnn        nn        nn.n%
   3:00      nnn        nn        nn.n%
   4:00      nnn        nn        nn.n%
   5:00      nnn        nn        nn.n%

Total actions for the day: nnnn
```

Chapter 10—Linked Lists—Double

Introduction

In chapter 9 the single linked list provides basic support for simple lists of items. Each node in the list contained a forward pointer to the next node in the list. Thus, one can traverse the list in the forward direction, beginning with the first node that is pointed to by the head of the list pointer. However, there is no way to easily traverse in the reverse direction, that is, to get the previous node to the current one.

A **double linked list** contains both a forward and a back pointer. Any node then points both forward to the next node in the list and points backwards to the previous node in the list. When either of these pointers are null or 0, such indicates that there is no previous or no next node. We are either at the beginning of the list or the end.

The class that implements a double linked list would have both a head pointer as well as a tail pointer that points to the last node in the list. The current pointer member can be used to traverse the list in either direction. This general situation is shown in Figure 10.1.

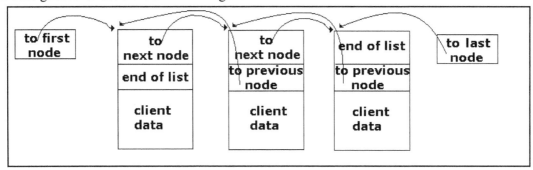

Figure 10.1 The Double Linked List Layout

Designing a Double Linked List Class

The data members of a double linked list class are obvious. Such a class would have a head pointer, a tail pointer and a current node pointer for iteration purposes. These pointers are of the data type of the "node." The class could also maintain a count of the number of nodes in the list for convenience. However, specification of the client's data that is to be stored in a node is the variable factor. Let's begin by exploring some possibilities for storing that client's data in the node.

Methods of Storing the Client Data in a Node

In chapter 9, the node contained a duplicate copy of the client's data structure, a **Student** structure. Although I used a **Student** structure in the program in chapter 9, I could have designed a **Student** class and used a duplicate copy of it in the node as well. The client's data to be stored in the nodes of the list could also be intrinsic types or even arrays of types. It is whatever the client needs to have stored in the list. Quite commonly, it is structure or a class instances that the client program wishes to store in the list.

Method A. Storing a Copy of the Client's Data in the Node

Here is the first approach that with which we are familiar. The client's data is stored in either a structure or class instance, here called **Student**.

```
struct Student {    // or class Student {
    ...
};
```

The **LinkNode** definition that defines the nodes can be either a structure or a class. Since the **LinkNode** has no member functions, it is more often just a structure. Notice the instance of the client's data within the **LinkNode**.

```
struct LinkNode {
    LinkNode* fwdptr;
    LinkNode* backptr;
    Student s;
};
```
or
```
class  LinkNode {
public:
    LinkNode* fwdptr;
    LinkNode* backptr;
    Student s;
};
```

The benefits of hardwiring the link node to the client's data is that many client-specific functions can be provided by the **LinkedList** class itself. Since **LinkedList** class knows all about the client's data, functions to find or match on a specific field, such as student id, can be included. Other functions, such as load the list from a file, write the list to a file, display the contents of the list—all can be provided by the **LinkedList** class itself. Very specific functions can be included, such as **DeleteStudentWithIdNumber()**. This can occur because the **LinkedList** class is completely aware of what the client's data actually is. In other words, we can move a good deal of list-processing complexity from the client program into the **LinkedList** class. This results in smaller, easier to maintain client programs. This is precisely what occurred in **Pgm09a** in the last chapter. Additionally, lists can easily be copied, unless there are dynamically allocated memory items within the **Student** structure or class itself.

Since we are storing copies of the client's data, there is no need for the client to dynamically allocate Student instances to pass into the **LinkedList** class to store. Thus, there are no clean up activities that the client programs must perform.

Are there any penalties or drawbacks of this method? Consider for a moment the memory requirements of a larger client data structure. Suppose that it had two dozen fields that occupied nearly 4k of memory. Each node would then be over 4k in size! Worse still, consider the impact at runtime for the compiler to make all the necessary copy structure operations. This penalty of size and runtime speed is a serious one indeed on larger client data structures and lengthy lists.

What about reusability of the **LinkedList** class when written using this method? There is none! If another application needed to store a list of boats, the entire class would have to be rewritten and then debugged. The next method handles the performance penalty but not the reusability issue.

Method B. Storing a Pointer to the Client's Data in the Node

To reduce any memory and speed of execution penalties, the **LinkNode** can store a pointer to the client's data instead. We change the structure or class as follows.

```
struct LinkNode {
      LinkNode* fwdptr;
      LinkNode* backptr;
      Student*  dataptr;
};
```

How many bytes does this structure occupy independently of however large the **Student** structure actually is? **LinkNode** consists of three pointers which are each 4 bytes in size. Each node occupies twelve bytes. How fast can the assignment of the client's data be done? All **LinkedList** must do is copy a pointer. Thus, any speed and memory requirements are removed, from the viewpoint of the **LinkedList** class proper.

This method retains all of the benefits of Method A in which specific functions to assist client programs can be included as part of the class itself. This is because the **LinkedList** class still knows all about the client's data, **Student** in this case. We can still provide an easy copy list operation duplicating each node by dynamically allocating new instances of the **Student** structure or class and copying the data from the old list.

However, by storing pointers to the client's data in the nodes, we have introduced an additional complexity level for all client programs. The client program must now dynamically allocate instances of the data and give a pointer to this memory instance to the **LinkedList** class to be stored in the nodes. However, since we know the data type of these pointers, we can provide for their removal when **EmptyList()** or the destructor is called. We can specifically call the **delete** function for each **dataptr** in each node. Hence, forcing client programs to dynamically allocate each data instance is not too terrible a price to pay in the client programs.

Of course, this method does nothing to address the reusability factor. Both Method A and B are closely tied to the client's data and are not reusable without a total rewrite.

Method C. Storing a void Pointer to the Client's Data in the Node

To reduce any memory and speed of execution penalties as well as to make a reusable double linked list class, the **LinkNode** can store a **void** pointer to the client's data instead. We change the structure or class as follows.

```
struct LinkNode {
     LinkNode* fwdptr;
     LinkNode* backptr;
     void*     dataptr;
};
```

Once again, the **LinkNode** structure consists of three pointers which are each 4 bytes in size. Any speed and memory requirements are once again removed, from the viewpoint of the **LinkedList** class proper.

By storing **void** pointers to the client's data, we have removed all dependencies upon client data. Thus, we can write a single implementation of the double linked list that can be used to store any kind of client data. This is the approach the **Pgm10a** follows. I am a firm believer in writing code once and then being able to just plug it into another application, as-is with no changes.

Once more, by storing **void** pointers to the client's data, we are normally forcing the client program to dynamically allocate instances of their data to be stored in the list. However, now we no longer know the data type of the client's data. And this factor does indeed impact the client programming significantly. Let's see how.

One of the more significant results of using **void** pointers is that the linked list class can no longer be responsible for the deletion of the client's data portions whenever **EmptyList()** or the destructor is called. All that the linked list class can do is delete the **LinkNode** instances. Thus, it becomes the full responsibility of the client program to traverse the list and delete all of the client's data before the client program calls **EmptyList()** or a linked list destructor!

There is another major impact on client programs. When copying lists either by use of the copy constructor or the assignment operator, a deep copy cannot be performed. The linked list class can only make duplicate copies of the **LinkNode** instances. Each of these new copies will contain the original client's data pointers. There is no way we can make duplicate copies of the actual client's data in the list. This is generally not a serious problem as long as the client program is aware of this side effect.

Thus, by placing a bit more of the burden on the client programs, we are able to write a reusable double linked list class. There are other methods of writing a linked list class. One of these is to use a template class. Templates are covered in advanced data structures because templates represent an advanced feature of the C++ OOP language. I would point out that such a template container class could store specific instances of the client's data in the nodes. This approach allows for tight coupling with client data while still having a reusable class.

Designing the Reusable Double Linked List Class

The actual **LinkNode** structure comes from Method C above and is repeated here.
```
struct LinkNode {
    LinkNode* fwdptr;
    LinkNode* backptr;
    void*     dataptr;
};
```
The four private data members are as follows.
```
 LinkNode* headptr;      // points to first node in list
 LinkNode* currentptr;   // points to the current node
 LinkNode* tailptr;      // points to last node in list
 long      count;        // the number of nodes in list
```

The class should have a constructor and destructor, the latter of which calls the usual **EmptyList()** function which could also be called by client programs. What kinds of add new node functions are needed? Because the list has both a head and a tail pointer, additions can be made at both locations; these are called **AddAtHead()** and **AddAtTail()**. With the current pointer marking the current node in the list, the user may wish to add either before or after this specific node. This is often the case when they wish to maintain a sorted list. We have then another pair of functions: **InsertAfterCurrentNode()** and **InsertBeforeCurrentNode()**.

We should also provide a means of deleting the current node, **DeleteCurrentNode()**. We can add some convenience functions such as **GetSize()**, which returns the number of items in the list, **IsHead()**, which returns **true** if the current pointer is pointing to the first item in the list, and **IsTail()**, which returns **true** if the current pointer is pointing to the last item in the list.

What iterator functions are required for list traversal? They include **ResetToHead()**, **ResetToTail()**, **Next()**, **Previous()** and **GetCurrentNode()**. Thus, a client program can move both forward and backwards through the list.

Providing a Find Matching List Item Function

Look over the functionality that the linked list class provides. Is anything missing? Well, yes, as a matter of fact, there is something missing. How would a client program find a specific item in the list? Suppose that the list contained instances of the **Student** structure. How could a client program find the student whose id number was 123456789? As the class design currently stands, the client program would have to manually iterate sequentially through the list from either end looking for a matching id number in the list.

Can we provide a **FindNode()** function to assist client programs in locating a specific item? Yes, however, this single function poses a major problem in design. Certainly, we can iterate sequentially through the list, setting **currentptr** as we go along. But how do we compare the current node's user data with the user's matching criteria when we know nothing about the client's data? In fact, we cannot. Instead, we must rely on the user to notify our **FindNode()** function if a specific node matches their criteria. The user criteria can be anything so **FindNode()** must accept that criteria using a constant **void** pointer. The user can typecast it back into the actual matching criteria data type. For each node in the list, we must call a function back in the client program and give it the current user data and the criteria in use on this search. This is known as a **call back function** because our function (which is viewed as "system" coding by the client program) must repeatedly call a function back in the client program to perform the actual comparison list item by list item. This process is diagramed in Figure 10.2 below.

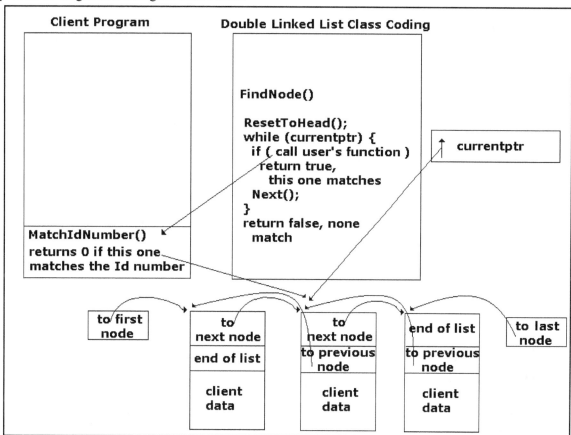

Figure 10.2 The Callback Function Process

What would the user call back function prototype be? It is given two constant **void** pointers, the pointer to the specific criteria for matching and the pointer current node's item. For example, suppose that the client program needed to match on student id numbers. They would have coded the function **MatchOnId()**.

```
int MatchOnId (const void* ptrmatchData,
                const void* ptrthis);
```

On the other hand, suppose the client program wanted to match on the student's name. The matching function prototype is

```
int MatchOnName (const void* ptrmatchData,
                const void* ptrthis);
```

Sample client coding to perform these actions might be as follows.

319

```
long idToFind;
char nameToFind[NAMELEN];
...
if (roster.FindNode (&idToFind, MatchOnId)) {
...
if (roster.FindNode (nameToFind, MatchOnName) {
...
```

Notice how the client must pass the address of the matching data item as the first parameter. However, it is the second parameter that causes the complexity. The client must pass into our **FindNode()** function the function for us to actually use.

This raises a most interesting question. What is the data type of the name of a function? We need this information to code our own prototype for **FindNode()**. The data type of the name of a function is a pointer to a function that has the same prototype. In the following prototype of the matching function, the parentheses around the * are required.

```
int (*FINDFUNCT) (const void* ptrmatchData, const void* ptrthis);
```

This reads, **FINDFUNCT** is a pointer to a function that returns an **int** and is passed two constant **void** pointers. If the parentheses (*) are omitted as in this next one,

```
int *OOPS (const void* ptrmatchData, const void* ptrthis);
```

This says that **OOPS** is a function that returns a pointer to an **int**!

Ok. Then how do we code our **FindNode()** prototype. The easiest way is to use the **typedef** statement to define **FINDFUNCT** as a new kind of data, one that is a pointer to a function that returns an **int** and is passed two constant **void** pointers.

```
typedef int (*FINDFUNCT) (const void* ptrmatchData,
                          const void* ptrthis);
```

Then, the **FindNode()** prototype in our class is simply

```
    bool  FindNode (const void* ptrmatchData, FINDFUNCT Find);
```

Within **FindNode()**, how do we actually call the passed function pointer, **Find()**?

Ok. Now how do we actually call this passed function pointed to by parameter **Find**? Normally, to get to the value pointed to by a pointer, we dereference the pointer; again the parentheses are required.

```
    (*Find) (x, y); // the hard way to invoke the Find function
```

If we had coded it as

```
    *Find (x, y); // error
```

The dereference operator is applied to the return value of the **Find()** function, a **bool** in this case, causing a compile-time error.

But wait a minute. All names of all functions in C/C++ are pointers to the coding that they represent. We never do the following.

```
    x = (*sqrt) (z);
    y = (*sin) (angle);
```

The compiler automatically performs function pointer dereference for us. Thus, we can call the passed **Find()** function by coding just this.

```
    Find (x, y); // the easy way to invoke the Find function
```

In reality, by having the **typedef** for the call back function, the **FindNode()** function is easily implemented. Here is the shell of our generic **DoubleLinkedList** class showing the implementation of **FindNode()**.

```
typedef int (*FINDFUNCT) (const void* ptrmatchData,
                          const void* ptrthis);
class DoubleLinkedList {
 bool  FindNode (const void* ptrmatchData, FINDFUNCT Find);
...
bool  DoubleLinkedList::FindNode (const void* ptrmatchData,
                                  FINDFUNCT Find) {
 if (!count)       // is the list is empty
   return false;   // yes, so leave doing nothing with no match
 ResetToHead ();  // begin at the first node in the list
 while (currentptr) { // for each node, see if it matches
  if (Find (ptrmatchData, currentptr->dataptr) == 0)
   return true; // yes, this one matches, return true to caller
  Next ();        // move to the next item in the list
 }
 return false;   // here no item matched the user's criteria
}
```

Handling the Insertions into the List

Now let's examine how items are added to the list with the four functions. The functions **AddAtHead()** and **AddAtTail()** are the simpler ones to implement because we are always at one end of the list, never in the middle. Adding at the head of the list presents only two circumstances—either the list is empty or there are one or more items already in the list. Figures 10.3 and 10.4 illustrates what must be done to insert a new node at the head. For both cases, allocate a new node and fill it as shown.

```
LinkNode* ptrnew = new (std::nothrow) LinkNode;
ptrnew->dataptr = ptrdata; // copy the passed client pointer
ptrnew->backptr = 0;       // back pointer is 0 because at head
count++;                   // increment total number of nodes
```

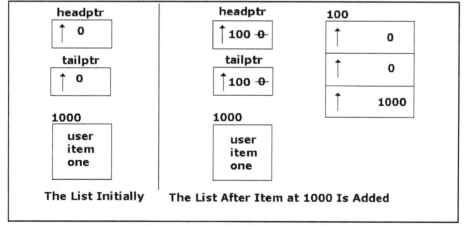

Figure 10.3 Adding a New Item at the Head to an Empty List

For an empty list, we just set the head and tail pointers to the new node.

```
headptr = tailptr = ptrnew; // this new node
ptrnew->fwdptr = 0;         // and no forward nodes yet
```

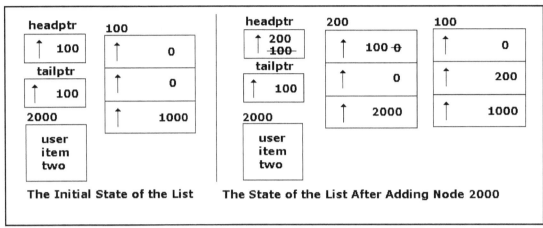

Figure 10.4 Adding a New Item at the Head with Items Already in the List

If there are items in the list, we must set the new node's forward pointer to the previous node that was at the front of the list. We must also set the previous first node's back pointer to point to the new first node. And **headptr** now stores the new node's address.

```
ptrnew->fwdptr = headptr; // fwdptr contains the previous one
headptr->backptr = ptrnew;// prev node's backptr is us now
headptr = ptrnew;         // set headptr to newly added node
```

When adding at the tail, once again, two cases arise: an empty list and a list with items in it. The situation of an empty list is the same as it is with adding at the head when the list is empty. When there are items in the list, adding at the tail is shown in Figure 10.5.

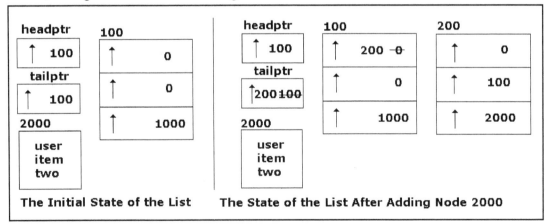

Figure 10.5 Adding a Node at the Tail of the List When There Are Items in the List

The current last node's forward pointer must now point to the new one being added at the tail. The new one being added must have its backwards pointer pointing to the previous last node. And the **tailptr** is updated to point to the new one being added at the tail.

```
tailptr->fwdptr = ptrnew; // yes, prev tail node points to us
ptrnew->backptr = tailptr;// us points back to the prev node
tailptr = ptrnew;          // tail is now us
```

Handling the insertion either before or after the current node raises additional complexities because a node could exist on either side of the insertion point. If the list is empty, **headptr** is 0, then reuse the **AddAtHead()** function. If the current pointer is 0, then I chose to also call **AddAtHead()**. However, one could signal an insertion error in this case if you so desire or even add at the tail. That leaves two remaining possibilities.

If we are inserting after the current node, then there must be a previous node from the viewpoint of this new one we are adding. If the current pointer is actually the last node in the list, then in effect we are adding at the tail and I chose to simple call **AddAtTail()** to carry out the insertion. That leaves only the one remaining possibility, we are inserting between two nodes. Figure 10.6 shows this more complicated case. Notice carefully how the forward and back chains on the list must be broken as the new node is inserted in between them. The code begins by allocating a new node and storing the user's data pointer and incrementing the count of the number of items in the list.

```
LinkNode* ptrnew = new (std::nothrow) LinkNode;
ptrnew->dataptr = ptrdata;
count++;
```

The new node must point forward to the node on the right and back to the node on the left of it. The node to its left must point forward to this new node while the node to its right must point back to the new node.

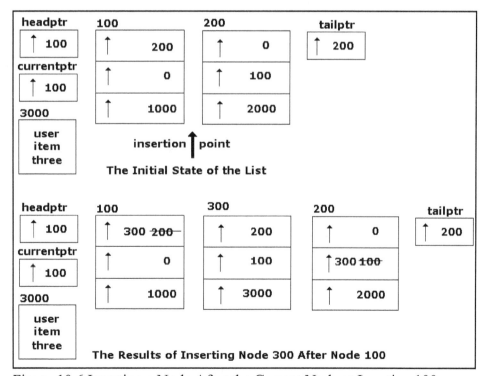

Figure 10.6 Inserting a Node After the Current Node at Location 100

The first two assignments are easy. Remember that **currentptr** is pointing to the node just before the new node.

```
ptrnew->backptr = currentptr;
ptrnew->fwdptr = currentptr->fwdptr;
```

The next two lines break the existing chain, inserting the new node into the chain.

```
currentptr->fwdptr = ptrnew;
ptrnew->fwdptr->backptr = ptrnew;
currentptr = ptrnew;
```

The insert before the current node is handled in a similar fashion. If the list is empty or the current pointer is 0, I call **AddAtHead()** to insert the new node. This leaves two remaining cases to handle. Since we are inserting before the current node, then there will always be a node to the new node's right. But if the current node is actually the first node, then there is no node to its left and we are in effect adding at the head once again. The coding begins the same way as before. Allocate a new node, copy the user's pointer and increment the number of items in the list.

```
LinkNode* ptrnew = new (std::nothrow) LinkNode;
ptrnew->dataptr = ptrdata;
count++;
```

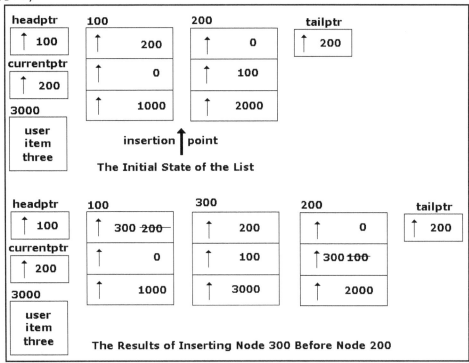

Figure 10.7 Inserting Node 300 Before Node 200

The new node's forward pointer is set to **currentptr** while the new node's back pointer is set to the current node's back pointer.

```
ptrnew->backptr = currentptr->backptr;
ptrnew->fwdptr = currentptr;
```

Then, the current pointer's back pointer must be set to point to the new node. And the previous node's

forward pointer must now point to the new node.
```
currentptr->backptr = ptrnew;
ptrnew->backptr->fwdptr = ptrnew;
currentptr = ptrnew;
```

Deleting the Current Node

When we wish to delete the current node, five situations arise. If the current node is 0, then there is nothing to do. The function should return **false** to alert the client program. Next, suppose that there is only one node in the list which is the current one to delete. This case is easy, we simply delete the node and reset all pointers and the count to 0. The remaining three cases deal with the location of the current node to delete in the list. The current node to delete could be the first node or the last node or one in the middle. Let's examine each of these three remaining cases in detail beginning with the node to delete being the first node in the list. Figure 10.8 illustrates the deletion process for the first node in the list.

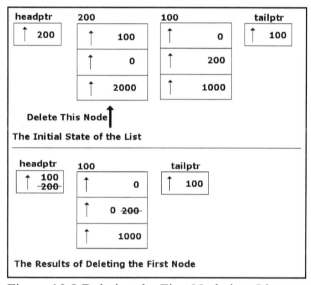

Figure 10.8 Deleting the First Node in a List

To delete the first node in the list, we must set the next node's back pointer to 0 and the **headptr** to the next node in order to remove the first node from the chain.
```
LinkNode* ptrtodelete = currentptr;
if (IsHead()) {                      // deleting first node? if so,
  currentptr->fwdptr->backptr = 0;// set next node's back to none
  headptr = currentptr->fwdptr;   // set head to next node
  currentptr = headptr;           // and current to next node
}
```

Next, suppose we are deleting the last node in the list. Figure 10.9 shows the situation. We must set the previous node's forward pointer to 0 and reset the tail pointer to that one.

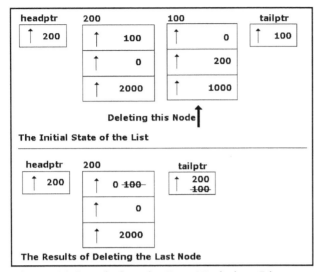

Figure 10.9 Deleting the Last Node in a List

```
else if (IsTail()) {              // deleting last one, if so,
  currentptr->backptr->fwdptr = 0;// set prev node's fwd to none
  tailptr = currentptr->backptr;  // set tail to prev node
  currentptr = tailptr;           // set current to prev node
}
```

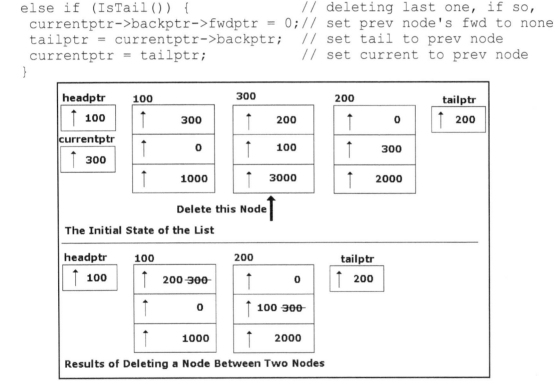

Figure 10.10 Deleting a Node from the Middle of the List

The final situation is deleting a node that is in the middle with a node on either side. Figure 10.10 illustrates how the chain of pointers must be adjusted to remove a middle node.

Examine the following two key coding lines and compare them to the above figure. Make sure you understand how the node at 300 is removed from the forward and back chains.

```
else { // here the node to delete is in the middle
  // set next node's back to previous node
  currentptr->fwdptr->backptr = currentptr->backptr;
  // set previous node's fwd to next node
  currentptr->backptr->fwdptr = currentptr->fwdptr;
  // leave current pointing to previous node
  currentptr = currentptr->backptr;
}
delete ptrtodelete; // now delete the requested node
return true;
```

Adding a Debugging Feature

When one has a class such as this which is storing generic user data, how can the class be tested? With the single linked student roster class of chapter 9, the class knew about the data it was storing. Consequently, the class could provide some nice displays of the list contents at any point in time. When we have a generic class which knows nothing about the data it is storing, other techniques can be used. In this case, the list involves numerous pointers, and worse still, chains of pointers that should be checked for accuracy. If something is coded incorrectly, then the various pointers might not be what we had hoped they would be.

To assist debugging this class, I added a simple **DebugDisplay()** function that displays all items in the list, which are the pointers and node contents. Here is what the display looks like.

```
Test of Three Items Each Added At the Head
head: 0x002F2568   Node At: 0x002F2568   Node At: 0x002F2530
tail: 0x002F1100      fwd: 0x002F2530      fwd: 0x002F1100
curr: 0x002F2568      bck: 0x00000000      bck: 0x002F2568
count:        3      dat: 0x0012FC64      dat: 0x0012FC5C

                   Node At: 0x002F1100
                      fwd: 0x00000000
                      bck: 0x002F2530
                      dat: 0x0012FC54
```

When pointers are displayed, the output is shown as hexadecimal numbers. In this sample, I added three successive items to the list at the head of the list each time. Visually, we can inspect the various chains and see they are correct. That is, head points to the first node, whose forward pointer points to the second node, whose forward pointer points to the third node, whose forward pointer is 0 indicating the end of list.

This technique is useful in debugging classes which use large amounts of dynamic memory allocations. We have a clear visual picture of the pointers and what they are pointing to.

The Generic DoubleLinkedList Class

Here is the header file for our generic **DoubleLinkedList** class. Notice that I placed numerous comments and some coding samples for the users in the header file.

```
Double Linked List Class Definition
```

```
 1 #pragma once
 2 #include <iostream>
 3 using namespace std;
 4
 5 /*************************************************/
 6 /*                                               */
 7 /* DoubleLinkedList Class: a reusable double linked list */
 8 /*                                               */
 9 /*************************************************/
10
11 // LinkNode: the link list node structure
12 struct LinkNode {
13  LinkNode* fwdptr;  // points to the next node in the list
14  LinkNode* backptr; // points to the previous node
15  void*     dataptr; // points to the client data stored
16 };
17
18 typedef int (*FINDFUNCT) (const void* ptrmatchData,
19                           const void* ptrthis);
20
21 class DoubleLinkedList {
22
23 private:
24  LinkNode* headptr;     // points to first node in list
25  LinkNode* currentptr;  // points to the current node
26  LinkNode* tailptr;     // points to last node in list
27  long      count;       // the number of nodes in list
28
29 public:
30         // constructs an empty list
31         DoubleLinkedList ();
32
33         // deletes the list but not the user's items stored
34      ~DoubleLinkedList ();
35
36         // removes all nodes, but not the user's items stored
37  void  EmptyList ();
38  /* Note: client program must ensure that all client data are
39   deleted before calling EmptyList() or the destructor
40   Example: suppose the list contains CostRec structures
41   list.ResetToHead();
42   CostRec* ptrdata = (CostRec*) list.GetCurrentNode();
```

328

```
43    while (ptrdata) {
44      delete ptrdata;
45      list.Next();
46      ptrdata = (CostRec*) list.GetCurrentNode();
47      }
48    list.EmptyList();*/
49
50          // add user's data at the head
51    void  AddAtHead (void* ptrdata);
52
53          // add user's data at the tail
54    void  AddAtTail (void* ptrdata); // add node at the tail
55
56          // add it after the current node - if current node is 0,
57          // it is added at the head
58    void  InsertAfterCurrentNode (void* ptrdata);
59
60          // add it before the current node - if the current
61          // node is 0, it is added at the head
62    void  InsertBeforeCurrentNode (void* ptrdata);
63
64          // deletes the current node, but not the user's data
65          // returns false if there is no current node
66    bool  DeleteCurrentNode ();
67
68          // sets the current pointer to the node whose data matches
69          // the matching criteria set by the caller
70    bool  FindNode (const void* ptrmatchData, FINDFUNCT Find);
71    /* example of usage. Suppose that user data are double pointers
72     client's prototype is:
73      int MatchDbl(const void* ptrmatchData, const void* ptrthis);
74     double findThis = 2;
75     if (test.FindNode (&findThis, MatchDbl)) {
76      double* ptrMatched = (double*) test.GetCurrentNode();
77      cout << "Found: " << *ptrMatched << " should find 2\n";
78      }
79     and the user's function is coded:
80     int MatchDbl (const void* ptrmatchData, const void* ptrthis){
81      double* ptrMatchThisOne = (double*) ptrmatchData;
82      double* ptrQuery = (double*) ptrthis;
83      if (*ptrQuery == *ptrMatchThisOne) return 0;
84      if (*ptrQuery > *ptrMatchThisOne) return -1;
85      return +1;
86      } */
87          // returns the number of items in the list
88    long  GetSize () const;
89
90          // returns true if current pointer is list at the start
91    bool  IsHead () const;
92
```

```
 93           // returns true if current pointer is list at the tail
 94  bool   IsTail () const;
 95
 96           // set current pointer to start of the list
 97  void   ResetToHead ();
 98
 99           // set current pointer to the end of the list
100  void   ResetToTail ();
101
102            // moves current pointer to the next item
103  void   Next ();
104
105           // moves current pointer to the previous item
106  void   Previous ();
107
108           // returns user data stored in the current node, 0 if none
109  void* GetCurrentNode () const;
110
111  // makes a copy of this list, but not the user's data stored
112  DoubleLinkedList (const DoubleLinkedList& r);
113
114      // makes a copy of this list, but not the user's data stored
115  DoubleLinkedList& operator= (const DoubleLinkedList& r);
116
117          // debugging display of all nodes and their values
118  void   DebugDisplay (ostream& os, const char* title) const;
119
120  protected:
121   // duplicates the list
122   void   CopyList (const DoubleLinkedList& r);
123  };
```

Here is the actual implementation. The major coding has already been discussed. You should look over the smaller functions as well as the more complex ones.

```
Implementation of a Generic DoubleLinkedList Class

 1  #include <iomanip>
 2  using namespace std;
 3  #include "DoubleLinkedList.h"
 4
 5  /***********************************************************/
 6  /*                                                         */
 7  /* DoubleLinkedList: constructs an empty list              */
 8  /*                                                         */
 9  /***********************************************************/
10
11  DoubleLinkedList::DoubleLinkedList () {
```

```
12  headptr = tailptr = currentptr = 0;
13  count = 0;
14  }
15
16  /*****************************************************/
17  /*                                                 */
18  /* ~DoubleLinkedList: destructor to remove all nodes  */
19  /*                                                 */
20  /*****************************************************/
21
22  DoubleLinkedList::~DoubleLinkedList () {
23   EmptyList ();
24  }
25
26  /*****************************************************/
27  /*                                                 */
28  /* EmptyList: remove all nodes from the list       */
29  /*                                                 */
30  /*****************************************************/
31
32  void  DoubleLinkedList::EmptyList () {
33   if (!headptr) return;
34   LinkNode* ptrnext = headptr; // pointer to traverse the list
35   LinkNode* ptrdel;            // the node to delete
36   // traverse the list - ends when there are no more nodes
37   while (ptrnext) {
38    ptrdel = ptrnext;           // save the current one to be deleted
39    ptrnext = ptrnext->fwdptr;// point to the next node
40    delete ptrdel;              // and delete the previous node
41   }
42   headptr = currentptr = tailptr = 0;
43   count = 0;
44  }
45
46  /*****************************************************/
47  /*                                                 */
48  /* AddAtHead: insert new node at the beginning of list  */
49  /*                                                 */
50  /*****************************************************/
51
52  void  DoubleLinkedList::AddAtHead (void* ptrdata) {
53   // allocate a new node and fill it up
54   LinkNode* ptrnew = new (std::nothrow) LinkNode;
55   if (!ptrnew) {
56    cerr << "DoubleLinkedList::AddAtHead - out of memory\n";
57    exit (1);
58   }
59   ptrnew->dataptr = ptrdata; // copy the passed client pointer
60   ptrnew->backptr = 0;       // back pointer is 0 because at head
61   count++;                   // increment total number of nodes
```

331

```
62  // now chain this one into the list
63  if (headptr) {                // if headptr exists, then the new
64   ptrnew->fwdptr = headptr; // fwdptr contains the previous one
65   headptr->backptr = ptrnew;// prev node's backptr is us now
66   headptr = ptrnew;          // set headptr to newly added node
67  }
68  else {                        // empty list, so all ptrs point to
69   headptr = tailptr = ptrnew; // this new node
70   ptrnew->fwdptr = 0;         // and no forward nodes yet
71  }
72  currentptr = ptrnew; // leave the current one at the new one
73 }
74
75 /***********************************************************/
76 /*                                                         */
77 /* AddAtTail: insert new node at the end of the list       */
78 /*                                                         */
79 /***********************************************************/
80
81 void  DoubleLinkedList::AddAtTail (void* ptrdata) {
82  LinkNode* ptrnew = new (std::nothrow) LinkNode;
83  if (!ptrnew) {
84   cerr << "DoubleLinkedList::AddAtTail - out of memory\n";
85   exit (1);
86  }
87  count++;                      // increment total number of nodes
88  ptrnew->dataptr = ptrdata; // store the client pointer in node
89  ptrnew->fwdptr = 0;         // at end, cannot be forward node
90  if (tailptr) {                // is there anything in the list yet?
91   tailptr->fwdptr = ptrnew; // yes, prev tail node points to us
92   ptrnew->backptr = tailptr;// us points back to the prev node
93   tailptr = ptrnew;          // tail is now us
94  }
95  else {                        // no - list is empty,
96   headptr = tailptr = ptrnew; // so set all to point to us
97   ptrnew->backptr = 0;        // and there is no prev node
98  }
99  currentptr = ptrnew;          // leave with current node set to us
100 }
101
102 /***********************************************************/
103 /*                                                         */
104 /* InsertAfterCurrentNode: add new node after the          */
105 /*                    current node                         */
106 /*                                                         */
107 /***********************************************************/
108
109 void  DoubleLinkedList::InsertAfterCurrentNode (void* ptrdata) {
110  if (!headptr)          // list is empty so add at head
111   AddAtHead (ptrdata);
```

```
112 else if (!currentptr) // current ptr is 0, so also add at head
113  AddAtHead (ptrdata);
114 else if (IsTail())    // current ptr is the last node, so
115  AddAtTail (ptrdata); // reuse add at the tail
116 else {                // here we are inserting in the middle
117  LinkNode* ptrnew = new (std::nothrow) LinkNode;
118  if (!ptrnew) {
119   cerr << "DoubleLinkedList::InsertAfterCurrentNode -"
120       << "out of memory\n";
121   exit (1);
122  }
123  ptrnew->dataptr = ptrdata;
124  count++;
125  // set new node's back pointer to current node to insert us
126  ptrnew->backptr = currentptr;
127  // set new node's forward ptr to the next node to the right
128  ptrnew->fwdptr = currentptr->fwdptr;
129  // set current's forward ptr to us to insert us
130  currentptr->fwdptr = ptrnew;
131  // set the node to the right of us to point back to us
132  ptrnew->fwdptr->backptr = ptrnew;
133  currentptr = ptrnew; // make the newly added node the current
134  }
135 }
136
137 /****************************************************/
138 /*                                                  */
139 /* InsertBeforeCurrentNode: add new node before current  */
140 /*      node.                                       */
141 /*                                                  */
142 /****************************************************/
143
144 void  DoubleLinkedList::InsertBeforeCurrentNode (void* ptrdata) {
145  if (!headptr)         // no nodes in list - so add at head
146   AddAtHead (ptrdata);
147  else if (!currentptr)// no current ptr, so add at head too
148   AddAtHead (ptrdata);
149  else if (IsHead())   // current ptr is the last node - so
150   AddAtHead(ptrdata); // add this one at the tail
151  else {                // here we are adding in the middle of list
152   LinkNode* ptrnew = new (std::nothrow) LinkNode;
153   if (!ptrnew) {
154    cerr << "DoubleLinkedList::InsertBeforeCurrentNode -"
155        << "out of memory\n";
156    exit (1);
157   }
158   ptrnew->dataptr = ptrdata;
159   count++;
160   // set new node's back ptr to pcurrents back
161   ptrnew->backptr = currentptr->backptr;
```

333

```
162    // set new node's forward ptr to current node
163    ptrnew->fwdptr = currentptr;
164    // set current node's back ptr to point to us
165    currentptr->backptr = ptrnew;
166    // set prevous node's forward ptr to point to us
167    ptrnew->backptr->fwdptr = ptrnew;
168    currentptr = ptrnew; // set current pointer to the new node
169  }
170 }
171
172 /********************************************************/
173 /*                                                      */
174 /* DeleteCurrentNode: removes the current node          */
175 /*     returns false if there is no current node        */
176 /*                                                      */
177 /********************************************************/
178
179 bool  DoubleLinkedList::DeleteCurrentNode () {
180  if (!currentptr) // if no current node, abort
181    return false;
182  count--;
183  if (!count) { // will list now be empty? if so reset to 0
184    delete currentptr;
185    headptr = tailptr = currentptr = 0;
186    return true;
187  }
188  LinkNode* ptrtodelete = currentptr;
189  if (IsHead()) {                    // deleting first node? if so,
190    currentptr->fwdptr->backptr = 0;// set next node's back to none
191    headptr = currentptr->fwdptr;    // set head to next node
192    currentptr = headptr;            // and current to next node
193  }
194  else if (IsTail()) {               // deleting last one, if so,
195    currentptr->backptr->fwdptr = 0;// set prev node's fwd to none
196    tailptr = currentptr->backptr;   // set tail to prev node
197    currentptr = tailptr;            // set current to prev node
198  }
199  else { // here the node to delete is in the middle
200    // set next node's back to previous node
201    currentptr->fwdptr->backptr = currentptr->backptr;
202    // set previous node's fwd to next node
203    currentptr->backptr->fwdptr = currentptr->fwdptr;
204    // leave current pointing to previous node
205    currentptr = currentptr->backptr;
206  }
207  delete ptrtodelete; // now delete the requested node
208  return true;
209 }
210
211 /********************************************************/
```

```
212  /*                                                              */
213  /* GetSize: returns the number of nodes in the list             */
214  /*                                                              */
215  /***************************************************************/
216
217  long   DoubleLinkedList::GetSize () const {
218   return count;
219  }
220
221  /***************************************************************/
222  /*                                                              */
223  /* IsHead: returns true if current node is the first node*/
224  /*                                                              */
225  /***************************************************************/
226
227  bool   DoubleLinkedList::IsHead () const {
228   return currentptr == headptr;
229  }
230
231  /***************************************************************/
232  /*                                                              */
233  /* IsTail: returns true if current node is the last one  */
234  /*                                                              */
235  /***************************************************************/
236
237  bool   DoubleLinkedList::IsTail () const {
238   return currentptr == tailptr;
239  }
240
241  /***************************************************************/
242  /*                                                              */
243  /* ResetToHead: sets current pointer to start of list    */
244  /*                                                              */
245  /***************************************************************/
246
247  void   DoubleLinkedList::ResetToHead () {
248   currentptr = headptr;
249  }
250
251  /***************************************************************/
252  /*                                                              */
253  /* ResetToTail: sets current pointer to last node in list*/
254  /*                                                              */
255  /***************************************************************/
256
257  void   DoubleLinkedList::ResetToTail () {
258   currentptr = tailptr;
259  }
260
261  /***************************************************************/
```

```
262 /*                                                        */
263 /* Next: move forward one node in the list                */
264 /*                                                        */
265 /**********************************************************/
266
267 void  DoubleLinkedList::Next () {
268  if (currentptr)
269    currentptr = currentptr->fwdptr;
270 }
271
272 /**********************************************************/
273 /*                                                        */
274 /* Previous: backs up one node in the list                */
275 /*                                                        */
276 /**********************************************************/
277
278 void  DoubleLinkedList::Previous () {
279  if (currentptr)
280    currentptr = currentptr->backptr;
281 }
282
283 /**********************************************************/
284 /*                                                        */
285 /* GetCurrentNode: returns user data at current node or 0 */
286 /*                                                        */
287 /**********************************************************/
288
289 void* DoubleLinkedList::GetCurrentNode () const {
290  return currentptr ? currentptr->dataptr : 0;
291 }
292
293 /**********************************************************/
294 /*                                                        */
295 /* DoubleLinkedList: copy constructor - duplicate a list  */
296 /*                                                        */
297 /**********************************************************/
298
299 DoubleLinkedList::DoubleLinkedList (const DoubleLinkedList& r) {
300  CopyList (r);
301 }
302
303 /**********************************************************/
304 /*                                                        */
305 /* operator=: Make a duplicate copy of a list             */
306 /*                                                        */
307 /**********************************************************/
308
309 DoubleLinkedList& DoubleLinkedList::operator= (
310                   const DoubleLinkedList& r) {
311  if (this == &r) return *this; // avoid a = a; situation
```

```
312  EmptyList ();  // remove all items in this list
313  CopyList (r);  // make a copy of r's list
314  return *this;
315 }
316
317 /*****************************************************/
318 /*                                                 */
319 /* CopyList: Make a duplicate copy of a list        */
320 /*                                                 */
321 /*****************************************************/
322
323 void  DoubleLinkedList::CopyList (const DoubleLinkedList& r) {
324   // handle the empty list first
325   if (!r.headptr) {
326    headptr = currentptr = tailptr = 0;
327    return;
328   }
329   count = r.count;
330   LinkNode* ptrRcurrent = r.headptr;
331   // previousptr tracks our prior node so we can set its
332   // forward pointer to the next new one
333   LinkNode* previousptr = 0;
334   // prime the loop so headptr can be set one time
335   currentptr = new (std::nothrow) LinkNode;
336   if (!currentptr) {
337    cerr << "DoubleLinkedList::CopyList - out of memory\n";
338    exit (1);
339   }
340   headptr = currentptr;  // assign this one to the headptr
341
342   // traverse list r's nodes
343   while (ptrRcurrent) {
344    // copy r's student info into our new node
345    currentptr->dataptr = ptrRcurrent->dataptr;
346    currentptr->fwdptr = 0;  // set our forward ptr to 0
346a   currentptr->backptr = 0; // set our back ptr to 0
347    // if previous node exists, set its forward ptr to the new one
348    if (previousptr) {
349     previousptr->fwdptr = currentptr;
349a    currentptr->backptr = previousptr;
349b   }
350    // save this node as the prevous node
351    previousptr = currentptr;
352    // and get a new node for the next iteration
353    currentptr = new (std::nothrow) LinkNode;
354    if (!currentptr) {
355     cerr << "DoubleLinkedList::CopyList - out of memory\n";
356     exit (1);
357    }
358    // move to r's next node
```

```
359    ptrRcurrent = ptrRcurrent->fwdptr;
360    }
360a   tailptr = previousptr ; // save tail
361   delete currentptr; // delete the extra unneeded node
362   // leave list at the beginning
363   ResetToHead ();
364   }
365
366   /***************************************************/
367   /*                                                 */
368   /* FindNode: find the node whose data matches users    */
369   /*           specifications - calls user's Find Function */
370   /*                                                 */
371   /***************************************************/
372
373   bool  DoubleLinkedList::FindNode (const void* ptrmatchData,
374                                     FINDFUNCT Find) {
375   if (!count) // empty list => not found
376    return false;
377   ResetToHead ();        // begin at the start of the list
378   while (currentptr) {  // examine each node in turn
379    if (Find (ptrmatchData, currentptr->dataptr) == 0)
380     return true;        // return true if this one matches
381    Next ();             // move to the next node in the list
382    }
383   return false;         // did not find it in whole list
384   }
385
386   /***************************************************/
387   /*                                                 */
388   /* DebugDisplay: make nicely formatted display of list   */
389   /*                                                 */
390   /***************************************************/
391
392   void  DoubleLinkedList::DebugDisplay (ostream& os,
393                                         const char* title) const {
394   os << endl << title << endl << dec;
395   if (!headptr) {
396    os << "head: " << setw(10) << headptr << endl;
397    os << "tail: " << setw (10) << tailptr << endl;
398    os << "curr: " << setw(10) << currentptr << endl;
399    os << "count: " << setw(9) << count << endl << endl << endl;
400    return;
401    }
402   LinkNode* ptr1, *ptr2, *ptrcur = headptr;
403   os << "head: " << setw(10) << headptr;
404   ptr1 = ptrcur;
405   ptr2 = ptr1->fwdptr;
406   os << "   Node At: " << setw(10) << ptr1;
407   if (ptr2)
```

```
408   os << "   Node At: " << setw(10) << ptr2;
409   os << endl;
410   os << "tail: " << setw (10) << tailptr;
411   os << "        fwd: " << setw (10) << ptr1->fwdptr;
412   if (ptr2)
413    os << "        fwd: " << setw (10) << ptr2->fwdptr;
414   os << endl;
415   os << "curr: " << setw(10) << currentptr;
416   os << "        bck: " << setw(10) << ptr1->backptr;
417   if (ptr2)
418    os << "        bck: " << setw(10) << ptr2->backptr;
419   os << endl;
420   os << "count: " << setw(9) << count;
421   os << "        dat: " << setw(10) << ptr1->dataptr;
422   if (ptr2)
423    os << "        dat: " << setw(10) << ptr2->dataptr;
424   os << endl << endl;
425   while (ptr2 && ptr2->fwdptr) {
426    ptr1 = ptr2->fwdptr;
427    if (ptr1)
428     ptr2 = ptr1->fwdptr;
429    else
430     ptr2 = 0;
431    os << "                    ";
432    os << "   Node At: " << setw(10) << ptr1;
433    if (ptr2)
434     os << "   Node At: " << setw(10) << ptr2;
435    os << endl;
436    os << "                    ";
437    os << "        fwd: " << setw (10) << ptr1->fwdptr;
438    if (ptr2)
439     os << "        fwd: " << setw (10) << ptr2->fwdptr;
440    os << endl;
441    os << "                    ";
442    os << "        bck: " << setw(10) << ptr1->backptr;
443    if (ptr2)
444     os << "        bck: " << setw(10) << ptr2->backptr;
445    os << endl;
446    os << "                    ";
447    os << "        dat: " << setw(10) << ptr1->dataptr;
448    if (ptr2)
449     os << "        dat: " << setw(10) << ptr2->dataptr;
450    os << endl << endl;
451   }
452   os << endl << endl;
453  }
454
```

A Testing Oracle and Program

To thoroughly test the **DoubleLinkedList** class, we must design a testing oracle. This one is a bit on the complex side because of off the possibilities among the functions. Some of the simpler functions can be tested implicitly because other functions that call them work. For example, the functions **IsHead()** and **IsTail()** are both called from other functions.

One should verify that a series of nodes can be added at the head and at the tail. When testing the **InsertAfterCurrentNode()** function, one should try to insert into an empty list, to insert after the first node in the list, to insert after the last node in the list as well as to insert into the middle of a list. These should be tested with one or more nodes already in the list as well. Likewise, when testing the **InsertBeforeCurrentNode()** function, one should try to insert into an empty list, before the first node, in the middle of a list and before the last in the list. Also, the list should have one, two, or more nodes as the tests are done.

DeleteCurrentNode() must be tested in many situations. With one item in the list, it should delete that one which is the current node. Then with two items in the list, it should be able to delete either node successfully. With three nodes in the list, it should be able to delete the one in the middle.

GetSize() and the iteration functions, both forward and backwards should be checked. The **FindNode()** function should be checked in a variety of ways, including attempts to find items that are not in the list. The assignment operator and copy constructor must be tested. And the **EmptyList()** and destructor should be verified as working.

As you look over my **Pgm10a** tester program and its results, see if you can spot some additional combinations that ought to have been tested.

In **Pgm10a**, I again took the expediency route and created an array of **double**s; each element's value is one greater than the previous element. The linked list stores the address of one element in this array as the client's data. In this manner, the client program does not have to worry about constantly dynamically allocating items to be stored in the list. The tester program can concentrate on debugging the list class.

Here are the tester program, **Pgm10a**, and the output from the test run.

```
Pgm10a - Tests the DoubleLinkedList Class

 1 #include <iostream>
 2 #include <iomanip>
 3 #include <fstream>
 4 #include <crtdbg.h>
 5 #include <string>
 6 using namespace std;
 7
 8 #include "DoubleLinkedList.h"
 9
10 /**********************************************************/
```

```
11 /*                                                              */
12 /* Pgm10a: Testing the Double Linked List Class                 */
13 /*                                                              */
14 /***************************************************************/
15
16 const int MAX = 100;
17
18 int MatchDouble (const void* ptrmatchData, const void* ptrthis);
19
20 int main () {
21  double data[MAX];
22  long i;
23  for (i=0; i<MAX; i++) {
24   data[i] = i;
25  }
26  double* ptrdata;
27  {
28   DoubleLinkedList test;
29   test.DebugDisplay (cout, "Test of Empty List");
30
31   test.AddAtHead (&data[0]);
32   test.AddAtHead (&data[1]);
33   test.AddAtHead (&data[2]);
34   test.DebugDisplay (cout,
35    "Test of Three Items Each Added at the Head");
36   test.EmptyList ();
37
38   test.AddAtTail (&data[0]);
39   test.AddAtTail (&data[1]);
40   test.AddAtTail (&data[2]);
41   test.DebugDisplay (cout,
42    "Test of Three Items Each Added at the Tail");
43   test.EmptyList ();
44
45   test.InsertAfterCurrentNode (&data[0]);
46   test.DebugDisplay (cout,
47    "Test of InsertAfter in Empty List");
48   test.InsertAfterCurrentNode (&data[1]);
49   test.DebugDisplay (cout,
50    "Test of InsertAfter First Item in the List");
51   test.InsertAfterCurrentNode (&data[2]);
52   test.DebugDisplay (cout,
53    "Test of InsertAfter Last Item in the List");
54
55   test.DeleteCurrentNode ();
56   test.DebugDisplay (cout,
57    "Test of DeleteCurrent - Last Item in the List");
58
59   test.Previous ();
60   test.InsertAfterCurrentNode (&data[2]);
```

```
61    test.DebugDisplay (cout,
62     "Test of InsertAfter Middle Item in the List");
63
64    test.DeleteCurrentNode ();
65    test.DebugDisplay (cout,
66     "Test of DeleteCurrent - Middle Item in the List");
67
68    test.DeleteCurrentNode ();
69    test.DebugDisplay (cout,
70     "Test of DeleteCurrent - First Item in the List");
71
72    test.DeleteCurrentNode ();
73    test.DebugDisplay (cout,
74     "Test of DeleteCurrent - When One Item Is in the List");
75
76    test.InsertBeforeCurrentNode (&data[0]);
77    test.DebugDisplay (cout,
78     "Test of InsertBefore in Empty List");
79    test.InsertBeforeCurrentNode (&data[1]);
80    test.DebugDisplay (cout,
81     "Test of InsertBefore First Item in the List");
82    test.Next ();
83    test.InsertBeforeCurrentNode (&data[2]);
84    test.DebugDisplay (cout,
85     "Test of InsertBefore Adds Middle Item to the List");
86
87    test.EmptyList ();
88    test.AddAtTail (&data[0]);
89    test.AddAtTail (&data[1]);
90    test.AddAtTail (&data[2]);
91    test.DebugDisplay (cout,
92     "Test of Three Items Each Added at the Tail");
93    test.ResetToHead ();
94    cout << "Testing GetSize(): " << test.GetSize ()
95         << " should = 3\n\n";
96    cout << "Testing forward iteration through list\n";
97    while ((ptrdata = (double*) test.GetCurrentNode ())) {
98     cout << *ptrdata << endl;
99     test.Next ();
100   }
101   test.ResetToTail ();
102   cout << "Testing backwards iteration through list\n";
103   while ((ptrdata = (double*) test.GetCurrentNode ())) {
104    cout << *ptrdata << endl;
105    test.Previous ();
106   }
107
108   cout << endl << "Testing FindNode Function\n";
109   double findThis = 2;
110   if (test.FindNode (&findThis, MatchDouble)) {
```

```
111      double* ptrMatched = (double*) test.GetCurrentNode();
112      cout << "Found: " << *ptrMatched << " should find 2\n";
113    }
114    findThis = 1;
115    if (test.FindNode (&findThis, MatchDouble)) {
116     double* ptrMatched = (double*) test.GetCurrentNode();
117     cout << "Found: " << *ptrMatched << " should find 1\n";
118    }
119    findThis = 3;
120    if (test.FindNode (&findThis, MatchDouble)) {
121     double* ptrMatched = (double*) test.GetCurrentNode();
122     cout << "Found: " << *ptrMatched << " should find 1\n";
123    }
124    else
125     cout << "No item matched\n";
126    cout << "  Should find no items matching\n\n\n";
127
128    cout << "Testing the assignment operator\n";
129    test.DebugDisplay (cout, "The List to be copied");
130    DoubleLinkedList copy;
131    copy = test;
132    copy.DebugDisplay (cout,
133     "The copied list - should match above list");
134
135    cout << "Testing the copy constructor\n";
136    DoubleLinkedList copy1 (test);
137    copy1.DebugDisplay (cout, "The copied list should also match");
138
139    cout << "Testing Destructor - leaving with items in the list\n"
140         << "Should produce no memory leaks\n\n";
141   }
142
143   if (_CrtDumpMemoryLeaks())
144    cout << "\nOops! Memory Leaks!!\n";
145   else
146    cout << "\nNo Memory Leaks\n";
147
148   return 0;
149 }
150
151 int MatchDouble (const void* ptrmatchData, const void* ptrthis) {
152  double* ptrMatchThisOne = (double*) ptrmatchData;
153  double* ptrQuery = (double*) ptrthis;
154  if (*ptrQuery == *ptrMatchThisOne)
155   return 0;
156  if (*ptrQuery > *ptrMatchThisOne)
157   return -1;
158  return +1;
159 }
```

```
Testing Results from Pgm10a

 1
 2 Test of Empty List
 3 head:   00000000
 4 tail:   00000000
 5 curr:   00000000
 6 count:          0
 7
 8
 9
10 Test of Three Items Each Added at the Head
11 head:   00355CC8   Node At:   00355CC8   Node At:   00355C90
12 tail:   00355C58      fwd:    00355C90      fwd:    00355C58
13 curr:   00355CC8      bck:    00000000      bck:    00355CC8
14 count:          3      dat:    0012FC48      dat:    0012FC40
15
16                      Node At:   00355C58
17                         fwd:    00000000
18                         bck:    00355C90
19                         dat:    0012FC38
20
21
22
23
24 Test of Three Items Each Added at the Tail
25 head:   00355C58   Node At:   00355C58   Node At:   00355C90
26 tail:   00355CC8      fwd:    00355C90      fwd:    00355CC8
27 curr:   00355CC8      bck:    00000000      bck:    00355C58
28 count:          3      dat:    0012FC38      dat:    0012FC40
29
30                      Node At:   00355CC8
31                         fwd:    00000000
32                         bck:    00355C90
33                         dat:    0012FC48
34
35
36
37
38 Test of InsertAfter in Empty List
39 head:   00355C58   Node At:   00355C58
40 tail:   00355C58      fwd:    00000000
41 curr:   00355C58      bck:    00000000
42 count:          1      dat:    0012FC38
43
44
45
46
47 Test of InsertAfter First Item in the List
```

```
48 head:    00355C58    Node At:    00355C58    Node At:    00355C90
49 tail:    00355C90       fwd:     00355C90       fwd:     00000000
50 curr:    00355C90       bck:     00000000       bck:     00355C58
51 count:          2       dat:     0012FC38       dat:     0012FC40
52
53
54
55
56 Test of InsertAfter Last Item in the List
57 head:    00355C58    Node At:    00355C58    Node At:    00355C90
58 tail:    00355CC8       fwd:     00355C90       fwd:     00355CC8
59 curr:    00355CC8       bck:     00000000       bck:     00355C58
60 count:          3       dat:     0012FC38       dat:     0012FC40
61
62                       Node At:    00355CC8
63                          fwd:     00000000
64                          bck:     00355C90
65                          dat:     0012FC48
66
67
68
69
70 Test of DeleteCurrent - Last Item in the List
71 head:    00355C58    Node At:    00355C58    Node At:    00355C90
72 tail:    00355C90       fwd:     00355C90       fwd:     00000000
73 curr:    00355C90       bck:     00000000       bck:     00355C58
74 count:          2       dat:     0012FC38       dat:     0012FC40
75
76
77
78
79 Test of InsertAfter Middle Item in the List
80 head:    00355C58    Node At:    00355C58    Node At:    00355CC8
81 tail:    00355C90       fwd:     00355CC8       fwd:     00355C90
82 curr:    00355CC8       bck:     00000000       bck:     00355C58
83 count:          3       dat:     0012FC38       dat:     0012FC48
84
85                       Node At:    00355C90
86                          fwd:     00000000
87                          bck:     00355CC8
88                          dat:     0012FC40
89
90
91
92
93 Test of DeleteCurrent - Middle Item in the List
94 head:    00355C58    Node At:    00355C58    Node At:    00355C90
95 tail:    00355C90       fwd:     00355C90       fwd:     00000000
96 curr:    00355C58       bck:     00000000       bck:     00355C58
97 count:          2       dat:     0012FC38       dat:     0012FC40
```

345

```
 98
 99
100
101
102  Test of DeleteCurrent - First Item in the List
103  head:    00355C90    Node At:    00355C90
104  tail:    00355C90       fwd:    00000000
105  curr:    00355C90       bck:    00000000
106  count:          1       dat:    0012FC40
107
108
109
110
111  Test of DeleteCurrent - When One Item Is in the List
112  head:    00000000
113  tail:    00000000
114  curr:    00000000
115  count:          0
116
117
118
119  Test of InsertBefore in Empty List
120  head:    00355C58    Node At:    00355C58
121  tail:    00355C58       fwd:    00000000
122  curr:    00355C58       bck:    00000000
123  count:          1       dat:    0012FC38
124
125
126
127
128  Test of InsertBefore First Item in the List
129  head:    00355C90    Node At:    00355C90    Node At:    00355C58
130  tail:    00355C58       fwd:    00355C58       fwd:    00000000
131  curr:    00355C90       bck:    00000000       bck:    00355C90
132  count:          2       dat:    0012FC40       dat:    0012FC38
133
134
135
136
137  Test of InsertBefore Adds Middle Item to the List
138  head:    00355C90    Node At:    00355C90    Node At:    00355CC8
139  tail:    00355C58       fwd:    00355CC8       fwd:    00355C58
140  curr:    00355CC8       bck:    00000000       bck:    00355C90
141  count:          3       dat:    0012FC40       dat:    0012FC48
142
143                         Node At:    00355C58
144                            fwd:    00000000
145                            bck:    00355CC8
146                            dat:    0012FC38
147
```

```
148
149
150
151 Test of Three Items Each Added at the Tail
152 head:    00355C58    Node At:    00355C58    Node At:    00355C90
153 tail:    00355CC8        fwd:    00355C90        fwd:    00355CC8
154 curr:    00355CC8        bck:    00000000        bck:    00355C58
155 count:          3        dat:    0012FC38        dat:    0012FC40
156
157                      Node At:    00355CC8
158                          fwd:    00000000
159                          bck:    00355C90
160                          dat:    0012FC48
161
162
163
164 Testing GetSize(): 3 should = 3
165
166 Testing forward iteration through list
167 0
168 1
169 2
170 Testing backwards iteration through list
171 2
172 1
173 0
174
175 Testing FindNode Function
176 Found: 2 should find 2
177 Found: 1 should find 1
178 No item matched
179   Should find no items matching
180
181
182 Testing the assignment operator
183
184 The List to be copied
185 head:    00355C58    Node At:    00355C58    Node At:    00355C90
186 tail:    00355CC8        fwd:    00355C90        fwd:    00355CC8
187 curr:    00000000        bck:    00000000        bck:    00355C58
188 count:          3        dat:    0012FC38        dat:    0012FC40
189
190                      Node At:    00355CC8
191                          fwd:    00000000
192                          bck:    00355C90
193                          dat:    0012FC48
194
195
196
197
```

```
198 The copied list - should match above list
199 head:    00355E68    Node At:    00355E68    Node At:    00355EA0
200 tail:    00355ED8        fwd:    00355EA0        fwd:    00355ED8
201 curr:    00355E68        bck:    00000000        bck:    00355E68
202 count:          3        dat:    0012FC38        dat:    0012FC40
203
204                      Node At:    00355ED8
205                          fwd:    00000000
206                          bck:    00355EA0
207                          dat:    0012FC48
208
209
210
211 Testing the copy constructor
212
213 The copied list should also match
214 head:    00355F10    Node At:    00355F10    Node At:    00355F48
215 tail:    00355F80        fwd:    00355F48        fwd:    00355F80
216 curr:    00355F10        bck:    00000000        bck:    00355F10
217 count:          3        dat:    0012FC38        dat:    0012FC40
218
219                      Node At:    00355F80
220                          fwd:    00000000
221                          bck:    00355F48
222                          dat:    0012FC48
223
224
225
226 Testing Destructor - leaving with items in the list
227 Should produce no memory leaks
228
229
230 No Memory Leaks
231 Press any key to continue . .
```

Writing Client Programs that Use the Double Linked List Class

With our generic class written and tested, let's turn our attention to how client programs are written using this generic list class. Now we get to deal with the client side dynamic memory allocation of items to be stored in the list.

Acme has a contract to produce an inquiry/update type of program to process telephone directory information. Initially, the directory should contain the person's first and last names, the area code and phone number. If the concept proves acceptable to their client, then the additional fields that a phone directory has will be added. The specifications call for drawing a text box graphic around the actual listing. A sample is shown below.

```
                            My Phone Directory
```

Record Number	First Name	Last Name	Area Code	Phone Number
1	Tom	Jones	(309)	699-9999
2	Betsy	Smith	(309)	699-4444
3	Annie	Cringle	(309)	696-4242
4	Henry	Albright II	(309)	694-5555
5	Lorri Ann	Spieldt	(309)	676-6666
6	Harry	Durch	(309)	688-4325
7	Rusty	Earls	(309)	676-5551
8	Jennifer	Smallville	(309)	688-5321

The ASCII codes to use when drawing the box are from the upper ASCII sequence and thus must be defined as **unsigned char**. Each of these displays one character, such as the upper left corner angle.

```
unsigned char upleft = 218;
unsigned char upright = 191;
unsigned char botleft = 192;
unsigned char botright = 217;
unsigned char horiz = 196;
unsigned char vert = 179;
unsigned char leftright = 195;
unsigned char rightleft = 180;
unsigned char cross = 197;
unsigned char topdown = 194;
unsigned char botup = 193;
```

The program, upon startup, loads the current test file of directory entries and displays the above report. Next, the main menu is shown as follows.

```
Friends Phone Book

1 Add new friend
2 Delete an entry
3 Display the phone listing
4 Display phone listing to a file
5 Save into a new file
6 Exit

Enter the number of your choice: 1
```

The program should only accept a valid menu choice. The entry of a non-numeric character should not halt the program but be rejected and the menu re-shown.

When "Add new friend" is chosen, the following is a sample of the conversational dialog required.

```
Enter first name (10 characters):  Jenny
Enter last name (20 characters):   Heart-Smith
Enter the area code (3 numbers):   309
```

```
Enter the phone number (999-9999): 699-7777
Addition was successful
```

When "Delete an entry" is chosen, a new problem arises. How should the user indicate which directory entry is to be deleted? Rather than asking the user to enter the person's name (first and last), the program should maintain a record number id that begins at one. Thus, when the original file is loaded, as the records are being added to the list, the program adds a consecutive numerical id to each directory record. Thus, to delete an entry, the user is prompted to enter the record number id. The conversational dialog is shown below.

```
Enter the number of the phone book entry to delete: 8
Confirm deletion of the following entry
    8   Jennifer    Smallville          (309)   688-5321

Enter Y to confirm deletion or N to abort: y

Record deleted
```

If a matching list entry matches the user's number, that directory entry is then displayed and a "confirm deletion" query is made. The only acceptable reply is Y or N; the user is re-prompted until either y or n is entered. When the deletion is made, a new problem arises with the record numbers. To avoid a "hole" in the numbers, all records that come after the deleted one in the list must be renumbered.

When "Display phone listing to a file" is chosen, prompt the user for the filename. However, the program should accept long filenames and filenames that contain blanks. To handle the blanks, force the user

to surround the filename with double quote marks.

```
Enter the filename on which to display the report
If there are blanks in the filename,
place double quotemarks around the whole filename.
for example, "My Phone Book.txt"
"My Phone Book.txt"

Report written to: My Phone Book.txt
```

When "Save into a new file" is chosen, use a similar dialog to obtain the new filename.

```
Enter the new filename to use
If there are blanks in the filename,
place double quotemarks around the whole filename.
for example, "My Phone Book.txt"
NewPhoneBook.txt
File Saved
```

Finally, if any changes have been made to the original data, then any attempt to exit the program should force a query of the user as shown below.

```
Note: you have made changes to the phone database
and have not yet saved those changes
Do you want to quit and discard those changes?
Enter Y or N: n
```

Again, accept only y or n and re-prompt until a valid entry is made. If the user does not want to quit, re-show the main menu.

I began the solution to the problem by using Top-down design to functionally decompose the problem into functional modules. Figure 10.11 shows the design I used.

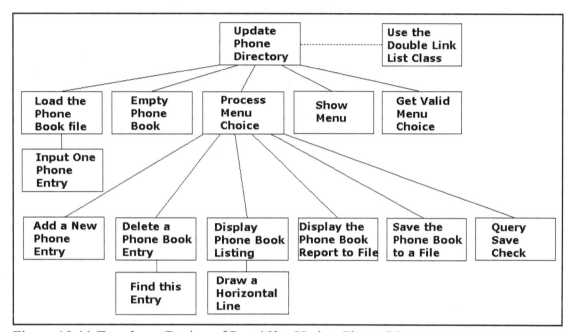

Figure 10.11 Top-down Design of Pgm10b - Update Phone Directory

Here is the completed **Pgm10b**, Update Phone Directory program. Examine the **main()** function first to see how the instance of the list is created. Next, look over the **LoadPhoneBook()** and **EmptyPhoneBook()** functions to see how **PhoneDirectory** structures are dynamically allocated, inserted into the list and finally deleted prior to program termination to avoid memory leaks.

Next, examine **DeleteEntry()** and its call back function **FindEntry()** to see how entries are found and deleted from the list. If you are interested in how the box is drawn around the reports, study the function **DisplayPhoneListing()**.

```
Pgm10b - Update Phone Directory Program

 1 #include <iostream>
 2 #include <iomanip>
 3 #include <fstream>
 4 #include <crtdbg.h>
 5 #include <string>
 6 using namespace std;
 7
 8 #include "DoubleLinkedList.h"
 9
10 /**********************************************************/
11 /*                                                      */
```

```
12 /* Pgm10b: Maintaining a Phone Directory Application      */
13 /*                                                        */
14 /**********************************************************/
15
16 const int MAX_FNAME_LEN = 11;
17 const int MAX_LNAME_LEN = 21;
18
19 // Phone Directory Information
20 struct PhoneDirectory {
21  int  recordNumber; // these are added by the pgm for id purposes
22  char firstName[MAX_FNAME_LEN];
23  char lastName[MAX_LNAME_LEN];
24  char areaCode[4];
25  char phoneNumber[9];
26 };
27
28 // the prototypes
29 bool LoadPhoneBook (DoubleLinkedList& pb, const char* filename);
30 istream& InputPhoneData (istream& is, PhoneDirectory& pd);
31
32 ostream& DisplayPhoneListing (DoubleLinkedList& pb, ostream& os);
33 void DrawLine (ostream& os, unsigned char c, int count);
34 void DisplayPhoneBookToFile (DoubleLinkedList& pb);
35
36 void EmptyPhoneBook (DoubleLinkedList& pb);
37
38 void ShowMenu ();
39 int  GetMenuChoice ();
40 bool ProcessMenuChoice (DoubleLinkedList& pb, int choice,
41                         bool& needToSave, ostream& os);
42
43 void AddEntry (DoubleLinkedList& pb, bool& needToSavePb);
44 void DeleteEntry (DoubleLinkedList& pb, bool& needToSavePb);
45 int  FindEntry (const void* ptrmatchData, const void* ptrthis);
46 void SavePhoneBook (DoubleLinkedList& pb, bool& needToSavePb);
47 bool SaveCheck (DoubleLinkedList& pb, bool needToSavePb);
48
49
50 int main () {
51  {
52   DoubleLinkedList phoneBook; // create the phonebook list
53
54   // load the book from a file
55   if (!LoadPhoneBook (phoneBook, "phoneBook.txt"))
56    return 1;
57   // display the listing using fancy box drawing characters
58   DisplayPhoneListing (phoneBook, cout);
59
60   bool needToSavePb = false; // true when data has been changed
61   bool quit = false;         // true when it is safe to quit
```

```
 62
 63   // main loop shows a menu, gets a valid choice and process it
 64   while (!quit) {
 65    quit = ProcessMenuChoice (phoneBook, GetMenuChoice (),
 66                               needToSavePb, cout);
 67    }
 68
 69    // remove all items from list
 70    EmptyPhoneBook (phoneBook);
 71   }
 72
 73   if (_CrtDumpMemoryLeaks())
 74    cout << "\nOops! Memory Leaks!!\n";
 75   else
 76    cout << "\nNo Memory Leaks\n";
 77
 78   return 0;
 79  }
 80
 81  /**********************************************************/
 82  /*                                                        */
 83  /* LoadPhoneBook: loads the list from a database file     */
 84  /*                                                        */
 85  /**********************************************************/
 86
 87  bool LoadPhoneBook (DoubleLinkedList& pb, const char* filename) {
 88   ifstream infile (filename);
 89   if (!infile) {
 90    cerr << "Error: unable to open file: " << filename << endl;
 91    return false;
 92   }
 93
 94   int i = 1; // this will be the record id number value
 95
 96   // allocate a new phone directory structure
 97   PhoneDirectory* ptrpd = new (std::nothrow) PhoneDirectory;
 98   if (!ptrpd) {
 99    cerr << "Out of memory in LoadPhoneBook\n";
100    exit (1);
101   }
102
103   // for each set of input data, insert the id number, add to list
104   // and allocate another phone directory structure for the next
105   // input opperation
106   while (InputPhoneData (infile, *ptrpd)) {
107    ptrpd->recordNumber = i++;
108    pb.AddAtTail (ptrpd);
109    ptrpd = new (std::nothrow) PhoneDirectory;
110    if (!ptrpd) {
111     cerr << "Out of memory in LoadPhoneBook\n";
```

```
112      exit (1);
113    }
114  }
115
116  delete ptrpd;    // delete the unneeded structure - eof was found
117  infile.close ();
118  return true;
119  }
120
121  /*****************************************************/
122  /*                                                   */
123  /*  InputPhoneData: input a single phone directory entry  */
124  /*                                                   */
125  /*****************************************************/
126
127  istream& InputPhoneData (istream& is, PhoneDirectory& pd) {
128    char c;
129    is >> c;   // input the leading " of first name
130    if (!is)
131      return is;
132    is.getline (pd.firstName, sizeof (pd.firstName), '\"');
133    is >> c; // get leading " of last name
134    is.getline (pd.lastName, sizeof (pd.lastName), '\"');
135    is >> pd.areaCode >> pd.phoneNumber;
136    return is;
137  }
138
139  /*****************************************************/
140  /*                                                   */
141  /*  DisplayPhoneListing: display in a fancy fashion the  */
142  /*                       complete phone listing     */
143  /*                                                   */
144  /*****************************************************/
145
146  ostream& DisplayPhoneListing (DoubleLinkedList& pb, ostream& os){
147    // the text graphics codes to draw fancy boxes
148    unsigned char upleft = 218;
149    unsigned char upright = 191;
150    unsigned char botleft = 192;
151    unsigned char botright = 217;
152    unsigned char horiz = 196;
153    unsigned char vert = 179;
154    unsigned char leftright = 195;
155    unsigned char rightleft = 180;
156    unsigned char cross = 197;
157    unsigned char topdown = 194;
158    unsigned char botup = 193;
159
160    os << "                     My Phone Directory\n\n";
161
```

```
162  // draws the top line
163  os << upleft;
164  DrawLine (os, horiz, 6);
165  os << topdown;
166  DrawLine (os, horiz, 12);
167  os << topdown;
168  DrawLine (os, horiz, 22);
169  os << topdown;
170  DrawLine (os, horiz, 7);
171  os << topdown;
172  DrawLine (os, horiz, 10);
173  os << upright << endl;
174
175  // display a pair of column heading lines
176  os << vert << "Record" << vert << " First     " << vert
177     << " Last                  " << vert << " Area   "
178     << vert << " Phone    " << vert << endl;
179  os << vert << "Number" << vert << " Name      " << vert
180     << " Name                 " << vert << " Code   "
181     << vert << " Number    " << vert << endl;
182
183  // display another horizontal line
184  os << leftright;
185  DrawLine (os, horiz, 6);
186  os << cross;
187  DrawLine (os, horiz, 12);
188  os << cross;
189  DrawLine (os, horiz, 22);
190  os << cross;
191  DrawLine (os, horiz, 7);
192  os << cross;
193  DrawLine (os, horiz, 10);
194  os << rightleft << endl;
195
196  // for each set of data, display all values within the boxes
197  pb.ResetToHead ();
198  PhoneDirectory* ptrpd = (PhoneDirectory*) pb.GetCurrentNode ();
199  while (ptrpd) {
200   os << vert << ' ' << setw(4) << ptrpd->recordNumber << ' '
201      << vert << ' ';
202   os.setf (ios::left, ios::adjustfield);
203   os << setw(10) << ptrpd->firstName << ' ' << vert << ' '
204      << setw(20) << ptrpd->lastName << ' ' << vert << " ("
205      << setw(3) << ptrpd->areaCode << ") " << vert << ' '
206      << setw(8) << ptrpd->phoneNumber << ' ' << vert << endl;
207   os.setf(ios::right, ios::adjustfield);
208   pb.Next ();
209   ptrpd = (PhoneDirectory*) pb.GetCurrentNode ();
210  }
211
```

```
212  // display the bottom line of the box
213  os << botleft;
214  DrawLine (os, horiz, 6);
215  os << botup;
216  DrawLine (os, horiz, 12);
217  os << botup;
218  DrawLine (os, horiz, 22);
219  os << botup;
220  DrawLine (os, horiz, 7);
221  os << botup;
222  DrawLine (os, horiz, 10);
223  os << botright << endl;
224  os << endl;
225  return os;
226  }
227
228  /***************************************************************/
229  /*                                                           */
230  /* DrawLine: helper function to draw a horizontal line    */
231  /*                                                           */
232  /***************************************************************/
233
234  void DrawLine (ostream& os, unsigned char c, int count) {
235  // displays character c count times to the stream
236   for (int i=0; i< count; i++) {
237    os << c;
238   }
239  }
240
241  /***************************************************************/
242  /*                                                           */
243  /* ShowMenu: displays the main menu of choices           */
244  /*                                                           */
245  /***************************************************************/
246
247  void ShowMenu () {
248   cout << "\n\n"
249        << "Friends Phone Book\n\n"
250        << "1 Add new friend\n"
251        << "2 Delete an entry\n"
252        << "3 Display the phone listing\n"
253        << "4 Display phone listing to a file\n"
254        << "5 Save into a new file\n"
255        << "6 Exit\n"
256        << "\nEnter the number of your choice: ";
257  }
258
259  /***************************************************************/
260  /*                                                           */
261  /* GetMenuChoice: gets a valid menu choice               */
```

```
262 /*                                                        */
263 /**********************************************************/
264
265 int GetMenuChoice () {
266  // get only a valid number between 1 and 6
267  int choice = 7;
268  while (choice < 1 || choice > 6) {
269   ShowMenu ();
270   cin >> choice;
271   if (!cin) {      // check for non-numeric data entered
272    cin.clear (); // yes, so reset cin state flags to good
273    char c;
274    cin.get(c);    // and get the offending character
275   }
276  }
277  cout << endl;
278  return choice;   // choice is a number between 1 and 6
279 }
280
281 /**********************************************************/
282 /*                                                        */
283 /* ProcessMenuChoice: driver to process that menu choice */
284 /*                                                        */
285 /**********************************************************/
286
287 bool ProcessMenuChoice (DoubleLinkedList& pb, int choice,
288                         bool& needToSavePb, ostream& os) {
289  switch (choice) {
290   case 1:
291    AddEntry (pb, needToSavePb);
292    return false;
293   case 2:
294    DeleteEntry (pb, needToSavePb);
295    return false;
296   case 3:
297    DisplayPhoneListing (pb, os);
298    return false;
299   case 4:
300    DisplayPhoneBookToFile (pb);
301    return false;
302   case 5:
303    SavePhoneBook (pb, needToSavePb);
304    return false;
305   case 6:
306    return SaveCheck (pb, needToSavePb);
307  };
308  return false;
309 }
310
311 /**********************************************************/
```

```
312 /*                                                            */
313 /* AddEntry: Adds a new person to the phone directory         */
314 /*                                                            */
315 /***********************************************************/
316
317 void AddEntry (DoubleLinkedList& pb, bool& needToSavePb) {
318  PhoneDirectory* ptrpd = new (std::nothrow) PhoneDirectory;
319  if (!ptrpd) {
320    cerr << "Out of memory in AddEntry - ignoring add\n";
321    return;
322  }
323
324  char c;
325  cin.get (c); // eat the crlf from the previous cin
326
327  // acquire the data on the new person to be added
328  cout << "Enter first name (10 characters):  ";
329  cin.get (ptrpd->firstName, sizeof(ptrpd->firstName));
330  cin.get (c);
331  cout << "Enter last name (20 characters):   ";
332  cin.get (ptrpd->lastName, sizeof(ptrpd->lastName));
333  cin.get (c);
334  cout << "Enter the area code (3 numbers):   ";
335  cin.get (ptrpd->areaCode, sizeof(ptrpd->areaCode));
336  cin.get (c);
337  cout << "Enter the phone number (999-9999): ";
338  cin.get (ptrpd->phoneNumber, sizeof(ptrpd->phoneNumber));
339  cin.get (c);
340
341  // set its record id to one larger than is in the list
342  ptrpd->recordNumber = pb.GetSize() + 1;
343
344  // and add it to the list
345  pb.AddAtTail (ptrpd);
346
347  // set the data has been modified flag
348  needToSavePb = true;
349  cout << "Addition was successful\n";
350 }
351
352 /***********************************************************/
353 /*                                                            */
354 /* DeleteEntry: removes a person from the phone directory */
355 /*    Note: use the record id number as the key id field  */
356 /*                                                            */
357 /***********************************************************/
358
359 void DeleteEntry (DoubleLinkedList& pb, bool& needToSavePb) {
360  char c;
361  cout << "Enter the number of the phone book entry to delete: ";
```

Beginning Data Structures in C++

```
362  int num;
363  cin >> num;
364
365  // now see if that number is in the list
366  if (pb.FindNode (&num, FindEntry)) {
367
368   // here we found the number in the list, so get that set
369   // and display it to the user and get a verification that
370   // they really do want to delete this one
371   PhoneDirectory* ptrpd = (PhoneDirectory*) pb.GetCurrentNode ();
372   cout << "Confirm deletion of the following entry\n";
373   cout << setw(4) << ptrpd->recordNumber << "   ";
374   cout.setf (ios::left, ios::adjustfield);
375   cout << setw(10) << ptrpd->firstName << "  "
376       << setw(20) << ptrpd->lastName << "  ("
377       << setw(3) << ptrpd->areaCode << ")  "
378       << setw(8) << ptrpd->phoneNumber << endl;
379   cout.setf(ios::right, ios::adjustfield);
380
381   // do not accept anything but a Y or N
382   c = ' ';
383   while (c != 'Y' && c != 'N') {
384    cout << endl << "Enter Y to confirm deletion or N to abort: ";
385    cin >> c;
386    c = toupper (c);
387   }
388   if (c == 'N')
389    cout << endl << "Nothing done\n";
390   else {
391    // here it has been verified as the one to delete, so do it
392    delete ptrpd;
393    pb.DeleteCurrentNode ();
394    // now handle renumbering all list items....
395    if (pb.IsHead()) // if deleted first one,
396     num = 1;        // renumbering begins at 1
397    else             // if we have not deleted the first one,
398     pb.Next ();     // move current to the first that may need it
399
400    // get current next one after the deleted one, if any
401    ptrpd = (PhoneDirectory*) pb.GetCurrentNode ();
402    while (ptrpd) { // for each phone directory, change its record
403     ptrpd->recordNumber = num++; // id number down one
404     pb.Next ();
405     ptrpd = (PhoneDirectory*) pb.GetCurrentNode ();
406    }
407    cout << endl << "Record deleted\n";
408    // set the data has been modified flag
409    needToSavePb = true;
410   }
411  }
```

359

```
412  else
413    cout << endl
414         << "No such number in the phone book - try again\n";
415  }
416
417  /**********************************************************/
418  /*                                                        */
419  /* FindEntry: call back function to see if this one       */
420  /*            the one we are looking for                  */
421  /*                                                        */
422  /**********************************************************/
423
424  int FindEntry (const void* ptrmatchData, const void* ptrthis) {
425    int* ptrnum = (int*) ptrmatchData;
426    PhoneDirectory* ptrpd = (PhoneDirectory*) ptrthis;
427    if (*ptrnum == ptrpd->recordNumber)
428      return 0;
429    if (*ptrnum > ptrpd->recordNumber)
430      return 1;
431    return -1;
432  }
433
434  /**********************************************************/
435  /*                                                        */
436  /* DisplayPhoneBookToFile: displays report to a file      */
437  /*            Note: can handle long filenames and those   */
438  /*            with blanks in them                         */
439  /*                                                        */
440  /**********************************************************/
441
442  void DisplayPhoneBookToFile (DoubleLinkedList& pb) {
443    char filename[_MAX_FNAME];
444    char c;
445    cin.get(c); // eat the crlf from previous cin
446
447    cout << "Enter the filename on which to display the report\n";
448    cout << "If there are blanks in the filename,\n"
449         << "place double quotemarks around the whole filename.\n"
450         << "for example, \"My Phone Book.txt\" \n";
451    cin.get (filename, sizeof(filename));
452
453    // check for long filename with quotemarks
454    if (filename[0] == '\"') {// doesn't check for required ending "
455      int len = (int)strlen (filename) - 2;
456      strncpy_s (filename, sizeof(filename), &filename[1], len);
457      filename[len] = 0;
458    }
459
460    // attempt to open the file
461    ofstream outfile (filename);
```

```
462  if (!outfile) {
463   cerr << "Error: cannot open output file: " << filename << endl;
464   return;
465  }
466
467  // now display the fancy report to this file
468  DisplayPhoneListing (pb, outfile);
469  outfile.close();
470  cout << endl << "Report written to: " << filename << endl;
471 }
472
473 /******************************************************************/
474 /*                                                              */
475 /* SavePhoneBook: saves the list to a new phone book file */
476 /*                Note: it allows long filenames with      */
477 /*                blanks as part of the filename           */
478 /*                                                              */
479 /******************************************************************/
480
481 void SavePhoneBook (DoubleLinkedList& pb, bool& needToSavePb) {
482  char filename[_MAX_FNAME];
483  char c;
484  cin.get(c); // eat crlf from previous cin
485
486  cout << "Enter the new filename to use\n";
487  cout << "If there are blanks in the filename,\n"
488       << "place double quotemarks around the whole filename.\n"
489       << "for example, \"My Phone Book.txt\" \n";
490  cin.get (filename, sizeof(filename));
491
492  // check for leading "
493  if (filename[0] == '\"') {          // this code doesn't check for
494   int len =(int)strlen (filename) - 2; // the required trailing "
495   strncpy_s (filename, sizeof (filename), &filename[1], len);
496   filename[len] = 0;
497  }
498
499  // attempt to open the file
500  ofstream outfile (filename);
501  if (!outfile) { // here we cannot, bad name or possibly bad path
502   cerr << "Error: cannot open output file: " << filename << endl;
503   return;
504  }
505
506  // now save all data, but do not save the record Id number
507  pb.ResetToHead ();
508  PhoneDirectory* ptrpd = (PhoneDirectory*) pb.GetCurrentNode ();
509  while (ptrpd) {
510   outfile << "\"" << ptrpd->firstName << "\" "
511        << "\"" << ptrpd->lastName  << "\" "
```

```
512              << ptrpd->areaCode << " "
513              << ptrpd->phoneNumber << endl;
514    pb.Next ();
515    ptrpd = (PhoneDirectory*) pb.GetCurrentNode ();
516  }
517
518  pb.ResetToHead ();        // leave list at a valid location
519  outfile.close ();
520  needToSavePb = false;  // turn off any need to save the data
521  cout << "File Saved\n";
522 }
523
524 /**********************************************************/
525 /*                                                      */
526 /* SaveCheck: query the user - saving the data on exit  */
527 /*                                                      */
528 /**********************************************************/
529
530 bool SaveCheck (DoubleLinkedList& pb, bool needToSavePb) {
531  if (needToSavePb) { // has the data been modified and not saved?
532   char yn = ' ';      // yes, so ask user if they want to quit
533   while (yn != 'Y' && yn != 'N') {
534    cout << "Note: you have made changes to the phone database\n"
535         << "and have not yet saved those changes\n"
536         << "Do you want to quit and discard those changes?\n"
537         << "Enter Y or N: ";
538    cin >> yn;
539    yn = toupper (yn);
540   }
541   return yn == 'Y' ? true : false;
542  }
543  else // here it has not changed, so it is save to quit
544   return true;
545 }
546
547 /**********************************************************/
548 /*                                                      */
549 /* EmptyPhoneBook: removes out phone directory items     */
550 /*                 before the list gets destroyed        */
551 /* Note: once this function is done, the list is trashed */
552 /*                                                      */
553 /**********************************************************/
554
555 void EmptyPhoneBook (DoubleLinkedList& pb) {
556  pb.ResetToHead ();
557  PhoneDirectory* ptrpd = (PhoneDirectory*) pb.GetCurrentNode ();
558  while (ptrpd) {
559   delete ptrpd;
560   pb.Next ();
561   ptrpd = (PhoneDirectory*) pb.GetCurrentNode ();
```

```
562   }
563   }
```

Finally, notice just how easily the generic **DoubleLinkedList** class actually is. It required no changes whatsoever to implement this client program. We have a very reusable list class.

Review Questions

1. Explain the concept of a double linked list. How does it work? Illustrate your answer with a drawing of how it operates.

2. What are the benefits of using a double linked list over a single linked list? Give two examples of applications in which a double linked list is more desirable than a single linked list.

3. What is the impact on client programs when the linked list class stores a copy of the client's data in the link nodes versus storing only a **void*** to that data? Be specific.

4. If a linked list class is storing only **void** pointers to the user's data, how can the linked list class ever be able to find any node that matches the user's criteria? Illustrate your answer with a drawing showing how this works.

5. What is meant by a call back function?

6. Describe how a new node can be inserted between two existing nodes. What pointers must be reset? Show an illustration of this process.

7. Describe how a node that lies between two other nodes can be removed from the list. What pointers must be reset? Show an illustration of this process.

8. When loading data from a file into a linked list, what is the difference between always calling **AddAtHead()** versus always calling **AddAtTail()**?

9. When using a linked list class that stores only **void** pointers to the client's data, how does the client program manage to avoid memory leaks when the list class instance is destroyed?

Stop! Do These Exercises Before Programming

1. This time our programmer decided to be wise and use our **DoubleLinkedList** class as his container class in his latest programming project. He thought, "What can possibly go wrong this time?" His application needs to perform real time inquiry and update of automobile parts for Acme's Finest Cars company. He created an initial test data file, corresponding structure and then attempted to load the input file into the array. The following coding failed miserably. Why? How can it be repaired so that it works?

```
...
struct PARTS {
 long partNum;
 int qtyOnHand;
 double cost;
};

int main () {
 DoubleLinkedList parts;
 ifstream infile ("parts.txt", ios::in | ios::nocreate);
 PARTS part;
 while (infile >> part.partNum >> part.qtyOnHand >> part.cost) {
  parts.AddAtTail (&part);
 }

 parts.ResetToHead();
 PARTS* ptrp = parts.GetCurrentNode ();
 while (ptrp) {
  cout << ptrp->partNum << " " << ptrp->qtyOnHand << endl;
  parts.Next();
  ptrp = parts.GetCurrentNode ();
 }
 return 0;
}
```

2. With your assistance, he now has encapsulated the loading of the file in a function and gotten it to load properly and display fine. However, he now finds that he has a memory leak. He tried to fix it as follows. It did not work. Help the programmer out, correct his errors.

```
int main () {
 DoubleLinkedList parts;
 LoadParts (parts, "parts.txt");
 DisplayParts (parts);
 parts.EmptyList ();
 return 0;
}
```

3. Having gotten his program to load, display and clean up properly, he now has written the main menu and has embarked upon implementing the various menu choices. He has written the following for his **FindAPart()** function. It does not work and he begs you for assistance once more. Find his errors so that this function works properly.

```
int main () {
 DoubleLinkedList parts;
...
 FindAPart (parts);
...
 parts.EmptyList ();
 return 0;
}

void FindAPart (DoubleLinkedList p) {
 char c;
 long num;
 cout << "Enter the number of the part to find: ";
 cin >> num;
 if (p.FindNode (&num, FindPart)) {
  PARTS* ptrpart = (PARTS*) p.GetCurrentNode ();
  cout ... this ptrpart fields...
 }
 else
  cout << "Error: part not found\n";
}

int FindPart (const void* ptrmatch, const void* ptrthis) {
 LinkNode* ptrpart = (LinkNode*) ptrthis;
 long* ptrnum = (long*) ptrmatch;
 if (ptrnum == ptrpart->ptrdata)
  return 0;
 else
  return 1;
}
```

4. With the find operation now working, he decided to make a very fancy display of the items in the list. He now has an infinite loop. Please help him out and fix his code so that it does not run forever.

```
void FancyDisplay (DoubleLinkedList& p) {
 p.ResetToHead ();
 PARTS* ptrpart = (PARTS*) p.GetCurrentNode ();
 while (ptrpart) {
  cout << ...fancy display of ptrpart items;
  ptrpart = (PARTS*) p.GetCurrentNode ();
 }
}
```

5. Claiming that it was sure a silly mistake in Problem 4, he now embarks on an ambitious method of adding items to the list such that all items in the list are in increasing numerical order on part number. His **AddSortedItem()** function does not work. After much experimentation, he again asks for your assistance. Correct his function so that items are added to the list in the proper order.

```
void AddSortedItem(PARTS* ptrp, DoubleLinkedList& p) {
 long matchNum = ptrp->partNum;
 p.ResetToHead ();
 PARTS* ptrlist = (PARTS*) p.GetCurrentNode ();
 while (ptrlist && ptrlist->partNum > matchNum) {
  p.Next ();
  ptrlist = (PARTS*) p.GetCurrentNode ();
 }
 p.InsertAfterCurrentNode (ptrp);
}
```

Programming Problems

Problem Pgm10-1 The Revised Update Phone Directory Program

Use Pgm10b as the beginning point for this problem. Acme wishes to add an "Undo" feature to all actions that can be performed on the Phone Book list. Add another item to the main menu, "Undo previous changes." To handle the undo process, Acme decided to create a second instance of the **DoubleLinkedList** class called **Undos**. Each time a change is made to the list, the original **PhoneDirectory** structure is copied and placed at the head of the **Undos** list.

When the user chooses the "Undo previous changes" menu item, begin at the head of the undo list and display each original **PhoneDirectory** instance in turn. Ask the user if they wish to revert this change. If yes is entered, go ahead and undo that change in the main phonebook list. Continue showing successive undo instances until the user chooses to quit the undo process.

Also add another menu choice "Update a phone entry." This option first asks the user for the record id number and then finds that record in the list. If the record is in the list, display it on the screen and ask if they want to change any of this information. If yes is chosen, allow the user to change any of the four main fields but not the record id number.

Thoroughly test your program.

Problem Pgm10-2 The Revised Suspect Matcher Program

Revise problem **Pgm06-1** to store all of the suspect structures in a doubly linked list. In your program, use the **DoubleLinkedList** class from **Pgm10b** exactly as-is with no changes. The behavior and functionality of the original Pgm06-1 program remain unchanged. For ease of work, I have included the specifications here.

      Your local law enforcement agency has requested that you write them a suspect matcher program. The program should load a file of suspect information into a double linked list of **Suspect** structures. Then, the program prompts the user to enter the characteristics of the perpetrator of the crime as described by the witness. The program then displays the suspects that match the perpetrator's characteristics. After waiting for an "Ok to Continue" message, the program prompts for another set of perpetrator characteristics and so on until the end of file is signaled.

      The Suspect structure should contain the following fields.

Field	Type	Description
First Name	first name of a person	a 12-character string including the null terminator
Last Name	last name of a person	a 25-character string including the null terminator
Height	height in inches	0 is unknown, 44 to 90 is valid
Eye Color	eye color	0 is unknown, 1 is brown, 2 is blue, 3 is hazel
Hair Color	hair color	0 is unknown, 1 is brown, 2 is black, 3 is red, 4 is gray
Hat Size	an integer	0 is unknown
Shoe Size	an integer	0 is unknown
Teeth Marks	a characteristic	0 is unknown, 1 is normal, 2 is crooked, 3 is gold filled, 4 is partial, 5 is missing
Facial Scar	a yes/no field	0 is unknown, 1 is yes, 2 is no
Hand Scar	a yes/no field	0 is unknown, 1 is yes, 2 is no
Eye Patch	a yes/no field	0 is unknown, 1 is yes, 2 is no
Bald Patch	a yes/no field	0 is unknown, 1 is yes, 2 is no
Leg Limp	a yes/no field	0 is unknown, 1 is yes, 2 is no
Tattoo	a yes/no field	0 is unknown, 1 is yes, 2 is no

      First, make up a test **suspects.txt** data file. The file should contain at least 12 suspect records. One of the records should have all information filled out with none marked as unknown; one should contain all 0's except the first and last name fields. The remainder should contain a variety of values. Assume that all information in the **suspects.txt** file is correct—there can be no invalid data in this data file.

You may use enumerated data types for program maintenance purposes or you may use **#define** values or **const int** values. While the program does not have to check for invalid data in the input file, it will have to detect invalid perpetrator entries being entered and re-prompt the user accordingly.

The matching process is done on all fields except the first and last names. No one characteristic is given more weight than another. If the perpetrator's twelve items match a particular suspect record, then the matching percentage is 100%. If none match, it is 0%. After calculating the matching percentage of the perpetrator to all of the suspects, display first the perpetrator's data followed by the suspects that match with a percentage above 0% in percentage order from highest to lowest. Your output should allow the user to see at a glance which characteristics are matching and which are not. There are many ways this can be done; columnar aligned fields is one way.

Problem Pgm10-3 The Acme Music Store's Sheet Music in Stock Program

Acme Music Store carries a wide line of sheet music, much of which is always in stock. They desire a program to allow them to perform real time inquiries while the customer is waiting.

Each piece of sheet music carries their stock number on it. They maintain a data base of sheet music in stock called **music.txt** located in the **TestDataForAssignments chapter10** folder. Each line contains the stock number (4 numerical digits), composer's name (21 characters), the title (31 characters), the quantity in stock at the moment and the cost of the music.

When the program begins, it should allocate an instance of the **DoubleLinkedList** class from **Pgm10b**. Make no changes in that class. Input the file of music in stock into that linked list instance, always adding at the tail. Then display the main menu.

```
Acme Music Store - Sheet Music Inventory Program

1. Check on availability of a piece of music by stock number
2. Find a piece of music given the composer
3. Find a piece of music given the title
4. Exit the program

Enter the number of your choice: _
```

When choice 1 is made, prompt the user to enter the four digit stock number and then look it up in the list. If the item is found, display its information nicely formatted on the screen. If it is not found, so state.

When choice 2 or 3 is made, prompt the user to enter the composer or music title. Then search the list for any matches. The search should be case insensitive. If one is found, display that item's information nicely formatted along with an option to continue the search. Remember, that there can be more than one piece of music written by any specific composer and some works may have duplicate titles.

Thoroughly test your program. You may add additional data to the music.txt file to ensure that your program is working perfectly.

Problem Pgm10-4 The Revised Student Roster Program

In chapter 9, program Pgm09b performed some student roster activities using a single linked list that stored the roster information in the actual nodes. Rewrite that main client program to use our new generic double linked list class. The revised program should produce the same output as Pgm09b. Make no changes to the **DoubleLinkedList** class of **Pgm10b**.

Problem Pgm10-5 The Boat Docking Application

Rewrite program Pgm09-1, the Boat Docking Application to use our new **DoubleLinkedList** class of **Pgm10b**. Make no changes to the **DoubleLinkedList** class of **Pgm10b**. The program specifications are otherwise the same.

Problem Pgm10-6 The Sorted List Class

Sometimes, a sorted list is a preferable container for the client's items. Add a new function to the **DoubleLinkedClass** called **AddSortedAscending()** that is passed a **void** pointer to the new client's data to be added to the list along with a **void** pointer to the client's sorting criteria and and the client's **Find()** call back function to use.

The **void** pointer to the client's sorting criteria and the prototype of the call back function are used exactly the same as in the **FindNode()** function. Traverse the list, calling **Find()** on each passing it the criteria pointer and the user's data contained in that node. When the user's call back function tells you that this current node's value is greater than his matching criteria, insert this new node before the current node. To test your new function, use Pgm10b and its data file as a starting point. Load the file of phone directory entries into the list in alphabetical order on last name. Then display the list to verify that the entries are in the proper order.

Chapter 11—Stacks

Introduction

In chapter 5 the concept of a stack was introduced and the properties and operations of a stack were presented. Let's review them before attempting to implement stack containers.

A stack is a linear, sequential access data structure. Recall that the last item pushed or stored onto the stack is the first item that can be popped or removed from the stack, that is, it is LIFO. A stack can be thought of as a very restricted version of a linked list in which all additions and removals occur at one end of the list.

The two major operations that a stack provides are called **Push()** and **Pop()** which puts a new item onto the top of the stack and removes the top item from the stack. Table 11.1 shows the definition of a stack data structure.

Data Type	Stack
Domain	A stack is a collection of component whose values are all of the same data type
Structure	A list that is maintained in LIFO order so that only the most recently added item is available
Operations	
Initialize()	Creates an empty stack
Push()	Place a new item on the top of the stack
Pop()	Remove the current item from the top of the stack
IsEmpty()	Returns true if the stack is empty

Table 11.1 The Definition of the Stack Data Structure

Notice that the number of operations that can be performed on a stack is much smaller than the number that can be done on a list data structure. Figure 5.3 in chapter 5 showed a stack in operation. It is reproduced here as Figure 11.1 below. Initially the stack contains one red block which is at the top of the stack. Next, a yellow block is pushed onto the top of the stack. Then a blue block is pushed onto the top of the stack. Finally, a block is popped off from the top of the stack leaving the yellow and red blocks still on the stack.

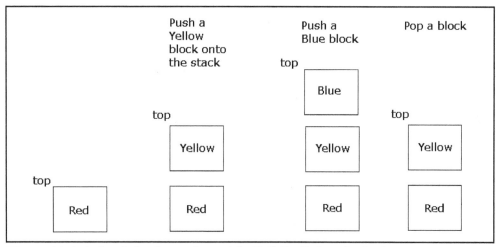

Figure 11.1 A Stack in Operation with Child's Colored Blocks

Stacks have many uses in programming. Indeed, in C++, automatic and parameter variables are stored on a stack that is called a **Stack Frame**. When a function is called or invoked, C++ stores the needed information in a Stack Frame for that function. The Stack Frame contains the return address to go back to in the calling program along with the parameter variables being passed to the function. As the function body is then entered, C++ stores all of the automatic storage variables for that block into the Stack Frame as well. When the function returns, after retrieving its return address, the Stack Frame with all of this information is then removed from the top of the stack.

From an application point of view, implementing "Undo Last Changes" is perhaps the most common usage of a stack. Nearly every major application that permits a user to alter information implements some means for the user to undo the last change(s) made to the data. The more flexible applications do not have any preset limits on the number of "undos" that can be made. Other applications only permit a finite number of changes to be undone.

Stacks are also widely used in game applications. Handling the traversal of a maze by trial and error is one such use of a stack. We will explore this one shortly. However, to begin our examination of stack coding, let's take a simpler example. Why?

In teaching data structures, I have found that beginning programmers often have a great deal of difficulty visualizing and solving programs that require the use of a stack. Perhaps it is because they are not as familiar such kinds of application logic that is being required in these solutions. Hence, let's begin with a very simple situation.

The Palindrome Analysis Program and a Simple Letter Stack

A palindrome is any word, verse, sentence, or numerals which read the same forward and backwards. The music group Abba is a palindrome as is Madam. The sentence, "Madam, I'm Adam." is also a palindrome, if we discount the punctuation and blanks. The numerical series, 123454321 is likewise.

Suppose that the user is asked to enter a series of characters. We are to say whether or not that series is a palindrome. There are a number of ways it can be done, but let's see how it can be done using stacks. Suppose that the user enters the series "abcd" which is not a palindrome. Suppose further that as each character is entered, we store that character in a stack. Figure 11.2 shows the stack after the user has entered "abcd." Notice that "d" is at the top of the stack and if we did a series of pop actions, we get the characters in the reverse order that the user entered them.

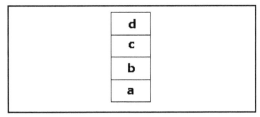

Figure 11.2 Reverse Order of Entry

Now suppose that we pop each letter in turn off of this stack and push them onto another stack. Figure 11.3 shows the final results. Notice that this new stack now contains the letters in the same order as they were entered, from the top of the stack downward.

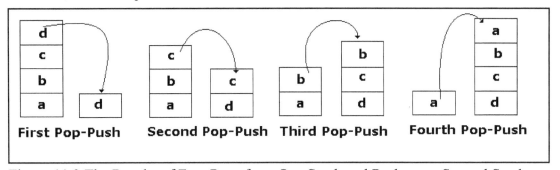

Figure 11.3 The Results of Four Pops from One Stack and Push on to Second Stack

Of course, the initial stack is now empty, but the new stack does have the characters stored in the original order they were entered by the user. If we keep a copy of the original stack, then we can compare each current entry. If all are the same, then the user entry is a palindrome. (Yes, there certainly are more efficient ways to detect palindromes, but this illustrates the usage of a stack in a particularly simple way.)

The LetterStack Class

To implement the **LetterStack** class, let's use a simple single linked list because with a stack, there is never any need to traverse in the reverse direction. The actual **StackNode** is specific to this problem.

```
struct StackNode {
  StackNode* fwdptr;
  char letter;
};
```

The design is very straightforward. Look over the definition of the **LetterStack** below. The only extra feature that I added was some assistance when debugging. The function **DebugDisplay()** traverses the entire stack, displaying the contents of each node on the passed stream. Thus, if the volume of display becomes too large for the screen, it can be passed an opened file stream instead.

The LetterStack Class Definition

```
 1 #pragma once
 2 #include <iostream>
 3 using namespace std;
 4
 5 /*****************************************************************/
 6 /*                                                               */
 7 /* StackNode: Single linked list node containing a char letter */
 8 /*                                                               */
 9 /*****************************************************************/
10
11 struct StackNode {
12   StackNode* fwdptr;
13   char letter;
14 };
15
16 /*****************************************************************/
17 /*                                                               */
18 /* LetterStack: Single linked list stack holding a char letter */
19 /*                                                               */
20 /*****************************************************************/
21
22 class LetterStack {
23 protected:
24   StackNode* headptr; // pointer to top of stack - head of list
25   long        count;   // number of nodes in the list
26
27 public:
28   LetterStack ();      // initialize an empty stack
29   ~LetterStack ();     // removes all items from the stack
30
31   void Push (char l); // store a new letter on top of the stack
32   char Pop ();          // remove a letter from top of stack
```

```
33
34  long GetCount () const; // returns the number of nodes on stack
35  bool IsEmpty () const;  // returns true when stack is empty
36
37  void RemoveAll ();  // empties the stack - remove all nodes
38
39  // debugging aid to display whole stack
40  ostream& DebugDisplay (ostream& os) const;
41 };
42
```

The implementation follows that of a single linked list. All of the coding is quite straightforward.

```
The LetterStack Class Implementation

 1 #include "LetterStack.h"
 2
 3 /**************************************************************/
 4 /*                                                          */
 5 /* LetterStack: Constructs empty letter stack               */
 6 /*                                                          */
 7 /**************************************************************/
 8
 9 LetterStack::LetterStack () {
10  headptr = 0;
11  count = 0;
12 }
13
14 /**************************************************************/
15 /*                                                          */
16 /* ~LetterStack: Empties the letter stack                   */
17 /*                                                          */
18 /**************************************************************/
19
20 LetterStack::~LetterStack () {
21  RemoveAll ();
22 }
23
24 /**************************************************************/
25 /*                                                          */
26 /* RemoveAll: Helper function to remove all items from stack */
27 /*                                                          */
28 /**************************************************************/
29
30 void LetterStack::RemoveAll () {
31  while (!IsEmpty()) Pop ();
32 }
33
```

```
34 /*******************************************************************/
35 /*                                                                 */
36 /* Push: Store a new letter on the top of the stack               */
37 /*                                                                 */
38 /*******************************************************************/
39
40 void LetterStack::Push (char l) {
41  StackNode* ptrnew = new (std::nothrow) StackNode; // make node
42  if (!ptrnew) {
43   cerr << "Error out of memory in Push\n";
44   exit (1);
45  }
46  ptrnew->letter = l;                  // store user's letter
47  ptrnew->fwdptr = headptr;            // store next node's address
48  headptr = ptrnew;                    // make this node the top
49  count++;                             // increment number of nodes
50 }
51
52 /*******************************************************************/
53 /*                                                                 */
54 /* Pop: Remove the top node from the stack; return that letter*/
55 /*                                                                 */
56 /*******************************************************************/
57
58 char LetterStack::Pop () {
59  if (IsEmpty ()) // if the list is empty, return a 0 character
60   return 0;
61  StackNode* ptrtodel = headptr; // save the top node for deletion
62  headptr = headptr->fwdptr;     // reset the next node as the top
63  char c = ptrtodel->letter;     // save the letter to return
64  delete ptrtodel;               // remove the node
65  count--;                       // decrement the number of nodes
66  return c;                      // give the user the letter
67 }
68
69 /*******************************************************************/
70 /*                                                                 */
71 /* IsEmpty: Returns true if the stack is empty - no nodes         */
72 /*                                                                 */
73 /*******************************************************************/
74
75 bool LetterStack::IsEmpty () const{
76  return headptr ? false : true;
77 }
78
79 /*******************************************************************/
80 /*                                                                 */
81 /* GetCount: Returns the number of items on the stack             */
82 /*                                                                 */
83 /*******************************************************************/
```

```
 84
 85 long LetterStack::GetCount () const {
 86  return count;
 87 }
 88
 89 /***************************************************************/
 90 /*                                                             */
 91 /* DebugDisplay: Display the contents from top to bottom       */
 92 /*                                                             */
 93 /***************************************************************/
 94
 95 ostream& LetterStack::DebugDisplay (ostream& os) const {
 96  os << "Debug display of the stack from top to bottom\n";
 97  StackNode* ptrnext = headptr;   // begin at the top of the stack
 98  while (ptrnext) {               // traverse all items in stack
 99   os.put (ptrnext->letter) << " "; // display that node's letter
100   ptrnext = ptrnext->fwdptr;     // point to the next node
101  }
102  os << "\nDebug display finished\n";
103  return os;
104 }
```

Finally, we must write the actual client program that determines if a user entry is a palindrome. When the user enters a keystroke, it is pushed onto the backwards stack and onto the temporary stack. Once all the characters have been entered, the temporary stack is emptied and placed onto the forward stack as shown in Figure 11.3 above. Finally, examine the detection loop. It is ended whenever there is a pair of characters that do not match or one of the stacks is empty.

```
Pgm11a - The Palindrome Analysis Program

 1 #include <iostream>
 2 #include <iomanip>
 3 #include <fstream>
 4 #include <cctype>
 5 using namespace std;
 6 #include <crtdbg.h>
 7 #include "LetterStack.h"
 8
 9 /***************************************************************/
10 /*                                                             */
11 /* Pgm11a: Palindrome Analysis program                         */
12 /*                                                             */
13 /***************************************************************/
14
15 int main () {
16  {
17  LetterStack forward;  // stack holds letters in order entered
18  LetterStack temp;     // stack to help reverse the characters
```

```
19  LetterStack backward; // stack holds reverse order of chars
20
21  cout << "Palindrome Analysis Program\n"
22      << "Enter a word or phrase and press enter when done\n"
23      << "Don't enter any punctuation or blanks between words\n";
24  char letter;
25
26  // note: if we push user letters as entered onto a stack, then
27  // the letter on the top of that stack will be the last letter
28  // entered - ie the backwards order.
29
30  while (cin.get(letter) && letter != '\n') {
31   backward.Push (letter); // save reverse order of letters
32   temp.Push (letter);     // save for later reversal of letters
33  }
34
35  while (!temp.IsEmpty ()) { // reverse all letters entered by
36   letter = temp.Pop ();      // popping the last letter and
37   forward.Push (letter);     // pushing it on the new stack
38  }
39
40  // display a debug series of messages to verify stack integrity
41  cout << "\nLetters as entered stack:\n";
42  forward.DebugDisplay (cout);
43  cout << "\nReverse order of letters stack:\n";
44  backward.DebugDisplay (cout);
45
46  // now check to see if the entry is a Palindrome
47  // guard against end of file with nothing entered
48  if (!forward.IsEmpty()) {
49   bool done = false;
50   bool matched = true;// assume they match until proven otherwise
51
52   // quit on first mis-match or when stack is empty
53   while (!done && !forward.IsEmpty()) {
54    char letterf = forward.Pop ();  // get next forward letter
55    char letterb = backward.Pop (); // get next backwards letter
56    if (toupper (letterb) != toupper(letterf)) {// letters differ?
57     done = true;
58     matched = false;
59    }
60   }
61   if (matched)
62    cout << "This is a palindrome\n";
63   else
64    cout << "This is not a palindrome\n";
65  }
66  else
67   cout << "No letters entered to check\n";
68  }
```

```
69
70  if (_CrtDumpMemoryLeaks())
71   cout << "\nOops! Memory Leaks!!\n";
72  else
73   cout << "\nNo Memory Leaks\n";
74
75  return 0;
76 }
```

Here are a few sample test runs.

```
Output from Pgm11a - The Palindrome Analysis Program

 1 Palindrome Analysis Program
 2 Enter a word or phrase and press enter when done
 3 Don't enter any punctuation or blanks between words
 4 Abba
 5
 6 Letters as entered stack:
 7 Debug display of the stack from top to bottom
 8 A b  b a
 9 Debug display finished
10
11 Reverse order of letters stack:
12 Debug display of the stack from top to bottom
13 a b  b A
14 Debug display finished
15 This is a palindrome
16
17 No Memory Leaks
18
19 Palindrome Analysis Program
20 Enter a word or phrase and press enter when done
21 Don't enter any punctuation or blanks between words
22 MadamImAdam
23
24 Letters as entered stack:
25 Debug display of the stack from top to bottom
26 M a d a m I m A d a m
27 Debug display finished
28
29 Reverse order of letters stack:
30 Debug display of the stack from top to bottom
31 m a d A m I m a d a M
32 Debug display finished
33 This is a palindrome
34
35 No Memory Leaks
```

```
36
37
38 Palindrome Analysis Program
39 Enter a word or phrase and press enter when done
40 Don't enter any punctuation or blanks between words
41 Abbd
42
43 Letters as entered stack:
44 Debug display of the stack from top to bottom
45 A b b d
46 Debug display finished
47
48 Reverse order of letters stack:
49 Debug display of the stack from top to bottom
50 d b b A
51 Debug display finished
52 This is not a palindrome
53
54 No Memory Leaks
55
56
57 Palindrome Analysis Program
58 Enter a word or phrase and press enter when done
59 Don't enter any punctuation or blanks between words
60 Dbba
61
62 Letters as entered stack:
63 Debug display of the stack from top to bottom
64 D b b a
65 Debug display finished
66
67 Reverse order of letters stack:
68 Debug display of the stack from top to bottom
69 a b b D
70 Debug display finished
71 This is not a palindrome
72
73 No Memory Leaks
74
75
76 Palindrome Analysis Program
77 Enter a word or phrase and press enter when done
78 Don't enter any punctuation or blanks between words
79 123454321
80
81 Letters as entered stack:
82 Debug display of the stack from top to bottom
83 1 2 3 4 5 4 3 2 1
84 Debug display finished
85
```

```
86 Reverse order of letters stack:
87 Debug display of the stack from top to bottom
88 1 2 3 4 5 4 3 2 1
89 Debug display finished
90 This is a palindrome
91
92 No Memory Leaks
```

Stacks do not always have to be implemented using a linked list. If there are a known maximum number of nodes that could be placed on the stack, then using an array would provide a faster executing implementation. This is explored in depth in the Stop! Exercises at the end of this chapter.

Traversing a Maze Problem—A More Complicated Stack Example

Consider the typical maze problem consisting of a grid of cells. The objective is to find the path from the entrance of the maze to the exit point of the maze. Of course, there are many dead ends that may be encountered. Traversing a maze is basically a trial-and-error process. The usual method employed is consistency of turn choices to avoid taking branches one has already tried.

For example, when one enters a cell that has more than one exit point, besides the one just entered, one always tries the right side path, then the forward or top path, and then the left side path, should these exist. By being consistent, one is guaranteed to eventually find the correct path through the maze.

Suppose the problem to solve is to write an artificial intelligence type of routine that can be used with a robot mouse. The mouse is placed at the entrance point of a maze and the program triggered. Our program controls the mouse's choice of motion and should guide the mouse out of the maze. (Note: our program does not actually control the mechanical aspects of the mouse, rather it provides overall guidance on the next move to make.)

To implement the maze, I chose to represent it as a two-dimensional array of cells. Strictly for convenience, I also chose to make it a square matrix. For this sample, the maze is an array of 5x5 cells. Figure 11.4 shows the maze and the path that the mouse must make to successfully traverse the maze.

The identity of a cell is the pair of subscripts required to access it in the two-dimensional array. Each cell can have one or more passages out of it as indicated by the broken side walls or door ways. I assume that the mouse is moved into cell at (4,1) which is the entrance and the starting point for our solution.

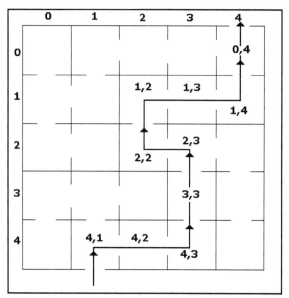

Figure 11.4 The Maze and the Correct Path

Next, how can we identify the existence of a door or free passage out of a side of any given cell? I chose to represent this as a boolean value—**true** or **false**, there is/is not a passage out of a cell on this side. The sides are called top, bottom, left, and right. I made a structure to store this information that is called **CellData**.

```
struct CellData {
 bool Bottom;
 bool Right;
 bool Top;
 bool Left;
};
```

The definition of the maze is then a two-dimensional array of **CellData**. The actual definition of the maze shown in Figure 11.4 is as follows.

```
CellData maze[5][5] = {

 {{true, false, false, false}, {true, true, false, false},
  {false, true, false, true}, {false, true, false, true},
  {true, false, true, true}},

 {{true, true, true, false}, {false, false, true, true},
  {true, true, false, false}, {false, true, false, true},
  {false, false, true, true}},

 {{false, true, true, true}, {false, false, false, true},
  {false, true, true, false}, {true, true, false, true},
  {true, false, false, true}},

 {{true, true, false, false}, {true, true, false, true},
```

```
  {false, false, false, true}, {true, false, true, true},
  {true, false, true, false}},

 {{false, false, true, false}, {true, true, true, false},
  {false, true, false, true}, {false, false, true, true},
  {false, false, true, false}}
};
```

A move consists of specifying the row and column subscript of the cell and the corresponding **CellData** for that specific cell. I stored this information in another structure called **CellMove**.

```
struct CellMove {
  int row;
  int col;
  CellData cd;
};
```

The algorithm I used is when moving into a cell, block off the entrance doorway just entered. For example, when entering the very first cell, the entrance, the cell definition says that there is an exit at the top, bottom and right. I block off the bottom by setting the corresponding **bool** called **bottom** to **false**. That then leaves two other exits to try. When we take one of the branches, there is no way of knowing in advance if this one is the correct one or if it leads to a dead end. Should all the sides be **false**, or no more doors out, then this is a dead end. Thus, if it is a dead end, I need a way to back up. Therefore, a stack that saves each move made is the ideal solution.

When entering a cell, I block off the entrance way (set it to **false**) and choose a path out. I then set the exit side to **false** and place this move onto the stack. Should the cell I move into be a dead end, then I can pop the previous cell off of the stack to return to the cell in which I originally was located and try another exit side.

To facilitate access of the **CellMove** instance that is at the top of the stack, I chose to provide an access function, **GetCurrentData()** which returns a pointer to this one. And the **Pop()** function only removes the top item and does not return a pointer to the original data.

```
CellMove* GetCurrentData () const;
```

Otherwise, the stack class itself is totally parallel to the **LetterStack** we have just seen. The final solution is represented by each **CellMove** instance that is stored on the stack when the mouse is out of the maze on the exit side. Thus, a **DebugDisplay()** shows the actual path to traverse the maze, but in reverse order, from the exit side to the entrance side.

Here is the output from **Pgm11b** showing the solution.

```
Test Run of Pgm11b Showing the Maze Solution

1 Path found is:
2 Debug display of the stack from top to bottom
3 CellMove row and column: 0, 4        Data: B=F R=F T=T L=T
4 CellMove row and column: 1, 4        Data: B=F R=F T=F L=F
5 CellMove row and column: 1, 3        Data: B=F R=F T=F L=F
```

```
 6 CellMove row and column: 1, 2        Data: B=F R=F T=F L=F
 7 CellMove row and column: 2, 2        Data: B=F R=F T=F L=F
 8 CellMove row and column: 2, 3        Data: B=F R=F T=F L=F
 9 CellMove row and column: 3, 3        Data: B=F R=F T=F L=T
10 CellMove row and column: 4, 3        Data: B=F R=F T=F L=F
11 CellMove row and column: 4, 2        Data: B=F R=F T=F L=F
12 CellMove row and column: 4, 1        Data: B=F R=F T=T L=F
13
14 Debug display finished
15
16 No Memory Leaks
17
```

Here is the main program that solves the maze, **Pgm11b**. The coding is straightforward. Examine how a move is actually made when going left or up and so on.

```
Pgm11b - Maze Problem

 1 #include <iostream>
 2 #include <iomanip>
 3 #include <fstream>
 4 #include <cctype>
 5 #include <crtdbg.h>
 6 using namespace std;
 7
 8 #include "MazeStack.h"
 9
10 // helper function that returns true when outside the maze
11 bool IsOutside (int row, int col);
12
13 /*****************************************************************/
14 /*                                                             */
15 /* Pgm11b: Find a path through a maze                          */
16 /*                                                             */
17 /*****************************************************************/
18
19 int main () {
20   {
21     // the actual definition of the maze
22     CellData maze[5][5] = {
23       {{true, false, false, false}, {true, true, false, false},
24        {false, true, false, true}, {false, true, false, true},
25        {true, false, true, true}},
26
27       {{true, true, true, false}, {false, false, true, true},
28        {true, true, false, false}, {false, true, false, true},
29        {false, false, true, true}},
30
```

383

```
31      {{false, true, true, true}, {false, false, false, true},
32       {false, true, true, false}, {true, true, false, true},
33       {true, false, false, true}},
34
35      {{true, true, false, false}, {true, true, false, true},
36       {false, false, false, true}, {true, false, true, true},
37       {true, false, true, false}},
38
39      {{false, false, true, false}, {true, true, true, false},
40       {false, true, false, true}, {false, false, true, true},
41       {false, false, true, false}}
42    };
43
44    int row = 4;        // the entrance cell
45    int col = 1;        // coordinates
46
47    MazeStack moves;   // the stack containing the moves
48
49    CellData thisone = maze[row][col]; // data of the entrance cell
50    thisone.Bottom = false;            // block the maze entrance point
51
52    CellMove save; // save info of the current cell we just entered
53    save.row = row;
54    save.col = col;
55    save.cd = thisone;
56
57    moves.Push (save); // save the initial move onto the stack
58
59    CellMove* ptrsaved;
60    int numberOfMoves = 0;
61    // solve the maize - repeat until no additional moves to undo
62    // are on the stack and we are not outside the maze (ie. done)
63    // or have tried 50 times (only 25 cells in the maze)
64    while (!moves.IsEmpty () && !IsOutside (row, col)
65          && numberOfMoves < 50) {
66     numberOfMoves++;
67     // see if we can go right into another cell?
68     if (thisone.Right) {
69      col++;                             // move to right cell
70      if (IsOutside (row, col)) break;   // see if we are outside
71      ptrsaved = moves.GetCurrentData ();// retrieve prior move and
72      ptrsaved->cd.Right = false;        // mark exit that we try
73      thisone = maze[row][col];          // grab defn of next cell
74      thisone.Left = false;              // block exit we entered
75      save.row = row;                    // fill up save with this
76      save.col = col;                    // move we are making
77      save.cd = thisone;
78      moves.Push (save);                 // store it onto the stack
79     }
80     // no, so see if we can go up into another cell
```

```
 81      else if (thisone.Top) {
 82       row--;                                    // move to the top cell
 83       if (IsOutside (row, col)) break;    // see if we are outside
 84       ptrsaved = moves.GetCurrentData ();// retrieve prior move and
 85       ptrsaved->cd.Top = false;           // mark exit that we try
 86       thisone = maze[row][col];           // grab defn of next cell
 87       thisone.Bottom = false;             // block exit we entered
 88       save.row = row;                     // fill up save with this
 89       save.col = col;                     // move we are making
 90       save.cd = thisone;
 91       moves.Push (save);                  // store it onto the stack
 92      }
 93      // no, so see if we can go left into another cell
 94      else if (thisone.Left) {
 95       col--;                                    // move to the left cell
 96       if (IsOutside (row, col)) break;    // see if we are outside
 97       ptrsaved = moves.GetCurrentData ();// retrieve prior move and
 98       ptrsaved->cd.Left = false;          // mark exit that we try
 99       thisone = maze[row][col];           // grab defn of next cell
100       thisone.Right = false;              // block exit we entered
101       save.row = row;                     // fill up save with this
102       save.col = col;                     // move we are making
103       save.cd = thisone;
104       moves.Push (save);                  // store it onto the stack
105      }
106      // no, so see if we can go out the bottom into another cell
107      else if (thisone.Bottom) {
108       row++;                                    // move to the bottom cell
109       if (IsOutside (row, col)) break;    // see if we are outside
110       ptrsaved = moves.GetCurrentData ();// retrieve prior move and
111       ptrsaved->cd.Bottom = false;        // mark exit that we try
112       thisone = maze[row][col];           // grab defn of next cell
113       thisone.Top = false;                // block exit we entered
114       save.row = row;                     // fill up save with this
115       save.col = col;                     // move we are making
116       save.cd = thisone;
117       moves.Push (save);                  // store it onto the stack
118      }
119      // no move is possible from here - dead end - so backup to
120      // previous cell and try other ways
121      else {
122       moves.Pop ();                       // remove this dead end
123       ptrsaved = moves.GetCurrentData ();// retrieve prior move
124       if (ptrsaved) {                     // if there was one, then
125        thisone = ptrsaved->cd;            // reset our cell from it
126        row = ptrsaved->row;
127        col = ptrsaved->col;
128       }
129      }
130     }
```

```
131
132   // now check the results.
133   // If the stack is empty, there was no solution.
134   if (moves.IsEmpty ())
135    cout << "No solution\n";
136   else {
137    if (numberOfMoves >= 50)
138     cout << "Maximun tries exceeded - the stack contains:\n";
139    cout << "Path found is:\n";
140    moves.DebugDisplay (cout);
141    }
142   }
143   if (_CrtDumpMemoryLeaks())
144    cout << "\nOops! Memory Leaks!!\n";
145   else
146    cout << "\nNo Memory Leaks\n";
147
148   return 0;
149 }
150
151 /****************************************************************/
152 /*                                                              */
153 /* IsOutside: returns true if this row and col is outside maze */
154 /*                                                              */
155 /****************************************************************/
156
157 bool IsOutside (int row, int col) {
158   if (row < 0 || row >= 5) return true;
159   if (col < 0 || col >= 5) return true;
160   return false;
161 }
```

Finally, here are the **MazeStack** definition and implementation files.

```
MazeStack Definition

 1 #pragma once
 2 #include <iostream>
 3 using namespace std;
 4
 5 /****************************************************************/
 6 /*                                                              */
 7 /* CellData: defines the exit sides of a maze cell              */
 8 /*           true if there is an exit on this side              */
 9 /*                                                              */
10 /****************************************************************/
11
12 struct CellData {
```

```
13  bool Bottom;
14  bool Right;
15  bool Top;
16  bool Left;
17  };
18
19  /**************************************************************/
20  /*                                                          */
21  /* CellMove: defines the exit sides of a maze cell          */
22  /*            true if there is an exit on this side         */
23  /*                                                          */
24  /**************************************************************/
25
26  struct CellMove {
27   int row;
28   int col;
29   CellData cd;
30  };
31
32  /**************************************************************/
33  /*                                                          */
34  /* StackNode: contains the forward pointer and this item data */
35  /*                                                          */
36  /**************************************************************/
37
38  struct StackNode {
39   StackNode* fwdptr;
40   CellMove CellMove;
41  };
42
43  /**************************************************************/
44  /*                                                          */
45  /* MazeStack: a stack class to solve the Maze problem       */
46  /*                                                          */
47  /**************************************************************/
48
49  class MazeStack {
50  protected:
51   StackNode* headptr;       // the top of the stack pointer
52   long        count;        // the number of items in the stack
53
54  public:
55   MazeStack ();             // construct an empty stack
56   ~MazeStack ();            // delete the stack
57   void Push (CellMove s);   // store a new node on the stack
58   void Pop ();              // removes top node from the stack
59   CellMove* GetCurrentData () const; // returns user's data on top
60   long GetCount () const;   // returns the number of nodes in stack
61
62   bool IsEmpty () const;    // returns true if stack is empty
```

387

```
63  void RemoveAll ();        // removes all nodes in the stack
64
65  // display all items on the stack nicely formatted
66  ostream& DebugDisplay (ostream& os) const;
67  };
```

MazeStack Implementation

```
 1  #include <iomanip>
 2  using namespace std;
 3  #include "MazeStack.h"
 4
 5  /*******************************************************************/
 6  /*                                                               */
 7  /* MazeStack: create an empty stack                             */
 8  /*                                                               */
 9  /*******************************************************************/
10
11  MazeStack::MazeStack () {
12   headptr = 0;
13   count = 0;
14  }
15
16  /*******************************************************************/
17  /*                                                               */
18  /* ~MazeStack: deletes the stack                                */
19  /*                                                               */
20  /*******************************************************************/
21
22  MazeStack::~MazeStack () {
23   RemoveAll ();
24  }
25
26  /*******************************************************************/
27  /*                                                               */
28  /* RemoveAll: deletes all nodes of the stack                    */
29  /*                                                               */
30  /*******************************************************************/
31
32  void MazeStack::RemoveAll () {
33   while (!IsEmpty()) Pop ();
34  }
35
36  /*******************************************************************/
37  /*                                                               */
38  /* Push: store new node on the top of the stack                 */
39  /*                                                               */
40  /*******************************************************************/
41
```

```
42 void MazeStack::Push (CellMove s) {
43  StackNode* ptrnew = new (std::nothrow) StackNode;
44  if (!ptrnew) {
45   cerr << "MazeStack: Push out of memory\n";
46   exit (1);
47  }
48  ptrnew->CellMove = s;
49  ptrnew->fwdptr = headptr;
50  headptr = ptrnew;
51  count++;
52 }
53
54 /****************************************************************/
55 /*                                                              */
56 /* Pop: remove the top item from the stack                      */
57 /*                                                              */
58 /****************************************************************/
59
60 void MazeStack::Pop () {
61  if (!headptr) return;
62  StackNode* ptrtodel = headptr;
63  headptr = headptr->fwdptr;
64  delete ptrtodel;
65  count--;
66 }
67
68 /****************************************************************/
69 /*                                                              */
70 /* GetCurrentData: returns a pointer to user data on the top    */
71 /*                 of the stack or 0 if it is empty             */
72 /*                                                              */
73 /****************************************************************/
74
75 CellMove* MazeStack::GetCurrentData () const {
76  return !IsEmpty () ? &headptr->CellMove : 0;
77 }
78
79 /****************************************************************/
80 /*                                                              */
81 /* IsEmpty: returns true when there are no items on the stack   */
82 /*                                                              */
83 /****************************************************************/
84
85 bool MazeStack::IsEmpty () const{
86  return headptr ? false : true;
87 }
88
89 /****************************************************************/
90 /*                                                              */
91 /* GetCount: returns the number of nodes on the stack           */
```

```
 92 /*                                                          */
 93 /*******************************************************/
 94
 95 long MazeStack::GetCount () const {
 96  return count;
 97 }
 98
 99 /*******************************************************/
100 /*                                                          */
101 /* DebugDisplay: display all items on stack nicely formatted  */
102 /*                                                          */
103 /*******************************************************/
104
105 ostream& MazeStack::DebugDisplay (ostream& os) const {
106  os << "Debug display of the stack from top to bottom\n";
107  StackNode* ptrnext = headptr;
108  while (ptrnext) {
109   os << "CellMove row and column: " << ptrnext->CellMove.row
110      << ", " << ptrnext->CellMove.col << "      ";
111   os << "     Data: B="
112      << (ptrnext->CellMove.cd.Bottom ? "T " : "F ")
113      << "R=" << (ptrnext->CellMove.cd.Right ? "T " : "F ")
114      << "T=" << (ptrnext->CellMove.cd.Top ? "T " : "F ")
115      << "L=" << (ptrnext->CellMove.cd.Left ? "T " : "F ") <<endl;
116   ptrnext = ptrnext->fwdptr;
117  }
118  os << "\nDebug display finished\n";
119  return os;
120 }
```

A Generic Stack Class

Now that we have some familiarity with stack design and usage, is there anything amiss with the design of both the **LetterStack** and the **MazeStack** classes? There are two major problems. Can you spot them?

The first problem occurs when a user codes the following.
```
LetterClass a, b;
...
b = a;
```
Neither class is robust since neither the copy constructor nor the assignment operator is supported! This may yield catastrophic results in client programs. They must be implemented.

The second problem is that neither class is generic. Both are specific to the problem to be solved. True, there is not much coding in either class so that a reuse by recoding is not a major hurdle. But our design goals include making reusable container classes.

Beginning Data Structures in C++

Our **StackNode** structure must store a **void** pointer to the user's data to be stored.

```
struct StackNode {
  StackNode*  fwdptr;
  void*       dataptr;
};
```

Next, we change the member function prototypes to use the **void*** instead of the application specific items. Then, add in support for the copy constructor and assignment operator. As usual, I added a helper function to perform the actual copy operation since it is needed in both functions.

However, the **DebugDisplay()** function represents a major design problem. Its purpose is to make a nicely formatted display of the user's items on the stack. However, we now know nothing at all about the user's data! At this point, the solution that can be followed should be obvious from the preceding chapters. We need a call back user function to assist us. Such a function ought to have a prototype of

```
ostream& Display (ostream& os, const void* ptrdata);
```

Here is the generic **Stack** class definition file.

```
The Generic Stack Definition File

 1 #pragma once
 2 #include <iostream>
 3 using namespace std;
 4
 5 typedef ostream& (*DISPLAY) (ostream& os, const void* ptrdata);
 6
 7 /*******************************************************/
 8 /*                                                     */
 9 /* StackNode: contains the forward pointer and this item data */
10 /*                                                     */
11 /*******************************************************/
12
13 struct StackNode {
14   StackNode*  fwdptr;
15   void*       dataptr;
16 };
17
18 /*******************************************************/
19 /*                                                     */
20 /* Stack: a generic stack class                        */
21 /*                                                     */
22 /*******************************************************/
23
24 /*******************************************************/
25 /*                                                     */
26 /* Usage Notes: This class stores client data in void pointers */
27 /*    thus, before the destructor is called, the client pgm    */
28 /*    must delete the actual data being stored.                */
29 /*                                                     */
30 /*    A sample destruction sequence might be as follows        */
31 /*    MyData* ptrd;                                            */
```

```
32 /*    while (!stack.IsEmpty()) {                          */
33 /*     ptrd = (MyData*) stack.Pop();                      */
34 /*     delete ptrd;                                       */
35 /*    }                                                   */
36 /*                                                        */
37 /* If a copy of the stack is made, a shallow copy is done. */
38 /* Only the pointers to the client data are copied.       */
39 /* The actual client data being stored is not duplicated. */
40 /*                                                        */
41 /**********************************************************/
42
43 class Stack {
44 protected:
45  StackNode* headptr;      // the top of the stack pointer
46  long       count;        // the number of items in the stack
47
48 public:
49  Stack ();                // construct an empty stack
50  Stack (const Stack& s);  // the copy constructor
51  Stack& operator= (const Stack& s); // the assignment operator
52
53  ~Stack ();               // delete the stack
54
55  void Push (void* ptrdata); // store this new node on the stack
56  void* Pop ();            // removes top node from the stack
57  void* GetCurrentData () const; // returns user's data on top
58  long GetCount () const;  // returns the number of nodes in stack
59
60  bool IsEmpty () const;   // returns true if stack is empty
61  void RemoveAll ();       // removes all nodes in the stack
62
63  // display all items on the stack nicely formatted
64  ostream& DebugDisplay (ostream& os, DISPLAY Display) const;
65
66 protected:
67  // helper function to duplicate the stack
68  void CopyStack (const Stack& s);
69 };
```

Here is the actual implementation of the generic stack class.

```
The Generic Stack Implementation File

 1 #include "Stack.h"
 2
 3 /**********************************************************/
 4 /*                                                        */
 5 /* Stack: create an empty stack                           */
```

```
 6 /*                                                               */
 7 /*****************************************************************/
 8
 9 Stack::Stack () {
10   headptr = 0;
11   count = 0;
12 }
13
14 /*****************************************************************/
15 /*                                                               */
16 /* ~Stack: deletes the stack                                     */
17 /*                                                               */
18 /*****************************************************************/
19
20 Stack::~Stack () {
21   RemoveAll ();
22 }
23
24 /*****************************************************************/
25 /*                                                               */
26 /* RemoveAll: deletes all nodes of the stack                     */
27 /*                                                               */
28 /*****************************************************************/
29
30 void Stack::RemoveAll () {
31   while (!IsEmpty()) Pop ();
32 }
33
34 /*****************************************************************/
35 /*                                                               */
36 /* Push: store new node on the top of the stack                  */
37 /*                                                               */
38 /*****************************************************************/
39
40 void Stack::Push (void* ptrdata) {
41   StackNode* ptrnew = new (std::nothrow) StackNode;
42   if (!ptrnew) {
43     cerr << "Stack Push: out of memory\n";
44     exit (1);
45   }
46   ptrnew->dataptr = ptrdata;
47   ptrnew->fwdptr = headptr;
48   headptr = ptrnew;
49   count++;
50 }
51
52 /*****************************************************************/
53 /*                                                               */
54 /* Pop: remove the top item from the stack                       */
55 /*                                                               */
```

```
56 /*****************************************************************/
57
58 void* Stack::Pop () {
59  if (!headptr) return 0;
60  StackNode* ptrtodel = headptr;
61  headptr = headptr->fwdptr;
62  void* ptrdata = ptrtodel->dataptr;
63  delete ptrtodel;
64  count--;
65  return ptrdata;
66 }
67
68 /*****************************************************************/
69 /*                                                             */
70 /* GetCurrentData: returns a pointer to user data on the top   */
71 /*                 of the stack or 0 if it is empty            */
72 /*                                                             */
73 /*****************************************************************/
74
75 void* Stack::GetCurrentData () const {
76  return !IsEmpty () ? headptr->dataptr : 0;
77 }
78
79 /*****************************************************************/
80 /*                                                             */
81 /* IsEmpty: returns true when there are no items on the stack  */
82 /*                                                             */
83 /*****************************************************************/
84
85 bool Stack::IsEmpty () const{
86  return headptr ? false : true;
87 }
88
89 /*****************************************************************/
90 /*                                                             */
91 /* GetCount: returns the number of nodes on the stack          */
92 /*                                                             */
93 /*****************************************************************/
94
95 long Stack::GetCount () const {
96  return count;
97 }
98
99 /*****************************************************************/
100 /*                                                             */
101 /* Stack: copy constructor - make a duplicate copy of passed s */
102 /*                                                             */
103 /*****************************************************************/
104
105 Stack::Stack (const Stack& s) {
```

```
106  CopyStack (s);
107 }
108
109 /******************************************************************/
110 /*                                                                */
111 /* operator=: assignment op - makes a copy of passed stack      */
112 /*                                                                */
113 /******************************************************************/
114
115 Stack& Stack::operator= (const Stack& s) {
116  if (this == &s) return *this; // avoid a = a; situation
117  RemoveAll ();   // remove all items in this stack
118  CopyStack (s);  // make a copy of stack s
119  return *this;
120 }
121
122 /******************************************************************/
123 /*                                                                */
124 /* CopyStack: helper that makes a duplicate copy                */
125 /*                                                                */
126 /******************************************************************/
127
128 void Stack::CopyStack (const Stack& s) {
129  if (!s.headptr) { // handle stack s being empty
130   headptr = 0;
131   count = 0;
132   return;
133  }
134  count = s.count;
135  StackNode* ptrScurrent = s.headptr;
136  // previousptr tracks our prior node so we can set its
137  // forward pointer to the next new one
138  StackNode* previousptr = 0;
139  // prime the loop so headptr can be set one time
140  StackNode* currentptr = new (std::nothrow) StackNode;
141  if (!currentptr) {
142   cerr << "Stack Copy - error out of memory\n";
143   exit (1);
144  }
145  headptr = currentptr;  // assign this one to the headptr
146
147 // traverse s stack's nodes
148  while (ptrScurrent) {
149   // copy node of s into our new node
150   currentptr->dataptr = ptrScurrent->dataptr;
151   currentptr->fwdptr = 0;  // set our forward ptr to 0
152   // if previous node exists, set its forward ptr to the new one
153   if (previousptr)
154    previousptr->fwdptr = currentptr;
155   // save this node as the prevous node
```

```
156    previousptr = currentptr;
157    // and get a new node for the next iteration
158    currentptr = new (std::nothrow) StackNode;
159    if (!currentptr) {
160      cerr << "Stack Copy - error out of memory\n";
161      exit (1);
162    }
163    // move to s's next node
164    ptrScurrent = ptrScurrent->fwdptr;
165    }
166  delete currentptr; // delete the extra unneeded node
167  }
168
169  /********************************************************/
170  /*                                                      */
171  /* DebugDisplay: display all items on stack nicely formatted */
172  /*                                                      */
173  /********************************************************/
174
175  ostream& Stack::DebugDisplay (ostream& os, DISPLAY Display)const{
176    os << "Debug display of the stack from top to bottom\n";
177    StackNode* ptrnext = headptr;
178    while (ptrnext) {
179      Display (os, ptrnext->dataptr);
180      ptrnext = ptrnext->fwdptr;
181    }
182    os << "\nDebug display finished\n";
183    return os;
184  }
```

Finally, we need a tester program. For simplicity, I chose to resolve the Palindrome problem using our new generic stack. In this version, I need to dynamically allocate a new character to store the letter on the stack. However, for simplicity with these various stacks, I chose to only dynamically allocate one character and store its address as the data pointer in all the remaining stack instances. Thus, come deletion time, I only need to actually delete the data pointers from one of these stack instances for the other instances just contain a copy of these original pointers. Note that I cannot just delete them as they come off in the comparison pop section, since the two stacks contain the same pointers only in reverse order. I must clean up after the comparison is done. Here is the implementation of **Pgm11c** that also tests the assignment operator and copy constructor.

```
Pgm11c - The Palindrome Problem Using the Generic Stack

  1 #include <iostream>
  2 #include <iomanip>
  3 #include <fstream>
  4 #include <cctype>
  5 #include <crtdbg.h>
  6 using namespace std;
  7
```

```
 8 #include "Stack.h"
 9
10 /*****************************************************************/
11 /*                                                               */
12 /* Pgm11c: Palindrome Analysis program using generic stack       */
13 /*                                                               */
14 /*****************************************************************/
15
16 ostream& Display (ostream& os, const void* ptrdata);
17
18 int main () {
19  {
20  Stack forward;  // stack holds letters in order entered
21  Stack temp;      // stack to help reverse the characters
22  Stack backward; // stack holds reverse order of chars
23  // note I am only going to delete the data pointers in backward
24  // stack. All others will contain a copy of those pointers
25  Stack assign;    // stack to test assignment operator
26
27  char* ptrc;              // a pointer to handle new character
28
29  cout << "Palindrome Analysis Program\n"
30      << "Enter a word or phrase and press enter when done\n"
31      << "Don't enter any punctuation or blanks between words\n";
32  char letter;
33
34  // note: if we push user letters as entered onto a stack, then
35  // the letter on the top of that stack will be the last letter
36  // entered - ie. the backwards order.
37
38  while (cin.get(letter) && letter != '\n') {
39   ptrc = new char;        // allocate a new char to store letter
40   *ptrc = letter;         // copy the letter and
41   backward.Push (ptrc); // save reverse order of letters
42   temp.Push (ptrc);       // save for later reversal of letters
43  }
44
45  while (!temp.IsEmpty ()) {  // reverse all letters entered by
46   ptrc = (char*) temp.Pop ();// popping the last letter and
47   forward.Push (ptrc);       // pushing it on the new stack
48  }
49
50  // display a debug series of messages to verify stack integrity
51  cout << "\nLetters as entered stack:\n";
52  forward.DebugDisplay (cout, Display);
53  cout << "\nReverse order of letters stack:\n";
54  backward.DebugDisplay (cout, Display);
55
56  assign = backward;
57  Stack copyToDelete (backward); // saved copy to use to delete
```

397

```
58
59   // now check to see if the entry is a Palindrome
60   // guard against end of file with nothing entered
61   if (!forward.IsEmpty()) {
62    bool done = false;
63    bool matched = true;// assume they match until proven otherwise
64
65    char* ptrf;  // the forward character
66    char* ptrb;  // the backward character
67
68    // quit on first mis-match or when stack is empty
69    while (!done && !forward.IsEmpty()) {
70     ptrf = (char*) forward.Pop ();  // get next forward letter
71     ptrb = (char*) backward.Pop (); // get next backwards letter
72     if (toupper (*ptrb) != toupper(*ptrf)) { // letters differ?
73      done = true;
74      matched = false;
75     }
76    }
77    if (matched)
78     cout << "This is a palindrome\n";
79    else
80     cout << "This is not a palindrome\n";
81   }
82   else
83    cout << "No letters entered to check\n";
84
85   // now remove all user allocated data
86   while (!copyToDelete.IsEmpty()) {
87    char* ptrb = (char*) copyToDelete.Pop (); // get next letter
88    delete ptrb;                              // and delete it
89   }
90  }
91
92  if (_CrtDumpMemoryLeaks())
93   cout << "\nOops! Memory Leaks!!\n";
94  else
95   cout << "\nNo Memory Leaks\n";
96
97  return 0;
98 }
99
100 // a display call back function from Stack::DebugDisplay
101
102 ostream& Display (ostream& os, const void* ptrdata) {
103  char* ptrc = (char*) ptrdata;
104  os.put (*ptrc) << " "; // display that node's letter
105  return os;
106
```

How to Dynamically Allocate a 2-D Array and Use Pointers to Access the Elements

To allocate a 2-d array, one cannot allocate it as one chunk of contiguous memory. Instead, one allocates a single dimensioned array of row pointers. Next, in a loop, for each row, one allocates the single dimensioned array of columns for that row, storing its address in the row pointer.

Once allocated, the array then acts like a normal 2-d array. Normal subscripting can be used. However, if speed of access is an issue, one can use a pair of pointers to speed up the array accesses, one is the row pointer and the other is the column pointer.

Deletion of the array is the reverse of allocation. First, one goes through each row and deletes the column array to which it points. Second, one array deletes the row pointers. Pgm11d illustrates these principles. The key lines are in boldface.

```
Pgm11d - Dynamic Allocation of a 2-D Array - Using pointer access

 1 #include <iostream>
 2 #include <iomanip>
 3 using namespace std;
 4
 5 /***********************************************************/
 6 /*                                                         */
 7 /* Pgm11d: Illustrates Dynamically Allocating a 2-D Array  */
 8 /*         and Using Pointers to Access the Elements       */
 9 /*                                                         */
10 /***********************************************************/
11
12 const int MAXROWS = 10;
13 const int MAXCOLS = 9;
14
15 int main () {
16  // an automatic - local array on the stack
17  int x[MAXROWS][MAXCOLS];
18
19  int row, col, count;
20  for (row=0; row<MAXROWS; row++ ) {
21   count = 1;
22   for (col=0; col<MAXCOLS; col++) {
23    x[row][col] = row*10 + count++;
24    cout << setw(3) << x[row][col];
25   }
26   cout << endl;
27  }
28
29  // Accessing that local 2-d array using a row pointer
30  int* ptrRow = x[0];
```

```
31   for (row=0; row<MAXROWS; row++ ) {
32    for (col=0; col<MAXCOLS; col++) {
33     cout << setw(3) << ptrRow[col];
34    }
35    cout << endl;
36    ptrRow++;
37   }
38
39   // dynamically allocating a 2-d array
40   // first allocate an array of row pointers
41   int** y = new int*[MAXROWS];
42   // second, allocate all the columns for each row
43   for (row=0; row<MAXROWS; row++) {
44    count = 1;
45    y[row] = new int[MAXCOLS];
46    //use normal subscripts to access elements
47    for (col=0; col<MAXCOLS; col++) {
48     y[row][col] = row*10 + count++;
49     cout << setw(3) << x[row][col];
50    }
51    cout << endl;
52   }
53
54   // use a row pointer and a column pointer to access
55   int** ptrRow2 = y;
56   int** ptrEndRow = y + MAXROWS;
57   int* ptrCol;
58   int* ptrEndCol;
59   while (ptrRow2<ptrEndRow) {
60    ptrCol = *ptrRow2;
61    ptrEndCol = ptrCol + MAXCOLS;
62    while (ptrCol < ptrEndCol) {
63     cout << setw(3) << *ptrCol++;
64    }
65    cout << endl;
66    ptrRow2++;
67   }
68
69   // deleting the dynamically allocated array
70   for (row=0; row<MAXROWS; row++) delete [] y[row];
71   delete [] y;
72
73   return 0;
74
```

Review Questions

1. Explain the concept of how a stack works. Illustrate your answer with a drawing of what happens when an item is pushed onto the stack and when an item is popped from the stack.

2. A stack is often implemented as a linked list. What are the differences between a linked list and a stack? How does this affect operations on the list and stack?

3. Give three examples not mentioned in this chapter that would be prime examples of when a stack would make an ideal data structure to use in the problem solution.

4. Diagram the steps required to Push an item onto a stack.

5. Diagram the steps required to Pop an item off of a stack.

6. What is the effect on a client program when the stack nodes are storing a copy of the user's data (or pointer to) or storing a **void** pointer to the user's data? Is there any impact on the client program's clean up activities?

7. The **LetterStack** class does not support either the assignment operator or the copy constructor. Show a client program that would use both of these actions. What would happen if the user actually ran such a client program?

8. Sketch how a copy constructor could be written for the **LetterStack** class.

9. Under what circumstances would a programmer opt to implement a stack class using an array of stack nodes whose array bounds was fixed at compile-time?

Stop! Do These Exercises Before Programming

1. Our programmer is confronted with a time-critical application. In real-time, his application helps predict space shuttle engine burns to move the shuttle out of the way of space debris that is on a collision course with the shuttle. That is, his application must execute quickly or there would be insufficient time for the shuttle to dodge the debris. He knows that his stack will never hold any more than 100 items. Thus, he has chosen to implement his **SpaceStack** by using an array of **StackNodes**. He began his class definition as follows.

```cpp
struct SpaceData {
... // contents are not important to the problem at hand
};

struct SpaceNode {
 int forward;
 SpaceData spaceData;
};

const int MAX = 100;

class SpaceStack {
protected:
 SpaceNode array[MAX];
 int headIdx;
public:
   SpaceStack ();
  ~SpaceStack ();
   void Push (SpaceData& data);
   SpaceData Pop ();
   bool IsEmpty () const;
};
```

His documentation indicates that the **headIdx** stores the subscript of the top item on the stack. The stack is empty when the **headIdx** contains –1. The stack is full when it contains the value of **MAX**. He has written the following thus far.

```cpp
SpaceStack::SpaceStack () {
   headIdx = -1;
}

bool SpaceStack::IsEmpty () const {
   return headIdx < 0 ? true : false;
}
```

Unfortunately, just at this point in the programming project, he became ill and the project manager has asked you for some assistance on this critical program.

Write the coding required to implement the **Push()** function.

2. Write the coding to implement the **Pop()** function.

3. Write the coding to implement the destructor.

4. Management is worried that under some extreme circumstances more than 100 nodes could be needed. But rather than arbitrarily setting **MAX** to some larger value, they have asked you to insert a new function, **IsFull()**, into the class and implement it. Then, make any needed changes to the **Push()** function to make use of the **IsFull()** function. If the stack is ever full, display an error message to **cerr**.

5. Since there is some chance the stack may need to be duplicated, management has asked you to go ahead and supply the copy constructor and the assignment operator and implement them.

Programming Problems

Problem Pgm11-1 The Eight Queens Problem

The objective is to place eight queen chess pieces on an 8x8 chess board such that no two queens lie in the same row, same column, or same 45-degree diagonal. Write a program to position the queens on any size board from 1 to 15. On a board of dimension 2, there are 2 queens to place. On a board of dimension n, there are n queens to position. The program should display either "For a board size of nxn, there is no solution" or display a chess board diagram showing the locations of the queens. (If you desire, you can use the upper ASCII text box drawing codes as was done in the last chapter.) Turn in a printout of the fifteen different test cases.

To illustrate the algorithm to use, consider placing four queens onto a 4x4 chess board. In what is called a **depth-first search**, we place queens one row at a time until we arrive at a solution or an impossible situation. If we reach an impossible, dead-end situation, then we back track to the last place where we had a choice of placing a queen and choose a different position. The stack data structure is ideal for keeping track of the choices so that the most recent queen position is readily available. The data to be stored on the stack is an ordered pair of row and column numbers.

The following eight figures illustrate the step by step process that yields the solution. In Step 1, we place the 1st in (1,1). Step 2 handles the second row. Notice that location (2,1) is in the same column as the initial queen (1,1) and location (2,2) is on a diagonal with (1,1). Thus, we choose to position the 2nd queen in location (2,3).

Now when we try to place the 3rd queen into row 3, there is no position for it to occupy. Every column in row 3 is now on a diagonal or in the same column as the other two queens. Thus, we must back track and pop the 2nd queen off the stack and try another position for it. Moving down one column, we can try placing the 2nd queen into location (2,4) shown in Step 3.

Next, we can then place the 3rd queen into location (3,2) as shown in Step 4.

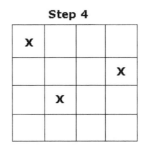

But when we go to place the 4th queen onto the board, there is no acceptable location for it. So we must back track again. However, we have used up all possible locations for the 2nd queen, so we must pop the 1st queen's location and try another location, (1,2) as shown in Step 5.

Step 5

Step 6

The 2nd queen now has only one location that is possible, (2,4), as shown in Step 6. Now place the 3rd queen onto the board. It can go in location (3,1). Then place the 4th queen onto the board. Likewise, there is only one location for it, (4,3). And thus Step 8 represents the final solution.

Step 7

Step 8

For extra credit, you might take this problem one step further and count all possible solutions—however, only display the first possible solutions for a given dimension. That is, pop all of the queens off of the stack and try the next location for the 1st queen, location (1,3) and then later on, location (1,4). With eight queens, there are 92 solutions, but for 12 queens on a 12x12 board, there are 14,200 solutions. At 15x15, there are 2,279,184 solutions!

The program must consist of a stack definition header file, a stack implementation cpp file and a client cpp file. Print out the results for all board sizes from 1 to 15.

Problem Pgm11-2 The Updated Phone Directory Program

Use Pgm10b as the beginning point for this problem. Acme wishes to add an "Undo" feature to all actions that can be performed on the Phone Book list as well as a "Redo" feature. Add a pair of items to the main menu, "Undo previous changes" and "Redo previous changes."

Add another menu choice "Update a phone entry." This option first asks the user for the record id number and then finds that record in the list. If the record is in the list, display it on the screen and ask if they want to change any of this information. If yes is chosen, allow the user to change any of the four main fields but not the record id number.

Both the undo and redo processes are best handled by a pair of stacks. Initially, both are empty. When an update is made to an existing record, push the **PhoneDirectory** structure onto the undo stack. Thus, as updates are done, the undo stack grows. Next, whenever the user chooses to undo the previous update, place the updated **PhoneDirectory** structure onto the redo stack and then pop the undo stack and undo that change. If a redo is chosen, pop the redo item off the redo stack and put the to be changed onto the undo stack.

Further, in the display menu and get choice functions, provide support for the these two new menu items. That is, if the undo stack is empty, do not display the "Undo" menu choice. Likewise for the"Redo" menu. These two menu choices are only available when there is something to undo or redo.

For both actions, display the current **PhoneDirectory** instance and then the proposed undo or redo changes. Ask the user if they wish to revert this change. If yes is entered, go ahead and undo or redo that change in the main phonebook list. Continue showing successive undo or redo instances until the user chooses to quit the undo or redo process.

Thoroughly test your program.

Problem Pgm11-3 Balanced () and [] in a C++ Program

One coding problem that sometimes occurs in writing expressions or a program statement is that of mismatched pairs of parentheses or square brackets. Acme wishes you to develop a "Programmer's Helper" program that finds mismatched items. The program is given a file consisting of one or more lines of coding of any type. The program then identifies the mismatched pairs.

Create a stack to hold one character which can be (or) or [or]. Input the data line by line. Then, process each character of that line. If the current character is a begin symbol (or [, then push it onto the stack. If the current character is an ending parenthesis, then pop the current symbol off the stack. Match the current ending one with the beginning one. If they form a matching pair, all is well. If they do not match, such as a [with), then display an error message that is appropriate. The following is an example of how the results can be displayed.

```
X = (y[2[ + (x - y) * (sin(angle))));
         ^                        ^
expected ]
extra )
```
Here is another example.
```
if ((x == (y/2)] && a]2] > (x - y)) {
                ^       ^ ^           ^
expected )
expected )
expected )
extra )
   R = s * 42 * sin[angle));
                       ^^
expected ]
extra )
}
```
Sometimes there is no real way you can easily tell what is really wrong as in the series of "expected)" messages where the] brackets are out of sync with each other.

You may place the error messages onto another message list instance to facilitate their proper display after the line and the ^ line are displayed.

Consider each line as a separate entity—that is, do not attempt to continue the process across line boundaries. The following is an example.
```
R = s * 42 * sin(angle)(;
                       ^
missing )
```

Thoroughly test your program.

Problem Pgm11-4 Announcing the Galactic Treaty Game

The Galactic Omega Confederation, consisting of a number of planets scattered across a vast space, was at war. However, at Planet X, a peace treaty was signed. However, none of the rulers of the various planets will believe the treaty unless they see it with their own eyes. Thus, you have been hired to fly a space ship to each planet and show the signed treaty to each planetary ruler. The objective is to travel the minimum total distance and thus complete the process in the shortest amount of time thereby ending the war as fast as possible. Simplifying the process, all of the planetary systems lie in a common two-dimensional plane of the galaxy.

Each planet is located by its (x, y) coordinates. The distance between planet1 and planet2 whose coordinates are (x1, y1) and (x2, y2) respectively, is given by the following formula.
```
Distance = sqrt ( (x2-x1)² + (y2-y1)² )
```
The program inputs a file of planet information and then displays the minimum total distance traveled along with the order of the planets.

Each line contains the planet's name, x and y coordinates. All coordinate values are in the same units. The name is abstract, such as "Planet 1" and can contain nine characters maximum. All coordinates are doubles. Further, the very first line is the location of Planet X, the starting point where the treaty was signed.

The program output should be something like the following.
```
Planet Visited     Total Distance Thus Far
Planet X                   0.0
Planet A                  10.3
Planet E                  15.3
...
Total Distance Traveled: 1000.2
```

Test your program using the provided file called **Planets.txt** which is located in the **TestDataForAssignments** folder under the **Chapter11** folder.

Chapter 12—Queues

Introduction

In chapter 5 the concept of a queue was introduced and the properties and operations of a queue were presented. Recall that a queue is a linear, sequential data structure with the properties that new items are added at one end of the list, the front, while items are removed from the other end of the list, the rear of the list. Queues are usually implemented as a variation of a double linked list data structure. A queue supports two key operations, **Enqueue()** and **Dequeue()** for the insertion of a new item and the removal of an existing item.

Examples of queues abound in the real world. The line of ticket purchasers at a movie theater is a queue. New arrivals are enqueued at the rear of the line. Tickets are sold only to those at the front of the queue. When purchasing your flight tickets at an airport, you stand often in a long queue waiting your turn. Similarly, the waiting room of a doctor can be modeled as a queue.

Programs that model assembly line operations use queues to simulate the line's action. A new car's engine appears at the end of the line. Workers then do various actions to it as it moves along the line. It is then removed from the other end of the line when they are finished.

Farmers who are loading cattle into a cattle truck force the cows into a queue to enter the truck. Students registering for school classes are formed into queues. Your car is forced into a queue behind the teller window when you go to the drive up window of a bank to make a deposit or withdrawal.

Table 12.1 (which was Table 5.8) gives the definition of the queue data structure. Queues are often called FIFO, first in, first out lists.

Data Type	Queue
Domain	A queue is a collection of component whose values are all of the same data type
Structure	A queue is a list that is maintained in first in, first out order. That is, insertions are done at the rear of the list, and removals are done at the head of the list.
Operations	
Initialize()	Create an empty queue
Enqueue()	Add an item at the rear of the queue
Dequeue()	Remove an item from the head of the queue
IsEmpty()	Returns true if the queue is empty

Table 12.1 The Queue Data Structure Definition

Figure 12.1 shows a queue in operation.

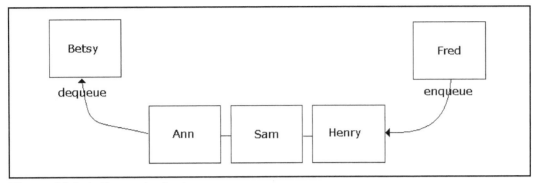

Figure 12.1 A Queue in Action

In Figure 12.1, Betsy has just purchased her ticket to the movie and is being dequeued from the queue of ticket purchasers. Fred has just arrived and is being enqueued at the end of the queue.

Designing a Reusable Generic Queue Class

A robust queue class cannot be limited by an arbitrary number of nodes. Thus, a queue is often implemented as a linked list. I have chosen to use a double linked list so that it can be extended easily with additional functions. I hate having a working single-linked list only to find that later uses require the use of a double linked list.

For the last several chapters, we have studied principles of linking lists together in various ways. Hence, the principles should be familiar to you at this point. Indeed, we can reuse much of the coding from the generic double linked list class from chapter 10.

The enqueue function is basically adding a new node at the tail. So we really have **AddAtTail()** renamed to **Enqueue()**. The **Dequeue()** function is just removing a node from the head of the list which is simpler to do than removing a node from the middle of the list. Hence, a queue class based on a double linked list is actually much simpler to implement than a double linked list. There are far fewer functions and possibilities.

To make it a totally reusable queue class, we should store the client's data using a **void** pointer. Thus, the **QueueNode** structure is simply the following.

```
struct QueueNode {    // a double linked list
  QueueNode* fwdptr;
  QueueNode* backptr;
  void*      dataptr; // the user's object being stored
};
```

In addition to the constructor, **Enqueue()**, and **Dequeue()** functions, we must support list traversal. The functions **ResetToHead()**, **GetCount()** and **GetNext()** allows anyone to write loops to process all items in the queue. The destructor removes all items from the queue as usual, However, I provide a **RemoveAll()** function to actually empty the queue. The destructor calls this function and a client program can also invoke it to empty the queue for its reuse.

To be robust, the **Queue** class must also support the copy constructor and the assignment operator. As usual, since both must copy a given queue, the helper function **CopyQueue()** actually does the work of duplicating a queue. However, since the **Queue** class is storing void pointers to the client's data, only a shallow copy can be performed.

Here is the Queue class definition file.

```
The Queue Definition File

 1 #pragma once
 2
 3 /********************************************************************/
 4 /*                                                                  */
 5 /* QueueNode: stores the double linked list's fwd/back ptrs    */
 6 /*            and the user's data ptr                          */
 7 /*                                                                  */
 8 /********************************************************************/
 9
10 struct QueueNode {   // a double linked list
11   QueueNode* fwdptr;
12   QueueNode* backptr;
13   void*      dataptr; // the user's object being stored
14 };
15
16 /********************************************************************/
17 /*                                                                  */
18 /* Queue Container Class                                       */
19 /*                                                                  */
20 /* stores void pointers to user's objects                     */
21 /* before deleting an instance, the user MUST traverse and     */
22 /* delete any objects whose pointers are being stored         */
23 /*                                                                  */
24 /********************************************************************/
25
26 class Queue {
27
28 private:
29   QueueNode* headptr;      // pointer to first node
30   QueueNode* tailptr;      // pointer to last node
31   QueueNode* currentptr; // the current node when traversing
32   long       count;      // the number of nodes
33
34
35 public:
36   Queue ();                              // makes an empty queue
```

411

```
37   Queue (const Queue& q);              // copy constructor
38   Queue& operator= (const Queue& q);  // assignment operator
39   // VITAL NOTE: when a copy is made, the copy contains the SAME
40   // pointers as the original Queue - be careful not to delete
41   // them twice
42
43   ~Queue ();              // the destructor removes the queue
44   void   RemoveAll ();  // but not the user objects being stored!
45
46   void   Enqueue (void* ptrdata);// add another object to the queue
47   void*  Dequeue ();              // return and remove current node
48   long   GetSize () const;        // returns the size of the queue
49
50   void   ResetToHead (); // reset current to the start of the queue
51   void*  GetNext ();      // returns next user object or 0 when at
52                          // the end of the queue
53   // for cleanup operations, traverse the queue and delete the
54   // objects the queue is saving for you before you destroy or
55   // empty the queue
56
57 private:
58   // helper function to copy a Queue
59   void   CopyQueue (const Queue& q);
60 };
61
```

The Queue Class Implementation

Let's begin with the **Enqueue()** function which is really the old **AddAtTail()** function of a double linked list. There are two possibilities: the list is empty or there are existing node(s). The **tailptr** identifies which case is present. If it is 0, the list is empty. So the sequence begins by allocating a new **QueueNode** and storing the client's data pointer in the new node. Then we test **tailptr** to determine which case is present.

```
void   Queue::Enqueue (void* ptrdata) { // Add at Tail
 QueueNode* ptrnew = new QueueNode;     // make new node
 ptrnew->dataptr = ptrdata;        // insert user's object
 count++;                          // increment number of nodes
 if (tailptr) {                    // if there are other nodes,
```

If **tailptr** is not zero, then there are already one or more nodes in the queue. Figure 12.1 illustrates an enqueue request. Here we are requested to store the client's data that is located at memory location 2000 onto the end of the queue. Notice that the previous node at the tail, located at memory location 100 must have its forward pointer changed to point to the new node at location 200. And the new node must have its back pointer set to the previous node at location 100.

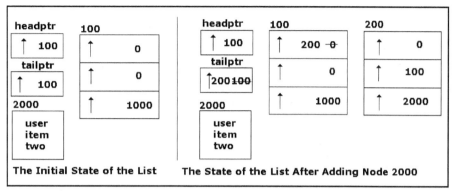

Figure 12.1 Enqueue a Node at the Tail

Thus, the coding becomes
```
tailptr->fwdptr = ptrnew;
ptrnew->backptr = tailptr;
ptrnew->fwdptr = 0;
tailptr = currentptr = ptrnew;
}
```
And the coding for an empty list addition is just
```
else { // queue is currently empty, so just add us
headptr = tailptr = currentptr = ptrnew;
ptrnew->fwdptr = ptrnew->backptr = 0;
}
```

The dequeue operation removes the current node from the head of the list, returning to the client the data pointer that the queue was storing. There are only two situations that can occur. Either the node at the head is the last node in the queue or there are additional nodes remaining. The **headptr**'s forward pointer distinguishes between these two situations. If the first node is the only node, then its forward pointer is 0. Thus, there is no back pointer to reset to 0. Figure 12.2 shows a dequeue request. Here we must delete the node at memory location 200 and return the client's data pointer that was stored in this node, address 2000.

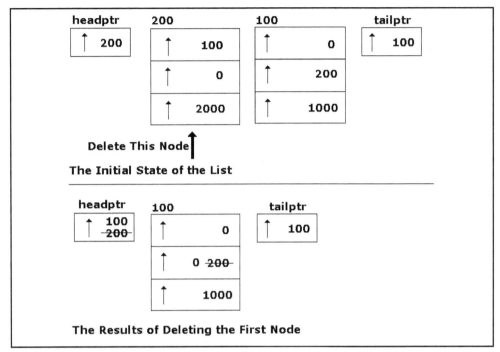

Figure 12.2 Dequeue — Deletion of the Node at the Head of the Queue

Notice that **headptr**'s forward pointer is not 0. Thus, that node, **headptr->fwdptr,** which is at location 100 in the figure, must have its back pointer reset to 0. And **headptr** is reset to point to this next node at location 100.

```
void* Queue::Dequeue () {
  if (!headptr) return 0;
  currentptr = headptr;
  if (headptr->fwdptr)
    headptr->fwdptr->backptr = 0;
  headptr = headptr->fwdptr;
  count--;
  if (count == 0) tailptr = 0;
  void* retval = currentptr->dataptr;
  delete currentptr;
  currentptr = headptr;
  return retval;
}
```

Here is the complete **Queue** class implementation. It is very straightforward.

```
The Queue Implementation File

1 #include <iostream>
2 using namespace std;
3 #include "queue.h"
```

414

```
 4
 5  /*************************************************************/
 6  /*                                                           */
 7  /* Queue: construct an empty queue                           */
 8  /*                                                           */
 9  /*************************************************************/
10
11  Queue::Queue () {
12   headptr = currentptr = tailptr = 0;
13   count = 0;
14  }
15
16  /*************************************************************/
17  /*                                                           */
18  /* ~Queue: remove all QueueNode objects - but does not delete */
19  /*         any user objects                                  */
20  /*                                                           */
21  /*************************************************************/
22
23  Queue::~Queue () {
24   RemoveAll ();
25  }
26
27  /*************************************************************/
28  /*                                                           */
29  /* RemoveAll: removes all QueueNode Objects, leaving the queue */
30  /*            in an empty but valid state                    */
31  /*                                                           */
32  /*************************************************************/
33
34  void Queue::RemoveAll () {
35   if (!headptr) return;            // nothing to do case
36   QueueNode* ptrnext = headptr;    // start at the front of the queue
37   QueueNode* ptrdel;
38   while (ptrnext) {                // for all QueueNodes,
39    ptrdel = ptrnext;               // save its pointer for later deletion
40    ptrnext = ptrnext->fwdptr;      // set for next node in the queue
41    delete ptrdel;                  // remove this node
42   }
43   // leave queue in a default, valid , empty state
44   currentptr = tailptr = headptr = 0;
45   count = 0;
46  }
47
48  /*************************************************************/
49  /*                                                           */
50  /* Queue Copy Constructor: duplicate the passed Queue object */
51  /*                                                           */
52  /* VITAL: we will not duplicate the user's actual data       */
53  /*                                                           */
```

415

```
54  /*****************************************************************/
55
56  Queue::Queue (const Queue& q) {
57   CopyQueue (q);              // call helper function to do the work
58  }
59
60  /*****************************************************************/
61  /*                                                             */
62  /* Operator= - Assignment operator: duplicate this Queue object*/
63  /*                                                             */
64  /* VITAL: we will not duplicate the user's actual data         */
65  /*                                                             */
66  /*****************************************************************/
67
68  Queue& Queue::operator= (const Queue& q) {
69   if (&q == this) return *this; // avoid silly case of x = x;
70   if (count != 0) RemoveAll (); // if we are not empty, empty us
71   CopyQueue (q);               // call helper function to do it
72   return *this;               // return us so user can chain
73  }
74
75  /*****************************************************************/
76  /*                                                             */
77  /* CopyQueue: make a shallow copy of the passed queue          */
78  /*                                                             */
79  /* VITAL: we will not duplicate the user's actual data         */
80  /*                                                             */
81  /*****************************************************************/
82
83  void  Queue::CopyQueue (const Queue& q) {
84   // initialize queue so that we can use Enqueue to add the nodes
85   currentptr = tailptr = headptr = 0;
86   count = 0;
87   if (!q.count) // if there are none, queue is now initialized
88     return;
89   QueueNode* ptrqcurrent = q.headptr;// point to their head
90   while (ptrqcurrent) {                 // while there's another node
91    Enqueue (ptrqcurrent->dataptr);   // add it to our queue
92    ptrqcurrent = ptrqcurrent->fwdptr;// point to next one to copy
93   }
94  }
95
96  /*****************************************************************/
97  /*                                                             */
98  /* Enqueue: Add a new node to the tail of the queue            */
99  /*                                                             */
100 /*****************************************************************/
101
102 void  Queue::Enqueue (void* ptrdata) { // Add at Tail
103  QueueNode* ptrnew = new (std::nothrow) QueueNode;//make new node
```

```
104  if (!ptrnew) {
105   cerr << "Queue::Enqueue - out of memory\n";
106   exit (1);
107  }
108  ptrnew->dataptr = ptrdata;        // insert user's object
109  count++;                          // increment number of nodes
110  if (tailptr) {                    // if there are other nodes,
111   tailptr->fwdptr = ptrnew;        // last one now points to us
112   ptrnew->backptr = tailptr;       // us points to previous last one
113   ptrnew->fwdptr = 0;              // us points to none
114   tailptr = currentptr = ptrnew;// reset tail to us
115  }
116  else { // queue is currently empty, so just add us
117   headptr = tailptr = currentptr = ptrnew;
118   ptrnew->fwdptr = ptrnew->backptr = 0;
119  }
120 }
121
122 /***************************************************************/
123 /*                                                           */
124 /* Dequeue: return object at the head and delete that node   */
125 /*                                                           */
126 /***************************************************************/
127
128 void* Queue::Dequeue () { // remove at head
129  if (!headptr) return 0;          // we are empty, so do nothing
130  currentptr = headptr;            // reset to the head object
131  if (headptr->fwdptr)             // is there more than one node?
132   headptr->fwdptr->backptr = 0;// yes, set next one's back to none
133  headptr = headptr->fwdptr;       // reset head ptr to the next one
134  count--;                         // decrement count of nodes
135  if (count == 0) tailptr = 0;   // reset tailptr if queue is empty
136  void* retval = currentptr->dataptr;// save object to be returned
137  delete currentptr;               // remove previous head object
138  currentptr = headptr;            // reset the current node ptr
139  return retval;                   // give the user their object
140 }
141
142 /***************************************************************/
143 /*                                                           */
144 /* GetSize: returns the number of items in the queue         */
145 /*                                                           */
146 /***************************************************************/
147
148 long  Queue::GetSize () const {
149  return count;
150 }
151
152 /***************************************************************/
153 /*                                                           */
```

```
154 /* ResetToHead: reset currentptr to head pointer for queue    */
155 /*                traversal operations                         */
156 /*                                                             */
157 /***************************************************************/
158
159 void  Queue::ResetToHead () {
160   currentptr = headptr;
161 }
162
163 /***************************************************************/
164 /*                                                             */
165 /* GetNext: returns next user object & sets currentptr for next*/
166 /*                                                             */
167 /***************************************************************/
168
169 void* Queue::GetNext () {
170   if (!currentptr) return 0;        // queue is empty, so do nothing
171   void* retval = currentptr->dataptr;// save object to be returned
172   currentptr = currentptr->fwdptr;// set currentptr to next in one
173   return retval;                    // give the user the current obj
174 }
```

A Modification to the Queue Class—A Priority Queue

The basic **Queue** class is actually fairly easy to implement. From this generalized implementation, more specialized types of **Queue** classes can be written. One of these is called a **priority queue**.

In a **priority queue**, the **Enqueue()** function is modified to permit some means of prioritizing of the client's data. For example, if we had a list of patients visiting a doctor's office, usually, the next person serviced comes from the head of the queue and new arrivals are enqueued at the tail. However, what happens if an emergency case arrives? Emergency situations must be placed at the very head of the queue for obvious reasons.

True, a doctor's office application could maintain two separate queues, one for normal patients and one for emergency cases. However, if we make the **Enqueue()** function a bit smarter, one priority queue can service the entire application. Let's call this function **PriorityEnqueue()**.

What information would we require to process a priority enqueue operation? With the doctor's office example, suppose that the **PriorityEnqueue()** function was given a priority integer along with the new client's data pointer. The higher the priority number, the higher in the queue it should be placed. Suppose the current patient queue contained several normal patients called say priority 1. Now a new patient arrives who is given a priority of 2. The **PriorityEnqueue()** should place that new node at the head of the queue. If another priority 2 patient arrives next, that one should be placed second in the queue, right after the first priority 2 patient. If a priority 3 patient is added next, then that one would become the first one in the list.

418

Thus, **PriorityEnqueue()** must traverse the list and place this new node after the last node of an equal priority or just ahead of one of a lesser priority when no existing nodes are at its priority level. If our **Queue** class was not a generic one, but was storing **Patient** structure instances or pointers to such in the **QueueNode**, then we could immediately implement the **PriorityEnqueue()** function. Unfortunately, the class is storing **void** pointers.

How can a **PriorityEnqueue()** function be written? The problem is similar in nature to the **FindNode()** function from the double linked list class in **Pgm10b**. To determine if a node matched the user's criteria, the **FindNode()** member function was passed a call back function along with a pointer to the user's matching criteria. The **FindNode()** function then called the user's call back function presenting each node in turn until the call back function indicated a match. We can use this same approach to implement a **PriorityEnqueue()** function.

The **PriorityEnqueue()** function must be presented with a void pointer to this new node's priority criteria, whatever that may be. It must also be given a call back function that it can use to assist it in finding the correct location in the queue. Thus, the prototype for **PriorityEnqueue()** could be as follows.

```
void PriorityEnqueue (void* ptrdata,
                      void* ptrPriorityForThisOne,
                      PRIORITYFUNCT FindPriority);
```

And the **typedef** for the **FindPriority()** function would be

```
typedef int (*PRIORITYFUNCT) (const void* ptrPriorityThis,
                              const void* ptrdata);
```

How would the **PriorityEnqueue()** function actually be implemented? If the queue were empty, then the priority of this request is irrelevant, just add this first node. If there are nodes in the queue, then begin at the head of the queue. Look for the first node whose priority criteria was less than this new one's priority criteria. If one such node is found, add this new one just before this found node. If the end of the list is encountered, add this new one at the end of the list.

Hence, the design calls for the **FindPriority()** function to return a negative integer whenever the priority of this one is greater than that of the node that was passed. (It should return 0 if the priorities are the same and a positive integer otherwise.)

```
void PriorityEnqueue (void* ptrdata,
                      void* ptrPriorityForThisOne,
                      PRIORITYFUNCT FindPriority) {
 if (headptr == 0) { // empty queue, so just add this one
  Enqueue (ptrdata); // reuse normal Enqueue function
  return;
 }
 // here, we must find the spot in which to insert this one
 ResetToHead ();
 while (currentptr) {
  if (FindPriority (ptrPriorityForThisOne,
      currentptr->dataptr) < 0)
   break; // we found where it goes, before currentptr
  GetNext ();
 }
```

419

```
if (currentptr == 0) { // add at tail
  Enqueue (ptrdata);     // so use normal Enqueue
}
else { // adding at the head or in the middle of 2 nodes
  QueueNode* ptrnew = new QueueNode; // make new node
  ptrnew->dataptr = ptrdata;      // insert user's object
  count++;                        // increment number nodes

  if (currentptr == headptr) { // adding at the head?
   ptrnew->fwdptr = headptr; // fwdptr contains the prev one
   headptr->backptr = ptrnew;// prev node's backptr is us
   headptr = ptrnew;          // set headptr to new node
  }
  else { // adding in the middle of the queue between nodes
   // set new node's back ptr to current's back
   ptrnew->backptr = currentptr->backptr;
   // set new node's forward ptr to current node
   ptrnew->fwdptr = currentptr;
   // set current node's back ptr to point to us
   currentptr->backptr = ptrnew;
   // set prevous node's forward ptr to point to us
   ptrnew->backptr->fwdptr = ptrnew;
   currentptr = ptrnew; // set current pointer to new node
  }
 }
}
```

Programming Problem 12-1 below will explore this implementation of creating a priority queue for a client application.

The Full-Course Waiting List Client Program, Pgm12a

We need a client program to test our new **Queue** class. This time we handle an administration problem. During student registration, sometimes a course becomes full: that is, the maximum number of students allowed into a section is reached. Additional students who wish to get into that specific section are put on a student waiting list. Then, as some students withdraw from that section or are dropped for not paying the tuition, those on the waiting queue are added to the course roster.

Throughout the day, the administrative personnel create and add to a log of transaction's to be applied that night to the waiting list itself. When a drop occurs in the course, a new line is added to the transaction's file, "Signup Student." During the day, when a student requests to be placed on the waiting list for the course, their information is added on another line in the transaction's file. For example,

```
Add 234234789 "Thomas Wainthrop" 309 699 9999
```

The information collected consist of the student's id number (his/her social security numbers), his/her name surrounded by double quote marks, and his/her area code and phone number. This information is stored in the following way.

```
const int MaxNameLen = 31;

struct PhoneNumber {
 short   areaCode;
 short   prefix;
 short   number;
};

struct WaitingList {
 long         ssno;
 char         name[MaxNameLen];
 PhoneNumber number;
};
```

Instances of the **WaitingList** structure are stored in the queue.

At the end of the day, **Pgm12a** is run. It begins by calling a function to load the waiting list queue from a file of people already on the waiting list. Then it calls another function to print the current contents of the waiting list. Next it calls a process transactions function which inputs the day's transactions, line by line, either enqueuing a new student onto the end of the waiting list or dequeuing a student. (In reality, the program would have to then add the dequeued student to the actual class roster.) Finally, the program displays the new waiting list. To test the copy constructor and assignment operator, I inserted some additional actions.

Here are the listing for **Pgm12a** and the test run.

```
Pgm12a - Process Waiting List Transactions

 1 #include <iostream>
 2 #include <fstream>
 3 #include <iomanip>
 4 #include <crtdbg.h>
 5 #include <string>
 6 //#include <stdlib> // if using vc6
 7 using namespace std;
 8
 9 #include "Queue.h"
10
11
12 /****************************************************************/
13 /*                                                            */
14 /* Pgm12a - Handle a Course Waiting List - Queue Application  */
15 /*                                                            */
16 /****************************************************************/
17
18 const int MaxNameLen = 31;
19
20 struct PhoneNumber {
```

```
21  short   areaCode;
22  short   prefix;
23  short   number;
24  };
25
26  struct WaitingList {
27  long          ssno;
28  char          name[MaxNameLen];
29  PhoneNumber number;
30  };
31
32  void LoadCurrentList (Queue& list, const char* filename);
33  void PrintWaitingList (Queue& list, ostream& out);
34  void ProcessTransactions (Queue& list, const char* filename);
35
36  int main () {
37  {
38   Queue waitingList;
39   LoadCurrentList (waitingList, "WaitingList.txt");
40
41   cout << "There are " << waitingList.GetSize()
42       << " students on the list\n"
43       << "Current Waiting List Contains:\n\n"
44       << "StudentID  Name                        Phone Number"
45       << endl << endl;
46
47   PrintWaitingList (waitingList, cout);
48   cout << endl << endl;
49
50   ProcessTransactions (waitingList, "WaitingTransactions.txt");
51
52   cout << "\n\nThere are " << waitingList.GetSize()
53       << " students on the list\n"
54       << "Current Waiting List Contains:\n\n"
55       << "StudentID  Name                        Phone Number"
56       << endl << endl;
57   PrintWaitingList (waitingList, cout);
58   cout << endl << endl;
59
60   // test copy and assignment operators
61   Queue copy (waitingList);
62   Queue asgn;
63   asgn = waitingList;
64   cout << "The copy constructor list contains:\n";
65   PrintWaitingList (copy, cout);
66   cout << endl << endl;
67   cout << "The assigned list contains:\n";
68   PrintWaitingList (asgn, cout);
69   cout << endl << endl;
70
```

```
71    // delete all WaitingList instances stored in the queue
72    WaitingList* ptrstudent;
73    waitingList.ResetToHead ();
74    while ((ptrstudent = (WaitingList*)waitingList.GetNext())!=0) {
75     if (ptrstudent) delete ptrstudent;
76     }
77    }
78
79    if (_CrtDumpMemoryLeaks())
80     cout << "\nOops! Memory Leaks!!\n";
81    else
82     cout << "\nNo Memory Leaks\n";
83
84    return 0;
85   }
86
87   /****************************************************************/
88   /*                                                            */
89   /* LoadCurrentList - load the queue from the current waiting  */
90   /*                   list file                                */
91   /*                                                            */
92   /****************************************************************/
93
94   void LoadCurrentList (Queue& list, const char* filename) {
95    ifstream in (filename);
96    if (!in) {
97     cerr << "Error: cannot open file: " << filename << endl;
98     exit (1);
99     }
100   WaitingList* ptrnew = new (std::nothrow) WaitingList;
101   if (!ptrnew) {
102    cerr << "Error - out of memory\n";
103    exit (1);
104    }
105   char junk;
106   while (in >> ptrnew->ssno >> junk) {
107    in.getline (ptrnew->name, MaxNameLen, '\"');
108    in >> ptrnew->number.areaCode >> ptrnew->number.prefix
109       >> ptrnew->number.number;
110    list.Enqueue (ptrnew);
111    ptrnew = new (std::nothrow) WaitingList;
112    if (!ptrnew) {
113     cerr << "Error - out of memory\n";
114     exit (1);
115     }
116    }
117   delete ptrnew;
118   in.close ();
119   }
120
```

```
121 /****************************************************************/
122 /*                                                              */
123 /* PrintWaitingList - display a report of all students on the  */
124 /*                    waiting list from front to rear          */
125 /*                                                              */
126 /****************************************************************/
127
128 void PrintWaitingList (Queue& list, ostream& out) {
129  WaitingList* ptrstudent;
130  list.ResetToHead ();
131  while ( (ptrstudent = (WaitingList*) list.GetNext()) != 0) {
132   out << setw(8) << ptrstudent->ssno << "   " << left << setw (30)
133       << ptrstudent->name << right << " (" << setw (3)
134       << ptrstudent->number.areaCode << ") " << setw(3)
135       << ptrstudent->number.prefix << "-" << setw (4)
136       << ptrstudent->number.number << endl;
137  }
138 }
139
140 /****************************************************************/
141 /*                                                              */
142 /* ProcessTransactions: handle the transactions against the   */
143 /*                      queue                                   */
144 /*                                                              */
145 /****************************************************************/
146
147 void ProcessTransactions (Queue& list, const char* filename) {
148  ifstream in (filename);
149  if (!in) {
150   cerr << "Error: cannot open the file " << filename << endl;
151   exit (2);
152  }
153  char type[30];
154  while (in >> type) {
155   if (_stricmp (type, "Signup") == 0) {
156    in >> type; // input rest of text "Student"
157    WaitingList* ptrstudent = (WaitingList*) list.Dequeue ();
158    if (ptrstudent) {
159     cout << "Signed up: " << ptrstudent->name << endl;
160     delete ptrstudent;
161    }
162   }
163   else if (_stricmp (type, "Add") == 0) {
164    WaitingList* ptrnew = new (std::nothrow) WaitingList;
165    if (!ptrnew) {
166     cerr << "Error - out of memory\n";
167     exit (1);
168    }
169    char junk;
170    in >> ptrnew->ssno >> junk;
```

424

```
171   in.getline (ptrnew->name, MaxNameLen, '\"');
172   in >> ptrnew->number.areaCode >> ptrnew->number.prefix
173       >> ptrnew->number.number;
174   list.Enqueue (ptrnew);
175   cout << "Added Student: " << ptrnew->name << endl;
176   }
177   else {
178   cerr << "Error: invalid transaction code encountered.\n"
179       << "It was: " << type << endl;
180   in.close ();
181   exit (3);
182   }
183 }
184 in.close ();
185 }
```

```
Output from Pgm12a

 1 There are 4 students on the list
 2 Current Waiting List Contains:
 3
 4 StudentID   Name                        Phone Number
 5
 6 123456789   Abbey Jones                 (309)  699-9999
 7 233345443   Billy J. Smith              (309)  699-9999
 8 454534534   Freddy Bolger               (309)  699-9999
 9 345343453   Kathy Sharpe                (309)  699-9999
10
11
12 Signed up: Abbey Jones
13 Signed up: Billy J. Smith
14 Added Student: Thomas Wainthrop
15 Signed up: Freddy Bolger
16 Added Student: Zoe Delmar
17
18
19 There are 3 students on the list
20 Current Waiting List Contains:
21
22 StudentID   Name                        Phone Number
23
24 345343453   Kathy Sharpe                (309)  699-9999
25 234234789   Thomas Wainthrop            (309)  699-9999
26 342323489   Zoe Delmar                  (309)  699-9999
27
28
29 The copy constructor list contains:
30 345343453   Kathy Sharpe                (309)  699-9999
31 234234789   Thomas Wainthrop            (309)  699-9999
```

```
32 342323489  Zoe Delmar                    (309) 699-9999
33
34
35 The assigned list contains:
36 345343453  Kathy Sharpe                  (309) 699-9999
37 234234789  Thomas Wainthrop              (309) 699-9999
38 342323489  Zoe Delmar                    (309) 699-9999
39
40
41
42 No Memory Leaks
```

Review Questions

1. Explain the concept of how a queue works. Illustrate your answer with a drawing of what happens when an item is enqueued and when an item is dequeued.

2. Discuss three applications that are ideal for a queue container which have not been discussed in this book thus far. Be sure to show why these applications could benefit from queue processing.

3. Since a queue is implemented using a double linked list, how does queue processing differ from that of a linked list?

4. Assume that a stack class and a queue class are both based upon a linked list. Describe the differences in operation between these two variations of a linked list.

5. What is the difference between a stack's **Push()** function and a queue's **Enqueue()** function? What functions of a double linked list class correspond to these two functions?

6. Why is it sometimes reasonable to implement a queue with a built-in array instead of a linked list of dynamically allocated nodes?

7. Why is the implementation of a queue easier to do when the actual client's data is stored as a structure instance within the queue nodes? What complexities arise when only a void pointer to the client's data is stored in the nodes?

Stop! Do These Exercises Before Programming

1. Our programmer is once again confronted with a time-critical application. In real time, his application must perform enqueues and dequeues as rapidly as possible. The nodes are to store void pointers to the client's data, however. He has chosen the concept of a **circular array** to implement the queue.

The idea of a circular array is that when the end of the array is encountered, we make the next element be subscript 0 once again. It is rather like taking a linear array and bending it around to form a circle with [0] coming after [n] where n is the last element. In the next figure, four items have been enqueued. Two indexes track the head and the end of the queue in terms of subscripts.

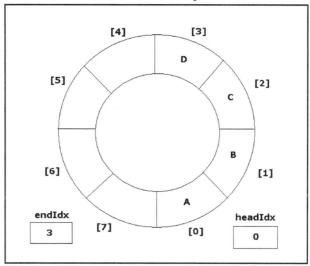

Next, 4 more items were enqueued, the original 4 dequeued and 2 more enqueued.

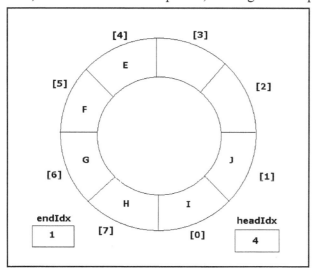

Notice how the head index is now properly pointing to [4] while the end index has wrapped around and points to [1].

The programmer has gotten the **RingQueue** definition file coded as follows.

```
struct QueueNode {    // a double linked list
 int   fwdIdx;  // index of next item or -1 for none
 int   backIdx; // index of previous item or -1 for none
 void* dataptr; // the user's object being stored
};

const int MAX = 100; // maximum number of nodes

class RingQueue {
private:
 int  headIdx;    // index of start of list
 int  endIdx;     // index of last node
 int  currentIdx; // index of current node
 long count;      // the number of nodes

 QueueNode array[MAX]; // the actual ring queue

public:
 RingQueue ();
~RingQueue ();
 void  RemoveAll ();

 bool  Enqueue (void* ptrdata);
 void* Dequeue ();

 long  GetSize () const;
 void  ResetToHead ();
 void* GetNext ();
};
```

He has implemented the following functions. His idea was to let −1 represent end of chain or no node, since values 0 and above could be valid subscripts.

```
RingQueue:: RingQueue () {
 count = 0;
 headIdx = endIxd = currentIdx = -1;
}

RingQueue::~RingQueue () {
 RemoveAll ();
}

void RingQueue::RemoveAll () {
 count = 0;
 headIdx = endIxd = currentIdx = -1;
}
```

428

Beginning Data Structures in C++

```
long RingQueue::GetSize () const {
 return count;
}

void RingQueue::ResetToHead () {
 currentIdx = headIdx;
}

void* RingQueue::GetNext () {
 if (currentIdx == -1)
  return 0;  // queue is empty, so do nothing
 void* retval = array[currentIdx].dataptr;
 currentIdx = array[currentIdx].fwdIdx;
 return retval;
}
```

At this point in the project development, the programmer had to go out of town on an emergency service call and has asked you to finish up his class for him.

Write the coding required for the **Enqueue()** function. If the member **count** is less than **MAX**, then there is more room in the array. If the queue should happen to be full, return **false**. The idea he has expressed is to add one to the **endIdx** and if it should equal **MAX**, then set it back to 0, starting over with the empty element 0 of the array. The following handles this wraparound action.
```
endIdx = (endIdx + 1) % MAX;
```

2. Write the coding for the **Dequeue()** function.

3. Using the generic **Queue** class of Pgm12a, implement a new function, **BailOut()**. Sometimes when people are involved in a queue situation, they decide not to wait it out and just leave the queue. Thus, applications need a method of removing an arbitrary node from the queue. The function's prototype is
```
void* BailOut (void* ptrMatchCriteria,
               BAILFUNCT FindThisNode);
```
and the **typedef** for the user call back function is
```
typedef int (*BAILFUNCT) (const void* ptrMatchCriteria,
                          const void* ptrdata);
```
Specifically, the **FindThisNode()** function returns 0 if this data matches the criteria, a negative value if this data is less than the matching criteria and a positive number if greater.

BailOut() should find the matching node and delete it, returning a pointer to the user's data. This way, the client can then delete their data. If the node is not found, return 0.

429

4. Graph the amount of memory that a queue implementation requires as a function of the number of elements in the queue. Specifically, compare an array-based implementation versus a double linked list version. Assume that the array has a maximum of 200 elements in it. Make the following assumptions.

> A pointer occupies 4 bytes.
>
> An index occupies 4 bytes.
>
> The client's data being stored in each node occupies 20 bytes.
>
> Each linked list node contains two pointers and the client data.
>
> Each array element contains two indexes and the client data.

The horizontal axis runs from 0 to 200 elements in the queue. The vertical axis runs from 0 bytes up to the amount for the largest point. Hint, the amount of memory required for the array version is independent of the number of elements in the queue.

With the graph plotted and for nodes of this size, what conclusions can be inferred?

Programming Problems

Problem Pgm12-1 The Veterinarian's Patient Processing Program

A veterinarian needs a program to manage his processing of his patients. When a person arrives with their pet, the pet information is input into a **Pet** structure. Next, the pet record is entered into his queue of patients at the proper location. The pet information consists of the owner's name (20 characters), the pet's name (20 characters), and an integer emergency code (0 = normal, 1 = emergency).

When the vet finishes with a patient, that animal is removed from the queue. The vet then takes the next patient in the queue unless there is an emergency patient in the queue. His algorithm to choose the next patient is to take the next patient in the queue unless there is another patient in the queue whose emergency code is 1. Should there be more than one emergency, he handles them in the order that they arrived.

To simulate the day's operations, a transaction file is used. Each record in the file consists of four fields:

> action code (1 character) A (add this patient) or H (handle next patient)
>
> owner's name
>
> pet's name
>
> emergency code (0 or 1)

If the action code is H, then the other three fields are not present. If the action code is A, then the other three fields are present.

In the **TestDataForAssignments** folder under the **Chapter12** folder is a test data file called **patients.txt**. Your program should input this file and process them. Your program output should be similar to the following.

```
Added:    Samuel Spade          Fido                0
Added:    John Jones            Rover               0
Added:    Betsy Ann Smithville  Jenny               0
Treated:  Samuel Spade          Fido                0
```

```
Treated: John Jones              Rover              0
Added:   Lou Ann deVille         Kitty              1
Treated: Lou Ann deVille         Kitty              1
Added:   Tom Smythe              Fifi               0
Added:   Marie Longfellow        Jack               1
Treated: Marie Longfellow        Jack               1
Treated: Betsy Ann Smithville    Jenny              0
Treated: Tom Smythe              Fifi               0
```

Each patient should be enqueued by calling **PriorityEnqueue()**. Use the sample coding given in the section above called "A Modification to the Queue Class—A Priority Queue" to implement this.

Problem Pgm12-2 DJ Swinging Annie's Morning Show Program

Annie, a disk jockey for a local radio station, has a morning two-hour program. Each day, she must pick songs from the station's library to play on the air. Her routine is to arrive ten minutes early and quickly pick a few songs and enter them into the program's queue. When she goes live on the air, she presses the Get Next Song button and the next song information is dequeued and displayed so that the engineer can cue up the song and she can announce it. While the song is playing, she then adds new songs to the queue.

The information that is entered for each song consists of the following data.
the CD id number as assigned by the station library manager
the artist name (20 characters)
the song name (20 characters)
the total playing time in minutes and seconds
Create a **Song** structure to encapsulate this information. Use the **Queue** class as given in **Pgm12a** with no changes.

The program should input the file **songs.txt** located in the **TestDataForAssignments Chapter12** folder. Each line in the file represents an action. The first character contains the action code. If the action code is P for play, your program should dequeue the next song and display the Song data nicely formatted. The remainder of the line is empty. If the action code is A for "Add new song," then this line contains the song data to be enqueued into the play queue. Following the A character comes the cd number which is followed by the artist and song names and the duration of the song in minutes and seconds.

When the program begins, prompt the user to enter the date as three integers and display a title line similar to this.

```
DJ Annie's Morning Show for 01/10/2001 - Play List

CD Num  Artist               Song              Duration (mm:ss)

  101   Jethro Tull          Aqualung             5:30
```
When the end of the file is reached, display the total duration time of the music played this day. This print out then serves as her play list that she then gives to management when she leaves.

Problem Pgm12-3 The Elevator Analysis Program

A local fancy diner is relocating to the 12th floor of a new building that is currently under construction. They have to make a decision on the number of very expensive, glass-lined, outside elevators to purchase. Each of these new elevators can carry ten people. Over the last few days, they have studied the arrival times of their customers and have prepared a sample data file with this information.

Acme Consulting has been given the task of evaluating the number of these elevators they require. The assumption is that the elevator makes a complete circuit from the ground floor to the diner and back to the ground floor in four minutes, including loading and unloading times.

Write a program to simulate the elevator operations using the provided **elevator.txt** data file. Each line in the file contains first an arrival time (hh and mm) and the number of persons. Consider the start time of the simulation to be the time of the first set of data. Load the elevator with the number of people that are there during that initial minute of time. That is, consider the elevator loaded with the people in the first line of data.

Add four minutes to the time and enqueue all data records up to that time. Then, the elevator can accept up to ten more from the queue. Load as many as will fit and dequeue them from the queue. Add another four minutes to the time and input and enqueue all new arrivals until the elevator arrives once more. Ignore the fact that if the elevator could take one more person and the next party contains four people, the party of four would likely wait for the elevator to return empty rather than split up. Note you will need to keep track of the number of people dequeued that did not fit in the elevator and load them first on the return trip.

Each time the elevator arrives to pick up more diner guests, display the current length of the queue in terms of waiting people and the time. Do not forget to count any left overs from a split party that are awaiting the return elevator. When the end of the file has been reached and the queue is empty, display the number of times during this evening that the queue length exceeded ten waiting customers. The diner has specified that a wait of four minutes by ten people is the maximum acceptable goal. Display a message stating whether or not a single elevator will meet their goals.

Chapter 13—Binary Files and Hashing Techniques

Introduction

A **binary file** is a file of data which are stored in internal numeric format rather than in the ASCII text format. Traditionally, the concepts and usage of binary files either are not presented or are not well covered in traditional beginning programming courses. However, virtually all company master files are in the binary format; very few, if any, data files contain text that can be streamed in using the usual extraction operator. This chapter is an attempt to remedy this situation. This chapter begins with a thorough discussion of what binary files are, how they are commonly used and finally some significant processing methods employed with binary files.

Dealing with Binary Files

Normal files are text files usually with the .txt file extension. Other names used for text files are ASCII files and DOS text files. These files contain only ASCII displayable or printable characters and are fully visible using Notepad, for instance. The end of the file is marked by a single byte that contains a ^Z (Ctrl-Z). This EOF byte is normally never visibly displayed by editors. Text files can be displayed on the screen or printed exactly as is.

    For example, if a text file contained the line
    ABC 1234<cr>
Then the file would contain ten bytes with the following ASCII decimal values.

    65, 66, 67, 32, 49, 50, 51, 52, 13, 10 <- ASCII values
     A   B   C   b   1   2   3   4   CR LF <- the text line
To input this line, we must define two variables as follows.

    char name[10];
    int qty;
Then, we can use **cin** to input the line.

    cin >> name >> qty;
The **istream** must therefore perform internal data conversion to convert this line into the way the data is to be stored in these variables in memory as shown in Figure 13.1.

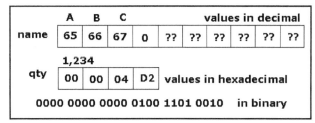

Figure 13.1 Internal Form of name and qty

In the above figure, the character string's contents are shown using the decimal values of the corresponding ASCII codes. The byte that contains the 0 is the null terminator. The integer **qty** occupies four bytes on a Win32 platform. I have shown the contents of each byte in the hexadecimal format which is usually used to show binary values. I also gave the contents of **qty** in binary. The leftmost 0 bit is the sign: 0 indicates a positive number. The 1 bit represents corresponding powers of 2. Or

$$1x2^1 + 1x2^4 + 1x2^6 + 1x2^7 + 1x2^{10} = 2 + 16 + 64 + 128 + 1024 = 1234$$

Notice then, that the **istream** must convert the ASCII digits into the binary number form before it can store the value into the integer. Likewise, on output, the internal forms must be converted back into a series of ASCII values. This data conversion is slow, particularly so for floating point types.

A binary file consists of data stored as a memory image of that data. Thus, if an **int** occupies four bytes and contains 00 00 04 D2 in hex, then, when written to a binary file, the binary file contains four bytes containing 00 00 04 D2 in hex.

Rule: No data conversion of any kind is ever done to binary files.

With binary files, data is transferred to and from memory precisely as it is/or will be in memory. The result is a tremendous increase in the speed of I/O operations.

Also, the end of file in a binary file is really tracked by the system and occurs when the file size number of bytes has been read into the computer.

Most all production data files will be binary files! Why? I/O speed is dramatically faster.

C++ Mechanics of Binary File Operations

When you open a binary file, you MUST tell the **iostreams** that this is a binary file. The **iostreams** default to a text file. All manner of ills will befall I/O operations if the binary file is opened as text and vice-versa. To tell the streams that this file is a binary file, OR in the **ios::binary** flag:

```
ifstream infile ("myfile.dat",
                 ios::input | ios::binary);
ofstream outfile ("newfile.dat", ios::output | ios::binary);
```

The input and output operations are much simpler. The **read()** and **write()** functions are used.

```
ifstream& read (char* inputarea,
                int number of bytes to input);
ofstream& write (char* outputarea,
                 int number of bytes to output);
```

If we are inputting or outputting something other than a string, we must use a typecast of the pointers.

```
infile.read ( (char*) &qty, sizeof (qty));
outfile.write ( (char*) &qty, sizeof (int));
```

Note that **sizeof (qty)** is better than **sizeof (int)** because, if you change its data type, it automatically gets the correct new size.

Here are some examples of their use. Suppose that we had an array of bounds 1000 which contained 950 elements and we wished to save that data to a binary file. The following writes all 950 elements in one write operation.

```
long array[1000];
int    count;
outfile.write ( (char*) array, sizeof (long) * count);
```

Character strings in a binary file are a bit peculiar. The binary file is a memory copy of the variable. So if **name** is defined to contain a maximum of 10 characters (including the null) and if it contains "Sam" (S, a, m, 0) at the moment, then, when written to a binary file, all ten bytes are written. When read in from a binary file, all ten bytes are input. However, C++ knows that the real contents of the string end at the null terminator.

Structures are commonly read or written to or from binary files. Suppose that we use the **CostRec** structure.

```
struct CostRec {
 int itemno;
 short qty;
 char descr[21];
 double cost;
};
...
CostRec crec;
...
outfile.write ((char*) &crec, sizeof (crec));
                        // or sizeof (CostRec)
...
infile.read ((char*) &crec, sizeof (crec));
```

In this example, an array of cost records is loaded from a binary file.

```
int LoadArray (CostRec arec[], int limit) {
 ifstream infile("master.dat",
                 ios::in | ios::binary);
 if (!infile) {
  cerr << "Error: Unable to open the input file!\n"
  exit (1);
 }
 int j = 0;
 while (j < limit &&
       infile.read ((char*) &arec[j], sizeof (CostRec))) {
  j++;
 }
 infile.close ();
 return j;
}
```

Physical I/O Versus Logical I/O Operations

The above examples have been logical I/O operations. That is, a program asks for the next cost record and the system "inputs" it into our designated input structure instance. However, in order to understand other I/O operations a program needs to make, the concepts of how the Windows/DOS system handles the physical I/O operations must be understood.

The smallest amount of data that the system will actually input or output to disk is called a **cluster**. The size of a cluster varies widely depending upon the size of the drive and the file system in use on that drive. Specifically, a cluster is **n** adjacent sectors of 512 bytes each. The number **n** varies depending upon the drive. For example, on the old 5¼ floppy disks, that held 360K of data, a cluster consisted of 2 adjacent sectors of data. Figure 13.2 shows the terminology of a track (a concentric circle of magnetic material that stores data) and a sector (a pie shaped section of a track).

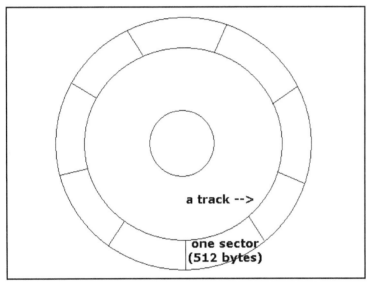

Figure 13.2 A Track and Sector of a 360k Floppy Disk

When running the FAT16 file system, Windows/DOS stores the number of clusters in an unsigned integer which is therefore limited to 65,536 clusters. The system identifies each cluster on the drive starting with cluster 0 and increases successive cluster numbers by one. On larger capacity drives, DOS must increase the number of sectors in a cluster to reduce the number of clusters to get their numbers to fit in range of the unsigned integer. Table 13.1 shows some cluster sizes for various disk drives or partitions.

Table 13.1 Cluster Sizes for Various Sized Partitions

Partition Size in MB	Type	Sectors Per Cluster	Cluster Size
16-127	FAT16	4	2K

436

128-255	FAT16	8	4K
256-511	FAT16	16	8K
512-1023	FAT16	32	16K
1024-2047	FAT16	64	32k
2048-4096	FAT16	128	64K
.256-8.01	FAT32	8	4K
8.02-16.02	FAT32	16	8K
16.03-32.04	FAT32	32	16K
>32.04	FAT32	64	32K

The cluster size is important. The significance is given by the following rule.

Rule: Windows/DOS physically inputs and outputs only clusters at a time.

In other words, DOS really only actually physically inputs or outputs a cluster. This is the smallest unit of I/O. Smaller requests are accumulated in a **buffer** staging area which is the size of a cluster. A buffer is a staging area for I/O operations. DOS stores smaller sized output requests in this buffer until it becomes full. When the buffer is full, DOS now actually writes that cluster. (When the file is closed, any partially filled buffers are also written. Also, there is a flush buffer instruction that a program may request.)

Suppose that you are running the FAT16 file system and have a 2G drive. The cluster size is 32K. Now suppose that you start writing a letter to me and get as far as entering the "D" (for Dear Vic) and then save the file. DOS reports that the file size is one byte. However, DOS can only write a cluster. So in fact this 1-byte file really occupies 32K of disk space!

I remember when I first got a large capacity drive and proceeded to copy all my data that was stored on several smaller drives onto this new big drive. The copy operation failed. The drive reported that there was 640M stored on a 1G drive! Most of the files were small C++ source files. I had wasted 360M of disk space because of the large cluster size.

Large cluster size also has a benefit—faster loading of data. For example, if Windows needed to load a system DLL file that was 64K in size, then only 2 physical I/O operations are required to input it if the cluster size is 32K. If I had a cluster size of say 4K instead of the 32K cluster size, then Windows would have to issue 16 I/O requests to load that same DLL file.

The vitally important fact is that a cluster is the smallest unit of information that Windows/DOS can physically I/O. Let's see how this physical I/O buffering operation works by following how the program that loads in cost records from a binary file on disk works. The main loop in **LoadArray()** was

```
int j = 0;
while (j < limit &&
       infile.read ((char*) &arec[j], sizeof (CostRec))) {
  j++;
}
```

Further, let's assume that the size of the **CostRec** structure is 100 bytes and that the cluster size of the drive holding the file is 2K or 2048 bytes. When the program issues its first read for the very first record, DOS must input the first cluster of data into its buffer and then copy the first 100 bytes into **arec[0]** as shown in Figure 13.3.

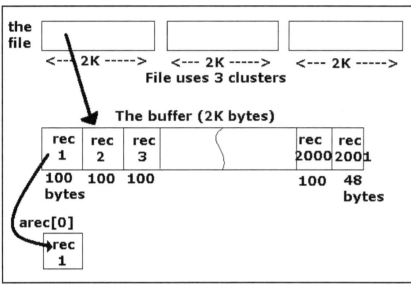

Figure 13.3 Input of the First Record

In order to input our first record, Windows/DOS inputs the first cluster into its internal buffer. Notice that there are 2000 complete 100 byte records and a partial last one of only 48 bytes. The remaining 52 bytes of the record 2001 are the first bytes in cluster 2. Next, the system copies the required 100 bytes from its buffer into our designated input area, here **arec[0]**.

However, when our program requests the next 1,999 records, Windows/DOS merely has to copy the required bytes from its buffer into our array elements. No physical I/O operations occur. However, when the program requests the 2001st record, after copying in the first 48 bytes of the data from its buffer, the system must again issue a physical I/O request to input the next cluster of data into its buffer. When that operation is complete, it can then move the remaining 52 bytes into our input area.

Note that smart disk cache controllers are highly likely to have (during some background processing time) already inputted the remaining clusters of the file and stored the data in cache memory. Thus, a real physical I/O operation might not need to be done. Instead, only a copy from cache memory is required in this case, speeding up the operation significantly.

As the system works its way through the buffer giving us our successive 100 byte records, DOS needs a pointer to keep track of where it is at in the buffer and file. This is called the **DOS File Offset**

Beginning Data Structures in C++

Pointer and is encapsulated by the **iostream** classes. The meaning of the DOS File Offset Pointer is this: the next input or output operation begins at this offset from the beginning of the file. And it is this DOS File Offset Pointer that we are vitally interested in understanding and using.

Figure 13.4 shows the DOS File Offset Pointer in operation during a series of successive input operations. Initially, when the file is first opened, the offset pointer is set to 0. In Figure 13.4, the first record has been input and stored in **arec[j]** and the file offset pointer has been incremented by the number of bytes just input. Figure 13.5 shows the situation after we input the second record.

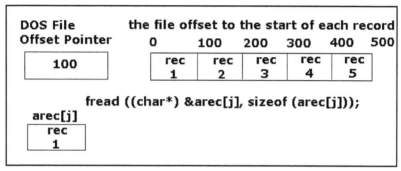

Figure 13.4 The File Offset Pointer After the First Read

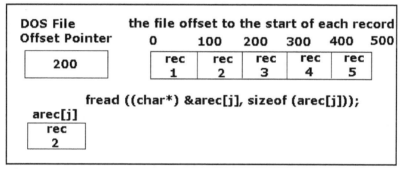

Figure 13.5 The File Offset Pointer after the Second Read

Now consider what would happen if somehow we placed 400 into the DOS file offset pointer and then issued another read instruction? Remember that the next file I/O operation will occur at this offset from the start of the file. We input record number 5. Further, what is the significance of the offset 500 in this example? It is the true DOS file size!

By adjusting the contents of the DOS file offset pointer, we can control which record in input by the next read instruction! Further, we can easily get the true file size of the file on disk. Finally, what results if we divide the file size by the size of the input record? This would be the number of records in the file! So this DOS file offset pointer is of vital importance when dealing with binary files.

Input streams have a pair of functions to read the contents of the DOS file offset pointer and to alter it. Output streams have a different pair of functions to read its contents and to alter it.
Input Streams:

```
pos_type tellg (); pos_type can be a long if filesize < 2G
istream& seekg (int offsetAmount, seekdir flag);
```

439

where the flag is

```
ios::beg - this offset from the beginning of the file
ios::cur - this offset from the current position in the file
ios::end - this offset from the end of the file
```

Output Streams:

```
pos_type tellp (); pos_type can be a long if filesize < 2G
istream& seekp (int offsetAmount, seekdir flag);
```

where the flag is the same as for input streams

The next series of examples illustrates some of the things we can do using binary files and the DOS file offset pointer.

Example 1: Reading and Writing Several Arrays to/from One Binary File

When the binary file contains several unrelated members, such as the contents of two different arrays that can contain differing number of elements, the current number in each array can be written first followed by that many elements of the corresponding array. Next, the number of elements in the second array is written followed by the second array.

```
long array1[1000];
int   count1;
double array2[2000];
int   count2;
...
outfile.write ((char*) &count1, sizeof (count1));
outfile.write ((char*) array1, sizeof (long) * count1);
outfile.write ((char*) &count2, sizeof (count2));
outfile.write ((char*) array2, sizeof (double) * count2);
```

To input the data, we code

```
infile.read ((char*) &count1, sizeof (count1));
infile.read ((char*) array1, sizeof (long) * count1);
infile.read ((char*) &count2, sizeof (count2));
infile.read ((char*) array2, sizeof (double) * count2);
```

Example 2: Processing an Array of Cost Records Blazingly Fast

Hard disks transfer data at very high rates. Some of today's faster disks transfer something like 120M per second or better. Let's say your drive can transfer 40M per second, roughly. How much data is 40M? To give you an appreciation for that volume, consider how many characters are in a large, fat novel. I wrote one once and it had 1,250,000 characters. How long would it take to type that many characters into the computer? Suppose that you can type as fast as the keyboard can accept data, 10 characters per second which corresponds to about 150 words per minute! This yields 125,000 seconds. How long is that? Well, let's divide by 50 seconds per minute (you need a breather each minute). This yields 2500 minutes. So let's divide by 50 minutes per hour (you will need a food break). This gives 50 hours or 2 days nonstop typing at 150 words per minute just to get the large novel entered. But in one second, the drive can give us 40M. Thus, if we had to type in that amount of data by hand, it would take us over 2 months continuous typing at 150 words per minute!

We can harness this incredible speed in our programs. There is no need for message boxes to pop up saying "10 seconds remaining" on copying a 10M file. It should take only a fraction of a second.

Here, the array **arec** can contain up to 100,000 records and **count** contains the current number in the array. To output the entire array of **count** elements, we code the following.

```
CostRec arec[100000];
long    count;
outfile.write ((char*) arec, sizeof (arec[0]) * count);
```

However, to input an array of an unknown number of cost records is more complex. We must find the number of elements that are actually in the binary file. We can use the **seekg()** and **tellg()** functions as follows.

```
// first, position file offset ptr to eof
infile.seekg (0, ios::end);
// get that offset and divide by size to get count
// note: if infile.tellg () % sizeof (CostRec) is not 0,
// then the file is somehow corrupt as we have a partial
// record in the file somewhere...
count = infile.tellg () / sizeof (CostRec);
// vitally important: reposition file offset to beginning!
infile.seekg (0, ios::beg);
// one read request inputs entire file at blazing speed
infile.read ((char*) arec, sizeof (CostRec) * count);
```

Just how fast is this going to be? It depends on the size of the file and available memory and the state of file fragmentation. But it will be a very dramatic speed up. I once had a student who was maintaining a production program that needed to input a very large two-dimensional array of long integers. It was a drafting type of program. However, every time the program needed to load the array, it took over three minutes! Likewise, when the user chose the save option, another three minutes elapsed. After this presentation, he rewrote the load operation to use the blazing fast approach. He wrapped a **cout** pair of messages around the new loading code: Starting the load and End of load. This way, he figured he could time how long it now took to load. When he first ran it, the two messages went by almost instantaneously so he figured the data failed to load. But upon checking, it was all there! He ran it again to be sure. His three minute delay was cut down to virtually no observable time at all!

Example 3: Using Dynamic Allocation for an Array of Unknown Number of Records

Dynamic memory allocation is very often used to load arrays of unknown numbers of elements. The idea is to determine the file size and hence the number of elements actually present in the file. Then, allocate an array sufficiently large enough to hold that data. Finally, issue a single read to load the entire file in a blaze.

```
CostRec* arec;
int   count;
infile.seekg (0, ios::end);
count = infile.tellg () / sizeof (CostRec);
infile.seekg (0, ios::beg);
arec = new CostRec [count];
infile.read ((char*) arec, sizeof (CostRec) * count);
...
delete [] arec;
```

However, the above coding is mostly working. What happens if the amount of memory the program asks for is not available? What happens if the file is corrupt? We can insert a bit of error checking as follows.

```
count = infile.tellg () / sizeof (CostRec);
if (infile.tellg () % sizeof (CostRec) != 0) {
 cerr << "Error: the input file may be corrupt\n";
 infile.close();
 exit (2);
}
infile.seekg (0, ios::beg);
arec = new CostRec [count];
if (!arec) {
 cerr << "Error: insufficient memory to load the array\n";
 infile.close();
 exit (1);
}
infile.read ((char*) arec, sizeof (CostRec) * count);
```

Example 4: Binary File Processing—the StudentRoster Single Linked List—Pgm13a

Returning to our single linked list of students from chapter 9 (**Pgm09c**), the Student Roster Program can be updated to support reading and writing binary files of student data. Of course, the real problem is that the binary master file must be built before it can be read. One cannot use a text editor to build a binary file. Rather, a program must write the binary data to the file. Usually, these are called data entry front end programs. Such programs input the text information and edit it, thereby guaranteeing only valid data is written to disk.

Pgm13a solves this problem by reading in the text file of student data and loading up the **StudentRoster** list. Then, it writes the list to a binary file. Finally, **Pgm13a** loads that binary file of data into the roster list.

I have added only three new member functions to the existing **StudentRoster** class. One is to load the binary file, one is a helper function read a single student data record from the binary file, one is to write the entire list to a binary file. Here is the revised **StudentRoster** class definition. I have highlighted (in boldface) the three new functions. Following the definition, I include only these three new functions from the implementation class. All other member functions are unchanged from chapter 9.

```
StudentRoster Class Definition

 1 #pragma once
 2
 3 /****************************************************/
 4 /*                                                  */
 5 /* StudentRoster class                              */
 6 /*                                                  */
 7 /* Maintain a list of students who are enrolled in a */
 8 /* course                                           */
 9 /*                                                  */
10 /* Ability to read and write a binary master file added */
11 /*                                                  */
12 /****************************************************/
13
14 const int NAME_LEN = 21;
15
16 /****************************************************/
17 /*                                                  */
18 /* Student: contains the client's student data      */
19 /*                                                  */
20 /****************************************************/
21
22 struct Student {
23   char name[NAME_LEN];
24   long ssno;
25   char grade;
26 };
27
28 /****************************************************/
29 /*                                                  */
30 /* StudentNode: the list node structure             */
31 /*                                                  */
32 /****************************************************/
33
34 struct StudentNode {
35   StudentNode* fwdptr;  // points to the next node in the list
36   Student      student; // contains the actual client data
37 };
38
39 class StudentRoster {
40
41   /****************************************************/
42   /*                                                  */
43   /* class data                                       */
44   /*                                                  */
45   /****************************************************/
46
47 private:
```

```
48  StudentNode* headptr;      // the list pointer
49
50  StudentNode* currentptr;  // the pointer to the current node
51
52  /***********************************************************/
53  /*                                                         */
54  /* class functions                                         */
55  /*                                                         */
56  /***********************************************************/
57
58 public:
59            StudentRoster ();  // constructs an empty roster
60            StudentRoster (const StudentRoster& r);  // copy roster
61 StudentRoster& operator= (const StudentRoster& r); // copy roster
62          ~StudentRoster ();  // deletes the roster
63  void     EmptyList ();        // removes all items from the list
64
65  // loads all students from a file - items are in reverse order
66  void     LoadAllStudents (const char* filename);
67  // loads all students from a binary file
68  void LoadAllStudentsBinaryFile (char* filename);
69  // adds a new student to the list at the head of the list
70  void     AddStudentAtHead (const Student& s);
71
72  // displays all students in the list
73  void PrintAllStudents (ostream& outfile);
74  // displays a single student
75  void PrintThisStudent (ostream& outfile, const Student& s)const;
76  // outputs the whole list to a new student roster file
77  void WriteNewFile (const char* filename);
78  // outputs a new binary master file of student data
79  void SaveFileBinary (char* filename);
80
81  // finds a specific student, returns 0 if ssn is not found
82  Student* FindThisStudent (long ssn);
83
84  // inserts a new student into list after this specific student
85  // or inserts thenew one at the head if this ssn is not found
86  void     InsertAfter (long ssn, const Student& s);
87  // remove this student from the list, does nothing if not found
88  void     DeleteThisStudent (long ssn);
89
90  // list iterator functions
91  void     ResetToHead ();              // set to start of the list
92  void     Next ();                     // moves to the next item
93  Student* GetCurrentStudent () const;  // gets the current student
94                                        // or 0 if there is none
95 protected:
96  StudentNode* Find (long ssn, StudentNode* &ptrprevstud);
```

```
 97  istream&   InputStudentData (istream& infile, Student& s);
 98  istream&   InputStudentDataBinary (istream& infile, Student& s);
 99  void          CopyList (StudentRoster& r);
100  };
101
```

StudentRoster Class Implementation

```
 1 #include <iostream>
 2 #include <iomanip>
 3 #include <fstream>
 4 using namespace std;
 5
 6 #include "StudentRoster.h"
 7
 8 /*****************************************************/
 9 /*                                                   */
10 /* SaveFileBinary: save list to a binary master file */
11 /*                                                   */
12 /*****************************************************/
13
14 void StudentRoster::SaveFileBinary (char* filename) {
15  ofstream out (filename, ios::out | ios::binary);
16  if (!out) {
17   cerr << "Error: cannot open the binary output file\n";
18   exit (1);
19  }
20  ResetToHead ();
21  while (currentptr) {
22   out.write ((char*) &currentptr->student, sizeof (Student));
23   Next ();
24  }
25  out.close ();
26 }
27
28 /***********************************************************/
29 /*                                                         */
30 /* InputStudentDataBinary: input one student's data from   */
31 /*                         a binary master file            */
32 /*                                                         */
33 /***********************************************************/
34
35 istream& StudentRoster::InputStudentDataBinary (istream& infile,
36                                                 Student& s) {
37  return infile.read ((char*) &s, sizeof (Student));
38 }
39
40 /***********************************************************/
```

```
41 /*                                                          */
42 /* LoadAllStudentsBinaryFile: load list from a binary       */
43 /*                          master file of data             */
44 /*                                                          */
45 /************************************************************/
46
47 void StudentRoster::LoadAllStudentsBinaryFile (char* filename) {
48  Student s;
49  ifstream infile (filename, ios::in | ios::binary);
50  if (!infile) {
51   cerr << "Error: cannot open input file\n";
52   exit (2);
53  }
54  while (InputStudentDataBinary (infile, s)) {
55   AddStudentAtHead (s);
56  }
57  infile.close ();
58  currentptr = headptr;
59 }
```

...

Pgm13a main() function coding is very simple indeed. The resulting output is shown below as well.

```
Pgm13a - Load and Save Using a Binary Master File

 1 #include <iostream>
 2 #include <iomanip>
 3 #include <crtdbg.h>
 4 #include <string>
 5 using namespace std;
 6
 7 #include "StudentRoster.h"
 8
 9 /**********************************************************/
10 /*                                                        */
11 /* Pgm13a: illustrate saving and loading a binary master */
12 /*         file                                           */
13 /*                                                        */
14 /**********************************************************/
15
16 int main () {
17
18  {
19   StudentRoster roster;
20   // first load from the text file of data
21   roster.LoadAllStudents ("Roster.txt");
22   cout << "\n\n    My Class Roster - loaded from text file\n\n"
23       << "    Name                        StudentID  Grade\n\n";
24   roster.PrintAllStudents (cout);
```

446

```
25
26    // now save to a binary file - ie. builds the binary master
27    roster.SaveFileBinary ("master.dat");
28    roster.EmptyList ();
29
30    // now load from a binary master file
31    roster.LoadAllStudentsBinaryFile ("master.dat");
32    cout << "\n\n    My Class Roster - loaded from binary file\n\n"
33        << "    Name                        StudentID  Grade\n\n";
34    roster.PrintAllStudents (cout);
35  }
36
37  if (_CrtDumpMemoryLeaks())
38    cout << "\nOops! Memory Leaks!!\n";
39  else
40    cout << "\nNo Memory Leaks\n";
41
42  return 0;
43 }
```

```
Output from Pgm13a

 1
 2
 3     My Class Roster - loaded from text file
 4
 5     Name                        StudentID  Grade
 6
 7     Jennifer Smallville         234234333    A
 8     Allan Adaire                324234234    C
 9     Thomas J. Jones             345344344    A
10     Annie Smith                 324233456    A
11     Sam Spade                   234565677    B
12     Betsy                       123456789    A
13
14
15     My Class Roster - loaded from binary file
16
17     Name                        StudentID  Grade
18
19     Betsy                       123456789    A
20     Sam Spade                   234565677    B
21     Annie Smith                 324233456    A
22     Thomas J. Jones             345344344    A
23     Allan Adaire                324234234    C
24     Jennifer Smallville         234234333    A
25
26 No Memory Leaks
```

Overview of Direct Access File Processing Operations

The ability to access the DOS file offset pointer becomes the basis for all types of direct access file processing operations. Direct access refers to the ability to input or output one specific record out of all others. In an Inquiry type of program, when the user enters some kind of key identification value, the program retrieves directly the record in the file that corresponds to that key. In a direct access update type of program, in addition to accessing a record with a specific identification key value, the program can rewrite just that corresponding record.

Direct access processing then differs from sequential access. The only way a sequential access operation could find a record that corresponded to a specific key identification value would be to input every record in turn looking for a match. With larger files, this is unworkable.

This section deals with the general theory of the more common methods that are employed.

The Relative Record Number Method

The most fundamental method of direct access is known as the relative record number method. Every record in the file must have the same length. The first record in the file is arbitrarily assigned relative record number of 0. Each successive record in the file has a relative record number that is one greater than the previous record. Figure 13.6 illustrates this with the five cost records. The key identifier value becomes the relative record number.

To access the cost record whose relative record number is 1, we must multiply the key by the size of the records, seek to that position from the beginning of the file and input that data.

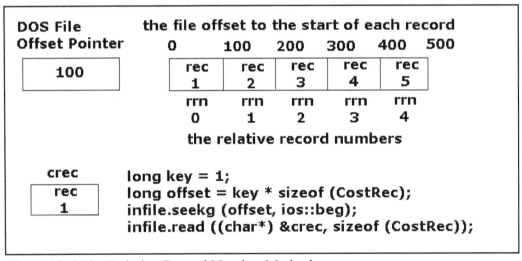

Figure 13.6 The Relative Record Number Method

Thus, given the key (which is the relative record number), one can directly access this data by the following.

```
CostRec crec;
long key;
long offset = key * sizeof (CostRec);
infile.seekg (offset, ios::beg);
infile.read ((char*) &crec, sizeof (crec));
```

The relative record number method is the fastest of all the methods for directly accessing a specific record in a binary master file. It is also the foundation of all the other more advanced methods. However, it has two serious drawbacks.

First, relative record numbers make terrible key identifier fields. Suppose your relative record number was 0. How many checks do you suppose you could cash if your account number was 0? These kinds of keys have nothing to do with real world identifiers, such as a person's social security number that is so often used as the key identifier.

Second, relative record numbers make deletion of records a total mess. Consider the following scenario as shown in Figure 13.7. Our company has five accounts. We use the relative record number as each account's id number. Now we delete Tom's account for failure to pay the balance due. What happens to the relative record numbers for those accounts that follow the deleted Tom account? They all change! Betsy's id, which was 3, now becomes 2. Fred's id, which was 4, now becomes 3. Thus, we have to issue new account numbers every time a record is deleted—reprint checks or issue a new plastic charge card and so forth.

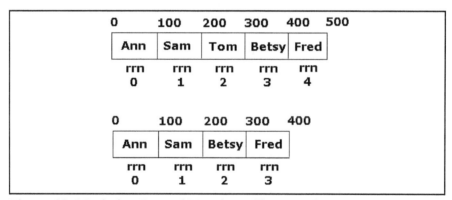

Figure 13.7 Relative Record Numbers Change After a Deletion

The Remainder Method

The remainder method is a vast improvement over the relative record number method because any numerical key can be used. Thus, one could use keys such as a person's social security number. With this method, one must know the absolute maximum number of records the binary master file is to contain. And a file containing this many records must be built. Initially all the records are dummies and contain dummy data. The procedure goes as follows.

Beginning Data Structures in C++

1. Determine the maximum number of records.
2. Find the largest prime number that does not exceed this maximum number.
3. Let key equal the individual's key id number % this prime number.
4. The resulting key becomes the relative record number of that record on disk.

Suppose that we decide that our company will never have more than 3 clients. So the maximum number is three. The largest prime number that does not exceed 3 is 3. Now we decide to add Ann as a client. We assign her an id number of 1. The key becomes 1 % 3 or 1. Thus, her data goes into relative record number 1 in the file. This process is shown in Figure 13.8. In a similar manner, we add clients Tom (id = 2) and Betsy (id = 3).

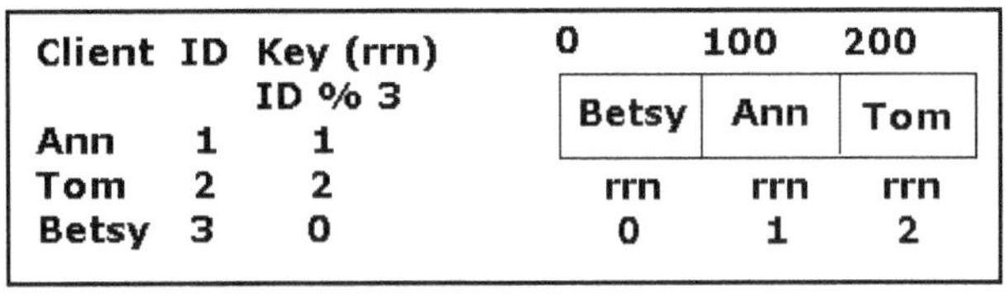

Client	ID	Key (rrn) ID % 3
Ann	1	1
Tom	2	2
Betsy	3	0

0	100	200
Betsy	Ann	Tom
rrn 0	rrn 1	rrn 2

Figure 13.8 The Remainder Method in Action

So far, all is working perfectly. But what happens when we decide to expand and add another client, say Sam? We assign Sam the id number of 4. The remainder is 1 and so the relative record number is 1. However, there already is a record at that location, Ann. Oops. Now what do we do? This is the common problem of duplicate remainders. The solution is to store all duplicate remainder records sequentially in an overflow area that begins immediately after the maximum number of records. Figure 13.9 shows the situation after adding three more clients.

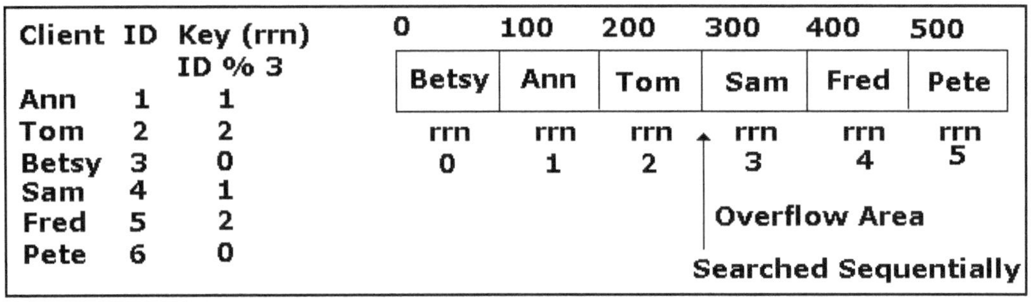

Client	ID	Key (rrn) ID % 3
Ann	1	1
Tom	2	2
Betsy	3	0
Sam	4	1
Fred	5	2
Pete	6	0

0	100	200	300	400	500
Betsy	Ann	Tom	Sam	Fred	Pete
rrn 0	rrn 1	rrn 2	rrn 3	rrn 4	rrn 5

Overflow Area

Searched Sequentially

Figure 13.9 Three Records in the Overflow Area

The coding to access a remainder method file is as follows.

```
long idNumber;          // the person's id number just input
long key = idNumber % Max; //Max is the max number of recs
long offset = key * sizeof (CostRec);
infile.seekg (offset, ios::beg);
infile.read ((char*) &crec, sizeof (crec));
if (crec.idNumber != idNumber) {
  // oops, the record must be in the overflow area
  infile.seekg (Max * sizeof(CostRec));
  while (idNumber != crec.idNumber && infile) {
```

```
  infile.read ((char*) &crec, sizeof (crec);
  }
  if (infile) {
  // here we have the desired record
  }
  else {
   cerr << "Error: record not found in data base\n";
  }
}
else {
  // here we have the desired record
}
```

Since the overflow area must be searched sequentially, the more records that are in the overflow area, the poorer the program's performance. Consider what would have occurred if I had used these clients' social security numbers as their identification keys. We might have had the following.

```
Ann     333 33 3333
Tom     333 33 3336
Betsy   333 33 3339
Sam     666 66 6666
Fred    999 99 9999
Pete    333 66 9999
```

All of these yield the same exact relative record number of 1!

To get the best results from the remainder method, one needs a good guess of the maximum number of records ever to be needed. Secondly, one should assign id numbers beginning with 1 up to that maximum number. This would avoid as many duplicate remainders as possible.

The Indexed Sequential Access Method (ISAM)

The Indexed Sequential Access Method, or ISAM for short, permits one to have any type of key identifiers desired, including characters as well as numerical digits. The ISAM scheme then stores a table of id keys versus the relative record number assigned to that record. Figure 13.10 illustrates this approach for our three clients.

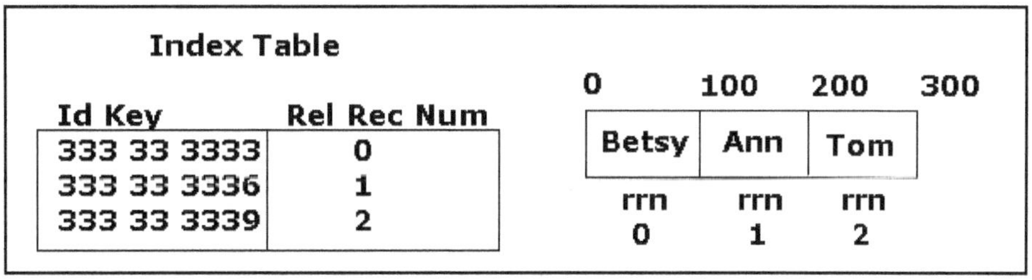

Figure 13.10 The ISAM Method with Three Clients

Notice that the key id numbers can be anything. To find any record, one searches the index table's Id Key array looking for an exact match. When found, the key to use becomes the corresponding relative record number. One would then proceed to input the data as before by finding the offset, seeking to that location and reading in the record.

Of course, one must save this index table on disk as well as the binary master file. Often the file extension .idx or .id is used. Sometimes the index file gets lost or accidentally deleted. Thus, the Id Key values must also be stored as a field within each record in the master file. Then, the index file can be recreated simply by reading in each record sequentially and adding another entry to the new index.

This method gets its name from the ability to read the file sequentially or by accessing a specific record directly. A monthly billing program certainly would access the file sequentially as it methodically printed a bill for each customer in turn.

However, of the three methods for direct access, the ISAM method is the slowest in execution because of the table lookup operation. Suppose that the Id Keys were actually character strings, such as part numbers AA-123-Z-42. How would the comparisons be done? We would have to use a **stricmp()** function call for each test! To speed up the searching operation when there are large numbers of records in the index, the index is maintained in a sorted manner, usually low to high. If the Id Keys are numeric and sorted, a binary search can be used to more rapidly find the matching entry.

Further, if the index is huge, then several layers of indices can be constructed. One might have a top-level index table such as shown below.

Master Index

Id Range	Use this index file next
100 00 0000 to 199 99 9999	Index1.idx
200 00 0000 to 299 99 9999	Index2.idx
...	
900 00 0000 to 999 99 9999	Index9.idx

Then in the nine additional index tables, only the indicated range of id values are present.

Handling Variable Length Records

Implicit in the entire discussion thus far is the fact that all records must be fixed in length. That is, all records contain the same number of bytes so that we can calculate the file offset by multiplying the relative record number by the constant fixed size. However, in the real world, not all records are fixed in length. How can a binary file contain variable length records and still provide direct access to them?

When a variable length record is written to disk, uniformly across all platforms, the first two or four bytes of that record contain the total length of the record. Without some idea of the length of the current record, it is impossible to effectively input it.

A trick that is often used to provide a method of direct access to a set of varying length records in a binary master file is to modify the ISAM index table. Instead of storing the relative record number, let's store the actual file offset to get to that record. It is also valuable to store the length of that record in the table as well. For example, we could have the following index table.

```
Id Number      Offset Length
111 11 1111       0      50
122 34 4444      50     100
344 43 6456     150     200
344 55 5555     350      50
555 55 5555     400     100
```
Now when a match is found, we seek to that offset and input the length number of bytes.

Handling Update Files in C++

When a program is to perform a binary file update, a record with a specific key is read into memory, changes are made to its contents, and the record rewritten back to disk at the same location in the file. This means that we need a file stream that can be both read and written. Such streams are instances of the **fstream** class.

Further, we must use **seekg()** and **tellg()** on the input side and **seekp()** and **tellp()** on the output side. However, another problem is likely to occur. Suppose we are reading records and reach the end of file. The stream goes into the end of file state. No further I/O operations are allowed because it is at the end of file. After handling any processing required because the end of file was reached, we need a way to reset the file back into the good state so that further I/O operations can be performed. The **clear()** function does this for us. We pass it the flag **ios::good** as the state in which we wish the stream to be. For example,

```
file.clear (ios::good);
```
would reset all flags to the good state for the resumption of I/O operations. Note that if no parameter is passed, it defaults to **ios::good**.

Pgm13b—the Master File Update Program—Relative Record Method

Pgm13b is designed to illustrate the methods required to handle update files using **fstream** instances. Acme Credit Card Company has a master file of card holders. During the day, three types of transactions can occur. A new card holder can be added. An existing card holder can have an increase in their credit limit. An existing card holder's balance can be changed because of payments or additional charges.

Initially, the binary master file must be constructed from a text file. The file contains the person's name surrounded by double quote marks. This is followed by their balance and their credit limit. The id number of each client is the relative record number. Thus, the program begins by building the binary master file.

Next, a file of new transactions must be applied to the master file. The first character in the transaction's file determines what type of transaction this line contains. If the character is an "a," then this is an add new client request. The new client's name follows next and is surrounded by double quote marks. Then comes the balance and finally the limit for that client. If the character is a "b," then we are to modify the balance. In this case, the next number is the relative record number id field which is followed by the relative change in their balance, a positive or negative number. If the first character is an "l," then we are to change their credit limit. The client's id number again comes next followed by the relative change in their

Beginning Data Structures in C++

credit limit.

When the transactions have been processed, a new binary master file is written. Here is what the output from the program looks like.

```
Output from Pgm13b - Binary Master File Update Program

 1  File initially contains 4 records
 2
 3
 4   Acme Credit Master File
 5
 6  Id Number   Name                    Balance   Limit
 7
 8      0       Annie Jones-Smith       4500.00   5000.00
 9      1       Betsy Smith             3000.00   4000.00
10      2       Samuel Spade            2500.42   3000.00
11      3       Thomas Dunhill          3500.00   4500.00
12
13
14  Transaction Log
15
16      4       Joe Smythe              4242.00   5000.00   Added
17      0       Annie Jones-Smith       4750.00   5000.00   Balance +250.00
18      2       Samuel Spade            2542.42   3000.00   Balance + 42.00
19      1       Betsy Smith             3000.00   6000.00   Limit + 2000.00
20      5       Henry P. Jones          4000.00   5000.00   Added
21
22
23  File now contains 6 records
24
25
26   Acme Credit Master File
27
28  Id Number   Name                    Balance   Limit
29
30      0       Annie Jones-Smith       4750.00   5000.00
31      1       Betsy Smith             3000.00   6000.00
32      2       Samuel Spade            2542.42   3000.00
33      3       Thomas Dunhill          3500.00   4500.00
34      4       Joe Smythe              4242.00   5000.00
35      5       Henry P. Jones          4000.00   5000.00
```

Here are the original **Accounts.txt** input file from which the master file is constructed and the **transactions.txt** file that defines the day's operations to be performed on the master file.

```
The Original Text Accounts Input File
```

```
1 "Annie Jones-Smith" 4500 5000
2 "Betsy Smith" 3000 4000
3 "Samuel Spade" 2500.42 3000
4 "Thomas Dunhill" 3500 4500
```

```
The TransactionsText File
```
```
1 a "Joe Smythe" 4242 5000
2 b 0 250
3 b 2 42
4 L 1 2000
5 a "Henry P. Jones" 4000 5000
```

In the **main()** function, notice how the update file is defined and opened.

```
fstream inout (masterfile, ios::in | ios::out | ios::binary);
```

Also, notice how the current number of records in the binary master file is obtained.

```
inout.seekg (0, ios::end);
maxCountOfRecs = inout.tellg () / sizeof (AccountRec);
cout << "File initially contains " << maxCountOfRecs
     << " records\n";
inout.seekg (0, ios::beg);
```

Remember to always keep the DOS file offset pointer at the beginning of the file. This is because **MakeReport()** reads the file sequentially from beginning to end. Also notice how the update file is passed to other functions. It is a reference to a **fstream** instance.

```
void MakeReport (fstream& inout);
void ProcessTransactions (fstream& inout, int& count);
```

Notice in the **MakeReport()** function, which reads the binary file sequentially until the end of file is signaled, that there must be a call to the **clear()** function to reset the EOF flag.

```
in.seekg (0, ios::beg);
// and clear the eof flag so more I/O to file can occur
in.clear (ios::goodbit);
```

To add a new record to the binary master file, we must position the file offset pointer to the end of the file so that the next write is appended to the end of the file.

```
inout.seekp (0, ios::end);
// and write new data at the current end of the file
inout.write ((char*) &rec, sizeof (rec));
```

The update sequence starts with the input of the id number, that is, the relative record number. This number is multiplied by the size of the records to obtain the offset for this record in the file. The file offset pointer is then set and the original data read. Once the changes have been made, the file offset pointer is repositioned back to the start of this record and the new data is written over the top of the old data in the file. If we did not reposition, then the rewrite would write over the next record after this one in the master file because the read operation adds the number of bytes just read to the file offset pointer.

```
infile >> findId >> num;
long offset = findId * sizeof (AccountRec);
```

```
inout.seekg (offset, ios::beg);
inout.read ((char*) &rec, sizeof (rec));
rec.creditBalance += num;
inout.seekp (offset, ios::beg);
inout.write ((char*) &rec, sizeof (rec));
```

Here is the complete Pgm13b update program.

```
Pgm13b - Master File Update Program - Relative Record Number

 1 #include <iostream>
 2 #include <fstream>
 3 #include <iomanip>
 4 #include <string>
 5 using namespace std;
 6
 7 /********************************************************************/
 8 /*                                                                  */
 9 /* Pgm13b: Acme Credit Update - binary file update program         */
10 /*                                                                  */
11 /********************************************************************/
12
13 const int MaxNameLen = 42;
14
15 struct AccountRec {
16   int    idNum;
17   char   name[MaxNameLen];
18   double creditBalance;
19   double creditLimit;
20 };
21
22 void InitialBuildOfMasterFile (const char* filename);
23 void MakeReport (fstream& inout);
24 void ProcessTransactions (fstream& inout, int& count);
25
26 int main () {
27   // setup floating point output for dollars and cents
28   cout << fixed << setprecision (2);
29
30   int maxCountOfRecs;
31   const char* masterfile = "AcmeCredit.dat";
32
33   // one time only, build the binary master file from a text file
34   InitialBuildOfMasterFile (masterfile);
35
36   // open the binary master file as an updat file
37   fstream inout (masterfile, ios::in | ios::out | ios::binary);
38   // calculate the number of records in the master file
39   inout.seekg (0, ios::end);
```

```
40  maxCountOfRecs = inout.tellg () / sizeof (AccountRec);
41  cout << "File initially contains " << maxCountOfRecs
42      << " records\n";
43  inout.seekg (0, ios::beg);
44
45  // display a report of all clients - read the binary master file
46  MakeReport (inout);
47
48  // handle all additions and updates to master file
49  ProcessTransactions (inout, maxCountOfRecs);
50
51  // now recalculate the number of records in the file
52  inout.seekg (0, ios::end);
53  maxCountOfRecs = inout.tellg () / sizeof (AccountRec);
54  inout.seekg (0, ios::beg);
55  cout << "\n\nFile now contains " << maxCountOfRecs
56      << " records\n";
57
58  // display a report of all clients after the update process
59  MakeReport (inout);
60  inout.close ();
61  return 0;
62 }
63
64 /***************************************************************/
65 /*                                                             */
66 /* InitialBuildOfMasterFile: make binary master from txt file  */
67 /*                                                             */
68 /***************************************************************/
69
70 void InitialBuildOfMasterFile (const char* filename) {
71  AccountRec rec;
72  // open text and the binary file
73  ofstream outfile (filename, ios::out | ios::binary);
74  ifstream infile ("accounts.txt");
75  if (!infile || !outfile) {
76   cerr << "Error: cannot open files\n";
77   exit (1);
78  }
79
80  char c;
81  int i = 0;
82
83  while (infile >> c && c == '\"') {
84   infile.getline (rec.name, sizeof (rec.name), '\"');
85   infile >> rec.creditBalance >> rec.creditLimit;
86   rec.idNum = i++;
87   if (infile)
88    outfile.write ((char*) &rec, sizeof (rec));
89  }
```

```
90
91   if (infile.good ()) {
92     cerr << "Error inputting initial data\n";
93     exit (2);
94   }
95
96   infile.close ();
97   outfile.close ();
98 }
99
100  /**************************************************************/
101  /*                                                          */
102  /* MakeReport: read binary file sequentially to eof         */
103  /*                                                          */
104  /**************************************************************/
105
106  void MakeReport (fstream& in) {
107   AccountRec rec;
108   int count = 0;
109   cout << "\n\n Acme Credit Master File\n\n"
110        << "Id Number  Name                         Balance"
111        "  Limit\n\n";
112
113   while (in.read ((char*) &rec, sizeof (rec))) {
114     cout << setw (5) << rec.idNum << "       " << left << setw (30)
115          << rec.name << right << setw (9) << rec.creditBalance
116          << setw (9) << rec.creditLimit << endl;
117   }
118
119   // here it is eof, so reset file offset pointer back to start
120   in.seekg (0, ios::beg);
121   // and clear the eof flag so more I/O to file can occur
122   in.clear (ios::goodbit);
123  }
124
125  /**************************************************************/
126  /*                                                          */
127  /* ProcessTransactions: add, update limit or update balance  */
128  /*                                                          */
129  /**************************************************************/
130
131  void ProcessTransactions (fstream& inout, int& count) {
132   AccountRec rec;
133   char transType;
134   char c;
135   double num;
136   int findId;
137
138   cout << "\n\nTransaction Log\n\n";
139
```

```
140  ifstream infile ("transactions.txt");
141  if (!infile) {
142   cerr << "Error: cannot open transactions file\n";
143   exit (3);
144  }
145
146  // handle all transactions in the file
147  while (infile >> transType) {
148   transType = toupper (transType);  // change code to upper case
149
150   if (transType == 'A') { // add a new record to master file
151    rec.idNum = count;
152    infile >> c;
153    infile.getline (rec.name, sizeof (rec.name), '\"');
154    infile >> rec.creditBalance >> rec.creditLimit;
155    // first point file offset pointer to eof mark
156    inout.seekp (0, ios::end);
157    // and write new data at the current end of the file
158    inout.write ((char*) &rec, sizeof (rec));
159    // display results of addition
160    cout << setw (5) << rec.idNum << "        ";
161    cout.setf (ios::left, ios::adjustfield);
162    cout << setw (30) << rec.name;
163    cout.setf (ios::right, ios::adjustfield);
164    cout << setw (9) << rec.creditBalance << setw (9)
165       << rec.creditLimit << " Added\n";
166    count++;
167   }
168   else if (transType == 'B') { // do a balance update
169    infile >> findId >> num;
170    // calculate the file offset of this id
171    long offset = findId * sizeof (AccountRec);
172    // position file offset pointer to this record's location
173    inout.seekg (offset, ios::beg);
174    // and input the record with this id
175    inout.read ((char*) &rec, sizeof (rec));
176    // update its balance
177    rec.creditBalance += num;
178    // reposition to this record in the master file
179    inout.seekp (offset, ios::beg);
180    // and rewrite this updated record
181    inout.write ((char*) &rec, sizeof (rec));
182    // display results
183    cout << setw (5) << rec.idNum << "        " << left << setw (30)
184       << rec.name << right << setw (9) << rec.creditBalance
185       << setw (9) << rec.creditLimit << " Balance + " << num
186       << endl;
187   }
188   else if (transType == 'L') { // here update credit limit
189    infile >> findId >> num;
```

```
190     // calculate the file offset for this id
191     long offset = findId * sizeof (AccountRec);
192     // position file offset to point to this record
193     inout.seekg (offset, ios::beg);
194     // input the record with this id
195     inout.read ((char*) &rec, sizeof (rec));
196     // update its credit limit
197     rec.creditLimit += num;
198     // reposition to this record in the master file
199     inout.seekp (offset, ios::beg);
200     // and rewrite this record in the master file
201     inout.write ((char*) &rec, sizeof (rec));
202     // display the results
203     cout << setw (5) << rec.idNum << "        " << left << setw (30)
204         << rec.name << right << setw (9) << rec.creditBalance
205         << setw (9) << rec.creditLimit << " Limit + " << num
206         << endl;
207   }
208   else {
209     cerr << "Error: invalid transaction code: " << transType
210         << endl;
211     exit (4);
212   }
213  }
214 }
```

Structure Alignment

When dealing with binary files, there is another architectural concern that must be understood and used. This is the principle of structure or data alignment in memory. Applications should align structure members and data values at addresses that are "natural" for the data type. A 4-byte type should be aligned on an address evenly divisible by 4. An 8-byte type should be aligned on an address evenly divisible by 8. The reason for this is how the circuitry fetches data from memory. No matter how you have the data stored in memory, the circuitry will retrieve that data. It is a matter of how efficiently it gets that data.

When inputting data from disk, remember that DOS first inputs an entire cluster of data into its internal buffer in memory. Then, it extracts what has been requested from the buffer and moves it into the destination variable. Thus, binary files on disk mirror this structure alignment.

Suppose that we wished to access a **long** whose 4-byte value began at memory location 2 in the DOS buffer, which is an address not evenly divisible by 4. The circuitry must fetch 2 4-byte memory locations and then extract the desired 4-byte long from the two 4-byte locations. This is shown in Figure 13.11. This is action causes a hardware fetch fault to occur. The hardware proceeds to get the two pieces from memory and join them into the 4-byte resulting **long** value.

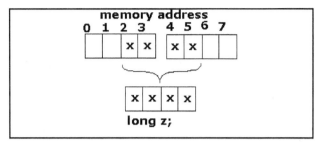

Figure 13.11 Fetching Unaligned Data

This faulting operation slows the memory accessing down significantly. But it guarantees that the requested data is retrieved. If the data is properly aligned, no fault occurs and the data is fetched normally and quickly.

When you make a new project, Visual Studio sets the structure alignment to 8 bytes by default. The guideline is "a structure should begin on address boundaries of the worst type of data in the structure." In our case of **AccountRec** structure, the **double** is the worst type. Thus, each instance of the structure in memory should be aligned on 8-byte addresses.

However, how many bytes does our structure contain? It is 4 + 42 + 8 + 8 bytes or 62 bytes long. And this value is NOT evenly divisible by 8. If we look into the data file or the DOS internal buffer when that cluster containing the data has been input, successive records are not back to back in memory since 62 is not an even multiple of 8. If the structure alignment is 8 bytes, then the compiler adds some additional **gas** or **slack** or **pad** bytes to each structure instance so that the total size ends up a multiple of 8 bytes. That is, gas, pad, or slack bytes are added by the compiler to enforce the alignment.

On a computer with only 32-bit or 4-byte high speed registers, then the computer cannot fetch a 64-bit or 8-byte value directly from memory with one fetch: its registers are too small. In this case, 8-byte alignment becomes really 4-byte alignment. If however, you do have one of the new 64-bit PCs which has a 64-bit memory bus access, then the data will be aligned on an 8-byte boundary because the high speed work registers are indeed 8 bytes in size and can handle it.

I am running a 32-bit computer. Thus, the binary master file Pgm13b wrote is aligned on 4-byte addresses. Since each structure instance that was written to disk contained only 62 bytes, the compiler automatically inserts two additional gas fill bytes. When you ask for the size of the **AccountRec**, the compiler returns 64 bytes not 62 bytes! When one looks at the actual data stored in the binary file, each record has an additional 2 bytes appended to it containing garbage.

When you are going to input a binary file, you **must** know what the structure alignment was in the program that wrote the binary file in the first place. Your program must match that structure alignment. If the original data was aligned on a byte boundary and your program inputs it aligned on a 4-byte boundary, then your program will input scrambled data! In the case of the **AccountRec** structure, each input would result in 64 bytes being input while the actual byte aligned data on disk had only 62 bytes.

Structure alignment is set through the project settings—Project Settings—C++ tab—Code Generation Category combo box choice—struct member alignment combo box—make your choice.

Rule: if the data was created with older DOS programs, the data is very likely to have been only byte aligned.

Corollary: if an older DOS program will be reading the data your program creates, then make sure that your project uses 1-byte alignment or the older DOS program will be inputting scrambled data.

To view a binary file, one needs an editor that can display the bytes in hex. Figure 13.12 shows the binary master file made by Pgm13b using 8-byte structure alignment.

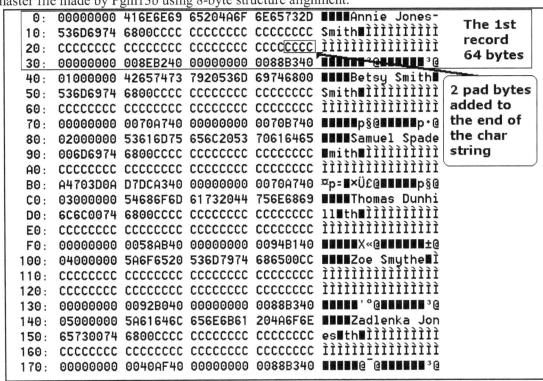

Figure 13.12 The Binary File (values in hex) Using 8-Byte Structure Alignment

Each line in Figure 13.12 shows the precise contents of 16 bytes or 10 in hexadecimal. Each byte consists of two hexadecimal nibbles. Each line shows groups of 4 bytes separated by a blank column. On the far right side of each line are the corresponding ASCII equivalent characters if there are any. Notice that on the right side we can read the contents of the string name because those are ASCII characters. I also noted where the compiler inserted the two gas bytes, right after the end of the string in the structure. It added the gas bytes here so that the next two doubles would be aligned on an 8-byte boundary. I boxed in one record which occupies 64 bytes on disk.

Beginning Data Structures in C++

In Figure 13.13, I rebuilt the project and binary master file using 1-byte alignment. Now each record is only 62 bytes long.

```
  0:  00000000 416E6E69 65204A6F 6E65732D  ████Annie Jones-    The 1st
 10:  536D6974 6800CCCC CCCCCCCC CCCCCCCC  Smith■ÌÌÌÌÌÌÌÌÌÌ    62-byte
 20:  CCCCCCCC CCCCCCCC CCCCCCC CCCC0000  ÌÌÌÌÌÌÌÌÌÌÌÌÌÌ■■     record
 30:  0000008E B2400000 00000088 B3400100  ████²@█████■³@██
 40:  00004265 74737920 536D6974 6800536D  ■■Betsy Smith■Sm
 50:  69746800 CCCCCCCC CCCCCCC CCCCCCCC  ith■ÌÌÌÌÌÌÌÌÌÌÌ
 60:  CCCCCCCC CCCCCCCC CCCCCCC 00000000  ÌÌÌÌÌÌÌÌÌÌÌÌ████
 70:  0070A740 00000000 0070B740 02000000  ■p§@█████p·@████
 80:  53616D75 656C2053 70616465 006D6974  Samuel Spade■mit
 90:  6800CCCC CCCCCCCC CCCCCCC CCCCCCCC  h■ÌÌÌÌÌÌÌÌÌÌÌÌÌ
 A0:  CCCCCCCC CCCCCCCC CCCCA470 3D0AD7DC  ÌÌÌÌÌÌÌÌÌÌ¤p=■×Ü
 B0:  A3400000 00000070 A7400300 00005468  £@█████p§@████Th
 C0:  6F6D6173 2044756E 68696C6C 00746800  omas Dunhill■th■
 D0:  CCCCCCCC CCCCCCCC CCCCCCC CCCCCCCC  ÌÌÌÌÌÌÌÌÌÌÌÌÌÌÌÌ
 E0:  CCCCCCCC CCCCCCC 00000000 0058AB40  ÌÌÌÌÌÌÌÌ█████X«@
 F0:  00000000 0094B140 04000000 5A6F6520  ██████±@████Zoe
100:  536D7974 686500CC CCCCCCC CCCCCCCC  Smythe■ÌÌÌÌÌÌÌÌÌ
110:  CCCCCCCC CCCCCCCC CCCCCCC CCCCCCCC  ÌÌÌÌÌÌÌÌÌÌÌÌÌÌÌÌ
120:  CCCCCCCC CCCC0000 00000092 B0400000  ÌÌÌÌÌÌ████'°@██
130:  00000088 B3400500 00005A61 646C656E  ████³@████Zadlen
140:  6B61204A 6F6E6573 00746800 CCCCCCCC  ka Jones■th■ÌÌÌÌ
150:  CCCCCCCC CCCCCCCC CCCCCCC CCCCCCCC  ÌÌÌÌÌÌÌÌÌÌÌÌÌÌÌÌ
160:  CCCCCCCC 00000000 0040AF40 00000000  ÌÌÌÌ█████@¯@████
170:  0088B340                             ■■³@
```

Figure 13.13 The Binary Master File Using 1-Byte Structure Alignment

Here is one final detail about structure alignment. Suppose that your structure was 9 bytes long and you saved the data to a binary file. Suppose further that there were 100,000 records in that file. If we used 1-byte structure alignment, how many bytes would the file occupy on disk? 900,000. However, if we used 8-byte alignment on a computer that could handle 8-byte aligned data, how many bytes would the file size report? Since 9 is not evenly divisible by 8, the compiler would add an additional 7 gas bytes to each structure instance. Now the file size on disk would be 1,600,000 bytes. This is a substantial difference in file size.

Hence, because of larger file sizes, many production applications that utilize large binary master files use 1-byte alignment to conserve disk space.

Implementing the Remainder Method of Direct File Processing—Hashing Theory

This last example, **Pgm13c**, illustrates how to create and use a direct file based upon the remainder method. With the remainder method, the key identifiers can be any numerical value. Here, I use the social security number as the key id field required to directly access the data.

Methods of performing a direct access to data are crucial to inquiry and update type programs. This applies not only to arrays of things but also to binary files on disk. Given an identifier, such as student id, a program needs to be able to directly access that student's data whether it is currently contained in an array or in a binary file on disk.

Consider the basic problem. Suppose we have an array of student records stored in memory and we need to find the information for a given student. The program is given the student id to match. We can make a simple **MatchId()** function as follows.

```
const int NoMatch = -1;
struct Student {
 int id;
 char name[21];
 char grade;
};
...
Student array[1000];
int numStudents;
int findId;
int matchIdx;
cin >> findId;
matchIdx = MatchId (array, numStudents, findId);
...
int MatchId (Student array[], int num, int findId) {
 for (j=0; j<num; j++) {
   if (findId == array[j].id) return j;
 }
 return NoMatch;
}
```

If there are only a few elements in the array or records on disk, there is not a problem with sequential searching. However, if there are thousands of elements or records and if the **findId** happens to contain the id for the last student in the array, then the program experiences a severe performance degradation.

The next improvement we can do is to have the array sorted into increasing **studentId** order. When the file or array is sorted into alphabetic order on the search key, a **binary search** can be performed. The idea is to first check the element in the middle. If you are lucky to have an exact match, you are done. If not, then decide if the **findId** lies in the upper or lower half. Now divide that half into half and search the middle once again, and so on.

```
bool  BinarySearch (Student array[], int num,
                        long findId, long& foundIdx) {
  int firstidx = 0;
  int lastidx = num - 1;
  int middleidx;
  bool foundMatch = false;
  while (lastidx >= firstidx && !foundMatch) {
   middleidx = (firstidx + lastidx) / 2;
   if (findId < id[middleidx].studentId)
      lastidx = middleidx - 1;
   else if (findId > id[middleidx].studentId)
      firstidx = middleidx + 1;
   else foundMatch = true;
  }
  foundIdx = middleidx
  return foundMatch;
}
```

The **main()** program calls it as follows.
```
if (BinarySearch (array, num, findId, matchIdx)) {
  // use array[matchIdx]
}
```
How effective is the binary search? Table 13.1 shows the array size and the number of number of loop iterations required to find it in the worst case.

Table 13.1 Binary Search Effectiveness

Array Size	# iterations
1	1
3	2
7	3
15	4
31	5
63	6
127	7
255	8

Notice that the number of loop iterations to find the data varies as the $\log_2$ of array size. There is a substantial difference between 255 loop iterations versus 8 iterations for the binary search. However, with large arrays or large binary files, even this is too many iterations. We need an even faster method to quickly find a specific element in the array or in the binary master file.

Thus, the concepts of hashing are needed.

Hashing

(**Hash**: the word has several meanings from a dinner food, to chopping into small bits.) In computer terminology, **hashing** means to take a user-friendly key or id number and perform some transformations to it to yield the subscript or index of that data in the array or on disk.

Microsoft defines hash as "To be mapped to a numerical value by a transformation known as a hashing function."

Hashing is used to convert an identifier or key into a value for the location of the corresponding data in a structure, such as a table. For example, given the key MOUSE and a hashing function that 1) added up the ASCII values of the characters, 2) then divided the total by 127 and 3) took the remainder as the final key value, MOUSE would hash to 12. The data identified by MOUSE would be found at entry 12 in the table.

The ultimate goal is, of course, a **perfect hash function** which is one that maps each potential search key to the unique position in the file or array.

If you have total control over what the keys' numeric values are to be and total control over the hashing algorithm, a perfect hash function can usually be made. Consider the remainder method of dividing the key by the largest prime number that does not exceed the largest key. In my earlier example above, the Id keys values were 1, 2 and 3. The corresponding hash function says that the key on disk is given by taking the Id key % 3. That is, the remainders are the indexes or relative record numbers. In this case, the indexes are 1, 2 and 0. And this is then a perfect hash function for this very tiny range of Id values. We also saw that as soon as we add even one more Id value, the perfect hash function breaks down. For example, we add Id 4 and the hash function returns a key or relative record number of 1 which is already in use.

However, suppose that the hashing function remained the same but that the keys were social security numbers: 333-33-3333, 333-33-3336 and 333-33-3339. This hashing function would yield the indexes 0, 0, 0. These duplicates are called **collisions** or **synonyms**.

Collisions are usually unavoidable. Normally, the number of entries in the table or binary file is less than the number of possible key values. If we expect to use social security numbers as the key and yet expect to have only 1000 students, one can expect collisions to occur. How are collisions resolved? There are many ways, but none are great.

First of all, when you are going to store a set of data with a specific key and you discover that the hashed index is already occupied by a synonym, where do you put that new one?

Linear Probing is one answer. The idea is to search the array from that point where the data should have been found on down for the first empty, unoccupied slot. If you reach the end of the array, start back over at element 0 until an empty available location is found and store the data there. Then, to look up this record, when you hash the key, look up the data at that key and discover that the data there is not the correct one, you then begin to search the array linearly down looking for it. Again, if you reach the last element in the array, begin with element 0 and continue looking until you arrive back at the original subscript. If you arrive back at the original subscript without having found the required item, it is not in the table or file. This process is called linear probing and is quite slow as you might expect.

Linear probing is highly susceptible to a phenomenon called **clustering of synonyms**. As the table is initially built, what happens frequently is that a large batch of synonyms ends up in a bunch of successive indexes somewhere beyond the index of the intended index. This of course then messes up all of those records that hash to these already occupied locations forcing them downward as well. To see this in operation, assume the hashing function to turn an Id number into the relative record number is % 3. When the file is built with the data below, notice the clustering effect.

```
Name   Id  Relative  Stored in
           Record    Array Element
           Number    of Subscript
Ann    1   1         [1]
Tom    4   1         [2]<-[1] is occupied, use the next available
Pete   7   1         [3]<-[1],[2] occupied, this is next free one
Betsy 10   1         [4]<-[1],[2],[3] occupied
Fred  11   2         [5]<-should be [2] but it is occupied by
                         clustering from [1] items
```

A grandiose scheme to handle synonyms and clustering is called **chained hash tables**. Here, we add one new data member to the structure instances that are being stored, a **fwdptr**. We link list all the synonyms together into a chain based on this common subscript or relative record number. Suppose that 10 keys yield the same hash index. The first one actually stored at that location contains a pointer to the second one, which points to the third and so on in a single linked list fashion.

When the data is on disk, another possibility to handle collisions is to add all the collision records into an overflow area located at the end of the theoretical end of the table as given by the hash keys. The direct file's remainder method does just this using linear probing to find any record in the overflow area. If you do not have a large number of records in the overflow area, this is fine.

How do hashing keys apply to a binary file? Clearly, the resulting hash key is the index into the array when it is in memory. But how do we translate that subscript into something meaningful when the array is really a binary file? It is usually done by computing the file offset of where the record begins. That is, consider the subscript or hash key to be the relative record number and multiply the hash key by the size of the record and setting the DOS file offset pointer to that value.

However, when dealing with binary files and hash keys, all potential entries MUST be in the binary file. That is, suppose that your hashing algorithm always results in a hash key between 0 and 255. Then, in the binary file, there must be 256 records actually in the file, even if there are no actual records stored in the file as yet! In other words, an empty file of 256 dummy records must be pre-built. These dummy records or place holders for the real data records have a dummy key id field set to −1 to indicate it is not yet in use. When adding a record to the file, one computes the hash key and then the file offset and retrieves the record currently stored there. If that record's id key is −1, then it is empty and you can store this new one there. If that id key is greater than 0, then you have a collision and must seek to the end of the file and add the new record there.

When doing an inquiry or update, you must first compute the hash key and then retrieve the record that corresponds to that relative record number. If that record's id matches the one you are looking for, you have found it; process it. However, if it does not match, then you must seek to the overflow area and begin a sequential search of all the records in the overflow area looking for a matching id.

Pgm13c—Direct File Processing in Action

To see this all in action, let's return to the previous example using the **AccountRec** binary file. Let's redo that program using hashing and make the master file be a direct access type of file. Initially, the file must be constructed with a known number of empty records. I call it the **InitialSize**. This value is also used to compute the offset of the overflow area.

Here are the input pair of files. I have now added lengthy id fields for each record.

```
The Revised Input Data to Build the Binary Direct Master File

1 12312341 "Annie Jones-Smith" 4500 5000
2 34234243 "Betsy Smith" 3000 4000
3 45435345 "Samuel Spade" 2500.42 3000
4 23442344 "Thomas Dunhill" 3500 4500
```

```
The Revised Transactions File

1 a 33453457 "Joe Smythe" 4242 5000
2 b 12312341 250
3 b 45435345 42
4 L 34234243 2000
5 a 33453453 "Henry P. Jones" 4000 5000
```

When we run the previous version of the program, recall that it printed a report of all the records in the master file. The same holds true in **Pgm13c**, however, now there are at least 100 records in the initial master file. The ones not yet in use are denoted as "empty." The next listing shows the output from the program when a bad hashing algorithm is used. The particular one I chose ends up generating duplicate has keys for all of the records!

```
The Output of Pgm13c with a Bad Hashing Algorithm

1 Built empty master file of 100 records
2 Hash for 12312341 is 0
3 Hash for 34234243 is 0
4 Hash for 45435345 is 0
5 Hash for 23442344 is 0
6 The number of records in the overflow area: 3
7 File initially contains 103 records
```

```
  8
  9
 10  Acme Credit Master File
 11
 12 Id Number   Name                       Balance  Limit
 13
 14  12312341         Annie Jones-Smith    4500.00  5000.00
 15         0         empty                   0.00     0.00
 16         0         empty                   0.00     0.00
...
113         0         empty                   0.00     0.00
114  34234243         Betsy Smith          3000.00  4000.00
115  45435345         Samuel Spade         2500.42  3000.00
116  23442344         Thomas Dunhill       3500.00  4500.00
117
118
119 Transaction Log
120
121 Hash for 33453457 is 0
122 33453457       Joe Smythe          4242.00   5000.00 Added
123 Hash for 12312341 is 0
124 12312341       Annie Jones-Smith   4750.00 5000.00 Balance+250.00
125 Hash for 45435345 is 0
126 45435345       Samuel Spade        2542.42   3000.00 Balance+42.00
127 Hash for 34234243 is 0
128 34234243       Betsy Smith         3000.00   6000.00 Limit+2000.00
129 Hash for 33453453 is 0
130 33453453       Henry P. Jones      4000.00   5000.00 Added
131
132
133 File now contains 105 records
134
135
136  Acme Credit Master File
137
138 Id Number   Name                       Balance  Limit
139
140  12312341         Annie Jones-Smith    4750.00  5000.00
141         0         empty                   0.00     0.00
142         0         empty                   0.00     0.00
143         0         empty                   0.00     0.00
...
239         0         empty                   0.00     0.00
240  34234243         Betsy Smith          3000.00  6000.00
241  45435345         Samuel Spade         2542.42  3000.00
242  23442344         Thomas Dunhill       3500.00  4500.00
243  33453457         Joe Smythe           4242.00  5000.00
244  33453453         Henry P. Jones       4000.00  5000.0
```

469

Beginning Data Structures in C++

Notice that all the records but one are in the overflow area. This atrocious algorithm consists of adding the ASCII values of all digits in the id key and then **% 1** to get the relative record number.

```cpp
char string[30];
ostrstream os (string, sizeof (string));
os << id << ends;
int i;
int sum = 0;
for (i=0; i<(int)strlen(string); i++) {
 sum += string[i];
}
int hash = sum % 1;
```

This coding is commented out in **Pgm13c** so that you can experiment. If you use **% 127**, then this becomes a more viable hashing algorithm

The good hashing algorithm I used consists of finding the largest prime number that does not exceed 100, the number of records in the direct file.

```cpp
int hash = id % 97;
```

Here are the results from a good hashing algorithm.

```
The Output of Pgm13c with a Good Hashing Algorithm

 1 Built empty master file of 100 records
 2 Hash for 12312341 is 34
 3 Hash for 34234243 is 33
 4 Hash for 45435345 is 60
 5 Hash for 23442344 is 63
 6 The number of records in the overflow area: 0
 7 File initially contains 100 records
 8
 9
10   Acme Credit Master File
11
12 Id Number   Name                         Balance   Limit
13
14          0        empty                    0.00      0.00
...
46          0        empty                    0.00      0.00
47   34234243        Betsy Smith           3000.00   4000.00
48   12312341        Annie Jones-Smith     4500.00   5000.00
49          0        empty                    0.00      0.00
...
73          0        empty                    0.00      0.00
74   45435345        Samuel Spade          2500.42   3000.00
75          0        empty                    0.00      0.00
76          0        empty                    0.00      0.00
77   23442344        Thomas Dunhill        3500.00   4500.00
78          0        empty                    0.00      0.00
...
113         0        empty                    0.00      0.00
```

470

```
114
115
116 Transaction Log
117
118 Hash for 33453457 is 0
119 33453457      Joe Smythe              4242.00   5000.00 Added
120 Hash for 12312341 is 34
121 12312341      Annie Jones-Smith       4750.00  5000.00 Balance+250.00
122 Hash for 45435345 is 60
123 45435345      Samuel Spade            2542.42  3000.00 Balance+42.00
124 Hash for 34234243 is 33
125 34234243      Betsy Smith             3000.00   6000.00 Limit+2000.00
126 Hash for 33453453 is 93
127 33453453      Henry P. Jones          4000.00   5000.00 Added
128
129
130 File now contains 100 records
131
132
133  Acme Credit Master File
134
135 Id Number   Name                      Balance   Limit
136
137  33453457       Joe Smythe             4242.00   5000.00
138         0       empty                     0.00      0.00
...
169         0       empty                     0.00      0.00
170  34234243       Betsy Smith            3000.00   6000.00
171  12312341       Annie Jones-Smith      4750.00   5000.00
172         0       empty                     0.00      0.00
...
196         0       empty                     0.00      0.00
197  45435345       Samuel Spade           2542.42   3000.00
198         0       empty                     0.00      0.00
199         0       empty                     0.00      0.00
200  23442344       Thomas Dunhill         3500.00   4500.00
201         0       empty                     0.00      0.00
...
229         0       empty                     0.00      0.00
230  33453453       Henry P. Jones         4000.00   5000.00
231         0       empty                     0.00      0.00
...
236         0       empty                     0.00      0.00
```

Now let's examine a few details of **Pgm13c**. With a direct access type of binary master file, space must be reserved for the maximum number of records the data base is being designed to hold. The overflow area then comes after this number of records. In this example, I have set that maximum number to 100 account records. Since the records in the overflow area must be searched for matching ids and since we must detect collisions in the main portion of the file, the id number must be a part of the account record. It is now defined as follows.

```
struct AccountRec {
  int     idNum;
  char    name[MaxNameLen];
  double  creditBalance;
  double  creditLimit;
};
```

In the dummy place holder records, I used 0 for the **idNum** members because no social security number has that value. If 0 would be a valid id number, then one could use any negative number to indicate this is an empty, unused dummy record.

In the **InitialBuildOfMasterFile()** function, one merely writes the maximum number of these dummy records to the file.

```
for (i=0; i<initSize; i++) {
  outfile.write ((char*) &rec, sizeof (rec));
}
```

Next, the real account records can be input one by one from the text file. As each one is input, the **AddRecord()** function is called to add in this record.

AddRecord() begins by finding what the theoretical hash number or relative record number should be for this Id number. **GetHashKey()** returns the id number % 97 where 97 is the largest prime number less than or equal to 100, the maximum number of records. Next, given this proposed relative record number, one then inputs the account record at that location in the file.

```
int hash = GetHashKey (rec.idNum);
long offset = hash * sizeof (rec);
AccountRec frec;
inout.seekg (offset, ios::beg);
inout.read ((char*) &frec, sizeof (frec));
```

If this inputted record is indeed a dummy record, the new record is added at this relative record number here in the main section of the file.

```
if (frec.idNum == 0) {
  inout.seekp (offset, ios::beg);
  inout.write ((char*) &rec, sizeof (rec));
}
```

However, if there is already another real record in this location, a collision has occurred. We must then add the new record to the end of the overflow area or append this new record to the end of the file.

```
else {
  inout.seekp (0, ios::end);
  inout.write ((char*) &rec, sizeof (rec));
}
```

When processing the update transactions, either a change in limit or balance, we are given the id number. The first step is to find the relative record number of this record in the file. **FindThisRecord()** first calls **GetHashKey()** to get the proposed relative record number, assuming that no collisions have occurred. The record stored at this location is retrieved and its Id number is compared to the one for which we are looking. If they match, then we have the correct relative record number to use.

```
int hash = GetHashKey (findid);
AccountRec rec;
long offset = hash * sizeof (rec);
inout.seekg (offset, ios::beg);
inout.read ((char*) &rec, sizeof (rec));
if (rec.idNum == findid)
 return hash;
```

However, if the Id numbers do not match, then the record we are looking for lies in the overflow area. To begin searching the overflow area, we must first position the file offset pointer to the beginning of that area.

```
offset = initialSize * sizeof (rec);
hash = initialSize;
inout.seekg (offset, ios::beg);
while (inout.read ((char*) &rec, sizeof (rec))) {
 if (rec.idNum == findid)
  return hash; // yes, so return this rel rec num
 else hash++;
 }
return NotFound;
```

Once the relative record number is found and returned, then the update can proceed as before by positioning to the record and inputting it, modifying the data and rewriting this record. Here is the complete **Pgm13**.

```
Pgm13c Accounts Update Program - Using a Direct Access File

 1 #include <iostream>
 2 #include <fstream>
 3 #include <strstream>
 4 #include <iomanip>
 5 #include <string>
 6 using namespace std;
 7
 8 /*********************************************************************/
 9 /*                                                                 */
10 /* Pgm13c: Acme Credit Update - Using a Direct File with           */
11 /*         the Remainder Method                                    */
12 /*                                                                 */
13 /*********************************************************************/
14
15 const int MaxNameLen = 42;
16 const int NotFound = -1;
17 const int InitialSize = 100;
18
19 struct AccountRec {
20  int    idNum;
21  char   name[MaxNameLen];
22  double creditBalance;
23  double creditLimit;
24 };
```

```
25
26
27  void InitialBuildOfMasterFile (const char* filename,
28                                    int initialSize);
29  void AddRecord (fstream& inout, AccountRec& rec,
30                    int& countCollisions);
31  int  GetHashKey (int id);
32  void MakeReport (fstream& inout);
33  void ProcessTransactions (fstream& inout, int& count,
34                               int initialSize);
35  int  FindThisRecord (fstream& inout, int findid,
36                         int initialSize);
37
38
39  int main () {
40   // setup floating point for dollars and cents
41   cout.setf (ios::fixed, ios::floatfield);
42   cout.setf (ios::showpoint);
43   cout << setprecision (2);
44
45   int maxCountOfRecs;
46   const char* masterfile = "AcmeCredit.dat";
47
48   InitialBuildOfMasterFile (masterfile, InitialSize);
49
50   fstream inout (masterfile, ios::in | ios::out | ios::binary);
51   inout.seekg (0, ios::end);
52   maxCountOfRecs = inout.tellg () / sizeof (AccountRec);
53   cout << "File initially contains " << maxCountOfRecs
54       << " records\n";
55   inout.seekg (0, ios::beg);
56
57   MakeReport (inout);
58
59   ProcessTransactions (inout, maxCountOfRecs, InitialSize);
60
61   inout.seekg (0, ios::end);
62   maxCountOfRecs = inout.tellg () / sizeof (AccountRec);
63   inout.seekg (0, ios::beg);
64   cout << "\n\nFile now contains " << maxCountOfRecs
65       << " records\n";
66
67   MakeReport (inout);
68   inout.close ();
69   return 0;
70  }
71
72  /****************************************************************/
73  /*                                                            */
74  /* InitialBuildOfMasterFile: build a Direct Access file with  */
```

```
75 /*           initSize dummy records and input the accounts file  */
76 /*           into the binary master file                          */
77 /*                                                                 */
78 /*****************************************************************/
79
80 void InitialBuildOfMasterFile (const char* filename,
81                                      int initSize) {
82 // Step 1: setup empty file of initSize number of records
83 int i;
84 AccountRec rec;
85 rec.idNum = 0; // we could use -1 if any id could be 0
86 strcpy_s (rec.name, sizeof (rec.name), "empty");
87 rec.creditBalance = rec.creditLimit = 0;
88
89 ofstream outfile (filename, ios::out | ios::binary);
90 if (!outfile) {
91  cerr << "Error: could not open the output file: "
92       << filename << endl;
93  exit (1);
94 }
95
96 for (i=0; i<initSize; i++) {
97  outfile.write ((char*) &rec, sizeof (rec));
98 }
99 outfile.close ();
100
101 cout << "Built empty master file of " << initSize
102      << " records\n";
103
104 // now load in the accounts file into the empty master file
105 ifstream infile ("accounts.txt");
106 fstream inout (filename, ios::in | ios::out | ios::binary);
107
108 if (!infile || !inout) {
109  cerr << "Error: cannot open accounts file and/or the master\n";
110  exit (2);
111 }
112
113 char c;
114 int countCollisions = 0; // tracks the number of collisions
115 // input each set of account data and add to master file
116 while (infile >> rec.idNum >> c && c == '\"') {
117  infile.getline (rec.name, sizeof (rec.name), '\"');
118  infile >> rec.creditBalance >> rec.creditLimit;
119  if (infile) AddRecord (inout, rec, countCollisions);
120 }
121 // if still in good state, something is wrong...
122 if (!infile.eof ()) {
123  cerr << "Error inputing initial data\n";
124  exit (3);
```

```
125  }
126  // here all is ok
127  infile.close ();
128  inout.close ();
129  cout << "The number of records in the overflow area: "
130       << countCollisions << endl;
131  }
132
133  /****************************************************************/
134  /*                                                            */
135  /*  GetHashKey: given the account Id, returns the hash key or  */
136  /*              the relative record number proposed for this   */
137  /*              set of data                                    */
138  /*                                                            */
139  /****************************************************************/
140
141  int GetHashKey (int id) {
142   int hash = id % 97;  // mod by largest prime number <= 100
143
144   // comment out the above line and uncomment out the following
145   // block to generate a bad hashing algorithm to see its effect
146  /* char string[30];
147   ostrstream os (string, sizeof (string));
148   os << id << ends;
149   int i;
150   int sum = 0;
151   for (i=0; i<(int)strlen(string); i++) {
152    sum += string[i];
153   }
154   int hash = sum % 1;
155   */
156   cout << "Hash for " << id << " is " << hash <<endl;
157   return hash;
158  }
159
160  /****************************************************************/
161  /*                                                            */
162  /*  AddRecord: adds a new record to the Direct Access file     */
163  /*             by finding the proposed hash key, reading in    */
164  /*             record and if empty, rewriting that one         */
165  /*             If collision occurs, add to overflow area       */
166  /*                                                            */
167  /****************************************************************/
168
169  void AddRecord (fstream& inout, AccountRec& rec,
170                  int& countCollisions) {
171   // get the hash key equivalent of this Id number
172   int hash = GetHashKey (rec.idNum);
173   // calculate the file offset for this record
174   long offset = hash * sizeof (rec);
```

```
175  AccountRec frec;
176  // position the file to this offset
177  inout.seekg (offset, ios::beg);
178  // and input the record that's there
179  inout.read ((char*) &frec, sizeof (frec));
180  // see if this record is then an empty record
181  if (frec.idNum == 0) {
182   // yes, is empty, so rewrite it with the new record to be added
183   inout.seekp (offset, ios::beg);
184   inout.write ((char*) &rec, sizeof (rec));
185  }
186  else { // here, that spot is occupied - so append to overflow
187   countCollisions++;
188   // position to eof
189   inout.seekp (0, ios::end);
190   // and write this new record at the end of the file
191   inout.write ((char*) &rec, sizeof (rec));
192  }
193 }
194
195 /******************************************************************/
196 /*                                                                */
197 /* MakeReport: display a report of the contents of every          */
198 /*             record in the file                                 */
199 /*                                                                */
200 /******************************************************************/
201
202 void MakeReport (fstream& in) {
203  AccountRec rec;
204  int count = 0;
205  cout << "\n\n Acme Credit Master File\n\n"
206   << "Id Number  Name                    Balance  Limit\n\n";
207  while (in.read ((char*) &rec, sizeof (rec))) {
208   cout << setw (9) << rec.idNum << "      " << left << setw (19)
209        << rec.name << right << setw (9) << rec.creditBalance
210        << setw (9) << rec.creditLimit << endl;
211  }
212  in.seekg (0, ios::beg);  // reset to beginning of the file
213  in.clear (ios::goodbit); // clear the eof flag
214 }
215
216 /******************************************************************/
217 /*                                                                */
218 /* ProcessTransactions: process the additions, limit and          */
219 /*                      balance updates                           */
220 /*                                                                */
221 /******************************************************************/
222
223 void ProcessTransactions (fstream& inout, int& count,
224                           int initialSize) {
```

```
225    AccountRec rec;
226    char transType;
227    char c;
228    double num;
229    int findId;
230    int countCollisions = 0;
231
232    cout << "\n\nTransaction Log\n\n";
233
234    ifstream infile ("transactions.txt");
235    if (!infile) {
236     cerr << "Error: cannot open transactions file\n";
237     exit (3);
238    }
239    while (infile >> transType) {
240     transType = toupper (transType);
241     if (transType == 'A') { // here it is an addition
242      // get the new data
243      infile >> rec.idNum >> c;
244      infile.getline (rec.name, sizeof (rec.name), '\"');
245      infile >> rec.creditBalance >> rec.creditLimit;
246      // and add this record to the file
247      AddRecord (inout, rec, countCollisions);
248      cout << setw (5) << rec.idNum << "        " << left << setw (19)
249           << rec.name << right << setw (9) << rec.creditBalance
250           << setw (9) << rec.creditLimit << " Added\n";
251      count++;
252     }
253     else if (transType == 'B') { // here it is a balance change
254      infile >> findId >> num;
255      // find the relative record number of this record
256      int id = FindThisRecord (inout, findId, initialSize);
257      if (id == NotFound) {
258       // if it is not found, display an error msg and ignore it
259       cerr << "Error: cannot find id " << findId << endl;
260      }
261      else {
262       // here it is present so input the desired record
263       long offset = id * sizeof (AccountRec);
264       inout.seekg (offset, ios::beg);
265       inout.read ((char*) &rec, sizeof (rec));
266       // update the balance
267       rec.creditBalance += num;
268       // rewrite the record
269       inout.seekp (offset, ios::beg);
270       inout.write ((char*) &rec, sizeof (rec));
271       cout << setw (5) << rec.idNum << "        " << left <<setw (19)
272            << rec.name << right << setw (9) << rec.creditBalance
273            << setw (9) << rec.creditLimit << " Balance + " << num
274            << endl;
```

```
275      }
276    }
277    else if (transType == 'L') { // here it is a limit update
278      infile >> findId >> num;
279      // find the relative record number of this record
280      int id = FindThisRecord (inout, findId, initialSize);
281      if (id == NotFound) {
282        // if it is not found, display an error msg and ignore it
283        cerr << "Error: cannot find id " << findId << endl;
284      }
285      else {
286        // here it is present so input the desired record
287        long offset = id * sizeof (AccountRec);
288        inout.seekg (offset, ios::beg);
289        inout.read ((char*) &rec, sizeof (rec));
290        // change the limit
291        rec.creditLimit += num;
292        // and rewrite the record
293        inout.seekp (offset, ios::beg);
294        inout.write ((char*) &rec, sizeof (rec));
295        cout << setw (5) << rec.idNum << "      " << left <<setw (19)
296             << rec.name << right << setw (9) << rec.creditBalance
297             << setw (9) << rec.creditLimit << " Limit + " << num
298             << endl;
299      }
300    }
301    else {
302      cerr << "Error: invalid transaction code: " << transType
303           << endl;
304      exit (4);
305    }
306  }
307 }
308
309 /***************************************************************/
310 /*                                                           */
311 /* FindThisRecord: Given the Id to find and the max number of  */
312 /*                 records (which pin points the start of the  */
313 /*                 overflow area, find the relative record     */
314 /*                 number of this record                       */
315 /*                                                           */
316 /*   returns the rrn or NoMatch if not found                   */
317 /*                                                           */
318 /***************************************************************/
319
320 int FindThisRecord (fstream& inout, int findid, int initialSize){
321   // get the proposed hash key (rel rec num)
322   int hash = GetHashKey (findid);
323   AccountRec rec;
324   // position to this proposed record
```

```
325  long offset = hash * sizeof (rec);
326  inout.seekg (offset, ios::beg);
327  // and input the record at the proposed rel rec num
328  inout.read ((char*) &rec, sizeof (rec));
329  // is this the correct record with this Id?
330  if (rec.idNum == findid)
331   return hash; // yes, so return this rel rec num
332
333  // no, so now we must search the overflow area sequentially
334  // position to start of the overflow area
335  offset = initialSize * sizeof (rec);
336  hash = initialSize; // hash will hold the rel rec num, if
337                      // we find this record in the overflow
338  inout.seekg (offset, ios::beg);
339  // search all records in the overflow area
340  while (inout.read ((char*) &rec, sizeof (rec))) {
341   // is this record the correct one with the right Id number?
342   if (rec.idNum == findid)
343    return hash; // yes, so return this rel rec num
344   else hash++;
345  }
346  return NotFound; // here no record matches this Id num
347 }
```

Review Questions

1. Explain the concept of a binary file. How does the storage of a **double** differ between a text file and a binary file? What would happen if you attempted to extract a **double** from a binary file? What would happen if you attempted to read in a **double** from a text file?

2. Under what circumstances is data conversion performed on data in a binary file?

3. How is a binary file opened in C++?

4. What functions can be used to I/O to or from a binary file? Under what circumstances can the insertion and extraction operator be used with a binary file?

5. How would an inventory structure be written to a binary file? How would it be read back in?

6. What is the most significant difference between the following two methods for outputting an array of **double**s? What will be in the file in both cases? Is there any significant benefit for using one of these in preference to another?

```
double array[10000];
for (i=0; i<10000; i++)
  outfile.write ((char*) array[i], sizeof (double));
```
and
```
outfile.write ((char*) array, sizeof (array));
```

7. What is a cluster? On a Windows/DOS platform, what is the significance of a cluster?

8. Explain what is meant by Physical I/O. Explain what is meant by Logical I/O.

9. What is the purpose of the DOS file offset pointer? How can a program make use of this pointer? What functions provide access to it?

10. Explain the instruction sequence required to obtain the DOS file size of a binary file.

11. Would there be any real benefit to inputting an entire text file in one I/O operation into an array of characters which is the same size as the binary file?

12. What is wrong with the following sequence to input a file of data?
```
infile.seekg (0, ios::end);
long sz = infile.tellg ();
char* buf = new char [sz];
infile.read (buf, sz);
```

13. Explain how the relative record number method for direct access of a specific record in a binary master file works. Why is this approach exceedingly fast at data retrieval?

14. Why do relative record numbers make poor values for client Id numbers?

15. A binary file is supposed to contain a series of **InventoryRec** structures. How can a program tell if the file either is corrupt or may contain other items besides these structure instances?

16. A direct access file uses the remainder method for locating where a record with a specific key id is located. Explain how this method works. Why does the file have to be pre-built with enough dummy records to equal the maximum number of records the file is designed to hold?

17. What kind of user id key fields can be used with a direct access type of file?

18. Explain how the ISAM method works. What kind of user id key fields can be used?

19. Why is the ISAM method slower at retrieving a specific record on disk?

20. What **iostream** class is used to create an update file—that is, a file instance that can be both read and written?

21. What is meant by structure alignment? How does it work? What is the impact of structure alignment on a program?

22. Program 1 writes a binary master file and uses 1-byte structure alignment. Program 2 inputs the data from that binary master file but uses 8-byte structure alignment. Explain what occurs at run time with Program 2 and why.

23. What is meant by a hashing algorithm? What is the purpose of a hash number?

24. Explain how a hash number can be used to access a specific record or element of an array?

25. How can collisions of hash numbers be handled?

26. What is meant by linear probing?

27. What is a chained hash table? How does such work?

Stop! Do These Exercises Before Programming

1. Our programmer has been asked to write an inventory update program for Acme Manufacturing Corporation. The binary master file is an ISAM type of file that contains inventory records that are defined as follows.

```
const int PARTNO_LEN = 16;
const int DESCR_LEN = 46;
const int LOC_LEN = 11;
struct InvRec {
  char    partNo[PARTNO_LEN];
  char    description[DESCR_LEN];
  int     qtyOnHand;
  double  unitCost;
  char    locationBin[LOC_LEN];
};
```

The key id field is the **partNo**. The master file itself is called **parts.dat** and was built using 8-byte structure alignment. The index file is called **parts.idx** and consists of instances of the structure **Index**.

```
struct Index {
  char partNo[PARTNO_LEN];
  long relRecNum;
};
```

The index records are stored in increasing ASCII sequence on the **partNo** field.

The programmer decided to implement the **FindRecord()** function whose purpose is to find the relative record number of the inventory record that corresponds to a given part number. Of course, he also had to write a **LoadIndex()** function to load the index file into an array. He also wrote a small driver program to test his new function. It fails completely. He has asked you for your assistance. Find his errors so that both the new function and driver work as expected. Is there anything grossly inefficient about his **FindRecord()** function?

```
const int NoMatch = -1;
int main () {
 InvRec rec;
 char partNo[PARTNO_LEN];
 fstream masterfile ("parts.dat", ios::in | ios::out);
```

```
fstream indexfile ("parts.idx", ios::in | ios::out);
long count;
Index* index = LoadIndex (indexfile, count);
while (cin >> partNo) {
 long relRecNum = FindRecord (index, count, partNo);
 if (relRecNum == NoMatch)
  cout << "Record not found - part number: " << partNo << endl;
 else {
  masterfile.seekg (relRecNum * sizeof (InvRec), ios::beg);
  masterfile.read ((char*) &rec, sizeof (rec));
  cout << "Found part number: " << rec.partNo << endl;
 }
}
...
}

Index* LoadIndex (fstream& file, long& count) {
 file.seekg (0, ios::end);
 long size = file.tellg ();
 count = size / sizeof (Index);
 Index* index = new Index [count];
 file.read ((char*) index, count * sizeof (index));
 return index;
}

long FindRecord (Index index[], long count,
                 const char* findThis) {
 for (long j=0; j<count; j++) {
  if (findThis == index[j].partNo)
   return j;
 }
 return NoMatch;
}
```

2. The programmer, after singing praises to you for your assistance, embarks on a total rewrite of the **FindRecord()** function. He has decided to implement a binary search for the id value.

```
bool FindRecord (Index id[], long num,
                 const char* findId, long& foundIndex) {
 int firstidx = 0;
 int lastidx = num - 1;
 int middleidx;
 bool foundMatch = false;
 while (lastidx >= firstidx && !foundMatch) {
  middleidx = (firstidx + lastidx) / 2;
  if (findId < id[middleidx])
   lastidx = middleidx - 1;
  else if (findId > id[middleidx])
```

```
      firstidx = middleidx + 1;
   else foundMatch = true;
 }
 foundIndex = middleidx;
 return foundMatch;
}
```

He changed the call in **main()** to the following.

```
long relRecNum;
if (FindRecord (index, count, partNo, relRecNum)) {
```

When it runs, the program does not find any records. After spending hours debugging it, he humbly begs you for your assistance. Fix his function so that it correctly finds matching records.

3. His enthusiasm returns when you point out his errors; his find function is working properly. So next he embarks on writing the code to perform the updates of specific inventory records. The relevant parts of his tester program now appear as follows.

```
... performing an update of partNo record
... the needed new values have been input
long relRecNum;
if (FindRecord (index, count, partNo, relRecNum)) {
 masterfile.seekg (relRecNum * sizeof (InvRec), ios::beg);
 masterfile.read (&rec, sizeof (rec));
 // ... made changes to rec fields
 masterfile.write (&rec, sizeof (rec));
 }
 else
  cerr << "Error: unable to find part: " << partNo << endl;
```

Unfortunately, the above coding does not compile or work properly. Find his errors in syntax and the two major logic blunders.

4. After profusely apologizing for making such a stupid blunder, he then begins the design for the addition of new records to the master file. Now he encounters a new problem. While it will be easy to add the new record to the master file, the index is another matter entirely. The new part number must be inserted into the index table in sorted order. He decides that he must add the new record to the master file first so that he knows the new relative record number of that new record. This time, he writes only the couple of lines needed to store the new record in the master file. But when he tests it, he discovers that the new record is not where it should be located and has indeed wiped other data out!

```
// rec contains the new data, so write it at the end of the file
masterfile.seekg (0, ios::end);
masterfile.write ((char*) &rec, sizeof (rec));
```

After spending hours playing with this error, he comes to you once more stating the computer must be broken because these two simple lines of coding do not work! The record is not added at the end of the file! Point out his error and fix this error for him.

5. Humbled and in awe of your programming prowess, the programmer now attempts to update the index file. He is absolutely certain that he will bungle this one too. And his postulate holds. His coding does not work. Rescue the programmer once more, please. Fix this coding so that it properly adds a new entry to the index in the proper location.

```
long newRelRecNum; // contains the new relative record number
// for the added record while partNo contains its Id value
long newIndex; // the location in the index
if (!FindRecord (index, count, partNo, newIndex)) {
 // here, newIndex contains the location in index where this
 // partNo should be located. so move all entries from here
 // down one slot and insert this new one
 long j, k;
 for (j=count-1; j>=newIndex; j--) {
  index[j] = index[j-1];
 }
 index[newIndex].partNo = partNo;
 index[newIndex].relRecNum = newRelRecNum;
 count++;
 indexfile.write ((char*) index, sizeof (Index) * count);
}
```

In fact, just before he came to you this last time, his computer started doing funny things after he had run the program, forcing him to reboot.

Programming Problems

Problem Pgm13-1 The Duplicate File Finder Program

You have been collecting some terrific scenery jpg images from the Internet. However, you notice that there are what appears to be duplicate files in your collection. That is, different filenames, but what appears to be the same images. The objective is to find out if two specific files are identical or not.

Write a function called **IsDuplicate()** that takes two constant character string filenames and returns a bool, true if the two files are precisely identical. You do not need to know what the contents of the image file actually contain, just that they are identical byte for byte. The approach to take is to open each file as a binary file and get the DOS file size of each. If the file sizes do not match, return false as they cannot be byte-by-byte duplicates.

Next, dynamically allocate memory to hold each file's contents. Use arrays of unsigned char. Input both files into these two arrays. Make sure you are using binary I/O. Now compare the two arrays, byte-by-byte. At the first unequal byte result, return false as they do not match. Return true if the end of the two equal length arrays occurs as they are the same.

Verify that you have not leaked any memory. Be sure to close all opened files. Write a simple driver program to thoroughly test the function.

Problem Pgm13-2 The CD Stock Update Program

Acme Music Store wants a program written that they can use to maintain their stock inventory of CDs. The main menu consists of the following.

```
Acme CD Inventory Program

1. Display CD Inventory
2. Update CD Inventory
3. Add a New CD
4. Exit the Program

Enter the number of your choice: _
```

The file **CDinventory.dat** is located in the **Chapter13** folder of **TestDataForAssignments**. It is a binary file of the current inventory and was built using 8-byte structure alignment. The inventory record consists of

```
struct Inventory {
  char cdNum[11];
  char cdTitle[41];
  long qtyOnHand;
  double cost;
};
```

487

Initially, open this file using a **fstream** instance and open it for update operations. Before the main menu is displayed, construct an instance of a growable array container to store an array of **CD_to_RRN** structure instances. This structure stores the **cdNum** and its corresponding relative record number. So read each record in the master file and build this conversion array. When updates are done, the user provides the **cdNum** and you look it up in the **CD_to_RRN** array to obtain the relative record number of the data in the master file.

When Display CD Inventory is chosen, read the file sequentially displaying each item nicely formatted on the screen.

When Update a CD Inventory is chosen, prompt the user for the cd number. Then look it up in the **CD_to_RRN** to obtain the relative record number on disk. If that cd is not in the file, display an error message to the user. If it is, read in that cd's inventory data and display it onscreen. Prompt the user for any changes in quantity or cost. Then rewrite that record on disk.

When Add a New Cd is chosen, prompt the user for the relevant information. Then, verify that the cd number is not already in the data base. If it is, display an error message to the user. If it is not in the file, then add this record to the master file and add a new entry to the **CD_to_RRN** array.

Thoroughly test your program.

Problem Pgm13-3 Modify Pgm13c to use an ISAM Master File

Revise Pgm13c to build and then use an ISAM master file instead of the Direct Access file. Store the index in a separate file with the .idx extension. Since the original data are not in any particular social security number order, make the searching of the index table be a simple sequential search. Test the program using the same data as was used in Pgm13c.

Problem Pgm13-4 Building and Reading a Binary File

Write a program that inputs the text file **cd.txt** located in the **Chapter13** folder of **TestDataForAssignments**. It contains cd inventory records. Make a structure called **CD** as follows.

```
struct CD {
  char cdNum[11];
  char cdTitle[41];
  long qtyOnHand;
  double cost;
};
```
Input each record from the text file into a **CD** record and then write that record to a binary output file.

Then, open the binary output file and input each record and display all four fields onscreen in a nicely formatted report.

Beginning Data Structures in C++

Chapter 14—Trees

Introduction

The data structures we have examined up to this point have been **linear** in nature. That is, the structures had unique first and last elements with each element having a unique element both preceding and following it (except for the very first and last elements). However, not all data are best presented in such a linear fashion. Consider the Explorer's tree view of the folders on a disk drive. Here the data is better presented in a **hierarchical** format commonly called a **tree**.

A tree is nonlinear in nature because each element may have more than one successor. The organizational chart of a company begins with the leader or CEO or president and below him/her are several vice presidents. Below each VP are several managers and so on. The Executive Branch of our government can be viewed as a tree structure with the President at the top and the numerous department heads below him/her and so on down. Genealogy makes extensive use of tree structure showing the parents at the top, their children below them and so on down the line.

In general, a tree is a structure in which each element in below only one other element but may have none or many elements immediately below it. That is, a node of a tree has only one predecessor but many successors. Only the top node has no predecessors.

Tree Notation

The notation or terminology of tree structures borrows from the real world of trees, such as oak or maple trees. The topmost node is called the **root** of a tree. It is the single element at the top or beginning of the hierarchical structure. For example, the president of a company would be at the root of the company's organizational chart. Elements with no successors are called **leaves**. In the company analogy, the individual employees would form the leaves below their boss or manager. A tree must have only one root and should branch out into many leaves which gives the appearance of an upside down tree.

Each of the elements of a tree are called **nodes** similar to linked lists. Each node has only one predecessor called its **parent**. The potentially many nodes that succeed it are called its **children**. And two nodes with the same parent are called **siblings**. In the company organizational chart analogy, all of the vice presidents are siblings and are the children of the parent, the president. The terms **ancestor** and **descendant** also can be applied to nodes. The vice presidents are the descendants of the president's node and the president is the ancestor of the vice presidents.

How can a tree be defined? We define a general tree using the following recursive definition.
A. An empty tree, without any nodes, is a tree.
B. A single node all by itself is a tree – this is the root.
C. The structure formed by taking a node N and one or more existing trees and making

489

node N be the parent of all the other existing tree roots is a tree. Figure 14.1 shows three different trees.

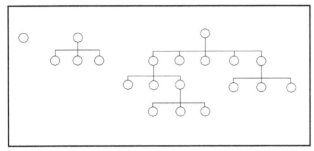

Figure 14.1 Three Trees

A subtree is a tree itself but is also part of a larger tree. Indeed, rule C above can be used to construct trees from existing trees. After the construction is done, the original trees are now subtrees of the larger tree. Figure 14.2 shows many of the subtrees of the more complex tree of Figure 14.1.

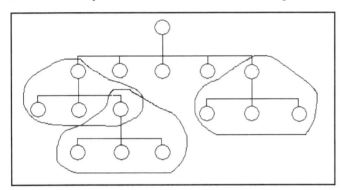

Figure 14.2 Three of the Subtrees of the Larger Tree

The term **level of a node** is often used to pin down the vertical location of that node within the entire tree. The level of the root node is defined to be 0.

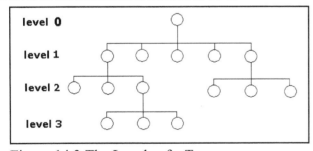

Figure 14.3 The Levels of a Tree

Its immediate children are at level 1. In Figure 14.2, the level of the lowest children on the left side is 3. This is shown in Figure 14.3.

Beginning Data Structures in C++

The term **degree** of a node refers to the number of subtrees associated with that node. A leaf of a tree has degree zero since there are no subtrees below it.

The term **height (or depth) of a tree** is defined to be the maximum level of the tree's leaves. The depth of the tree shown in Figure 14.3 above is 4. In Figure 14.1 above, the middle tree's height is 2 and the leftmost tree's depth is 1.

The term **path** is defined as the non-empty sequence of nodes from the root to the desired location. In Figure 14.3, there are 15 separate paths. The topmost path is of length 0 containing only the root node. Then there are five paths to each of the nodes on level 2. Imagine the Figure 14.3 is defining the folder structure with the root node containing C:\. Each lower circle represents another folder. The 15 separate paths would represent all the possible file specification paths on that drive. In Figure 14.4, I have arbitrarily assigned a letter to each element.

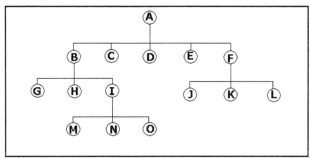

Figure 14.4 A Tree with Letter Elements

An alternate graphical representation of this same tree (Figure 14.4) is called a **Venn** diagram, which represents the tree as a series of nested regions in a plane as a series of sets. This is shown in Figure 14.5. In this form, it appears much like an outline of a chapter of a book.

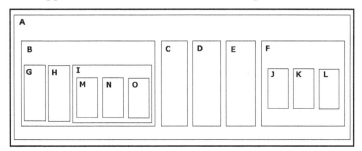

Figure 14.5 The Tree as a Venn Diagram

This same tree could be represented as a block of C++ coding as shown below!

```
A:    {
    B:  {
        G:  statement;
        H:  statement;
        I:  {
            M:  statement;
```

```
            N:  statement;
            O:  statement;
        }
    }
C:  statement;
D:  statement;
E:  statement;
F:  {
        J:  statement;
        K:  statement;
        L:  statement;
    }
}
```

Therefore, it is not surprising that tree structures play an important role in the compiler writing, word processing and many other computer applications other than searching for matching key applications.

Trees can come in many different forms. In the general tree case, each node can have a different number of subtrees or each node can be of a different degree. The tree shown in the above series of figures is a general tree. The root node has five subtrees while each of the others has three or none. However, there are many kinds of more specialized trees.

An **N-ary tree** is a tree in which all of its nodes have the same degree. That is, every node that has children has the same number of children. In Figure 14.4, if we deleted nodes C and D, then the resulting tree would be an N-ary tree.

Binary Trees

An especially important N-ary tree is one that has degree 2, or N is 2. This is called a **binary tree**. Each node has at most two subtrees below it. They are called the **left child** and the **right child**. Thus, every node of a binary tree has zero, one, or two children. Or a parent can have at most two children. Sometimes only the left child is present; others, only the right child is present. Figure 14.6 shows five binary trees. Note that the two trees with only nodes A and B are different binary trees. One has only a left child; the other has only a right child. However, if these were defined to be general trees, these two would be the same tree.

Suppose that we wished to create a **BinaryTree** class or ADT. How can we implement it? There are many ways, but in keeping with the concept of code reusability, let's store the user data for each node as a **void***. This way, we can write the class one time and reuse it for many applications. Each node should be dynamically allocated so that there is no arbitrary maximum number of nodes in the tree.

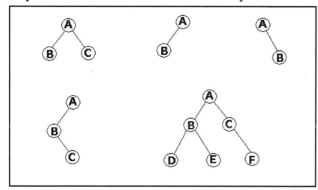

Figure 14.6 Five Binary Trees

The tree node structure could be defined then as follows.
```
struct TreeNode {
 void*      ptrData;
 TreeNode* ptrLeftChild;
 TreeNode* ptrRightChild;
};
```
What data members are needed? The only required data member is a pointer to the root node, **ptrRoot**. Here is the start of a relatively simple **BinaryTree** class definition.

```
struct TreeNode {
 void*      ptrData;
 TreeNode* ptrLeftChild;
 TreeNode* ptrRightChild;
};
class BinaryTree {
protected:
 TreeNode* ptrRoot;
public:
         BinaryTree ();
```

```
            ~BinaryTree ();
bool        IsEmpty () const;
void        BuildRoot (void* dataptr);
TreeNode*   GetRootNode () const;
void AppendLeftChild (TreeNode* ptrParent, void* dataptr);
void AppendRightChild (TreeNode* ptrParent, void* dataptr);
void*       GetNodeData (TreeNode* ptrNode) const;
void        SetNodeData (TreeNode* ptrNode, void* dataptr);
TreeNode*   GetLeftChild (TreeNode* ptrNode) const;
TreeNode*   GetRightChild (TreeNode* ptrNode) const;
bool        IsLeaf (TreeNode* ptrNode) const;
void        DeleteLeaf (TreeNode*& ptrNode);
};
```

The **BinaryTree** constructor sets **ptrRoot** to 0. **IsEmpty()** returns **true** if **ptrRoot** is 0. **BuildRoot()** allocates a new **TreeNode** and sets the **ptrdata** member to the user's data pointer and sets the two child pointers to 0. The two append functions perform basically the same operations. First, each function allocates a new **TreeNode** and copies in the user's data pointer to be stored in this node. Then each function sets the two child pointers to 0. Finally, each function stores the address of this new node in the passed **TreeNode** pointer's left or right child pointer. The access functions, **Get/SetNodeData()** returns or changes the data that this node is storing for the user. The pair **GetLeftChild()** and **GetRightChild()** return the child pointer of the passed **TreeNode** pointer. The **IsLeaf()** function returns **true** if both of the child pointers of the passed TreeNode are 0. **DeleteLeaf()** deletes the passed node, setting the reference pointer to 0.

However, there are some basic problems with this design. First, if **DeleteLeaf()** removes this leaf, how do we guarantee that the parent **TreeNode**'s appropriate child pointer is reset to 0? And how do we implement the destructor? The destructor some how must traverse the entire tree deleting all **TreeNodes**?

Methods of Binary Tree Traversal

Traversal means to visit each node of the binary tree. Binary trees can be traversed in several manners depending upon the requirements of the task. With a double linked list, traversal could be from the head sequentially to the end of the list or from the tail to the beginning of the list. However, a binary tree presents several different possibilities. Should ancestors be visited before the descendants or vice versa? Should siblings be visited from the right to the left or from the left to the right? There are three common traversal algorithms for binary trees.

Inorder Traversal

The **inorder** traversal method visits each node by first visiting all nodes in the left subtree of the root, then visit the root, and then visit all nodes in the right subtree. Of course, each subtree can be either nonexistent, a leaf or a subtree itself. Thus, the definition is actually a recursive one. One could define the recursive function as follows.

```
void BinaryTree::InorderTraversal (TreeNode* ptrNode) {
  if (ptrNode) {
    InorderTraversal (ptrNode->ptrLeftChild);
    Visit (ptrNode);
    InorderTraversal (ptrNode->ptrRightChild);
  }
}
```

The **Visit()** function would perform whatever action was needed. Examine Figure 14.6 again and find the bottom right tree with nodes labeled A to F. What would the inorder traversal produce? Assuming that **Visit()** displayed the letter of the node visited, the following represents the sequence followed.

D, B, E, A, F, C

The Preorder Traversal

The **preorder** traversal visits the node itself before visiting the left and then the right subtrees. One could define the recursive preorder traversal function as follows.

```
void BinaryTree::PreorderTraversal (TreeNode* ptrNode) {
  if (ptrNode) {
    Visit (ptrNode);
    PreorderTraversal (ptrNode->ptrLeftChild);
    PreorderTraversal (ptrNode->ptrRightChild);
  }
}
```

Look at the tree with nodes A-F in Figure 14.6 once more. Here is the preorder traversal order.

A, B, D, E, C, F

The Postorder Traversal

The **postorder** traversal visits the node itself after visiting both the left and then the right subtrees. One could define the recursive postorder traversal function as follows.

```
void BinaryTree::PostorderTraversal (TreeNode* ptrNode) {
  if (ptrNode) {
    PostorderTraversal (ptrNode->ptrLeftChild);
    PostorderTraversal (ptrNode->ptrRightChild);
    Visit (ptrNode);
  }
}
```

Look at the tree with nodes A-F in Figure 14.6 once more. Here is the postorder traversal order.

D, E, B, F, C, A

The ~BinaryTree() Function

Ok. So which of these traversal methods do we need to implement the class destructor whose task is to delete all of the dynamically allocated **TreeNode**s? A postorder traversal is needed because it guarantees that the actual node itself is visited last so that it is then safe to delete that node at that point. Here is how the destructor could be implemented.

```
BinaryTree::~BinaryTree () {
 DeleteAllNodes (ptrRoot);
}
void BinaryTree::DeleteAllNodes (TreeNode* ptrNode) {
 DeleteAllNodes (ptrNode->ptrLeftChild);
 DeleteAllNodes (ptrNode->ptrRightChild);
 delete ptrNode;
}
```

Binary Search Trees

A **binary search tree** is a specialized binary tree in which three additional properties hold true.
   A. No two nodes can contain the same user data value.
   B. The user data values have a means of determining the relations greater than and less than. This often means numeric data, but could also apply to string comparisons as well.
   C. The data value in every node in the tree is both greater than every data value in its left child subtree and less than every data value in its right side subtree.

With these criteria met, such binary trees are very useful for searching and for sorting operations. Because there are no duplicates, when a match is found, we can be certain we have the correct user data. Also, the actual matching algorithm can take advantage of the third rule. If we have a user value to find, we can compare it to that stored in the root of the tree. If the value we are to find is greater than that value in the root node, we know for certain that it lies only in the right child subtree, if it is there at all. Thus, we can rapidly traverse the tree to find the matching node.

For example, suppose that **TreeNode** was not storing **void** pointers to the client's data but rather was storing a **long** id number and the corresponding relative record number of that data in a direct access file. That is, suppose that it had been defined as follows.

```
struct TreeNode {
 long       id; // user key
 long       userRelativeRecordNumber;
 TreeNode* ptrLeftChild;
 TreeNode* ptrRightChild;
};
```

We could then implement a fast binary search of the tree for the matching item's relative record number as follows.
```
const int NoMatch = -1;
```

496

```
long BinaryTree::FindId (long matchKey) {
 TreeNode* ptrNode = ptrRoot;
 while (ptrNode && ptrNode->id != matchKey) {
 if (matchKey < ptrNode->id)
   ptrNode = ptrNode->ptrLeftChild;
 else
   ptrNode = ptrNode->ptrRightChild;
 }
 return ptrNode ? ptrNode->userRelativeRecordNumber : NoMatch;
}
```

The maximum number of iterations in the worst case would be the height of the binary tree. The worst case would occur when all nodes except a single bottom level leaf node contained only one child node. This is known as a **degenerate binary tree**. A search of a degenerate binary tree cannot ignore any nodes and thus must search all nodes. Similarly a binary tree with all nodes present is called a **full binary tree**. That is, if a tree has a height of N, then it has 2^N-1 nodes. It is a full binary tree. Finally, a **balanced tree** (sometimes called a **b-tree**) is nearly a full binary tree but does have a few scattered nodes that do not have two children. Many algorithms have been developed for b-tree processing. It is an extremely important type of tree widely used with data base processing. Figure 14.7 shows three binary search trees.

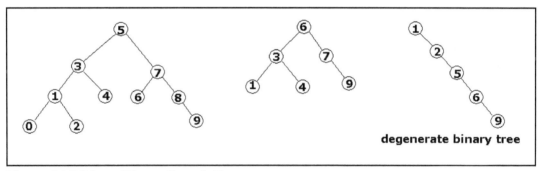

Figure 14.7 Three Binary Search Trees

However, inserting a new node into a full binary tree or a balanced tree requires some analysis. Before we tackle this more difficult problem, let's examine one last type of tree.

The Heap Tree

The C++ heap is that region of unused memory from which dynamic memory can allocate space. With trees, there is a specialized meaning. A **heap tree** is a complete binary tree in which the data stored in its nodes is arranged such that no child has a larger value than its parent. Figure 14.8 shows a heap tree. Notice that it is a binary tree but not a searchable binary tree since all of the right child nodes are not less than the parent node and all of the left child nodes are not greater than the parent.

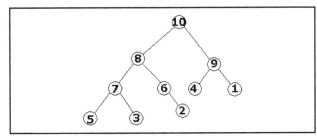

Figure 14.8 A Heap Tree

The heap type of tree can be used in sorting an array of items very quickly. In the above figure, the largest value of the integers is currently in the root node. If one saved that value in a temporary area and removed the value from the root node, one gets the situation shown in Figure 14.9.

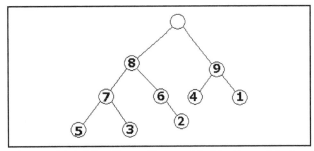

Figure 14.9 The Heap Tree with No Root Node

Next, the heap must be restructured as a binary tree. To replace the value in the empty root node, remove and use the value in the rightmost node at the lowest depth or height of the tree. In this case, it is the node containing the value of 2 since it is the rightmost node of nodes 5, 3, and 2. This yields the tree shown in Figure 14.10.

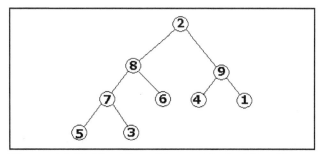

Figure 14.10 The Heap Tree with the New Root

Of course, the tree now does not satisfy the requirement that no child has a value greater than its parent. Obviously the two nodes containing the 8 and 9 are greater than the parent root node. Now a process called **Reheapify** or **RebuildHeapDownwards** must be done. This process consists of starting at the root and repeatedly exchanging its value with the larger value of its children until no more exchanges are possible. The reheapify process first compares the 2 to its two children, the 8 and 9, choosing the larger value, the 9. The 9 replaces the 2 and we get the results shown in Figure 14.11

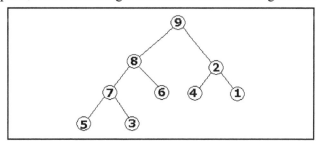

Figure 14.11 The Heap Tree After One Swap

The process must be recursive since now the node containing the value of 2 is not proper for a heap. So beginning with the new node containing the value 2, we find which of its children contain the larger value and swap once more. This yields the final reheapified tree shown in Figure 14.12.

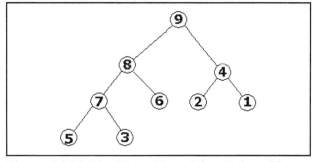

Figure 14.12 The Heap Tree After Reheapify

This process is implemented in the next chapter as a part of the fast executing sort known as the Heapsort. (See the function in **Pgm15a** called **RebuildHeapDownwards()**.) However, the ideas presented here for the heap tree can be utilized to solve the problem we are facing – how to actually build a binary search tree.

Building a Binary Search Tree

The real problem we must solve in order to make use of a binary search tree is how to load it in the first place. With a double linked list, we could call the **AddAtHead()**, **AddAtTail()**, **InsertBefore()**, or **InsertAfter()** functions to initially build the list say from a file of data. We need a similar mechanism to load the binary search tree. Suppose we call it the **InsertAnItem()** function. It can be implemented simply as follows.

```
bool BinaryTree::InsertAnItem (void* dataptr) {
 if (IsEmpty () ) {
  BuildRoot (dataptr);
   return true;
 }
 return Insert (ptrRoot, dataptr);
}
```

If the tree is empty, build the root node with this user item and return true, the insertion was successful. If there are items in the tree, we must find the location within the tree in which to store the new data. The **Insert()** function is a recursive function that locates where within the tree this item should be located and so places it there.

However, if this item is already in the tree, placing this new one, a duplicate, would violate the criteria for a binary search tree. Should this happen, **Insert()** must not add it but return **false** instead. Thus, one of the first actions of **Insert()** must be to compare this node's data with the data to be inserted. However, since the data is stored as a **void** pointer, a user call back function must be used, here called **Compare()**. Its prototype is

```
    int Compare (const void* ptrnodedata, const void* ptrnewdata);
```

If the two user data are equal, the function returns 0. If the node data is less than the new data, it should return a negative number. If the node data is larger than the new data, it should return a positive number.

So if the node pointer exists, then **Compare()** is called to determine the situation. If the new data is the same as an existing set, then the **Insert()** function returns **false**, ending the entire process. Otherwise, the **Insert()** function is recursively invoked passing this node's right or left child. If, however, the node is null, then this is the location for this entry. A new **TreeNode** is allocated and filled with the user data. Finally, notice that in order for us to be able to set the caller's right or left child pointer, the **Insert()** function must be passed a reference to that pointer. This is a crucial point. **ptrNode** is null, it is the contents of some node's left or right child pointer and that pointer must be set to point to the new node. It must be passed by reference.

```
bool BinaryTree::Insert (TreeNode*& ptrNode, void* dataptr) {
 if (ptrNode) {
  int retcd = Compare (ptrNode->ptrdata, dataptr);
  if (retcd == 0)
   return false;
  else if (retcd < 0)
   return Insert (ptrNode->ptrLeftChild, dataptr);
  else
   return Insert (ptrNode->ptrRightChild, dataptr);
 }
 else {
  ptrNode = new TreeNode;
  ptrNode->ptrData = dataptr;
  ptrNode->ptrRightChild = ptrNode->ptrLeftChild = 0;
  return true;
 }
}
```

Let's examine just how the **Insert()** function would insert data and build the tree, given several sets of input data. This is shown in Figure 14.13.

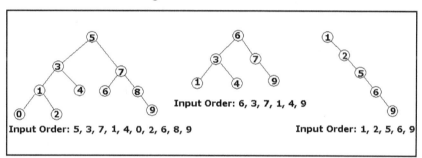

Figure 14.13 Insertion Order of Three Trees

The left two trees in Figure 14.13 look very nicely built. However, the tree shape is totally determined by the order of the input values. The rightmost tree in the figure shows what happens if the data is not input in the correct order to build a tree properly – it ends up a degenerate tree! Oops indeed. So the **Insert()** function works just fine if the data is already in the right order to build a proper tree. So we just have to educate the users to know how to determine the proper order to enter their data. Oh no! That would never do for at the very least, he/she would immediately ask you to write some kind of sorting program to get his/her data into the "proper" order **Insert()** requires.

If, however, the data values to be added to the tree are in random order, then very often the resulting tree built using the **Insert()** function is acceptable. Only if the data values are sorted into order does a degenerate tree result. In practice, the **Insert()** is reasonably acceptable practice. An advanced data structures course should continue from here and present methods for balancing the tree.

Determine the Height and the Number of Nodes in a Tree

To calculate the number of nodes in a tree, a recursive **CountNodes()** function can be used. Again, begin with a definition of the function. Assume the function is passed a **TreeNode** pointer.

A. If the **TreeNode** pointer is null, return 0 as the number of nodes.

B. Otherwise, return the sum of the number of nodes in the left child plus the number of nodes in the right child plus one for this node.

The recursive **CountNodes()** is called from the **GetNumberOfNodes()** function which passes it the root node with which to begin operations. Here is the simple coding.

```
long BinaryTree::GetNumberOfNodes () const {
 return CountNodes (ptrRoot);
}

long BinaryTree::CountNodes (TreeNode* ptrNode) const {
 return ptrNode ?
  CountNodes (ptrNode->ptrLeftChild) +
  CountNodes (ptrNode->ptrRightChild) + 1 : 0;
}
```

To find the height of a tree, we need to find the maximum height of the deepest leaves. Again, this can be done by using a recursive function. Assume the height of a null tree is 0; the height of only a root node is 1 and so on. The recursive definition of the **HeightOfNodes()** recursive function that is passed a **TreeNode** pointer is as follows.

A. If the **TreeNode** pointer is null, return 0 height.

B. Otherwise, return the maximum of the number of nodes in the left child branch of the tree and the number of nodes in the right child branch and add one more for this node itself.

The **HeightOfNodes()** function is called from the **GetHeightOfTree()** function which passes it the root pointer with which to start.

```
long BinaryTree::GetHeightOfTree () const {
 return HeightOfNodes (ptrRoot);
}
```

However, we need to write coding to find the maximum of the pair of return values from **HeightOfNodes()** of the left and right children. Rather than writing a function **max()**, I chose to code a simple C macro to do this.

```
#define max(a,b) (((a) > (b)) ? (a) : (b))

long BinaryTree::HeightOfNodes (TreeNode* ptrNode) const {
 if (ptrNode == 0)
  return 0;
 else
  return max (HeightOfNodes (ptrNode->ptrLeftChild),
            HeightOfNodes (ptrNode->ptrRightChild)) + 1;
}
```

Pgm14a – The BinaryTree Class and Tester Program

All of the details of binary trees that we have examined have been implemented in the **BinaryTree** class that follows. First, here is the definition of the **BinaryTree** class followed by its implementation. Notice that as usual, I have stored the user data with **void*** making the class reusable in many applications. Also notice that by making the assignment operator and the copy constructor protected functions, then client programs cannot copy a tree.

```
BinaryTree Class Definition

 1 #pragma once
 2
 3 /********************************************************************/
 4 /*                                                                  */
 5 /* BinaryTree: a class encapsulating Binary Trees                   */
 6 /*                                                                  */
 7 /********************************************************************/
 8
 9 /********************************************************************/
10 /*                                                                  */
11 /* TreeNode: contains the user data and two child pointers          */
12 /*                                                                  */
13 /********************************************************************/
14
15 struct TreeNode {
16   void*     ptrData;
17   TreeNode* ptrLeftChild;
18   TreeNode* ptrRightChild;
19 };
20
21 /********************************************************************/
22 /*                                                                  */
23 /* Call back functions required by the client application           */
24 /*                                                                  */
25 /********************************************************************/
26
27 typedef int (*FIND) (const void* ptrThis, const void* ptrToFind);
28 typedef int (*COMPARE) (const void* ptrnodedata,
29                         const void* ptrnewdata);
30 typedef void (*VISIT) (TreeNode* ptrNode);
31
32 /********************************************************************/
33 /*                                                                  */
34 /* BinaryTree class                                                 */
35 /*                                                                  */
36 /********************************************************************/
37
38 class BinaryTree {
```

```
39   protected:
40    TreeNode* ptrRoot; // pointer to the root node of the tree
41
42   public:
43             BinaryTree (); // construct the tree
44           ~BinaryTree (); // remove all nodes and destroy tree
45   protected:
46    void       DeleteAllNodes (TreeNode* ptrNode);
47
48   public:
49    bool       IsEmpty () const;          // returns true if empty
50    void       BuildRoot (void* dataptr); // builds the root node
51    TreeNode* GetRootNode () const;       // returns ptr to the root
52
53    // adds a new node at the specified location
54    void       AddNode (TreeNode*& ptrNode, void* dataptr);
55
56    // user access functions to get and set the data of a node
57    void*      GetNodeData (TreeNode* ptrNode) const;
58    void       SetNodeData (TreeNode* ptrNode, void* dataptr);
59
60    // user access functions to acquire ptrs to a node's children
61    TreeNode* GetLeftChild (TreeNode* ptrNode) const;
62    TreeNode* GetRightChild (TreeNode* ptrNode) const;
63
64             // returns true if this node is a leaf
65    bool       IsLeaf (TreeNode* ptrNode) const;
66
67             // manually delete a specific node
68    void       DeleteLeaf (TreeNode*& ptrNode);
69
70             // returns the number of nodes in the entire tree
71    long       GetNumberOfNodes () const;
72   protected:
73    long       CountNodes (TreeNode* ptrNode) const;
74
75   public:    // gets the height of the binary tree
76    long       GetHeightOfTree () const;
77   protected:
78    long       HeightOfNodes (TreeNode* ptrNode) const;
79
80   public:    // search tree for this data item
81             // caller must provide Find call back function
82             // returns 0 if not found or the user data ptr
83    void*      FindThisData (void* ptrDataToFind, FIND Find);
84
85    // three traversal functions to traverse the tree
86    // user must provide a Visit call back function
87    void       InorderTraversal (TreeNode* ptrNode, VISIT Visit);
88    void       PreorderTraversal (TreeNode* ptrNode, VISIT Visit);
```

```
 89   void          PostorderTraversal (TreeNode* ptrNode, VISIT Visit);
 90
 91   // inserts a new item into tree at the proper location
 92   // user must provide a Compare call back function
 93   // error displayed if item is already in the tree
 94   bool          InsertAnItem (void* dataptr, COMPARE Compare);
 95  protected:
 96   bool Insert(TreeNode*& ptrNode, void* dataptr,COMPARE Compare);
 97
 98   // class instances cannot be duplicated
 99   // disallow these operations
100   BinaryTree (const BinaryTree&) {} // copy ctor
101   BinaryTree& operator= (const BinaryTree&) {} //assignment op
102 };
103
```

```
BinaryTree Class Implementation
```

```
 1 #include <iostream>
 2 using namespace std;
 3
 4 #include "BinaryTree.h"
 5
 6 // max macro to return maximum of two values
 7 #define max(a,b) (((a) > (b)) ? (a) : (b))
 8
 9 /****************************************************************/
10 /*                                                            */
11 /* BinaryTree: initializes tree to null                       */
12 /*                                                            */
13 /****************************************************************/
14
15 BinaryTree::BinaryTree () {
16  ptrRoot = 0;
17 }
18
19 /****************************************************************/
20 /*                                                            */
21 /* IsEmpty: returns true if tree has no nodes at all          */
22 /*                                                            */
23 /****************************************************************/
24
25 bool BinaryTree::IsEmpty () const {
26  return ptrRoot ? false : true;
27 }
28
29 /****************************************************************/
30 /*                                                            */
31 /* BuildRoot: allocates the root node of the tree             */
```

```
32 /*                                                              */
33 /****************************************************************/
34
35 void BinaryTree::BuildRoot (void* dataptr) {
36  AddNode (ptrRoot, dataptr);
37 }
38
39 /****************************************************************/
40 /*                                                              */
41 /* GetRootNode: returns a pointer to the root node of the tree */
42 /*                                                              */
43 /****************************************************************/
44
45 TreeNode* BinaryTree::GetRootNode () const {
46  return ptrRoot;
47 }
48
49 /****************************************************************/
50 /*                                                              */
51 /* AddNode: allocates a new node storing user's data in it     */
52 /*                                                              */
53 /****************************************************************/
54
55 void BinaryTree::AddNode (TreeNode*& ptrNode, void* dataptr) {
56  ptrNode = new (std::nothrow) TreeNode;
57  if (!ptrNode) {
58   cerr << "AddNode - error out of memory\n";
59   exit (1);
60  }
61  ptrNode->ptrData = dataptr;
62  ptrNode->ptrLeftChild = ptrNode->ptrRightChild = 0;
63 }
64
65 /****************************************************************/
66 /*                                                              */
67 /* GetNodeData: returns a ptr to user data stored in this node */
68 /*                                                              */
69 /****************************************************************/
70
71 void* BinaryTree::GetNodeData (TreeNode* ptrNode) const {
72  return ptrNode ? ptrNode->ptrData : 0;
73 }
74
75 /****************************************************************/
76 /*                                                              */
77 /* SetNodeData: replaces the user data stored in this node     */
78 /*                                                              */
79 /****************************************************************/
80
81 void BinaryTree::SetNodeData (TreeNode* ptrNode, void* dataptr) {
```

```
82  if (ptrNode)
83    ptrNode->ptrData = dataptr;
84  }
85
86  /*****************************************************************/
87  /*                                                             */
88  /* GetLeftChild: returns ptr to this node's left child node    */
89  /*                                                             */
90  /*****************************************************************/
91
92  TreeNode* BinaryTree::GetLeftChild (TreeNode* ptrNode) const {
93    return ptrNode ? ptrNode->ptrLeftChild : 0;
94  }
95
96  /*****************************************************************/
97  /*                                                             */
98  /* GetRightChild: returns ptr to this node's right child node  */
99  /*                                                             */
100 /*****************************************************************/
101
102 TreeNode* BinaryTree::GetRightChild (TreeNode* ptrNode) const {
103   return ptrNode ? ptrNode->ptrRightChild : 0;
104 }
105
106 /*****************************************************************/
107 /*                                                             */
108 /* IsLeaf: returns true if this node is a leaf - no child nodes*/
109 /*                                                             */
110 /*****************************************************************/
111
112 bool BinaryTree::IsLeaf (TreeNode* ptrNode) const {
113   return ptrNode ? (ptrNode->ptrLeftChild == 0 &&
114    ptrNode->ptrRightChild == 0 ? true : false) : false;
115 }
116
117 /*****************************************************************/
118 /*                                                             */
119 /* DeleteLeaf: removes this node only                          */
120 /*             does not delete user data                      */
121 /*             does not delete child nodes                    */
122 /*                                                             */
123 /*****************************************************************/
124
125 void BinaryTree::DeleteLeaf (TreeNode*& ptrNode) {
126   if (!ptrNode) return;
127   delete ptrNode;
128   ptrNode = 0;
129 }
130
131 /*****************************************************************/
```

```
132 /*                                                                    */
133 /* GetNumberOfNodes: returns the total number of nodes in tree */
134 /*                                                                    */
135 /********************************************************************/
136
137 long BinaryTree::GetNumberOfNodes () const {
138  return CountNodes (ptrRoot);
139 }
140
141 /********************************************************************/
142 /*                                                                    */
143 /* CountNodes: recursive protected function to count nodes     */
144 /*                                                                    */
145 /********************************************************************/
146
147 long BinaryTree::CountNodes (TreeNode* ptrNode) const {
148  return ptrNode ?
149   CountNodes (ptrNode->ptrLeftChild) +
150   CountNodes (ptrNode->ptrRightChild) + 1 : 0;
151 }
152
153 /********************************************************************/
154 /*                                                                    */
155 /* GetHeightOfTree: returns the total height of the tree      */
156 /*                                                                    */
157 /********************************************************************/
158
159 long BinaryTree::GetHeightOfTree () const {
160  return HeightOfNodes (ptrRoot);
161 }
162
163 /********************************************************************/
164 /*                                                                    */
165 /* HeightOfNodes: recursive protected function to get node's ht*/
166 /*                                                                    */
167 /********************************************************************/
168
169 long BinaryTree::HeightOfNodes (TreeNode* ptrNode) const {
170  if (ptrNode == 0)
171   return 0;
172  else
173   return max (HeightOfNodes (ptrNode->ptrLeftChild),
174            HeightOfNodes (ptrNode->ptrRightChild)) + 1;
175 }
176
177 /********************************************************************/
178 /*                                                                    */
179 /* FindThisData: search tree to find this user item          */
180 /*    requires Find call back user function                  */
181 /*    returns the user data pointer of matching item         */
```

508

```
182 /*            or 0 if not found                          */
183 /*                                                        */
184 /**********************************************************/
185
186 void* BinaryTree::FindThisData (void* ptrDataToFind, FIND Find) {
187  int retcd;
188  TreeNode* ptrNode = ptrRoot;
189  while (ptrNode &&
190         (retcd = Find (ptrNode->ptrData, ptrDataToFind)) != 0) {
191  if (retcd < 0)
192    ptrNode = ptrNode->ptrLeftChild;
193  else
194    ptrNode = ptrNode->ptrRightChild;
195  }
196  return ptrNode ? ptrNode->ptrData : 0;
197 }
198
199 /**********************************************************/
200 /*                                                        */
201 /* ~BinaryTree: deletes all nodes and the tree            */
202 /*              Note: does not delete the contained user data */
203 /*                                                        */
204 /**********************************************************/
205
206 BinaryTree::~BinaryTree () {
207    DeleteAllNodes (ptrRoot);
208 }
209
210 /**********************************************************/
211 /*                                                        */
212 /* DeleteAllNodes: recursive function to delete all nodes */
213 /*                                                        */
214 /**********************************************************/
215
216 void BinaryTree::DeleteAllNodes (TreeNode* ptrNode) {
217  if (!ptrNode) return;
218  DeleteAllNodes (ptrNode->ptrLeftChild);
219  DeleteAllNodes (ptrNode->ptrRightChild);
220  delete ptrNode;
221 }
222
223 /**********************************************************/
224 /*                                                        */
225 /* InorderTraversal: traverses the tree inorder method    */
226 /*                   requires Visit user call back function */
227 /*                                                        */
228 /**********************************************************/
229
230 void BinaryTree::InorderTraversal (TreeNode* ptrNode,
231                                    VISIT Visit) {
```

```
232   if (ptrNode) {
233     InorderTraversal (ptrNode->ptrLeftChild, Visit);
234     Visit (ptrNode);
235     InorderTraversal (ptrNode->ptrRightChild, Visit);
236   }
237 }
238
239 /******************************************************************/
240 /*                                                              */
241 /* PreorderTraversal: traverses the tree preorder method        */
242 /*                    requires Visit user call back function     */
243 /*                                                              */
244 /******************************************************************/
245
246 void BinaryTree::PreorderTraversal (TreeNode* ptrNode,
247                                     VISIT Visit) {
248   if (ptrNode) {
249     Visit (ptrNode);
250     PreorderTraversal (ptrNode->ptrLeftChild, Visit);
251     PreorderTraversal (ptrNode->ptrRightChild, Visit);
252   }
253 }
254
255 /******************************************************************/
256 /*                                                              */
257 /* PostorderTraversal: traverses tree postorder method          */
258 /*                     requires Visit user call back function    */
259 /*                                                              */
260 /******************************************************************/
261
262 void BinaryTree::PostorderTraversal (TreeNode* ptrNode,
263                                      VISIT Visit) {
264   if (ptrNode) {
265     PostorderTraversal (ptrNode->ptrLeftChild, Visit);
266     PostorderTraversal (ptrNode->ptrRightChild, Visit);
267     Visit (ptrNode);
268   }
269 }
270
271 /******************************************************************/
272 /*                                                              */
273 /* InsertAnItem: inserts user item in proper location in tree   */
274 /*                                                              */
275 /******************************************************************/
276
277 bool BinaryTree::InsertAnItem (void* dataptr, COMPARE Compare) {
278   if (IsEmpty () ) {
279     BuildRoot (dataptr);
280     return true;
281   }
```

```
282   return Insert (ptrRoot, dataptr, Compare);
283 }
284
285 /*****************************************************************/
286 /*                                                             */
287 /* Insert: recursive function to find proper location of the   */
288 /*         insertion and to insert this new item there         */
289 /*                                                             */
290 /*****************************************************************/
291
292 bool BinaryTree::Insert (TreeNode*& ptrNode, void* dataptr,
293                          COMPARE Compare) {
294  if (ptrNode) {
295   int retcd = Compare (ptrNode->ptrData, dataptr);
296   if (retcd == 0)
297    return false;
298   else if (retcd < 0)
299    Insert (ptrNode->ptrLeftChild, dataptr, Compare);
300   else
301    Insert (ptrNode->ptrRightChild, dataptr, Compare);
302  }
303  else {
304   ptrNode = new (std::nothrow) TreeNode;
305   if (!ptrNode) {
306    cerr << "AddNode - error out of memory\n";
307    exit (1);
308   }
309   ptrNode->ptrData = dataptr;
310   ptrNode->ptrRightChild = ptrNode->ptrLeftChild = 0;
311  }
312  return true;
313 }
```

Now we need a tester program to test all of these functions. **Pgm14a.cpp** defines two 10-element arrays of integers that are used to build the trees. The first set yields a uniform binary tree but the second, which is in sorted order, yields a degenerate binary tree. Most of the coding is very straight forward. The only tricky coding is that that is required to produce the graphical display of the tree. First, examine the basic coding and the output from the program. Second, examine how the graphical display appears in the output. Then, after the listings, let's examine how that graphical listing is produced and its limitations.

```
Pgm14a - Tester of BinaryTree Class

 1 #include <iostream>
 2 #include <strstream>
 3 #include <iomanip>
 4 using namespace std;
 5 #include <crtdbg.h>
 6
```

```
 7 #include "BinaryTree.h"
 8
 9 /**************************************************************/
10 /*                                                          */
11 /* Pgm14a: BinaryTree tester program                        */
12 /*                                                          */
13 /**************************************************************/
14
15 // array bounds for graphical display of tree
16 const int ROWS = 20;
17 const int COLS = 61;
18
19 // needed call back functions
20 int  Compare (const void* ptrnodedata, const void* ptrnewdata);
21 void Visit (TreeNode* ptrNode);
22 int  Find (const void* ptrThis, const void* ptrToFind);
23
24 // functions to provide a graphical display of the tree
25 void InsertValue (int x, char msg[][COLS], int row, int col);
26 void DisplayGraphicalTree (BinaryTree& tree);
27 int  DisplayGraphNode (TreeNode* ptrNode, char msg[][COLS],
28                        int row, int col);
29
30
31 int main () {
32  // two arrays of integers to use to build the trees
33  int testNumbers[10] = {5, 3, 7, 1, 4, 0, 2, 6, 8, 9};
34  int testNumbers2[10] = {0, 1, 2, 3, 4, 5, 6, 7, 8, 9};
35  int i;
36  {
37   BinaryTree tree;
38   cout << "Number of Nodes (should be 0): "
39        << tree.GetNumberOfNodes () << endl;
40   cout << "Height of Empty Tree (should be 0): "
41        << tree.GetHeightOfTree () << endl;
42
43   // add 10 integers to the tree
44   for (i=0; i<10; i++) {
45    tree.InsertAnItem (&testNumbers[i], Compare);
46   }
47   cout << "Number of Nodes: "
48        << tree.GetNumberOfNodes () << endl;
49   cout << "Height of Tree: " << tree.GetHeightOfTree () << endl;
50   // test the three traversals
51   cout << "Inorder Traversal: ";
52   tree.InorderTraversal (tree.GetRootNode(), Visit);
53   cout << "\nPreorder Traversal: ";
54   tree.PreorderTraversal (tree.GetRootNode(), Visit);
55   cout << "\nPostorder Traversal: ";
56   tree.PostorderTraversal (tree.GetRootNode(), Visit);
```

```
57    cout << endl;
58    // make a graphical display of the tree
59    DisplayGraphicalTree (tree);
60    int findThis = 2;
61    void* ptrfound = tree.FindThisData (&findThis, Find);
62    if (!ptrfound) {
63     cout << "Find Error: should have found 2 in the tree\n";
64    }
65    else {
66     int* ptrd = (int*) ptrfound;
67     cout << "Find 2 succeeded and found " << *ptrd << endl;
68    }
69    findThis = 42;
70    ptrfound = tree.FindThisData (&findThis, Find);
71    if (!ptrfound) {
72     cout << "Find: correct - could not find 42 in the tree\n";
73    }
74    else {
75     int* ptrd = (int*) ptrfound;
76     cout << "Find Error looking for 42 and found "
77          << *ptrd << endl;
78    }
79
80
81    cout << endl << endl;
82    // make the second tree from the sorted integer array
83    BinaryTree tree2;
84    for (i=0; i<10; i++) {
85     tree2.InsertAnItem (&testNumbers2[i], Compare);
86    }
87    cout << "Number of Nodes: "
88          << tree2.GetNumberOfNodes () << endl;
89    cout << "Height of Tree: " << tree2.GetHeightOfTree () << endl;
90    cout << "Inorder Traversal: ";
91    tree2.InorderTraversal (tree2.GetRootNode(), Visit);
92    cout << "\nPreorder Traversal: ";
93    tree2.PreorderTraversal (tree2.GetRootNode(), Visit);
94    cout << "\nPostorder Traversal: ";
95    tree2.PostorderTraversal (tree2.GetRootNode(), Visit);
96    cout << endl;
97    DisplayGraphicalTree (tree2);
98   }
99
100  if (_CrtDumpMemoryLeaks())
101   cout << "\nOops! Memory Leaks!!\n";
102  else
103   cout << "\nNo Memory Leaks\n";
104  return 0;
105 }
106
```

```
107 /***************************************************************/
108 /*                                                             */
109 /* Compare: call back function to compare this node's data to  */
110 /*          the new data being inserted into the tree          */
111 /*                                                             */
112 /***************************************************************/
113
114 int Compare (const void* ptrnodedata, const void* ptrnewdata) {
115   // build intelligent pointers from the void pointers
116   int* ptrNodeData = (int*) ptrnodedata;
117   int* ptrNewData = (int*) ptrnewdata;
118   // check the three cases
119   if (*ptrNodeData == *ptrNewData)
120     return 0;
121   if (*ptrNodeData > *ptrNewData)
122     return -1;
123   else
124     return 1;
125 }
126
127 /***************************************************************/
128 /*                                                             */
129 /* Visit: call back function displays user data from traversal */
130 /*                                                             */
131 /***************************************************************/
132
133 void Visit (TreeNode* ptrNode) {
134   // display the integer being stored in this node
135   int* ptrx = (int*) ptrNode->ptrData;
136   cout << *ptrx << "   ";
137 }
138
139 /***************************************************************/
140 /*                                                             */
141 /* Find: call back function to see if this node is a match     */
142 /*                                                             */
143 /***************************************************************/
144
145 int  Find (const void* ptrThis, const void* ptrToFind) {
146   int* ptrthis = (int*) ptrThis;
147   int* ptrfind = (int*) ptrToFind;
148   if (*ptrthis == *ptrfind)
149     return 0;
150   else if (*ptrfind < *ptrthis)
151     return -1;
152   return 1;
153 }
154
155 /***************************************************************/
156 /*                                                             */
```

```
157 /* DisplayGraphicalTree: make a graphical display of the tree  */
158 /*                                                              */
159 /***************************************************************/
160
161 void DisplayGraphicalTree (BinaryTree& tree) {
162  int numRows = tree.GetNumberOfNodes();
163  if (numRows > ROWS) {
164   cerr << "DisplayGraphicalTree: Increase the number"
165        << " of ROWS in the display strings from "
166        << ROWS << " to " << numRows << endl;
167   return;
168  }
169  // simple array of strings - one node per line - init to blanks
170  char msg[ROWS][COLS];
171  int i, j;
172  for (i=0; i<ROWS; i++) {
173   for (j=0; j<COLS-1; j++)
174    msg[i][j] = ' ';
175   msg[i][COLS-1] = 0;
176  }
177
178  TreeNode* ptrNode = tree.GetRootNode();
179  if (!ptrNode) return;
180  i = 0;
181  j = 1;
182  DisplayGraphNode (ptrNode, msg, i, j);
183
184  // now display all the filled up lines
185  for (i=0; i<numRows; i++) {
186   cout << msg[i] << endl;
187  }
188 }
189
190 /***************************************************************/
191 /*                                                              */
192 /* DisplayGraphNode: displays one node's worth of info         */
193 /*                                                              */
194 /***************************************************************/
195
196 int DisplayGraphNode (TreeNode* ptrNode, char msg[][COLS],
197                       int row, int col) {
198  int ct = 0;
199  if (!ptrNode) return 0;
200  int i = row;
201  int j = col;
202  int* ptrd = (int*) ptrNode->ptrData;
203  // display this node's integer
204  InsertValue (*ptrd, msg, i, j);
205  ct++;
206  i++;
```

```
207  unsigned char c;
208  // display all left children
209  if (ptrNode->ptrLeftChild) {
210   // insert proper graphic depending on whether or not there is a
211   // right child
212   c = ptrNode->ptrRightChild ? 195 : 192;
213   msg[i][j] = c;
214   msg[i][j+1] = (char) 196;
215   msg[i][j+2] = (char) 196;
216   msg[i][j+3] = (char) 196;
217   int num =DisplayGraphNode(ptrNode->ptrLeftChild, msg, i, j+4);
218   ct += num;
219   // insert needed number of | lines
220   for (int k=0; k<num; k++) {
221    i++;
222    msg[i][j] = (char) 179;
223   }
224  }
225  // display all right children
226  if (ptrNode->ptrRightChild) {
227   c = 192;
228   msg[i][j] = c;
229   msg[i][j+1] = (char) 196;
230   msg[i][j+2] = (char) 196;
231   msg[i][j+3] = (char) 196;
232   int num =DisplayGraphNode(ptrNode->ptrRightChild, msg, i, j+4);
233   ct += num;
234  }
235  return ct;
236 }
237
238 /****************************************************************/
239 /*                                                              */
240 /*  InsertValue: stores the integer into the mgs string        */
241 /*                                                              */
242 /****************************************************************/
243
244 void InsertValue (int x, char msg[][COLS], int row, int col) {
245  char val[10];
246  ostrstream os (val, sizeof (val));
247  os << setw(2) << x << ends;
248  msg[row][col] = val[1];
249  msg[row][col-1] = val[0];
250 }
```

```
Output of Pgm14a - Tester of BinaryTree Class

  1 Number of Nodes (should be 0): 0
  2 Height of Empty Tree (should be 0): 0
```

```
 3 Number of Nodes: 10
 4 Height of Tree: 4
 5 Inorder Traversal: 0  1  2  3  4  5  6  7  8  9
 6 Preorder Traversal: 5  3  1  0  2  4  7  6  8  9
 7 Postorder Traversal: 0  2  1  4  3  6  9  8  7  5
 8 5
 9 ├── 3
10 │   ├── 1
11 │   │   ├── 0
12 │   │   └── 2
13 │   └── 4
14 └── 7
15     ├── 6
16     └── 8
17         └── 9
18 Find 2 succeeded and found 2
19 Find: correct - could not find 42 in the tree
20
21
22 Number of Nodes: 10
23 Height of Tree: 10
24 Inorder Traversal: 0  1  2  3  4  5  6  7  8  9
25 Preorder Traversal: 0  1  2  3  4  5  6  7  8  9
26 Postorder Traversal: 9  8  7  6  5  4  3  2  1  0
27 0
28 └── 1
29     └── 2
30         └── 3
31             └── 4
32                 └── 5
33                     └── 6
34                         └── 7
35                             └── 8
36                                 └── 9
37
38 No Memory Leaks
```

The graphical display of the tree is just a quick and dirty approach to showing the nodes. I needed a fast way to visually verify that the nodes I had intended to be built were in fact being built. There is nothing rigorous about the solution and it is limited. The approach is to define an array of strings sufficiently large enough to hold all of the needed lines. Since one node's value is placed on one line, the number of lines is actually given by the number of nodes in the tree. Rather than dynamically allocating an array of strings, I chose to use a fixed sized array:

```
char msg[ROWS][COLS];
```

where ROWS is 20 and COLS is 61. I do display an error message if more than 20 rows are needed.

The lowest level function, **InsertValue()** is given the integer to display, the array of strings, and the row and column subscripts of the destination location within the array. It inserts the two-digit number into

517

the correct two characters of the array of strings.

DisplayGraphicalTree() gets the number of rows needed, in other words, the number of nodes and aborts if it exceeds 20. Next it fills the 20 strings with blanks and inserts the null terminator. It calls the recursive function **DisplayGraphNode()** passing it the root node and the coordinates for the first node's integer, row 0, column 1. When the recursive function has finished, the proper number of strings or lines are then displayed to **cout**.

DisplayGraphNode() does nothing if this is a null node. Otherwise, it begins by displaying the integer value it is storing. Next, it must determine if there are any left child nodes. If so, it must figure out which graphic character to display: a "tee" or an "L" depending on whether or not there is also a right child node present or not. It then inserts into the correct line the "tee" or "L" character and three "-" characters. Then, it can call itself passing the left child node pointer. Notice that it increases the column subscript by 4 to account for the graphics already inserted.

```
int num =DisplayGraphNode(ptrNode->ptrLeftChild, msg, i, j+4);
```

The **DisplayGraphNode()** function returns the number of rows in which it has inserted data. This number is then used to control how many vertical "|" characters are also inserted in those lines, forming the connector from the parent node. Finally, if the right child node exists, the four graphics characters are inserted, an "L" and three "-" and the function calls itself passing the right child node. When everything is done, it returns the total number of lines in which insertions are made. The previous invocation then uses this number to insert the outer graphics characters providing the connections between nodes.

While the method is crude, it makes it easy to verify that the correct node structure has been created. Next, we need to utilize the **BinaryTree** class in an application.

Pgm14b—the Account Inquiry Application
Loading a Binary Search Tree from a Sorted ISAM Index File

One usage of binary search trees is to find records in a database or master file. In this example, I reuse the simple accounting record example we utilized in the binary files chapter. Acme Credit Corporation stores their account records in a binary master file. The key id field that is used to directly access a specific record is the client's social security number. An ISAM index, whose entries contain the client's key and the relative record number, has been created to allow direct access to the records. Here is the definition of both the master records and the index records.

```
Accounts.h Definition File

 1 #ifndef ACCOUNTH
 2 #define ACCOUNTH
 3
 4 const int NAMELEN = 31;
 5
 6 // the data base records
 7 struct AccountRec {
 8   long    ssno;         // social security number = key id field
 9   char    name[NAMELEN]; // customer name
10   double creditLimit;   // limit of credit on this account
11   double balance;       // current account balance
12 };
13
14 // the index records to allow direct access to accounts
15 struct IndexRec {
16   long ssno;        // social security number = key id field
17   long relRecNum; // corresponding relative record number on disk
18 };
19
20 #endif
```

The objective is to write an inquiry program – that is, given a client's social security number, the program displays that client's account information. Realistically, this program would display a menu prompting the operator to enter a client's social security number. Then, it would display the corresponding accounting data for that person or an error message and then wait for another look up request. However, because our emphasis is on how to build and use a binary search tree to find the records, I have made a batch file of these requests and will just have the program display the results in a columnarly aligned report.

For best results, the binary search tree should be as balanced as possible among its nodes. The incoming index records are sorted into increasing social security number order. If we just add each entry to the binary tree as it is input from the index file, the resulting tree would be degenerate, each key is larger than the previous and would be added to the right side of the node above it. In this case, any tree search would degenerate into a sequential search of keys. So the real problem we face is how to easily and quickly load a sorted set of values into a binary search tree such that it is fairly well balanced. In the actual index data file, I have 32 entries.

Suppose that I sequentially number each node and leaf beginning with 1, where 1 represents the first index record in the index file. Our desired tree should look like figure 14.14.

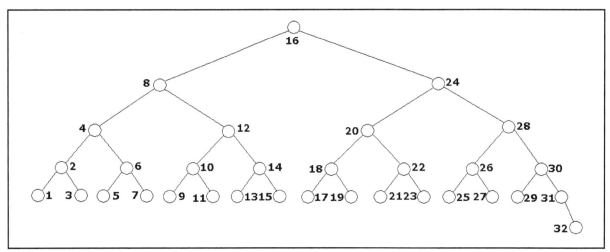

Figure 14.14 The Desired Binary Tree of 32 Index Records

This is our ideal binary search tree whose data values are **void** pointers to **IndexRec** instances containing the social security numbers and corresponding relative record numbers. There are several interesting points to note about this tree structure, given the numbering scheme I used. Notice that all nodes immediately above the bottom leaves have a number that is evenly divisible by two, ignoring leaf 32. Further, the nodes directly above those are also evenly divisible by 4. The two nodes above them are also evenly divisible by 8. This yields a crucial principle that we can exploit.

Rule: in a complete binary search tree whose nodes are numbered in sequence beginning with 1, each node is exactly as many levels above the leaves as the highest power of two that divides its number.

Since we must input the actual index data file, assume that the entire array of index records has been input into an array in memory and that we also know the exact number of items in the array with which to populate the tree. Further, theses index records are sorted into increasing social security number order. Given these facts and the rule above, a really simple algorithm immediately appears. Suppose that we choose the element in the middle of the array and use that item as the root of the tree. Numbering the elements beginning at 1 instead of 0, let **N** be the one in the middle. Now which elements should become the left and right children of this first node? If we let **factor** represent **N/2**, then the left child would be **N-factor** while the right child is given by **N+factor**. (The actual index of these is always 1 less, of course.)

Ok. Once these two children have been added, what would be the left and right children of the root's left node at **N/2-factor**? This new **factor** would be the previous **factor/2** or **(N/2)/2**. For example, if there were 31 index records, numbered from 1 to 32, then the root would be 16 and its left and right children would be 8 and 24. The left and right children of 8 would be 4 and 12, while the left and right children of 24 would be 20 and 28. What would the left and right children of the node at 4 be? 2 and 6. And finally, what would they be for the node at 2? 1 and 3. This is ideal for a recursive function, **Add()**.

Beginning Data Structures in C++

The recursive **Add()** function is given the array of index records and the maximum number in that array along with the current node, and the values for **N** and **factor**. It calculates the numbers for the left and right child nodes – **N-factor** and **N+factor**. It then adds those two new nodes into the tree. Finally, the function would call itself twice, once to fill its left node and once to fill its right node. For the left node call, it passes **(N-factor)** as the new left **N** and **factor/2** as the new factor. For the right node call, it passes **(N+factor)** and **factor/2**.

Of course, the actual subscripts are always one less than these **N** values. Certainly we must guard against a subscript becoming less than zero and greater than or equal to the maximum number of elements. But what about the recursion ending condition? When we are adding the left and right children of node number 2, **factor** is 1, yielding node 1 and 3. The new **factor** is now 0, or 1/2. This is the ending condition, when **factor** is less than 1.

Of course, this process is not going to add every element if the number of elements in the array does not form a perfectly balanced binary tree. We cannot force every tree to have 3, 7, 15, 31 and so on number of elements. So we also need some final addition method for the extra leaves.

The problem of the extra leaves is not trivial or easily solved with our basic data structure's theory. In advanced data structures, there are other forms of trees that handle just such situations. These routines are often called "balancing the tree." Here we need something fool proof and very easy to implement. Remember that the tree nodes are storing **void** pointers to the index records. To add a new node, I allocate a new **IndexRec** structure and copy the correct index array structure element into this new instance and link the new instance into the tree. Thus, once the data has been copied from the index array into the new node instance, I no longer need that array instance. So I chose to replace the social security number in that used array instance with a unique value, a -1. When the node addition process is finished, we only need to loop through the index array looking for social security numbers that are not -1. Those few that are found can be added to the tree using the normal **AddNode()** function which places them into the correct position in the tree. There will only be a few of these to add in any case so the process is not going to be time-consuming at all.

Here is the output of Pgm14b which reads a transactions file of clients to find and display. I actually requested that each client in the file to be found for debugging purposes. Also, I adapted the graphic display to also show us the resultant tree. Notice the location of the 32nd node on the bottom right of the far right node. I also requested the program find three clients that are not in the data base – one that would appear before the very first social security number, one that would be after the last one in the file, and one number that would be located somewhere in the middle of the tree if it were present.

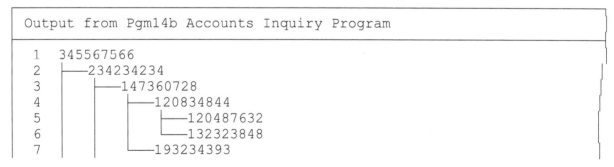

```
Output from Pgm14b Accounts Inquiry Program

  1   345567566
  2   ├──234234234
  3   │   ├──147360728
  4   │   │   ├──120834844
  5   │   │   │   ├──120487632
  6   │   │   │   └──132323848
  7   │   │   └──193234393
```

521

```
 8                    ┌──173763483
 9                    └──193293934
10          └──289784744
11              ┌──280482793
12              │   ┌──237473650
13              │   └──289573072
14              └──333937457
15                  ┌──333333333
16                  └──343455545
17      └──645343545
18          ┌──376360873
19          │   ┌──348893489
20          │   │   ┌──345994595
21          │   │   └──349672503
22          │   └──482874743
23          │       ┌──384720984
24          │       └──545564665
25          └──894378238
26              ┌──838747653
27              │   ┌──745645534
28              │   └──892893298
29              └──934887474
30                  ┌──898932833
31                  └──943847344
32                      └──958274873
33
34                  Acme Credit Inquiry
35
36  ID Number   Customer Name                    Limit     Balance
37
38  333333333   Annie Jones                    5000.00     2500.00
39  343455545   Tom Jones                      9000.00     5000.00
40  345567566   Betsy Smyth                   10500.00     6700.00
41  545564665   Henry Jasper                   6700.00     5344.50
42  645343545   William Smith                  7500.00     5555.55
43  745645534   Thomas Albert                  4500.00     4300.00
44  234234234   Lola L. Lorraine               5500.00     5000.00
45  193234393   Jeremie Jones                  4500.00     4242.42
46  943847344   Sam Spade                      5500.00     5432.11
47  345994595   Larime Smith                   6500.00     4500.00
48  934887474   Jerome Jones                   7000.00     6500.00
49  173763483   Ally Shows                     4500.00     4000.00
50  894378238   B. B. Jones                    5500.00     5323.50
51  120834844   DJ Smith                       6000.00     5400.00
52  898932833   Lou Anne Jones                 8000.00     7400.00
53  193293934   Albert Smith                   6800.00     4500.00
54  348893489   Thomas Thoms                   1500.00     1000.00
55  838747653   Bertha Bottles                 3500.00     2500.00
56  958274873   Ruth Smithe                    5500.00     4368.55
57  132323848   Lenard Jones                   8000.00     4568.47
```

```
58 892893298   Louis Louie                    9000.00    8888.88
59 333937457   Nancy Smith                   10500.00    9999.99
60 237473650   Mertle Jones                  11000.00   10000.00
61 280482793   Frodo Backwater                9500.00    8888.50
62 482874743   Hank Albert                    5800.00    4800.00
63 147360728   Cecil Smith                    8700.00    7777.77
64 349672503   Larime Jones                   9700.00    8877.55
65 289573072   Herbert Smith                  7800.00    7788.99
66 384720984   Frank Jones                    5600.00    5555.55
67 120487632   Sammy Smith                    6500.00    5600.00
68 289784744   Doc Smith                      7800.00    7744.11
69 376360873   Lea Ann Jones                  8900.00    8765.42
70 Error: 444444444 is not in the master file
71 Error: 1111 is not in the master file
72 Error: 999999999 is not in the master file
73
74 No Memory Leaks
75 Press any key to continu
```

Here is the coding for the **Pgm14b**. For brevity, I have not shown the very slightly modified coding for the graphic display of the tree. The **BinaryTree** class is identical to that in **Pgm14a**. Please study the coding to build the binary tree.

```
Pgm14b - Accounts ISAM File Inquiry Program Using Binary Search Tree

 1 #include <iostream>
 2 #include <iomanip>
 3 #include <fstream>
 4 #include <strstream>
 5 using namespace std;
 6 #include <crtdbg.h>
 7
 8 #include "Account.h"
 9 #include "BinaryTree.h"
10
11 const int ROWS = 50;
12 const int COLS = 79;
13
14 // functions to build the index tree
15 void BuildTree (BinaryTree& tree);
16 void Add (IndexRec* irec, long maxRecs, TreeNode*& ptrParent,
17           long N, long factor);
18 int  Compare (const void* ptrnodedata, const void* ptrnewdata);
19
20 // cleanup action
21 void DeleteVisit (TreeNode* ptrNode);
22
23 // perform the set of inquiries
24 void ProcessInquiries (BinaryTree& tree);
```

```
25 int  Find (const void* ptrThis, const void* ptrToFind);
26
27 // functions to provide a graphical display of the tree
28 void InsertValue (long x, char msg[][COLS], int row, int col);
29 void DisplayGraphicalTree (BinaryTree& tree);
30 int  DisplayGraphNode (TreeNode* ptrNode, char msg[][COLS],
31                        int row, int col);
32
33 /**************************************************************/
34 /*                                                            */
35 /* Pgm14b: Accounts data base Inquiry with ISAM and binary tree*/
36 /*                                                            */
37 /**************************************************************/
38
39 int main () {
40  {
41  BinaryTree index;
42
43  BuildTree (index); // load index into a binary search tree
44
45  DisplayGraphicalTree (index); // debug display the tree
46
47  ProcessInquiries (index); // process all inquiries
48
49  // remove all user data from tree prior to destruction
50  index.InorderTraversal (index.GetRootNode (), DeleteVisit);
51  }
52
53  if (_CrtDumpMemoryLeaks ())
54   cout << "\nOops! Memory Leaks!!\n";
55  else
56   cout << "\nNo Memory Leaks\n";
57
58  return 0;
59 }
60
61 /**************************************************************/
62 /*                                                            */
63 /* BuildTree: convert an IndexRec array into a binary tree    */
64 /*            the array is sorted into increasing ssno (key)  */
65 /*            order                                           */
66 /*                                                            */
67 /**************************************************************/
68
69 void BuildTree (BinaryTree& tree) {
70  // open the Index file
71  ifstream index ("Accounts.idx",
72                  ios::in | ios::binary);
73  if (!index) {
74   cerr << "Error: cannot open Accounts.idx file\n";
```

```
 75    exit (1);
 76  }
 77
 78    // get the total file size and thus the number of records in it
 79    index.seekg (0, ios::end);
 80    long maxRecs = index.tellg () / sizeof (IndexRec);
 81    index.seekg (0, ios::beg);
 82
 83    if (maxRecs < 1) { // if no records, quit, nothing to do
 84      index.close();
 85      return;
 86    }
 87
 88    // allocate an array of Index records to hold them
 89    IndexRec* irec = new (std::nothrow) IndexRec [maxRecs];
 90    if (!irec) {
 91      cerr << "Error: out of memory\n";
 92      exit (2);
 93    }
 94
 95    // input the entire sorted ISAM index
 96    index.read ((char*) irec, maxRecs * sizeof (IndexRec));
 97    index.close ();
 98
 99    // get the middle element as the root node
100    long N = (maxRecs + 1) / 2;
101    long rootIdx = N - 1;              // the subscript of root node
102    // create a new Index rec
103    IndexRec* ptri = new (std::nothrow) IndexRec;
104    if (!ptri) {
105      cerr << "Error: out of memory\n";
106      exit (2);
107    }
108    *ptri = irec[rootIdx];            // copy this one into new one
109    irec[rootIdx].ssno = -1;          // mark this one as used
110    tree.BuildRoot (ptri);            // set this one as the root node
111
112    TreeNode* ptrNode = tree.GetRootNode ();
113
114    long factor = N / 2; // calc the +- factor to get to next nodes
115
116    // add in both left and right children recursively
117    Add (irec, maxRecs, ptrNode, N, factor);
118
119    // now manually add in all those entries not yet in nodes
120    for (long i=0; i<maxRecs; i++) {
121      if (irec[i].ssno != -1) {
122        IndexRec* ptri = new (std::nothrow) IndexRec;
123        if (!ptri) {
124          cerr << "Error: out of memory\n";
```

```
125     exit (2);
126     }
127     *ptri = irec[i];
128     tree.InsertAnItem (ptri, Compare);
129     }
130   }
131
132   delete [] irec; // and remove the index array
133 }
134
135 /********************************************************************/
136 /*                                                                  */
137 /* Add: add the left and right nodes to this node                   */
138 /*                                                                  */
139 /********************************************************************/
140
141 void Add (IndexRec* irec, long maxRecs, TreeNode*& ptrParent,
142           long N, long factor) {
143   long lIdx = N - factor - 1; // index of the left irec to add
144   long rIdx = N + factor - 1; // index of the right irec to add
145   TreeNode* ptrNode;
146   IndexRec* ptri;
147   // add the left index record at iLdx if it is 0 or above
148   if (lIdx >= 0) {
149    ptrNode = new (std::nothrow) TreeNode;
150    if (!ptrNode) {
151     cerr << "Error: out of memory\n";
152     exit (2);
153    }
154    ptrParent->ptrLeftChild = ptrNode;
155    ptri = new (std::nothrow) IndexRec;
156    if (!ptri) {
157     cerr << "Error: out of memory\n";
158     exit (2);
159    }
160    *ptri = irec[lIdx];
161    irec[lIdx].ssno = -1;    // mark this index record as used
162    ptrNode->ptrData = ptri;
163    ptrNode->ptrLeftChild = ptrNode->ptrRightChild = 0;
164   }
165   // add the right index record at rIdx if it is < max in array
166   if (rIdx < maxRecs) {
167    ptrNode = new (std::nothrow) TreeNode;
168    if (!ptrNode) {
169     cerr << "Error: out of memory\n";
170     exit (2);
171    }
172    ptrParent->ptrRightChild = ptrNode;
173    ptri = new (std::nothrow) IndexRec;
174    if (!ptri) {
```

```
175    cerr << "Error: out of memory\n";
176    exit (2);
177   }
178   *ptri = irec[rIdx];
179   irec[rIdx].ssno = -1;     // mark this index record as used
180   ptrNode->ptrData = ptri;
181   ptrNode->ptrLeftChild = ptrNode->ptrRightChild = 0;
182  }
183  // calculate next left and right node locations
184  long newLN = N - factor;
185  long newRN = N + factor;
186  // calculate the reduced gap size for the next pair of nodes
187  long newfactor = factor / 2;
188  if (newfactor == 0)
189   return; // no more nodes left
190  // recurively add left and right children of this node
191  if (newLN >= 0)
192   Add (irec, maxRecs, ptrParent->ptrLeftChild, newLN, newfactor);
193  if (newRN < maxRecs)
194   Add (irec, maxRecs, ptrParent->ptrRightChild, newRN,newfactor);
195 }
196
197 /****************************************************************/
198 /*                                                            */
199 /* Compare: call back function to match this ssno with that in */
200 /*          the passed tree node in order to find correct      */
201 /*          location in the tree at which to add this one      */
202 /*                                                            */
203 /****************************************************************/
204
205 int Compare (const void* ptrnodedata, const void* ptrnewdata) {
206  // build intelligent pointers from the void pointers
207  IndexRec* ptrNodeData = (IndexRec*) ptrnodedata;
208  IndexRec* ptrNewData = (IndexRec*) ptrnewdata;
209  // check the three cases
210  if (ptrNodeData->ssno == ptrNewData->ssno)
211   return 0;
212  if (ptrNodeData->ssno > ptrNewData->ssno)
213   return -1;
214  else
215   return 1;
216 }
217
218 /****************************************************************/
219 /*                                                            */
220 /* DeleteVisit: remove this tree node's index data            */
221 /*                                                            */
222 /****************************************************************/
223
224 void DeleteVisit (TreeNode* ptrNode) {
```

```
225   IndexRec* ptri = (IndexRec*) ptrNode->ptrData;
226   delete ptri;
227 }
228
229 /****************************************************************/
230 /*                                                            */
231 /* ProcessInquiries: Display account info for customer requests*/
232 /*                                                            */
233 /****************************************************************/
234
235 void ProcessInquiries (BinaryTree& tree) {
236  // open master data base binary file
237  ifstream master ("Accounts.dat",
238                      ios::in | ios::binary);
239  if (!master) {
240   cerr << "Error: cannot open Accounts.dat\n";
241   exit (3);
242  }
243
244  // open the inquiries transactions file
245  // normally, this would really be some kind of real time menu
246  // driven process
247  ifstream trans ("Inquiries.txt", ios::in);
248  if (!trans) {
249   cerr << "Error: cannot open Inquiries.txt\n";
250   master.close ();
251   exit (4);
252  }
253
254  // set up for dollars and cents and display headings
255  cout.setf (ios::fixed, ios::floatfield);
256  cout << setprecision (2);
257  cout << endl << "                     Acme Credit Inquiry\n\n"
258       << "ID Number  Customer Name                    Limit"
259       << "    Balance\n\n";
260
261  IndexRec* ptrirec;
262  AccountRec arec;
263  long findId;
264  while (trans >> findId) { // for all requests,
265   // find their relative record number from the Index tree
266   ptrirec = (IndexRec*) (tree.FindThisData (&findId, Find));
267
268   if (!ptrirec) { // invalid ssno
269    cout << "Error: " << findId << " is not in the master file\n";
270   }
271   else {
272    // find the file offset of this account
273    long offset = sizeof (AccountRec) * ptrirec->relRecNum;
274    master.seekg (offset, ios::beg);
```

528

```
275    // input this account
276    master.read ((char*) &arec, sizeof (arec));
277    // display this account
278    cout << setw (9) << arec.ssno << "  ";
279    cout.setf (ios::left, ios::adjustfield);
280    cout << setw (30) << arec.name;
281    cout.setf (ios::right, ios::adjustfield);
282    cout << "  " << setw (8) << arec.creditLimit
283        << "  " << setw (8) << arec.balance << endl;
284    }
285  }
286  trans.close ();
287  master.close ();
288  }
289
290  /******************************************************************/
291  /*                                                                */
292  /* Find: call back function to match ssno to index in tree        */
293  /*                                                                */
294  /******************************************************************/
295
296  int  Find (const void* ptrThis, const void* ptrToFind) {
297  long* ptrthis = (long*) ptrToFind;
298  IndexRec* ptri = (IndexRec*) ptrThis;
299  if (ptri->ssno == *ptrthis)
300   return 0;
301  if (ptri->ssno > *ptrthis)
302   return -1;
303  return 1;
304  }
305
306  /******************************************************************/
307  /*                                                                */
308  /* DisplayGraphicalTree: make a graphical display of the tree     */
309  /*                                                                */
310  /******************************************************************/
... nothing changed here on down from the previous version
```

Once you are satisfied that you understand the build tree coding, examine how the tree is deleted. Remember that it is storing **void** pointers to index records. When the class destructor is called, all of the tree nodes are deleted. But how do we get the index records that we allocated deleted? Before the destructor **~BinaryTree()** is called at line 51, the end block, I called one of the traversal methods. Each node is then visited with our call back function, **DeleteVisit()**, being passed each instance found. Here is where I delete them.

Multiple Projects in the Same Workspace

How did the original ISAM master file and index get created in the first place? I had to write a short program to input a text file of client data and write it to the binary master file. I had to create the corresponding index records and sort them and write the index file. Since the initial build program and Pgm14b are so closely related, I chose to have them in the same workspace.

To add additional projects to the same workspace, when you choose Add New Project, instead of making a new project folder, click the "Add to current workspace" radio button. I chose to have the additional project in a separate subfolder from Pgm14b. Thus, I needed to manually copy the two master binary files that were built from the subfolder to the main Pgm14b folder. Likewise, I copied the Account.h header file as well. The project workspace appears as shown in Figure 14.15.

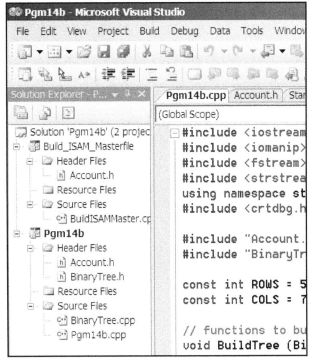

Figure 14.15 Projects in the Same Workspace

Only one of the projects can be the current project that is compiled and debugged. Which one is the current one is selected using the menu choice Project – Set as Startup Project – and selecting which is to be the current project. Also, selecting the project in the Solution Explorer window will also switch the active project.

Review Questions

1. Why is a tree a nonlinear data structure?

2. Give an example of a tree structure not mentioned in the text.

3. What is the difference between the root of a tree and a node of a tree and a leaf of a tree?

4. In Figure 14.4, what letter does the root node contain? What letters do the siblings of node B contain? What are the children of node I? What node is the parent of K?

5. What are the heights of the three trees shown in Figure 14.1?

6. Draw a Venn diagram of the bottom right tree shown in Figure 14.6 which contains nodes A through F.

7. What is meant by an N-ary tree?

8. What is a binary tree? How is it different from a general tree?

9. Describe the difference between an inorder, postorder, and preorder tree traversals?

10. What is a binary search tree? How is it different from a binary tree? What is the difference between a full binary tree and a balanced tree? What is a degenerate binary tree?

11. What is a heap tree? How is it different from a binary search tree?

12. Describe how a new node is added to a binary tree?

Stop! Do These Exercises Before Programming

1. The Acme Corporation programmer has been given a new programming assignment – the team leader of the Folder Tree Project. You, of course, have been assigned to his team of programmers. The task is to create a **FolderTree** class to encapsulate the directory tree structure of a disk drive. The root node contains the Drive's root folder. For example, it might be the string "D:\" or "C:\". There can be zero, one or more folders beneath the root folder and each of these can have any number of child folders as well. Thus, a general tree form is to be used.

       Assume the following directory layout.

D:\

    Testing
            GroupA
            GroupB
    Production
            Daily
            Weekly
            Monthly

Then the tree contains the root folder with two children and the first child node also contains two children while the other child of the root contains three of its own. The data to be stored in a node is the character string folder name. When allocating a new tree node, dynamically allocate memory for the string and copy the passed folder name into the new string. The destructor and any node deletion functions should delete the node's character string. In other words, the nodes are not storing **void** pointers but character strings.

       Our programmer has decided that to handle the varying number of child nodes beneath any given node a single linked list should be used. Here is his start of the **FolderTree** class definition.

```
#ifndef FOLDERTREEH
#define FOLDERTREEH

struct TreeNode {
 char*      folder;
 TreeNode* fwdptr;   // points fwd to next child in linst
 TreeNode* ptrChild; // head pointer of a linked list of children
};

/******************************************************************/
/*                                                                */
/* Call back functions required by the client application         */
/*                                                                */
/******************************************************************/

typedef int (*FIND) (const char* string, const char* findString);
typedef int (*COMPARE) (const char* nodeString,
                        const char* newString);
typedef void (*VISIT) (TreeNode* ptrNode);

class FolderTree {
```

```
protected:
  TreeNode* ptrRoot; // pointer to the root node of the tree

public:
             FolderTree (); // construct the tree
            ~FolderTree (); // destroy tree
protected:
    void       DeleteAllNodes (TreeNode* ptrNode);

public:
    bool       IsEmpty () const;
    void       BuildRoot (const char* string);
    TreeNode*  GetRootNode () const;

    // adds a new node at the specified location
    void       AddNode (TreeNode*& ptrNode,
                        const char* newString);

    // user access functions to get a node's folder string
    char*      GetNodeData (TreeNode* ptrNode) const;

    void       DeleteLeaf (TreeNode*& ptrNode);

public:    // search tree for this data item
           // caller must provide Find call back function
           // returns 0 if not found or the user folder string
const char* FindThisFolder (const char* findString, FIND Find);

   // three traversal functions to traverse the tree
   // user must provide a Visit call back function
   void       InorderTraversal (TreeNode* ptrNode, VISIT Visit);
   void       PreorderTraversal (TreeNode* ptrNode, VISIT Visit);
   void       PostorderTraversal (TreeNode* ptrNode, VISIT Visit);

   // class instances cannot be duplicated
   // disallow these operations
   FolderTree (const FolderTree&) {} // copy ctor
   FolderTree& operator= (const FolderTree&) {} //assignment op
};

#endif
```

Our programmer has implemented the easy functions as follows.

```
FolderTree::FolderTree () {
 ptrRoot = 0;
}

FolderTree::~FolderTree () {
 DeleteAllNodes (ptrRoot);
}
```

```
bool FolderTree::IsEmpty () const {
 return ptrRoot ? false : true;
}

void FolderTree::BuildRoot (const char* string) {
 ptrRoot = new TreeNode;
 ptrRoot->folder = new char [strlen(string)];
 strcpy (ptrRoot->folder, string);
 ptrRoot->ptrChild = ptrRoot->fwdptr = 0;
}

TreeNode* FolderTree::GetRootNode () const {
 return ptrRoot;
}

void FolderTree::AddNode (TreeNode*& ptrNode,
                          const char* newString) {
 ptrNode = new TreeNode;
 ptrNode->folder = new char [strlen(newString)];
 strcpy (ptrNode->folder, newString);
 ptrNode->ptrChild = ptrNode->fwdptr = 0;
}

char* FolderTree::GetNodeData (TreeNode* ptrNode) const {
 return ptrNode->folder;
}

void FolderTree::DeleteLeaf (TreeNode*& ptrNode) {
 delete folder;
 delete ptrNode;
 ptrNode = 0;
}
```

As usual, the coding has many problems with it. Correct the syntax and logical errors thus far. He explains that at the root node, the **ptrChild** points to the first child folder of the root and **fwdptr** is 0. Following that pointer chain to the child of the root, the **fwdptr** points to the next child of the root or is 0 if there are no more. If this child of the root has children in turn, then its **ptrChild** points to the first of its children.

2. Since you have been instrumental in fixing the beginning coding, our programmer assigns you the task of implementing the **FindThisFolder()** function.

```
// search tree for this data item
// caller must provide Find call back function
// returns 0 if not found or the user folder string
const char* FolderTree::FindThisFolder (const char* findString,
                                         FIND Find) {

}
```

534

3. Next, you are assigned to write the **DeleteAllNodes()** function.
```
void FolderTree::DeleteAllNodes (TreeNode* ptrNode) {


}
```

4. Next, you are assigned to write the **InorderTraversal()** function. Our programmer has decided that means you should traverse the siblings first and then their children and then this node.
```
void FolderTree::InorderTraversal (TreeNode* ptrNode,
                                   VISIT Visit) {


}
```

5. With your excellent work on the first of the traversal functions completed, our programmer assigns the other traversal functions to the junior programmer on the team, asking him to emulate your implementation. He then embarks on the far more important function to build the tree from the folder structure on a given disk drive. He sketches out the coding to visit all folders on the drive, indicating where new nodes must be allocated. You are assigned to implement the tree portion where indicated in the following coding.
```
void FolderTree::BuildTreeFromDisk (const char* driveString) {
 if (strlen (driveString) == 0) {
  cerr << "Error: no folder to remove\n";
  return 0;
 }
 BuildRoot (driveString);
 AddChildren (ptrRoot, driveString);
}

void FolderTree::AddChildren (TreeNode*& ptrNode,
                              const char* folderString) {
 char mdir[_MAX_PATH];
 strcpy (mdir, folderString);
 // guatantee no trailing backslash
 if (mdir[strlen(mdir)-1] == '\\') mdir[strlen(mdir)-1] = 0;

 long hFind;          // used by _findxxx functions
 _finddata_t fd;      // filled in by _findxxx functions
 char idir[_MAX_PATH]; // the search string with *.* appended
 strcpy (idir, mdir);
 strcat (idir, "\\*.*");
 // attempt to find the first entry in this folder
 if ((hFind = _findfirst (idir, &fd)) == -1L )
  return ct; // failed, so abort
 // for each file found in this folder,
 // check its file attributes - is it a subdir
 // then if so, bypass . and .. system entries
 do {
  if (fd.attrib & _A_SUBDIR) { // is it a subdir?
   if (fd.name[0] != '.') {    // yes, is it not . or ..
```

```
    // here add a new child to the ptrNode
    // whose name is fd.name);

    char xdir[_MAX_PATH];       // yes, so remove
    strcpy (xdir, mdir);        // anything under it
    strcat (xdir, "\\");
    strcat (xdir, fd.name);

    // now add all children of this folder to the new folder
    AddChildren (ptrNode->????, xdir);
   }
  }
} while (_findnext (hFind, &fd) == 0);
// repeat for all files in the folder

// now close the find operation
_findclose (hFind);
}
```

Programming Problems

Problem Pgm14-1 The Binary Formula Evaluator Program

The add, subtract, multiply, and divide operators are binary in nature. If an expression is written like this
>A + B

then a binary tree can be created with the operator+ in the root node and A and B in the left and right child nodes. Thus, the following tree represents this expression.

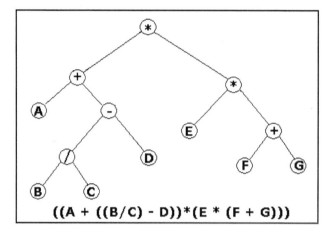

$$((A + ((B/C) - D))*(E * (F + G)))$$

Write a program that prompts the user to input an equation in the above format using uppercase letters A through G. From that equation, construct a binary tree to store the expressions as shown in the above figure. Then prompt the user for numerical values of the doubles A through G. Then, using the binary expression tree, evaluate the formula.

The user must always use the seven variables, A-G. Thoroughly test the program. Hint: a stack can be very useful in backtracking.

Problem Pgm14-2 The Artificial Intelligence Learning Program

This program is a classic artificial intelligence program; it learns new things by asking yes/no questions. The program uses a binary tree structure as its main data structure. All nodes which are not leaves contain a question that can be answered yes or no. The children of this node are either subtrees or leaves. The left child is contains the no results, while the right node contains the yes result. If it is a leaf, then it contains the object or answer. If it is a subtree, it contains a refining yes/no question. For example, the root question might be, "Is this object considered to be living or alive?" If the answer is "No", then the left node might have the question "Is this object in the animal kingdom?" However, if the answer had been yes, then the right child might contain the computer's guess, "a Rock."

Initially, construct the binary tree with the following questions and objects.
Root: Is this object considered to be living or alive?"

No
>   rock
Yes
>   Is this object in the animal kingdom?
>   No
>   tree
>   Yes
>   Does it have legs?
>   No
>   fish
>   Yes
>   person

When the program begins, display the following message to the player.

```
Welcome to the teach your computer game. I am here to learn from you. You
think of an object and I will ask you some questions that can be answered
yes or no and based on your reply, I will guess your object. Please think
of an object. When you are ready, answer my first question.

Question: Is your object considered to be living or alive? Enter y or n
__
```

The general format is
Question: <u>question from the tree node</u>? enter y or n __

Suppose the user enters n for the first question. The program should display the following.
Is your object a/an tree? Enter y or n _
where the format is
Is your object a/an <u>item from leaf</u>? Enter y or n _

Now if the user replies with 'y', then display the following message.
```
Great! See how smart your computer is becoming? Do you want to continue?
If so, think of another object and enter y. If you want to quit, enter
n. Enter y or n __
```

However, if the user replies with 'n', then display the following message.
`What object were you thinking of?` And after inputting the object, ask
`Now specify a yes/no question which if answered yes would be your object
but if no would be my object.` And input the user's question. Add the question and the two answers into the binary tree at the correct position. Finally, display the following. `Do you want to continue? If so, think of another object and enter y. If you want to quit, enter n. Enter y or n __`

Accept y or n in either upper or lower case. If the yes/no entry is not valid, display an error message and get a new yes/no response. Thoroughly test your program.

538

Problem Pgm14-3 Loading and Saving an Artificial Intelligence Tree

Familiarize yourself with the specifications of **Pgm14-2** above. In this problem, you are to design two **BinaryTree** member functions, **LoadTree()** and **SaveTree()**, that load the binary artificial intelligence tree as used in **Pgm14-2** or save the tree to a disk file. Devise some method to easily store the data in a text file. If you have written **Pgm14-2**, modify it to test your load and save operations. If not, modify the graphical display functions used in the sample programs **Pgm14a** and **Pgm14b** to display your resultant tree.

Chapter 15—Sorting Algorithms

Introduction

Sorting refers to rearranging all elements in an array or in a set of records on disk or some unordered collection of keys into some kind of order, either ascending or descending on some value. For instance, sorting an array of cost records might be done based on the item number. Or it might be sorted into alphabetical order based on the product description. Or it might be sorted into increasing quantity purchased. Or it might be sorted into increasing total order cost. Sorting an array of phone numbers would likely be done in increasing numerical order. If one had an ISAM data base, one would need to sort the index table's keys into increasing key value order. Wherever one looks in the data processing industry, sorting can be found.

Many different algorithms exist for sorting items into order. The problem of sorting has captivated the attention of theoretical computer scientists over the years. As a result, much is now known about the efficiency of different approaches to sorting. Sometimes an approach works well on arrays in memory, but is terrible when it is used to sort large arrays stored on disk. Some methods work fast on totally unsorted data. Other methods work drastically faster when most of the data is already in sorted order and only one or a few elements are out of order - such as the problem of adding a new key into a sorted array of keys.

Within the business industry, for those companies that use main frames, sorting can be a very important and vital process. One national insurance company spends nearly 25% of all of its processing time each month sorting its insurance records in various ways in order to produce all of its needed reports. When one has 26 million records to sort, any sorting method that can do the job fast is highly desired and sought after. On the PC side, if a company's server has a large data base that must be sorted, similar considerations apply.

Indeed, various sorting packages are readily available for both the main frame and PC computer environments. And a company, which has a lot of data to sort, generally purchases just such a package. So why do we need to study sorting algorithms if, in reality, one would just purchase a package to handle it for us?

We are studying the sorting methods just to make the theoreticians at the four-year universities happy. No, just kidding. Familiarity with the performance characteristics of various sorting methods may be of value to you in selecting a sorting technique that is well-matched to your company's needs. A proficient software engineer must be able to know how to choose the best available methods to solve a problem. Additionally, one ought to have an intuitive feel for the execution speed of alternative blocks of coding that accomplish the same task.

The theoreticians have developed a complex set of mathematics to describe and discuss the relative efficiencies of the various sorting algorithms. However, my experience has shown that the average student at our junior college does not yet have a sufficient math background to understand or follow these discussions. Thus, this chapter will not be presenting the complex mathematical discussions that are often found with texts on sorting.

Beginning Data Structures in C++

This chapter will present various common sorting algorithms and examine their relative efficiencies, their strengths and weaknesses. As we study these methods, let's also see if we can get an approximation of how fast the approaches will perform their task. This information can easily be applied to gaining an understanding of how other non-sorting loops and methods will perform.

The Straight Selection Sort

The straight selection sort is one of the easiest sorting methods for a beginner to remember and be able to code. It makes repeated passes through the array from top to bottom. On the initial pass, it finds the smallest element in the array and places it in the topmost element of the array. This is shown in the next two figures, Figure 15.1 and 15.2.

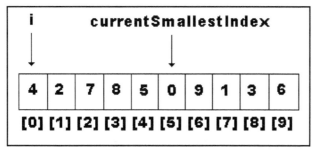

Figure 15.1 Straight Selection Sort Pass 1

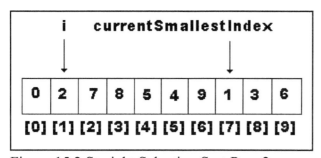

Figure 15.2 Straight Selection Sort Pass 2

On the next pass, it finds the next smallest and places it in the second element of the array and so on. It can also be done in reverse, that is, place initially the largest value in the last element of the array. Then, look through the remaining elements and place the next largest into the next to the last position and on up to the top. It gets its name from the idea that it is selecting the next largest or smallest element and placing it where it belongs. Here is the coding for the straight selection sort which is sorting an array of **count** integers.

```
void StraightSelectionSort (int array[], long count) {
  long currentSmallestIndex; // stores idx of current smallest one
  int  temp;
  long j, k;
  // outer loop traverses all elements except the last one
  for (j=0; j<count-1; j++) {
```

```
// assume that the current j contains the smallest value
currentSmallestIndex = j;
// inner loop traverses all elements below j looking for the
// next smallest one - notice we avoid swapping each time a
// smaller one is found - just keep track of its index
for (k=j+1; k<count; k++) {
 if (array[k] < array[currentSmallestIndex])
  currentSmallestIndex = k;
}
// now see if the new smallest one is in the correct position
if (currentSmallestIndex != j) {
 // no, so one time only, swap the smallest into the correct
 // position in the array
 temp = array[j];
 array[j] = array[currentSmallestIndex];
 array[currentSmallestIndex] = temp;
 }
 }
}
```

Now let's analyze this coding and see what we can determine about its performance characteristics. How many times does the outer loop execute? It is done **count-1** times. How many times is the inner loop performed? Well, the first time, it is done **count-1** times, then **count-2**, then **count-3**. This yields the total number of inner loop iterations as approximately **count**^{2} times.

Sorting algorithms are often analyzed for two separate measures:
> 1. The number of times two array elements are compared.
> 2. The number of times two array elements are swapped or moved.

With the straight selection sort, the number of comparisons is about **count**^{2} and the maximum number of swaps is about **count**. Of course, if the array was already in sorted order, there would be no swaps at all. Notice that the number of comparisons is independent of the actual state of the data values. If the array was already mostly in the correct order, the same number of comparisons must be done, **count**^{2}. Thus, an important consideration with this approach is that, independent of the data values, we are always going to do **count**^{2} comparisons.

The Bubble Sort

The bubble sort makes repeated passes through the elements. However, each time it finds a consecutive pair of elements out of order, it swaps them into the correct order. At the end of the first traversal of the array, the largest value has been bubbled all the way to the bottom of the array. Thus, the second pass does not need to go all the way to the bottom, just to the next to the last element. This is illustrated in the next seven figures. Notice how the '9' is bubbled on down into its final resting place.

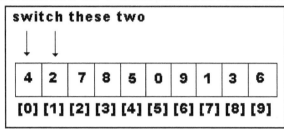

Figure 15.3 Bubble Sort - Step 1

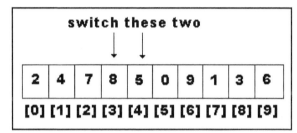

Figure 15.4 Bubble Sort - Step 2

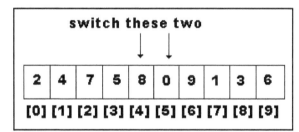

Figure 15.5 Bubble Sort - Step 3

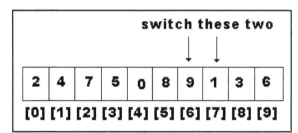

Figure 15.6 Bubble Sort - Step 4

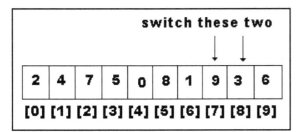

Figure 15.7 Bubble Sort - Step 5

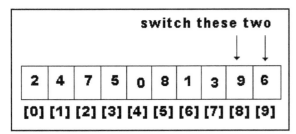

Figure 15.8 Bubble Sort - Step 6

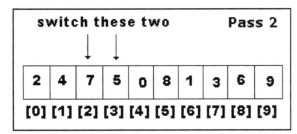

Figure 15.9 Bubble Sort - Step 7

```
void BubbleSort (int array[], int count) {
 int  temp;
 long j;
 long lastSwapIndex;         // the idx of the last one swapped
 long bottomIdx = count - 1; // the current ending idx

 while (bottomIdx > 0) { // repeat until only the top idx is left
  lastSwapIndex = 0;
  // rearrange all elements to current bottom
  for (j=0; j<bottomIdx; j++) {
   if (array[j] > array[j+1]) {
    // swap these two into increasing order
    temp = array[j];
    array[j] = array[j+1];
    array[j+1] = temp;
    lastSwapIndex = j; // reset the last idx swapped
   }
  }
```

```
    // since several lower ones might already be in increasing
    // order, we may not need to further check these - thus,
    // reposition bottom accordingly
    bottomIdx = lastSwapIndex;
  }
}
```

Notice that the bubble sort makes **count-1** total passes through the array independent of the original ordering of that data. In other words, even if the array was already in the correct order, it still makes **count-1** passes to determine this fact. In such a case, **lastSwapIndex** remains at 0 because nothing got swapped. Thus, **bottomIdx** ends up at 0 after one full pass and the while loop terminates then. So the best case scenario is if the data is already sorted into order. In this case, **count-1** comparisons are done and no swaps are done.

What would be the worst case for a bubble sort? If all the values were in descending order, then everyone would have to be swapped repeatedly to bubble the largest to the bottom and so on. Again we have the result that in the worst case, the bubble sort would need **count^2** swaps and **count^2** comparisons.

The Quicksort Method

The Quicksort algorithm was created by the British computer scientist C.A.R. Hoare. It is the method that the C built-in library **qsort()** function utilizes. This method uses recursion to sort the array. Quicksort partitions the array into two sub arrays in which all elements of one sub array are greater than all the elements in the other sub array. Then it recursively calls itself to partition each sub array into two more sub arrays in which all elements in one half are greater than the other. It continues to recursively call itself on these new partitions until the array is sorted.

Since recursion is involved, we should begin by making a recursive definition of the solution. The function prototype is

```
    void Quicksort (int array[], long lowIndex, long highIndex);
```
Our definition is
if there are no items or one item to sort, return - we are done
if there are two items to sort then
  swap them if needed and return done
else do the following
  rearrange the array so that all values in array[lowIndex through midIndex-1] are
    less than all values in array[midIndex through highIndex]
  Quicksort the array from lowIndex to midIndex-1
  Quicksort the array from midIndex to highIndex
  return done

The tricky part of the coding is actually the rearranging of the array into two pieces such that all values in the lower portion are less than those in the upper portion. On the initial pass, **lowIndex** is index 0 and **highIndex** is **count-1**. The method to partition into two pieces requires choosing an array value to be the **pivot** value. One portion will then contain all elements whose values are greater than this pivot value and the other portion contains all those values that are less than or equal to this **pivot** value. For best results, we should choose for the **pivot** value the element in the array that lies in the middle of the range from **lowIndex** to **highIndex**. And we then swap that **pivot** value into the array at **lowIndex**. This is shown in Figure 15.10.

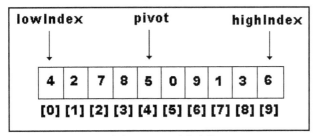

Figure 15.10 Quicksort - Initial Setup

Given this starting point, here is the coding down to this point.

```
void QuickSort (int array[], long count, long lowIndex,
                long highIndex) {
 int  pivot;
 int  temp;
 long lowSwapIndex;
 long highSwapIndex;

 if (lowIndex >= highIndex) // 0 or 1 item to sort, we are done
  return;

 if ((highIndex - lowIndex) == 1) { // only two items to sort
  if (array[lowIndex] > array[highIndex]) { // we must swap them
   temp = array[lowIndex];
   array[lowIndex] = array[highIndex];
   array[highIndex] = temp;
  }
  return;
 }

 // here we have 3 or more items to swap
 // pick the value in the middle to be the pivot value for the
 // dividing vlaue between the two portions
 long mid = (lowIndex + highIndex) / 2;
 pivot = array[mid];
 // and swap this value into lowIndex postion
 array[mid] = array[lowIndex];
 array[lowIndex] = pivot;
```

The next figure, 15.11, shows the situation after we have placed the '5' into element 0.

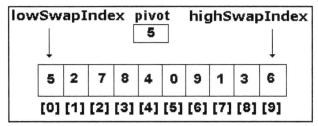

Figure 15.1 Quicksort - Ready for the First Loop

Now we set up a **lowSwapIndex** to point to the next element at index 1, and a **highSwapIndex** set to the right bounds, index 9. The first half pass, we continue checking until the **lowSwapIndex** increases to beyond the **highSwapIndex** and as long as each element pointed to by **lowSwapIndex** belongs in this half, that is, is less than or equal to the **pivot** value. At index 1, 2 is smaller than 5, so we continue. At index 2, the 7 is not, so the first loop ends with **lowSwapIndex** pointing to index 2; this element does not belong in the lower half partition.

The next loop begins at a **highSwapIndex** of 9 and continues as long as the value there is greater than the pivot element of 5. When **highSwapIndex** id decremented to 9, the array element of 3 is not greater than the **pivot** element and thus this element does not belong in the higher portion. This is shown in Figure 15.12.

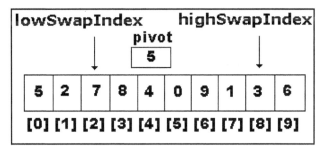

Figure 15.12 Quicksort - End of Inner Loops

```
// divide into two portions in which one portion's array values
// are all greater than the pivot value and the other one's
// values are all <= to it
lowSwapIndex = lowIndex + 1;
highSwapIndex = highIndex;
do {
 while (lowSwapIndex <= highSwapIndex &&
         array[lowSwapIndex] <= pivot) {
  lowSwapIndex++;
 }
 while (array[highSwapIndex] > pivot) {
  highSwapIndex--;
 }
```

Beginning Data Structures in C++

Since the two swap indexes have not yet crossed, we need to swap the two array elements to get them into their correct portions of the two halves of the array.

```
if (lowSwapIndex < highSwapIndex) {
  // here we have encountered an array value that belongs in the
  // other partition, so we must swap these two array values to
  // get them into the correct portions
  temp = array[lowSwapIndex];
  array[lowSwapIndex] = array[highSwapIndex];
  array[highSwapIndex] = temp;
}
```

Here is what the array looks like once the swap is completed. We now repeat the entire loop because the two swap indexes have not yet crossed. This is shown in Figure 15.13.

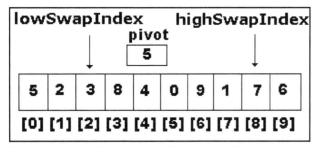

Figure 15.13 Quicksort - Swapping Values

```
  // and repeat the process until these two points cross
} while (lowSwapIndex < highSwapIndex);
```

When the two inner loops end this time, **lowSwapIndex** is at element 3 whose value of 8 is larger than the **pivot** of 5. The **highSwapIndex** is at element 7 whose value of 1 is less than the **pivot** of 5. Once again, we swap these two array values to get them into their respective portions and is shown in Figure 15.14.

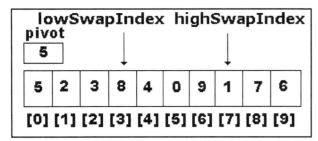

Figure 15.14 Quicksort - Second Swap

The results are shown in the next figure. Since the two swap indexes have not yet crossed, we continue the two inner loops again. This time they cross before finding their respective elements.

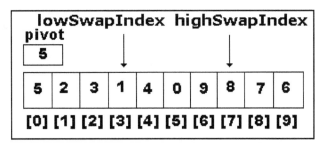

Figure 15.15 Quicksort - Next Swap Point

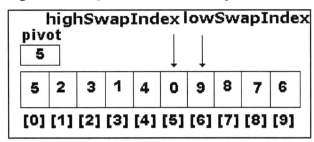

Figure 15.16 Quicksort - Indexes Have Crossed

```
// here highSwapIndex has crossed, so all values in the
// range of highSwapIndex through highIndex, are larger than
// pivot. Thus, we put the value of pivot into its correct
// position at point highSwapIndex. It is currently stored in
// position lowIndex

array[lowIndex] = array[highSwapIndex];
array[highSwapIndex] = pivot;
```

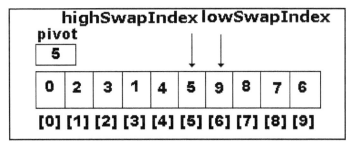

Figure 15.17 Quicksort - Placing Pivot in Destination

Now we perform the recursive call twice, once on the lower portion bounded by indexes 0 through 4 and once on the upper portion bounded by 6 through 9.

```
QuickSort (array, count, lowIndex, highSwapIndex-1);
QuickSort (array, count, highSwapIndex+1, highIndex);
}
```

And the process continues until the array is sorted. How can we analyze the performance of this algorithm? It certainly is more difficult. If the pivot does not divide the array evenly, the performance suffers.

What happens if at the indicated pivot element we always end up finding the largest value or the smallest value? In such as case, we end up with one partition of size 0 and the rest of the array in the other partition! In this situation, we would end up with a running time proportional to **count**^{2} once again. The best case situation can be described by **count log count**. A major benefit of Quicksort is that it handles large arrays much more quickly than the other versions.

Shellsort

The Shellsort was discovered by Donald Shell in 1959. His idea was to avoid the large amounts of data movement. It compares elements that are far apart first and then those that are less far apart, gradually shrinking the gap toward successive elements. Thus, it is also known as the diminishing gap sort.

The outer loop begins at **count/2** or the middle. On each iteration, the gap is reduced by an arbitrary value that has been tested empirically to give good performance, 2.2. The new value of the gap is given as
```
gap = (gap==2) ? 1 : (long)(gap/2.2);
```

Next, the middle loop sweeps across all elements from gap to the end of the array. Within this middle loop, the inner loop then checks all elements separated by the gap value with the current middle loop element, swapping when necessary.

Shellsort works very fast on large arrays. It is an example of simplicity in coding but complexity in analysis. Theoreticians predict its efficiency as **count log count** as opposed to **count**^{2}.
```
void ShellSort (int array[], long count) {
 long gap, i, j;
 int temp;
 for (gap=count/2; gap>0;
      gap = (gap==2) ? 1 : (long)(gap/2.2)) {
  for (i=gap; i<count; i++) {
   temp = array[i];
   for (j=i; j>=gap && temp<array[j-gap]; j-=gap) {
    array[j] = array[j-gap];
   }
   array[j] = temp;
  }
 }
}
```

Heapsort

The Heapsort gets its name from pretending that the array is really a b-tree (balanced tree) with nodes or a heap or linked tree. In a b-tree, each node can contain at most two leaves below it. Often a b-tree is used to rapidly find a specific key. Figure 15.18 shows what one would normally consider to be a b-tree to rapidly find a matching key. Notice that all values on the right side of the root node are greater than the root node's value while all values on the left side of the root node are less than the root node's value.

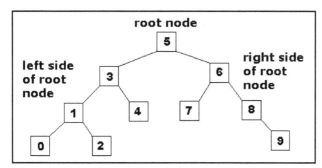

Figure 15.18 A Balanced Tree

The Heapsort pretends the original array is a b-tree that is out of order. Figure 15.19 shows the initial array that the tester program uses viewed as a b-tree.

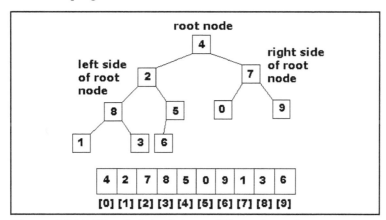

Figure 15.19 The Original Array Viewed as a b-tree

Of course, the nodes are out of order. That is, all values on the right side of a node are not all greater than that node's value while all nodes on the left side of a node are not all less than that node's value. Heapsort must then perform a "rebuild the heap downward" action to get the nodes in their proper order. The proper order is dictated by **array[node] >= array[node*2+1]** for the left side and **array[node] >= array[node*2+2]** for the right side. The action consists of going down each node and moving the elements around such that all the nodes on the right side of a given node are greater than the node and similarly with the left side. It begins at the top node and works its way to the bottom.

The **RebuildHeapDownwards** function is passed the current root node. It compares the two leaves below it to find which one is the greater value and whose index is then stored in **maxChild**. If that found largest value is greater than the root's value, it swaps that **maxChild**'s value with the root's value. Then it recursively calls itself using the index of **maxChild** as the next downward node.

```
void RebuildHeapDownward (int array[], long root, long bottom) {
  int temp;
  long maxChild;
  long leftChild  = root * 2 + 1;
```

```
long rightChild = root * 2 + 2;
if (leftChild <= bottom) {
 if (leftChild == bottom)
  maxChild = leftChild;
 else {
  if (array[leftChild] <= array[rightChild])
   maxChild = rightChild;
  else
   maxChild = leftChild;
 }
 if (array[root] < array[maxChild]) {
  temp = array[root];
  array[root] = array[maxChild];
  array[maxChild] = temp;
  RebuildHeapDownward (array, maxChild, bottom);
 }
}
}
```

The Heapsort itself begins by choosing as the root node that node located in the middle of the array, **count/2**. It calls **RebuildHeapDownward** from this point to the end of the array. When those are finished, it decrements the index of the root node and repeats the process. When the first loop is finished, here is what the original array has become. The original array is on the first line, the rebuilt one on the second line.

```
4  2  7  8  5  0  9  1  3  6
9  8  7  3  6  0  4  1  2  5
```

The second loop first stores the largest value which is at index 0 into its proper slot, index 9 and then rebuilds the heap downward again. Here is a consecutive display after each rebuild is completed.

```
8  6  7  3  5  0  4  1  2  9
7  6  4  3  5  0  2  1  8  9
6  5  4  3  1  0  2  7  8  9
5  3  4  2  1  0  6  7  8  9
4  3  0  2  1  5  6  7  8  9
3  2  0  1  4  5  6  7  8  9
2  1  0  3  4  5  6  7  8  9
1  0  2  3  4  5  6  7  8  9
0  1  2  3  4  5  6  7  8  9
```

```
void HeapSort (int array[], long count) {
 int temp;
 long i;
 for (i=count/2 - 1; i>=0; i--) {
  RebuildHeapDownward (array, i, count-1);
 }
 for (i=count-1; i>=1; i--) {
  temp = array[0];
  array[0] = array[i];
  array[i] = temp;
  RebuildHeapDownward (array, 0, i-1);
```

```
    }
}
```

With such a complex algorithm, does it actually execute with speed? The answer is yes, it does indeed run significantly faster than the straight selection and bubble sorts. Theoreticians predict its efficiency as **count log count**, similar to the Quicksort and Shellsort methods.

Pgm15a—Tester Program for the Different Sorting Methods

To test these sorting functions, **Pgm15a** has an array of **COUNT** integers initialized to some non-sorted order. Before each sorting function is called, it copies the unsorted array into a new array and passes the new array to the sorting function. When the sorting function returns, it displays the contents of the sorted array.

```
Pgm15a - Sort Methods Tester Program

 1 #include <iostream>
 2 #include <iomanip>
 3 using namespace std;
 4
 5 void CopyArray (int src[], int des[], long count);
 6 ostream& PrintArray (ostream& os, int array[], long count);
 7
 8 void StraightSelectionSort (int array[], long count);
 9 void BubbleSort (int array[], int count);
10 void QuickSort (int array[], long count, long lowIndex,
11                 long highIndex);
12 void HeapSort (int array[], long count);
13 void RebuildHeapDownward (int array[], long i, long num);
14 void ShellSort (int array[], long count);
15
16 /******************************************************************/
17 /*                                                              */
18 /* Pgm15a - Tester Program to Test the Sorting Functions        */
19 /*                                                              */
20 /******************************************************************/
21
22 const int COUNT = 10;
23
24 int main () {
25   int x[COUNT] = {4, 2, 7, 8, 5, 0, 9, 1, 3, 6};
26   int xx[COUNT];
27   CopyArray (x, xx, COUNT);
28   cout << "Original Array: ";
29   PrintArray (cout, x, COUNT);
30
31   StraightSelectionSort (xx, COUNT);
```

```
32  cout << "St. Selection:   ";
33  PrintArray (cout, xx, COUNT);
34  CopyArray (x, xx, COUNT);
35
36  BubbleSort (xx, COUNT);
37  cout << "Bubble Sort:     ";
38  PrintArray (cout, xx, COUNT);
39  CopyArray (x, xx, COUNT);
40
41  QuickSort (xx, COUNT, 0, COUNT-1);
42  cout << "Quicksort:       ";
43  PrintArray (cout, xx, COUNT);
44  CopyArray (x, xx, COUNT);
45
46  HeapSort (xx, COUNT);
47  cout << "Heap Sort:       ";
48  PrintArray (cout, xx, COUNT);
49  CopyArray (x, xx, COUNT);
50
51  ShellSort (xx, COUNT);
52  cout << "Shell Sort:      ";
53  PrintArray (cout, xx, COUNT);
54
55  return 0;
56 }
57
58 /****************************************************************/
59 /*                                                            */
60 /* CopyArray: Helper function to make a duplicate array copy  */
61 /*                                                            */
62 /****************************************************************/
63
64 void CopyArray (int src[], int des[], long count) {
65  for (long i=0; i<count; i++)
66   des[i] = src[i];
67 }
68
69 /****************************************************************/
70 /*                                                            */
71 /* PrintArray: Helper function to display the array's contents */
72 /*                                                            */
73 /****************************************************************/
74
75 ostream& PrintArray (ostream& os, int array[], long count) {
76  for (long i=0; i<count; i++) {
77   os << setw(4) << array[i];
78   if ((i % 60) == 0 && i != 0)
79    os << endl;
80  }
81  os << endl;
```

```
 82  return os;
 83 }
 84
 85 /*****************************************************************/
 86 /*                                                               */
 87 /* StraightSelectionSort:                                        */
 88 /*                                                               */
 89 /*****************************************************************/
 90
 91 void StraightSelectionSort (int array[], long count) {
 92  long currentSmallestIndex; // stores idx of current smallest one
 93  int  temp;
 94  long j, k;
 95  // outer loop traverses all elements except the last one
 96  for (j=0; j<count-1; j++) {
 97   // assume that the current j contains the smallest value
 98   currentSmallestIndex = j;
 99   // inner loop traverses all elements below j looking for the
100   // next smallest one - notice we avoid swapping each time a
101   // smaller one is found - just keep track of its index
102   for (k=j+1; k<count; k++) {
103    if (array[k] < array[currentSmallestIndex])
104     currentSmallestIndex = k;
105   }
106   // now see if the new smallest one is in the correct position
107   if (currentSmallestIndex != j) {
108    // no, so one time only, swap the smallest into the correct
109    // position in the array
110    temp = array[j];
111    array[j] = array[currentSmallestIndex];
112    array[currentSmallestIndex] = temp;
113   }
114  }
115 }
116
117 /*****************************************************************/
118 /*                                                               */
119 /* BubbleSort:                                                   */
120 /*                                                               */
121 /*****************************************************************/
122
123 void BubbleSort (int array[], int count) {
124  int  temp;
125  long j;
126  long lastSwapIndex;        // the idx of the last one swapped
127  long bottomIdx = count - 1; // the current ending idx
128
129  while (bottomIdx > 0) { // repeat until only the top idx is left
130   lastSwapIndex = 0;
131   // rearrange all elements to current bottom
```

```
132    for (j=0; j<bottomIdx; j++) {
133     if (array[j] > array[j+1]) {
134      // swap these two into increasing order
135      temp = array[j];
136      array[j] = array[j+1];
137      array[j+1] = temp;
138      lastSwapIndex = j; // reset the last idx swapped
139     }
140    }
141    // since several lower ones might already be in increasing
142    // order, we may not need to further check these - thus,
143    // reposition bottom accordingly
144    bottomIdx = lastSwapIndex;
145   }
146  }
147
148  /******************************************************************/
149  /*                                                                */
150  /* QuickSort:                                                     */
151  /*                                                                */
152  /******************************************************************/
153
154  void QuickSort (int array[], long count, long lowIndex,
155                  long highIndex) {
156   int  pivot;
157   int  temp;
158   long lowSwapIndex;
159   long highSwapIndex;
160
161   if (lowIndex >= highIndex)// 0 or 1 item to sort, so we are done
162    return;
163
164   if ((highIndex - lowIndex) == 1) { // only two items to sort
165    if (array[lowIndex] > array[highIndex]) { // we must swap them
166     temp = array[lowIndex];
167     array[lowIndex] = array[highIndex];
168     array[highIndex] = temp;
169    }
170    return;
171   }
172
173   // here we have 3 or more items to swap
174   // pick the value in the middle to be the pivot value for the
175   // dividing vlaue between the two portions
176   long mid = (lowIndex + highIndex) / 2;
177   pivot = array[mid];
178   // and swap this value into lowIndex postion
179   array[mid] = array[lowIndex];
180   array[lowIndex] = pivot;
181   // now divide into two portions in which one portion's array
```

```
182  // values are all greater than the pivot value and
183  // the other's is <= to it
184  lowSwapIndex = lowIndex + 1;
185  highSwapIndex = highIndex;
186  do {
187   while (lowSwapIndex <= highSwapIndex &&
188          array[lowSwapIndex] <= pivot) {
189    lowSwapIndex++;
190    }
191   while (array[highSwapIndex] > pivot) {
192    highSwapIndex--;
193    }
194   if (lowSwapIndex < highSwapIndex) {
195    // here we have encountered an array value that belongs in the
196    // other partition, so we must swap these two array values to
197    // get them into the correct portions
198    temp = array[lowSwapIndex];
199    array[lowSwapIndex] = array[highSwapIndex];
200    array[highSwapIndex] = temp;
201    }
202   // and repeat the process until these two points cross
203  } while (lowSwapIndex < highSwapIndex);
204
205  // here highSwapIndex has crossed, so all values in the
206  // range of highSwapIndex through highIndex, are larger than
207  // pivot. Thus, we put the value of pivot into its correct
208  // position at point highSwapIndex. It is currently stored in
209  // position lowIndex
210
211  array[lowIndex] = array[highSwapIndex];
212  array[highSwapIndex] = pivot;
213
214  // now we repeat the process on each half - note that
215  // array[highSwapIndex] is in its correct final position and
216  // does not need to be further used
217
218  QuickSort (array, count, lowIndex, highSwapIndex-1);
219  QuickSort (array, count, highSwapIndex+1, highIndex);
220 }
221
222 /****************************************************************/
223 /*                                                            */
224 /* HeapSort:                                                  */
225 /*                                                            */
226 /****************************************************************/
227
228 void HeapSort (int array[], long count) {
229  int temp;
230  long i;
231
```

```
232  for (i=count/2 - 1; i>=0; i--) {
233   RebuildHeapDownward (array, i, count-1);
234  }
235
236  for (i=count-1; i>=1; i--) {
237   temp = array[0];
238   array[0] = array[i];
239   array[i] = temp;
240   RebuildHeapDownward (array, 0, i-1);
241  }
242 }
243
244 /*****************************************************************/
245 /*                                                             */
246 /* RebuildHeapDownward: used by HeapSort                       */
247 /*                                                             */
248 /*****************************************************************/
249
250 void RebuildHeapDownward (int array[], long root, long bottom) {
251  int temp;
252  long maxChild;
253  long leftChild  = root * 2 + 1;
254  long rightChild = root * 2 + 2;
255
256  // find which leaf is larger
257  if (leftChild <= bottom) {
258   if (leftChild == bottom)
259    maxChild = leftChild;
260   else {
261    if (array[leftChild] <= array[rightChild])
262     maxChild = rightChild;
263    else
264     maxChild = leftChild;
265   }
266
267   // replace root element with the larger and rebuild the heap
268   if (array[root] < array[maxChild]) {
269    temp = array[root];
270    array[root] = array[maxChild];
271    array[maxChild] = temp;
272    RebuildHeapDownward (array, maxChild, bottom);
273   }
274  }
275 }
276
277 /*****************************************************************/
278 /*                                                             */
279 /* ShellSort:                                                  */
280 /*                                                             */
281 /*****************************************************************/
```

```
282
283 void ShellSort (int array[], long count) {
284  long gap, i, j;
285  int temp;
286  for (gap=count/2; gap>0;
287      gap = (gap==2) ? 1 : (long)(gap/2.2)) {
288   for (i=gap; i<count; i++) {
289    temp = array[i];
290    for (j=i; j>=gap && temp<array[j-gap]; j-=gap) {
291     array[j] = array[j-gap];
292    }
293    array[j] = temp;
294   }
295  }
296 }
```

Here is the output from the tester program.

```
Output from Pgm15a - Sort Methods Tester Program

1 Original Array:    4  2  7  8  5  0  9  1  3  6
2 St. Selection:     0  1  2  3  4  5  6  7  8  9
3 Bubble Sort:       0  1  2  3  4  5  6  7  8  9
4 Quicksort:         0  1  2  3  4  5  6  7  8  9
5 Heap Sort:         0  1  2  3  4  5  6  7  8  9
6 Shell Sort:        0  1  2  3  4  5  6  7  8  9
```

Benchmarks

In order to properly evaluate these sorting algorithms, one must time how long each takes to sort the same array. By varying the array size and the degree that the initial array is already sorted, we can get a good feel for their performance.

The starting point is how to create a large array of "random" values. I would not want to build a file of 100,000 numbers by hand. Instead, C++ had a random number generator function that can be used to provide as many "random" numbers as we require. The built-in random number generator requires the use of a "seed" value. For any given seed value, the random number function returns the same sequence of "random" numbers. Thus, it really is not creating true random numbers. This is actually a useful property. If you are creating a game program based upon random events, by using the same seed and thus obtaining the same series of random numbers, you can debug the program. If each run created a truly different set of numbers, debugging would become much more difficult since it would be hard to reproduce the error situations.

The C++ function is called **rand()**. I wrote a small helper function, **GetRandom()** that is passed the maximum value of the generated numbers. The function then returns a random number between zero and that maximum.

```
unsigned  GetRandom (int maxVal) {
 return rand () % maxVal;
}
```

For a seed value, game programmers often use the current time as a seed because from one execution of the program to another, it is nearly impossible to launch the program at the same exact instant. The C++ **time()** function returns the number of seconds elapsed since midnight (00:00:00), January 1, 1970, coordinated universal time, according to the system clock. (The function is passed a zero for the pointer to the time location to set to the current time; we just need the return value.) The C++ function to set the initial seed value of the random number generator is called **srand()**. I invoke it this way.

```
srand ((unsigned) time (0));
```

To use these, include the **iostream** and **ctime** header files. Here is the start of the program. It defines two arrays of 100,000 integers and fills the first with the random numbers and then copies that array into the working array **xx**. It is array **xx** that will be sorted by the various methods.

```
const int MAX = 100000;
int main () {
 srand ((unsigned) time (0));

 int x[MAX];
 for (int i=0; i<MAX; i++)
  x[i] = GetRandom (MAX);

 int xx[MAX];
 CopyArray (x, xx, MAX);
```

How do we know how long it takes for any sorting method to execute? The C++ function **clock()** returns the number of clock ticks that has elapsed since the machine was turned on. If you divide by the constant, **CLOCKS_PER_SEC**, the number is converted into seconds. Thus, if we call **clock()** before calling the sort function and then immediately after the function returns, we can subtract the two values and divide by the constant to determine the total elapsed time that sort function executed. The return value of **clock()** is really a long but has been type defined as a **clock_t** data type.

This gives us the basic logic behind all of the timings.

```
clock_t timeStart, timeEnd;
timeStart = clock ();
StraightSelectionSort (xx, max);
timeEnd = clock ();
cout << setw (10)
     << ((double)(timeEnd-timeStart))/CLOCKS_PER_SEC;
```

I want to benchmark how long it takes these five sorting functions to execute as a function of the number of elements in the array. Thus, I created another array that provided the number of elements to sort.

```
const long amts[NUM] = {100, 200, 500, 1000, 2000, 5000, 10000,
```

Beginning Data Structures in C++

20000, 50000, 100000};

So the program then times each of the sorting functions for each of these array sizes.

For variation, I also performed the whole series on an array that was already in sorted order, but in high to low or backwards order. Then, I performed the whole series on an array in which all elements were already in their proper order except the last element. This might be the situation facing an update program which must add a new record to the array in its proper position.

Here are the output benchmark timings I obtained from a Release Build of Pgm15b.

```
Output of Pgm15b - Sort Efficiencies Program

 1 Times in seconds for a random order array
 2
 3   Count  Straight    Bubble      Quick      Heap       Shell
 4          Selection    Sort        Sort       Sort       Sort
 5
 6    100     0.000      0.000      0.000      0.000      0.000
 7    200     0.000      0.000      0.000      0.000      0.000
 8    500     0.000      0.000      0.000      0.000      0.000
 9   1000     0.000      0.020      0.000      0.000      0.000
10   2000     0.030      0.060      0.000      0.000      0.000
11   5000     0.190      0.371      0.000      0.000      0.010
12  10000     0.791      1.582      0.000      0.010      0.010
13  20000     3.145      6.259      0.020      0.010      0.020
14  50000    31.365     62.560      0.040      0.050      0.080
15 100000   165.568    315.263      0.070      0.141      0.180
16
17
18
19 Times for an already sorted array - last element new
20   Count  Straight    Bubble      Quick      Heap       Shell
21          Selection    Sort        Sort       Sort       Sort
22
23    100     0.000      0.000      0.000      0.000      0.000
24    200     0.000      0.000      0.000      0.000      0.000
25    500     0.000      0.000      0.000      0.000      0.000
26   1000     0.010      0.000      0.000      0.000      0.000
27   2000     0.050      0.000      0.000      0.000      0.000
28   5000     0.190      0.000      0.000      0.000      0.000
29  10000     0.782      0.000      0.000      0.010      0.000
30  20000     3.144      0.000      0.000      0.010      0.000
31  50000    31.405      0.000      0.010      0.050      0.041
32 100000   165.808    165.969      0.030      0.090      0.090
33
34
35
36 Times in seconds for backwards sorted array
37   Count  Straight    Bubble      Quick      Heap       Shell
```

38		Selection	Sort	Sort	Sort	Sort
39						
40	100	0.000	0.000	0.000	0.000	0.000
41	200	0.000	0.000	0.000	0.000	0.000
42	500	0.000	0.000	0.000	0.000	0.000
43	1000	0.010	0.010	0.000	0.000	0.000
44	2000	0.040	0.040	0.000	0.000	0.000
45	5000	0.291	0.250	0.000	0.000	0.000
46	10000	1.182	0.941	0.000	0.000	0.010
47	20000	5.037	3.806	0.000	0.020	0.010
48	50000	45.345	52.776	0.020	0.040	0.050
49	100000	226.155	310.647	0.040	0.080	0.100

As you examine these results, notice how dramatic the time variations between the first two methods (straight selection and bubble) and the last three (Quicksort, Heapsort, and Shellsort) are. Then compare the times for the straight selection and bubble sorts in the three different circumstances; there is quite a difference in speed depending upon the initial state of the data to be sorted. This is also true with Quicksort. However, the Heapsort and Shellsort show much less of a dependency on this effect.

Here is the benchmark program, **Pgm15b**.

```
Pgm15b - Sort Efficiencies Program

 1 #include <iostream>
 2 #include <iomanip>
 3 #include <ctime>
 4 using namespace std;
 5
 6 unsigned GetRandom (int maxVal);
 7
 8 void CopyArray (int src[], int des[], long count);
 9 ostream& PrintArray (ostream& os, int array[], long count);
10
11 void StraightSelectionSort (int array[], long count);
12 void BubbleSort (int array[], int count);
13 void QuickSort (int array[], long count, long lowIndex,
14                 long highIndex);
15 void HeapSort (int array[], long count);
16 void RebuildHeapDownward (int array[], long root, long bottom);
17 void ShellSort (int array[], long count);
18
19 const int MAX = 100000;
20 const int NUM = 10;
21
22 /******************************************************************/
23 /*                                                              */
24 /* Pgm15a - Tester Program to Test the Sorting Functions        */
25 /*                                                              */
```

```
26  /*************************************************************/
27
28  int main () {
29   cout.setf (ios::fixed, ios::floatfield);
30   cout << setprecision (3);
31
32   srand ((unsigned) time (0));
33
34   int x[MAX];
35   for (int i=0; i<MAX; i++)
36    x[i] = GetRandom (MAX);
37
38   int xx[MAX];
39   CopyArray (x, xx, MAX);
40
41   clock_t timeStart, timeEnd;
42
43   long max;
44   const long amts[NUM] = {100, 200, 500, 1000, 2000, 5000, 10000,
45                           20000, 50000, 100000};
46
47   cout << "Times in seconds for a random order array\n\n"
48     << "  Count    Straight    Bubble     Quick      Heap      Shell"
49     << "\n"
50     << "           Selection     Sort      Sort       Sort      Sort"
51     << "\n\n";
52   for (i=0; i<NUM; i++) {
53    max=amts[i];
54    cout << setw(7) << max;
55    timeStart = clock ();
56    StraightSelectionSort (xx, max);
57    timeEnd = clock ();
58    cout << setw (10)
59        << ((double)(timeEnd-timeStart))/CLOCKS_PER_SEC;
60    CopyArray (x, xx, max);
61
62    timeStart = clock ();
63    BubbleSort (xx, max);
64    timeEnd = clock ();
65    cout << setw (10)
66        << ((double)(timeEnd-timeStart))/CLOCKS_PER_SEC;
67    CopyArray (x, xx, max);
68
69    timeStart = clock ();
70    QuickSort (xx, max, 0, max-1);
71    timeEnd = clock ();
72    cout << setw (10)
73        << ((double)(timeEnd-timeStart))/CLOCKS_PER_SEC;
74    CopyArray (x, xx, max);
75
```

```
 76    timeStart = clock ();
 77    HeapSort (xx, max);
 78    timeEnd = clock ();
 79    cout << setw (10)
 80         << ((double)(timeEnd-timeStart))/CLOCKS_PER_SEC;
 81    CopyArray (x, xx, max);
 82
 83    timeStart = clock ();
 84    ShellSort (xx, max);
 85    timeEnd = clock ();
 86    cout << setw (10)
 87         << ((double)(timeEnd-timeStart))/CLOCKS_PER_SEC;
 88    CopyArray (x, xx, max);
 89
 90    cout << endl;
 91  }
 92
 93  cout << endl << endl << endl;
 94  cout <<"Times for an already sorted array -last element new\n"
 95    << " Count   Straight     Bubble       Quick        Heap       Shell"
 96    << "\n"
 97    << "          Selection     Sort        Sort         Sort        Sort"
 98    << "\n\n";
 99  QuickSort (xx, MAX, 0, MAX-1);
100  for (i=0; i<MAX-1; i++) {
101   x[i] = xx[i+1];
102  }
103  x[MAX-1] = 42;
104  CopyArray (x, xx, max);
105
106  for (i=0; i<NUM; i++) {
107   max=amts[i];
108   cout << setw(7) << max;
109   timeStart = clock ();
110   StraightSelectionSort (xx, max);
111   timeEnd = clock ();
112   cout << setw (10)
113        << ((double)(timeEnd-timeStart))/CLOCKS_PER_SEC;
114   CopyArray (x, xx, max);
115
116   timeStart = clock ();
117   BubbleSort (xx, max);
118   timeEnd = clock ();
119   cout << setw (10)
120        << ((double)(timeEnd-timeStart))/CLOCKS_PER_SEC;
121   CopyArray (x, xx, max);
122
123   timeStart = clock ();
124   QuickSort (xx, max, 0, max-1);
125   timeEnd = clock ();
```

```
126    cout << setw (10)
127        << ((double)(timeEnd-timeStart))/CLOCKS_PER_SEC;
128    CopyArray (x, xx, max);
129
130    timeStart = clock ();
131    HeapSort (xx, max);
132    timeEnd = clock ();
133    cout << setw (10)
134        << ((double)(timeEnd-timeStart))/CLOCKS_PER_SEC;
135    CopyArray (x, xx, max);
136
137    timeStart = clock ();
138    ShellSort (xx, max);
139    timeEnd = clock ();
140    cout << setw (10)
141        << ((double)(timeEnd-timeStart))/CLOCKS_PER_SEC;
142    CopyArray (x, xx, max);
143
144    cout << endl;
145  }
146
147
148  cout << endl << endl << endl;
149  cout << "Times in seconds for backwards sorted array\n"
150    << "  Count    Straight     Bubble      Quick       Heap       Shell"
151    << "\n"
152    << "            Selection     Sort       Sort       Sort       Sort"
153    << "\n\n";
154  QuickSort (xx, MAX, 0, MAX-1);
155  for (i=0; i<MAX-1; i++) {
156   x[i] = xx[MAX-1-i];
157  }
158  CopyArray (x, xx, max);
159
160  for (i=0; i<NUM; i++) {
161   max=amts[i];
162   cout << setw(7) << max;
163   timeStart = clock ();
164   StraightSelectionSort (xx, max);
165   timeEnd = clock ();
166   cout << setw (10)
167        << ((double)(timeEnd-timeStart))/CLOCKS_PER_SEC;
168   CopyArray (x, xx, max);
169
170   timeStart = clock ();
171   BubbleSort (xx, max);
172   timeEnd = clock ();
173   cout << setw (10)
174        << ((double)(timeEnd-timeStart))/CLOCKS_PER_SEC;
175   CopyArray (x, xx, max);
```

```
176
177    timeStart = clock ();
178    QuickSort (xx, max, 0, max-1);
179    timeEnd = clock ();
180    cout << setw (10)
181        << ((double)(timeEnd-timeStart))/CLOCKS_PER_SEC;
182    CopyArray (x, xx, max);
183
184    timeStart = clock ();
185    HeapSort (xx, max);
186    timeEnd = clock ();
187    cout << setw (10)
188        << ((double)(timeEnd-timeStart))/CLOCKS_PER_SEC;
189    CopyArray (x, xx, max);
190
191    timeStart = clock ();
192    ShellSort (xx, max);
193    timeEnd = clock ();
194    cout << setw (10)
195        << ((double)(timeEnd-timeStart))/CLOCKS_PER_SEC;
196    CopyArray (x, xx, max);
197
198    cout << endl;
199    }
200
201  return 0;
202 }
203
204 /******************************************************************/
205 /*                                                                */
206 /* GetRandom: gets a random number from 0 to maxVal              */
207 /*                                                                */
208 /******************************************************************/
209
210 unsigned  GetRandom (int maxVal) {
211  return rand () % maxVal;
212 }
... the actual sorting functions are unchanged from Pgm15a
447 }
```

Review Questions

1. Explain in your own words how the straight selection sort works.

2. Explain in your own words how the bubble sort works.

3. Explain in your own words how the Quicksort works.

4. Explain in your own words how the Heapsort works.

5. Explain in your own words how the Shellsort works.

6. In the benchmark runs, the straight selection sort ran twice as fast as the bubble sort when the data was in random order. Yet, when the array was already in sorted order except for the last element, the two methods took about the same amount of time to sort the array. How do you explain this difference?

7. In the benchmark runs, why should the straight selection sort run times be nearly identical for the random order array and the array in which the data is already in order except for the last element?

8. In the benchmark runs, the Heapsort times for the backwards sorted array and the array that was already in sorted order except for the last element were nearly identical. Why should this be the case? Why is the random order case running slower?

9. Using the benchmark runs as a guideline, suppose that your company needed to sort an array of 6,000,000 cost records. Which sort method would you recommend? Why? What is the impact of recursion when the array size becomes huge?

Stop! Do These Exercises Before Programming

1. Our programmer has had his ISAM inventory update program for Acme Consolidated accepted and put into production. While it was running in the production environment, a speed issue has arisen. The company has in excess of 500,000 parts to track in the ISAM data base. They are constantly adding new parts. It was discovered that the add new part function and the find this record functions were consuming huge amounts of execution time. Management has asked our programmer to speed these operations up significantly.

The index file is called **parts.idx** and consists of instances of the structure **Index**.
```
struct Index {
  char partNo[PARTNO_LEN];
  long relRecNum;
};
```
The index records are stored in increasing ASCII sequence on the **partNo** field.

The **FindRecord()** function he currently has does a binary search to find the matching item in the index array. Its prototype is
```
bool FindRecord (Index id[], long num,
                 const char* findId, long& foundIndex);
```
It returns **true** if it finds a match and **false** if not. Of course, with a binary search, if there was no match, the **foundIndex** contained the subscript of where this item should have been located. That meant the programmer could also use this routine when adding new items to the index as well as matching existing ones.

The programmer has decided that a better way to handle the addition problem is to just add the new index element to the end of the already sorted index array and call a sort function to properly resort the index. Since your prowess as a programmer is now widely known, our programmer has gotten management approval to have you assist him in this project.

Write a **Quicksort()** function to sort the array of index elements. Its prototype should be
```
void QuickSort (Index array[], long count, long lowIndex,
                long highIndex);
```

2. Write a **Shellsort()** function to sort the array of index elements. Its prototype should be
```
void ShellSort (Index array[], long count);
```

3. With these new changes for sorting the Index array, the speed of the add new parts operation has improved. Why does this not affect the speed of the other operations, update this part and delete this part?

4. Look back over the implementation of the **FindRecord()** binary search function presented in the Stop! Exercises for chapter 13. What is the real reason the **FindRecord()** function is running slowly with this many records in the index? What would you recommend to management for drastically speeding up this matching operation?

Programming Problems

Problem Pgm15-1 The Benchmark Program Revised

When a program has a huge amount of automatic storage defined in **main()** or another function, to avoid a runtime stack overflow, there is a project setting that can be made. Project Settings—Link tab—Output choice in the Category combobox—Stack Allocations edit control—enter the basic amount needed, such as 4000000 for close to 4M of memory.

Revise the benchmark program, Pgm15b, as follows. Remove the Straight Selection and Bubble sorts completely. Set the total array size to 4000000. Run a series of speed tests on random data for the Quicksort, Heapsort, and Shellsort. Test with 100,000 elements, 500,000 elements, 1,000,000 elements.

Problem Pgm15-2 Write a Shellsort Function to Sort Inventory Records

An **InventoryRec** structure is defined as follows. The **itemNumber** consists of two letters, a dash, and three numerical digits.

```
const int DESCRLEN = 21;
const int ITEMLEN = 7;

struct InventoryRec {
 char    itemNumber[ITEMLEN]; // format aa-nnn
 char    descr[DESCRLEN];
 short   quantity;
 double  cost;
};
```

The DOS command line provides two filenames for the program. The first filename is the name of the input file to use. The input file is a binary file of inventory records that was built using **1-byte** structure alignment. The output file should also be a binary file.

The program loads the binary file into an array, sorts them into increasing order on **itemNumber**, and writes a new sorted binary file. Since the number of elements in the array is not known, use dynamic memory methods to allocate the array. That is, determine the input file size and divide by the size of an **InventoryRec** to get the number of elements. Then, dynamically allocate the array. Next, invoke a **LoadArray()** function followed by **ShellSort()** function followed by **WriteArray()** function. Also, make a printed report of the first 20 and the last 20 records in the sorted array. However, if the array is smaller than 40 elements, display all the sorted elements.

Use the **invmast.dat** file provided in the **Chapter15** folder under **TestDataForAssignments** for your input file.

Problem Pgm15-3 Write a Quicksort Function to Sort Inventory Records

An **InventoryRec** structure is defined as follows. The **itemNumber** consists of two letters, a dash, and three numerical digits.

```
const int DESCRLEN = 21;
const int ITEMLEN = 7;

struct InventoryRec {
 char    itemNumber[ITEMLEN]; // format aa-nnn
 char    descr[DESCRLEN];
 short   quantity;
 double  cost;
};
```

The DOS command line provides two filenames for the program. The first filename is the name of the input file to use. The input file is a binary file of inventory records that was built using **1-byte** structure alignment. The output file should also be a binary file.

The program loads the binary file into an array, sorts them into increasing order on **itemNumber**, and writes a new sorted binary file. Since the number of elements in the array is not known, use dynamic memory methods to allocate the array. That is, determine the input file size and divide by the size of an **InventoryRec** to get the number of elements. Then, dynamically allocate the array. Next, invoke a **LoadArray()** function followed by **QuickSort()** function followed by **WriteArray()** function. Also, make a printed report of the first 20 and the last 20 records in the sorted array. However, if the array is smaller than 40 elements, display all the sorted elements.

Use the **invmast.dat** file provided in the **Chapter15** folder under **TestDataForAssignments** for your input file.

Appendix A—A Review of Array and Structure Processing

This appendix covers the basic principles of single dimensioned array processing, two-dimensional array processing and the use of structures in programming with which you should already be familiar.

A Review of Single Dimensioned Array Operations

This section is a general review of single dimensional array operations.

Using an Array for Direct Lookup Operations

When working with dates, one often needs to know how many days there are in a given month. Using an array can streamline such operations. Given the month number (1 through 12), the program can access directly the array element that contains the number of days in that month. If the month number is 1 for January, then **days_in_month[1]** should contain 31 days. When setting up the **days_in_month** array, since all arrays begin with element 0 and since 0 is not normally a month number, it is permissible to make the array one element larger, placing a dummy value in the never-to-be-used element 0. The array could be defined as follows

```
const int days_in_month[13] = {0, 31, 28, 31, 30, 31, 30,
                               31, 31, 30, 31, 30, 31}
```

Notice also the usage of the **const** keyword. Once the array elements are given their initial values, they should never be changed. Making the array constant ensures that no accidental changes to these values can be made.

In this example, the month number is used as the subscript to directly access the correct number of days in that month. The following illustrates this.

```
int month;
cout << "Enter a month number: ";
cin >> month;
while (month < 1 || month > 12) {
 cout << "Invalid month number - please re-enter: ";
 cin >> month;
}
cout << "Month " << month << " contains "
     << days_in_month[month] << " days\n"
```

Parallel Arrays and Sequential Searches – Inquiry Programs

Consider two single-dimensioned arrays, one contains the student id number and the other contains his/her course grade. Clearly, the two arrays must be kept synchronized at all times. The grade stored in element 1 of the **grade** array corresponds to the student whose id is stored in element 1 of the **id** array. Once the information is loaded into the two arrays, then the inquiry operations can begin. An **inquiry program** is one in which the user is prompted to enter a specific id of some kind and the program then finds the corresponding data and displays it. Inquiry programs are widespread in the modern world. Checking on your bank account balance, credit card limit, and even the grade that you received in a course—all are inquiry type programs.

Let's first examine how the inquiry array is loaded and then how it is used or searched. Assume that each line of input contains a long student id number followed by the letter grade they received. The following loads both arrays

```
long id[MaxStudents];
char grade[MaxStudents];
int numberStudents;
int j = 0;
while (j < MaxStudents && cin >> id[j] >> grade[j]) {
  j++;
}
numberStudents = j;
```

Notice the **while** test condition checks first to see if there is still another available element and if so, attempts the input operation and if successful, increments the subscript for the next iteration. Assume that the following Illustration A.1 represents the arrays after all the data have been input. The variable **numberStudents** contains the number actually input into the arrays and is 5.

Illustration A.1 The Id and Grades Arrays

```
subscript    id array   grade array
    0         111111111       A
    1         444444444       B
    2         222222222       A
    3         555555555       C
    4         333333333       B
```

Next, the inquiry program prompts the user to enter the id of the student whose grade is to be found.

```
long studentId;
char studentGrade;
cout << "Enter student id number: ";
cin >> studentId;
```

Now the objective is to search the id array looking for a match on **studentId**, obtain the subscript of the matching id and use that subscript to get at that student's grade. Let's encapsulate the matching process in a function, **MatchId()**, whose header begins

```
int  MatchId (long id[], int num, long findId) {
```

MatchId() must be passed the array of id numbers and the current number in the array along with the id number to find, **findId**. It should return the subscript of that element of the id array that matched **findId**.

Look over Illustration A.1 above; suppose that the user enters an id number of 555555555. Counting down the array elements, the **MatchId()** function should return 3. But what would happen if the user asks **MatchId()** to find a student id of 666666666? That id number is not in the list. Thus, when **MatchId()** ends, if there is no match on the **findId**, **MatchId()** must have a way to notify the caller of that fact. Because no subscript can ever be a negative integer, we can adopt some negative number to return to indicate no match found. Commonly –1 is used for this purpose.

Following good programming practice, define a constant integer to represent it and place it in the global namespace above the **main()** function.

```
const int NoMatch = -1;
```

The logic of the **MatchId()** function is

```
int  MatchId (long id[], int num, long findId) {
 for (int j=0; j<num; j++) {
  if (findId == id[j])
    return j;
 }
 return NoMatch;
}
```

The **main()** program then invokes **MatchId()** as follows.

```
int match = MatchId (id, numberStudents, studentId);
if (match != NoMatch) {
 studentGrade = grade[match];
 cout << studentID << "received a grade of "
      << studentGrade << endl;
}
else {
 cout << "Error: invalid student id\n";
}
```

Inserting Another Element into an Unsorted Array

Suppose that a student with an id number of 666666666 takes a make-up exam and scores a grade of B. One could alter the input file to add this sixth line and rerun the program. However, in some applications, it is neither possible nor desirable to terminate the program and restart it just to reload the arrays. Instead, the new information is additionally inserted into the array. In an unsorted array, the new information added into the first empty element. Make sure that the total number of elements in the array is incremented. The following **InsertStudent()** function illustrates how this may be done.

```
bool  InsertStudent (long id[], char grade[],
                     int& num, int maxlimit,
                     long newid, char newgrade) {
 if (num >= maxlimit) return false;
 id[num] = newid;
```

```
grade[num] = newgrade;
num++;
return true;
}
```

Notice that the function returns **false** if there is no more room left in the array. Observe that the number in the array, **num**, must be passed by reference so that the number in **main()** can be incremented. The two arrays now appear as follows as shown in Illustration A.2.

Illustration A.2 Updated Id and Grade Arrays
numberStudents is 6—**main()**'s variable

```
subscript     id array   grade array
    0          111111111       A
    1          444444444       B
    2          222222222       A
    3          555555555       C
    4          333333333       B
    5          666666666       B
```

Ordered (Sorted) Lists

One problem of unsorted lists is the time that it takes to search through the array sequentially looking for a matching value in the array. If there are only a few elements, the amount of time is negligible. However, suppose that these arrays contained a store's inventory numbers, quantity on hand and unit cost. Further, suppose that the store handles 100,000 separate items. If the item number desired was the last one in the list, a significant amount of time is needed to find that match. The answer is not "Get a faster computer" but rather devise a better algorithm. If the list is sorted into numerical or alphabetical order depending upon the type of data the array contains, then far faster searches can be devised. Returning to the student id and grades arrays, let's assume that the arrays have been sorted into increasing numerical order on the ids. The arrays appear as shown in Illustration A.3.

Illustration A.3 Sorted Id and Grade Arrays
numberStudents is 6—**main()**'s variable

```
subscript   id array  grade array
    0        111111111       A
    1        222222222       A
    2        333333333       B
    3        444444444       B
    4        555555555       C
    5        666666666       B
```

The array of ids can still be matched sequentially. However, we can take advantage of the ordered nature to detect no matching id number more quickly. Suppose that the **findId** this time was 345678999. Notice that when we are at subscript 3 which contains id 444444444, we know for certain that this id is not in the array and can return **false** at once without having to check any further subscripts. The slight modification is in boldface.

574

```
int  MatchSortedId (long id[], int num, long findId) {
 for (int j=0; j<num && findId >= id[j]; j++) {
  if (findId == id[j])
    return j;
 }
 return NoMatch;
}
```

On the average, some increase in speed results. However, for items near the end of the array are still going to take a large number of iterations through the loop to find them.

The Binary Search Method

The **binary search** method uses a different searching algorithm, one that drastically reduces the number of comparisons that need to be done to find the match. Before looking at the coding for the search, let's examine in detail how the binary search works. Let N represent the number of ids in the array. The first subscript to use in the search is N/2—the midpoint. We compare the **findId** to the element in the middle. If we are lucky, we have an exact match and are done. More likely it does not match, but if the **findId** is smaller than the one in the middle, we can eliminate the entire higher half of the array from further consideration. Likewise if the **findId** is greater than that in the middle, we can eliminate all those values in the lower half. Thus, on one test, we have eliminated one-half of the array from further consideration! Now that same process is repeated, halving the new interval and testing the one in the middle again, and so on until we find the match or run out of array, indicating no match.

Let's do a concrete example using the student data above in Illustration 2.4. Say the **findId** is 22222222. The first subscript to try is $(0 + 5) / 2$ or index 2 which stores id 333333333. The **findId** is smaller so if this one is in the array it must lie in the lower half, between indexes 0 and 1. The new index to try is halfway between. At subscript 1, we have our match.

The binary search function should be designed so that it returns **true** if it finds a match; the index of the match is stored in a reference parameter for use by the caller. However, if it does not find a match, the index stored in the passed reference parameter should be the index of where that value ought to have been if it was in the list. Why? Code reuse. True, for a simple query, match this id, just a return value of **false** for not present is sufficient. But the next feature one might need to implement is to add this id into the sorted list where it belongs. Thinking ahead, when an id is not in the list, it is a simple matter to also provide the index of where this element should be if it were in the list. Then only one **BinarySearch()** function need be written.

```
bool  BinarySearch (long id[], int num,
                    long findId, int& foundIndex) {
 int firstidx = 0;
 int lastidx = num - 1;
 int middleidx;
 bool foundMatch = false;
 while (lastidx >= firstidx && !foundMatch) {
  middleidx = (firstidx + lastidx) / 2;
  if (findId < id[middleidx])
```

```
      lastidx = middleidx - 1;
    else if (findId > id[middleidx])
      firstidx = middleidx + 1;
    else foundMatch = true;
  }
  foundIndex = middleidx;
  return foundMatch;
}
```

Inserting New Data into a Sorted List

Inserting new elements into a sorted array is more difficult. Consider the above **id** and **grade** arrays with the six elements currently in it, Illustration A.3. Suppose that a student id of 255555555 with a grade of B needs to be inserted. What would have to be done to actually insert this new student?

First, we would have to find the subscript where that id would be the proper sequence. In this case, 255555555 belongs in the element with a subscript of 2, between the values 222222222 and 333333333. Since element 2 is already occupied, that element and all others must be moved down one element. That is, the data at index 2 must be moved into subscript 3; 3 must be moved into index 4; 4 into 5 and 5 into the unoccupied 6.

Caution. The movement of elements must be done in reverse order. If we move 33333333 into the **id** array at subscript 3, it replaces the data that is there, id 444444444. Thus, the movement must be 5 into 6, 4 into 5, 3 into 4 and finally 2 into 3. Once the data in the element of index 2 has been copied into element 3, we can then copy in the new id of 255555555 into the element at index 2.

Of course, nothing can be inserted if all the elements are used. To be robust, the insert function should also make sure the requested id is not already in the list. Remember, too, when parallel arrays are involved, what is done to one array must be echoed in the other parallel array(s).

For this example, assume the following **const int** definitions are available in the global namespace.
```
const int InsertErrorBoundsExceeded = -1;
const int InsertErrorDuplicateId = -2;
const int InsertSuccess = 0;
```
Further assume that the new data to be inserted into the list are contained in the following **main()** program's variables.
```
long newId;
char newGrade;
```
The **main()** function invokes the **InsertStudent()** function as follows
```
int retcd = InsertStudent (id, grade, numberStudents,
                           MaxStudents, newId, newGrade);
if (retcd == InsertErrorBoundsExceeded) {
  cout << "Error: Cannot add more students\n"
       << "The list is full\n";
}
else if (retcd == InsertErrorDuplicateId) {
  cout << "Error: student id " << newId
```

```
            << " is already present in the list\n";
}
```

The coding for the robust **InsertStudent()** function is as follows.

```
int InsertStudent (long id[], char grade[],
                   int& num, int maxlimit,
                   long newId, char newGrade) {
  if (num >= maxlimit) // out of elements
    return InsertErrorBoundsExceeded;
  int index; // subscript where id belongs
  if (BinarySearch (id[], num, newId, index))
    return InsertErrorDuplicateId; // found this id
  if (index != num) {
  // move all items down one index
  for (int j=num-1; j >= index; j--) {
    id[j+1] = id[j];
    grade[j+1] = grade[j];
  }
  // copy new data into lists
  id[index] = newid;
  grade[index] = newgrade;
  num++;
  return InsertSuccess;
}
```

A Review of Two-dimensional Array Processing

One common application of two-dimensional arrays is a spreadsheet. In a monthly budget spreadsheet, for example, the rows represent the income and expenses while the columns represent the monthly expenses. Consider the following budget.

```
item              June      July     August
income          1500.00   1550.00   1500.00
rent             500.00    500.00    500.00
utilities        200.00    200.00    200.00
phone             40.00     40.00     40.00
movies            20.00     30.00     25.00
```

All of the above numerical values are **double**s. While one could create five single-dimensioned arrays, each containing three elements to hold the sets of monthly values, a single two-dimensional array of five rows each with three columns greatly simplifies the programming logic.

Defining Multidimensional Arrays

The above budget two-dimensional array is defined as

```
double budget[5][3];
```

577

In general, the syntax is

```
datatype name[limit1][limit2][limit3]...[limitn];
```

The number of dimensions is unlimited; however, for practical purposes, the amount of memory available for a program to use on a specific platform becomes the limiting factor. How much memory does the above budget array occupy? Assuming that a **double** occupies 8 bytes, then budget takes 5 x 3 x 8 bytes, or 120 bytes.

When defining multidimensional arrays, each array bound or limit should be either a **#define** value or a **const int**. These limit values are likely to be used throughout the program. If a symbolic limit is used, it is easier to later modify the limits to allow for more data. The above budget array can be defined as follows.

```
const int NumberItems = 5;
const int NumberMonths = 3;
...
double budget[NumberItems][NumberMonths];
```

Consider another example. Suppose that we needed to accumulate the total sales from various cash registers located in three different stores and that each store had four departments each. We could define three separate total arrays, one for each store; each array would have four elements, one for each department. However, defining one two-dimensional array of three stores each with four departments greatly simplifies programming. The **totals** array could be defined as follows.

```
#define STORES 3
#define DEPTS 4
...
double totals[STORES][DEPTS];
```

Suppose further that, within each department, there are always two cash registers. Now the array would contain a third dimension.

```
#define REGS 2
...
double regtotals[STORES][DEPTS][REGS];
```

How are the individual elements within a multidimensional array accessed? By providing all the needed subscripts. Remember that all subscripts begin with element 0. The following are valid.

```
totals[0][1] = 5.;   // store 0, dept 1
totals[1][3] = 10.;  // store 1, dept 3
totals[0][0] = 0;    // the first element in the array
x = totals[2][3];    // the last element in the array
regtotals[1][2][0] = 42; // store 1, dept 2, reg 0
```

The following are invalid.

```
totals[0,1] = 5; // each subscript must be within []
totals[1] = 1;   // this only specifies row 1 -
                 // which has 4 columns
totals = 0;      // unfortunately not allowed either
```

Beginning Data Structures in C++

Normally, the subscripts are variables and not constants. The subscripts may also be integer expressions. The following are valid.

```
totals[i][j]++;  // increments this specific total
totals[k][0] = 5;
totals[k+j][j/2] = 5;
```

The following are invalid.

```
totals[k++][0]; // incs k not the element in total
totals++[k][0]; // ++ op comes after the subscripts
totals[.5][.3] = 5; // subscripts must be integers
```

Physical Memory Layout Versus Logical Layout

The physical memory layout always follows the same sequence. In a two-dimensional array, all of the columns of row 0 come first followed by all the columns for row 1 and so on. This is called **row-major order**. Figure A.2 shows how memory is laid out for the **totals** array while Figure A.2 shows how the **regtotals** array is stored in memory.

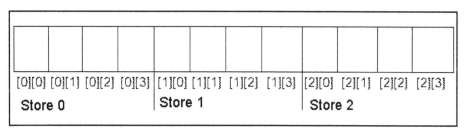

Figure A.2 Memory Layout for **totals**

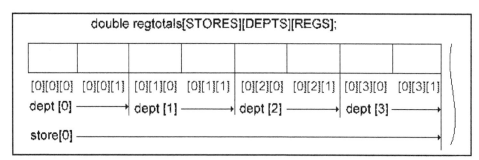

Figure A.3 Memory Layout for **regtotals**

Programmatically, two-dimensional arrays are often thought of as having rows and columns, rather like a table. It is more useful to take the following logical viewpoint of the **totals** array, where the x-axis represents the columns and the y-axis represent the rows. This is shown in Figure A.4.

In a similar manner, a three-dimensional array has the first or leftmost dimension on the z-axis (coming into or out of the page) and its second dimension is along the y-axis and the rightmost

579

dimension is along the x-axis.

columns→ 0	1	2	3
rows 0 totals[0][0]	totals[0][1]	totals[0][2]	totals[0][3]
1 totals[1][0]	totals[1][1]	totals[1][2]	totals[1][3]
2 totals[2][0]	totals[2][1]	totals[2][2]	totals[2][3]

Figure A.4 The logical Rows and Columns View

Initialization of Multidimensional Arrays

The basic concept of single-dimensioned array initialization is extended in a similar fashion to multidimensional arrays. Consider the totals array of 3 rows by 4 columns. First, all of row 0 is initialized. However, since row 0 is an array of 4 columns, the array notation is used.

```
double totals[3][4] = { {1, 2, 3, 4}, {11. 12. 13. 14},
                          row 0                row 1

                        {21, 22, 23, 24} };
                          row 2
```

If all of the elements of a single-dimensioned array are not initialized, the default value of 0 is used for the remaining unspecified elements. Thus, if **totals** were to be initialized to 0, it could be done as follows.

```
double totals[3][4] = { {0}, {0}, {0} };
```

To initialize all the elements of **regtotals** to 0, one could do the following.

```
double regtotals[3][4][2] = { { {0}, {0}, {0}, {0} },
//                              dept 0    1    2    3
//                                 -- store 0 ---------
  { {0}, {0}, {0}, {0} }, { {0}, {0}, {0}, {0} } };
// ----- store 1 -----       ----- store 2 -----
```

As the number of dimensions increases, the initialization syntax becomes awful! Frequently, it is much simpler just to write some loops to initialize the arrays at run time. The **regtotals** array can be initialized as follows.

```
for (int i=0; i< STORES; i++) {
  for (int j=0; j<DEPTS; j++) {
    for (int k=0; k<REGS; k++) {
      regtotals[i][j][k] = 0;
    }
  }
}
```

Passing Multidimensional Arrays to Functions

With single-dimensioned arrays, the name of the array is a constant pointer or memory address of the first element of the array. The same is true of a multidimensional array; its name is a constant pointer or memory address of the first element. If the **totals** array were to be passed to a function, say **calcs()**, the prototype is

```
void calcs (double totals[][DEPTS]);
```

It would not be wrong to provide all dimensions though, as in

```
void calcs (double totals[STORES][DEPTS]);
```

However, the compiler always ignores the leftmost dimension's value. However, all other dimensions must be specified. The **main()** function would then invoke the **calcs()** function by

```
calcs (totals);
```

The following is in error – why?

```
void calcs (double totals[][]);
```

To see why, suppose that within **calcs()** one coded the following.

```
totals[1][0] = qty * sales;
```

How does the compiler locate the specific element to assign the calculation result? The compiler finds the start of the 2nd row (subscript 1) by multiplying the number of elements in any row times the size of the data type of the array. This is called the **row offset** from the start of the array. It then finds the **column offset** by multiplying the column number by the size of the data type of the array. Finally, the compiler adds the starting address of the array with the row offset and then the column offset to yield the memory address of the requested element. Thus, to find the row offset, the compiler must know how many elements are in a row, that is, the second dimension.

Suppose that the array **regtotals** is to be passed to the **calcs2()** function. The prototype is

```
void calcs2 (double regtotals[][DEPTS][REGS]);
```

In all cases, it is permissible to omit only the leftmost dimension. However, it is always permissible to provide all the dimension limits; this is also less error prone.

```
void calcs2 (double regtotals[STORES][DEPTS][REGS]);
```

The **main()** function would then invoke **calcs2()** by the following.

```
calcs2 (regtotals);
```

Loading a Multidimensional Array from an Input File

Consider again the **budget** array with which the chapter began. It was defined as

```
double budget[NumberItems][ NumberMonths];
```

Suppose that the data were stored in a file called **budget.txt** and that a **LoadArray()** function is to read this data filling up the **budget** array. Recall with a single-dimensioned array, typically, not all potential elements were used in a given execution of a program. We commonly track the number of elements actually input with an integer, **numElements**, for example. The input of a multidimensional array presents some additional complications.

Suppose in true generality that not every column of every row was present. That is, for row 0, we might only have the first two columns; for row 1, all three columns are present; for row 2, only the first column's data is present; and so on. How could this be represented in the input data and worse still, how would the program know when accessing a specific row how many columns of data were actually in that row? True, we could input on a line by line basis and say all columns for a given row were on one line so that line breaks ended that row's input, but there is no easy way to "remember" how many elements each row has. If this needed to be done, a parallel second array of integer column counts would have to be constructed in which the number of elements actually in row 0 of the budget array was stored in element 0 of the counts array. Notice how fast the complexity is rising!

In reality, very often the input of multidimensional arrays is simplified to one of two approaches:

All elements of every row and all rows are entered

All elements of every row are entered, but not all rows are input

In other words, only the leftmost dimension can have a variable number input. For instance, with the **budget** array, we could store the number of rows of budget items actually input in the integer **numItems**. However, every row entered must have all three monthly values present.

The **main()** function calls **LoadBudget()** as follows.

```
int numItems = LoadBudget (budget, NumberItems,
                           NumberMonths);
```

Here is the **LoadBudget()** function that returns the number of items or rows actually input.

```
int LoadBudget (double budget[NumberItems][NumberMonths],
                int itemLimit, int monthLimit) {
 ifstream infile ("budget.txt");
 if (!infile) {
  cerr << "Error: cannot open budget.txt\n";
  exit (1);
 }
 int j = 0;
 int k;
 while (j<itemLimit && infile >> ws && infile.good()) {
  for (k=0; k<monthLimit; k++) {
   infile >> budget[j][k];
  }
  j++;
 }
 infile.close ();
 return j;
}
```

Working with Multidimensional Arrays

When working with two-dimensional arrays, a programmer is frequently called upon to sum the contents of an entire row (summing all the columns of that row) or to sum the contents of a specific column (summing that column in all the rows). Let's examine the straightforward approach to these two problems and then see what can be done to improve execution speed of the operations. The **main()** function defines the array to use and calls the simple **sumrow1()** function to sum all of the values in a row and display that sum.

```cpp
#include <iostream.h>
const int NUMROWS = 3;
const int NUMCOLS = 4;

int sumrow1 (int x[][NUMCOLS], int whichrow);
int sumrow2 (int x[NUMCOLS]);

int sumcol1 (int x[][NUMCOLS], int whichcol);
int sumcol2 (int x[NUMCOLS], int whichcol);

int main() {
 int n;
 int array[NUMROWS][NUMCOLS] = { {1,2,3,4}, {11,12,13,14},
                                  {21,22,23,24} };
 // Method 1: normal sumrow function
 for (n=0; n<NUMROWS; n++) {
   cout << "sumrow1 = " << sumrow1(array,n) << endl;
 }
```

The function **sumrow1()** is straightforward.

```cpp
int sumrow1 (int x[][NUMCOLS], int whichrow) {
 int i, sum = 0;
 for (i=0; i<NUMCOLS; i++) {
  sum += x[whichrow][i];
 }
 return sum;
}
```

How can this coding be speeded up at execution time? First of all, if the bounds are small and the sum is invoked only one time, there is no need to try to improve its efficiency. However, if the bounds are large and this function is to be invoked many times, then a speed up is in order. What is slowing down the **sumrow1()** function is the need for two subscripts. Remember that to find the current element to add to the sum, the compiler must first calculate the row offset and then the column offset and add those to values to the beginning memory address of the array in order to find the requested element. Both offset calculations involve multiplying by the size of the data type, the **sizeof** a **double** or 8 in this case. The multiplication machine instruction is fairly slow, though on the Pentium class chips, it has been drastically speeded up. If we can reduce the number of multiplies, the function executes more quickly.

Beginning Data Structures in C++

When summing a row, all the columns of that row are in consecutive memory locations, that is, it can be thought of as a single-dimensioned array of four columns in this case. Thus, we pass only the current row **n** of four columns. The notation is

```
array[n]
```

Here I have provided only the first subscript of the two-dimensional array. The compiler assumes that I am specifying only the nth row, which is a single-dimensioned array of four **doubles**.

The **main()** function now does the following.

```
// results in 25% less code, 4% faster execution
for (n=0; n<NUMROWS; n++) {
  cout << "sumrow2 = " << sumrow2(array[n]) << endl;
}
```

The **sumrow2()** function is now very simple indeed.

```
int sumrow2 (int x[NUMCOLS]) {
  int i, sum = 0;
  for (i=0; i<NUMCOLS; i++) {
  sum += x[i];
  }
  return sum;
}
```

The other common operation is summing columns. For a specific column, find the sum of that column by accumulating the sum of that column in every row. The **main()** function calls **sumcol1()** illustrating the straightforward approach. Note that no matter which vertical column whose sum is desired, the entire array is passed.

```
for (n=0; n<NUMCOLS; n++) {
  cout << "sumcol1 = " << sumcol1(array,n) << endl;
}
```

The basic **sumcol1()** function is as follows.

```
int sumcol1 (int x[][NUMCOLS], int whichcol) {
  int i, sum = 0;
  for (i=0; i<NUMROWS; i++) {
  sum += x[i][whichcol];
  }
  return sum;
}
```

If performance requires the **sumcol()** function to be more efficient, how can it be improved? The objective is once more to reduce the number of multiplication machine instructions it takes to find the desired element. In this case, we cannot just pass the needed row as an array of four column values; we need to go vertical through the rows summing the specific column in each row. However, there is a trick that we can use. Recall that the compiler never checks for the "subscript out of range" condition. Assume that we have passed only the very first row of the two-dimensional array, so that the **sumcol2()** function sees only a single-dimension array of four elements, those of row 0. Set the initial subscript to the desired column that we are to sum - for example column 2. Then, to get to the next row's corresponding column, to our subscript add the number of columns in a row. In this case there are four columns per row. The next subscript is 2 + 4 or 6 which is, in fact, really in column 2 of the next row.

```
// The results: it has 2% faster execution
for (n=0;n<NUMCOLS;n++) {
 cout << "sumcol2 = " << sumcol2(array[0],n) << endl;
}
```

The improved **sumcol2()** function is shown below.

```
int i, j = whichcol, sum = 0;
for (i=0; i<NUMROWS; i++) {
 sum += x[j];
 j = j + NUMCOLS;
}
```

A Review of Structures

A **structure** is a grouping of related fields of information into one group which is often called a record of data. Many convenient operations can be performed using this structure aggregate. The structure also provides means for us to access the individual member fields as needed.

Defining Structures

The starting point is to define the model or blueprint that the compiler uses when it needs to create an actual instance of the structure in memory. This model is called the **structure template** or definition. The template includes the keyword **struct** followed by the **structure tag** which is the name that is used to identify this structure from all others. This is followed by all of the member field definitions surrounded by braces {…} and ends with a semicolon.

Suppose that the program is to process cost records. Each cost record includes the item number, quantity on hand, product description and its cost. Here is what the structure template looks like.

```
const int DescrLen = 21; // max length of description

struct COSTREC {
   long    itemNum;          // item number
   short   qty;              // quantity on hand
   char    descr[DescrLen];  // item description
   double  cost;             // item cost
};
```

The structure tag, **COSTREC** in this case, is used to identify this particular structure. By convention, all structure tags either are wholly uppercase names (usually) or are capitalized.

The four data items contained between the braces { } are called the **structure members**. Each structure member is a normal variable data definition. Constant integers or **#define**s should be used for array bounds, but those definitions must precede the structure template, following the "defined before first use" rule.

When any instance of **COSTREC** is created or used, the member fields are always created and stored in the order shown in the template. For most problems, the fields can be in any order you choose.

Suppose that when recording weather statistics, data is measured and recorded every hour. A daily weather record might be defined as follows.

```
const int NumObs = 24;
const int StationLen = 21;
struct WEATHER {
  char    stationName[StationLen]; // reporting location
  float  temps[NumObs];           // degrees Centigrade
  float  humidity[NumObs];         // such as 50%
  float  rainfall[NumObs];         // in millimeters
  float  windspeed[NumObs];        // in m/s
};
```

Notice that a structure can contain arrays.

Creating Instances of a Structure

With the structure template defined, how are instances of it created? The data type precedes the desired name of the variable. Structure instances follow the same pattern. The data type is the structure tag in C++. The following creates a **structure variable** called **costRec** and a structure variable called **weaRec**. A structure variable is just an instance of a structure in memory.

```
COSTREC costRec;
WEATHER weaRec;
```

What does the structure variable **costRec** look like in memory when it is created by the compiler? Figure A.1 shows the memory layout of **costRec** and its member fields. Notice that the fields are in the same order as in the **COSTREC** template.

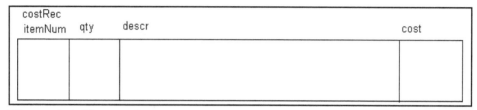

Figure A.1 The **costRec** Memory Layout

One can have arrays of structures as well. Suppose that the program needed to store a maximum of 1000 cost records and a maximum of 500 weather records. The following defines these two arrays and also shows the location of all the parts of the structure definitions.

File: CostRec.h

```
#ifndef COSTREC_H
#define COSTREC_H

#define MAXRECS 1000
const int DescrLen = 21;   // max length of description

struct COSTREC {
   long   itemNum;          // item number
   short  qty;              // quantity on hand
   char   descr[DescrLen];  // item description
   double cost;             // item cost
};
#endif
```

File: main.cpp

```
#include "CostRec.h"
int main () {
 COSTREC arec[MAXRECS];   // array of 1000 cost records
 ...
```

or

File: WeatherRec.h

```
#ifndef WEATHERREC_H
```

587

```
#define WEATHERREC_H

#define LIMIT 500
const int NumObs = 24; // number observations per day
const int StationLen = 21; // max len of station

struct WEATHER {
 char  stationName[StationLen]; // reporting location
 float temps[NumObs];           // degrees Centigrade
 float humidity[NumObs];        // such as 50%
 float rainfall[NumObs];        // in millimeters
 float windspeed[NumObs];       // in m/s
};
#endif
```

File: main.cpp

```
#include "WeatherRec.h"
int main () {
 WEATHER weaArray[LIMIT];
```

A Structure Can Contain Instances of Other Structures

A structure can also contain instances of other structures and arrays of other structures. For example, consider a **DATE** structure which represents a calendar date. Using instances of a **DATE** structure would make passing dates very convenient. Further, consider an employee record that contained the employee's id number, his/her salary and the date that he/she was hired. The **EMPLOYEE** structure contains an instance of the **DATE** structure as shown below.

```
struct DATE {
   char month;
   char day;
   short year;
};

struct EMPLOYEE {
   long id;
   double salary;
   DATE hireDate;
};
```

Suppose that a **CARMAINT** structure must be defined to represent the periodic maintenance requirements for a new car. Here the **CARMAINT** structure contains an array of **DATE** structures.

```
const int numMaint = 10;
struct CARMAINT {
 bool maintenanceDone[numMaint];   // true if the work was done
 int  maintenanceCode[numMaint];   // manufacturer's maint. codes
 DATE maintenanceDueDate[numMaint];// date maintenance is due
};
```

How are Structure Instances Initialized?

An instance of a structure can be initialized when it is defined, just as any other variable. However, since a structure typically has a number of data members, the values are surrounded by braces {} as are single dimensioned arrays. The following structure represents a quarter coin initialized as it is defined within **main()**.

```
const int MaxLen = 10;
struct COIN {
 int denomination;
 char singular[MaxLen];
 char multiple[MaxLen];
};
int main () {
 COIN quarter = {25, "Quarter", "Quarters"};
```

How are Structure Members Accessed?

Having defined the structure template and created instance(s) of it, the next action is to utilize the members within the structure. This is done by using the **dot (.)** operator. To the left of the **dot** operator must be a **structure variable** and to the right must be a **member variable** of that structure.

To access the **qty** member of the **costRec** instance, one codes

```
costRec.qty
```

To calculate the **totalCost** using the **cost** and **qty** members of the **costRec** instance, do the following.

```
double totalCost = costRec.qty * costRec.cost;
```

To display the description, use

```
cout << costRec.descr;
```

To increment the **costRec**'s quantity member or add another variable to it, one can code

```
costRec.qty++;
costRec.qty += orderedQty;
```

To input a set of data into the **costRec** variable, there are a number of ways. Here is one.

```
cin >> costRec.itemNum >> costRec.qty >> ws;
cin.get (costRec.descr, DescrLen);
cin >> costRec.cost;
```

The above assumes that no description field in the input data contains all blanks. It also assumes that all descriptions contain **DescrLen – 1** number of characters.

As you look these over, notice that there are no differences at all on input or output of structure members, other than the requisite **dot** operator qualification with the structure variable.

Rules of Use for Structure Variables

Structure variables can be used for only five actions. These are the following.

A structure variable can be used to access structure members.

A structure variable or reference to one can be passed to a function.

A function can return a structure variable.

The address operator & returns the memory address of a structure variable

A structure variable can be assigned to another structure variable as long as they both have the same structure tag.

We have already examined the first one, using the structure variable to access the individual members, as in **costRec.qty**. The **address** operator & returns the address of the structure variable. If one codes

```
&costRec
```

then the compiler provides the memory location where the instance begins. Normally, the compiler does this automatically for us when we use reference variables.

Assume that the program also had defined another instance of the **COSTREC**.

```
COSTREC previousRec;
```

The fifth rule says that a complete copy of a structure variable can be done as follows.

```
previousRec = costRec;
```

This is very powerful indeed. Consider the alternative if this were not allowed. One would have to write an assignment for each of the three numeric fields and then use **strcpy()** to copy the string as shown below.

```
previousRec.itemNum = costRec.itemNum;
previousRec.qty = costRec.qty;
previousRec.cost = costRec.cost;
strcpy (previousRec.descr, costRec.descr);
```

Clearly, the ability to assign one structure variable to another instance can be a terrific operation when it is needed.

A structure variable can be passed to a function or a reference or pointer to one can be passed. Passing by reference is the best approach to take. However, passing by use of a pointer is also fine. Likewise, a function can return a copy of a structure. However, in reality, returning a structure and passing a structure and not using reference to a structure instance is generally avoided. Let's examine these two issues in detail.

Suppose that the **main()** program defined the cost record structure as we have been using it thus far. Suppose further that the **main()** function then wanted to call a **PrintRec()** function whose task is to print the data nicely formatted. The **main()** function does the following.

```
int main () {
COSTREC crec;
...
PrintRec (outfile, crec);
```

The **PrintRec()** function begins as follows.

```
void PrintRec (ostream& outfile, COSTREC crec) {
   outfile << crec.itemNum...
```

Beginning Data Structures in C++

When the compiler generates the instructions to make the call to **PrintRec()**, it must make a new parameter instance of the **COSTREC** structure and then spend execution time to copy all the data from the **main()**'s **costRec** instance into **PrintRec()**'s **crec** parameter instance. For structures that contain a large number of members, this is wasteful of both memory (the parameter copy) and execution speed (making the copy every time the function is called).

A far better approach is to pass the structure variable by reference. A simple change to **PrintRec()** vastly improves both memory utilization and execution speed.

```
void PrintRec (ostream& outfile, const COSTREC& crec) {
   outfile << crec.itemNum...
```

Here the compiler actually passes only the memory address of **main()**'s **costRec**. **PrintRec()**'s **crec** parameter is now a reference variable (usually occupying 4 bytes of memory). No copy of the data is made. Further, since the print operation does not change the data, it is passed as a constant reference.

If the instance was passed using a pointer, the programmer must remember to carry out all the actions that the compiler does when a reference variable is used.

```
void PrintRec (ostream& outfile, const COSTREC* ptrcrec) {
   outfile << ptrcrec->itemNum...
```

and main() would call it this way

```
PrintRec (cout, &crec);
```

This brings up the **ReadRec()** function whose job it is to input the data and somehow fill up the **main()**'s **costRec** with that data. One way that the **ReadRec()** function can be defined is to have it return a **COSTREC** structure. This is not a good way to do it, but let's see how a function can return a structure instance. Then, we will see how to better design the **ReadRec()** function. If **ReadRec()** returns a structure, then **main()** would have to assign it to **main()**'s **costRec** variable. From a design point of view, since **main()** is passing **ReadRec()** a reference to the input stream, **ReadRec()** lets the **main()** function decide on what to for I/O errors, bad data and EOF detection. The coding for **main()** is as follows.

```
int main () {
 COSTREC costRec;
 costRec = ReadRec (infile);
 // now check on infile's state
```

Now in **ReadRec()**, the coding can be done this way.

```
COSTREC ReadRec (istream& infile) {
 COSTREC temp = {0};
 if (infile >> ws && !infile.good()) {
  return temp;
 }
 infile >> temp.itemNum >> and so on
 return temp;
}
```

Here the structure variable **temp** is filled with the input file's next set of data and then a complete copy of **temp** is returned to **main()**. However, since EOF can occur as well as bad data and since we have to return an instance of the **COSTREC** structure, **temp** is initialized to zeros. Back in **main()**, when the function call to **ReadRec()** is completed, the compiler then must copy that returned copy of **temp** into **main()**'s **costRec** variable. If the structure contained a large number of member fields, memory is being wasted. In all cases, execution speed is going to suffer because of all the copying operations needed to move the data from **temp** into **costRec**.

While there can be times when this overhead cannot be avoided, usually the answer is to pass a reference to the **ReadRec()** function and have the function fill up **main()**'s **costRec** directly. This then frees up the return value for other uses. And by now returning a reference to the input stream being used for input, the caller of the **ReadRec()** function can make more effective use of the language.

Suppose that **ReadRec()** was rewritten to be passed a reference to the caller's **COSTREC** structure variable to be filled with the input data. The improved function is shown below.

```
istream& ReadRec (istream& infile, COSTREC& crec) {
 if (infile >> ws && !infile.good()) {
  return infile;
 }
 infile >> crec.itemNum >> and so on
 return infile;
}
```

Now the **main()** function has more ways that it can utilize the **ReadRec()** function. Here is the improved **main()** function.

```
int main () {
 COSTREC costRec;
 ...
 while (ReadRec (infile, costRec)) {
```

Certainly **main()** benefits from the change. The **while** clause is basically testing the goodness of the input stream after the input operations are complete. Also, **ReadRec()** now avoids both the extra memory overhead of returning a structure instance and the execution time needed to make the copies.

www.ingramcontent.com/pod-product-compliance
Lightning Source LLC
LaVergne TN
LVHW060119070326
832902LV00019B/3038